Ethnographies of U.S. Empire

Ethnographies of U.S. Empire

Carole McGranahan & John F. Collins,
EDITORS

DUKE UNIVERSITY PRESS *Durham & London* 2018

Printed in the United States of America on acid-free paper ∞
Designed by Matt Tauch
Typeset in Minion Pro by Westchester Publishing Services

Library of Congress Cataloging-in-Publication Data
Names: McGranahan, Carole, editor. | Collins, John F., [date–], editor.
Title: Ethnographies of U.S. empire / Carole McGranahan and John F. Collins, editors.
Description: Durham : Duke University Press, 2018. | Includes bibliographical references and index.
Identifiers: LCCN 2017060940 (print) | LCCN2018001556 (ebook)
ISBN 9781478002086 (ebook)
ISBN 9781478000099 (hardcover : alk. paper)
ISBN 9781478000235 (pbk. : alk. paper)
Subjects: LCSH: Ethnology. | Imperialism. | Postcolonialism. | Ethnicity—Political aspects—United States. | United States—Foreign relations—History.
Classification: LCC GN316 (ebook) | LCC GN316 .E78 2018 (print) | DDC 305.800973—dc23
LC record available at https://lccn.loc.gov/2017060940

Cover art: Andrea Coronil, *Papi's jokes didn't cover this part / Papá nunca contó chistes de esto*, 2015. Wax pencil on acetate, metallic paint on inkjet print on acetate (of a declassified FBI file on Fernando Coronil).

Portions of chapter 13 appear in Erin Fitz-Henry, "'But There's No American Base Here': Becoming Domestic in a Foreign Sense," in *U.S. Military Bases and Anti-Military Organizing: An Ethnography of An Air Force Base in Ecuador*, 47–80 (New York: Palgrave Macmillan, 2015).

An earlier version of chapter 20 appeared as, "Reporting Cambodian Refugees: Youth Activism, State Reform, and Imperial Statecraft," in *Positions: East Asia Cultures Critique* 20, no. 3 (2012): 737–62.

Contents

Acknowledgments

This volume had its beginnings in a Wenner-Gren workshop held in April 2011, in New York City. Fifteen of us gathered in the Empire State for several days of intense debate about U.S. empire. Since then, our conversations have continued over email and in panels at the annual American Anthropological Association conference and elsewhere. And we have invited other colleagues to join in to help us extend the depth and breadth of our coverage of U.S. imperial reach. Like all ethnographies, this volume is a work in progress that draws on stories that continue to unfold, that are not yet over, that shift and duck and dodge at times, and that we hope speak boldly into an imperial wind tunnel whose effects may become strangely visible if engaged creatively and carefully.

We are deeply grateful to the Wenner-Gren Foundation for Anthropological Research for funding our workshop, and for its support in the years since. We also appreciate the support for our initial meeting in New York offered by the Union Theological Seminary and the Queens College and CUNY Graduate Center Departments of Anthropology. Most of all, we thank the contributors to this volume, both the original workshop participants and those who joined the project soon after. Your collective insights, commitments to the volume, and recognition of the importance of considering empire beyond individual cases or types were crucial in building our overall arguments. Your scholarship makes up a formidable ethnographic force—impactful on its own, but truly powerful in this side-by-side format that pulls together so many perspectives on U.S. empire. The perspective achieved by juxtaposing and grouping these ethnographies and histories has permitted us, as editors, to appreciate individual cases and their details in novel ways. We hope the same is true for readers of this volume. And we hope those readers might begin to make out U.S. empire in its full and devastating—and thus at times partial and disaggregated—force across time and around the world: from the Mohawk and Osage Nations to Puerto Rico and Samoa, from the Philippines to Hawaiʻi and on to U.S. military bases and prisons at home and abroad, to Tibet and "highland" New Jersey, to Korea and Vietnam, to company towns in Suriname and rocket bases in Brazil, and to immigrants, refugees, and military dissenters in the United States.

Duke University Press has been a generous partner throughout the process of producing this volume. Thank you to all at Duke who made this volume a reality, especially Elizabeth Ault and Editorial Director Ken Wissoker. We are grateful for your wisdom and patience, for your confidence in the importance of the text, and for engaging stellar reviewers who were both critical and insightful in ways that improved the end result. Ben Joffe was an excellent research assistant and Alison Hanson contributed detailed, thoughtful work on the entire manuscript.

Here it is important to note that the ideas for this volume were sparked well before 2011. Yet as ethnographers have emphasized in so many ways, the contours of historical events are typically open to disagreement, and too much of a focus on the event itself may obscure the processes that cause that figure to take on its symbolic weight. A related insight girds our approach to empire and its ethnography, a journey that began in different forms much earlier, in Ann Arbor, Michigan, in the mid-1990s. There, while students at the University of Michigan, we had the privilege of immersing ourselves in what was then called "colonial studies" in dialogue with Ann Laura Stoler. In spite of the fact that both of us worked mostly outside of the accepted parameters of that colonial studies—Carole in Tibet and John in Brazil—Ann's fearless, rigorous brilliance shaped how we understood empire through both anthropological and historical perspectives, as well as how we understood anthropology through an uncompromising imperial critique. Ann has long thought through and beyond anthropology's limits and possibilities, struggling to make out archives as ethnographic spaces and always emphasizing the importance of forms of critique that depend on a constant turning over and refinement of one's standpoints and fidelities. Within colonial studies in the 1990s, Ann's work charted out especially new terrain that would mark the critique produced across multiple disciplines. Her analysis brought the intimacies of race, class, gender, and sexuality into dialogue with intrusive colonial state policies marking who was "European" or "native"; opened a creative new page for analysis of the presence and policies toward white women, children, and poor white men in the European colonies; and highlighted (along with Fred Cooper in *Tensions of Empire*) the epistemological, and not just economic or political importance, of empire for the metropole. Or, put slightly better, Ann's interventions into accepted ways of doing colonial studies came to suggest not simply that intimate matters are indeed matters of state, but that empire as a political economic formation relies, and even piggybacks, on epistemological contests. For her students, Ann was, and remains always, a generous mentor. Her scholarship grounds this collection in relation to attempts at thoughtful and sometimes devastating detail, as well as in the new terrain she has opened up, and on which contributors to this volume seek to build. It was our honor and pleasure to have Ann participate in the initial Wenner-Gren workshop for this project, and to conclude the volume with an afterword in the form of a conversation with her.

We dedicate this volume to the late Fernando Coronil—teacher, interlocutor, colleague, and inspiration. Fernando was one of our first professors in graduate school, coteaching with Nicholas Dirks "Traditions I," or the theory seminar required of all incoming anthropology graduate students. In Fernando's hands, anthropology included poetry and history as well as both classical and iconoclastic readings on capitalism and the state. His insights on U.S. empire were both academic and personal, something captured powerfully in his article from 1996 "Beyond Occidentalism: Toward Nonimperial Geohistorical Categories." Fernando was supposed to have participated in the original "Ethnographies of U.S. Empire Workshop" held at Union Theological Seminary. But illness prevented him from doing so, and he passed away soon after. Then as now, he is greatly missed. We are grateful for all we learned from him and touched to showcase the art of his daughter Andrea Coronil on the cover. With much respect, we offer this volume in the spirit of political intervention so clearly embodied in Fernando's anthropology.

Finally, as is common at moments like this, we thank the members of both our families for putting up with the long hours spent crafting a volume that, in spite of its size and attention to comparison, never pretends to be encyclopedic. Ana, John, Riley, Liya, and Gabriel—thank you. Thanks also to John J. Collins, whom the world lost as this book was nearing completion. Such thanks, and personal stakes, are emblematic not simply of the multiple influences and supporters that have structured this book, but of our hopes for a future whose outlines must necessarily engage, and emanate in some way in relation to, the structures of U.S. empire we seek to make apparent in the pages that follow. A volume such as this one—necessarily flawed, partial, and scarred by the imperial formations it engages through an ethnography similarly marked by empire—seems especially important at a moment when U.S. electoral politics have come to turn ever more explicitly on a dizzying mix of foreign intervention and internal violence. It is our intention to make clearer not simply the components, but the often-missed processes, sediments, and precipitations so much a part of empire as a poisonously productive ecology of North American life.

INTRODUCTION Ethnography and U.S. Empire

JOHN F. COLLINS AND CAROLE McGRANAHAN

The United States of America has long been an empire in denial. If European incursions into the "New World" so often rested on an imperial bravado in which inhabited territories were construed as empty, available, or filled with ostensible primitives awaiting missionization, the foundation of the United States rested on a rejection of British rule and an inauguration of an anti-imperial politics that continues to do much to define the country and its discourses of freedom today. Throughout U.S. history and historiography, then, political actions are often situated against empire and discussed in seemingly empire-neutral registers.[1] Engaged from such well-camouflaged blinds, the occupation of Native American lands takes form as destiny or "expansion" rather than "colonization." Attempts by the United States to piggyback upon Latin American independence movements become wars against European colonial powers rather than a usurpation of slaves' and creole pioneers' struggles for emancipation. The cultivation of global influence during the Cold War emerges as "politics as needed" rather than the seizure of a gap opened by decolonization. And overseas military interventions were (and remain) a paternalistic or even "democratic" responsibility rather than linked strategies within shifting constellations of imperial aggression. Nonetheless, in settler colonialism as in slavery, in territorial "acquisitions" and in hemispheric empire in the Americas since 1898, and during the Cold and Vietnam Wars as well as the current period of renewed militarism around presidential decree, a series of contradictory imperial formations arise, structure political possibilities, and are nonetheless denied or rendered deniable. The imperial bluster evident during the early stages of Donald Trump's presidency seems to enunciate publicly the imperial volition we argue has so often been occluded. And yet, the Trump administration couples imperial bluster and violent politics at home and abroad with a rhetoric of turning inward, of responsibility, and of caring for one's own while excluding and leaving ostensible others to what come to be configured as their self-adminstered fates. Once again, the fundaments and ongoing practices of U.S. nation-state consolidation and imperial politics fail to cohere as a linear history of clear perception, easily partible epochs, stable forms, and heroic actors. Instead, they form something akin to what Ann Stoler, resituating Clifford Geertz's insight, calls "blurred genres," or an ensemble of colonizing practices and policies full of contradictions, hubris, and imperial refusals.[2]

If political discourse, academic geography, and historiography have conspired to energize and legitimate denials of empire that operate alongside the sporadic celebration of the importance of empire to what the United States is and does, anthropology as a discipline has played at least a supporting role. Over the last century our scholarship has engaged U.S. empire erratically and inconsistently. Empire hovers in the shadows of many ethnographies. It is untended to, even when hiding in plain sight or cohabiting with critique in murky bundles of practices and epistemological initiatives so much a part of the everyday life and disciplinary norms accepted as fully North American, and productive of new, even politically aware, analysis today. Nonetheless, and in what might be read as yet another aspect of imperial formations' ability to shape-shift so as to deceive while nonetheless motivating long-standing global inequities, over the last four decades anthropology as a discipline has turned a critical eye toward European empires. In conjunction with the work of Edward Said and the rise of postcolonial studies, anthropologists have issued sustained and often searing critiques of the discipline's imperial genealogies.[3] They have sought to expand and decolonize by rethinking accepted or acceptable subjects of research; subject/object binaries and the limits of the human; representational strategies; methodological and theoretical approaches to the past; and personal relationships to, and especially researchers' emplacements within, particular communities and intellectual traditions.[4] This work has added substantially to the interdisciplinary study of empire, especially in relation to the transport of ethnographic sensibilities to the writing of histories.[5] Yet engagements with empire and its contemporary forms suggest a need to augment analyses of the past, even as analyses of the past are never simply interpretations of what has passed.[6]

For some time now, anthropologists have launched serious political protests against U.S. imperialism and the use of anthropological scholarship in wartime.[7] This has been most notable in relation to the Cold War, Vietnam, and the more recent invasions of Iraq and Afghanistan.[8] And yet, in spite of this increasingly sustained disciplinary engagement with empire, the ethnographic—as opposed to historical—scholarship on U.S. empire at home and abroad remains thin, at least in relation to the world historical gravity of its object of inquiry.

Contributors to the present volume engage contemporary U.S. empire from an ethnographic perspective. This means that we hope to add field-based anthropological research findings, questions, contradictions borne of embodied experience, and manners of examining systems of knowledge and social ontologies to the historical and political analyses that have dominated the field of colonial and imperial studies. But it also means that we are seeking to do more than "add ethnography and stir," or inject some facile, presentist perspective into the sort of interrogation that requires analysts to consider empire as not simply an object, but as an assemblage of shifting conjugations that alter the grammars within and through which we find ourselves making claims. Therefore, in taking up calls for more and sharper ethnographies of empire, and in agreeing that empire "is in the details," we seek to perform a collective double move.[9] This involves bringing anthropology and its established methods to bear on U.S. empire, but also considering carefully how empire in turn shapes and reshapes ethnography, and thus those methods. What, we ask, does it mean to examine empire ethnographically? How might an apparently enduring or reanimated imperial present be addressed and contested through painstaking, self-reflexive, and empirically grounded anthropological research; and what might *empiricism* look like in such contexts? How might anthropologists develop ethnographic questions, agendas, and methods adequate to considerations of contemporary imperial formations? What might such an anthropological project mean in relation to broader politics and knowledge practices outside academia? Most basically, then, how does the study of empire alter what ethnography is and does, and how might such shifts contribute to political change in the world?

We seek to encourage, and perform, a social science that is up to the task of producing new knowledge about the diffuse and yet sometimes tightly bundled practices and phenomena that make up the slippery entity dubbed *empire*. In doing so, then, we hope to inflect the very nature of ethnography and its place in imperial knowledge practices. This is not a detached activity or a historical project that considers where we may have been and what we have gotten wrong so that we may seek absolution in the present. It is instead a program undertaken in the present that considers how we as ethnographers might alter what anthropologists think they know already, so as to clarify the stakes of that present, the retrospective histories it produces, and the futures it may engender. This effort involves taking into account the quandaries of a modern knowledge spawned by what is today a United States–dominated imperial order, while continuing to develop the powerful forms of intercourse, debate, embodied and affective practice, and personal engagements that are so much a part of contemporary ethnography.[10]

How might the ethnographic study of empire change ethnography without doing away with the incompletely and tentatively shared horizons of ethnography's different forms, or what we see as its ongoing and productively ragged potential for questioning shifting political rationalities, and thus the "contemporary"?[11] The authors included in this volume see ethnography as providing four much-needed methodological and theoretical approaches: (1) studying empire as it actually unfolds, (2) capturing the rhythms, sentiments, logics, and violence of U.S. empire as lived and experienced by its agents, subjects, and objects, (3) considering the historic and geographic range of U.S. imperial formations and the perspectives in the present from which they arise and do so much to gird, and (4) revealing how arenas of North American life previously analyzed as separate from empire may both contribute to and develop from the United States' role as an imperial power. This fourth point is especially important in light of what Ann Stoler has referred to, in another context, as "historical negatives."[12] These are social forms, objects, and ideas whose very inconsequentiality, incompleteness, or subservience to habitual epistemologies or the business of empire might give rise to unexpected perspectives and deeper insights into the slippages that make empire both so invisible, and yet so easy to talk about. In this volume, then, we seek not only to read empire against the grain, but also "with the grain."[13] If the first approach is one of confronting empire, the second means getting inside it; both strategies are needed in order to ask and answer questions of U.S. empire and its multiple logics. In this way we strive to come closer to apprehending its contradictory, obvious, and yet so often easily deniable impacts on lives, institutions, politics, and the grounds from which they emanate.

At a juncture at which empire is more a "way of life" than a discrete aspect of foreign policy—even as it is fundamental to that policy—research is needed that will enable us to assess empires *in and as* the present, and not solely as either precursors or novel entities to that present or to a United States taken as a stable geographical entity onto which foreign ventures taken as the real or demonstrable form of empire boomerang, to return in new form.[14] In bringing together an interdisciplinary group of ethnographers conducting fieldwork on empire, our intent in this volume is to tend to the specific formations and types of linked experiences engendered by empire on a global scale and within North American communities. We seek to interrogate not simply the construction of the United States as an empire, but the extent to which this nation-state has become unthinkable except in relation to an array of patterned denials that appear to coexist with a scattered recognition of what living in and with empire has wrought. Our focus is thus on classically "deep" fieldwork, rather than historical-archival research or a discursive analysis of politics and readily available public representations. Such ethnographic insights, and engagements with the intimacies of everyday life and the production of shared representations, are needed in this current moment so as to sharpen understandings of U.S. imperial formations as they are forged, resisted, celebrated, and lived around the world.

EMPIRE AND ETHNOGRAPHY

Despite their similarities in modern English, *empire* and *empiricism* are not closely related in an etymological sense. However, in terms of a social, intellectual, or political history, the two are bound tightly, and ethnography is thus, we hope, a disciplinary practice that might be put to use to confound the borders between social, intellectual, and political work without doing away with existing insights. Anthropology's relationship with empire dates to its earliest days as a discipline, when armchair anthropologists turned to reports and travelogues from colonial officials and informal agents such as missionaries, traders, and explorers. As it developed into a field-based science, anthropology relied heavily on relatively privileged, if often disaffected, access to colonial territories—Franz Boas among Native Americans, Bronisław Malinowski in the Trobriand Islands, E. E. Evans-Pritchard in the Sudan, Alfred Radcliffe-Brown in India and Kenya, Julian Steward in Puerto Rico, and Margaret Mead in American Samoa to name just a handful of well-known, pioneering fieldworkers. It is important to remember that these scholars did not necessarily see themselves as imperial actors any more than do scholars today who head to the field with a Fulbright grant or other government funding. Such fieldwork, and associated insights and forms of blindness, have been a cornerstone of the discipline since its inception, weathering paradigm shifts and providing a consistent ground for a discipline often inconsistent in other ways. In short, "being there" enabled and enables anthropologists to get at the quotidian, the lived, the vital, and, it has been argued forcefully, an elusive "real."

If, as social scientists, we are committed to pushing social ontologies and modern institutions severed from empire and disaggregated from one another back into a more global, albeit multiplex, field of analysis, then embodied, fieldwork-based attempts to disentangle naturalized evidentiary paradigms and truth claims would seem a powerful step. But in light of the well-developed literature on a "classical" European colonialism, one that has emphasized the extent to which colonists' most modern of social scientific methods served as key accessories to colonial expansion, this ethnography cannot be simply a resolution or panacea for the contradictions faced by anyone who analyzes empire today.[15] In this volume, then, we join others in working to decolonize anthropology, and we do so through a study of empire itself.[16]

The ethnographic turn enacted in this volume rests on recognizing that empire is a moving target and that this mobility is a prime source of its enduring yet oft-denied influence. Imperial formations are always polities of deferral, dislocation, and dispersion, but not always polities of denial.[17] Thus, one challenge involves thinking through and expanding collectively upon ways for uncovering—if this recourse to depth is really the correct metaphor for the problem at hand—that which is not apparent.[18] One strategy involves exploring the often contradictory matrices that gird historical junctures and the political rationalities that both structure and emerge from them.[19] Here Europe and its possessions, economies and politics, metropoles and peripheries, and empire and the nation-state emerge as what pass for qualitatively different entities in spite of their coconstruction.[20] One goal, then, is to make the historical sundering of empires' complementary parts more clearly analyzable in relation to mobile techniques of governance, exploitation, and even enjoyment and emotional identification.

Yet an emphasis on mobility, however descriptive of actually existing empire, seems also to require a certain temporal distance. How, we ask, does one make out movement when one is caught within that movement? Field-based ethnographic research on contemporary empire is not necessarily the same as mapping the shared logics of ostensibly competing agendas on the basis of work in colonial archives. But nor is it necessarily separate or separable from such tasks. One of our starting points is joining with E. E. Evans-Pritchard and his evocation of F. W. Maitland in asserting that anthropology must be historical, if it is to be anything.[21] No ethnography of contemporary empire can ignore the past or claims about its influence and ongoing production in relation to presentist concerns. But how anthropologists might build upon such productive openings is something still to be worked out.

Basic to the approach we seek to put into practice across this volume's chapters are issues of availability, appearance, and thus, at least implicitly, a "problem of presence" more typically ascribed to overarching, puzzling phenomena such as religious belief and its material instantiations.[22] While anthropologists have long defetishized, deconstructed, and denaturalized, it is clear that we continue to miss and misinterpret much that surrounds us, and much that we might otherwise make apparent. If empire is indeed about a blurring of boundaries that plays out alongside the determined policing of those borders, and thus involves, for example, the movements of capital and the machinations of capitalists, the love of families, the very epistemological formations brought to bear in its analysis, and the overlaps of differently conceived forms of value, how might an engaged ethnography keep up with or describe such shifts in scale and object?

Scholarship on U.S. empire, seemingly even more so than in many other areas of political analysis, makes up a literature in formation. Newly energized in the post-9/11 period of roiling exceptions that when examined closely are not necessarily novel, and with a president who in 2016 argued that his predecessor erred by not holding onto more of Iraq's oil, anthropologists have increasingly applied an imperial framework to work on and in the United States.[23] In so doing, they bring into dialogue peoples, places, and politics long considered independent of one other and subject to particular analytic frameworks indebted to more regional debates. We are not the first to make such connections. Indeed, one pivotal earlier moment was the late 1960s/early 1970s. Among a group of scholars calling attention to U.S. empire in that time was Vine Deloria. In *Custer Died for Your Sins: An Indian Manifesto* (1969), Deloria mocked President Johnson's promises to Southeast Asian allies in the Vietnam War, positing them as the latest version of centuries of broken treaties the U.S. government made with American Indian groups. Out of this key moment in linking identity, territory, and empire in relation to the politics of the present, scholarship expanded into formations such as the Black Atlantic or considerations of Aztlán.[24] Yet such redefinition of world regions and scholarly intervention was not always approached ethnographically, or via an imperial lens. More recently, however—in ethnic studies and cultural studies, in anthropology and sociology, in history and literature—frames for investigation have once again begun to congeal around empire through genealogies both shared and specific, such that we may now return in new ways to Deloria's prescient focus on imperial connections in the face of ongoing denial.

What new questions can we raise now about colonial experiences and exchanges, about citizenship and sovereignty, by apprehending empire as a political phenomenon and analytic framework that brings together ostensibly distinct topics and peoples? A central element in this move involves claiming U.S. empire historically as a colonizing force, as Alyosha Goldstein and a group of interdisciplinary scholars do in *Formations of United States Colonialism*.[25] Colonialism was not solely the province of European empires. Other imperial polities were colonial as well as imperial, including the United States of America.[26] A colony of the United States for almost fifty years, from 1898 through 1946, the Philippines now has both an imperial and postcolonial relationship with the United States of America.[27] The relationship is postcolonial in its well-worn routes to and from former metropole and colony, in a linking of sensibilities and practices, and in the sense that an end of some sort was reached in the relationship. And it is imperial in that the relationship continues, not as a sort of benevolent colonialism, but as a putatively friendly or generous form of assistance made manifest in numerous national obligations and expectations, most visibly the massive U.S. military presence in the Philippines. As Vernadette Vicuña Gonzalez argues, the post-9/11 period has involved the reterritorialization of the Philippines as "an American laboratory for technologies and techniques of surveillance, discipline, and war."[28] For Filipinos, the colonial period might be over, but the imperial continues. And this insight might do something to resituate our interpretations of Filipino President Rodrigo Duterte's recent brutal, nationalistic, and U.S.-DEA–snubbing shift in illegal drug policy.[29]

How might thinking of U.S. imperial *and* colonial formations alter contemporary approaches to belonging and political struggle for peoples of Native North America, Guam, Hawai'i, Puerto Rico, Samoa, and beyond, including most recently, Muslim immigrants to the United States?[30] Could such a cross-border and imperial perspective be brought to bear more fully on class formation and labor struggle in ways that augment understandings of the making of particular working classes?[31] Might this and other nascent strategies help social scientists, citizens, and policymakers think through experiences and histories that take shape around a U.S. military presence such as in Japan, Diego Garcia, Korea, the Philippines, Vietnam, Iraq, and so many other places around the world?[32] One intellectual and political move we make in this volume involves presenting scholarship from across a breadth of U.S. imperial formations—settler colonialism, overseas territories, communities throughout Latin America impacted by U.S. military and capitalist interventions, Cold War allies and enemies around the world and the post-imperial milieu they now experience, the many societies and territories around the world occupied by the U.S. military, and most recently, new forms of U.S. empire after 9/11. That we bring these together in one analytical move is especially important given the glaring omission of discussions of empire in related scholarship. Why has empire been so absent, in particular or even patterned ways, from our conversations?

Described by some as a phantom traveling in disguise, one of the many covers with which U.S. empire cloaked itself was decolonization.[33] Cold War politics, for example, married anticommunist rhetoric with new global and older, North American anti-imperialist discourses.[34] This period shelters forms of empire that boast most openly about its covert nature: CIA operations; innumerable unnamed political and military interventions, assassinations, and coups in corners of the globe far and wide; the development of nuclear power at home; and continuing from earlier periods, the cultivation of markets abroad; and certain nations or regions as "rent-capturing" or "nature-intensive" commodity producers.[35] Many such endeavors involve unofficial agents of empire who, as with European colonialism, may be

Christian missionaries, or other familiar figures of liberal humanism such as teachers, health professionals, or development workers.[36] Living in empire, after all, is not just something that happens elsewhere, but is rather something cultivated and normalized at home within the United States.[37] At the same time, this everyday life of empire provokes a questioning of the boundaries of the nation-form that mimics the uncertain yet palpable borders between individual subjects and the imperial nation-state.[38]

In moving to apprehend distributed imperial experiences, we are indebted to scholars who have led the way in raising questions via cases that challenge the conventions of the imperial register. We think of Amy Kaplan and Donald E. Pease's groundbreaking volume *Cultures of US Imperialism* (1993), of Fernando Coronil's persistent pressing on questions of capitalism and imperialism across the Americas, of Ann Stoler's provocative volume *Haunted by Empire* (2006), which set the predominantly European-focused colonial studies literature in dialogue with U.S. histories of empire, the Social Science Research Council's volume *Lessons of Empire: Imperial Histories and American Power*, historical sociologist Julian Go's work on thinking through colonized political culture in the Philippines and Puerto Rico, Greg Grandin's historicization of U.S. hegemony in relation to what he describes as a longstanding development of techniques of imperial control across Latin America in *Empire's Workshop: Latin America, the United States, and the Rise of the New Imperialism* (2006), and Alfred McCoy and Francisco Scarano's volume *Colonial Crucible: Empire in the Making of the Modern American State* (2009). We understand these works in dialogue with numerous other examples of novel approaches to empire ranging from legal studies to American studies, and on to a new roster of anthropological scholarship on militarism in the present.[39]

The above-mentioned works help lay out U.S. empire in its sprawl and its histories of denial. They thus provoke the question: What sort of empire is the North American variant? Is it even an empire? Or is this query, and its responses, yet another way of veiling the reach of imperial violence through a compartmentalization of terms and a dogged recourse to exceptionalisms?[40] Can we as ethnographers make powerful contributions to a phenomenon we cannot define? If so, how might we conduct such an investigation? And if not, shall we move to define it?

U.S. IMPERIAL FORMATIONS

There is no single modality of U.S. empire. That is, there is no unitary form or even genealogy of U.S. empire, but instead a series of chronological and coeval imperial formations. If we consider empires to be plural, and to rest on different series of moving and even contradictory parts, then U.S. empire is plural in the most simple of senses: it is composed of plural forms, strategies, justifications, and disguises. This is an empire in place, one in which settler colonialism obscures the very ground of imperial expansion in the form of the fifty states of the United States of America. It is an empire abroad, one in which territories and peoples are tethered to the metropole and suspensions of sovereignty mark indelibly the Native American communities directly and territorially incorporated into it. It is a military empire, claiming space and bodies and redefining territorial sovereignty in the name of democracy and freedom. In fact, imperial technologies cultivated over the centuries are familiar to students of empires, as well as democracies, across the globe. U.S. imperial formations drew, and continue to draw, on the spread of capitalism and Christianity, on truncated possibilities for citizenship, on historiographic rewrites of particular political moments, and on a clunky flexibility, not so much agile in form as adept in distraction, and thus skilled in redirecting narrative, attention, and desire. The United States is an empire still unfolding, with populations both colonial and imperial, in a world supposedly decolonized and postcolonial. Today's U.S. empire is neither singular nor past, but instead persists, continuing to incorporate new peoples and practices while leaving behind others, in ruins.

Our volume's organizational logic is both chronological and thematic, designed to establish the diffuse and discrete parts of U.S. empire as imperial and linked. This is thus an exercise in making U.S. empire recognizable and easy to think, albeit in new ways. We start with "Settlement, Sentiment, Sovereignty," and essays on issues of settler colonialism, new indigenous demands, and the empire that will not go away. From here we move to "Colonialism by Any Other Name" and discussions of the territories of 1898 of the Philippines, Puerto Rico, and Samoa. Colonial in another era, these polities and their residents remain imperial, though not directly incorporated into the United States as was Hawai'i.

War, Christianity, and capitalism have been central to U.S. imperial formations from the beginning. Our next section, "Temporality, Proximity, Dispersion," explores these and other technologies of imperialism with essays on mining in South America, Korean Christian proselytization in the Muslim world, Cold War empire, and time as an imperial standard. Making the world safe for U.S. corporate and government interests is the job of the military. It is a job it has long done without apology, and yet with sometimes devastating repercussions at home and abroad. The next section, "Military Promises," takes an ethnographic approach to military empire, including the semantics and wordplay involved in military operations and service. "Residue, Rumors, Remnants" next brings us to questions of an aftermath of empire that is not quite over, via contemporary explorations of the Korean War, CIA involvement in the Tibetan resistance movement, the Iran-Contra War, and persistent U.S. interventions in Latin America. The final section is "9/11, the War on Terror, and the Return of Empire," in which we directly confront subjects newly recognized as imperial: Muslim youth, Cambodian refugees, working-class white hunters in New Jersey, and political prisoners in the Global War on Terror. From settler colonialism to Guantánamo, the volume covers the pliant reach of U.S. empire, and does so through a methodological and theoretical commitment to ethnography demonstrated in each of its chapters.

Settlement, Sentiment, Sovereignty

Living within empire is not a singular experience. Of all North American peoples, however, indigenous peoples of what is now the United States have lived with the longest duration and closest proximity to U.S. empire. What are the effects of this duration and proximity? For the Osage, Jean Dennison shows that imperial authority works through both structural and affective forces. Osage modes of relations and governance are entangled with imperial ones in ways that foreclose alternative forms and futures. Writing a Constitution, managing a mineral estate trust, trusting in the familiar, determining who is and is not Osage, and even what such a determination means, all reverberate with a fear cultivated over generations. This is a fear, Dennison claims, that is deeply rooted through domestication and discipline in which the language available to speak back to empire shifts over time. Claims to sovereignty return, and rights discourse is appropriated by colonizers, as J. Kēhaulani Kauanui demonstrates in the case of Hawaiʻi. There, New Right activists work in racist ways against the Hawaiian sovereignty movement, deploying a form of what Kauanui, building on the work of Renato Rosaldo, calls "imperial resentment." What drives resentment among these conservative activists, and what does that resentment perform in relation to national politics? Discourses of U.S. exceptionalism herald not only the desirability of association with the United States, but also a long-standing refusal to see Hawaiʻi as a "site of ongoing colonial and racial domination." Instead, Hawaiʻi appears as "part of" the United States, a designation which dismisses the imperial in favor of the shared and the codified. It is, after all, a right.

Nonetheless, the rights of settler societies are not those of indigenous societies. Plowing through existing boundaries and communities, rewriting a history of conquest as one of discovery, and declaring an imperial society to be one of immigrants—these are the rights of settlers. This is true in both Canada and the United States of America, as experienced by the Kahnawake Mohawk and other peoples whose indigenous lands precede imperial boundaries. Building in part on Patrick Wolfe's scholarship, and joining Kauanui in refusing to reduce indigenous difference to a racial logic, Audra Simpson contends that the operations and secrets of dispossession that are part of settler colonialism are persistent structures, not onetime events. The imperial work of keeping indigenous sovereignty in the past tense is ongoing, and is troubled by indigenous peoples' insistence in the present that they are indigenous and not just Canadian or American. As Simpson shows from the standoff at Oka to the residential schools' sexual abuse scandal to the need to perform forgiveness in the face of imperial apology, this is life lived through an "idiom of pain" that rejects the suggestion that the forms of settlement and attendant political technologies that have produced the United States present liberal, representation-based resolutions to historical violence.

Colonialism by Any Other Name

Pain is often at the heart of empire. If colonialism creates certain sorts of subjects, colonial discourses pathologize them in certain ways—the lazy, indolent native, for example, or ideas of poverty, lack of ambition, and addiction. In the case of colonialism denied, as Adriana Garriga-López argues for Puerto Rico, drug addiction is a part of the island's colonial history. This is a history not located only on the island, but also in the well-worn routes connecting Puerto Rico to the U.S. East Coast and its illegal as well as corporate-led drug markets. Yet an ability to narrate this history, as well as possibilities for independence, is not held back by addiction. It is not necessarily drugs in one's system that shut down narrative coherence, but the indeterminacy of a status neither independent nor fully incorporated. In this light, Garriga-López asks whether numbness to empire might be a strategy of resistance. What possibilities exist for Puerto Ricans to engage the political in the neither foreign nor domestic space of the "oldest colony in the world"? Ambivalence, a register found not only in addiction, might be one available strategy.

Waiting is a well-honed practice of imperial subjects. Waiting for change, waiting for something better, waiting for independence. As an element of decolonial praxis, Melissa Rosario suggests that at times Puerto Rican activists locate freedom in the apparent banality of waiting, developing anti-imperialist politics through individual autonomy and a valorization of process as a critique of expected forms of resistance. In the case of activists squatting on a beach slated for private ownership, activism "requires comfort with not-knowing, and not-deciding what the solution may be before arriving." This is a protest composed not out of, but in the experience of the banal, of still-undetermined everyday life in a beachside camp. Here, squatting in empire takes form as a passage that opens up an ambivalent but persistent call to reclaim territory and time. Such structures of feeling are found across U.S. territories. American Samoa, for example, shares issues of deferred possibilities and the particular pains of becoming certain sorts of subjects of U.S. empire.

What does empire look and feel like in "American" Samoa? Fa'anofo Lisaclaire Uperesa contends that neither macroanalyses nor surface-level perspectives reveal "how empire is sustained in and through nonstate activities and micropractices of the body." Turning to an ethnography of football, she asks how capitalism and colonialism collude to produce an unexpected range of imperial figures in the form of football coaches and clinics. Training for empire might be supported by different interests—Christian, humanitarian, community—all maneuvering within a tight, but never simple, space of imperialism. Samoans serve empire on the football field, or by performing exceptionalism through a cultivation of a certain type of masculine body. In the postcolonial Philippines, imperial service is performed through similarly exceptional skills, in this case, the ability to speak English in a U.S.-friendly, and thus recognizable, affective register. In fact, Jan Padios argues that some seven decades after the end of direct U.S. rule in the Philippines, Filipinos are "still suspended . . . within U.S. imperialism." Call center labor epitomizes this continuing relationship as desired qualities such as a certain accent or an ability to perform compassion are linked to both modern Americana *and* the ability to be oneself, to be Filipino. The creativity and exceptionalism—and thus, strangely enough, the recognizability—of the Filipino subject or the Samoan one or the Puerto Rican one "underwrites U.S. imperialism" in an important way, and has since at least 1898.

Temporality, Proximity, Dispersion

The technologies of empire are no surprise: naming, mapping, converting, conquering, extracting, rewriting, recalibrating. They are not new, but instead shared and inherited across empires, generated in moments of comparison and competition within and across imperial formations. For example, U.S. empire and its reach stretch through multinational corporations, across the Americas, to Mexico and Central America, and on to Suriname and Maroon communities. There, fieldwork among the descendants of escaped slaves recognized as indigenous peoples of the Amazon by both the Dutch colonial state and the United Nations today permits Olívia Maria Gomes da Cunha to write an ethnographic history of Ndyuka Maroons in Moengo, Suriname, as a formation drawn into, and yet capable of mobilizing in a very different vein, colonial activities as well as U.S. imperial history. Maroons drawn originally to Moengo by Dutch and U.S. bauxite mining, like their descendants today, conceptualized the arrival from afar of an extractive industry not as a circumscribed event, but as part of their own, ongoing reconfigurations of landscape, life, and spirits. Reflecting on such divergent ontologies, Gomes da Cunha's ethnographic vantage point mitigates against both a facile enrollment of Maroon histories into an ostensibly larger, global history of empire and an anthropological erection of a "radical opposition between the geometric, disciplinary, and colonial model of Moengo and the spatiotemporal configurations of place in which spirits, kin, non-kin, and other agents dialogue with each other." Even now, so many years later, the territorializations that accompany and fill in empire in Suriname are not just about geography or spatial relations. Instead, Gomes da Cunha contends, they remain a sanction as well as an occupation of agency and of possible modes of existence and enunciation that resist the totality of U.S. empire.

Imperial efforts to shape and order populations are often undertaken by imperial proxies, such as influential capitalists. Yet of the many individuals and groups who have claimed to act on behalf of U.S. and European empires, one of the most persistent are Christian missionaries. But are all missionaries acting as imperial proxies? Ju Hui Judy Han contends that U.S. empire serves as catalyst for Korean evangelical Christianity via a Cold War connection that grounds a certain sort of Korean Christian international vision. This is not just about religion. Han argues instead that the concept of "proxy" falls short in that Korean evangelicals are not seeking solely to carry Christianity to new domains in a sort of postimperial service to U.S. expansion. Instead, Korean Christians' goals extend to their own "neocolonial or subimperial ambitions." These goals include geopolitical reach, capitalist gain, humanitarian service, and a proselytizing heavily directed against Islam. As such, a twenty-first-century collusion between evangelical Christianity and U.S. imperialism offers a wide-angle lens for considering the spaces opened for an at times surprising array of imperial actors. Korean religious designs provide an especially important node for considering such imperial historicity, as well as the almost mythic accounts of good, evil, and global redemption that seemingly do so much to motivate action.

Was the Cold War imperial? Occupying historically the space of European decolonization and post–World War II realignment, the Cold War is commonly portrayed as a battle between two great powers—the USA and the USSR. According to Heonik Kwon, such a portrayal misses two key components: the plural and the global. Kwon identities these as (1) local-level, ethnographic experiences of the Cold War rather than just political or historical narratives and (2) experiences of the Cold War beyond Europe. His resultant reassessment of the Cold War through ancestor worship rituals in both Korea and Vietnam aims to provide an ethnographic rendering of U.S. empire, and to raise questions about the social orders, not only the geopolitical ones, of the

Cold War then and now. Kwon's optic gathers together the imperial and the postcolonial in order to consider local efforts "to come to terms with the ruins and enduring wounds" of U.S. empire during the Cold War.

The "post" to U.S. empire is coterminous with the imperial. In an example of the sorts of braidings that, contradictorily, so often accompany moments of imperial aphasia, many of the chapters in this volume suggest that temporal periods may be inhabited simultaneously. Perhaps unsurprisingly, one domain in which contests over empires' temporalities come to the fore is time itself, or more specifically, the setting of "standard" time by means of an international project dominated by the United States via satellites, GPS, and computer networks and examined ethnographically by Kevin Birth. Birth argues that the politics of actual time reveal important facets of the scientific infrastructure of contemporary U.S. empire. Aligning his research among U.S. government scientists with Prasenjit Duara's notion of a "new imperialism" in today's historical moment, Birth finds ethnographic evidence of complicity and coordination, as well as political divergences, in the science underlying U.S. approaches to the time standards so important to satellite, and thus financial as well as missile and cellular, technologies. The technologies of empire, then, are as important as the institutions; the one requires the other.

Military Promises

The U.S. empire is a military empire. Has there ever been a time this was not so? From the earliest days of settler colonialism on to the concrete lines and video cameras of Guantánamo Bay Detention Camp today, this militarism has taken different forms. David Vine's work illustrates how, and with what local effects, an extensive network of military bases grounds U.S. empire. This territorial model is not so much a new structure as a return to an earlier one, including that used by earlier European empires. In light of the spiraling productivity of never-implemented colonial blueprints, of colonizing schemes gone array, and of impossible attempts to separate out people and places, none of this can be taken as given: not the logics of bases such as Diego Garcia, nor the experiences of displaced and indigenous peoples such as the Chagossians, nor the contradictions of the U.S. government officials involved in administering and planning such bases. A politics of concealment and linguistic sleight of hand often accompanies U.S. military bases overseas. In Manta, Ecuador, Erin Fitz-Henry was repeatedly told "there is no U.S. military base in Manta." In fact, "legally" there was no base in Manta, since the United States rented space from the Ecuadorian military. As Fitz-Henry argues, this was strategic ambiguity at work, a geopolitical "interpretive gap exploited by agents of empire." In spite of the U.S. troops and material, there was no U.S. military base on Ecuador's north coast. Such denial and wordplay have purchase in imperial politics and military theaters.

What sort of institution is the military? One might approach the U.S. military ethnographically as an institution of "hierarchy, coercion, and obedience" in which an ironic rhetoric of choice also exists. This involves the "choice" to join, as well as the choice to leave and to choose dissent. Matthew Gutmann and Catherine Lutz argue that ideas of choice saturate U.S. discourses of citizenship, empire, and masculinity, and these play an important role in assigning particular values to military "service" to the nation, and the world. Why then, they ask, do U.S. soldiers abandon the military? What sort of moral and political crises and epiphanies arise for these lowest-level agents of the imperial military missions? The repercussions for some of the soldiers who choose to step away from empire involve a type of imperial debris, a state of cast-off being and, at times, uncanny insights.[41]

Residue, Rumors, Remnants

Militarized ecologies are an intrinsic, and yet thoroughly hybridized, part of empire.[42] Generative and destructive at the same time, war wreaks havoc on the natural landscape, and empire provides a particular sort of narrative—and even presence—that accompanies these destructive processes. Drawing on the work of Rob Nixon, Eleana Kim contends that the Demilitarized Zone, or DMZ, between the Koreas is still "armed and dangerous" due to the just barely concealed presence of landmines. These lie as a material token of U.S. imperial power, and work unexpectedly to keep the peace through their "material and affective traces." Even in its ruins, then, imperial power is efficacious, felt and feared, and generative of a range of responses including from the ethnographer. Ruined landscapes are also human ones.

Ruins offer new opportunities for action. In 1959, some Tibetans escaped the invasion and colonization of their country by Mao Zedong's People's Republic of China, fleeing to India, where they established a refugee community under the leadership of the Dalai Lama. Different groups mobilized to provide aid to these new refugees, including the CIA. Carole McGranahan explores the covert side of empire in assessing sympathy and sincerity in two CIA-Tibet operations: (1) a homegrown citizens' army that fought against the Chinese People's Liberation Army with help from the CIA, including secret training in Colorado, and (2) the American Emergency Committee for Tibetan Refugees, a CIA front operation that appeared publicly as a legitimate aid group. We cannot presume to know or to dismiss the sentiments involved in such covert humanitarianism, nor can we assign agency only to the CIA.

Instead, McGranahan argues, we need to consider how although humanitarianism "provides cover for empire," the covert is a space that is deeply human.

"What kinds of life are possible under imperial conditions? And whose knowledge of that life counts?" Joe Bryan asks such questions in the case of Miskito former soldiers supported and then discarded by the United States during the Contra War in late twentieth-century Nicaragua. Miskito Indians are not just "indigenous peoples," as they are often named. They are also imperial subjects who recognize and respond to the geohistorical *and* discursive power of U.S. empire, albeit from a position of marginalization and abandonment that nonetheless takes very different forms in relation to distinct locations within, or at what pass for the edges of, U.S. empire. Life in the space of imperial discard and disregard on Nicaragua's Atlantic coast thus involves continuing efforts to activate imperial connections, even those that appear fleeting and out of reach. Such encounters with empire in the field, especially when an ethnographer is ostensibly researching something else, have become an important trope within a number of recent studies around the world. The discursive power inherent in renaming empire as anything other than *empire* here becomes relatively more important, as do the secrets and denials that have long supported U.S. imperial formations. The realization that "conspiracy disrupts this discursive economy" propels Bryan into an ethnographic account that "does not explain imperialism so much as provide pause for reflection on how knowledge of it adheres to a discursive economy that sets limits on whose knowledge counts."

What, then, if one cannot visualize empire? In his research on Brazil's spaceport and the circulation of accusations and disavowals of empire, Sean T. Mitchell explains that U.S. empire did not have a clear presence in his ethnographic data. In an argument reminiscent of Peter Redfield's focus on scale and visibility in his ethnography of French rocket bases in French Guiana, Mitchell suggests that U.S. empire shape-shifted and came to impact unexpected processes and relations in hard-to-trace manners.[43] Specifically, U.S. imperial practices and discourses helped shape a nationalist and technocratic or military-linked paranoia about United States interference and the racial politics of Afro-Brazilian mobilization around the spaceport. Drawing on the work of Michel-Rolph Trouillot, Mitchell argues that postcolonial societies remain under the discipline of foreign entities in ways that ethnography helps us perceive as not just localized experiences, but as part of broader global epistemic conditions. In spite of, or perhaps due in part to its motility, the imperial remains a structural feature of the contemporary world system. As true of this is of places and peoples incorporated into the imperial domain outside of the United States, it also remains true in the metropole.

9/11, the War on Terror, and the Return of Empire

The events of 9/11 changed—or rendered more easily apparent—much about social power in the United States, perhaps more so for Muslim Americans than for any other group. How do Muslim youth experience everyday life in this political moment? What would it mean to put imperialism and its apperception, rather than ethnicity or religion, at the center of the story of Muslims in the contemporary United States? Drawing on ethnographic research in Silicon Valley, which is now more timely than ever, Sunaina Maira shows that Islamophobia, racism, and imperial violence at home and abroad are visible, tangible components of the lives of Muslim youth. This is not solely about being a target of empire, but also of building alliances within and against certain facets of empire. Maira argues that possibilities for political expression by Muslim youth in the United States take form around questions of empire, especially imperial intervention abroad. As such they exceed well established discourses of liberal "tolerance" and diversity that shape, as well as contain, cross-racial and interfaith affiliations. Such moments of excess beg for ethnographic analysis, for a dedication to making apparent the conjuncture of lived experience and cultural logics and political realities.[44] Here ethnography would seem to have the potential to disrupt history, to open up national amnesias about past and not-quite-past moments and the imperial subjects created within them.

Immigrants and refugees are two types of subjects produced in and by empire. Soo Ah Kwon argues that Cambodian refugees in the San Francisco Bay Area, when disciplined into a familiar imperial mode of gratitude, occupy a precarious sort of deportable citizenship. But community efforts to halt deportations connect Cambodian youth activists with other immigration activists revealing the broader scope of U.S. empire and tie Southeast Asians to the political struggles of Central Americans and others deemed "undesirable." The imperial heartland is no easier a space to reside in than its fringes and, indeed, one of the projects of the present volume is to peer into imperial folds rather than define cores and peripheries. Through an example of how such doublings take form, Kwon documents how imperial statecraft is implicated not only in deportation regimes in the United States, but also in "producing the contexts of violence from which Southeast Asian refugees fled in the first instance."

Soldiers and the nightly news bring war home with them too, from Vietnam and the Gulf, and from Iraq and Afghanistan. In this contemporary period, how does empire arise as a way of life in those parts of the United States usually not approached as imperial? In his research on human-animal relations among hunters of white-tail deer in New Jersey, John Collins considers how an emotional ecology tied tightly to empire permeates the changes taking place as different classes mark land in ways that halt the efforts of the others not just to hunt, or to gather berries or hike, but also to be good people in the ways they have been trained and forced by necessity to be, for so long. “It'll be all right,” a grandfather tells his grandson, easing the blow of a certain sort of pain. But, as Collins notes, “in an imperial United States” such an attempt at “making things ‘all right,’ or livable, rests on dislocations of violence.” Violences of history, and violences of class, can be hard to transcend. Serving one's country, helping the less fortunate, doing good, making things right: these are not just fantasies or legitimating props put forth by people invested in that which oppresses them, but moral discourses cultivated through imperial sentiments and even potentially violent practices at home and abroad. Such hybrid and untrustworthy but nonetheless influential sentiments developed through violent and often unwanted juxtapositions—on the battlefield, in the news media, and in the space from forest to food bank—mark a nation in which many “us” and “them” groups coexist. This is part of knowing, being, and being political in a contemporary United States in which resentment too often seems to replace engagement. In response, Collins follows the hunting of deer and the exchange of meat in order to reveal how denials of codependence, and thus denials of a coconstruction of ethics and environments by people who often configure themselves as standing on opposite sides of the hunt, are themselves effects of imperial violence, especially when they promise a neat redemption from that violence.

Claiming to be singular, to be exceptional, and then to produce such exceptions, has long been part of imperial formations from England to China to the United States and beyond.[45] As academics and citizens, we seem to know this. Yet we are still learning the ways in which such exceptions are forged anew in the twenty-first century through new sorts of extraterritorial arrangements and extralegal statuses. Drawing on his research with “out of place Muslims” in Bosnia-Herzegovina, Darryl Li suggests that plural and external conceptions of sovereignty are at work in the Global War on Terror that “exceed” current anthropological theory. Given that the Global War on Terror is both everywhere and nowhere, relying on logics of circulation in moving other countries' citizens through the well-traveled carceral routes of the post-9/11 world, U.S. “empire mobilizes multiple state sovereignties as a way of structuring and mediating unequal power relations.” Imperial subjects recognized such connections and networks early on, without waiting for theorists to catch up with them. Meeting with Abu Hamza, a detainee at the Reception Centre for Irregular Migrants outside of Sarajevo, Li finds him dressed in a bright orange *jalabiyya*, reminiscent of the orange jumpsuits prisoners at Guantánamo wear, and sporting a baseball cap with BOSNATANAMO inscribed upon it. Forcibly taken from the Spanish, Guantánamo Bay became part of U.S. empire in 1898 and now hosts Muslim and other imperial prisoners in its new post-9/11 guise as GTMO. This is one return of empire that illustrates, as part of a broad historical arc, how analysis of circulation may bring into clearer view the workings of the exception, and thus the inadequacy of that exception for explaining sovereignty in an imperial system in which power is so often exercised informally, and through third-party actors.

Finally, we close the volume with an afterword—Ann Laura Stoler in conversation with Carole McGranahan on disassemblage in rethinking U.S. imperial formations. How, asks Stoler, has the delinking of territories, peoples, and practices come to define U.S. empire? Taking disassemblage as an object of inquiry reveals the relational histories that gird imperial politics. We see this for example in practices of proxy and surrogate colonialism, in the ways histories of Israel and Palestine have and have not been written, and in the framings of histories of racism and slavery in relation to capitalism but not necessarily to empire. Instead, Stoler suggests, "naming those things we've been educated not to see allows us to get at the tensions of certain moments." Naming directly challenges denial, those denials of imperial actors as well as those of scholars, including our own expectations of what empire is and does.

CONTINGENCY AND CONCLUSION: A CAUTION

In setting out the problems and questions above, we have suggested not simply the importance of understanding empire, but the need to expand what counts as empire. Yet this involves certain dangers. Principal among these is a repetition of an earlier moment in which anthropological knowledge about putative Others was understood as but a means of improving the lives and perspectives of those within the metropole. While a duplication of such a perspective seems unlikely, or at least undesirable, in studying U.S. empire we do risk folding unrelated or particular struggles into an umbrella that is already too powerful, if still relatively undertheorized and understudied (at least in terms of direct study). But this points to some of the challenges at hand: If, as historian Greg Grandin posits, struggles in Latin America served to develop strategies later deployed by the United States elsewhere in the world, including at home, then how does one begin to understand such contacts and confrontations as anything but components of U.S. empire?[46] Here our study of empire touches upon familiar concerns enunciated in subaltern studies' critiques of colonial power in that, just as writing histories that are more than particular instantiations of a European, Christian, universal history presents a new series of conundrums, so too does expanding what counts as empire without adding to the power of imperial formations.[47] This is a fear, and a challenge, that sticks with all contributors to this volume as we consider the details of, and possibilities brought forth by, an expanded ethnography of empire.

NOTES

1 Chang, *The Color of the Land*; Kaplan, "Left Alone with America." We emphasize, however, that the widespread imperial myopia we associate here with U.S. claims about the United States is often punctured by historical, and even popular, analyses from different world regions, especially Latin America. See, for example, Escobar, "Beyond the Third World."

2 Stoler, *Haunted by Empire.*

3 Said, *Orientalism.* For an influential example of pioneering anthropological engagements, see especially Asad, *Anthropology and the Colonial Encounter.*

4 Dirks, *Colonialism and Culture*; Richard Price, *The Convict and the Colonel*; Redfield, *Space in the Tropics*; Stoler, *Race and the Education of Desire*; and Stoler, *Carnal Knowledge and Imperial Power.*

5 Cohn, *An Anthropologist among the Historians and Other Essays*; Cohn, *Colonialism and Its Forms of Knowledge*; Comaroff and Comaroff, *Ethnography and the Historical Imagination*; Dirks, *Colonialism and Culture*; Etienne and Leacock, *Women and Colonization*; Stoler, "Rethinking Colonial Categories"; Stoler, "Sexual Affronts and Racial Frontiers"; Taussig, "Culture of Terror—Space of Death"; Trouillot, *Silencing the Past.*

6 Foucault, *The Archaeology of Knowledge*; Stoler, "On Degrees of Imperial Sovereignty"; Stoler and Bond, "Refractions off Empire." On empire and temporality, see especially Wilder, *Freedom Time*; Scott, *Conscripts of Modernity* and *Omens of Adversity*; as well as Stoler, "The Rot Remains."

7 Diamond et al., "Anthropologists Speak Out on Nuclear Disarmament"; Frese and Harrell, *Anthropology and the United States Military*; Gusterson, "Anthropology and Militarism," "Project Minerva and the Militarization of Anthropology"; Gough, "Anthropology and Imperialism," "New Proposals for Anthropologists," "'Anthropology and Imperialism' Revisited"; Lucas Jr., *Anthropologists in Arms*; McFate, "Anthropology and Counterinsurgency"; Nader, "The Phantom Factor"; David H. Price, *Cold War Anthropology* and "Interlopers and Invited Guests"; Weltfish, "Racialism, Colonialism, and World Peace." For sociology, see Steinmetz, *Sociology and Empire.*

8 On the Cold War and Korea, see especially David H. Price, *Threatening Anthropology*; and Wax, *Anthropology at the Dawn of the Cold War.* Especially salient works related to the Vietnam War are Berreman, "Is Anthropology Alive?"; Sahlins, "The Destruction of Conscience in Vietnam"; and Wakin, *Anthropology Goes to War.* For more recent conflicts, ranging from Grenada to Iraq and Afghanistan, see especially

Gonzalez, *Anthropologists in the Public Sphere* and *American Counterinsurgency*; Network of Concerned Anthropologists, *The Counter-Counterinsurgency Manual*; and Sluka, "Curiouser and Curiouser."

9 Lutz, "Empire Is in the Details."

10 On U.S. geography and its imperial entanglements, see especially N. Smith, *American Empire.*

11 Rabinow et al., *Designs for an Anthropology of the Contemporary.*

12 Stoler, "Developing Historical Negatives."

13 Stoler, "Developing Historical Negatives."

14 Stoler, *Duress*; Williams, *Empire as a Way of Life.*

15 Asad, *Anthropology and the Colonial Encounter*; Comaroff and Comaroff, *Ethnography and the Historical Imagination*; Dirks, *Colonialism and Culture*; Cooper and Stoler, *Tensions of Empire.*

16 Harrison, *Decolonizing Anthropology.*

17 Stoler and McGranahan, "Introduction: Refiguring Imperial Terrains."

18 On the seductiveness, and importance to modern politics, of the representation of knowledge production as a hermeneutics of depth, see Collins, *Revolt of the Saints.*

19 D. Nelson, *Reckoning*; Stoler, *Race and the Education of Desire*; Stoler, *Haunted by Empire*; Stoler, "On Degrees of Imperial Sovereignty"; Wilder, *The French Imperial Nation-State.*

20 Adelman, *Sovereignty and Revolution in the Iberian Atlantic*; Coronil, "Beyond Occidentalism"; Wilder, *Freedom Time.*

21 Evans-Pritchard, "Social Anthropology."

22 Engelke, *A Problem of Presence*; Richard Price, *Travels with Tooy.*

23 Maskovsky and Susser, "Introduction: Rethinking America."

24 Influential works that mark and add to such redefinition of scholarly interests, political mobilization, and geographic areas include Anaya and Lomelli, *Aztlán*; and Gilroy, *Black Atlantic.*

25 A. Goldstein, *Formations of United States Colonialism.*

26 Stoler, McGranahan, and Perdue, *Imperial Formations.*

27 On the Philippines and U.S. imperialism, see Anderson, *Colonial Pathologies*; Choy, *Empire of Care*; David, "The Sexual Fields of Empire"; Espiritu, *Homeward Bound*; Go and Foster, *The American Colonial State in the Philippines*; Kramer, *The Blood of Government*; Manalansan, *Global Divas*; Rafael, *White Love*, "Translation, American English, and the National Insecurities of Empire," and "Translation in Wartime"; Rosaldo, "Imperialist Nostalgia"; Tadiar, *Fantasy-Production* and *Things Fall Away.*

28 V. Gonzalez, *Securing Paradise*, 219.

29 For a critical history of the importance to U.S. empire of efforts to control flows of illegal drugs, see Reiss, *We Sell Drugs.*

30 On colonialism and native peoples of North America, see especially Byrd, *The Transit of Empire*; Cattelino, *High Stakes* and "Anthropologies of the United States"; Dennison, *Colonial Entanglement*; A. Simpson, *Mohawk Interruptus*. Diaz, "Deliberating 'Liberation Day,'" is a fascinating analysis of politics in Guam, and Imada, *Aloha America*, and Kauanui, *Hawaiian Blood* and "Colonialism in Equality," offer

important contributions in relation to the United States' fiftieth state. Meanwhile, Derby, "Imperial Secrets," and Silver, "'Then I Do What I Want,'" offer critical perspectives on Puerto Rico as a territory, while Salesa, "Samoa's Half-Castes and Some Frontiers of Comparison," extends a complementary analysis to American Samoa. For valuable perspectives on issues faced by Muslim and Arab Americans, see especially Abraham, Howell, and Shryock, *Arab Detroit 9/11*; Maira, "Belly Dancing, Arab-Face, Orientalist Feminism, and U.S. Empire" and *Missing*; Mamdani, "Good Muslim, Bad Muslim"; Rana, *Terrifying Muslims*; Shryock, "Cracking Down on Diaspora"; and Shryock and Howell, "New Images of Arab Detroit."

31 Chomsky, *Linked Labor Histories*; Rodney, *A History of the Guyanese Working People*.

32 For Japan, Frühstück, *Uneasy Warriors*; Inoue, *Okinawa and the U.S. Military*; and C. Nelson, *Dancing with the Dead*. On Diego Garcia, see Vine, *Island of Shame*. For Korea, Höhn and Moon, *Over There*; J. Lee, *Service Economies*; and Oppenheim, "On the Locations of Korean War and Cold War Anthropology." For Vietnam, Espiritu, *Body Counts*; Kwon, *After the Massacre* and *Ghosts of War in Vietnam*; and Schwenkel, "Recombinant History" and "From John McCain to Abu Ghraib." Gutmann and Lutz, *Breaking Ranks*, deals with the trauma and the traumatic history of more recent conflicts in Iraq.

33 Ho, "Empire through Diasporic Eyes"; Stoler, *Haunted by Empire*.

34 Louis and Robinson, "The Imperialism of Decolonization"; McGranahan, "Empire Out-of-Bounds."

35 On interventions, Gill, *The School of the Americas*; and McGranahan, *Arrested Histories* and "Truth, Fear, and Lies." On nuclear development, Gusterson, *Nuclear Rites*; and Masco, *The Theater of Operations* and *The Nuclear Borderlands*. Mitman and Erickson, on markets, "Latex and Blood." On ground rent, oil, the Venezuelan nation-state, and imperial inequality, Coronil, *The Magical State* and "Towards a Critique of Globalcentrism."

36 Collins, "'But What if I Should Need to Defecate in *Your* Neighborhood, Madame?'"; Cueto, *Cold War, Deadly Fevers*; J. Han, "Missionary"; McAlister, "What Is Your Heart For?"

37 Feldman, "On Cultural Anaesthesia," "Securocratic Wars of Public Safety"; Fosher, *Under Construction*; Friedman, *Covert Capital*; E. Kim, *Adopted Territory*; Lutz, *Homefront*; Nugent, "Knowledge and Empire"; Wainwright, *Geopiracy*.

38 Fanon, *A Dying Colonialism* and *Black Skin, White Masks*.

39 See Burnett and Marshall, *Foreign in a Domestic Sense* in relation to critical legal studies. For American studies as a discipline, some of the more helpful, recent works include Campomanes, "New Formations of Asian American Studies and the Question of U.S. Imperialism"; Fujitani, White, and Yoneyama, *Perilous Memories*; J. Kim, *Ends of Empire*; Rafael, "Translation, American English, and the National Insecurities of Empire"; and Shigematsu and Camacho, *Militarized Currents*. And, finally, on militarization, see especially Borneman, "Responsibility after Military Intervention"; Forte, *The New Imperialism*, vol. 1; Kelly et al., *Anthropology and Global Counterinsurgency*; Kosek, "Ecologies of Empire"; Lutz, "Making War at Home in the United States" and *The Bases of Empire*; and Robben, *Iraq at a Distance*.

40 Stoler, *Haunted by Empire* and "On Degrees of Imperial Sovereignty."
41 See Stoler, "Imperial Debris," and the collected essays in Stoler, *Imperial Debris*.
42 Kosek, "Ecologies of Empire."
43 Redfield, *Space in the Tropics*.
44 Da Col and Graeber, "Foreword."
45 Stoler and McGranahan, "Introduction: Refiguring Imperial Terrain."
46 Grandin, *The Last Colonial Massacre* and *Empire's Workshop*.
47 Guha and Spivak, *Selected Subaltern Studies*.

I

Settlement, Sentiment, Sovereignty

01 The "Affects" of Empire

(Dis)trust among Osage Annuitants

JEAN DENNISON

Empires take shape through a series of entanglements. These ties manifest as strategic policies, premeditated institutions, and lingering affective flows that connect peoples, senses of materiality, and polities in irreducible and irreconcilable ways. The heterogeneous emotions generated by living within empire both mark and perpetuate the unequal power dynamics at play across the globe. Such affective linkages, while far less traceable than the policies and institutions that scholars usually refer to as imperialism, are no less powerful in giving empire authority.[1] As a result, we must understand empire not only as a power structure constituted through governmental policies and planned wars, but also as an entity kept in place by emotional disruptions.

Given both the duration and proximity of their experiences with the empire of the United States, Native nations provide particularly keen insights into the nature of such experiences.[2] Using the Osage Nation as a lens, this chapter demonstrates how the affective processes of empire are at work in the space of settler colonialism in the twenty-first century. Patrick Wolfe describes this process of settler colonialism as "an inclusive, land centered project that coordinates a comprehensive range of agencies, from the metropolitan centre to the frontier encampment, with a view to eliminating Indigenous societies."[3] Elimination, however, is just one of the many strategies at work within empire building that operate to redirect bodies, emotions, processes, structures, and laws. Within empire, affective flows are often directed toward the construction of a particular entity as central, federal, and ubiquitous.

Specifically, this chapter demonstrates how empire fosters a deep-seated pessimism about what change will bring, leading some Osages to trust in the current status quo, no matter how problematic it may be. Nowhere were such concerns more evident than in the 2006 Osage Nation constitutional discussions about the Osage Mineral Estate Trust. U.S. Code Title 25 defines the Osage Mineral Estate as "any right, title, or interest in any oil, gas, coal, or other mineral held by the United States in trust for the benefit of the Osage Tribe of Indians under section 3 of the Osage Tribe Allotment Act." This notion of a trust relationship between the U.S. government and American Indian nations is a particularly powerful entanglement of empire, worthy of further interrogation. It signals the way in which the government of the United States has positioned itself as "protector" of American Indian nations even as it is often their worst enemy.[4]

My central contention is that the imperial legacy of failed trusteeship creates distrust well beyond its source. The Osage Mineral Estate Trust has generated a legacy of cynicism so deep that when the colonial mandate for full U.S. control is removed, some Osages question the wisdom of increased Osage control. Trust, then, is more than a federal policy; it is an affective cord that works to bind an empire together. Signaling this dual movement of entrenching American authority and inculcating cynicism throughout indigenous governance, I will investigate how *(dis)trust* manifests within Osage politics in the twenty-first century. (Dis)trust thus signals not only how the federal government has continually failed its trust responsibility, but also how it has fostered wider pessimism, all the while maintaining the ultimate authority as trustee.

In following the debates concerning the Osage Mineral Estate, this chapter will mark the transformations at play within empire building, as well as the prospects that have been rendered almost unimaginable. In highlighting the affective manifestations present in several Osage Government Reform Meetings during the writing of the constitution of 2006 and the online blogs following the passage of the constitution, this chapter focuses an ethnographic eye on the entanglements of empire. This investigation illustrates that empire is not an organized or even wholly deliberate master plan, as much as it is a series of loosely associated and deeply layered interactions that disrupt polities in ways that limit their ability to challenge a particular axis of power.[5] Looking at empire as a disruption of resources, desires, bodies, loyalties, and securities can shed light on how the United States continues to maintain authority in the twenty-first century and, perhaps, even what is needed to disrupt this hegemony.

"YOU ALL STAY OUT OF IT"

The apprehension in the car was palpable as several of the reform commissioners, their lawyer, and I made the trek out to Grayhorse, the most remote Osage community, in January 2006. I was engaged in research on the Osage Nation reform process taking place in 2004–6 and I traveled almost everywhere with reform commissioners. While I got to hide behind my camera during the community meetings, they had to sit center stage, spearheading the citizenship and governmental reform process. The Grayhorse Indian camp was known not just for its isolation, but also for its inhabitants' fierce independence and skepticism, especially concerning issues of Osage governance. In the late nineteenth century, they were the last of the three Osage districts to settle on the Osage reservation, making the migration from the Kansas lands only with great trepidation.[6] Grayhorse community meetings were frequently contentious, often involving circular discussions that left little opportunity for finding common ground.

Additionally, this was the first community meeting to be held after the referendum vote of 2005, where all but one issue was decided by a large margin. From 2004 to 2006 the Osage Nation went through a government and citizenship reform process that led to the implementation of the Osage Nation Constitution of 2006. After the Osage Tribal Council (OTC) successfully lobbied the United States Congress to pass Public Law 108–431, "to reaffirm the inherent sovereign rights of the Osage Tribe to determine its membership and form of government," they appointed ten Oklahoman Osage Shareholders to the Osage Government Reform Commission (OGRC) to survey the Osage people and write a constitution. In their efforts to gain citizen input into the writing process, the OGRC held over forty community meetings around Oklahoma, Texas, and California; circulated a questionnaire; operated a web page with feedback forums; solicited individual Osage input; and held a referendum vote.

By January 12, 2006, the most contentious remaining issue the OGRC had to deal with was how the Osage Mineral Estate was going to be incorporated into the new government. For the Osage annuitants, or those individuals holding a share/headright in the nationally owned Osage Mineral Estate, this created consternation. Some Osage annuitants were deeply skeptical of any change to the original 1906 Osage Allotment Act (34 Stat. 539), arguing throughout the community meetings that the Osage Mineral Estate should be left alone. A desire to leave things alone, however, was at odds with the desires of a majority of Osages—annuitants and nonannuitants alike—who argued that nonannuitants be allowed to vote in Osage Nation elections. There was no way to include nonannuitants and not change the structure of the Osage government, especially because annuitants did not want nonannuitants having a say in Mineral Estate affairs. General Osage governance and the Osage Mineral Estate had to be separated, thus changing the current structure.

When we walked into the aluminum-sided community building in the center of Grayhorse, we were greeted by the stares of two dozen citizens who were already waiting for the meeting to begin. The long and narrow room was filled with tables and folding chairs facing a single table, reserved for the commissioners, at the front of the room. Behind the audience, the kitchen sat dark and empty, evidence that the meeting was held with little advance notice. Unlike the earlier meetings, when the commissioners went to great lengths to encourage participation, which included offering elaborately catered meals by well-known Osage cooks, this round of meetings had few such attractions and was solely intended to address the vocal minority of annuitants who had concerns about the proposed constitution.

From the beginning of the meeting, it was clear that the apprehension felt on the long drive across the reservation was well-founded. At Grayhorse, the concern surrounding the future of the Osage Mineral Estate took on even more force, with tensions reaching a peak. One middle-aged annuitant from Fairfax, the nearest town to Grayhorse, grew visibly upset, repeatedly pounding his fist on the table and yelling, "It's ours!," asserting that all of the natural resources on the Osage Reservation, and even the casino gaming proceeds, belonged to the Osage annuitants alone. Even though all of the commissioners were annuitants, he continued, yelling: "You all need to stay out of the Mineral Estate. You all stay out of it. You have no business in there." This stopped the room cold, leaving the reform commissioners unsure of how to proceed.

If not always as visible as in this moment, concerns that the new Osage Nation Constitution was going to do something to harm the Osage Mineral Estate were a constant roadblock throughout the Osage reform process of 2004–6, and continue to plague the Osage Nation to this day. While U.S. Public Law 108–431 acknowledged the Osage Nation's ability to create an entirely separate structure for governance from what had been imposed on the Osages for a hundred years, it could not erase the affective forces of empire still at play in the Mineral Estate. The policies undergirding U.S. empire work not just to insist that the United States has ultimate authority over the entire territory, but also to instill distrust so potent that moving toward self-control feels impossible. Such change is understood as a serious threat to existing Osage rights, authority, and income. This, then, is one of the real potencies of empire. While the structures themselves can be challenged and overturned, the (dis)trust accompanying empire is much more deeply rooted.

"AT ONE TIME WE OWNED EVERY INCH OF THIS GROUND— AND NOW WE HAVE HARDLY ANYTHING"

Throughout the reform process, most discussions of what an Osage Nation future should entail devolved into discussions about ongoing settler colonial processes. Specifically, a majority of the community meetings, no matter what their intended focus was, were spent discussing the Mineral Estate, with the commissioners repeatedly assuring those in attendance that their headrights were protected by the legislation itself. These declarations could never quite calm vocal annuitants, however, making it clear that these tensions were not just about the right to profit from the Mineral Estate. After almost a hundred years of colonial attempts at eliminating the Mineral Estate, vocal annuitants were convinced that any change would be detrimental to their livelihoods, the Osage Mineral Estate, and even the Osage Nation.

Cora Jean Jech, an annuitant who would in 2009 be the first plaintiff in a court case challenging the authority of the 2006 Osage Constitution over the Mineral Estate, frequently expressed her concern about the new government. During the question-and-answer period at the beginning of one government reform meeting, she drew a strong connection between past encroachments and the current reform effort. She argued: "There are several Osages that think that there is a plot going on to try to get the Minerals from underneath the Estate. [They think] that the [new Osage] government will actually end up with the Minerals and it will no longer be ours. [They think] that it will be turned over to somebody else because it goes back to greed. When you look at this land all around us and think at one time we owned every inch of this ground—and now we have hardly anything."[7] Referencing the greed that motivated settler colonial encroachment on Osage land, Jech here demonstrates powerfully the way (dis)trust works to stymie change.

To understand the logic of Jech's statements, it is vital to understand U.S. territorial and political expansion in the context of the Osage Nation. The U.S. government has continually made promises that Osage lands would remain intact, only to renege on its agreements, including most recently in the federal courts' denial that the Osage reservation continues to exist despite the existence of no federal legislation terminating it.[8] From 1808 until 1839, there were seven treaties under which the Osage Nation lost control of over 151 million acres of land in Oklahoma, Kansas, Missouri, and Arkansas, receiving only minimal compensation.[9] Loss of land, however, was just a small part of the U.S. empire's disruption of the Osage Nation.

The history of the Osage Mineral Estate itself marks a key disruption, especially its entanglement with corporate interests, which frequently work in tandem with empire. Oil production on Osage land began at the end of the nineteenth century, with a blanket lease to the entire reservation going to Kansas railroad man Henry Foster and his brother Edwin in 1896. The Osage agent H. B. Freeman, the Office of Indian Affairs (OIA), and Foster negotiated the deal. Only after the fact did the governing body of the 1881 Osage Constitution, the Osage National Council, put it to a vote. The initial lease passed by the narrow margin of 7 to 6, but a little over a year later the National

Council voted to annul the contract. William Pollock, Freeman's successor as Osage agent, overrode the National Council seven months later, reinstating the contract.[10] Given the competitive advantage lost with the blanket lease, it is hard to understand the OIA motivation here as anything but an example of early corporate lobbying, not unlike what happened later across Indian Country, and what continues to happen across the globe.[11]

During the allotment era (1887–1934), the United States government claimed control over almost a hundred million acres of American Indian land and, perhaps most problematically, encouraged white settlement directly within indigenous territories. Unlike other American Indian nations, the Osages were able to negotiate a unique deal. While they agreed to allow the allotment of the surface of the Osage reservation, the subsurface—including rights to oil, natural gas, and other minerals—was left in the communal ownership of the Osage Tribe. The most common narrative about this unique allotment is that Chief Bigheart was able to negotiate a better deal because the Osage Nation had purchased their reservation land and understood the importance of collective ownership. It is also likely that the oil lobby played a key role in preventing the allotment of the subsurface.[12] In the congressional hearings concerning allotment, they specifically discussed this unique arrangement, which included reference to both keeping costs low for the oil company and sharing the wealth equally among all Osages.[13]

As historian Alexandra Harmon points out, the argument of equity does not make sense given the strict cut-off date for the Osage allotment roll of 1906, which was used to determine who was eligible to vote, receive a land allotment, and a quarterly payment from the minerals proceeds.[14] In the last hundred years, the Osage Mineral Estate has created a deep divide between Osage "haves" and "have-nots." Osage descendants born after July 1, 1907, were not only landless and excluded from the proceeds of the communally owned Mineral Estate—which was distributed equally among all those listed on the roll of 1906—but they were also given no say in Osage politics. Tying Osage citizenship to the Mineral Estate created high tensions among Osage descendants, thwarted earlier attempts at reorganization, created many obstacles during the 2004–6 reform process, and greatly distracted the elected officials of the newly reconstituted Osage Nation. This history also worked to instill in many Osages a deep-seated concern that others, whether Osages or non-Osages, were going to take their annuity check away.

Like many legacies of empire, the creation of the Osage Minerals Estate had an impact far beyond shifting structures of power. My grandfather, George Orville Dennison, was born eighteen months before the July 1, 1907, cut-off date, and so he received three 160-acre parcels of land within the Osage reservation, a 1/2,230th share of all monies produced from the Mineral Estate, and, when he turned twenty-one, a vote in Osage elections.[15] His two brothers, who were born after the 1907 cut-off date, received nothing and had no voice in the government. This led my great-grandmother to distribute my grandfather's portion of Mineral Estate money among the three boys, until my grandfather married and his wife put an end to the redistribution. These Mineral Estate proceeds divided the family, leading my great-grandmother to favor the brothers' children at gift-giving occasions, rather than my grandfather's children. This estranged my father and his sister from the larger family, who as children did not understand why they were not receiving presents from their grandmother as the cousins did.

As a growing percentage of Osage descendants were disenfranchised, they began fighting for equal voting rights through organizations such as the Osage Nation Organization (ONO).[16] My grandfather—and more frequently my grandmother—often voiced disapproval of such nonannuitant Osages, especially within the family, by saying "they are just trying to get our money." In this way, the authority of U.S. empire was strengthened by connecting Osage livelihoods and political identities to a U.S. created structure and by breeding wider scale suspicion, even (especially) among family members. Such deep-seated (dis)trust stymied the ONO and all other Osage government reform efforts until 2004.[17]

The concern that the nonannuitants were going to find a way of accessing the Mineral Estate proceeds was only further reinforced by the troubles of the roaring 1920s. After the discovery of oil in 1897, the market for Osage oil grew dramatically, bringing much wealth to Osage annuitants. At its peak in 1925, when each annuitant earned $13,200 per quarter, many people came onto the Osage reservation as legal guardians, merchants, suitors, swindlers, and murderers in search of access to this wealth.[18] The Osage Nation eventually paid the FBI to investigate the murders of sixty Osages, which ended in several convictions.[19] This did not, however, end the millions of dollars being lost to price-gouging shop owners and legal guardians, who, as Harmon states, "could skim money from their charges' account with an ease too tempting for many to resist."[20] Such colonial legacies could not help but breed wide scale distrust. The terror from this period also created lasting legacies of suspicion within Osage families, as children have had to make sense of fathers who murdered aunts and uncles in search of additional Osage wealth.

(Dis)trust surrounding the Osage Mineral Estate was further deepened by the many battles the OTC had to fight for its own preservation. In the original Osage Allotment Act of 1906, the Mineral Estate, and the accompanying government to administer it, were only set up to last for twenty-five years. Through various creative tactics, the OTC was able to extend the Mineral Estate until 1958 and then again to 1983. In 1978, the OTC convinced the U.S.

government to change the language concerning the duration of the Mineral Estate from "until otherwise provided by an Act of Congress" to "in perpetuity."[21] Additionally, in 1953, the Osage Nation, along with over a hundred other American Indian nations, faced termination through House Concurrent Resolution 108 because the federal government saw them as successfully assimilated into American society. The Osage Nation, understanding the importance of federal recognition, sent representatives to Washington, where they were able to successfully negotiate for continued recognition by promising to pay their own operation costs through Osage Mineral Estate proceeds.

These battles for preservation took place even as the Mineral Estate fostered deeper entanglements with empire. In addition to the introduction of the oil lobby into Osage Nation affairs and the arrival of many non-Osages in search of Osage wealth, the Mineral Estate also increased the role of the U.S. government in Osage affairs. From the beginning of the oil production on the reservation, the OIA overrode Osage decisions and created policies that went against Osage desires and interests. In 1921, the U.S. Congress went so far as to pass a law that "noncompetent" Osages, generally those listed as having over one-half Indian blood, could have access to only $4,000 of their annuitant payments per year.[22] Withholding this money was justified as an attempt to obstruct Osage consumption patterns and the flagrant fraud occurring throughout the reservation. Both justifications, however, worked to strengthen the U.S empire. As Harmon points out, Osage consumption was on par with the spending habits of others in their income bracket during this time, but it was disconcerting because it challenged stereotypes of the poor Indian in need of U.S. protection. As for the outright fraud happening across the reservation, this would have more appropriately been dealt with by punishing the perpetrators rather than the victims.[23]

While many Osages did fight the rigid caps imposed on their funds, others developed an ambivalent relationship with U.S. guardianship. Given the murder and fraud brought on by the Mineral Estate, it is easy to understand why protection would be desirable. But there is a good deal of evidence suggesting that U.S. officials continually failed to live up to their trust responsibility. In 1917, the OTC complained that Superintendent George Wright was "more greatly concerned about and . . . favorable to the interests of big oil companies and men of large financial means and political influence than . . . to the interests of the Osage people."[24] The OTC went on to argue that the agency was spending Osage annuitant money needlessly and without their consent.[25]

This mismanagement is, sadly, not limited to the early twentieth century. On October 14, 2011, after the U.S. District of Columbia Court had heard extensive discovery, motions, and rulings, the Osage Nation and the U.S. government negotiated an agreement for $380 million to compensate for mismanagement of Osage Mineral Estate funds that occurred between 1972 and 2000.[26] This result, as well as continued evidence of mismanagement since the settlement, illustrates the failure of the United States to act as a responsible trustee of Osage affairs. However, many Osage annuitants point out that it is the trust relationship itself that forces the federal government to compensate the Osage for this mismanagement. The affective force of empire is thus built not on a trust in the aptitude of imperial systems, which is frequently questioned, but from concern that change is likely to bring about more loss. When the cards are so clearly stacked against you, few people are willing to bet the house.

Finally, the Osage Minerals Council became a less trustworthy structure over time, as a higher percentage of Osage descendants were without the right to vote. By 2004 only four thousand of the roughly sixteen thousand Osage descendants could vote, based solely on their possession of a headright. Furthermore, this system was focused primarily around the extraction of minerals, to the detriment of other issues such as territorial control. However, since the termination era, as well as the battles required to maintain the Osage Mineral Estate, many Osage had concerns that changing this system would only lead to further loss. By making the Osage Mineral Estate the primary system by which the U.S. government recognized Osages and by tying it to personal revenues, U.S. empire was able to establish overlapping affective ties that are hard for some Osages to remap.

Through these intertwined forces of (dis)trust, the Osage Mineral Estate has worked to bolster U.S. empire. It limited options for the Osage Nation, discouraged Osages from maintaining territorial control, and instilled deep skepticism of any change. The hidden ties to oil corporations; the fostering of divisive internal politics, privilege, status, U.S. guardianship; and the precarity surrounding the Mineral Estate were all still very much present during the Osage reform process of 2004–6. In light of this history, along with the money and authority at stake, it is little wonder that some Osages focused their energy and concern on the Mineral Estate trust, limiting the space available for other visions of an Osage future.

"OUR PEOPLE HAVE ALWAYS BEEN MOVING FORWARD"

Not all Osages, however, agreed that change was dangerous. By 2004, it was clear to most Osages that a structure focused on the Mineral Estate was limiting the potential of the Osage Nation. Only those who had inherited a share in the Mineral Estate, or a headright, had the right to vote for elected officials. Many voters had only a fraction of a vote, while a few had multiple votes.

Although all lineal descendants of the roll from 1906 were eligible for membership cards in 2004—in addition to eligibility for tribal services such as health care and partial college scholarships—they could not elect tribal officials or run for office unless they held a headright. Nonannuitant Osages were counted in order to gain access to more federal grant dollars, but these same individuals had no say in how those funds were spent. Furthermore, all informal institutions—from Osage naming ceremonies to the five-person committees in the districts—were open to and included all Osage descendants, not just headright holders. It was less clear whom the Bureau of Indian Affairs (BIA) recognized as the Osage Nation, with some evidence pointing only to the original annuitants (all but one of whom had died by this time), excluding even those who had inherited their headright. This led to a concern among some Osage officials that when the last original annuitant passed, the BIA would simply terminate its relationship with the Osage Nation.

Given these concerns, there were few during the reform process who argued for continued limitations on citizenship. One of the debates specifically treating this subject occurred during a Pawhuska community meeting. In response to the impassioned plea of an older Osage annuitant to leave the Mineral Estate voting system in place, one middle-aged annuitant responded: "We've been dealing with this for years and years. Like he said, the 1906 [Act] has been very good to us. But our people have always been moving forward and we always change, and change is needed. We have to make some changes because there are Osages that are totally estranged from their own nation."[27] While the Mineral Estate is presented here as a beneficial entity, this speaker also highlights the need for change because of the disenfranchisement of Osage descendants who, holding no headright, are disqualified from participating in the official Osage political structure. The majority of Osages embraced change as part of who the Osages are.

When the OGRC asked all lineal descendants of the original allottees who had addresses listed with the nation whether government reform was needed, 77.3 percent of the 1,379 respondents answered in the affirmative. Only 38.5 percent of the total respondents were nonannuitants, likely because this population had long been alienated from Osage politics. This meant that while several annuitants spoke vocally against reform, they did not represent the majority even of those Osages who held headrights. Change was ultimately embraced as a central part of the Osage story, something that even the affective entanglements of empire couldn't block.

In the Osage Nation Constitution of 2006, the Osage Mineral Estate was incorporated into the new government as a minerals council with limited authority. This meant that instead of acting as the sole authority of the nation, the officials elected by the annuitants served on a board within the larger government of the Osage Nation. Even though some Osage annuitants were wary of any change in the authority of the Mineral Estate, the constitution passed by a two-thirds majority of the Osage voters, placing the minerals squarely under the authority of a larger Osage government. Article XV, section 4, of the Osage Nation Constitution of 2006 created a minerals management agency, which was named the Osage Minerals Council. This agency was, as the constitution reads, "established for the sole purpose of continuing its previous duties to administer and develop the Osage Mineral Estate in accordance with the Osage Allotment Act of June 28, 1906, as amended, with no legislative authority for the Osage Nation government." In this way, the Osage Minerals Council was created as an independent board within the new Osage Nation government.

To assure that the Osage Minerals Council did not violate Osage law, the same section of the constitution includes this stipulation: "Minerals leases approved and executed by the Council shall be deemed approved by the Osage Nation unless, within five (5) working days, written objection is received from the Office of the Principal Chief that the executed lease or other development activity violates Osage law or regulation. Any dispute that arises through this process may be heard before the Supreme Court of the Osage Nation Judiciary." Particularly important here is the fact that those annuitants voting for the new system, including the members of the current OTC, voted for a system in which they were going to lose their monopoly over general Osage affairs.

Affective forces within empire can be understood as not denying possibilities completely, but instead rendering them much more cumbersome. Throughout the reform process, the majority of the energy was spent on what to do with the Minerals Estate, rather than on what structures made the most sense for the Osage Nation. (Dis)trust realigned the present focus into a discussion about the past, limiting the time and energy available for planning a future. In such spaces of colonization, efforts to build a stronger future are drained of energy, left to move forward with only part of the attention they deserve. Empire in such moments is best understood as a parasite, extracting not just resources, but the vitality needed to imagine alternative futures.

"KICK THAT HATEFUL LITTLE WHITE-MAN RIGHT OUT OF YOUR HEAD!"

While I followed online discussions during the reform process, it was not until I was away from the reservation that I truly appreciated the Osage territory that existed on the World Wide Web. No Osage group was more active on the web following the passage of the 2006 Osage Nation Constitution than the members of the Osage Shareholders Association (OSA). This group of Osage annuitants organized in 1994 in Pawhuska, Oklahoma, for the purpose of encouraging efficient management of the Osage Mineral Estate; protecting the federal trust relationship with the Mineral Estate; encouraging better management of the Mineral Estate by the BIA; and calling for laws to protect the Mineral Estate against theft, fraud, and conflicts of interest. They took a vocal stand against the 2006 constitution and have led multiple initiatives against its passage and for its reform.[28] Shortly after I began my research, the group created a web page with an online discussion forum. This forum was the home of the most aggressive criticisms of the Osage Constitution of 2006 until it was taken offline for financial reasons in 2012. Like the views expressed in the OSA meetings, the postings generally focused on finding a way to undo the changes made by the passage of the Osage Constitution of 2006. While certainly not representative of a majority of Osages, the group is made up of the most vocal and politically active of the citizens and therefore continues to play a formidable role in Osage politics.

Contributors to OSA's discussion page included discussions about potential and actual lawsuits, all of which argued that the Osage Mineral Estate had been diminished by its new placement within the larger Osage Nation. Contributors to the forum expressed their concerns that this new system gave the nation and the chief too much authority over the Mineral Estate, especially since it was not required that the chief be an annuitant. Other concerns were that the Minerals Council no longer had a chief or assistant chief, leaving it with just eight council members. Moreover, there had never been a vote by just the Osage annuitants that reform should even take place. They also expressed concerns similar to those expressed during the reform process, with a growing certainty that the Osage annuitants had been wronged by the 2006 constitution. The OSA web page became the primary space in which these assertions gained traction.

Maintaining the existing relationship with the United States was a central motivator behind many of the concerns found on the OSA web page about the changes the Osage Constitution had implemented. For example, Galen Crum, an annuitant who, after unsuccessfully running for the Osage Congress in 2006, was elected to the Osage Minerals Council in 2010 and 2014, took an early role in fighting against the changes that he felt had been imposed by the successful passage of the 2006 constitution. Crum was from Kansas and had made his name known among a wider Osage population through his presence on the OSA discussion board. He argued in a post to the OSA's web page in October 2006 that change might cause problems for the minerals trust held by the U.S. government:

> It's all about the legal concept of a trust and about keeping the Osage Trust intact, so that the special relationship the 1906 Act gives all the Osage people with the federal government, will not be destroyed. A trust can be thought of as a box in which something of value is kept safe for the owners. It is usually meant to keep the valuables safe not only from outside forces, but also from unauthorized use from the owners. So there are special rules as to its use and a trustee is placed in charge of both protecting the valuables and regulating their use. As long as the box is kept intact and all the rules are followed the trust itself can be thought of as being intact and unassailable. . . . I want agreements made that are consistent with the CFR.[29]

Crum's main point here is that changes made during the reform process would require a change in the Code of Federal Regulations (CFR), thus creating an opening for the federal government to dissolve the entire Mineral Estate trust and perhaps even the nation.[30] Because of the effort to extend the Mineral Estate in perpetuity, there is substantial historical evidence behind these concerns. Osage assertions of sovereignty, through the formation of the new government, were going to require the BIA to rework its laws, a process which historically had almost always led to further erosion of Osage authority.

The U.S. government in its earliest treaties established itself as "protector" of American Indian nations. The 1808 and subsequent Osage treaties are riddled with such phrases. For example, Article 10 of the 1808 Osage treaty reads: "The United States receives the Great and Little Osage nations into their friendship and under their protection; and the said nations, on their part, declare that they will consider themselves under the protection of no other power whatsoever." The Supreme Court first suggested the existence of a trust relationship in *Cherokee Nation v. Georgia* (1831). Chief Justice John Marshall's majority opinion characterized the Cherokee Nation as "a domestic dependent nation . . . in a state of pupilage . . . Their relation to the United States resembles that of a ward to his guardian."[31] Built out of settler colonial mentalities that indigenous people were fundamentally inferior to Europeans, the trust relationship has been a powerful tool of empire building. In 1942, the Supreme Court held that this promised protection created a unique bond between the United States and each recognized American Indian nation, imposing on the federal government "moral obligations of the highest responsibility and trust."[32] Since Congress claims plenary power, allowing it to change or negate any of its trust responsibilities, these are unenforceable "moral" obligations rather than any genuine guarantee of protection.[33]

Another clear example of how (dis)trust worked to limit indigenous futures occurred in July 2007, when the shareholders' listserv became embroiled in a battle over whether Chief Gray of the Osage Nation should assert more jurisdiction over the entire 1.47-million-acre Osage reservation. Gray had recently backed a bill in the Osage Congress to regulate environmental standards across the reservation, and he had kept Oklahoma state inspectors out of an Osage-owned grocery store, asserting accurately that they lacked jurisdiction and were thus violating Osage sovereignty. After having a government focused primarily on the extraction of minerals for almost 100 years, the state had taken over many jurisdictional functions that even the U.S. government recognized Native nations as having. Reasserting authority over these areas was going to be an uphill battle, but it was made even more complicated by a legacy of (dis)trust.

In response to the posts questioning the wisdom of asserting sovereignty over non-Osage living on the reservation, several people on the forum expressed outrage that any Osage would take the side of the "backward and superstitious" whites. They argued it was instead time to "civilize" the white population and educate them as to what having an Osage Nation would really mean. Such comments were arguing for Osages to put trust in Osage systems rather than systems that were so clearly designed to disenfranchise Osages. Furthermore, their aim was often to argue that a strong Osage Nation would be good for the entire area, particularly in terms of economic development.

To these and other accusations another contributor argued, "What's being ignored, by our leadership and those that follow, is that we are a little bitty fish in a big pond and we don't yet know if we even have any teeth. I don't think anyone here is saying that we shouldn't strive for sovereignty, inasmuch as the Yankee government in Washington will let us exercise it . . . It seems that the reality of our situation has been lost in the fervor of what we know to be right."[34] This statement demonstrates clearly the affective power of empire, especially the ways in which colonial processes create lasting (dis)trust. Here, concerns about potential ramifications are privileged over "what we know to be right." Even while this contributor accepts Osage National sovereignty as a fundamental truth, the possibility that the federal or state government would ever recognize fully this authority is rendered an impossibility. Such skepticism, allows U.S. empire to go unchallenged, furthering is hold on authority.

Twenty-first-century Osage nation building took place within the space of empire, where both structural and affective forces worked against assertions of Osage authority. Some Osages even went as far as to argue that the U.S. government's recognition of Osage self-determination, such as in Public Law 108-431, was really their latest tactic to terminate their trust responsibility to the Osage people. Given the long history of U.S. expansion, especially the termination period, concerns that the federal government was just using self-determination as one more strategy to be rid of their "Indian problem" were entirely reasonable. Within such a space of inequality and exploitation, (dis) trust is in fact the most logical response.

Not all of the Osage contributors to the Osage Shareholders Association web page agreed with this approach, however. To the above postings one person responded,

> How sad it is that you perceive yourself, and all Osages, in such a sad pathetic light! Seriously, I really feel bad for you. It can't be comfortable to live such a diminished, marginalized existence. Did you go to a government boarding school? Did they, the U.S. government, do this to you? It doesn't have to be this way. God isn't white and the whites aren't gods. They're no better than we Osages . . . Formerly oppressed native peoples can and do move beyond the mental artifacts which make them prisoners in their own skins. You can as well. Kick that hateful little white-man right out of your head![35]

For the writer, asserting Osage sovereignty is part of the process of decolonization and moving past the discourses of conquest inherent within empire. Rather than feeling oppressed by the limitations inherent in Osage nation-building today, this contributor looks forward to a sovereign Osage future beyond the limiting narratives of the U.S. empire. In naming this (dis) trust as part of the ongoing process of colonization, the posting not only recognizes the source of the problem, but also attempts to get outside the colonizing narrative itself.

In 2009 the OSA took their concerns to federal court. Eight Osage annuitants sued the U.S. Department of the Interior, alleging that the department "unlawfully failed to hold the election for the Osage Nation Constitution as it applied to the Mineral Estate; have further unlawfully failed to hold elections for Minerals Council in accordance with the 1906 Act and 25 C.F.R. Part 90, and are unlawfully recognizing the Osage Nation Constitution as applicable to the Mineral Estate."[36] By turning to the federal government to settle the internal power struggle that they had lost during the election of 2006, these annuitants hoped to reinstate the Mineral Estate's authority, which they felt had been usurped by the Osage Constitution. Such a move is a clear example of the affective force of empire, which works here to jeopardize sovereignty by fostering internal divisions and (dis)trust.

The problem remained, however, that such a focus on the Mineral Estate occurs at the expense of a focus on wider Osage governance. As another OSA contributor, whose online name was Southside Osage, put it: "I love the idea of Osage government taking care of Osage, but I have seen nothing in my lifetime, from nearly all governments, not just the Osage, to suggest that would be the case."[37] Given the limiting structure imposed on the Osage Nation, which focused on minerals extraction to the detriment of jurisdictional issues and infrastructure building, it is no wonder that many Osages are skeptical of the new constitution. This (dis)trust was deeply rooted, extending to all forms of governance that, as Southside Osage went on to explain, "reward people that have a self-interest."[38] From these discussions, it is clear that for these OSA members, governments simply could not be trusted, Osage or otherwise. In addition to limiting the infrastructure necessary to develop a flourishing Osage Nation, U.S. expansion has created an entrenched skepticism of government more generally. Empire can thus also be seen as eroding trust, weakening populations' faith in themselves, and humans more generally, to do what is right. By forcing trust in systems of exploitation and colonization, empires create much larger suspicion.

When heard by the District Court for the Northern District of Oklahoma, however, the case was quickly dismissed due to the plaintiffs' need to first exhaust administrative remedies. The U.S. 10th Circuit Court of Appeals upheld this decision in June 2012. In response, Galen Crum on the Minerals Council and Geoffrey Standing Bear on the Osage Congress put together a series of amendments to the Constitution. While controversial in nature, the intent of the amendments was generally to further protect the Mineral Estate from the influence of the Osage Nation.

The most extreme of the amendments proposed that "Article XV of the Osage Nation Constitution be amended to delete the existing language in its entirety and to replace Article XV with language on recognizing the authority of the Osage Minerals Council to manage the Osage Minerals Estate." The attached description states, "the purpose of the proposed amendment to the Osage Nation Constitution is to remove the responsibility for the Osage Minerals Estate from the Osage Nation generally and instead recognize the authority of the Osage Minerals Council to manage the Osage Mineral Estate, including providing for the election of Osage Minerals Council representatives and terms of office." This amendment would have created a separate entity from the Osage Nation in charge of overseeing the minerals estate.

Interestingly, other than the writers of the amendments, few Osages supported this legislation openly on the Osage Shareholders web page or the newly formed Facebook group "Osage Community for Responsible Citizenry." In both spaces, it was once again the trust relationship that most Osages worried was in danger. Osage annuitant and lawyer Wilson Pipestem posted, "I think it would be a bad idea to mess with the foundations of the federal trust system that's been in place since 1906. The 1906 Act, and amendments to it, protect the mineral estate and its trust status, which is why we still have it in its entirety over 100 years later. Changing the ownership, management, and control of the mineral estate would require an act of Congress, and

I have not heard any good arguments of why this would be a good idea."[39] As U.S. Code Title 25 states, the Osage Mineral Estate is held in trust for the Osage Tribe of Indians; it would thus require an act of Congress to change ownership, and thereby full control, to only the annuitant-elected Osage Minerals Council.

As this posting supports the constitution of 2006, it is a helpful example in illustrating the power that the trust relationship holds today. The importance placed on the trust, at least in this context, went beyond desire for exclusive authority by the Osage annuitants. These postings, while often signaling complex debates over authority, property, and privilege, also reveal the affective authority of the entanglements of empire. The federal trust relationship, a legal concept with a strong emotional undercurrent, is a telling example of how the U.S. empire creates and maintains authority through the fostering of (dis)trust.

While the amendments all received a majority approval, they did not pass by the required supermajority requirement of 65 percent. Geoffery Standing Bear, the Osage congressman who most actively spearheaded the amendments, later explained in an interview that all of the work he put into the amendments "took away from getting people together on the issues I am working on now . . . on rebuilding our child care, elder housing and community centers, rebuilding our reservation housing through opening access to financial markets for housing, rebuilding our arbors, education, and a lot of other matters."[40] Standing Bear, who went on to become Chief of the Osage Nation, has implemented such rebuilding efforts. They include taking over the running of the health clinic from the BIA, purchasing a 43,000-acre ranch, and creating an Osage Nation immersion language school. While some have critiqued the decision to dive into so many initiatives at once, Standing Bear argues that there is no reason to have an Osage Nation unless it is asserting sovereignty over and investing in Osage health, land, and cultural practices like language.

The Osage Minerals Council, however, continues to question the Osage Nation authority and puts its faith in the federal government to address its concerns. In September of 2017 the Osage Minerals Council passed a resolution to sue the Osage Nation in federal court over the ownership of the Osage Mineral Estate. During the meeting, Councilwoman Cynthia Boone said that she put her full faith in the 1906 Act of Congress and that she would be fine if this lawsuit meant the dissolution of the entire Osage Nation government. Given that there is no current evidence that the Osage Nation is doing anything to diminish the proceeds made from the Mineral Estate, the legacies of (dis)trust appear to be at work here. Not only does the majority of people sitting on the Osage Minerals Council in 2017 believe that the federal government is the best protector of its assets, but given the legacies of colonialism, they have no trust in their own system of government.

In investigating the space of empire, it is essential that we not only look for the material evidence of entanglement but that we also interrogate its affective flows. While brute force is powerful in creating a short-term restructuring of power, fostering (dis)trust has a much more long-lasting impact. There has been a long philosophical (and more recently societal) debate about whether or not humans are naturally trusting and what can be done to make people more trusting.[41] From the vantage of Osage politics, I have focused on a different question: What are the forces that impact our ability to trust?

The federal government's trust relationship with American Indian nations is a potent example of how empire fosters (dis)trust. Throughout Osage discussions during and subsequent to the decade following the 2006 Osage Constitution, it was (dis)trust far more than any other emotion that dictated the future of the Osage Nation. (Dis)trust limited conversations, focused energy on maintaining the status quo, and undermined efforts to build a stronger Osage Nation. It manifested in the form of fist pounding, yelling, and many stinging satirical comments. (Dis)trust was so powerful that it worked as a political impediment to nation-building efforts, limiting the time and energy that was available to discuss matters outside the Mineral Estate. (Dis)trust was in fact the primary motivation for much of the participation in the reform process, working to focus far too many of the conversations around what would best preserve the trust relationship, rather than what would best serve the Osage Nation. Tensions with the Osage Minerals Council will continue to take up Osage resources and energy. Given the continuance of empire, perhaps trust is not really a reasonable response. But the question remains, "How do we kick that hateful little white man out of our heads?"

NOTES

1 Stoler, McGranahan, and Perdue, *Imperial Formations*.

2 For a discussion of how indigeneity and empire are intertwined in the United States, see Goldstein, *Formations of United States Colonialism*.

3 Wolfe, "Settler Colonialism and the Elimination of the Native."

4 Tsosie, "Conflict between the Public Trust and the Indian Trust Doctrines," 271.

5 Stoler, McGranahan, and Perdue, *Imperial Formations*.

6 Burns, *A History of the Osage People*.

7 Government Reform Meeting, September 26, 2005.

8 Dennison, "Whitewashing Indigenous Oklahoma and Chicano Arizona: 21st-Century Legal Mechanisms of Settlement."
9 Burns, *A History of the Osage People.*
10 Wilson, *The Underground Reservation.*
11 See Weyler, *Blood of the Land*, for the U.S. context, and Coll, *Private Empire*, for a more global perspective
12 Moore, "The Enduring Reservations of Oklahoma."
13 Subcommittee of the Committee on Indian Affairs, "Division of Lands and Moneys of the Osage Tribe of Indians."
14 Harmon, *Rich Indians.*
15 The 2,230th share of the Mineral Estate was granted to a white woman for her lifetime because of her service to the Osage Nation. For more on the roll of 1906, see Wilson, *The Underground Reservation.*
16 The ONO was a group officially founded in 1964 that argued that the Osage Nation Constitution of 1881 had been illegally terminated by the Bureau of Indian Affairs (BIA) and thus still represented an active government. The ONO was unsuccessful in its reform efforts due to its insistence on a minimum blood requirement for citizenship and the perception that its intent was to do away with the headright system altogether.
17 In 1994 the Osage Nation implemented a federal-court-mandated constitution, which granted citizenship to all descendants of the Act of 1906, regardless of whether or not they held a headright. This constitution was, however, invalidated in 1997, when annuitants successfully challenged the process in another federal court.
18 Wilson, *The Underground Reservation.*
19 Federal Bureau of Investigation, "Osage Indian Murders."
20 Harmon, *Rich Indians*, 197.
21 Burns, *A History of the Osage People.*
22 *Competency* is a legal phrase developed during the allotment era, which indicates that an Indian had been deemed capable of handling her or his own affairs and could be issued a patent in fee, which in turn signaled that her or his land was owned outright and no longer had any federally imposed restrictions on its use or sale.
23 Burns, *A History of the Osage People.*
24 Burns, *A History of the Osage People*, 199.
25 Burns, *A History of the Osage People*, 199.
26 Myers, "Osage Nation, US Settle Legal Battle."
27 Pawhuska Community Meeting, January 19, 2006.
28 During the reform process, OSA meetings were attended by about thirty individuals and generally occurred once a month, depending on current issues of concern.
29 Crum, "Daily Oklahoman Editorial."
30 The Code of Federal Regulations (24 C.F.R. Part 91) was put in place to support the operation of the Osage Tribal Council and the distribution of the Osage Mineral Estate proceeds. These regulations were originally written to support the 1906 congressional act and have been amended many times by the federal government in the last hundred years to be in line with laws.
31 *Cherokee Nation v. Georgia* 30 U.S. 1 (1831), 20.

32 *Seminole Nation v. United States*, 316 U.S. 286 (1942), 296–97.

33 See *Lone Wolf v. Hitchcock*, 187 U.S. 553 (1903) for a full description of Congress's plenary power.

34 "Re: Daily Oklahoman Editorial," *Osage Shareholders Association*, accessed August 27, 2009, http://www.osageshareholders.org/disc50_frm.htm.

35 Proud Osage, "Internalization of Oppressor, a Legacy of Colonialism," *Osage Shareholders Association*, accessed August 27, 2009, http://www.osageshareholders.org/disc50_frm.htm.

36 *Jech v. United States*, 09 U.S. 818, 19.

37 "Re: Black & White World," *Osage Shareholders Association*, accessed September 30, 2010, http://www.osageshareholders.org/disc68_frm.htm.

38 Southside Osage, "Re: Thanks," *Osage Shareholders Association*, accessed December 14, 2010, http://www.osageshareholders.org/disc68_frm.htm.

39 Wilson Pipestem, "Osage Community for Responsible Citizenry," *Facebook*, accessed August 17, 2012, http://www.facebook.com/groups/yanman/.

40 John Moncraivie, "From StandingBear Post," *Osage Shareholders Association*, accessed August 27, 2012, http://www.osageshareholders.org/disc94_frm.htm.

41 Cook, *Trust in Society*; Jiménez, "Trust in Anthropology"; Liisberg, Pedersen, and Dalsgard, *Anthropology and Philosophy: Dialogues on Trust and Hope*.

02 Milking the Cow for All It's Worth

Settler Colonialism and the Politics of Imperialist Resentment in Hawai'i

J. KĒHAULANI KAUANUI

Native Hawaiians as cows? I first encountered this suggestion on the website of a local daily paper called the *Hawaii Reporter*, where it was featured as "cartoon of the week" in late January 2008 (see figure 2.1).[1] The cartoon is attributed to "ZeroShibai.com" (a Hawai'i-based political satire site), but the actual creator remains unknown. The *Hawaii Reporter*, the publication in which it appeared, is a relatively new paper. Its very emergence, along with the cartoon and accompanying text, are indicative of the New Right's entrenchment in Hawai'i, which operates by settler colonial logic, or elimination of the native.[2] Settler colonialism is the policy and process of conquering a distant land, sending settlers in order to reshape the land's demographics to resemble the metropole. As Patrick Wolfe argues: "Settler colonies were (are) premised on the elimination of native societies. This split tensing reflects a determinate feature of settler colonization: The colonizers come to stay—invasion is a structure not an event."[3] Racism is a central feature of settler societies, whose policies pushed for the destruction of indigenous societies and then assimilation for those who survived the process of conquest.[4]

Malia Zimmerman and Jay McWilliams launched the *Hawaii Reporter* in February 2002 while then state Governor Benjamin Cayetano (Democrat) was in his eighth year in office. The founders explain on their website that they founded the paper as a response to Cayetano's leadership, which they characterize as that of a "third world dictator," presumably because Cayetano is of Filipino ancestry. Zimmerman explains that the paper is an "alternative news source," one critical of government and pork barrel: "Whether about heroes or scoundrels, the *Hawaii Reporter* stories help to expose good deeds and wrongdoing. We'd like to think these stories empower the public and make them more aware of the actions by legislators and those in the executive branch, in the county governments, in the public education system, in the judiciary and in the media." While Governor Cayetano may have been

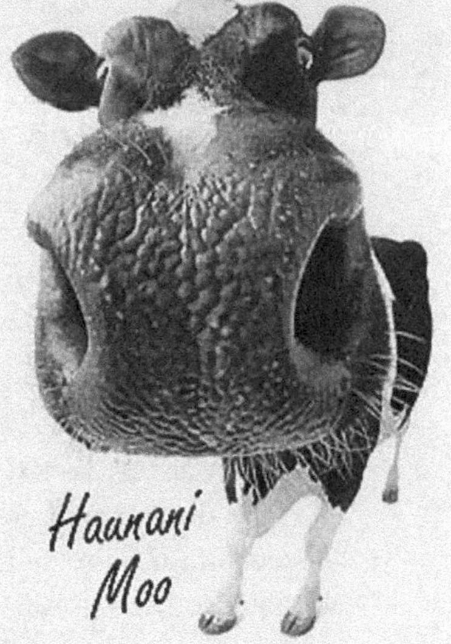
"Land, Money, and Grass for Graze, eh."
For years, you've taken our milk and our beef. Now it's time for some payback. We cows have been in Hawaii since the first volcanoes peeked their heads out of the Pacific Ocean. As native cows, we deeply resent all the cows that came to Hawaii after us. We were grazing in the fields of the Hawaiian Islands since time began. And in the spirit of aloha, we don't wish to share our grass with imported cows. Sure, we've been freely mating with these new cow arrivals for centuries. And sure, there are only a handful of purebred native cows left. And yes, the standard of living for all cows is better than in the old days thanks to the new cows; especially since we can do all our shopping at Costcow. But at the risk of being hypocritical, on behalf of all cows in Hawaii, I demand the right to send these Johnny-come-lately cows back where they came from. That's why all cows -- *even halfbreeds, quarterbreeds and one drop breeds* -- must put their hoof prints on the list of eligible bovines to get Hawaii's pastures divided between native cows and newcomer cows. As natives, we'll get to graze on both pastures, while the cows that stole our land will be limited to a shrinking supply of grass that the Office of Cow Affairs will keep purchasing from under their hoofs, by the authority of the Acowcow Bill.
COW INOA
Haunani Moo
TO GET BACK OUR NATIVE-ONLY GRAZING RIGHTS

FIGURE 2.1 Cow Inoa: Local Bovines Join In Sovereignty Push. Cartoon of the Week, by ZeroShibai.com, January 21, 2008, 10:47:31 AM.

the most hostile to Native Hawaiian concerns of any earlier elected governors, the *Hawaii Reporter* considered him too supportive of indigenous grievances. As such, the online news source became an outlet for anti-Hawaiian sentiments, neoconservative libertarian politics, and support of big business and neoliberal economic policies. Hence, it is a fitting and unsurprising place for bovine satire as "cartoon of the week."

The graphic begins with an accusation—what Kanaka Maoli (indigenous Hawaiians) supposedly think the settlers have taken from them. The complete text embedded within the image states:

> "Land, Money, and Grass for Graze, eh?" For years you've taken our milk and our beef. Now it's time for some payback. We cows have been in Hawaii since the first volcanoes peeked their heads out of the Pacific Ocean. As native cows, we deeply resent all the cows that came to Hawaii after us. We were grazing in the fields of the Hawaiian islands since time began. And in the spirit of aloha, we don't wish to share our grass with imported cows. Sure, we've been freely mating with these new cow arrivals for centuries. And sure, there are only a handful of purebred native cows left. And yes, the standard of living for all cows is better than in the old days thanks to the new cows; especially since we can do all our shopping at Costcow.

But at the risk of being hypocritical, on behalf of all cows in Hawaii, I demand the right to send these Johnny-come-lately cows back where they came from. That's why all cows—even *half-breeds*, *quarter-breeds*, and *one-drop* breeds—must put their hoof prints on the list of eligible bovines to get Hawaii's pastures divided between native cows and newcomer cows. As natives, we'll get to graze on both pastures, while the cows that stole our land will be limited to a shrinking supply of grass that the Office of Cow Affairs will keep purchasing from under their hoofs, by the authority of the Acowcow bill. COW INOA TO GET BACK OUR NATIVE-ONLY GRAZING RIGHTS.

The piece is written from the (imagined) perspective of the Kanaka Maoli supporters of Kau Inoa (here "Cow Inoa")—an initiative of the Office of Hawaiian Affairs (here the "Office of Cow Affairs") to register individuals on an official state "Native Hawaiian roll." Kau Inoa (literally "write name") was developed in anticipation of passage of federal legislation, the Native Hawaiian Government Reorganization Act, known as the Akaka Bill after its sponsor, then-senator Daniela Akaka (D-HI); here the "ACowCow bill"—a play on the official's Hawaiian surname. In March 2000, Hawai'i's congressional delegation formed a Task Force on Native Hawaiian Issues, chaired by Akaka. As its immediate goal, the task force aimed to clarify the political relationship between Hawaiians and the United States. Later that same year, during the 106th U.S. Congress, the senator first introduced federal legislation that proposes to recognize Hawaiians as indigenous people who have a "special relationship" with the United States and thus a right to internal self-determination. From the time that it was first introduced in 2000, until 2012 when it was last on the table, conservatives consistently blocked the proposal, even though it had been redrafted (watered down) many times to try to appease their concerns. Neoconservatives have cast indigenous Hawaiian self-determination as "race-based" government akin to apartheid.

"Haunani Moo" is a play on a brand of milk found in Hawai'i called Lani Moo directed at Haunani Apoliona, then chair of the Office of Hawaiian Affairs. While using the cow to characterize the Hawaiian people in general is problematic given that cow is often used as an epithet for those who are stupid and/or fat, the term is especially insulting when used toward women—in this case Apoliona in particular.[5] The piece draws on all the tropes settlers have used in the past; it sets up gathering rights as "free access" to natural resources and suggests overfarming—as in overdoing it. The title itself is quite interesting since grass here may have a double meaning perhaps as both staple and as drug, as in marijuana: *grass* for "graze," or *grass* for "days/daze." It refers to "grazing rights," not land rights per se, and certainly not nationhood. Thus, the right to occupancy is the central assertion attributed to the Kanaka cow, but even that limited claim is written off as extraordinary. The text mocks the quest for a Native Hawaiian Governing Entity even while framing it as a form of retribution—a debt for which settlers must pay that leads to their own supposed victimization. Further, it inadvertently illustrates some of the core questions about settler colonial articulations regarding land, blood, and property. The caricature also reveals some particular fears embedded within settler colonialism, especially the specters of anti-Hawaiian racism that loom through humor, sarcasm, and distortion. It also disavows the aggressive and unjust colonial processes by which Americans have subordinated and dispossessed the Native Hawaiian people.[6]

Herein I analyze this graphic as a prime example of what I term *imperialist resentment*, an aspect of settler colonialism at work in the islands today within the context of an expanding presence of the New Right. A contemporary manifestation of settler colonialism is the concept of "reverse racism" that undergirds the attacks on indigenous sovereignty, naturalizes imperialism, and effaces historical grievances by suggesting that indigenous peoples, in this case, Native Hawaiians, aim to dispossess settlers based on their own supposed racial supremacy. I theorize these developments as a form of imperialist resentment to describe the collective resentment among many non-Hawaiians in the concerted anti-Hawaiian backlash—a widespread negative reaction to the Hawaiian sovereignty movement. A backlash can also refer to "blaming the victim," which occurs when people in the surrounding environment shift blame, from the criminals, to their victims—in this case the dominant society targeting Kanaka Maoli. This can continue in relation to subsequent controversies and conflicts, sometimes long after the initial crime—such as the U.S.-backed overthrow of the Hawaiian Kingdom in 1893. It is imperialist in nature given that it is about the maintenance of an unequal economic, cultural, and territorial relationship—in this case, in support of U.S. empire—based on domination.

In *The Cultivation of Resentment,* Jeffrey Dudas examines how grassroots conservative activists use rights discourse to pursue their political goals.[7] Through an in-depth case study of opposition to Indian treaty rights, he argues that conservative activists engage in frequent and sincere mobilizations of "rights talk"—a discourse that includes accusations that socially marginal Americans are seeking un-American, "special" rights that violate the nation's commitment to equal rights. So here we have the formulation of rights, once a resource used by excluded groups to gain inclusion, now one of the most formidable tools used by dominant groups to regain their lost power to exclude. This co-optation by the New Right has had profound effects on our political and legal landscape. Dudas's analysis develops a framework for understanding the language of "special rights" and the cultivation of resentment.[8] As Lisa Duggan documents in *The Twilight of Equality? Neoliberalism, Cultural Politics, and the Attack on Democracy*, ongoing bipartisan sponsorship of free market economics has eclipsed social democracy and culture from the mid-'80s to the present.[9] She argues that neoliberalism's most insidious characteristic is its wolf-in-sheep's-clothing claim of multicultural neutrality. She examines the way conservatives have clamped down on social movements that threaten the current social order.

In my formulation of imperialist resentment, I draw on Renato Rosaldo's theory of *imperialist nostalgia*. As he advances, imperialist nostalgia is when agents of colonialism often display nostalgia for the colonized culture as it was "traditionally" (i.e., when they first encountered it). Imperialist nostalgia entails a commitment to a civilizing mission and a mourning of the the passing of traditional society. As Rosaldo notes, there is a "peculiarity of their yearning" in that they long for the very forms of life they intentionally altered or destroyed—and thus imperialist nostalgia revolves around a paradox. He further argues that the "mood of nostalgia makes racial domination appear innocent and pure," since imperialist nostalgia uses a pretense of guiltless yearning both to capture people's imagination and to conceal its complicity with often brutal power. Rosaldo further argues, "When the so-called civilizing process destabilizes forms of life, the agents of change experience transformations of other cultures as if they were personal losses."[10] It is this thread that links to what I am calling *imperialist resentment*—the destroyers experiencing, as if these were personal losses, the change in cultures that they themselves have a hand in transforming. Nostalgia and resentment go hand in hand in this case, since Kanaka Maoli demands disrupt imperialist nostalgia as the living also mourn the colonial destruction, but additionally call for culpability, accountability, and restitution. It is these demands that are resented by those committed to sustaining settler colonial norms. This resentment is both crucial to, and an index of, the expansion of pervasive ties between the New Right in the United States in general, and its development in Hawai'i as a neocolonial site in particular. The persistent ideology of American exceptionalism is at the heart of this problem of imperialist resentment—the refusal to see the islands as a site of ongoing colonial and racial domination.

The ascendancy of the largely white New Right in Hawai'i remains obscured due to a Democratic stranglehold on state politics in the post–World War II era, or a moment marked by the rise of Japanese American social and political power. In this context, the partially obscured New Right backlash comes as a response to Hawaiian nationalist activism in the 1980s and 1990s.[11] In tracing some formative moments, the watershed event of the

Apology Resolution of 1993 deserves attention in relation to the New Right as it is entrenched in the islands while simultaneously taking hold across the United States. The stated rationale for the legislative proposal is the joint-senate resolution of 1993, in which the U.S. Congress apologized to the Hawaiian people for its role in backing the overthrow of the Hawaiian Kingdom. The apology admits, "The indigenous Hawaiian people never directly relinquished their claims to their inherent sovereignty as a people or over their national lands to the United States, either through their monarchy or through a plebiscite or referendum."[12] After this resolution passed, the entire Hawaiian sovereignty movement shifted as this admission from the U.S. government seemed to clear a space for a new generation of independence activism. However, the state government rapidly co-opted this groundswell by trying to contain the movement with governor-appointed commissions and promises of settlements over land claims. In reaction to this combination, the non-Native residents of Hawai'i created a strong backlash against both the movement and the state, and by the late 1990s, there was something else in the works—a series of lawsuits by white Americans, and even some Asian Americans, attempting to take down Hawaiian-specific institutions in the name of civil rights.

The contemporary Hawaiian sovereignty terrain is made up of three main divisions. The first is made up of those who support Hawaiian political independence from the United States. The second includes those who supported the Native Hawaiian Government Reorganization Act in the hope that it would put Native Hawaiians on par with federally recognized tribal nations. Since a legislative approach has failed, this segment currently supports the federal drive to recognize a Native Hawaiian governing entity through a new administrative process being considered by officials within the U.S. Department of the Interior. The third is composed of neoconservatives who are against both these political goals and who have focused the majority of their time mobilizing against the legislation because they see it as "race-based government" that discriminates against non-Natives by offering "special privileges" to Kanaka Maoli.

I first provide a historical overview of the events that impact the current political situation. Then I briefly discuss a set of contemporary conditions that served to catalyze widespread support for the New Right. I discuss also the broader political campaign for recognizing Native Hawaiians as an indigenous people within the United States. I then highlight the expansion of the New Right in Hawai'i as context for my critical reading of the cartoon, with a focus on the legal assault on the Kanaka Maoli people through the targeting of institutions earmarked for Native Hawaiians. Next, I examine the establishment of one of the neoconservative organizations in Hawai'i that now leads political opposition to federal recognition for Native Hawaiians—Aloha for All. Finally, I show how both the guiding principles of Aloha for All, as well as the perspectives found in the cartoon and its accompanying text, evade a history of Hawaiian dispossession while inculcating imperialist resentment among nonindigenous peoples throughout the islands.

A HISTORY OF ILLEGALITY

A series of critical historical events provide a backdrop for understanding the complex terrain of contemporary Hawaiian sovereignty politics. In 1893, U.S. Minister of Foreign Affairs John L. Stevens, with the support of a dozen white settlers, organized a coup and overthrew Queen Lili'uokalani, the monarch of the Hawaiian Kingdom.[13] The queen yielded her authority under protest, as she was confident that the U.S. government and President Harrison would endeavor to undo the actions led by one of its ministers. However, Harrison found himself out of office soon after, and Grover Cleveland became the next president. Eventually, after sending an investigator to look into the matter, Cleveland declared the action an "act of war" and acknowledged that the overthrow, backed by U.S. marines, had been unlawful and should be undone. Specifically, he recommended that the provisional government (made up of those who had orchestrated the overthrow) should step down. But they refused. Cleveland did not compel them to do so and thus did not assist in restoring formal recognition to the queen. In the meantime, the provisional government established the Republic of Hawai'i on July 4, 1894, with Sanford Ballard Dole as president. As the de jure government, asserting jurisdiction over the entire island archipelago, this group seized roughly 1.8 million acres of Hawaiian Kingdom Government and Crown lands.[14]

In 1898, when the United States unilaterally annexed the independent state of Hawai'i, the republic then ceded these same lands, under the condition that they be held in trust for the inhabitants of the Hawaiian Islands.[15] In her pathbreaking research, Noenoe K. Silva has brought to light a powerful resistance history that reveals broad-based Hawaiian opposition to U.S. annexation—opposition so strong that it successfully defeated a proposed treaty of annexation in 1897.[16] Hawaiians organized into two key nationalist groups—Hui Aloha 'Āina (which had two wings: the men's group and the women's) and Hui Kālai'āina—each of which submitted petitions representing the vast majority of Hawaiian people alive in Hawai'i at the time. In those petitions, called the Kū'ē Petitions (*kū'ē* translates "to oppose, resist, protest"), Hawaiians clearly stated their opposition to becoming part of the United States "in any form or shape." The U.S. Senate accepted these petitions but found it impossible to secure the two-thirds majority vote required for a treaty. However, this did not stop the U.S. government. During U.S. president McKinley's term, the Republic of Hawai'i and other pro-annexationists proposed a joint resolution of Congress, which required only a simple majority in both houses—and so the Newlands Resolution passed in 1898.[17] Thus, the United States did not annex the Hawaiian Islands by treaty, as required under customary international law at the time.

To many outsiders today, the history of the illegal overthrow and annexation may seem irrelevant, given that Hawai'i is currently counted as one of the fifty states of the United States of America. But as many Hawaiian activists point out, statehood is also contestable. Like many other colonial territories, in 1946 Hawai'i was inscribed on the United Nations list of non-self-governing territories.[18] Although Hawai'i was on that list, and therefore entitled to a process of self-determination to decolonize, the U.S. government predetermined statehood as the status for Hawai'i by treating its political status as an internal domestic issue. The 1959 ballot in which the people of Hawai'i voted to become a state of the union included only two options: integration and remaining a U.S. colonial territory.[19] And settlers as well as military personnel outnumbered Hawaiians among those allowed to take part in the vote.[20] By citing the internal territorial vote, the U.S. State Department then misinformed the United Nations, which in turn considered the people of Hawai'i to have exercised their self-determination and chosen freely to incorporate themselves to the United States.[21]

By UN criteria established the following year in 1960, certainly known to the United States at the time, the ballot would have had to include independence and free association as choices. On December 14, 1960, the UN General Assembly issued a Declaration on the Granting of Independence to Colonial Countries and Peoples—resolution 1514 (XV).[22] Also in 1960, the assembly approved resolution 1541 (XV) that defined free association with an independent state, integration into an independent state, or independence as the three legitimate options of full self-government.[23] UN General Assembly Resolution 1541 refers to territories that are "geographically separate and distinct ethnically and/or culturally" without specifying what "geographically separate" must entail. Nonetheless, this chapter of the resolution has been accepted as applicable mainly to overseas colonization, while relegating indigenous peoples to a condition of "internal colonization."[24] At stake is the prohibition of the indigenous claim to the same self-determination granted to "blue water" colonies by Resolution 1514, "which can logically lead to independence."[25] Hence, the phrase "all peoples have the right of self-determination" has been applied mainly to inhabitants of territories destined for decolonization, rather than to indigenous peoples.[26]

For example, Guam as a U.S. territory is on the list, not the Chamoru people indigenous to Guam.

This exclusion changed some under the UN General Assembly's passage of the Declaration on the Rights of Indigenous Peoples in 2007, but even that has conditions to what constitutes "self-determination." On the one hand, Article 3 states, "Indigenous peoples have the right of self-determination. By virtue of that right they freely determine their political status and freely pursue their economic, social, and cultural development." But on the other hand, the last article, Article 46, states: "Nothing in this Declaration may be . . . construed as authorizing or encouraging any action which would dismember or impair, totally or in part, the territorial integrity or political unity of sovereign and independent States." This contradiction makes the question of self-determination somewhat paradoxical in that it works against Hawaiian claims to nationhood and self-government based on indigeneity, thus making it difficult for such claims to be enacted.

CONTEXT FOR THE COW AS CARICATURE

While there was massive opposition to the Akaka Bill from the conservative right in both Hawai'i and Capitol Hill, there exists also on-island resistance for the totally opposite reason—namely, a number of independence activists assert Hawai'i's national sovereignty under international law. Given the history of the U.S.-backed overthrow of the Hawaiian Kingdom in 1893, the model of internal self-determination for Native Hawaiians is problematic in multiple ways. For one, all major global powers throughout the nineteenth century recognized the Hawaiian Kingdom as an independent state. Also, the Kingdom had citizens who were not Native Hawaiian. Hence, the claim to sovereignty exceeds the model of self-governance based solely on indigeneity as the structuring element of the reconstituted polity. Although indigenous peoples, as collective entities, are entitled to self-determination under both U.S. domestic and international law, the political and racial categories wrought by U.S. colonialism in Hawai'i impinge on the question of Hawaiian sovereignty. Additionally, the conservative right framed its opposition to the Akaka Bill as legislation that would create a "race-based government," just as neoconservative assessments cast American Indian tribal governments as race-based governments, despite the fact that U.S. law acknowledges that tribal nations are political entities (not racial ones).

Any discussion of the backlash against Kanaka Maoli must be understood in relation to how this is playing out in Indian Country, even if one rejects the model of self-determination imposed on tribes. There is growing resentment among some Americans who see Indian gaming and treaty rights as an unfair advantage based on race privileges. As Joanne Marie Barker documents and analyzes, the Indian Gaming Regulatory Act of 1988 served as a catalyst for renewed political opposition to native sovereignty movements throughout the United States.[27] Furthermore, she notes that the use of reverse racism arguments challenges laws recognizing native rights to sovereignty and self-determination. As such, the racialization of native peoples as both "special interest groups" and "racial minorities" is used to undermine the unique status of indigenous peoples.[28]

The case of *Rice v. Cayetano* in 2000 exemplifies this bid to chip away at indigenous standing, and was a watershed ruling for the political climate in Hawai'i that gave rise to expanding right-wing institutional development. In this suit, a white American man named Harold F. Rice—a fourth-generation resident of Hawai'i—sued then-governor Cayetano because he was prohibited from voting for the elections for trustees to the state Office of Hawaiian Affairs. Prior to the ruling in the case, these elections had been restricted to Native Hawaiians (of any Kanaka ancestry) who resided in Hawai'i. Rice was denied the right to vote because he is not Hawaiian by any statutory definition (he is neither "native Hawaiian"—the definition of which means those who meet a 50 percent blood quantum rule—nor "Native Hawaiian," those of Kanaka ancestry who do not meet the 50 percent criterion). The Office of Hawaiian Affairs, established in 1978, is governed by a nine-member elected board of trustees and holds title to all real or personal property set aside or conveyed to it through the state Admission Act of 1959 as part of the "Ceded" Public Lands Trust (part of the 1.8 million acres of Kingdom Crown and Government Land). It is also meant to hold the income and proceeds derived from a portion of a trust for "native Hawaiians" as defined in the Hawaiian Homes Commission Act and granted to the State of Hawai'i at the time it was admitted to the union in 1959.[29] As the plaintiff, Rice charged that both the trust managed by the office and the OHA voting provisions were racially discriminatory and violated the Fourteenth and Fifteenth Amendments to the U.S. Constitution, which, respectively, are meant to provide equal protection, and to guarantee that the right of citizens to vote shall not be denied or abridged on account of race, color, or previous condition of servitude.

It should be noted that Rice was backed by the Center for Individual Rights, and the Pacific Legal Foundation (PLF). The Pacific Legal Foundation is a legal organization that claims it's the "legal watchdog for freedom." The PLF "litigates for property rights, limited government, free enterprise and a balanced approach to environmental regulation, in courts across the country" (e.g., in the 1970s, it supported Allan Bakke in his successful U.S. Supreme Court challenge to affirmative action). By 1996, the PLF opened the Hawai'i office in

Honolulu, and its attorneys had a role in shopping for a legal case that could challenge Hawaiian-only voting for trustee elections at the Office of Hawaiian Affairs. More recently, the PLF filed an amicus brief in December 2008 in support of the State of Hawai'i, characterizing the ceded lands issue as one of impermissible use of public land based on race-based exclusions that violate the equal protection clause of the Fourteenth Amendment of the U.S. Constitution. The Center for Individual Rights (CIR) is a law firm "dedicated to the defense of individual liberties against the increasingly aggressive and unchecked authority of federal and state governments." Although it claims to be nonpartisan, it is quite conservative, and sometimes libertarian, in outlook. Its work focuses on enforcement of constitutional limits on state and federal power, primarily through litigation. The CIR's primary focus for most of its existence has been challenges to what it regards as unconstitutional or unlawful preference based on race, sex, or another protected status (e.g., backing *Gratz v. Bollinger* and *Grutter v. Bollinger*) by Abigail Thernstrom and those of her political persuasion at the Manhattan Institute, a think tank devoted to shaping American political culture.[30]

In the ruling in the case, although the trust itself is for the benefit of "native Hawaiians," the U.S. Supreme Court's majority opinion decreed that the state's electoral restriction enacted race-based voting qualifications and thereby violated the Fifteenth Amendment. Although, in the end, the court did not rule on the Fourteenth Amendment in Rice, and thus did not affect the trust that the Office of Hawaiian Affairs is meant to manage, the ruling laid the essential groundwork for further assaults on Hawaiian lands and people through a rash of lawsuits across the next decade.

These new cases threatened the existence of all Hawaiian-specific funding sources and institutions, including the Office of Hawaiian Affairs; all federal funds for Hawaiian health, education, and housing; and the state Department of Hawaiian Home Lands and the lands it manages. Plaintiffs charged that these institutions are racially discriminatory because they violate the Fourteenth Amendment. Within the broader context of these legal assaults, in which any indigenous-specific program is deemed racist, many Native Hawaiians and their allies support Senator Akaka's original proposal for federal recognition, especially since he pitched the legislation as a protective measure against such lawsuits. Those engaging in reactionary opposition to indigenous sovereignty claims employ a twisted rhetoric of "civil rights" to assault and dispossess Native Hawaiians by arguing that non-Hawaiians are being discriminated against, and they have also raised the specter of apartheid by suggesting that the bill promotes Hawaiian "minority-rule" (discussed further below). This casting of the legislation is a false dilemma given that the Akaka Bill would merely authorize a Native Hawaiian governing entity—subject to both Hawai'i State and U.S. federal laws—with limited self-governance for Native Hawaiians. In other words, it would not empower Native Hawaiians to exercise any form of jurisdiction over non-Hawaiians.

Another major development during the post-*Rice* period was the founding of Aloha for All in 2003. The organization is a 501(c)(4) tax-exempt nonprofit corporation that was created by attorney H. William Burgess and former Honolulu *Advertiser* publisher Thurston Twigg-Smith with the support of Ken Conklin. Burgess has been instrumental in bringing two controversial lawsuits seeking to have such indigenous-specific programs declared unconstitutional. Thurston Twigg-Smith is a fifth-generation Hawai'i resident and the great-great grandson of Asa and Lucy Goodale Thurston as well as Lorrin Andrews—pioneer Calvinist missionaries to Hawai'i. He is also the grandson of Lorrin A. Thurston, who played a key role in the overthrow of the Hawaiian Kingdom in 1893. Twigg-Smith is an avowed opponent of the Hawaiian nationalist movement and wrote a book to debunk what he considers revisionist history: *Hawaiian Sovereignty: Do the Facts Matter?*[31] Conklin is a retired schoolteacher and an opponent of the Hawaiian sovereignty movement. He has also sought to overturn existing laws and practices earmarked for Native Hawaiians. He is a prolific writer of documents and essays regarding Hawaiian sovereignty, which he considers race-based politics. Conklin also authored *Hawaiian Apartheid: Racial Separatism and Ethnic Nationalism in the Aloha State.*[32] He was one of thirteenth plaintiffs in a controversial lawsuit *Arakaki v. State of Hawai'i* challenging the requirement that candidates for election to the Office of Hawaiian Affairs board of trustees be Hawaiian. The suit was argued by H. William Burgess (along with cocounsel Patrick W. Hanifin) and claimed that the restriction violated the equal protection clause of the Fourteenth Amendment, the Fifteenth Amendment, and the Voting Rights Act.[33] Although to date the lawsuit has been unsuccessful, it was part of a wave of anti-Kanaka political action.

It should also be noted that in July 2007, the U.S. Commission on Civil Rights filled vacancies on its Hawai'i advisory committee by choosing several outspoken activists against Native Hawaiian sovereignty. Under the Bush administration, the civil rights commission was a cruel joke. The commission itself is on record against the Akaka Bill for its sponsor, but the Hawai'i Advisory Committee has previously favored federal recognition for Native Hawaiians. Among the 14 new members to the 17-member advisory committee are H. William Burgess (attorney in the Arakaki case, and cofounder of Aloha for All) and Tom MacDonald (a retired investment executive who is on the board of scholars of the Grassroots Institute of Hawai'i, a libertarian public policy think tank formed in 2001 that opposes Hawaiian sovereignty claims on grounds that they are a threat to individual freedoms of

U.S. citizens and counter to private property rights), along with several other neoconservatives.

Aloha for All describes itself as "a multiracial, multi-ethnic group committed to the principle that aloha is for all people regardless of racial, ethnic, or national origin."[34] The name of the organization itself reveals the complicated—perhaps even imperialist nostalgic—relationship to Hawaiian cultural logics as the mandate of "aloha for all" is a gross cultural appropriation, as if to say love for all, or justice for all (and not just Native Hawaiians). This also speaks to broader neoliberal and neoconservative cultural appropriations purporting to speak to multiculturalism and "oneness."

Its stated mission is "to ensure that ALL citizens of Hawai'i are treated equally under law." Aloha for All stands against proponents of "Hawaiian sovereignty" because they are seen as supportive of political projects of Hawaiian "racial supremacy." Aloha for All asserts seven basic commitments in its political vision:

1. A UNITED STATE OF HAWAI'I. We favor keeping Hawai'i as a single, unified political entity as one of the States of the United States of America. We oppose partitioning the State of Hawai'i along racial or hereditary lines. We oppose creating any political subdivisions where members of any racial or ethnic group would have legally recognized supremacy of voting rights or property rights. We oppose seceding from the United States to create an independent nation of Hawai'i, or asking the United States to withdraw from Hawai'i.

2. ALL PERSONS ARE INHERENTLY EQUAL. We believe that all persons are inherently equal. We oppose giving special economic rights or political status to any group based on genetics.

3. KANAKA MAOLI ARE CULTURALLY FIRST AMONG EQUALS. We acknowledge that the kanaka maoli (Native Hawaiian people) came to Hawai'i centuries before people of other races and ethnicities came here. They established a complex culture with many beautiful aspects that continue to inspire people of all races who choose to learn about them. . . . Because of the special affection the people of Hawai'i feel toward the kanaka maoli and their culture, we freely support and encourage the preservation and thriving of that culture as first among equals—not because it has any legal or political entitlement to supremacy, but because it was historically first and continues to inspire us all.

4. ALL RACES WERE HISTORICALLY FULL PARTNERS IN THE KINGDOM OF HAWAI'I, AND REMAIN FULL PARTNERS TODAY. We note with pride that people of all races were welcomed into Hawai'i from the time of first contact in 1778 until now. Europeans, Americans of all races, and Asians became full partners who helped Kamehameha the Great unify the Kingdom of Hawai'i,

who brought written language and the rule of law, who helped Hawai'i become a thriving Kingdom, prosperous territory, and proud state . . . By the time of the overthrow and annexation, kanaka maoli were a minority, as demonstrated by the Census of 1900 showing that only 26% of the population had any kanaka maoli genetic heritage. . . .

5. GOVERNMENT ASSISTANCE SHOULD BE BASED ON NEED WITHOUT REGARD TO RACE. We believe that if federal, state, or local governments wish to give help to needy people, such help should be given on the basis of who needs it and not on the basis of their race. . . .

6. THERE ARE NO SPECIAL LAND RIGHTS BASED ON RACE. The government lands of the Kingdom of Hawai'i were held by government on behalf of all the people. . . . At the time of annexation, the government and crown lands were ceded to the United States subject to the requirement that all these ceded lands were to be held in trust for the benefit of all the people of Hawai'i. . . .

7. KANAKA MAOLI ARE NOT COMPARABLE TO AN INDIAN TRIBE. THEY ARE AN ETHNIC GROUP, NOT A POLITICAL ENTITY. Kanaka maoli eagerly welcomed newcomers since the moment of first contact in 1778. They freely intermarried and produced succeeding generations with lower and lower quanta of native blood. Today, 3/4 of all persons who have any native ancestry have less than 50% blood quantum; and many have very small portions of native ancestry. . . . Attempts to gain recognition as an indigenous political entity are motivated primarily by a desire for special welfare benefits, tax exemptions, and regulatory exemptions. . . . We oppose any governmental recognition of political status for people with kanaka maoli ancestry because it is unnecessary, historically inappropriate, racially divisive, and destructive to the Aloha Spirit. . . .

The quest for Hawaiian nationhood is explicitly framed as a bid to "partition" the state of Hawai'i along racial lines in the explanations that follow each of the seven principles on Conklin's website. The group also presumes that attempts to gain recognition as an indigenous political entity are "motivated primarily by a desire for special welfare benefits, tax exemptions, and regulatory exemptions." In other words, here Native Hawaiians are figured as always already "on the take." Also, the notion that Native Hawaiians remain "full partners" today under settler colonialism is an obscene contradiction in terms. There is no acknowledgment of indigeneity here; Aloha for All regards Native Hawaiians as a race in order to render invisible such land claims based on original occupancy and the sovereignty of the kingdom—and without further recourse to reclamation. It also positions whiteness (and its power dynamics) as parallel instead of hierarchical. Again, this appraisal denies the destructive processes by which colonial Americans subordinated and dispossessed the Hawaiian people.

Indigeneity is about connection to place and assertions of nationhood, not race and liberal multiculturalism. However, this inclusiveness has been exploited by those who incorrectly assume that since most Hawaiians are racially mixed, everyone in Hawai'i is therefore Hawaiian. Yet Native Hawaiians constitute only 20 percent of the population there, and are subject to a racial blood quantum legal standard. The rule operates through the logic of disappearance, which is central to the project of settler colonialism. The references to blood quantum in the principles of Aloha for All pervert the historical fact that the U.S. Congress requires Kanaka Maoli to prove they meet a 50 percent blood quantum rule in order to count as "native Hawaiian" under Hawai'i state law. As I detail in *Hawaiian Blood: Colonialism and the Politics of Sovereignty and Indigeneity*, the contemporary legal definition of "native Hawaiian" is guided by a 50 percent blood quantum rule: "descendant with at least one-half blood quantum of individuals inhabiting the Hawaiian Islands prior to 1778."[35] This criterion originated in the Hawaiian Homes Commission Act of 1921 (HHCA) in which the U.S. Congress allotted approximately 200,000 acres of land in small areas across the main islands to be leased for residential, pastoral, and agricultural purposes by eligible "native Hawaiians." In the quest to control Hawaiian land and assets, blood quantum classification emerged as a way to undermine Kanaka Maoli sovereignty claims—not only by explicitly limiting the number who could lay claim to the land, but also by reframing the Native connection to the land itself from a legal claim to one based on charity. In the context of the HHCA, and indeed U.S. policy in general, the logic of blood dilution through legal and popular discourses of race displaces indigeneity and erodes indigenous peoples' sovereignty claims. Hence, on the one hand, Kanaka Maoli endure a state-imposed blood racialization regime that purports to measure indigeneity, while on the other, some non-Hawaiians appropriate Native Hawaiian identities to assert their own place in Hawai'i while displacing Hawaiian claims to prior occupancy and national sovereignty.

BACK TO THE BOVINE: COW DUNG

In the cartoon's assertion of original occupancy, the irony (or is it the intention?) is that cows are not indigenous to the Hawaiian Islands. The use of the cow for this cartoon's caricature of the Native Hawaiian who supports Kou Inoa and the Akaka Bill is curious for several reasons. In 1793, Capt. George Vancouver gave King Kamehameha I six cows and a bull.[36] Popular historical narratives suggest that the king immediately placed a *kapu* (taboo/restriction) on them, which restricted Hawaiians and others from disturbing them in any way. The cows reproduced and eventually became central to the first ranching expedition in Hawai'i developed by John Palmer Parker, who was a white American sailor from Massachusetts who jumped ship in 1809. Eventually, he won the favor of Kamehameha I and married his granddaughter Kipikane in 1816. Through this union he secured land, and this became the basis for the enormous Parker ranch, which has been in continuous operation by the same family to the present day.[37]

Cows are domesticated, which seems to resonate with the anti-Hawaiian sovereignty sentiments that argue that Kanaka Maoli are not entitled to any distinct recognition given that Hawaiians have been "domesticated" by the United States. In other words, because Kanaka Maoli have supposedly been absorbed, there is no "unfinished business" to tend to in the way of the sovereignty question. But also, given that cows were imported to the islands, I take the use of the cow as a suggestion that even the indigenous claims of Kanaka Maoli are questionable. Indeed, many archaeologists continue to discredit the autochthonous claims of Kanaka Maoli by asserting that the Hawaiian people migrated from the South Pacific to Hawai'i. Thus, using a cow to represent the Hawaiian assertion of original occupancy mocks Kanaka Maoli claims to indigeneity. Here, the operative logic is that we are all animals off the boat—whether it is Noah's Christian ark, or the Polynesian double-hulled voyaging canoe. Hence the indigenous claim of occupancy and grazing since time immemorial is written off as farce. Moreover, the indigenous claim is framed as a position based on simple resentment, rather than social justice for a history of dispossession. The sarcastic evocation of the "spirit of aloha" marks Hawaiian claims as selfish and therefore a withholding and hording gesture vis-à-vis the newcomers, named here as "imported cows."

Now to the issues of blood, reproduction, and the state of the Hawaiian population: the text mentions that the cows have been "freely mating" for centuries and suggests that the "new cows" are simply a "new breed," none too different from the original stock. Of course the notion of "freely mating" already evokes a primitive animal-like quality with regard to sexual intercourse. Not surprisingly, most attacks on indigenous claims to land and nationhood typically point to any histories of racial mixing—regardless of the reasons we might consider this a form of survival—as evidence of inauthenticity without acknowledgment that settlers themselves create the main problem in the dynamic of mating in the first place. Here, the history of Hawaiian depopulation due to foreign intrusion remains unaccounted for, which has been estimated at a 95 percent population collapse within the first seventy-five years after Captain Cook's arrival in the Hawaiian Islands.[38] Also, nowhere in this inverted diatribe is there recognition, let alone understanding of, the strategic intermarrying with Hawaiian women on the part of European and white American men during the late eighteenth century and throughout the nineteenth, which facilitated their access to land and wealth in Hawai'i. Consequently, the double standard of racial intermingling remains in place in order to fortify white settler colonial claims. Thus we have the declaration that there are "only a handful" of purebreds in existence, as though those who are seen as racially pure are the only rightful claimants of indigeneity, land, and sovereignty. The use of racial categories here is also interesting given that, historically, the term *half-breed* has usually been reserved for American Indians of mixed European ancestry, while *one-quarter* happens to be the most common blood quantum standard for tribal membership within federally recognized tribes, whereas *one drop* is typically used to characterize the hypodescent rule whites imposed on African Americans.[39]

Here indigeneity gets dissolved into race, where Native Hawaiians are regarded as just one minority among others. On the one hand, Hawaiians endure a blood racialization regime that purports to measure our indigeneity. Meanwhile, on the other hand, non-Hawaiians appropriate our identities to assert their own place in Hawai'i while displacing Hawaiian claims to prior occupancy and national sovereignty. The term *eligible bovines* marks the fact that some cows are qualified, while others are not. Here, the catalogue of eligible animals will be counted in order to divide resources between those who are Kanaka Maoli and non-Hawaiians.

The graphic also advances an apologist position regarding colonialism in the mention of the cows' improved standard of living, thanks to the colonial cows. Due to the newcomers, things are far better than in the old days. Here, "Cost-Cow," or Costco, a membership-only wholesale warehouse club, stands in for white civilization and the notion of "progress," presented as inextricably tied to consumption. Note that the attempt to recuperate colonial virtue is coming directly from the mouth of the Hawaiian cow, in the "we must admit . . . ," which is construed as Hawaiian hypocrisy. Then there is the imagined demand for expulsion of newcomers, something that has never actually been part of the articulated goals (nor the rhetoric) of the Hawaiian sovereignty movement, despite the fact that many will admit in private that it is not such a bad idea. In any case, even as a fantastic desire among Kanaka Maoli, the scheme is derided as hypocritical. Here we have the notion of deceptive Hawaiians demanding the right to send them back (to where, we do not know).

Under the legislation, Natives would have supposedly gotten to "graze" on both pastures, as though only one pasture is ours and we are then portrayed as morally questionable because of our "double dipping"—or should I say double chewing the cud—while the colonizers who stole our land will be limited to a shrinking supply of grass. Note the anxiety regarding the purchase power of the Office of Hawaiian Affairs Corporation, as the so-called Office of Cow Affairs will keep purchasing from under the hoofs of the colonial cows—supposedly by the authority of the "Acowcow bill." This false notion is part of an ongoing misinformation campaign about the legislation stirred by scaremongers, since nothing in the proposal would have empowered the Office of Hawaiian Affairs.

Finally, the last line of the text that accompanies the cartoon, which reads "Cow Inoa: Local Bovines Join In Sovereignty Push," reveals an incongruity in that "local" is not even Kanaka Maoli-specific. In Hawai'i, the term *local* is typically used to refer to Hawaiians, Asians, other Pacific Islanders, Puerto Ricans, and others except whites. So, the use of the term here might be intended to position Hawaiians as further distanced from claims to indigeneity. In any case, the message here is that joining in with the "sovereignty" push in signing onto Kou Inoa is framed as simply going with the herd as part of a mindless form of groupthink. The graphic can be understood as a racial project that masks serious human violations, theft, and injustices. It represents a total disregard for indigenous sovereignty while legitimating settler colonial logics cloaked with satire and appearing to be totalizing.

Perhaps if the author of the graphic, the *Hawaii Reporter*, and groups such as Aloha for All understood why Hawaiian independence activists opposed the Akaka Bill, they might have supported the legislation after all. It would have set up a process whereby the U.S. federal government would authorize a Native Hawaiian Governing Entity, subject to the sovereign authority of the state of Hawai'i, and no provisions for land, civic, or criminal jurisdiction, or cash restitution. It is no coincidence that this bill was a federally driven proposal supported by Hawai'i's entire congressional delegation and the state's past Democrat and Republican governors.

The reactionary assessment of federal recognition as Hawaiian "minority-rule" is a joke—the Akaka Bill would have merely authorized a Native Hawaiian governing entity to govern its own membership in compliance with both Hawai'i State and U.S. federal laws, with limited self-governance for Native Hawaiians. Neoconservatives cast the Hawaiian national claim as a racial claim because they acknowledge *only* the advocates for federal recognition, while disregarding those like myself who rejected the Akaka Bill in favor of the restoration of Hawaiian nationhood under international law. Hence they misread the indigenous bid for federal recognition through an inversion of civil rights discourse in order to dismiss Native self-determination as a discriminatory "racial preference." They relied on this inverted logic to then dismiss all sovereignty claims as absurd. Here, imperialist resentment casts Hawaiian as ingrates—it is not enough that Kanaka Maoli come from such a beautiful place, now they want it back when instead they should just be grateful. The concept of "reverse racism" that undergirds the broad attacks on Hawaiian sovereignty naturalizes imperialism and effaces historical grievances by suggesting that Kanaka Maoli aim to dispossess settlers based on their own supposed racial supremacy. Yet, neither civil rights nor indigenous rights under U.S. federal law can account for the full Hawaiian sovereignty claim to independent nationhood. Federal protection is now being sold to Native Hawaiians as a defense against average citizens who challenge the Hawaiian trusts that the United States never upheld in the first place—trusts that are based on the theft of a nation.[40]

Under President Barack Obama, there was firm administration support for the Akaka Bill.[41] All versions of the bill reaffirmed the *delegation* of U.S. government authority to the State of Hawai'i in order to address the condition of Native Hawaiians under the Hawai'i state admissions act. With regard to negotiations, the legislation specified that after the Native Hawaiian governing entity is created, *both* the United States and the State of Hawai'i would enter into negotiations with the Native Hawaiian Governing Entity. This set the bill apart from most forms of federal recognition of tribal groups, which do not typically give state governments any part in the negotiations with the exception of matters related to Indian gaming. Furthermore, no land, jurisdiction, assets, or governmental power were guaranteed in any version of the bill; they were all up for negotiation, but without all parties having equal footing.

CONCLUSION

By July 2010, when the Akaka Bill seemed dead, the OHA trustees moved to work with the new governor, Neil Abercrombie (formerly a U.S. House Representative), to select state legislators to push for a law that would offer state recognition of a native Hawaiian governing entity while also getting the Akaka Bill reintroduced in Congress. Meanwhile, on July 6, 2011, Abercrombie signed into law the First Nation Government Bill.[42] Although the state version was modeled after the Akaka Bill, it did not authorize a government-to-government relationship between the U.S. federal government and a Native Hawaiian governing entity. Instead, it authorized a First Nation–to-fiftieth state relationship. But just like the Akaka Bill, this legislation was a pretense. The new law set up a commission to produce a "Native Hawaiian roll" (continuing the work of Kau Inoa), in which Kanaka Maoli sign on to take part in the formation of the "First Nation" within the state process.

In July 2011, Hawai'i governor Abercrombie appointed former governor John Waihe'e to lead a new commission to prepare and maintain a roll of qualified Native Hawaiians who would work toward the reorganization.[43] By July 20, 2012, the effort had come to be called "Kana'iolowalu" and it included an online registry to create a base roll of Native Hawaiians—individuals understood as eligible to participate in the formation of a governing entity.[44] According to OHA, these individuals would "then be eligible to participate in the formation of a sovereign government, and also gather signatures from Hawaiians and non-Hawaiians on petitions declaring support for the reunification of Native Hawaiians and recognition of Native Hawaiians' un-relinquished sovereignty." The goal of those driving the initiative was to register 200,000 Native Hawaiians and "Once the roll is finished, the Commission is required to publish the registry to start the process of holding a convention to organize a Hawaiian governing entity and then the Commission will be dissolved." Initially, Kanaʻiolowalu was to run through January 19, 2014, with certification of the roll to follow. But, due to low participation, on March 17, 2014, the Native Hawaiian Roll Commission reopened the registry and extended it to May 1, 2014, in the hope of securing more names.[45] At the time, advocates of the Akaka Bill vowed to press on and mobilize for federal recognition. However, with the death of high-ranking U.S. senator Daniel K. Inouye in December 2012, and the retirement of Akaka in January 2013, the legislation lost its greatest advocates in the U.S. Congress (even while the subsequent and current members of Hawaiʻi's delegation support federal recognition).

Since then, advocates have pursued additional paths to obtaining federal recognition through the U.S. Department of the Interior (DOI). In response, in June 2014, with only five days' notice, the DOI began hearings throughout the islands and in select places on the continental United States to get public input to consider procedures for "Re-establishing a Government-to-Government Relationship with the Native Hawaiian Community." By July 28, 2015, The Native Hawaiian Roll Commission posted online their certified list of 95,690 people of Hawaiian ancestry who could form the voting base to create a Native Hawaiian governing entity.[46] And by September 2016, the DOI announced that it had crafted a new rule for procedures for "reestablishing" this relationship.[47] But given the election of Donald Trump to the presidency, it remains to be seen what the full outcome with respect to the formation of a Native Hawaiian Governing Entity underwritten by the "50th" state and federal government will be.

In the Hawaiʻi context, opposition to Hawaiian sovereignty exemplifies the Right's mobilization of resentment against Kanaka Maoli as a politically marginalized people. The deployment of rights discourse by conservative activists such as William Burgess, Ken Conklin, and others expresses the imperialist resentment that saturates their politics while deflecting critical scrutiny. As with imperialist nostalgia, those who seethe with imperialist resentment—with its commitment to a "civilizing mission"—mourn the passing of traditional society, which demonstrates their part in settler colonial continuity in the guise of "equal rights," while they invoke the supposed demise of Kanaka Maoli integrity in terms of distinct peoplehood as justification for the denial of Hawaiian sovereignty.

Since Kanaka Maoli have more to lose than to gain from the Akaka Bill legislation, those who are hostile to Hawaiian sovereignty claims might instead push for its passage. However, they are simply too caught up in the settler colonial logic of racial resentment, where they can only imagine their own dispossession at the hands of those they themselves stole from. Further, all they can see is the proposal for creating a new governing entity, and since they are antigovernment they cannot see above the grass they wish to graze.

The word *cow* can also connote "for a very long time; indefinitely," as in: "some Americans say that Hawaiians can wait until the cows come home for the United States to relinquish its control over Hawai'i." But *cow* can also mean to frighten with threats or a show of force: "the Hawaiians cowed the settlers with the enduring sovereignty claim." And *cow* also can be used as slang for becoming angered, or upset. For example, "the settlers in Hawai'i had a cow when Kanaka Maoli started clouding title over their private land holdings."[48] Indeed, although in the United States and Hawai'i cows are raised as livestock for their meat, dairy products, and leather, and as labor, Kanaka Maoli need not be assessed merely for what they offer the colonizers.

Legal Documents

JOINT-SENATE RESOLUTION · To Provide for Annexing the Hawaiian Islands to the United States. Resolution No. 55, known as the "Newlands Resolution," 2nd Session, 55th Congress, July 7, 1898; 30 Sta. at L. 750; 2 Supp. R. S. 895

APOLOGY RESOLUTION · To acknowledge the 100th anniversary of the January 17, 1893, overthrow of the Kingdom of Hawaii, and to offer an apology to Native Hawaiians on behalf of the United States for the overthrow of the Kingdom of Hawaii. Resolution No. 19, known as the "Apology Resolution," 103d Congress, November 23, 1993; U.S. Public Law 103–150.

NOTES

1 The cartoon was originally located at http://www.hawaiireporter.com/story.aspx?d44d4c25-f8c904ff9-ae3c-c96610c811c6, but the link is no longer live and for this reason the cartoon is reproduced in this chapter, in figure 2.1.

2 See http://www.hawaiireporter.com/, accessed August 10, 2017.

3 Wolfe, *Settler Colonialism and the Transformation of Anthropology*, 2.

4 Elkins and Pederson, *Settler Colonialism in the Twentieth Century*.

5 "Cow," *Urban Dictionary*, accessed August 10, 2017, www.urbandictionary.com /define.php?term – cow.

6 It should be noted that the term *colonialism* itself is contested by many Hawaiian independence activists seeking the restoration of the Hawaiian Kingdom, because they insist that the United States has merely occupied Hawai'i. The distinction between *colonialism* and *occupation* has legal ramifications under international law, since to decolonize or deoccupy Hawai'i entails the reliance on different legal bases for the claim (i.e., The Laws of Occupation).

7 Dudas, *The Cultivation of Resentment*.

8 Bethan Loftus's work on an English police force explores how greater political recognition of cultural and gendered identities has impacted the interior culture. He found two broad, and opposing, perspectives on the contemporary working environment. The first is characterized by resistance and resentment toward the new diversity terrain and is articulated principally by white, heterosexual, male officers. The second contrasting standpoint—held by female, minority ethnic, and gay and lesbian officers—reveals the persistence of an imperious white, heterosexist, male culture. Loftus argues that "the narratives of demise and discontent put forward by the adherents of the former operate to subordinate the spaces of representation for emerging identities and sustain an increasingly endangered culture" (Loftus, "Dominant Culture Interrupted," 756).

9 Duggan, *Twilight of Equality?*

10 Rosaldo, "Imperialist Nostalgia," 107–8.

11 *Baehr v. Lewin*, 74 Haw. 645, 852 P.2d 44 (Hawai'i Supreme Court, May 5, 1993). Arguably, the debates regarding same-sex marriage and civil unions were also pertinent to the culture war in Hawai'i when the Hawaii State Supreme Court ruled in favor of same-sex marriage in the case of *Baehr v. Lewin*. Nina Baehr sued the state of Hawai'i, alleging that the state's refusal to issue her and her same-sex partner a marriage license amounted to illegal discrimination on the basis of gender, in violation of the state's Equal Rights Amendment. The Hawai'i Supreme Court ruled that the state's prohibition of same-sex marriages amounted to discrimination on the basis of sex. The court remanded the case to a lower court to determine whether the state could prove this compelling state interest in prohibiting same-sex marriage. The *Baehr v. Lewin* decision mobilized opponents of same-sex marriages, who feared that gay marriage would soon be legal in Hawai'i, and anti-gay-marriage legislation was passed on both the state and federal levels. Voters in Hawai'i adopted a constitutional amendment allowing legislators to ban same-sex marriages, thus making the state's Equal Rights Amendment no longer applicable. In late 1999, the Hawaiian Supreme Court determined that this new ban was effective and refused to recognize same-sex marriages in the state. In 1996, in response to the *Baehr* decision, the U.S. Congress passed the Defense of Marriage Act (DOMA).

12 "Apology Resolution." See this text as reproduced at the end of this chapter.

13 Fuchs, *Hawaii Pono*; Kent, *Hawai'i*; Trask, *From a Native Daughter*.

14 Coffman, *Nation Within.*

15 Hasager and Friedman, *Hawai'i Return to Nationhood.*

16 Silva, *Aloha Betrayed.*

17 Omandam, "Report." One hundred years later, the United Nations issued the findings of a nine-year treaty study and called the annexation of Hawai'i into legal question. More specifically, it assessed the so-called annexation as invalid.

18 Trask, "The Politics of Oppression."

19 Trask, "The Politics of Oppression," 68–87.

20 Trask, "The Politics of Oppression," 68–87. After a massive increase in American migration to Hawai'i, statehood emerged as a real prospect. As early as 1950, two special elections were held to choose sixty-three delegates who would draft a state constitution for Hawai'i. In addition, among those who were allowed to take part in the vote were settlers as well as military personnel—who together outnumbered Hawaiians.

21 Trask, "The Politics of Oppression," 68–87.

22 "Declaration on the Granting of Independence to Colonial Countries and Peoples," accessed November 9, 2017, http://www.un.org/Depts/dpi/decolonization/declaration.htm.

23 In 1962, the assembly established a special committee, now known as the Special Committee of 24 on Decolonization, to examine the application of the declaration and to make recommendations on its implementation.

24 Barsh, "Indigenous Peoples," 373.

25 Griswold, "State Hegemony Writ," 101n14.

26 Griswold, "State Hegemony Writ," 93.

27 Barker, "Recognition." This changing political terrain creates the need for multiple interventions on different fronts when challenging the logic and workings of settler colonialism and how the logic of capital functions in relation to settler colonialism.

28 Goldstein, "Where the Nation Takes Place."

29 MacKenzie, *Native Hawaiian Rights Handbook.*

30 See http://www.pacificlegal.org/ and http://www.cir-usa.org/.

31 Twigg-Smith, *Hawaiian Sovereignty.*

32 Conklin, *Hawaiian Apartheid.*

33 This case has gone up to the Ninth Circuit Court of Appeals in a decision over whether the plaintiffs had standing as state taxpayers. The judge removed the Hawaiian Homes Commission Act from the case and declared that element of the complaint a political question. In February 2007, the federal appeals court stopped short of dismissing the lawsuit of 2002 but overturned its own earlier decision by finding the plaintiffs lacked legal standing. The court sent the case back to U.S. District Court in Honolulu to determine if any of the plaintiffs are eligible "in any other capacity," and so it goes on. See Conklin's own website for details, accessed August 10, 2017, http://www.angelfire.com/bigfiles90/ConklinBio.html.

34 Kenneth R. Conklin, "Aloha for All: Basic Principles," 2001–8, accessed August 10, 2017, http://www.angelfire.com/hi2/hawaiiansovereignty/principles.html.

35 Kauanui, *Hawaiian Blood.*

36 Whitehead, "Hawai'i."

37 In the 1830s, Parker herded and slaughtered cattle for Kamehameha III in the Waimea region on the island of Hawai'i. In 1847, Parker received two acres of land from Kamehameha III (Whitehead, "Hawai'i," 160–61).

38 Stannard, *Before the Horror*.

39 Kauanui, *Hawaiian Blood*.

40 See Faludi, "Broken Promise"; Hawaii Advisory Committee to the United States Commission on Civil Rights, "A Broken Trust"; Federal-State Task Force on the Hawaiian Homes Commission Act, "Report"; Morse, "Home Lands Lawsuit to Be Filed Today"; Pang, "Land You Bought May Actually Be Home Lands"; Uyehara, *The Ceded Land Trusts, Their Use and Misuse*.

41 Since the start of the 111th Congress (January 3, 2009) three sets of proposals have made their way to the table, all titled the Native Hawaiian Government Reorganization Act of 2009: S 381 and HR 862 introduced on February 4, 2009; S 708 and HR 1711 introduced on March 25, 2009; and S 1011 and HR 2314 introduced on May 7, 2009. It was this last set of bills that saw the most political activity of the three sets. On May 7, 2009, when both were introduced, they were identical. For information on these bills and their predecessors, see http://thomas.loc.gov/cgi-bin/bdquery/D?d111:2:./temp/~bd4Kwa::|/bss/111search.html| for S. 1011 and http://thomas.loc.gov/cgi-bin/bdquery/D?d111:1:./temp/~bd4Kwa::|/bss/111search.html| for HR 2314, accessed August 10, 2017. There was standstill on all of these bills, and it wasn't until the next Congress that S 675 was reintroduced to the Senate Committee on Indian Affairs on March 30, 2011 (along with its companion, HR 1250). S 675 passed the Senate Committee on Indian Affairs on September 12, 2012. See http://www.indian.senate.gov/. For more details on this most recent action, see "Streamlined Akaka Bill Passes Committee," 2012, accessed August 10, 2017, http://www.hawaiinewsnow.com/story/19539550/streamlined-akaka-bill-passes-committee.

42 Hawaii Senate Bill 1520, "First Nation Government," July 6, 2011, accessed August 10, 2017, http://www.capitol.hawaii.gov/session2011/Bills/SB1520_CD1_.HTM.

43 Other members of the Native Hawaiian Roll Commission are Na'alehu Anthony, chief executive director of 'Oiwi TV and the principal of Paliku Documentary Films; Lei Kihoi, former staff attorney for Judge Walter Heen; Mahealani Perez-Wendt, executive director of the Native Hawaiian Legal Corporation; and Robin Puanani Danner, president and chief executive officer of the Council for Native Hawaiian Advancement.

44 The commission is funded by OHA and authorized to prepare and maintain a roll of qualified Native Hawaiians who meet specific criteria; each person must be at least eighteen years old, be able to trace ancestry back to 1778, show that she or he has maintained the indigenous culture, and be willing to participate. Native Hawaiian Roll Commission, "Kana'iolowalu Launches Online Registry for Native Hawaiians," press release, accessed November 11, 2017, https://www.oha.org/registry.

45 Kana'iolowalu, "Moving the Nation Forward." March 17, 2014, accessed November 10, 2017, https://www.kanaiolowalu.org/news/story/?id=47.

46 Susan Essoyan, "Certified Native Hawaiian roll posted online with 95,690 names," *Honolulu Star-Advertiser*, July 28, 2015, accessed July 29, 2017, http://www

.staradvertiser.com/2015/07/28/breaking-news/certified-native-hawaiian-roll-posted-online-with-95690-names/.

47 Department of the Interior, Press release, "Interior Department Finalizes Pathway to Reestablish a Formal Government-to-Government Relationship with the Native Hawaiian Community," September 23, 2016, accessed November 10, 2017, https://www.doi.gov/pressreleases/interior-department-finalizes-pathway-reestablish-formal-government-government; see especially the "final rule," which was published on September 22, 2016, accessed November 10, 2017, https://www.doi.gov/sites/doi.gov/files/uploads/all_agency_combined_9.22.16_final_clean.pdf.

48 http://www.answers.com/topic/cow, accessed August 10, 2017.

Sovereignty, Sympathy, and Indigeneity

03

AUDRA SIMPSON

SOVEREIGNTIES COLLIDE

This chapter builds on the political life of settlement, its operations, and its secrets. By *settlement* I mean the imagined goal of massive demographic and bodily displacement of Indigenous peoples in what is now the United States and Canada and the replacement of those people with others, or the smooth move to a consent-based, multicultural, and liberal society that has settled all of its accounts and has taken, successfully, legally, and ethically the land that it occupies. This is an ongoing project that is imagined to be in the past tense, to have had its primary work finished, as in the "settling of land, the settling of consciousness, the making of moral and political worlds" atop the worlds of others. The stories that North American nation-states tell themselves and others is that all matters in fact have been settled, that Indigenous people are no more, that if their sovereignties survive they are in an insignificant form, that their significance to both legal and ethical matters is so minimal that in fact, this is an "immigrant" society and is, from the visual likes of things, governmental things, suggested by the visuality of an African American president, a pretty tolerant place. America must then be a place that embraces the difference of others enough to allow one to be led by the formerly subjected and enslaved (Obama's specificity and biography aside) and so, things are somewhat OK in regards to the past posing an ethical problem upon the present. "Things are OK" as in "things are settled." Yet even if we were to take these thin signs as history and historical redress—which I think is what the fixation with his blackness is supposed to tell us, and were we somehow to ignore the preponderance of black deaths at the hands of cops and civilians in the United States, the preponderance somehow of what this signals and means not only to their families and communities but to the larger publics that comprise the United States, then we would be forced to ask how it is that Obama's person, his politics, and his skin were to resolve a historical violence, how was his *election* at the very level of the body, of the right literally, to live, to make significant inroads into corporeal justice for African American people?

The preponderance of both black and Native deaths at the hands of police in the United States might force the question of the presumed promise of representation and justice (and presumed fairness) offered by electoral politics itself and the territory that it governs and elaborates.[1] This false promise, brought to bare relief by the force of the state against bodies of color (perceived to be dangerous, lawless, criminal, in Sherene Razack's analysis of Native bodies in custody, as "already dead"),[2] pushes to deeper questions of history and of justice—the very concern of this analysis. If you were to ask, even of the present, how does this electoral system come to happen, and why does it hold such seemingly unquestioned, and promissory hope?, in tending to these questions you might consider the conditions under which these places came and still come into being, the interlocking processes of enslavement and Indigenous dispossession. And once you configure this interlocking of dispossession and enslavement, these alienations of labor and land, as foundational context, you might want to then ask, "What histories can make the break for an opening in political consciousness and what histories cannot?" What if the history that has been experienced is ongoing and concludes not with the narrative of immigration and newness, with the promise of signifying skin, but with an ongoing project of dispossession and denigration, of an ongoing process of colonization, where the signifier is not darkened skin and a (not) repaired system of human bondage and thus a restoration of a universal mode of humanity? What if the signifier is other systems of politics, other land tenure systems, normative and philosophical orders that predate this one here? It will then take more than a differently skinned person (vis-à-vis whiteness) to signal the break between a grievous past and a new present. I start this analysis with Obama's skin and what it is taken to signal to multiple publics because its presumed break with a grievous past and the impossibility of a correspondence between his skin and what it is taken to mean. Here my claim is actually much broader—the promise of "hope" that mobilized an unprecedented number of people of color voting in 2008 and 2012 was indeed, an impossible one, in part because the "hope" that was generated by his election, just the possibility of his election—a repaired past, reparations, justice, reconciliation, is impossible in a place that has not untethered itself from its initial imperative: to take land and live atop it as if it is fair. Further, the "difference" of Indigenous peoples is not their skin per se (although that can matter greatly), but their political lives as sovereigns away from whiteness and foreign-ness within their own territories.

The story that I am telling then is a history of multiple sovereignties, rather than races—sovereignties that push up and live within the present. And this story is one that is inassimilable or unsignalable to a nation-state whose ongoing life is predicated upon the elimination not only of their bodies, but also their political orders, their governmental systems, and their title to land. This process is what the comparative historian Patrick Wolfe calls cleanly, "a structure, not an event."[3] Yet their sovereignty wrestles with the ongoing tech niques of elimination as it remains intact in their consciousness, their lives, legal mandate, and so on. So my question then is how justice is to be rendered in such a tight spot, where politics are predicated upon a disavowal and a simultaneous dispossession? Where histories are selected for, where political consciousness knows scant forms of the past, but can celebrate, vigorously the "hope" of brown skin and of democratic interventions into the neoliberal and conservative excesses of republican presidents.[4] In this piece I argue that hope goes in a different direction when we go North of the border and look to a governance system that seeks to repair its past openly, vigorously and formally in the eyes of the public. I argue that this question on "finding justice" in the present finds its answer in a move to emotion, with recourse to sorrow and conciliation, but also within an inherently limited and limiting formulation—the form of a contract that will then repair and presumably cancel out the possibility of all further claims to harm. The cost of justice however, is pain and its value is set within a market of sympathy—a market that is inherently limited by the structural and thence, distributive model of a market and a juridical frame for making commensurate fundamentally different polities.

So how to do politics in these "tight spots"? Through affect, through the spectacular performance of contrition, of repair, of hope, and ultimately, of sympathy. Sympathy (like savagery) is a mode of identification that is based, Hume argues, in a fundamental sameness of shared bodily form and shared "parallel passions."[5] This bodily form and its passions are presumed, but are also read perspectivally upon those bodies, and the resemblances and disresemblances are registered accordingly. An "imagined" pain may be read, somatically as it would be felt, for one self. Humesean ethics, the eighteenth-century moral ethics of sympathetic passions, has an enduring life, and has explanatory power for contemporary liberal, settler politics, and in the contexts of the United States and Canada, as this is how they now operate. Here, *injury* has been constructed as legal and social and political cause for concern and passions, *sympathy* in particular, part of the remedy to this injustice of emotional, rather than political, injury. In order to think through that remedy, we must consider as well Indigenous subjects have not always been injured; they were sovereign nations that entered into treaties with other sovereign nations. And simultaneously they have served as savage and unruly foils of a sort, while also being explicitly for the settler, one's better self (or one's worse self). This identification as "savage," but "like me" or savage, and distasteful, reprehensible, uncontrollable (absolutely not "like me") may be generative, and I wish to argue, may itself operate as a field of force. "Savagery," more explicitly than sympathy, has been productively tracked by scholars within American Studies for years. Here I am thinking of the Indigenous savage in Pearce's *Savagism and Civilization*,[6] and the subsequent savages that proliferate the captivity literature, representing various forms of American anxiety, American longing, American horror. *Americans.* However, the more specified process I want to go after is that of sympathetic reasoning in politics. The question I wish to pose and to provide critical nourishment for elaborates an old one, and is one that animates Canadian politics today and forms an unspeakable and underlying grid in American democratic politics further: "What is the possibility of justice or political transformation when the idiom for meeting out must take the form of a wound?" (not the form of other sovereignties, but the wound of actual injury) and more specifically (and here I mean, ethnographically), "How are those wounds to be known, how do politics then take the form of claims, and how then may justice be met out with emotional and economic disbursement?"[7] What are the political possibilities afforded within such a framework?

Wendy Brown's *States of Injury* theorizes the necessity of an injured political subject, a subject who is reduced to the form of "political identity" and then makes herself apparent to the state through the work and the idiom of claiming.[8] What generates and lies beneath this claim is harm. The claim that she or he will make will have to provide proof of that injury, proof that takes the form of adjudicative, knowable, replicable, certain evidence. For the original social contract to be upheld between the party and her or his state, a state represented through a court and its attendant adjudications, for her or his injury to be (validated) to be compensated for, this evidence must be persuasive. When compensated, a value is attached to the claim, and that value also cancels out further claims to lingering injury and/or suffering. The contract stills time but also opens time into one critical, defining moment, an opening of sorts to the possibility that one's truth (often anchored in the body and requiring narration and testimony and triangulation) is in fact the truth and that in the meeting of that truth with punishment or with capital, the pain will be diminished, or will at least cease to visit itself upon the national (state) body through the form of further claims upon its purse and its reason.

Here the earlier question moves through this latticework of possibility, or impossibility that Brown maps out for us, and which I now wish to move more explicitly to the time-sensitive model of the contract.[9] What is then the space of politics that is afforded to those whose histories, selves, and aspirations are whittled to a space of an injured claimant, and a claimant whose "prior" is suffering, rather than sovereignty, or the injustice of stolen land and stolen selves? How does this play out when suffering is attributable fundamentally to state sovereignty (i.e., via boarding and residential schools, germ warfare)? Settler sovereignty, I have argued elsewhere, is precarious and yet hegemonic through its instantiation through law,[10] and is being heard and performed through a fundamental question of Indigenous rights and reparations repeatedly in the theater of court.[11] It is in the theater of the courts, in part, that settler sovereignty sets itself up in adversarial or bequeathing relationship to Indigenous sovereignty. In fact, it is through settler sovereignty that Indigenous sovereignty, in a legal sense, gets its form. In order to consider these broad questions I will assess parallel sovereignties as they brush up and against each other. I am arguing that these are juridicalized market forces of sympathy—a new order of affective politics, particular to liberal, settler states, for rendering justice. So this chapter will move to these following three manifestations of political life. Now this becomes a story in three parts, if you will: first, a story of Indian foment (or rather, unambiguous, rather classic armed "resistance") as an instantiation of their sovereignty; second, their bodily suffering as a negation of their sovereignty and reinstantiation of state sovereignty; and third, the state-driven project of truth and reconciliation as a failed commensuration of both.

SOVEREIGNTY

In the 1990s in Canada there were several national injuries to be adjudicated, all having to do with Native bodies, territorial or otherwise, and their urgent, spectacular, rupturing pain upon the settler nation's international image, an image we were told of one of the most "tolerant and beneficent countries."[12] This first rupturing episode occurred in the summer of 1990, rendered in popular English newspapers as the "Indian Summer." This long hot summer, we were repeatedly told (as we experienced it) was on another scale, an explosive summer when Mohawks and allied individuals took up AK-47s and held ground at Kanehsatà:ke, a reservation in Quebec, in a seventy-eight-day defense of their territory against state-sanctioned land expropriation. This land expropriation was to annex a Mohawk burial ground and sacred pine trees in order to extend a nine-hole golf course by nine more and construct luxury condominiums in place of, or on top of, the dead and in the horrified face of the living.

During that summer the Progressive Conservative (PC) prime minister of Canada, Brian Mulroney, explained to a Canadian Broadcasting Corporation journalist that the Warriors who defended these sacred pines and were encamped behind the barricades at Kanehsatà:ke were not a traditional Iroquois society. Instead, they were criminals and terrorists. And as criminals and terrorists there was no authorizing text for their action besides vice and violence. Yet the Warriors he spoke of argued in fact that they had an authorizing text, but that text can be known in very partial ways to those who watch the evening news. The "Warriors" were and still are a society of Mohawk men whose role is defense of territory. In order to do so their minds must be free from grief, inconsolability, or loss. They must think clearly in accordance to the Kaianere'kó:wa, the "Great Binding Law" of "The League of the Haudenosaunee"—or those who are known in more common parlance as the "Iroquois Confederacy." That duty, some would argue among them, is their authorizing text, not violence and vice.

The Mohawks of Kanehsatà:ke were never in a proper status of wardship vis-à-vis the federal government, and so their land was vulnerable to expropriation and their reactions to those expropriations vulnerable to such external interpretations. Given this, at times they needed to act even more defensively and persistently, and would appear also to act in unreasonable ways.[13] Prior to the summer of 1990 they endured two centuries of sustained land expropriation. In response to those alienations they petitioned Ottawa, they petitioned Quebec, they suffered incarceration(s) for their petitionings, and finally, in 1990, they resorted to peaceful protest, a protest that became decidedly violent. When their peaceful protest did not effect a response from Ottawa regarding "the most recent land situation," a situation whereby Jean Ouellette, the mayor of the neighboring town of Oka, moved to extend the neighboring Oka country club golf course, the Mohawks of Kanehsatà:ke moved militarily. This is because Ouellette's extension moved directly into Mohawk land and bodies, even if those bodies were dead. Perhaps even more egregiously because they were dead. After four months of peaceful protest the Warrior society convened at Kanehsatà:ke with AK-47 assault rifles.

Carl Schmitt argues that the power of the sovereign is such because he or she may determine what is needed and act accordingly, and so the major of Oka, Jean Ouellette, attempted to act as a sovereign.[14] He acted in accordance to what he deemed necessary, and in doing so incited a state of exception that distributed its effects through a ratcheting of tradition, Iroquois political theory, and a maelstrom of sensations and meanings that were sieved and mediated through the evening news—news that saturated a viewing world with two centuries of refusals, of misrecognitions. In this state of exception, there was no monopoly on violence nor was there a dense, recognizable moral cachet to reveal what "the good" was. The utility of every action was unclear, and everybody, in certain moments, looked really bad. However, some looked bad for more sustained moments than others. One thing that was certain was this: the land that was to be used to extend the golf course nine more holes was and still is precious to the Mohawks of Kanehsatà:ke as it held both the bodies of their dead as well as pines that were sacred to them.

Why did the Mohawks do what they did? In part because of their own constitutional framework, the Kaianere'kó:wa, which decrees that they have to defend their land from encroachment, but they also did what they did because of the vulnerable and contested nature of title to their land, land they could never properly or improperly own. Indians in Canada can never own land in a full sense, in a Lockean fashion, even when they have been encouraged by the state to farm it in preparation for title and for their own "civilization" and entry into a life of agriculture and settler citizenship.[15] Thus their bodies and the land that contained them were vulnerable beyond the notion of subsurface rights or the "aboriginal right to use"; their bodies had no integrity even as their genealogic property. Who was protected in this game of leisure? The gentleman's game of leisure—golf—trumped a seignorial obligation of protection, trumped imperfectly rendered use and occupancy, and trumped two centuries of active registrable protest, operating as the most recent affront to the territorial integrity of this northernmost tip of traditional Mohawk territory. The "law," settler *law*, revealed itself again to be precarious and fragile, never properly extending itself to them or their territory, enunciating in those moments a colonial past that refused to stay there, historically, *there* in a "before" state. Suddenly the largest deployment of troops in the history of Indigenous-settler relations in North America was deployed to Kanehsatà:ke, as this was the most unambiguous form of exceptional relations, that of warfare. Two thousand, six hundred and fifty soldiers were deployed to handle fifty-five people

I want to think now about what the law failed to contain in those moments and will do so with appeal to a brief sociological descriptor that will contain what I just described. This was a seventy-eight-day armed standoff, one that resulted in three deaths: a Sûreté du Québec officer, a Quebecois resident of the sister reservation Kahnawà:ke, and an English Canadian who died from tear gas poison outside of Kanehsatà:ke. Three arms of the law arrived, the Sûreté du Québec, the Royal Canadian Mounted Police, and finally, 2,650 regular and reserve troops from the 34th and 35th Canadian Brigade Groups and the 5th Canadian Mechanized Brigade Group. These were brought in a the height of tension, when Quebec premier Robert Bourassa requisitioned the assistance of the Canadian Forces in "aid to the civil power" by invoking the Emergencies Act. In that moment "The State of Exception" was official, and colonial law was strangely, violently, and very precariously reinscribed.

Simultaneously the Canadian viewing public and negotiators were forced to listen to sound bites that issued from the Kaianere'kó:wa, Iroquois peoples' "Constitution" or Great Binding Law that authorized their defense of territory.[16] This brief sociologic descriptor is a "watershed" moment so disorienting in this history of Indian–white relations in Canada that capital had to be released immediately to address, to redress, to assuage, to silence (some would say) once things came to a strange and immediate close. The federal government released $5.2 million afterward to buy the land in question for the federal government (finally to be purchased for the settler state, to then be held in trust for Mohawks), and another $51.2 million was released for a five-year Royal Commission to hold hearings around Canada on the issue of land and sovereignty and Indigenous rights.

The Mohawks burned their weapons (rather than bury them), peacefully surrendered, and were immediately incarcerated. This was a state of emergency that was not a state of exception for all. In this, the Salish scholar Luana Ross argues that for the United States genocide has never been murder,[17] and in a similar vein the legal scholar Sora Han argues, "alongside the newest images of America *at* war (over there, back then) there is, still, an image of America *as* war—even as this image is effectively invisible under the War on Terror's visual economy." Han writes from the vantage point of the "War on Terror," over there.[18] I wondered then (as I wonder now) if Canada fancied itself to be the United States? In Agamben's exhaustive review of the labor of philosophical, juridical, and congressional fiat after fiat that work to conceal the suspension of individual and collective rights in times of emergency,[19] forms of suspension that work insidiously to secure constitutional totalitarianism (under the ruse of democracy), we see here a precise correspondence. This is a precise accord to this sociology of event I have just offered. However, this suspension is the norm, the geopolitical norm of indigeneity in constitutional democracies. The exception is the norm for Indigenous peoples.

The state of exception is coterminous with the space we understand to be indigeneity (and the ongoing emergency that is making commensurate settlement and Indigenous sovereignty) as settler sovereignty requires the reformation of the indigenous as a *zoë* (a stripped, bare life)—the cadastral Indian registered and quantified in the eyes of the state. Perhaps we know this but too well. And this so their land may be taken, apportioned, and reformed as a camp for them. This state of exception, Agamben argues, is sovereignty, and perhaps we agree and want to modify this for the settler form that it may take and then say this is simply not surprising or perhaps an innovating concept when we consider the experience of Indigenous peoples in what is now the

United States and Canada. The very settlement of America required not only Jesuits, military force, violent and assimilative schooling, but a juridical move to disappear indigeneity, to make way for the ongoing emplacement of Europeans. Here the justificatory framework of the Doctrine of Discovery—the precedential practice from sixteenth-century Europe that is central to the dispossession and to political life here of seeing, claiming, and owning—does the great ideational and legal work of making this all possible.[20] And it works as a surprise, to put it lightly, upon indigenous people. Here, David Wilkins argues, law and the Supreme Court in particular work not according to a consistent logic of fairness, equity, and justice but rather "self-interest, political expediency and cultural arrogance" of the court.[21] In this, the persistence of the indigeneities of Mohawks of Kanehsatà:ke and many others necessitates techniques of power that work upon them to foment the exception not only through the ways in which law must respond to their actions, but also because they are themselves always a subject of failed elimination and juridic containment.

The land in Kanehsatà:ke was that problem writ large as they lived with their reservation so improperly configured; their land in a state of continued expropriation, their actions, ignored or vanquished, or incarcerated that they themselves recognized that they were in their own, constant state of historical emergency. This was what Jeremy Waldron and other political theorists sometimes gloss as *historic injustice.*[22] For the people of Kanehsatà:ke, it was most specifically, most grievously a sustained, not episodic or fitful or temporary problem; it was a *constant* of land expropriation.[23] Further to that, they could not achieve a colonial contortion that would allow for a recognition, and some degree of protection. Instead, the existing colonial contortions meant that their land did not appear the way it should *because* it was expropriated, because "it was sold out from under them." It would not and could not appear in a manner that would afford it proper recognition or protection. Their land did not appear to be theirs for use and occupancy, making it even more vulnerable to expropriation.

The seventy-eight-day standoff at Oka resulted in three deaths, a still-improper configuration of territory, national outrage (and shame), and the aforementioned five-year, $51.2 million Royal Commission on Aboriginal Peoples (RCAP) to investigate, to examine, and to textualize the problem of Indian-white relations.[24] Numbering five volumes and over 4,000 pages, this national exercise to document the "problem" created a multitude of recommendations, but none of those recommendations in this state-sponsored and state-driven research needed to be heeded.[25]

In 1992 Canada was ranked number one on the United Nations Human Development Index for the first time, hanging on to the top spot until 2001, when it dropped to third behind Norway and Sweden.[26] The drop was attributed in part to Aboriginal (or Indian, Metis, and Inuit) poverty and diminished life expectancy, forms of suffering that registered on agreed-upon indices of national well-being. The affront to these indices marked inequity in a manner that harmed the nation-state in an international imaginary of the moral good: the healthy life, the robust nation, the *caring* nation. This statistical drop in ranking was coterminous with the foment that I started to describe with "Oka." Just three months after Oka there was another rupturing incident, this one televised to the public, via a nationally televised "tell-all" confession/exposé by the Assembly of Manitoba Chiefs Grand Chief Phil Fontaine of emotional, physical, and sexual abuse while a student at Fort Alexander Residential School in Manitoba. Fontaine's confession was more of a testimonial, one that would not, in its nationally televised form, specify the *content* of his abuse, even after being asked twice by Barbara Frum about *sexual* abuse. He replied to her, "some things are private," but did say that all the boys in his third-grade class were abused and possibly sexually.[27] Fontaine's public interview created a national interest and furor in what became on those very moments the "scandal" of residential schools. Starting in Canada in the late nineteenth century and lasting until 1996, when the last school closed in Gordon, Saskatchewan, residential schools were entrusted to various churches, but were a state-driven mandate to civilize, whiten, and prepare Indian people for citizenship and private property. What they were in fact was a carceral system of violence.[28] Thus this "scandal" became knowable then through the currency of individual and then collective claims against the United Church of Canada, claims that have since bankrupted the church.[29] This process of adjudication, both on individual and collective levels, moved capital, sentiment, and possibility in different directions—it stood in contradistinction and contradiction to the image of masked warriors at Oka, who collectively and forcefully refused state encroachment; the impetus for that encroachment is what Elizabeth Povinelli theorizes and tracks in her work as "liberal power."[30]

Liberal power distributes itself in accordance to a moral good, but one that is economically determined. It moves capital and sentiment so that market of profitability and concurrent shame may collect for economic surplus but also collect for national absolution along nodal points of pain, of redemption, of disbursement that will take the form of a minimal, subsurface, "recognition." The recognition need not be deep; in the context of Australia, it is rendered through the impossibility of the formula itself. So for example, the *Wik* decision of 1996 seeks to address land use and rights in conflict. What should take precedence in a case where you have overlapping claims to land, Native title or pastoral leases? Pastoral leases constitute 70 percent of Australian land. We learn from Povinelli and Larissa Berhendt that post-*Wik*, the exercise of Native title is only possible for a small number of Native people.[31] The formula, with *Wik*, as with federal recognition here in the States as well as in Canada, is itself a contortion, one that for many Indigenous claimants is unachievable. But it appears as if it is just. In this, the very existence perhaps of a formula and the possibility of meeting its requirements offers a *chance* at justice—here access and repossession of traditional lands, not redress or compensation for their loss.

The "events" that I just detailed are in fact a logic of dispossession and accordant resistance or engagement that I do not wish to assign a spectacular space in studies of recognition, or resistances or rearticulations. It wants to be known according to the market for rendering legibility and sympathy in this setting that I speak of—Canada—a new space of settlement. The requirements that indigenous peoples be subject, that their subject status be known through the idiom of pain was impossible in those first moments in 1990, as AK-47s do not speak of pain, they speak of the potential to unleash pain. The language of sovereignty avails itself to us now as Mohawks spoke of their land, their governing system, their political and theoretical framework for asserting that system, their philosophical basis for refusing encroachment. Sovereignty then was made material, an impossibility within normative order that struggled with its own shaky, precarious sovereignty (we know this from Quebec's fitful partnership within confederation) and sought to realign itself with its own precarious beginnings: force, perhaps deceit, and the suspension of law.

FAILED COMMENSURATION

How to commensurate the life of Indigenous sovereignty with the settler expectation of pain? How to commensurate then with the pain of abuse, of rape, or of institutionalized pedophilia? I borrow the term *institutionalized pedophilia* from the written decision of Canadian Supreme Court justice Douglas Hogarth in his 1995 sentencing of especially egregious and now deceased Port Alberni residential school supervisor and pedophile Arthur Plint.[32] Plint sexually abused thirty Native boys at the Port Alberni residential school in British Columbia while he was dormitory supervisor there from 1948 to 1968, and the responsibility for this, the legal and fiscal responsibility, was curiously absorbed by the state. The case against Plint, *Blackwater v. Plint* (2001) first heard in the British Columbia Supreme Court in 1998[33] with twenty-one litigants was the first of its kind to disburse fiduciary responsibility from the individual, the monstrous Arthur Plint to the church (25 percent) and to the federal government (75 percent). The original $30 million claim against him actually amounted to much less and set up a scale for harm in the following way: a high of CAD$145,000 for a former student who had been subjected to "anal and oral rapes [that] were extremely violent and brutal and were accompanied by threats," and a low of CAD$10,000 for a student involved in "two instances where Plint took his hand and placed it on Plint's genital area while both were fully clothed. Although there were additional similar assaults by Plint," the court decided that this litigant had "not proved that any of the psychological difficulties he has experienced in his life after leaving the school were likely caused by the incidents he described." The other awards were for $125,000, $85,000, $20,000 and $15,000, bringing the total to CAD$400,000.[34] Recall that the original claim against him was $30 million.

How to commensurate the pain and agony and continued suffering of those whose live bodies, whose young bodies were considered of so little worth that they were subject to (state- and church-sanctioned) intrusion, to a *constant* of violation? Violation that occurred under the sign of civilization and white beneficence? The argument of repair is critical here—how do "we" commensurate "their" diminished bodily sovereignty (a restoration of it) to the market for adjudication? How can their new subjecthood, a status as (largely strangulated) indigenous nationals and simultaneous subjects of state violation and violence be made legible enough for adjudication? These children are now adults, and are referred to as "survivors."[35] Which, indeed they are. But they are also nationals of Indigenous political orders. One must ask if justice is then to be found in this resubjectifying process, and through the market of sympathy and narration found in the transnational model of the Truth and Reconciliation Commission (TRC)?[36] It states quite simply, "The truth of our common experiences will help set our spirits free and pave the way for reconciliation."[37] I quote the mandate of the commission as retold to the Canadian Broadcasting Corporation: "The purpose of the commission is not to determine guilt or innocence, but to create a historical account of the residential schools, help people to heal, and encourage reconciliation between aboriginals and non-aboriginal Canadians. The commission will also host events across the country to raise awareness about the residential school system and its impact." The Truth and Reconciliation Commission has a budget of $60 million. It was formally established on June 1, 2008, and will complete its work within five years.[38]

This commission is also predicated upon the contract, the time-sensitive model of disbursement, and in this, the form of liberal power theorized ethnographically by Elizabeth Povinelli. Here it is a power that opens memories and bodies up for inspection, expects and invites narratives (that notably are not legally binding, so perpetrators are excised from the archive, protecting them from legal action), and creates *yet another* national, settler archive of what has happened—recall the post-Oka Royal Commission. Who has been inspected but for whom and to what effect? The TRC was part of a massive 2006 Indian Residential School Settlement Agreement (IRSSA),[39] which included "common experience payments" as well as the establishment of a TRC. The disbursement here is of monetary funds that are supposed to be palliative, disbursed through prefigured indices of sympathy. A sympathy that performs the semblance of a listening state, a *caring* state, a state that says quite literally, as the then conservative prime minister Stephen Harper said in 2008, "I am sorry" (speaking as a state: "that I hurt you, that I took you from your parents, that I raped you"). Will the testimonial restore a body to its former state, will it remove the scars and wounds and ongoing suffering that mark indigenous bodies and communities today? Will land be given back and can bodies be given back; can they be restored to their former state? Can Indigenous sovereignty itself, stand up and be heard in these theaters of sympathy, shame, false adjudication?

I don't know if that really is the name of the game. But it seems for now to be the only game in town, a game that Denise da Silva might call the tyranny of the fetish of the transparent self, the modern subject.[40] It is one that works to be like the imagined, authorizing center, be it in this case the imagined "white man," the civilized self, the dispossessing rather than the dispossessed, and to accord to their ideal, to repair the wound so that their difference (raced, indigenous, perhaps queered . . . take your pick) will not stay outside the normative and territorial center of the moral universal and modal subject. *Restoration, repair, reconciliation*, "I am sorry" (. . . "that I raped you"). This is the gestural architecture of settler states, the idea that repair will allow a joining, a concurrence, an equality, an assimilation (a further swallowing?). For some, that would be really great, really ideal: "We said we are sorry—we can now reconcile." But what if some things are irreconcilable?[41] Because for some, perhaps actually for many, who form these differently subjected bodies and philosophical orders, life with this form of subjecthood has been in fact a living death and a fight for life—a fight even for the bodies of the dead and the land that nourishes those bodies to have an integrity, a concordant respect by the living.

What we have in this triangulation of events that I have just unpacked is a mapping of that impossibility, in part for "pragmatic" reasons and in part for the problem of commensuration itself. Robust Indigenous sovereignties are completely impractical, we will hear repeatedly, by (presumed) landowners who have assembled into such groups such as the "Upstate Citizens for Equality" when confronted with the reality of Cayuga land purchases in what is now Central New York State.[42] Indigenous sovereignty, Oneida sovereignty in particular, is time sensitive. It is not upheld by the force of their historical removal, or their purchase of their lands, but by the impracticality of what their return means for the current property owners of the town of Sherrill. Their sovereignty, the very specter of their return to their traditional territory after forcible removal is simply untenable for *economic and practical reasons.* This practicality is determined by the notion of *laches*, which Supreme Court Justice Ruth Ginsburg determined trumped historical use, occupancy, stewardship and a prior, rightful claim.[43]

When power takes a certain form and demands and requires that we line up in certain ways and presents then an impossibility of concordance, I wish to argue that it then requires instead a volley of spectacles and in this, the inducement to move public sentiment forward, *now. Right now*. Or, *right now* as it should have been *then*. Indigenous bodies were torn open way before Oka, but Oka and its quiet and then militarized reminders required a spectacular repair, to territorial and historical injuries of the settler's sovereignty, of the Indians' (young) bodies *fast*. That second injury, the one that seems to haunt us all, made itself known in part through Phil Fontaine's initial refusal to specify the content of his wound; however, the Truth and Reconciliation commission, a state-sponsored listening exercise that archives these narratives of deep suffering and pain, takes into its auditory arena all of these wounds. Oka, of course, will never be forgotten (in that territorial context). However, that land remains improperly rendered and Indigenous bodies remain themselves, and simultaneously outside of themselves, in this new market for their pain. And in this, the exteriority of their lives, from the West, from the points of reason, opened up a further space for settler instantiation and now, I want to note, with the cunning, and masking language of *reconciliation*—a settler absolution.

NOTES

1 For recent statistics on deaths at the hands of police, please see the *Center on Juvenile and Criminal Justice*. "The racial group most likely to be killed by law enforcement is Native Americans, followed by African Americans, Latinos, Whites,

and Asian Americans. Native Americans, 0.8 percent of the population, comprise 1.9 percent of police killings. African Americans, 13 percent of the population, are victims in 26 percent of police shootings. Law enforcement kills African Americans at 2.8 times the rate of white non-Latinos, and 4.3 times the rate of Asians" (Mike Males, "Who Are Police Killing?" *Center on Juvenile and Criminal Justice*, accessed October 31, 2015, http://www.cjcj.org/news/8113). For a book-length analysis of Native deaths in custody in Canada please see Razack, *Dying from Improvement.*

2 See Razack, *Dying from Improvement.*

3 Wolfe, "Settler Colonialism and the Elimination of the Native."

4 My argument will now ground itself in Canada, but please note that a similar excitement obtains to the youthful, newly elected liberal prime minister, Justin Trudeau. Trudeau is the son of Pierre Elliot Trudeau (and Margaret Trudeau), both extremely popular in Canadian politics and beyond, but most significantly for Native people Trudeau senior attempted to divest them of their rights as Indians via *The White Paper* of 1969. Trudeau used their presumed "assimilation" into Canadian society, after 100 years of aggressive and state-mandated assimilation, to mean that they should be automatically enfranchised and would lose their land base. This is not to say that the new Trudeau will operationalize the same arguments and theories of difference at the level of politics, but he is in support of neoliberal "development" (i.e., pipelines, fracking) that are located domestically on Indian land. Nonetheless, like Obama, his election saw unprecedented numbers of Native people go to the polls to vote out Stephen Harper, a conservative prime minister. Harper was in office for two terms and did all he could to secure capital accumulation and cut social programs. For an analysis of the assimilationist White Paper politics of Pierre Elliot Trudeau, see Turner, *This Is Not a Peace Pipe.*

5 I am drawing my interpretation from David Hume's *A Treatise of Human Nature.*

6 Pearce, *Savagism and Civilization.*

7 Formal apologies are paradigmatic forms of emotional, state-driven forms of emotional disbursement. On December 19, 2009, U.S. president Barack Obama signed an apology resolution to Native Americans that reads, "on behalf of the people of the United States to all Native peoples for the many instances of violence, maltreatment and neglect inflicted on Native peoples by citizens of the United States." The resolution however, was not publicized, and in spite of efforts on the part of specific Republican Party members (former senator Ben Nighthorse Campbell, Colorado, and Senator Brownback, Kansas) to move the bill since 2004, there was no announcement and no fanfare. This generated a response from Robert Coulter, executive director of the Indian Law Resource Center, who stated, "For an apology to have any meaning at all, you do have to tell the people you're apologizing to." See Capriccioso, "Native Apology Said Out Loud." For an analysis of the quiet of Obama's apology vis-à-vis Canada and Australia's apologies, see Simpson, "Settlement's Secret."

8 Brown, *States of Injury*. See in particular chap. 4, "Rights and Losses," 96–132.

9 Brown does discuss the liberal abstraction of the contract as an instantiation of power that is consolidating and signals a *consent* to be subordinated in an agreement whose ideational history (she moves briefly through Locke, Rousseau, and Hobbes) is the subjugation from nature to civil society (cf. 162–64). Brown then

genders this to discuss the predicament of women (as thus not consenting fully to be ruled by men), but does not consider the larger claims of the language of civilization upon those who are determined to be savage in new, settler states that require and yet make impossible the consent of those positioned in prior, Aristotelian terms as fundamentally without reason, or law, or other "fundamental" attributes of civilization. As a result, these actors are made impossible subjects, incapable of receiving full and proper consent. For thinking through the significance and work of contract theory in settler colonial contexts, please see Nichols, "Realizing the Social Contract," "Indigeneity and the Settler Contract Today," and "Contract and Usurpation"; and Razack, "The Murder of Pamela George."

10 See Simpson, *Mohawk Interruptus.* See chap. 5 (115–46) for settler state precariousness.

11 Simpson, *Mohawk Interruptus*, 143.

12 Please note that the following passages may also be found in edited form in my *Mohawk Interruptus* since this analysis follows directly from the book itself. I use my own earlier words to describe the *Oka Crisis* as it is the account and interpretation that feeds directly into this broader analysis of sympathy (*Mohawk Interruptus*, 150–54).

13 See John Pocock's "The Ideal of Citizenship Since Ancient Times" for a tidy summary of the relationship between rights and reason in Western political theory.

14 See opening arguments in Schmitt, *Political Theology*.

15 For historical studies that examine this paradox and even the force, violence, and sometimes profound loss and failure that attended to the settler colonial project to *make* Indians agriculturalists, see Sarah Carter, *Lost Harvests*; and James Daschuk, *Clearing the Plains*. Robert Innes's study of Cowessess kin and territorial history, *Elder Brother and the Law of the People*, also documents the starving force of agriculture in the Prairies.

16 See Parker's version of *The Constitution of the Five Nations*: the *Kaianere'kó:wa* has six wampum beads that deal explicitly with the conditions of war and force, and these conditions are most caught up with nations that do not accept the message of Peace. However, wampum 91 explicitly states that "A certain wampum of black beads shall be the emblem of the authority of the War Chief to take up weapons of war and with their men resist invasion. This shall be called a war in defense of territory" (54).

17 Ross, *Inventing the Savage*, 15.

18 Han, *Bonds of Representation*, 232.

19 Agamben, *State of Exception*.

20 Miller et al., *Discovering Indigenous Lands*.

21 Wilkins, *American Indian Sovereignty and the U.S. Supreme Court*, 4.

22 Waldron, "Superseding Historic Injustice," 4–28.

23 For an excellent visual summary, see the documentary film by Obomsawin, *Kanehsatà:ke: 270 Years of Resistance*. For a history of the community and land written by the people of Kanehsatà:ke, see Gabriel-Doxtator and Van den Hende, *At the Woods' Edge*.

24 This is from the RCAP website, where the entire report is available for download: "This report of the Royal Commission on Aboriginal Peoples concerns government policy with respect to the original historical nations of this country. Those

nations are important to Canada, and how Canada relates to them defines in large measure its sense of justice and its image in its own eyes and before the world" (*The Royal Commission on Aboriginal Peoples*, 1996, accessed October 27, 2017, https://www.bac-lac.gc.ca/eng/discover/aboriginal-heritage/royal-commission-aboriginal-peoples/Pages/final-report.aspx).

25 I quote extensively from Audrey Doerr's summary of events in the Canadian Encyclopedia under "Response and Legacy" of the Commission: "the federal government did not call a First Ministers' Conference within six months of the Report's release, as recommended by the Commission. Instead it issued a lengthy information document, 'Aboriginal Agenda: Three Years of Progress,' outlining government achievements from 1993. When the federal government did make a formal response on January 7, 1998, its proposals emphasized nonconstitutional approaches to selected issues raised by the report. The four objectives of the federal response were renewing partnerships; strengthening Aboriginal governance; developing a new fiscal relationship; and supporting strong communities, people, and economies. In particular, the federal government issued a Statement of Reconciliation in which it expressed profound regret for errors of the past and a commitment to learn from those errors." This precedes the formal apology for residential school abuses offered in Parliament in 2008 by former Prime Minister Stephen Harper. The Statement of Reconciliation was accompanied by a commitment of $350 million to be used to support community-based healing, especially to deal with the legacy of abuse in the residential schools system, resulting in a five-year research and community-driven healing projects funded by "The Aboriginal Healing Foundation." Doerr's entry continues, "Very little response was given by provincial governments, which viewed the report as a federal initiative" (Royal Commission on Aboriginal Peoples, thecanadianencyclopedia.com, accessed October 26, 2017, http://thecanadianencyclopedia.ca/en/article/royal-commission-on-aboriginal-peoples/).

26 The UN development index rankings include life expectancy, education, health, income, poverty, and the environment.

27 The Fontaine-Frum interview was originally broadcast on CBC's *The Journal* on October 30, 1990. The interview may be viewed on CBC digital archives online, accessed November 22, 2015, http://www.cbc.ca/archives/entry/phil-fontaines-shocking-testimony-of-sexual-abuse.

28 Million, "Telling Secrets."

29 The United Church of Canada operated 100 of the 130 residential schools and faced 100 civil lawsuits. For histories of the residential schools in Canada, see Milloy, *A National Crime*.

30 Povinelli, *The Cunning of Recognition*.

31 In her lecture on "The Promise of Mabo," Larissa Behrendt argues in general in relation to Native title and then specifically in relation to the *Wik* decision: "Native title is a very weak form of property interest. The Wik case, while recognising that Native title could co-exist determined that it only survives if it is not inconsistent with any other interest and there has been no intention to extinguish it. Whenever there is a conflict in the interests between leaseholders and Native title holders, the interest of the farmer will always triumph." See Larissa Behrendt, "Finding the Promise of Mabo."

32 See Lazaruk, "77 Year Pedophile Sentenced to 11 Years." The specificity of abuses at this residential school are reported here by Codlin, "Black Spot on the Hearts of Survivors Revealed."

33 This case was heard in British Columbia Courts twice before it was appealed by the United Church of Canada on the grounds of "charitable immunity" to the Supreme Court of Canada in 2005. The SCC upheld the fiscal liability of the Church (25%).

34 A summary of the "Alberni Residential School Case" may be found in Miller, "The Alberni Residential School Case: Blackwater v Plint." The case itself is Blackwater v Plint 2001 BCSC 997, accessed February 7, 2010, http://www.courts.gov.bc.ca/jdb-txt/SC/01/09/2001BCSC0997.htm.

35 See Niezen, *Truth and Indignation* for a tidy history of survivor discourse and organizing at a global and national (also local, indigenous level) in Canada, 18–20.

36 Also see Niezen, *Truth and Indignation*, for a recent, ethnographic account of the TRC that tends to the narratives as well of priests and government officials.

37 From the "Introduction," Truth and Reconciliation Commission of Canada website, its mandate, accessed October 31, 2015, http://www.trc.ca/websites/trcinstitution/index.php?p = 7.

38 From Canadian Broadcasting Corporation's "FAQs: Truth and Reconciliation Commission," accessed October 27, 2017, http://www.cbc.ca/news/canada/faqs-truth-and-reconciliation-commission-1.699883.

39 A detailed summary of the agreement, accessed October 28, 2017, may be found at http://www.aadnc-aandc.gc.ca/eng/1100100015576/1100100015577 under "Indian Residential Schools Settlement Agreement."

40 da Silva, *Toward a Global Idea of Race.*

41 Neither time nor space will allow me to incorporate the analysis of either of these cognate pieces of critical scholarship; please consult Coulthard, *Red Skin, White Masks*, for a critical analysis of the emotional demands of "reconciliation" upon Indigenous politics (esp. chap. 4), and Million, *Therapeutic Nations*, for a gendered and global history of the affective structure of this demand.

42 *Upstate Citizens for Equality*, accessed October 27, 2017, http://www.upstate-citizens.org/.

43 See Goldstein, "Where the Nation Takes Place," for an analysis of *City of Sherrill v. Oneida Indian Nation of New York.*

II Colonialism by Any Other Name

04

A School of Addicts

The Coloniality of Addiction in Puerto Rico

ADRIANA MARÍA GARRIGA-LÓPEZ

SCHOOL OF ADDICTS

Sitting on the low wall hugging the corner where I interviewed him, Edgar enumerated the jails where he had served time for drugs and petty theft. Pointing out ruefully that he had used drugs throughout his time in Puerto Rico's penal system, he named one infamous institution and blurted, "Damn! There is more dope in there than out on the street! When I got out of there, I was using more than before I went in."

"That is everyday life," he continued. "Drugs are what make the jail go around." Then he exclaimed, "Puerto Rico is a school of addicts!" But what does it mean to say that Puerto Rico is a "school of addicts"? If this is true, how do Puerto Ricans learn to be addicts and to what are we addicted? Does Edgar's provocative highlighting of tutelary relationships within colonialism point to new ways of considering addiction and identity formations in relationship to U.S. empire and Puerto Rico's status today? What is, after all, the coloniality of addiction in this context? What might such coloniality say to ethnographers and ethnography? And, perhaps, most important, what might ethnographers say and do in the face of such aspects of the imperial formations as make up and gird relations between the United States and its colonial possessions today, including within anthropology?

Frantz Fanon described colonialism as a "fertile purveyor for psychiatric hospitals."[1] He argued that even during periods of "successful" colonization, there is "a regular and important mental pathology which is the direct product of oppression."[2] After all, "colonialism has not simply depersonalized the individual it has colonized; this depersonalization is equally felt in the collective sphere, on the level of social structures."[3] To understand Edgar's story we need not rely on discourses of individual pathology. On the contrary, as Edgar emphasizes, we should approach his life trajectory as the result of social processes and institutions that teach people to be addicts. Following Fanon, then, we might locate the problem of addiction squarely within sociopolitical life in imperial formations.

Figurations of Puerto Rican psychological and social pathologies have been central to the development of knowledge across a broad range of disciplines, including psychology, anthropology, sociology, economics, and history.[4] Therein, representations of Puerto Rican suffering of a primarily individual order gain form in dialogical relation to representations of the whole society and culture as pathological. Puerto Rican laziness, vagrancy, and indolence have been at the heart of U.S. colonial discourse and local reformist preoccupations.[5] Narratives about the pathology of Puerto Rican culture are still prevalent today, not least of all among Puerto Ricans who have experienced steep economic decline and the erosion of community structures. Yet, culture is neither the cause, nor purely a reflection of conditions of oppression. In spite of the ubiquity of the move, merely positing Puerto Rican culture as problematic does not explain or account for the dialectic between colonial violence and forms of resistance.

Vagrancy as a category of state capture has been central to ideological treatments—often in a putatively benevolent, liberal-democratic, or even multiculturalist vein—of Puerto Rican labor and culture. "Anthropologists have noted the Puerto Rican's resistance to hierarchy [and] his/her reluctance to work in teams."[6] And cultural critics argue that forms of autonomy persist in practices that act as a limit to capitalism, including "subaltern disturbances" of normative social life and engagements with "popular illegalities ranging from petty thefts to homicides."[7] Criminality, then, is the nexus through which "the pathology of the Puerto Rican, [or] his/her 'docility' in terms of his/her subsumption within the real regime of labour" is constructed and/or problematized.[8] These socioeconomic processes continue to shape, albeit with changing effects, how addiction becomes visible or intelligible, and how drug use is managed in Puerto Rican society. Puerto Rican sociality, with its quotidian illegalities and ordinary disturbances, acts as a limit to U.S. colonial power and transnational capital, even while simultaneously mapping its rhizomatic effects.

The sharp rise of injecting-drug use in late twentieth-century Puerto Rico took place during a moment marked by the fracturing of the welfare state and the alienation of large numbers of the population from the formal labor market. To gain a critical purchase on addiction as a social process with roots in U.S. American empire requires an ethnographic approach to knowledge production in tandem with a resistance to individually stigmatizing or criminalizing narratives. This implies a consideration of the public health effects of colonial domination and the foreclosure of Puerto Rican self-determination at multiple levels. Public health is one of many points along a continuum of social differentiation and biopolitical domination that results, as Ann Stoler has noted, from gradated forms of sovereignty as "the hallmark feature of imperial formations."[9]

This chapter seeks a reorganization of the flow between science and street, wherein anthropologist and addict have a conversation by the side of the road that in turn situates all participants within a shared, yet lopsided social scientific field.[10] Knowledges hovering at the edges of consciousness become apparent in both the interviewee's storytelling and in the anthropologist's narrative of their encounter. Our identities are both in question. Something such as an impression or a hallucination floats in the space between us. At times, it takes form as a Puerto Rico painfully clinging to the imperial pleasures and myths of the voracious capitalism that cannibalizes us.

Relation as a concept is "*holographic* in the sense of being an example of the field it occupies, every part containing information about the whole and information about the whole being enfolded in each part."[11] In Edgar I found a lucid interlocutor. In what follows I narrate my relationship with him in order to reflect on the portrait of addiction as assemblage that emerges out of the motion of bodies and machines through San Juan, a former Iberian imperial outpost and today the capital of the United States' largest colony. Our incompletely shared text is part of the oppositional knowledge I seek to generate from ethnographic engagements that go beyond the administrative taxonomies of public health research on addiction. What emerged in my conversations with Edgar was both endless possibility and inescapable immobility—fixed or truncated positionalities alongside and in tension with expansive notions of life and labor.

MY LIFE IS NO DIFFERENT FROM ANYONE ELSE'S

> Because it is a systematic negation of the other person and a furious determination to deny the other person . . . humanity, colonialism forces the people it dominates to ask themselves the question constantly: "In reality, who am I?"
>
> —Fanon, *Wretched of the Earth*, 250

Edgar is a Puerto Rican man who was in his late thirties when I met him. Although born in a midsized town on the north coast, Edgar told me that he came of age in urban New Jersey. Tall and thin, with brown eyes and handsome features, his light-colored skin browned and crinkled by the sun, Edgar always looked tired standing at the streetlight. He toted a pasteboard sign, announcing to motorists that he was homeless and had AIDS. He asked for assistance, monetary or otherwise, while the traffic light shone red.

Bitingly hot, the sun hangs heavy over the city's concrete; the steamy asphalt refracts the light so it appears wet and tactile. The avenue undulates like a mirage of expectation. During morning and evening rush hours, traffic is heavy and thousands of cars go past this particular intersection. Most motorists passing by Edgar's corner watch anxiously, anticipating the green light, studiously ignoring him and others like him. Gleaned from such encounters, their skillfully averted gazes evoke neutrality or benign indifference with an acquired precision. Yet a few roll down their windows and hand over some coins, occasionally a dollar or more.

Edgar was only one of several guys asking for money from motorists at this intersection near my home. I drove past his corner every day on the way to work at a U.S. government-directed HIV study, or in order to get onto San Juan's major highway. Early one morning Edgar was crying as I approached the light. He tugged at his hair and sat down on the curb as I watched. He was shouting as he wept, gesturing toward the sky with his hands. He seemed utterly desperate and frustrated.

Other times he weaved between cars stopped at the light, as he slowly limped from driver to driver and held out a waxed paper soda cup to collect small donations. Edgar had seemed calm, or perhaps very high, filled with a warm resignation and a moist sense of purpose. He was addicted to heroin and dependent on what he collected on his corner to get his fixes, a fact he made no effort to disguise or hide from those who chose to help. His somewhat regular haircuts and shaves, and occasional, newly acquired hand-me-down clothes, suggested ongoing contact with social services or community-based organization outreach programs.

On a day soon after I had seen him crying, I rolled down my window while stopped at the light to offer some change. I put a few coins in Edgar's cup and he responded, "Thank you. God bless you." I thanked him in turn for his blessing. "How are you?" I then asked with concern, remembering the crying fit I had witnessed. He answered quickly, complaining, "I'm not very well. I'm sick. I feel bad." I was unsure as to how to answer him and I asked, "What is your name?" "Edgar," he answered. I replied, "Hi Edgar, I'm Adriana, it's a pleasure." While holding his muffled gaze, I added, "Take care of yourself." He thanked me for my "human warmth" and I waved goodbye. After this interaction, Edgar began to recognize me, and he would smile and wave when I passed him. Slowly, we developed a rhythm of interaction, each short conversation bringing forth new dimensions of relationality. "It's good to see you, Edgar," I would say each time, before asking how he was doing.

Over the two years I lived near his working station, I gave Edgar small sums of cash, bottles of drinking water, sandwiches, and a couple of used shirts while waiting for the light. When I asked whether he would be willing to be interviewed by me, he acceded warily, and only after ascertaining to his satisfaction that I was not a journalist or social worker, but (just) a student doing research for a school project, a practice he said he understood (Sí, yo entiendo eso).

Injecting-drug users living in the San Juan Metropolitan Statistical Area (MSA) have a higher rate of injection frequency than users in other MSAs under United States (U.S.) federal purview, as reported in a wealth of scientific literature.[12] This means that injecting-drug users living in Puerto Rico put drugs into their bodies more times in one day than their counterparts in other areas of the United States and its territories.[13] Such island-based users report a higher frequency of injection than users in the continental U.S. even when compared to those who inject mostly the same drugs and are also of Puerto Rican descent. Like most addicts living on the street in San Juan, Edgar injected a mix of heroin, cocaine, Ketamine, and other veterinary anesthetics and fillers an average of five to eight times a day. This cost him between fifty to a hundred or more dollars daily, though this figure was contingent on what he collected at the streetlight and elsewhere. Amassing this amount that is never enough, and that responds to an ascending demand, assumes the character of an unequally segmented necessity or a daily crisis that must be met with increasingly creative and flexible modes of accumulation.

When I asked Edgar how much he spent on drugs, he answered: "I try to save eleven to seventeen dollars to go down there [to the place where drugs are sold—the *punto*], but I am not satisfied. I come back sick." Here to be sick is to say that one is "fiending" for drugs, or in withdrawal from not having had a fix recently enough.[14] *Enfermo* as used by Edgar and in general by addicts in Puerto Rico indicates being sick with need and refers to a feeling of illness resulting from heroin withdrawal symptoms. This can appear as quickly as two hours after a fix.

Other users claimed that any and all addicts would consume as much heroin as they could get their hands on, or up to one or even two *paquetes* a day. This would mean ten to twenty decks of heroin, at approximately fifty dollars per *paquete*. But Edgar was emphatic in explaining that his use was not geared toward being what he described, in an accented but fluent-sounding English, as "high" or "happy." He said that heroin facilitated survival, "for me to be OK," that is, merely in order to be able to function, "to be able to be normal, able to walk, not have a headache. I am conscious," he said.

Edgar did not measure drug use in the way common in public health literature on addiction, which involves specifying units of use distributed at certain points along the day's axis. Nonetheless, influenced by the literature on addiction I had read in preparation for this research, I insisted on asking him, "And you shoot up about how often? Like five or six times a day?" He first mumbled something I couldn't make out, and then said,

> This vice is something different. This is . . . this is not a question of looking to get high, or get happy. Now heroin is something different. What one looks for is just to be able to be normal, to feel well, to be able to walk, not to have pain. Heroin gives you pain in your bones, it gives you nausea, it gives . . . Heroin is a . . . The brain creates these liquids which cause you to laugh, to yawn. One's feelings, one's sensations . . . I don't know how to say it, I am not very . . . I know what it is but I don't know specifically in words. Well, the brain creates those liquids. Heroin, when you inject heroin you supplement those liquids, and the brain stops producing them. When the brain stops producing those liquids, which are necessary for your well-being, for your own good, um, well that's when the problems come."

"Yes, that's when the dependence comes . . . and you need it just in order to be calm," I responded awkwardly, but impressed with his understanding of current paradigms for a neurochemical basis to addiction.

Edgar made a point of saying that he was not the kind of addict who injected as much as he could get. Again switching into English, he said, "I'm not greedy." Then in Spanish, "That's why I don't believe in being asleep. You're not going to see me like that." By saying that he did not believe in being asleep, he meant that by injecting heroin he did not seek a state of dormant hallucinatory meditation or "unconsciousness" that is not properly sleep, but a haze through which the sensations of the body are dissolved into the dreamy processes of the mind. In such a state a user, like a sleeping person, is unaware of his or her surroundings. As I listened, I remembered having seen Edgar at his station, staring off into the horizon with the drooping waxed cup and the pasteboard sign in his lax hands, with slackened jaw, nonreactive to the movement of the world around him, appearing almost fully anesthetized, but, indeed, still standing.

Sometimes Edgar's body, like those of other addicts begging on street corners, assumed implausible positions; the sleepy downwards drift of the intoxication known locally as "monkeydreaming" led toward the ground, but somehow never arrived there as muscles even in their slackness rested upon bones, keeping the body stacked mostly upright. Slouching or crouching, or bent over in ways that would seem impossible to sustain, this movement of contraction and expansion of bodies corresponds to the temporality of "nodding off" engaged by heroin use. This border between sleep and wakefulness is an angular and uncomfortable way to spend time, as when one nods off while sitting, and loses control of one's neck muscles, jerking back awake every so often. Such tumescence of bodies reveals something more than just the blissful or absent sleepiness of heroin. I had heard people in San Juan refer to heroin injectors' postures as "performance art," as "living sculptures," and as something akin to Michael Jackson's music video "Thriller" (1982). Torpidity and enervation seem here to act at once in the body, pulling it in different directions and producing performative sculptures of death in life and life in death.

I tracked Edgar down one evening in November 2006. I was on my bicycle, with a small notebook and a voice data recorder in my cloth backpack. Edgar saw me as I parked and locked my bike. I watched him work the traffic at the intersection. As I made voice comments into my digital recorder I noticed that I could smell the sea only a few blocks away. I was unsure how to approach. But then it was Edgar who approached me. He remembered that he had agreed to an interview, and he was prepared to talk. I explained my research and that I wanted to know who he was and what he did at the light every day, repeating the assurance that I was neither a reporter, nor a social service provider trying to recruit him for rehabilitation. I explained that I couldn't afford to pay him for his time, though in the end, when the interview was over, he asked me for five dollars, which I gave to him. Edgar thus agreed to the interview, but established that he would keep an eye on oncoming traffic and might interrupt our conversation. He clearly did not want to miss out on his collections.

Almost immediately after he sat down with me, another man took his place at the stoplight. Edgar got up to discuss the situation with him, apparently consenting to letting the other man borrow his station while we talked. My recording of his voice that day begins with him saying that he was at the time nearly perfectly disposed to help me. Yet when I thank him for talking with me, he begins again in a different tone that resonates with a willing vulnerability. This vulnerability was self-consciousness about being recorded, and not just by the cheap recording device that I held openly between us in the palm of my right hand, but by something like History with a capital H. He began his *testimonio*, and what would prove to be the first and last interview of its kind that I was able to perform, repeating the words: "I am in the best disposition to help you" (Estoy en la mejor disposición para ayudarte). And then, "My life is no different from anyone else's." Something seemed to cohere as Edgar began talking into the recorder. Fanon's insistent question reappeared, and the need of and for the colonized to produce a coherent narrative about them/ourselves once again came to the fore. And this question is multiply refracted and rearticulated in my own ethnographic engagement by means of the text that appears here, as part of an edited collection of essays about U.S. empire.

LA LUZ ESTÁ MALA / THE LIGHT IS NO GOOD

Edgar set about the task before him methodically and eloquently, offering his depressive character as an explanation for his addiction and tracing this trait to the influence of his mother's neglect of him as a boy, a neglect born from the pressure of economic demands on her migrant household in New Jersey. He told me that his father abandoned the family, reappearing only when Edgar was ten years old because he was dying and wanted forgiveness from his ex-wife and children. Meanwhile, Edgar's mother worked two jobs while raising four children, two of them her sister's children who had been sent to live with their aunt so that they would learn to speak English. Edgar was an adolescent by then, and he grew up mostly on the street looking after himself.

> My cousins lived with us for about four or five years and my mother's life became very difficult. She had to get two jobs, and I lost time with her then, you understand. That's when I got derailed a little bit, as such. I was alone, on the streets, in the United States. I was always an A student, with a four point average. I was always very intelligent, apparently my mother took that into consideration, like I would be able to manage my life on my own at thirteen or fourteen years of age. And as they say, my *teenage* [in English] time was . . . I spent it alone, you know, I never had attention from my mother.

Edgar's narrative was neutral, in the sense that he clearly did not want to be pitied. Instead, he stated plainly that these experiences left him lonely and alone on the rough urban streets of northern New Jersey. He described how years later he returned to Puerto Rico to care for his dying mother, who had retired to the island before being diagnosed with cancer. He came close to tears as he recounted bathing and feeding his mother for months while she underwent chemotherapy. But he was not complaining. In fact, he said regretfully, "She died quickly." And he expressed remorse for having refused to give his father the forgiveness he asked of his ten-year-old son just before he died, to which I offered some words of comfort. Edgar's mother died when he was twenty-six. Edgar told me that although he married and had children after her death, he continued to feel lonely and depressed. Edgar started using heroin when he was thirty-one years old. He blamed this turn to drugs on the stress from his job, the responsibilities of his domestic life, and his persistent loneliness.

Edgar's marriage ended because of his heroin use, and eventually he also lost his job refurbishing and expanding houses and buildings, something at which he claimed he was "the best." Edgar said he had worked too much, and this had led to arguments with his wife and to a generalized state of exhaustion. But given the passionate way he described his career in construction, his devotion to his mother, and his pride in schoolwork, it became evident that Edgar was proud of his accomplishments. He felt they revealed his intelligent and compassionate nature, and demonstrated that he was well mannered and worthy of respect. In the pain that it clearly caused him to speak of his parents, his children, and his ex-wife, who, he said, had already found another partner and was happy and stable, there was a manifest loss, a renunciation, and an acceptance of this loss—a suicidal abandonment, as well as a certain kind of tortured freedom from this history of himself. I kept my promise not to try and convince him to enter a rehabilitation program, letting a protracted silence pass between us. As the intensity of emotions subsided, he pointed out the construction and design flaws of buildings around us, as something in his eyes brightened and his manner quickened, while he explained he was a perfectionist for this sort of thing. Then he said, "I'm an Aquarius," as though this turn to astrology might explain his perfectionism.

Edgar went on, "You are lucky that you spoke with me, because if it had been one of these other guys . . ." This served as a warning that I should be careful when approaching addicts asking for money at traffic lights. Edgar wanted to help me get interviews with other people working at the light, but he said that I should let him approach the others, something that never came to pass. He told me that he was speaking in this open way with me because he understood what I was trying to do. But he warned me that other people would say whatever they thought I wanted to hear, or that they might rob me. At that moment, however, with so much traffic going by in what were still the remains of daylight, and without more than five dollars, my keys, a pen, some paper, and a voice recorder in my pocket, I didn't feel particularly endangered.

Edgar claimed to have no friends. "What about the other guys here at the light?" I asked. He said, "Those are not friends. If you go to sleep with a dollar in your hand, they take it. Or they see you sick, and they have [drugs] on them, and they don't say to you, 'here, I will give you a little.' I use drugs *por estrés,* because I found myself alone. I am the kind of person who needs a lot of attention. Not to be coddled. I am not a child, but I like attention."

"Did you feel alone even when you were with your family [his wife and children]?" I asked. He replied simply, "Yes." In the silence that gathered between us after his answer, fearing that he was becoming uncomfortable speaking so intimately, I tried to figure out what to ask next. After what seemed like a long pause, I said: "Do you take any medications for your HIV?" He said that he was not presently, nor had he ever. When I asked why, he answered enigmatically: "I require nothing."

As he said this, another man who worked at a different corner of the same streetlight approached us, and Edgar got up to go meet him. They spoke for a few seconds, and I waited, worrying about the indicator light on my recorder that announced the battery was running out. When he came back, Edgar complained, "Things are bad at the light," meaning there was not enough money to be made. "Before, I used to stand there and make twenty bucks in half an hour!" He sat back down on the low wall. As he settled in, we were both distracted by a car waiting in front of us. It blasted reggaetón music, every piece of glass, metal, and plastic vibrating and shaking to the rhythm.

I looked at Edgar as he watched and, noticing a grimace, asked him, "You don't like reggaetón?" "I didn't say that," he said. "Because it's like hip-hop and salsa; the only thing is there are no instruments. It is a machine that is playing, but it makes some sense. I used to play the trumpet," he continued. Edgar said that he didn't look down on reggaetón, "because that is something that is ours." In his comparison of reggaetón to hip-hop and salsa, he was making reference to the humble early years of both musical genres, when, like reggaetón, they were each declared by many to be worthless, mere noise, or somehow inauthentic as truly Puerto Rican music. Edgar saw reggaetón as a generational style, and I shared with him that I also valued this type of music as the product of the cultural sensibilities and aesthetic proclivities of Puerto Ricans in the diaspora and on the diasporized island. Edgar nodded in agreement and then exclaimed with a grin, "But . . . I love the Beatles!"

Edgar thought for a while and then exclaimed, "I see that we are creating a copied culture. Nothing is genuinely ours; everything is store-bought. We need something genuine; to work, to create our own things. Because we have the knowledge for that. I am too proud. I am too patriotic. Most intelligent people are pro-independence. I read the newspaper often to keep up with things." He continued, explaining why he was in favor of political independence from the United States for Puerto Rico: "I am pro-independence. I believe in earning things for yourself. I am antiquated and have always tried to be around older people," he said. Edgar was now on a roll. He didn't wait for my questions, and continued,

> The government itself has let a lot of things slide to be able to get away with theirs, because I say that it **is** possible to stop drug trafficking and all that, but it is a business. All this is a business! The biggest addicts, the biggest *tecatos* are the rich. Tons of eating and shopping . . . You're not going to see a rich people's party without drugs there or any of that. There are many hidden tecatos; so many lawyers and doctors go to La Milagrosa [the *punto* where he buys drugs]. Those are the best because they send me to go get them six hundred dollars' to eight hundred dollars' worth and that's fifty dollars or sixty dollars for me.

He then told me that these wealthy users are identifiable by their expensive cars, gleamingly out of place in the depressed zones that serve as puntos. Drug users living on the streets make large purchases for these drive-through users, and in return they often receive a percentage of drugs or money. They are motivated to deliver their charge and receive this percentage rather than simply taking off with the entire amount by the watchful eyes of the puntos' owners (*bichotes*) and their sentries and lookouts that would not hesitate to assault, rob, or kill users who interfere with wealthy clients.[15] Despite this, Edgar assured me that the motorists who deal with him are lucky, because other users will just take them for their money and run. Then he declares, "I'm getting sick." I realized he was saying that our interview was bound to end shortly, and I didn't want to forget to ask him what he thought of the term *tecato* (the local equivalent of *junky*). When I ask him, Edgar replies, "The word *tecato* is disrespectful. The correct word is *addict*. Addiction is a mental disease, [I know] because I am living it. I am an addict because of my severe depression." Despite his elaborate understanding of the related development of his depression and heroin addiction, Edgar claimed that he had never spoken with any kind of counselor or psychotherapist. When I pressed, he insisted that he had not talked with an HIV counselor either, even after he was diagnosed as HIV positive through a routine blood test during intake at one of the five local jails where he had served time.

The voice data recorder's battery had run out of power, and I had filled all the pages and the inside cover of my small notebook. Edgar looked tired. It was time to go. I thanked him for talking so openly, and the interview ended. I gave him the five dollars he asked of me and watched as he reclaimed his corner. I shoved the recorder, pen, and notebook into my backpack and hurried home on my bike in the descending darkness, feeling like I had finally done something I could call *fieldwork*.

A few weeks after our interview, Edgar began to deteriorate visibly. He seemed more stoned than previously. Often he just stood there, eyes half mast, staring off into nothing, not even moving among the cars at the red light. His mouth hung open and his body crumpled, in a half bent posture that looked uncomfortable. A few times I passed him, and he didn't see me. But when we spoke he mentioned he was not feeling well and wanted to quit using. I offered, tentatively, to find out about free detox treatment centers. Even though I worked for a community-based organization focused on services to drug addicts and people living on the streets, it was not easy to obtain this kind of information. After calling a number of centers, I found only one that was willing to admit a new resident.

I tried to give Edgar the numbers and addresses of places he could go to detox or get treatment for HIV. But then he simply disappeared. After about a month of not seeing him, I asked a different man working the stoplight, and he told me he thought Edgar had died. Stunned by this report, I did not believe him fully. The next person I consulted at the streetlight a few days later told me a different story. He said that Edgar had been caught stealing some windows from a nearby construction site and was in jail. After more than two months absent from his station, Edgar reemerged. He smiled widely when he saw me, and I was happy and relieved to see him. He had gained weight and looked healthier. His hair was short, his skin bright, and he wore relatively clean clothes. I was so glad he was alive.

The principal modes of treating drug addiction in Puerto Rico are religious group recovery programs, or "addiction ministries."[16] These operate as both voluntary and court-mandated treatment programs. Helena Hansen argues that in the context of economic depression in Puerto Rico, "[a]dopting the 'new masculinity' of addiction ministries might be seen as a strategy for male ex-addicts to insert themselves on a track to middle-class respectability by pursuing a spiritually-based, rather than economically-based patriarchy."[17] Vinh Kim Nguyen has described an analogous form of citizenship in West Africa that emerges in a parastate context through an engagement with the politics of respectability and decency among HIV-positive people made possible by the social effects of antiretroviral treatments distributed by nongovernmental organizations (NGOs).[18] This therapeutic citizenship is "a form of stateless citizenship whereby claims are made on a global order on the basis of one's biomedical condition, and responsibilities worked out in the context of local moral economies."[19] Because of Puerto Rico's liminal position within the global political order, however, Puerto Ricans cannot access treatment for addiction or HIV through NGOs. As a result, the (albeit limited) social benefits of this form of stateless citizenship are not available to Puerto Ricans. Instead, many seek social capital through spiritual reform or are mandated by the courts to participate in rehabilitation programs run by religious organizations. If you are an addict dependent on public health care in Puerto Rico, there are no secular alternatives for detox and rehabilitation.

Shared needles and paraphernalia are significant vectors of HIV infection. Insulin needles are sold individually in San Juan's *hospitalillos* (literally, "small hospitals") or *chooting* (a colloquial form of the English term *shooting gallery*) where the heaviest and poorest users go to inject. In these places, insulin needles are often sold by the manager at a price of a dollar or two per needle. Yet many respondents reported that needles sold in hospitalillos are sold as new but are often actually used needles rinsed out with water or bleach. Most addicts I spoke with reported repeated incidents when their dependence on and desire for heroin, or the combination of drugs described above (basically, a "speedball" mixed with anesthetics), overcame their safety concerns, even when they were well aware of the high risk of HIV. Fewer users had the same knowledge about the sharing of cookers and/or filters used in preparation for injecting heroin and cocaine, common practices that are likely to transmit HIV between users. Insulin needles are also generally available in pharmacies, but are usually sold in bundles rather than individually, except at the discretion of the pharmacist. Many pharmacists will not sell to addicts asking for individual needles, or at all. According to Edgar,

> ninety percent of times you go in a pharmacy, because of looking like this, because the pharmacist knows they're for using drugs, they don't want to sell them to you. Egotistically, stupidly, foolishly! Because it's a question of health, and they don't see it that way, even being a health professional, I don't know why they don't see it that way. The only thing they see is the drug, the street, and . . . the negative stuff. . . . He . . . will tell you they are out of needles.

Here Edgar was direct in his challenge to what he saw as the misapplied authority of the pharmacist. He appealed instead to what my reader may recognize as the logic underlying the theory of harm reduction, as based on his experience and the reality of life on the street.

Shooting galleries spring up in abandoned or semi-inhabited structures and spaces. The sale and use of improperly sanitized and reused needles is a serious and hard-to-contain public health problem in Puerto Rico, one that has never been properly addressed as a serious issue. Despite the preponderance of data about the central role of injecting-drug use in HIV transmission in the Puerto Rican context, there has never been a state-run prevention campaign aimed at injecting-drug users. This shocking neglect has had terrible consequences for public health in Puerto Rico.

One of the most disturbing aspects of the mix of heroin, cocaine, and Ketamine common in Puerto Rico is its apparent effect on the soft tissues of injectors. Although I was unable to find conclusive evidence, addicts and health-care workers remarked frequently that the preponderance of large ulcerations on the bodies of injecting-drug users in Puerto Rico results from adding Ketamine to the heroin mix. Heroin and cocaine-injecting drug users have lived on the streets of Puerto Rico for a long time, but nobody can remember an earlier moment when so many addicts had abscesses so large and deep that they seem to take over people's extremities until one can plainly see the bones underneath.

Ketamine was categorized a Schedule III Controlled Substance in 1999, after its unregulated status facilitated its becoming one of the most popular "club drugs" in the United States.[20] Ketamine is mixed into batches of heroin along with fillers that are used to "cut" and reduce the purity of the drug before it is put for sale on the streets of Puerto Rico. Where this mixing occurs and whether it is being transported to selling points in the United States is unclear. Officials from the Food and Drug Administration have testified before the U.S. Senate that Puerto Rico is an "excellent gateway" into the United States for illegal drugs and that "Puerto Rican customs procedures are minimal compared to those of other nations bordering the US."[21] But the interviews I conducted also show that a significant amount of heroin moves from the northern continent to the island.[22] Ketamine is purchased from the United States and imported by veterinarians to countries around the world. If the mix of Ketamine with heroin and other "street" drugs is specific to Puerto Rico, how can we understand such parallel economies of intoxication in the interaction of metropole and colony? And what does this dual economy indicate about addiction as pedagogy in the various infrastructures that link Puerto Rico and the United States?

How Ketamine goes from being a legally marketed product to a major component in the "cut" of Puerto Rican street heroin, and who profits from that mixture, was one of the questions that guided this research. But the question elicited few real answers from users and medical professionals. Some conceded that the underground drug market's dependence on Schedule III veterinary pharmacological products requires the collaboration of veterinarians willing to fake prescriptions, place illicit orders, or participate in improper distribution.[23] And this is not unusual, as sociologist Madeline Román has noted, "At present, drug trafficking expresses the ways in which legal and illegal sectors of capital are inter-related. Both sectors reproduce and complement each other."[24] Certainly the participation of federal, state, and municipal law enforcement in the illegal drug trade is everywhere in evidence in

Puerto Rico. Without collaborators in law enforcement, medicine, and international finance, large and constant shipments, sales, and distribution of illegal drugs would be impossible.

The presence of Ketamine has become so common that an intake counselor and case manager at one of the group homes run by the largest rehabilitation company in San Juan lamented that some of his clients test negative on intake toxicology screens and are not able to receive services because the tests do not measure the presence of anesthetics, but only of heroin and cocaine.[25] This means that some of the neediest addicts do not receive proper detoxification even when voluntarily sought. The situation is compounded by the absence of detoxification and rehabilitation protocols for Ketamine addiction in general, meaning that health providers do not have a recommended treatment regimen to address the effects of Ketamine withdrawal. Counselors and case managers do not have adequate guidelines to follow with regard to the specific psychological and social effects of Ketamine addiction, and its associated behaviors and symptoms.

CONCLUSION

My attempt to circumvent the routinized (in)efficiency of public health discourse, research design, and data collection practices led to some insights regarding the practice of research with injecting-drug users in Puerto Rico. Despite the central role of injection in the transmission and dissemination of HIV in Puerto Rico, the available health resources are grossly inadequate and—with the exception of a few community organizations who provide clean needles and other paraphernalia—prevention strategies among the injecting population are almost nonexistent. Doing ethnographic research with addicts on the streets of San Juan proved daunting because the modes of relationality within knowledge production about this population saturated my encounters, most of which were heavily overdetermined by normative and hypocritical moralities such as those decried by Edgar and others. Various modalities of thought regarding addiction are deeply and paradoxically interrelated in Puerto Rico, in part because all court-mandated rehabilitation programs are premised on religious ideologies that require faith conversions as a necessary step in the process of recovery. Meanwhile, community-based organizations founded by leftists or queer activists find themselves obligated to act as subcontractors for epidemiological technologies and research protocols designed elsewhere, with someone else in mind.

The blurry spaces where law, religion, biology, psychiatry, journalism, anticolonial activism, queer feminist politics, and social science converge to produce the figure of the addict as an object of research and rehabilitation share a common circumspection, namely, the congressional cap that limits federal funding for public health care in Puerto Rico. Since its inception in the late 1960s this funding cap has been one of the most crushing facets of U.S. colonialism on the island. The resulting state of permanent resource insufficiency undergirds and supports the assemblage of social, technical, and clinical knowledges, and speculative modalities mobilized in response to addiction.

In such a circumscribed sociopolitical space, community health projects mostly reiterate and reinforce the conditions of structural and semiotic violence that are the hallmark of U.S. colonialism on the island. Even when such projects operate expressly in opposition to structural violence, they generally are able to effect only palliative and fragmentary action. In contrast to this, or perhaps as a result of such opacity, my conversation with Edgar took form as the most human exchange I had during my time as a researcher among injecting-drug users in San Juan. Edgar offered an eloquent discourse that looked from the marginalized and stigmatized space of the street, addiction, and poverty out toward the rest of Puerto Rican society, to those rushing past him in their cars hurrying out to meet the demands of work, consumerism, and family. Edgar enunciated clearly a position of protest against the violence produced by the moralism of antidrug policing and propaganda. Crucially, he offered a critical assessment of the conditions of dependence and addiction not as personal or moral failures, or even solely as diseases or afflictions, but as part of generalized modes of consumption in contemporary Puerto Rico.

While there were limitations to my research model, the exchange that took place between us happened between two people, both taking risks while also being vulnerable in order to become intelligible to one another. In this holographic attempt, we agreed to discuss the relationship between addiction, HIV, and colonialism as a "formulation of a shared yet contested space in real time and alongside its production of materiality" around our very bodies.[26] Despite the ways in which the social terrain that lay between us marked us differently in significant ways as student and addict, we found common ground in quotidian experiences of being Puerto Rican and in epistemological affinities. We shared a desire to examine the relationship between addiction and conditions of structural violence in Puerto Rico. We were both indignant that addicts should be criminalized and marginalized by means of hypocritical logics that specify certain forms of substance use as pathological, while excusing or normalizing those of others, especially those of the privileged. We shared a desire to see Puerto Rico become politically independent from the United States. In navigating our differences and affinities, the terrain upon which we stood as differently positioned subjects of U.S. empire, as researcher and native, shifted continually. Our transient relationship would not keep still, as we each became refracted in the other.

Puerto Rico is one of the key places where the United States has tested and refined its strategies of imperial governance and control. The island and those people's bodies who are marked by their relationship to its members of the Puerto Rican diaspora have been made to act as legal, social scientific, clinical, and financial laboratories for forms of appropriation and domination that have become central to the contemporary global reach of U.S. biopolitical, military, and economic hegemony. In the introduction to the present volume, Collins and McGranahan contend that ethnography promises fresh insights into U.S. imperial formations even as the very existence of such formations is often denied, hidden, or disavowed, in part because "one of the many covers with which U.S. empire cloaked itself was decolonization." For Puerto Rico, the disavowal of actual colonialism occurring under the guise of putative decolonization (either from Spain, or through the adoption of a Constitution in 1952) has led to the island's predicament of remaining "like a disembodied shade, in an intermediate state of ambiguous existence for an indefinite period," as Chief Justice Fuller famously and presciently wrote in his dissenting opinion to one of the Insular Cases foundational to the congressional doctrine of territorial unincorporation.[27]

It seems many specters haunt this small island. Yet this kind of ethnographic research into addiction, homelessness, and poverty on the streets of San Juan begins to make apparent the historical interconnectedness (and incompleteness) of the project of social reformation begun by the doctrine of Americanization, and the necropolitical strategies that multiply relegate the socially marginalized to categories of political waste. This entanglement of culture, politics, and flesh produces the island as event or problem at the macro level, but it can also be understood to be intimately connected to Edgar's life, and to my own, as to all the particular forms of embodied suffering prevalent in Puerto Rico and among Puerto Ricans today. Addiction, although significantly common, is only one of many such deep sorrows.

NOTES

All translations are my own, unless otherwise noted, and all names used are pseudonyms.

1 Fanon, *Wretched of the Earth*, 249.

2 Fanon, *Wretched of the Earth*, 251.

3 Fanon, *Wretched of the Earth*, 293.

4 Gherovici, *The Puerto Rican Syndrome*; Lewis, *La Vida*; Marqués, *El puertorriqueño dócil*; Pabón, *Nación postmortem*; Santiago-Valles, *Subject People and Colonial Discourses.*

5 Briggs, *Reproducing Empire*; Godreau, *Scripts of Blackness*; Suárez Findlay, *Imposing Decency.*

6 López and Natarajan argue that this "peculiarity of [the] Puerto Rican insertion into the work regime" results from the incomplete "transition from the formal (imposed externally) to the real (internalised by the workers) subsumption of labour in Puerto Rico" ("American Colonialism and Puerto Rican 'Criminality,'" 2237).

7 López and Natarajan, "American Colonialism and Puerto Rican 'Criminality,'" 2236.

8 López and Natarajan, "American Colonialism and Puerto Rican 'Criminality,'" 2236.

9 Cited in Collins, "Ruins, Redemption, and Brazil's Imperial Exception," 185.

10 Bourgois, *Righteous Dopefiend*, 306. See also Collins, *Revolt of the Saints.*

11 Strathern, *The Relation*, 18.

12 Andía et al., "Peer Norms and Sharing of Injection Paraphernalia"; Colón et al., "Between-City Variation in Frequency of Injection among Puerto Rican Injection Drug Users"; Colón, Robles, and Marrero, "Frequency of Drug Injection in Puerto Rico and among Puerto Rican Injection Drug Users"; Estrada, "Drug Use and HIV Risks"; Selik et al., "Birthplace and the Risk for AIDS among Hispanics in the United States"; Singer, "Why Do Puerto Rican Injection Drug Users Inject So Often?"; Singer et al., "Variation in Drug Injection Frequency."

13 Intravenously, intramuscularly, or subcutaneously—what is also known as *skin popping*. As Bourgois notes, each of these practices carries its own symbolic and socially consequential meanings: "Mechanisms of administering injections (skin popping versus intravenous) are a technique of the body that inscribes ethnicity and propels symbolic violence" (*Righteous Dopefiend*, 298).

14 This word is also used in Puerto Rico in reference to sexuality. Calling someone an *enfermo sexual* (sexually sick) or *un(a) enfermito/a* (sick-ey, or sick-o with an added diminutive), connotes a perversity. But it is not necessarily a slight, in that it indicates an active sex drive—a trait valued in men and in some women. It can be seen as analogous to *lovesickness* in this sense, where the sickness is a pressing need for the object of desire.

15 *Bicho* in Puerto Rico means penis. *Bichote,* therefore, denotes a large penis, but actually refers to a drug kingpin or owner of the punto.

16 Hansen, "The 'New Masculinity,'" 1721. A handful of methadone programs also exist.

17 Hansen, "The 'New Masculinity,'" 1725.

18 Collins, "Patrimony, Public Health, and National Culture"; Nguyen, "Antiretroviral Globalism, Biopolitics, and Therapeutic Citizenship."

19 Nguyen, "Antiretroviral Globalism," 142.

20 When Ketamine emerged in the underground drug market in Puerto Rico in the 1990s, it largely skipped the club-drug status attained in the United States. Its psy-

chotropic and numbing effects, however, quickly became subsumed into the high (*la nota*) expected from street *manteca* (heroin; literally, "lard" or "butter"), even though its chemical properties are supposed to be far less addictive than heroin itself.

21 Hansen, "The 'New Masculinity,'" 1722.

22 Many users interviewed for this project, including Edgar, reported buying heroin that came from New York, suggesting that the flow of heroin may not be only up from South and Central America, but also "down" from the metropole.

23 Traces of Xylazine have been detected in Ponce, Puerto Rico, in hypodermics analyzed as part of a clinical research protocol involving needle exchange (N. Rodríguez et al., "GC-MS Confirmation of Xylazine"). Xylazine and other veterinary anesthetics are not as highly regulated as Ketamine.

24 Román, *Narcotráfico*, 89.

25 None of the injecting-drug users interviewed during the course of this research reported having ever used methamphetamine. At present, crystal meth has not reached Puerto Rico in large measure, and the prospect that it may arrive eventually presents an alarming possibility that would complicate significantly the epidemiological picture with regard to injecting-drug use, the concomitant risks of exposure to HIV/AIDS, and drug-related violence. The prevailing street wisdom on this matter holds that Puerto Rican drug kingpins themselves have prohibited the sale of crystal meth on the island, though this remains uncorroborated.

26 Collins, "Ruins, Redemption, and Brazil's Imperial Exception," 184.

27 See Torruella, "The Insular Cases," 309.

Inhabiting the Aporias of Empire 05

Protest Politics in Contemporary Puerto Rico

MELISSA ROSARIO

The question of what it means to rebel in Puerto Rico is a fraught one, with roots as deep as its ties to U.S. empire. While electoral politics on the island suggest that Puerto Ricans overwhelmingly support continued association to the U.S. and, thus, *don't want to rebel*, there has existed in parallel a vibrant and long-standing history of grassroots movements that suggests otherwise. As Félix Córdova argues, these few movements gather energy (*recoger la energía*) of another kind.[1] Resolutely driven by a sense of national patrimony, these movements convey a deep understanding of Puerto Ricanness: a sentiment that is resonant not just on the register of cultural identity, but also in terms of geographic spaces. One such space is the coastline. In Puerto Rico, the beaches are particularly considered to belong "to the people," reflecting a commonsensical understanding of their status as public space as per Article 6, Section 19 of the island's Constitution.[2]

Despite this popular and legal significance, the coast has long symbolized the less savory aspects of Puerto Rico's long-term subordinate position to U.S. empire. Although the coastline has been cemented in public and legal insular law as patrimony of the public, its unincorporated status, and mainland interests in the sand, sun, and beaches have involved selling sought-after coastal property. As Arnaldo Cruz-Malavé has argued, Puerto Rican literature is littered with references to "the island's coast, its ocean-swept ports and cities, with foreign invasion, penetration, prostitution, plagues [that serve as symbols of] . . . colonialism."[3] Indeed, one needs no fiction to be aware of these facts. Standing nearly anywhere on San Juan's shores reveals this asymmetry between outsider and insider exchanges. The saltwater, which can heal, also burns for those with historical insight, reminding them of an ever growing sense of deep ambivalence for what the future holds.

The construction of the Hilton Hotel in 1946 reflects this disjuncture between the coast as patrimony of the public and as a place that also operates as the seat of empire. Sitting at the very entrance to the Old San Juan islet, the Hilton was the first hotel built as part of a government plan to establish a high-end tourist industry on the island.[4] Typical of the economic vision heralded by it, the hotel's construction was paid for by Puerto Rico's government, and Hilton's profits were tax free. The deal to establish the Hilton is a particularly ironic case in the history of coastal privatization because it was struck at the same time that the local elites were involved in drafting the island's own constitution. At the exact moment coastal lands were being imagined as public space, a different reality was also born—the de facto privatization of the beaches.

In 2007–9, I visited multiple sites where local activists were struggling to prevent coastal privatization: Piñones (Costa Serena), El Corredor Ecológico del Noreste, Arecibo (el pozo del Obispo), Isabela (Rescate Playas de Isabela) and Carolina (El Campamento Playas Pa'l Pueblo). For the most part, their process of contesting privatization was similar. Activists often began by publicizing a controversy through mainstream media, and holding a press release that denounced the current development plans. The press release would end by asserting the right of the public (*el pueblo*) to the lands and would be followed up by efforts to educate a broad populace about the planned privatization, usually organized through loose coalitions. Often children were the target audience of such programming, but traditional protest forms such as picketing and marching were also part and parcel of this rebellion. In the majority of these aforementioned cases, proposed privatization meant the expropriation of uninhabited lands, but it could also mean displacing families who had lived on the lands for generations without title, as in the case of Piñones.[5]

I was most taken by the ongoing protest in the Carolina campsite (El Campamento Playas Pa'l Pueblo) for two reasons. In the first instance, the intersection of local government corruption with the more global problem of beaches and natural beauties of the Caribbean being reserved for the tourist industry perfectly reflected what one NGO journal, *Cumbre Social*, projected for the near future: *una isla sin costa* (an island without the sea). It highlighted government corruption because the five acres that were now a construction zone for luxury condominiums and a parking lot were a designated part of the municipality's public bathing area in public zoning maps dating back to 1965. In this way, it was not only public space in the abstract sense that all natural resources were destined for "the general welfare of the people" under the Constitution, but it was one of twelve coastal areas on the island that had been marked out for the public to use in perpetuity. The campsite was also fascinating because it was the longest direct action I'd ever heard of—made possible because activists' legal team succeeded in paralyzing the construction project, leaving the activists free to inhabit the space, which they had done since 2005. Having long since outlived the brief period of media attention and police confrontations so characteristic of direct action, the few men who continued on as residents were neither hopeful nor going anywhere, a kind of activism that was entangled with doubt and possibility.

CHILL OUT AND WAIT: RADICAL POLITICS IN NEOLIBERAL TIMES

When I arrived to El Campamento Playas P'al Pueblo (Campsite Beaches for the People), it was so quiet I wondered if anyone was even there. Unlike Amigos del M.A.R.'s other protest encampment, Paseo Caribe, this encampment was quiet, and removed from the street.[6] First, I noticed the tattered nationalist Puerto Rican flag marking the entrance to a sandy parking lot, which prompted me to examine the area more carefully. Upon further inspection, I noticed a *ceiba* tree located next to trailer that showed several caricatured local activist faces.[7] They each held small protest signs related to distinct environmental issues. Over their heads, the phrase *las playas son del pueblo* (the beaches belong to the people) was written in graffiti-style lettering. Looking to my left, I noticed the barricades between the Marriott and the campsite—short concrete blocks, reaching my knees—marked with faded spray paint advocating sustainability and protection of the beaches.

Once I passed through the parking lot, and under the first tarp, I found myself in the campsite proper. It looked like a makeshift home. The first space to the right resembled a living room. It housed a bookshelf on one end, and a couple of worn but comfy couches in a semicircle. In the open space between the bookshelf and seating was a coffee table. In the far corner, covered by two overlapping tarps, sat a moderately sized television on a stand protected from the rain. To the left, I could see the entrance to the trailer, which served as a storage area for food, supplies, and miscellaneous items and occasional sleep space for certain visitors and for all residents during hurricanes. Just ahead, I noticed a kitchen that consisted of a hot plate, powered by a propane tank, a makeshift counter of old plywood, painted various colors throughout the years, and a sink. Residents had used an old, discarded kitchen sink and hooked it up to a large water receptacle filled with rainwater that was collected by residents throughout the campsite. They sometimes had access to electricity (a mystery that I never inquired about), but the refrigerator stored there was essentially nonfunctional.

Ahead of the kitchen was an outdoor seating area that had the feel of a deck marked by mismatched metal chairs arranged around a table with a large tree branch hanging overhead, providing shade. A few steps closer to the beach led directly into the campsite proper—a mix of tents, each in its own area, interspersed between trees of various sizes and raised garden plots. Overall, it looked like a mix between a long camping trip and an improvised experiment in "off-the-grid" living. Over the three-year span of my research visits to this encampment, I was constantly surprised by the pace of life there, which displayed no attributes that I associated with direct action.

In the beginning, I pushed my interlocutors to tell me more about their plans for what would happen when the protest was over, but I was never successful. Then one day while talking to Watusi—an old surfer living at the site—who was again explaining the story that led to the occupation, Erizo intervened. Up until then, I hadn't realized he was listening. He was tinkering with an old vehicle while smoking a cigarette. Suddenly, he shrugged his shoulders and said, "We have no intention of moving. Until they force us to leave, we'll stay." Although I was hardly satisfied with his answer then, the ambivalence and disregard for the future he displayed was an orientation that activists shared. I would come to appreciate this openness to inhabiting spaces without a clear vision of what is to come as a radical response to the aporias left by Puerto Rico's political entanglement with U.S. empire.[8]

In what follows, I examine resident activists' interpretation of how their work responded to imperialism and to the unabated privatization of the coastline. I consider two sides to the ambivalence that they expressed. On the one hand, residents' comfort with the idea that a total win was impossible—"until they force us to leave"—signaled a rare kind of realist political possibility that emphasized present-oriented pursuits and personal transformation. On the other, it also served to justify practices that might be thought of as coping mechanisms for navigating the broken-down dream of an anti-imperial revolution in the neoliberal present. David Scott characterizes the neoliberal present as time stalled because we live with an awareness that the transcendental revolutionary projections of the 1960s–1980s associated with socialism have long since failed. This sense of time stalled is, for David Scott, evidence of a tragic realization that the future offers no certainty that things will change for the better.[9] I would add that this sense of broken time is even more intensely felt in Puerto Rico, given that it is inscribed in over more than 100 years of U.S. rule, to say nothing of its status as a colony and economic outpost for more than five hundred years.

Although most people are resigned to the United States' continued presence in the formal political sphere, grassroots movements offer us possibilities to examine how ambivalent affect—energies we normally catalogue as negative, or at the very least incapacitating—can be directed toward other imaginaries even as they coexist with its impossible total realization. I look to this campsite in order to investigate how the energy of political possibility, which can sometimes direct radical leftist attitudes, transforms in moments of decline.

Looking at the mundane experiences of inhabiting the campsite, I set out to establish that these activists' mode of inhabiting the protest space interrupted teleological discourses of progress and resistance. I situate their ambivalent attitude toward change, and their understanding of the time politics of resistance as a response to the ongoing court case to determine the legality of the ninety-nine-year rental contract for public coastal lands as well as to the larger histories of land expropriation in which the original founders of the mobilization are embedded. Building on Maria Josefina Saldaña-Portillo's analysis of the revolutionary imagination in the Americas proffered by the Zapatistas and Rigoberta Menchú, who operate from "a zone of occult instability . . . [that] . . . resists transcendent, stable definition and acquires its urgency . . . in the concrete materiality of everyday struggle,"[10] I examine how activists' practices of engaging with people and place produced an imagined sense of territorial sovereignty and individual autonomy. In short, I am interested in highlighting the dynamics of inhabiting the "zone of occult instability" in another space of radicalism that has emerged after the fall of socialism within the Americas. I expand Saldaña-Portillo's analysis to the case of Puerto Rico in order to contribute to etching a portrait of radical politics in the contemporary moment and to continue building a robust understanding of areas of the Americas whose political futures have long been protracted by the rise of U.S. empire.

THE LEGAL CASE: CIRCULAR LOGICS, STALLED TIME

As I alluded to in the introduction to this chapter, part of the reason activists were able to establish a quasi-permanent reforestation project on the lands in question was because of the legal case that existed in parallel with the protest itself. Three activists were largely responsible for bringing the issue to the public eye—attorney Jessica Rodríguez Martin; Wanda Colón, longtime leader of the Caribbean Project for Justice and Peace based in Vieques; and Ariel Lugo, director of the Institute of Tropical Forestry. In 2005, just nine days before the occupation began, they held a press conference on the lands to publicize the controversy. They highlighted two major inconsistencies regarding the development project. The first was that no environmental impact report had been filed or approved by La Junta de Planificación (planning board), a necessary stage for assuring that developers have done as much as possible to limit potentially harmful ecological consequences of proposed construction. The second issue was the measurement of *la zona marítimo terrestre* (maritime zone, or ZMT) which dated back to the 1990s, nearly ten years prior to the start of construction. Because the ZMT's boundaries can change quickly due to erosion and rising sea levels, the activists were concerned the measurements were no longer valid. Both of these inconsistencies, they charged, were a result of the secret and illegal plan to privatize lands that were clearly a part of the neighboring *balneario* (public bathing area).

The center point of the controversy was an agreement of lease entered into on March 11, 1996, between Desarrollos Hoteleros de Carolina (the Marriott's construction partner) and the now-defunct branch of the Puerto Rican Government—Fomento Recreativo—for a total period of ninety-nine years.[11] After Hurricane Hugo destroyed the infrastructure of the *balneario* in 1989, five acres were left undeveloped. These were the lands whose ownership was now being contested. Even the rental contract's developer changed multiple times over a five-year period, passing from Desarrollos Hoteleros to Sunshine Inn, LLC, to HR Properties, and finally, CH Properties in 2002.[12] While the reasons for this movement remained unclear to me, a long-term lease is a common loophole used by developers who are looking to acquire the security and rights of "real property," usually avoiding an outright sale, because it is forbidden.

Responsible parties were not forthcoming. The municipality of Carolina was the official custodian of these lands, since title was ceded to them by the now-defunct Recreation Division of the government in 2003. But the mayor, J. Aponte de la Torre, claimed he was unaware of the rental contract. After protests began, he requested that an investigation be carried out to ascertain the details of the deal. In the name of the municipality, Aponte filed a suit against HR/CH Properties, adding support to the activists' case. La Compañía de Parques Nacionales (National Parks) also filed a suit against HR/CH Properties in their capacity as official custodians of all balnearios on the island. The combination of institutional and activist claims against the Marriott lent much momentum and support for the movement, and within the first year a *primer instancia* (first-level) judge ruled the contract null and void.

The activists' victory was short-lived. FirstBank, the financial institution who had awarded the Marriott a mortgage for the lands, immediately contested the decision. As a third party who had an economic interest in the outcome, the bank's claim that it was unaware of the controversy undermined the win. The courts rescinded the decision, as is customary when the third party clause is invoked. However, the fact that money transfers were initiated between bank and developer in 2002 for sums over six million dollars makes it seem more than suspect that FirstBank was unaware of the controversy when the case finally went to court in 2005. Regardless, the case was sent back to the courts to be litigated again—this time with financial backing and coordination between the Marriott, First Bank, and CH Properties.

It was not until 2011 that a new decision was issued, this time in favor of the Marriott Corporation and its developer CH Properties. In part, this was a result of the rapidly increasing size of the team who opposed the development. The two other cases—*Municipio de Carolina v. HR y CH Properties* and *La Compañía de Parques Nacionales v. HR y CH Properties*—brought by the municipal government of Carolina and the National Parks Company respectively, were dropped before the original case presented by activists was decided upon. The first case was resolved in negotiations whereby HR/CH Properties rescinded its consult to build a hotel on the property. While this did not necessarily imply that they would not bring a new proposal to the island's planning board, it satisfied the municipality enough to drop the case. The second case, brought by National Parks (the custodian of all public bathing areas) against HR/CH Properties was withdrawn in 2010 after they received a payment for damages. This made the opposition much less diverse, leaving only the suit brought by El Comité de Vecinos de Isla Verde, aimed at contesting the legality of the rental contract.

The final (original) case brought by the Neighborhood Committee of Isla Verde was ultimately dismissed by the courts. The court never made an official pronouncement about the legality of the contract—the original issue that created the groundswell for the movement—and focused instead on the fact that no decision could be made because the protestors had no standing in the eyes of the court to contest the contract. That is to say, the court decided that the activists' interest in the future of the land was not directly proprietary, and thus it was not evident that developing the lands would affect them negatively. To allege that the project would impede public use of the beachfront was ultimately a claim based on abstract and hypothetical damages that the court could not substantiate.[13]

The court's claim about the weak standing of the protestors was bolstered by a shifting legal understanding of the meaning of *ownership* and *investments*, as well as a new permits law. Signed on December 19, 2009, Law 161 was one of the outcomes of El Programa de Cambio y Recuperación Económica, Governor Luis Fortuño's 2009–12 plan for alleviating a four-year recession. Four months before Law 161 was signed by the governor, he issued a statement on the necessity of the law. The problem, as he defined it, was of the decreasing global competitiveness of the island. His claims were based on two studies written by the World Economic Forum and the World Bank Group in 2008–9, where Puerto Rico was evaluated to have one of the most bureaucratic and "difficult" permitting processes.

The restructuring of the law amended and negated a whole series of laws intended to prevent environmentally harmful construction projects.[14] The new structure under Law 161 eliminated all the current recourses for challenging and checking the feasibility of a project, placing all decision-making power within the Gerencia de Permisos (Permits Management Office).[15]

One of the worst parts of the new law for environmental activists and community groups is that it strictly limits who can legitimately intervene in the process of permit granting. In order to call a proposed construction into question today, one must be able to demonstrate a clear and direct proprietary interest in the land in question. In the past, community groups or concerned citizens successfully blocked a number of questionable construction projects by mobilizing a claim directed at the general welfare of the public. Under the current structure, the only way a project can be halted is if it represents an imminent danger to the public health or security—a claim that is much harder to substantiate.

When the second decision was issued, I had already been back in the States for three months, nearly seven years after the occupation began. I wasn't around to witness what the residents had to say about the case, but I imagine it mattered little to them. After all, the occupation was still ongoing in 2015, three years after the decision. *Till they force us to leave, we'll stay.* It is with this understanding of the circular logics of the law that the resident-squatters' attitude toward resistance becomes even more profound.

ANTI-IMPERIALIST WAY(S): ON DANGER + ACCEPTANCE

Although I never asked explicitly whether residents of the encampment saw their mobilization as a direct affront to U.S. empire, the connection was clear in numerous ways. In large part, this is due to residents' relationship to Tito Kayak—an activist famous for his spectacular acts of civil disobedience[16]—and the organization Amigos del M.A.R., which began in Vieques during the late 1990s. They were one of the key groups who undertook campaigns of civil disobedience along with local Viequenses and international activist allies in opposition to the U.S. Navy war games and pollution of the island. Many of those who began sitting and camping in bombing zones on *la isla nena* (sister island) had a strong sense of Puerto Rico's suffering as a result of its geopolitical significance for the United States, and they carried it with them in this later mobilization.

The history of Vieques is probably about as hyperbolically imperial as you can get.[17] Once the United States decided to pursue a policy of permanent arms race against the Soviet Union, it began the military occupation of Vieques, displacing thousands of residents from the most fertile land on the island. Two-thirds of the island was taken over by the U.S. Navy and used for over six decades as a bombing zone, and site for hosting war games. While not formally members of the organization Amigos del M.A.R., all of the men who lived in the campsite had spent time in Vieques, and had worked with Tito in other protest spaces. They understood their presence at the encampment to support his work *para la patria* (for the nation). Moreover, nearly everyone I came to know at the campsite had some relationship to Vieques, especially the old-timers.

Despite the base's closure in 2002, the navy remains a very active player in the island's affairs and continually obstructs the process of rebuilding a healthy Vieques. The U.S. Navy marshals evidence from its own contracted experts to dispute military responsibility for heavy metal contamination and higher disease rates on the island. At the same time, new development projects consisting of exclusive gated communities and walled beachfront resorts are on the rise on Vieques's north coast.[18] Although the direct target was privatization of the coast, their concerns were deeply entangled with an understanding of the ecological damages the island had incurred through U.S. intervention, evidence of what Grandin calls "the perpetual war" that those who live within empire's workshop face daily.[19]

Activists' formation in Vieques shaped their attitudes toward their own occupation. The handful of men who lived in the campsite were resolutely nationalist, though they did not support political parties, and a few were even uncertain about whether achieving the nation-state would solve Puerto Rico's problems. Instead, their nationalism manifested as a fervent opposition to the mistreatment of the island and its inhabitants, and they constructed their identity in opposition to the imperial forces that created these present-day realities.

It was this resolutely nationalist attitude, combined with their ambivalence about the possibility of change, that heavily influenced their approach toward activism. Their attitude which was surprisingly laid back and not outwardly directed in most moments. One of the most insightful descriptions of how this peculiar view of nationalist identification intersected with the practice of rebelling against empire came from Miguel. He was notoriously difficult to get along with; I personally witnessed him embroiled in extremely intense verbal altercations with other members of the campsite and even some women he dated. For the majority of the time he lived in the encampment, before disappearing into Vieques, we got along well because I was a Nuyorican and he had fond memories of having lived in New York for a time. He took me around with him, mostly to hang out in the neighboring housing project—Torres Llorens—though we'd sometimes venture out into other areas in San Juan or

Carolina. In 2010, he helped to found *la granja ecológica* (the ecological farm) on-site and afterward led a brief, if powerful initiative to link the gardening project in the encampment to a gardening and consciousness-raising project in Torres Llorens.

Even before that project was designed, he and I would venture to Llorens and just hang out with residents. Miguel repeatedly underscored that this was part of the work itself. As someone who had himself been in jail and been in trouble with the law, he saw this as part of the vital work of social transformation. While he was living at the campsite, he always actively recruited participants for events there from Llorens. The links he made to anti-imperialism were profoundly mixed with a sentiment about the importance of waiting, and about the time politics of revolution. "To get to the people, you have to go with the flow. It's slower than you might imagine. You can't force-feed people. That's the imperialist way. It creates docile subjects, people who are willing to accept blows, who grow up expecting them. You build with them, burn with them, joke around [*vacilla*], flow." What I most appreciated about Miguel's approach is that it went beyond the dominant leftist attitude in Puerto Rico, which focuses heavily on impoverished people's dependency on the state in ways that create a sense of superiority for the activists and locks the lower classes into a narrative of victimization. To point the finger at others is much like the imperialist view, which stands outside and operates as an all-knowing subject who doesn't allow the encounter with another person to direct the conversation, the action, and the vision of social change. The imperialist way doesn't allow for the relational and the intersubjective to emerge.

Miguel posits another way, and it seems clear to me that rethinking the rhythms of resistance is important for revitalizing the study of and the practice of liberation in the contemporary moment. It's also important to underscore that Miguel's quote emerged within the specific context of working with *maleantes* (those who work in informal economies and often have criminal records). These groups are not normally directly targeted by activist organizing, in part because they are seen as part of the problem. This directionality was also astute, especially given that the poor communities on the island, especially in the housing project complexes, are notorious for supporting the statehood party (PNP). It's where the work of transformative praxis really needs to occur if an anti-imperial movement is to thrive in Puerto Rico.

Although other resident-squatters may not have framed their work in these exact terms, the hospitality they showed toward any guests who passed through the site was consistent with Miguel's claim that you had to flow with and connect to people in order to build an alternative politics. Indeed, their openness toward others was part of what made the space feel downright magical at times. To say that they were adept at connecting with people who came by and who tried to interact is an understatement. It became clear to me that this relational interest is one of the places that one's energy might go as we wait for conditions to change outside (but also inside) of us.

COPING STRATEGIES: VEILING (IN)CORRECT POLITICS IN UNCERTAIN TIMES

There was an underside to the beautiful practice of flowing with others that I just described as anti-imperialist practice of the resident-squatters who lived in the campsite. To get a fuller picture of it, one needs to realize that the men who lived in the campsite were homeless by choice. As each one described it to me, their anti-imperialist attitude also served as justification for their efforts to live outside the strictures or commitments of society. They didn't want to work full time, and avoided it at all costs. Although some had children, they did not want to be in monogamous relationships or have to answer to anyone about what they did, when, or how. Their number-one fear was to become incorporated into those day-to-day rhythms conditioned by capitalism, but it was a fear mixed with an unwillingness to cede to any structure at all.

Only two of the residents were permanently in this condition. The others were more like "floaters," shifting between the more regimented structures of everyday life—work, paying rent, living with partners, and raising children—settling into the campsite whenever things got a little too stressful at home, often tied to their ability to financially support themselves. They floated into and out of the campsite as their everyday living situations changed. In sum, the campsite members were resolutely antistructure, and that attitude also seemed to be not just reflective of their attitude toward empire, but their way of coping within the strictures of it.

Even though squatter-residents were more than happy to talk radical politics and the need for anti-imperialist work on the island, this attitude was underwritten by a cynicism and ambivalence about the time politics of resistance. For example, one day I got the dreaded question: What will the results be of your study? Miguel laughed at me as I stood there awkwardly trying to avoid answering what he probably only intended as a joke. Finally, he broke the silence by saying, "Okay, I'll save you some time. The conclusion of your report should be Puerto Rico is fucked" (*Puerto Rico está jodido*). I was taken aback by his answer—it seemed like something an apathetic people might say as justification for why they didn't bother protesting at all. Instead, he replied, "It was different in the beginning. It was far more interesting. Now we just chill out and enjoy the beach." While this period was by his own estimation, far less interesting, it did provide an avenue for engaging in a kind of open resistance—signaled by the desire to just relax and enjoy it. I have written about this reclamation of *el vacilón* (revelry) in another context, but what I want to underscore here is that it is embedded within a larger profound ambivalence about what the future holds for Puerto Rico.[20] In this space, experimentation and individual autonomy were upheld as the highest symbols of one's freedom and one's ability to enact anti-imperialist politics.

Although Miguel was the only one who expressed the issue in these dramatic terms—that the island couldn't be saved, as it was fucked—it appeared to me that others felt the same and consequently were reticent to spend any time discussing how to equitably share space with others. In other words, they shared a particularly acute desire to avoid acknowledging intragroup conflict. Without a transparent structure for reckoning with disagreements, residents would look to passive ways to push out the least agreeable of the crew. Although violent confrontations broke out only rarely, the space's affective energy could become palpably tense and threaten to radically upset the day-to-day dynamics.

A disguised structure is quite common in nonhierarchical movements that are not explicitly committed to direct democracy or another organizing principle. As Jo Freeman argued of the sixties, unacknowledged structures make for an unaccountable leadership since their very existence is systematically denied. When incidents occurred, battles over the legitimacy of one's actions hinged on whether one had acted as if he or she were the leader when that person in fact was not. These kinds of subterranean conflicts were never dealt with openly, because activists believed that individual actions could negatively shape the public opinion of the whole group. Collectively, they were on display, but to be oriented toward public perception over such a long period of time was detrimental.

Comfort with passively attending to conflict went along with *la política incorrecta* (incorrect politics). One resident used this term with me to describe the contradictory, or incompatible, practices that he engaged in outside the public gaze. The pressure was so high to be "perfectly correct" that activists were rather comfortable with (and treated it as a matter of course), hiding their contradictions from public scrutiny.

While I never directly experienced this pressure in the campsite—as it was so far from public scrutiny by the time I arrived—I felt something similar as I ran in the midst of a group of student strikers from the University of Puerto Rico during the early hours of *el paro* (a stoppage) in Feburary 2011. The campus had been occupied by private security officers from the company Capitol Security after the success of the 2010 strike and students had tried to prepare for a stoppage with the gates open by installing barricades the night prior to the start of their action. After the work was completed, they found that the private security agents from Capitol Security were driving around in a van, destroying the barricades. Furious, the group was in a frenzy, as we tried in vain to restore the barricades we had built. When some members of the group saw the officers driving in a van, they began chasing after the van and some students vandalized it as officers ran away. The group was roundly chastised by some of the coordinators of the event, who and yelled: "We have to think! That's our role! We're the ones who are knocking on this monster's door and we have to be perfect, or will be torn apart." The student coordinators understood that the public would not support them if their movement became violent, no matter that the context under which students were protesting had become more militarized and violent toward them. Ultimately, in this case, trying to suppress violence turned it into a form of incorrect politics. While the same fear may have originally brought about the need to engage in strategic moments of incorrect politics in El Campamento Playas P'al Pueblo, it no longer served a positive function. The irony was that by denying to look at the incorrect, or contradictory aspects, of their politics, they were torn apart anyway.

From my perspective, then, it seemed that these attitudes may have once worked, but the longer the campsite existed, the more exhausting these games became—and the harder it made it to coexist and just "chill out." While I was convinced by these protestors of the necessity of geographic space for creating the conditions for other ways of interacting, it seemed that something else was needed. What could be another way to protest while maintaining respect for the extreme ambivalence of the antiprivatization, quasi anti-imperial conflict in Puerto Rico? In my conclusion, I turn to some possibilities.

DECOLONIAL APORIAS

In Derrida's late work *Aporia*, he titles the first section of this treatise *finis*, the French word for a border. Indeed, the limit of truth is something that Derrida wants to reclaim as a space of possibility. He grapples at length with what the "beyond" in the crossing of the border between truth and the unknown might be. In the case of protest politics in contemporary Puerto Rico, I think that the question is how to move toward decolonization—something that is unknown, and that many doubt can ever come to pass. Derrida comes to the idea that transforming an aporia is a nonpassage, or at least, a movement that would no longer be what it was in the crossing itself, "a coming without *pas*."[21] It seems to me that is the challenge to those of us interested in enacting transformative practice within the purview of empire. To go beyond the colonial logics that have shaped the harsh realities and protracted future of island protest politics, we need processes that are aimed at simply going beyond the known—a practice that requires comfort with not-knowing, and not-deciding what the solution may be before arriving.

Many of the (in)actions that took place in the encampment on the beach might be thought of as a nonpassage, or an engagement with aporias of empire. But they also seemed at times to be stuck in the passage itself—not able to arrive at a limit, and, therefore, trapping the activists in a kind of enticing rhythm that locates the protestors outside of normative time, but also outside of radical transformative practice. Among the multiple antiprivatization struggles organized in Puerto Rico in the contemporary period, the student strikes of 2010 at the University of Puerto Rico stand out as one of the most successful for navigating this terrain. Perhaps most important of all was the way that the students' organization adhered to direct democratic principles, breaking with the usual fragmentation of the political sphere and securing the support of a broad sector of the public through creative interventions. As I traveled between these two occupations, I came to understand that direct democracy was especially compatible with decolonial praxis because it places great importance on the process—of how we live our politics. At its best, horizontality forces participants to rethink the logics that dominate our colonized world and minds.

Perhaps the issue in the campsite is simply related to that first thing that drew me to the space—its long duration. If system "breaks" are to be transformative, it seems to me that there must be a pulse—a link to the normative so that "delinking" from the limits imposed by living our lives according to the demands of a twenty-four-hour clock and abstract measurements that fit within it can find some meaning beyond refusal.[22] Delinking signals a possible future that is not merely bound up with changing the status quo on the level of the state but is interested in creating the future in the now/here—a decolonization of the terms of decolonization if you will, moving away from placing all one's attention on the political status in order to begin the long process of delinking with those structures that maintain both the island and one's very being in a sense of perpetual colonization.

Attention to process instead of end goals might lead us closer to producing the aporetic space that Derrida dreams of as a response to the impasse, the buildup of sheer inconsistencies and fears that no real change is possible in the present moment. One student, Ricardo Lora, who was a founding member of the self-documentation/news-making project Radio Huelga (strike radio), offered some insight into this practice of inhabiting aporia that focuses on the paradoxical play between inhabiting and passing through. In answering what he saw as an ideal future for the island or outcome of *la lucha* he said: "The significance or value of struggle is not in what we aspire to do but rather in the construction/in the doing itself. I don't want to arrive anywhere. Clearly, it's obvious that we need goals . . . but the process definitely changed my way of seeing things." Ricardo's reflection conveys a clear shift toward valorizing process over outcomes in his understanding of the goal of social struggle. His words suggest he has moved away from seeing things in a narrow mode, whereby struggles begin and die with the site where one is fighting. Instead of accepting the fragmentation, such thinking suggests, one vacillates through the process that moves toward a project of escaping certainties and familiar formulas.

As Ricardo suggested in his valorization of process over outcomes, taking a revolutionary posture within the aporias of empire rests less on the fact that there are achievements, and more on the fact of how things happen. To argue that revolution is not a bundle of accomplishments, but a process, makes it possible to understand where resident-squatters might fail. While they recognize that idea that it is necessary to think differently about time, they lack an interest in, or dedication to, interrogating process. Without it, we are merely creating a context that creates a fleeting sense of happiness, which cannot be tracked or crossed in a deep way.

NOTES

Unless otherwise noted, translations are my own.

1 G. Robert. "¿Podemos? . . . y nuestras preguntas," *80grados*, January 21, 2015, accessed October 20, 2017, http://www.80grados.net/podemos-y-nuestras-preguntas/.

2 The specific language of the clause reads, "The government declares outright that the public policy of the island will be to conserve, develop and use its natural resources for the general welfare of the community." Both laypeople and attorneys alike agree that this clause establishes the coastline as public space to be protected for the common good.

3 Cruz-Malavé, "The Oxymoron of Sexual Sovereignty," 52.

4 This plan to expand the tourist industry was a part of the island's industrialization project, Operation Bootstrap, which was formally initiated in 1947 by the Industrial Incentives Act. In the years following the passage of the act, Teodoro Moscosco ran Compañía de Fomento Industrial, the agency in charge of Puerto Rico's industrial promotions and economic development. Advocates of this plan believed that Puerto Rico could build its local economy by attracting foreign investors with federal and local tax exemption. The plan initially "worked," raising the standard of living on the island, increasing pay and job opportunities for a

small sector of society (mostly women), but within fifteen years, economic decline had returned and has continued unabated since.

5 In the thirty-year battle against development project Costa Serena, several families lived on the acres for generations, but their legal standing was in question given that the Katz family held title to the lands, giving them more legitimacy in the eyes of the court. See Morales, *Desalambrar*, for a discussion of *los rescates de terreno* (land rescue) projects in history.

6 Ironically, this direct action encampment was sited on the grounds adjacent to the Hilton hotel that began the de facto privatization of the coastline in the late 1940s. In 2007, activists were contesting the proposed Hilton expansion plans for two reasons. First, the plan to build luxury condominiums, parking garage, and shopping mall was within *la zona marítimo terrestre* (maritime zone—the area that can be covered by water in high tide). Moreover, it would block access to the Fort Jerónimo—a historic and public landmark. Paseo Caribe was intensely resisted by a wide array of actors in varied forms. Probably the most iconic and spectacular images from this protest is of environmental activist Tito Kayak, who climbed the construction crane on-site and halted building for one week with his solo occupation. A loose coalition came together to protest the action and set up a protest encampment just outside the property—between the road and the sidewalk. For an extensive discussion of this controversy, see Fernos, *De San Jerónimo a Paseo Caribe*.

7 Since it is illegal to cut down any Ceiba given its status as a national tree, activists understood this siting of the tree to be a practical way to secure the life of a small green space on the site no matter what the final outcome of their struggle would be. Some species of the Ceiba can grow to 230 feet tall, and they are distinguished by a straight, largely branchless trunk that culminates in a huge, spreading canopy and buttress roots that rise out of the ground, towering over six feet tall.

8 The term *aporia* originates in classical Greek philosophy, and signals an impasse in thought, or a problem for which there is no apparent solution. When the term was later taken up by Derrida, he sought to reframe this apparent "limit of truth" in more positive terms by highlighting that aporetic spaces heralded the possibilities that could not yet be thought. See Derrida, *Aporias*.

9 D. Scott, *Omens of Adversity: Tragedy, Time, Memory, Justice*, 6.

10 Saldaña-Portillo, *The Revolutionary Imagination*, 190.

11 The original contract was for a period of fifty years, with four extensions or prorogations totaling ninety-nine years.

12 For the sake of simplicity when describing the legal case, I will refer to the last developer, CH Properties, in the body of the chapter.

13 A special thank you to Pedro Saade for sharing Rocío de Félix Dávila's brief on the case. Since the decisions from this level of the court are not available for public record, I have relied on their analysis of the proceedings here.

14 This note lists all amended laws affected by the new permits process and indicates, more specifically, whether they were amended or eliminated. These are: el Artículo 5 y 6 de la Ley Núm. 374 de 14 de mayo de 1949 (amended); el Artículo 4 de la Ley Núm. 135 de 15 de junio de 1967 (eliminated); el Artículo 8 de la Ley Núm. 84 de 13 de julio de 1988 (amended); los Artículos 6 y 7 de la Ley Núm. 10 de 7 de agosto de 1987, known as the "Ley de Protección, Conservación y Estudio

de los Sitios y Recursos Arqueológicos Subacuáticos" (amended); las secciones 2 y 3 de la Ley Núm. 112 de 20 de julio de 1988, known as the "Ley de Protección del Patrimonio Arqueológico Terrestre de Puerto Rico" (amended); los incisos (c) y (d) del Artículo 10 de la Ley Núm. 8 de 8 de enero de 2004, known in the wake of its amendment as the "Ley Orgánica del Departamento de Recreación y Deportes" (amended); la Ley Núm. 313 de 19 de diciembre de 2003 (eliminated); el Artículo 4 de la Ley Núm. 416 de 22 de septiembre de 2004, known as the "Ley sobre Política Pública Ambiental" (amended); la Ley Núm. 76 de 24 de junio de 1975, known as the "Ley Orgánica de la Administración de Reglamentos y Permisos" (eliminated).

15 ARPE, JACL, TPI Tapell, tribunal de apelaciones, and the TSPR.

16 Although Tito's political interests are diverse, they most often respond to U.S. imperialism or to constructions that have ecological consequences. He not only is famous for his on-island protests, but he also hung the Viequenses' flag outside the crown of the Statue of Liberty in New York, and he hung a Palestinian flag off an Israeli security tower in the West Bank. He actually served as a member of the U.S. Coast Guard briefly, an experience that clearly shaped his understanding of how Puerto Rico was embroiled in U.S. empire. While his fame and popularity were key to the early success of the mobilization, he rarely stayed overnight, nor did he stay for days at a time by this time.

17 To engage this history fully is beyond the scope of this article, but César J. Ayala has written at length about the complex history of the occupation of Vieques. See, for example, Ayala and Bolívar, *Battleship Vieques: Puerto Rico from World War II to the Korean War.*

18 Davis et al., "Military Pollution and Natural Purity," 170.

19 Grandin, *Empire's Workshop*, 27.

20 Rosario, "Intimate Publics," 34.

21 Derrida, *Aporias*, 9.

22 Mignolo, "Delinking," 453.

06

Training for Empire?

Samoa and American Gridiron Football

FA'ANOFO LISACLAIRE UPERESA

On a 2010 stopover to Tutuila, the largest island of the entity known as "American Samoa," U.S. secretary of state Hillary Clinton was greeted with a traditional *'ava* ceremony performed for honored guests.[1] After acknowledging the "close relationship" and "deep ties" between the United States and Tutuila and Manu'a, she remarked, "I'm sure my husband will also be very disappointed if I didn't say how much he enjoys watching the young men from American Samoa play football."[2] Her comment gestured toward the visibility of Samoan football success, one of the central ways Samoans are known to the wider American populace today. The presence of the "Sunday Samoans" on the gridiron football field has been chronicled recently in a number of journalistic pieces, and has promoted a narrative of upward mobility wherein football represents a way out of underprivileged island conditions.[3]

Structural factors have shaped the current contexts in which football is increasingly seen as a beacon of future success on a pathway linking educational and sporting institutions across the Pacific and the continental United States. Over the course of the twentieth century, a combination of indigenous agitation and American initiative expanded industry, infrastructure, military contribution, and social and welfare institutions underwritten by the United States such that American appropriations or corporations provide the majority of employment in the islands today.[4] Still, jobs are hard to come by and are increasingly tied to educational credentials (although personal contacts are still primary). Meanwhile, for a variety of historical and structural reasons, Samoans in the continental United States and Hawai'i remain concentrated in low-income areas, have lower household incomes relative to other ethnic groups, and are overrepresented in juvenile courts and the penal system.[5]

Beginning slowly in the late 1970s and intensifying throughout the 1980s and 1990s, the increasing visibility of American football articulated with and built upon ideologies of sporting success and upward mobility in American society that promise rewards for hard work regardless of class, race, or familial wealth. Intergenerational success in football and the expansion of the sporting industry in the United States and American Samoa have produced potential sporting futures as real and viable for succeeding generations of Samoan youth. Among a resident population exceeding 55,500, with minimum wage ranging from $4.18 to $5.59 per hour and chronic underemployment, it is increasingly seen by young men as "a way out" of a stifled field of opportunity.[6]

The high-profile success of Samoans in football and the discourse of Samoans as natural-born and -bred athletes are a complex crystallization of subjective agency and particular politicoeconomic, ideological, and discursive formations infused with relations of power.[7] More specifically, this success and its representation in popular discourses are both shaped by distinct but connected processes, notably the twentieth-century political, economic, and social transformations in the islands, including territorial status and U.S. military presence, American-led development initiatives, and expansion of the cash economy. These processes intersect with long-standing U.S. racial frameworks and ethnographic imaginations of Samoan as a cultural group, which shape the way Samoans (as nonwhite, culturally marked athletes) were seen as they entered the late twentieth-century expansion of the football industry in the United States, and continue to impact the game today.[8] Yet the contemporary phenomenon of widespread Samoan participation in American football is not simply an effect of the growth of global sporting labor markets, but rather is fundamentally tied to the islands' territorial status within the constellation of American imperial formations.

The concept of imperial formations—as mobile and dependent on moveable populations, recognizable as "semblances of sovereignty," amorphous forms of power, and the proliferation of legal exceptions—is useful for examining the case of American Samoa.[9] Its political status as an "unincorporated, unorganized" overseas U.S. territory has shaped local structures of opportunity, routes of movement abroad, and imaginaries of the future. In this chapter I temper the celebratory vision of football success by analyzing how individuals engage the macropolitical and economic relations that structure possibilities for Samoan movement and mobility. I thus examine American football in Samoa as a complex practice that both accommodates Samoans to American empire and challenges conventional assumptions about how individuals engage imperial projects (and how imperial projects are constituted).

What do we gain analytically from calling American Samoa an "imperial outpost"?[10] How does ethnography here illuminate our understanding of empire? In this case, the lens of empire provides an important critical vantage point that highlights American juridical power and its importance in shaping contemporary possibilities in American Samoa. However, examining mechanisms of law and politics yields limited insight into how conditions of exceptionality, of attenuated sovereignty, and of deferral are sustained; that is, into why and how local residents accept legal judgments, government policies, and claims of jurisdiction today. Ethnography reveals macroanalyses as woefully insufficient in capturing the texture, slippage, durability, and incoherence of imperial relations. It also reveals how empire is sustained in and through nonstate activities and micropractices of the body. Focusing on the realm of sport reveals both regimes of truth that circulate more widely in social life (and are repeated in official events) and the processes of training and discipline that reflect a longer history of efforts aimed at transforming Samoans as subjects of U.S. empire.

Drawing on Michel Foucault's theory of the production of "docile bodies" through disciplinary practices of modern social institutions, as well as Loïc Wacquant's use of "bodily capital," I argue that the transformation of Samoan bodies and subjectivities in and through football training can be seen as part of an assemblage of American imperial institutions, discourses, and practices that simultaneously discipline and reward young Samoan men (and, by extension, their home communities). Still, my fieldwork reveals the practice of football to be a multivalent endeavor—at once a pedagogy of empire, a path of transnational mobility, a vehicle for community empowerment, a site of personal and collective expression, and a valued practice of self-fashioning.

INSTITUTIONALIZING MODERN AMERICAN SPORTS IN SAMOA

On a trip to Tutuila in the summer of 2012, I observed a series of announcements for youth sports activities—in the local newspaper, on the radio, on television. From an "Olympic Day" event with a fun run and variety of sport exhibitions to a two-day youth sports event for U.S. military families to football and softball camps to practices for the American Samoa Under-19 Football and Boy's Baseball team gearing up for trips to Texas and Utah/Canada, respectively, there was no shortage of sports activities for youth.[11] At the Olympic Day event, for example, current active athletes and future prospects participated in wrestling demonstrations on the beach, weightlifting under the tents, and volleyball on the grass amid wind and occasional rain showers. There was a mix of children, young adults, and parents and family members all present and taking part to varying degrees in the activities of the day. As the existence of multiple sporting associations in the islands suggests, organized sports activities are part of the social landscape of American Samoa today, and have been for some time.

While many of these activities are focused on promoting health and well-being in a time of shocking rates of noncommunicable diseases (NCD) such as diabetes and obesity among Samoans, football represents something different. In my interviews and observations, football participation was never couched in a health discourse. The issue of health in football did not often arise, but when it did it was in the language of risk management and injury avoidance. Unlike many other sporting activities in the islands that might be promoted as part of health and anti-NCD campaigns,[12] football cannot be depicted as a healthy activity (particularly with recent revelations about the link between repeated head trauma and mental illness). Rather, football is linked structurally and ideologically to mobility via U.S. educational and professional sporting institutions, as well as to local games of status and competition.

The emergence of gridiron football in American Samoa was rooted in the expansion in the 1960s to 1970s of the educational system as part of U.S. development and modernization policies. The expanded educational system drew American teachers and administrators from the continental United States and Hawai'i, many of whom had played football in the secondary, collegiate, and professional ranks in the United States and used their knowledge and networks to establish a football program on the island of Tutuila. The expansion was consonant with a larger effort at establishing sports and recreation activities for local residents and more generally with the growth of bureaucratic state institutions on Tutuila.[13]

Historically, competitive physical contests had long been part of the social landscape of Samoa, but government efforts expanded both formal community recreation programs and institutionalized sports as part of the schooling infrastructure. With its initial expansion in the early 1970s as part of larger efforts to develop the Department of Parks and Recreation, football became entwined with school-based sporting programs. In the years that followed, former college and professional players returned to coach and work in sport administration, spearheading the development of football as another avenue through which local people could pursue new opportunities for local recognition, travel, formal education, and migration. This sporting pathway, following the continental U.S. model, is tied to the K-12 and postsecondary educational system.

Schools have long been recognized as instruments of U.S. empire in its territories.[14] In Tutuila they are a site where students, teachers, and administrators negotiate American and Samoan visions of modernity and mobility in the context of increasing economic hardship. Samoan aesthetics or forms of sociality infuse schooling culture and instructional pedagogies in many schools; still, textbook adoption, curriculum content, and assessment follow that of stateside public schools. The educational common sense figures college degrees as what will enable hard-working students to avoid low-wage careers (in the tuna canneries or as taxi drivers, for example). In numerous conversations with coaches and administrative personnel, it became clear that they viewed the student-athlete's ability to effectively pursue dreams of upward mobility, individual growth, and supporting his family as dependent on him successfully navigating his educational pathway and mastering the sport. To do so requires submission to a process of discipline.

THE GRIDIRON AS A SITE OF DISCIPLINE, ACCUMULATION, AND CREATIVITY

In the late afternoon heat the scream of whistles punctuated the shuffling of cleats in the dirt. The players lined up again and again, catching their breath with their hands on their knees in between plays. Their teammates, coaches, and a few parents and random spectators stood on the grassy margins of the field, alternating between intent watching and laughing at a hushed joke or a mistake made on the field. The hard work of conditioning had already been completed, and in these last weeks before the American Samoa team left to represent Oceania in the International Federation of American Football's (IFAF) Under-19 World Championships, there was little time left to perfect the team's plays. Days were split between continued fundraising efforts, media events, and dawn or twilight practices. These practices were not primarily aimed at developing individual position skills, but rather focused on bringing the players who had been chosen as seniors and recent graduates from the island's high schools together to play as a team, coordinated and driven with one goal in mind: success in Texas. In these sessions that spanned several hours the players ran the drills over and over and over, in a pattern of constant repetition that was designed to move their action from thought to instinct, to eliminate hesitation, and to speed up the sharp movements—each an integral part of the performance. The endless repetition disciplined not only the body movements but the thought process as well, instructions internalized as body sense in the quest for superior performance and athletic success. Many of the players would go on to play for U.S. college teams in the fall as new or returning students. The games in Texas were a unique opportunity to play in a nationally televised game, representing the islands and all of Oceania.

The Gridiron as a Site of Discipline

The discipline involved in organized modern sport has been theorized by some as a condition of domination.[15] Others view it as an experience of freedom.[16] The case of Samoan success in American football embodies both viewpoints in relation to a complex engagement with American empire and personal and collective achievement and expression. The disciplinary training of football toward success on the field that is translatable to success off the field highlights the incoherence or instability of pedagogies of empire. The training regimens are laden with assumptions of meritorious masculinity and an ethos of achievement while their orientation toward export is fundamentally shaped by transnational capitalist ventures such as the NFL; they shape the body though apparatuses of power that are obscured by popularized "Friday night lights," but to uncertain ends.

In his influential book *Discipline and Punish* (1977), Michel Foucault theorizes what he sees as a shift in the eighteenth century in which the body becomes an "object and target of power."[17] Through a series of disciplinary institutions—the school, the hospital, and the military—power was exerted over individual bodies through the control over their movement through time and space. Arguing that "a body is docile that may be subjected, used, transformed and improved,"[18] he details the scale of control of individuals through widely dispersed practices of "subtle coercion" that obtain a hold on the individual at the "level of the mechanism itself—movements, gestures, attitudes, rapidity: an infinitesimal power over the active body."[19] In this process the target was economy of movement in which "the only truly important ceremony is that of exercise."[20] Foucault writes:

> The historical moment of the disciplines was the moment when an art of the human body was born, which was directed not only at the growth of its skills, nor at the intensification of its subjection, but at the formation of a relation that in the mechanism itself makes it more obedient as it becomes more useful, and conversely. What was then being formed was a policy of coercions that act upon the body, a calculated manipulation of its elements, its gestures, its behaviour. The human body was entering a machinery of power that explores it, breaks it down and rearranges it.[21]

Through this new "mechanics of power" individual bodies were trained not only in what to do, but in what way and how quickly. "Thus discipline produces subjected and practised bodies, 'docile' bodies. Discipline increases the forces of the body (in economic terms of utility) and diminishes these same forces (in political terms of obedience)," producing a link between increased aptitude and increased domination.[22] The imposition of new temporal regimes, exercise regimens, and precise system of command, reinforced by systems of surveillance, produced the "correct means of training."

While Foucault concentrated on the growth of social institutions and the extension of the state in conjunction with new technologies of power through which to exercise control over subject populations in eighteenth-century Europe, his theory of disciplinary power in producing docile bodies is useful for approaching the dynamics of power operating on the football field today. Through the combines, camps, and practices, and their associated disciplinary practices, gridiron players undergo the "correct means of training" that produce increased body force, obedience to the coach, and submission to intense training regimen.

The physical field is a measured and marked construction of space that is carved up by white lines and hash marks, notating a spatial relationship to the end goals. The social field of the gridiron is structured by hierarchical relations of power under which players must assume positions or roles within the team hierarchy, and conform to the wishes of the coaches or be punished. Participation is governed by elaborate systems of rules codified at the high school, college, and professional levels that determine when and in what capacity players may engage the team's training. Additionally, the disciplinary power at work dictates the proper use of one's body even when the players are not under direct surveillance of the coach. In some instances individuals work out on their own; in others "voluntary" off-season training and conditioning is not voluntary at all, but will be directed by team leaders and is aimed at facilitating individual fitness and team cohesiveness.

Foucault's discussion is useful for examining the process of discipline in sporting institutions and the larger context of education and society where hierarchy, inequality, and a mythology of achievement and mobility through sport are naturalized. Yet, while the transformations of body and subjectivity that produce docile bodies are crucial here, they are not the only issue: the experience of empowerment through this transformation still must be addressed. Given the rewards and status associated with football success, training cannot simply be a site of routine domination—we have to recognize the creative possibilities within it as well, in the sense of creative use of the body, but also in the ability to create one's future through valued performance and access to various forms of capital.

Accumulating Gridiron Capital

Over the past twenty-five years, football has become an important path of circular migration to Hawai'i and the continental United States for Samoan youth. Negotiating different sites of the football industry, young men must actively maximize their marketability as players and maneuver within constraints set by coaches, teams, owners, and fans. As noted above, an important part of the process is training, where players hone their skills in daily workouts in anticipation of the combines or team workouts.[23] During this training players turn themselves into high-value products that are then selected by coaches, and eventually—if one is both lucky and talented—idolized and consumed by fans.

Training is also the process by which one transforms the body through submission to the discipline of the coaches and the various drills designed to configure the body for football. In the training camps in which players participate, the body is broken down and reshaped while one's relationship to one's body and sense of self in the context of the field is remade. In the workouts players build muscle, gain speed, perfect their footwork, and build endurance; they *transform* both their bodies and subjective understanding of themselves as a player-products in order to compete at the best of their ability. This constant manipulation of the body is intended to produce a variety of abilities that are then measured not only during preseason camps, but also in different kinds of combines. Performance at these events illustrates the effectiveness of accumulated disciplinary procedures in maximizing the player's ability to perform sport labor on the field and potentially bring value to their future team. In the football combine we can see the importance of regimes of measurement and correct means of training by which players submit to the disciplinary regimen of football in order to succeed on the gridiron.

Yet even in circumstances over which they have limited control, the players as actors are empowered through their productive practice. In the context of submitting to this disciplinary regimen, football players also become entrepreneurs in bodily capital. Drawing on his ethnography of a boxing gym in Chicago, Loïc Wacquant describes a process of bodywork whereby boxers convert corporeal capital into pugilistic capital. Training imparts "to the fighter's body a set of abilities and tendencies liable to produce value in the field of professional boxing in the form of recognition, titles, and income streams."[24] For football players, the endless drills, workouts, scrimmages, camps, and combines together provide a slow and protracted experience of sedimentation through which individual players gain practical mastery over the sense and action-execution of various body parts, transforming their bodily sensitivity and accumulating what I call *gridiron capital*.[25] In the possibility of capital conversion, of reward, of success, and in the spaces of resistance and negotiation (from slowing down at practice to adopting different techniques to privately criticizing or praising the coaches), the players as actors shape their engagement with the sport.

If, following Foucault, football can be seen as a form of discipline by modern power that renders Samoan bodies docile in the service of U.S. sovereignty and American capitalism without the need for repressive colonial power, then the U.S. coaches that run intermittent training camps might perhaps be described as substitutes for the imperial agents of old, imposing these new body regimes on indigenous Samoan boys and young men. Yet a closer examination reveals a much more complex reality. The coaches from the United States are not an undifferentiated mass, but come to the coaching process with a variety of backgrounds, intentions, and attachments.

During the summer of 2008 three different football clinics were held on Tutuila, each run by a group of coaches from the United States. The three clinics varied widely in their duration, activity, publicity, perceived level of quality, and coaching expertise provided. A local church that had links to a church group on the east coast of the United States sponsored the first event, and the camp was staffed by a religious group of volunteers, coaches and non-coaches, who ran a series of drill stations at a local park. They were holding clinics for the local football players and softball players as well. Their stated goal (to me) was to evangelize, but they were ministering to a population well known for saturation of religion (particularly Christianity) in social life, and their short stay did not permit sustained contact with student-athletes. While appreciative of the distance traveled and effort put in to the clinic, a number of the players and coaches who participated offered mixed opinions on the scope and depth of the camp. If the camp coaches were agents of a disciplinary regime, their effectiveness could be questioned since the evangelical component was neither new nor revelatory, and the short duration of the camp (a matter of hours) meant limited impact on the players themselves. (In the years since this particular camp, its organizers have developed a nascent recruiting organization aimed at helping stateside coaches effectively recruit local athletes.)

In another camp, framed as part of a larger "goodwill mission," non-Samoan Division I college coaches and current and former Samoan professional players held half-day sessions with local players. Complete with television interviews, autograph signings, and free lunches, it generated a lot of publicity and excitement, but the actual instruction given to student players and coaches was limited. As an event with high-profile participants, it renewed social ties between off- and on-island coaches and sporting personnel (paid and volunteer) and reinvigorated the social and institutional networks that have long facilitated football routes of movement between the islands and the states of the (American) union.

The third camp I will discuss at more length because it further complicates the view presented so far of football as a site of imperial discipline. This camp was the first local meeting of a very successful summer camp held annually in the continental United States. In previous years, teams from some of the local high schools had raised funds (thousands of dollars) throughout the academic year to be able to attend. This year, the camp came to the island, and students paid a registration fee to help defray costs.

At the end of the camp on the third day, the mood was light. Everyone was happy; the camp had a good turnout and had gone smoothly. Players seemed pleased to have a chance to go full contact, suited up with helmets and pads. The field was wet, and the air was humid; rain had come down intermittently throughout the day alternating with the hot sun shining in a bright sky. The camp was held at the Veterans Memorial Stadium, built a few years before to host a regional sports competition. Throughout the practice, the sound of construction rang out, as workers continued to build the stage for the Festival of Pacific Arts to be held on island in a month's time. At the sound of the final whistle all the players hustled into the covered stands, grouped by their school and jersey colors. The coaches were lined up to speak to the player crowd, leaving them with words of wisdom to consider. Without exception, each stressed two key points: taking advantage of the opportunity football provides for earning your college degree, and that football will only be a small part of your life.

What was perhaps more salient for many of the players was the fact that, in contrast to the other clinics held that summer, the majority of coaches associated with this camp were of Polynesian descent, and most were Samoan. Several of the coaches who spoke to the players that last day had direct ties to Tutuila—three had graduated from local high schools, while two more were raised in local villages. Their ties to the island and to the Samoan community more broadly were reflected in how they spoke to the students and how they articulated their role as coaches. In interviews and informal discussions with many of these coaches, they drew upon a larger notion of service to the Samoan and wider Polynesian communities, in the ways they articulated their own work and why they felt it was important. This was particularly true of off-island Samoan coaches who have been working to support the development of football on the island and to recruit students from the islands to football scholarships in the United States. As one of them remarked to the students, "Our goal is to help you succeed." All of the Samoan coaches stressed the importance of using the opportunities available to put oneself in a position to support or "give back" to one's family. This is a recognizable script shaped by Samoan cultural values and general expectations of care, concern, and assistance. Whether the message was in all ways consistent with individual coaching practices is not relevant; the message itself was what was important because it resonated with culturally specific expectations of *tautua*, or service (to one's family, village, and nation).

The coaches' affiliation with the camp, as one coach expressed to me, is part of a larger commitment to Polynesian students, and serving the island and diasporic communities with the talents and resources available to them. These coaches are not undifferentiated agents of empire, but participate in the disciplining of young Samoan bodies with a variety of agendas and attachments. If their work facilitates the submission of players to the hierarchy of the team and the capitalist dictates of higher levels of the sport, they do so with a sober assessment of the opportunity structure open to these players (precisely because of its location on the margins of the U.S. national body).

Pacific scholars have written about the ways in which sports for Maori in Aotearoa/New Zealand, Hawaiians and other Polynesians in Hawai'i, and local people in Guam are not only part of historical legacies of colonialism, militarism, and domination of indigenous populations but are also key sites for personal expression, community pride, and transformation of social orders.[26] In these places Islander athletic excellence is multivalent: it indicates not only the presence of state projects of discipline; emergent nationalist discourses; and the reinforcement of class, race, and gender orders but also serves as a vehicle by which islanders may counter established hierarchies, enact individual and collective desires, express anticolonial sentiment, and validate nondominant masculinities. Evident in parts of the Pacific noted above, as well as in diasporic and transnational islander communities in the United States, sport is not simply transplanted but becomes transformed and resignified in the local context.

SITING EMPIRE IN SPORT

As a social institution, sport is enmeshed with relations of power and therefore is a very useful site in which to examine important social processes,[27] including how formations of and attachments to empire are brought to life, tensely sustained, and transformed. Recently, a number of scholars have examined the important geopolitical context within which many so-called big-time elite and highly commercialized sports are played;[28] still, the examination of sport and imperialism remains underdeveloped.[29] While work on British sport and empire is relatively well established, in analyses of U.S. imperialism critical examination of sport is typically absent.[30]

American football is part of a longer history of colonialism and sport. Gridiron football, as played in the United States, evolved from rugby football.[31]

In its early institution in the Victorian boarding schools of Britain, rugby was foundationally implicated in projects of discipline and transformation.[32] In the United States, secular organized sport was also thought to produce strong citizens and was bound up with the extension of U.S. colonialism on the continent and empire abroad: organized sport had been an important tool for assimilation and pedagogy at Native American boarding schools, as well as an important venue for physical and moral discipline aimed at reinvigorating American citizens in the absence of war. [33]

While football can be understood as symbolizing American modernity and nationhood, it would be a mistake to dismiss its appeal abroad and in the U.S. territories as a simple case of cultural imperialism. In its emergence as a path of mobility and access to capital predicated on the mastery of modern institutions of education and sport, and enmeshed with ideologies of achievement and prestige, it has become a pedagogy of U.S. American empire in island and stateside Samoan communities. As in other communities under the American flag, these subtle disciplinary processes are accomplished with intense effervescent affect as the rhythm of daily life for families, communities, and players accommodates the tempo of sporting activity. This affection fosters tender ties to the nation even for those whose belonging is not guaranteed (and in legal contexts requires tense negotiation).[34]

Narratives of Nation, Politics of the Present

As I stood in the stadium at the end of one of the football camps in the summer of 2012, we could hear the honking of horns as the motorcade for the *vili paelo* approached.[35] The delegate team for Oceania pulled into the stadium, with the players clothed in crisp new uniforms and carrying the American Samoa national flag. One of the camp organizers standing next to me exclaimed, "They look so American!" But they had a Samoan twist, as they paired their new jerseys with *ie lava lava*,[36] which had been printed for the team. Having prevailed over Australia in the Oceania tournament, the American Samoa team represented the entire region at the IFAF Under-18 World Championships. As the Oceania delegate, the players were not subsumed into the U.S. national team, but rather matched up against them in a televised broadcast (June 30, 2012) after having lost their first game.[37] During the broadcast, the USAF executive director pointed out, "Our friends from American Samoa made history—they are the first team to score a touchdown on team USA since this program started." This series was a unique opportunity for the players from American Samoa, many of whom would not play in another nationally televised contest. The games also represent the kinds of blurred boundaries produced by the "unincorporated territory" status. These unstable dynamics of incorporation and distinction permitted American Samoa to compete as an entity distinctively removed from the United States and part of Oceania, while in other arenas the islands are more closely linked to the United States than to any of its island neighbors.

Formally, American Samoa holds the unique status of "unincorporated territory" of the United States. American Samoans are considered "U.S. nationals" who may travel, work, and reside in the United States but who do not pay federal income taxes and may not vote in U.S. elections. Recognized on the international stage as a nonsovereign state, some might argue that the term American Samoa proclaims a clear relationship of dominance and submission that has been enshrined in law and inscribed in social life, from the ubiquity of American media, popular culture, and consumer products to the dependence on U.S. financial largesse. As one of seventeen territories that remain on the UN List of Non-Self-Governing Territories, it remains so designated because its inhabitants "have not yet attained a full measure of self-government."[38] Yet detractors, invoking an image of classic European-style colonialism, argue that it is not and never has been a colony since there was no concerted effort at settlement or resource extraction.[39] For over a decade, local government leaders have spoken out against this designation and advocated removal from the UN list. In island affairs the ambiguous legal distinction of unincorporation has enabled the uneven application of U.S. laws, left obscure the question of jurisdiction, and allowed for considerable freedom in local exercise of sovereignty.[40]

This ambiguity is narrated in ways that solidify what is an incoherent and unstable relationship of power. We return to Secretary of State Hillary Clinton's remarks on her trip to American Samoa in 2010: "The United States is aware of, and grateful for, our close relationship and our deep ties; made most evident by the long and noble history and sacrifice of the men and women of American Samoa. Not only as members of our military, serving with great distinction and honor, but as fellow travelers along life's path joined together by decisions that were made more than a hundred years ago, but which have stood the test of time." Reiterating the State Department's position in response to a local reporter's question about American Samoa's colonial status, Clinton said: "we reject this characterization. We think that it is not accurate and does not describe the relationship that we have had over all of these years. But I do think we have to work more closely together to meet the needs of the people of American Samoa. And that is my pledge to you, that we will do all that we can to ensure that we have a very close, respectful working relationship now and far into the future."[41] Here we see just one of many instances in which the relationship of dominance—the assertion of U.S. plenary power over the islands—is discursively recast in the language of "fellow travelers" and as "close, respectful working relationship" that is meant to imply a degree of equality that does not exist in the relationship between the federal government and U.S. territories. What also emerges in these remarks is a contrast between the language of tutelage that marked the American imperial imperative in Samoa in the early to mid-twentieth century, and the contemporary discourse of assistance that helps to create a "commonsense understanding of reality."[42]

At the same meeting, a local official stated: "More than a hundred years ago, our ancestors ceded our islands to the United States. With a mutual agreement made by men of impeccable integrity, honor and moral fortitude, we have enjoyed this relationship. It has provided us with a sense of respect and integrity in exercising the freedom and liberty throughout the years as part of the American family."[43] In this statement, the partition of the Samoan islands by Germany, the United States, and Great Britain at the Tripartite Convention of 1899 and the ensuing efforts to establish and extend U.S. sovereignty over the islands are recast as a "mutual agreement" that has allowed the exercise of "freedom and liberty."[44] The use of the familial not only calls forth the dominance of the patriarch (United States) over its children (Samoans) as in the nuclear family model but also invokes the relationships of extended family, the family chief (rendered in some idealized versions as foremost among equals), and norms of reciprocity rather than repressive power.

In this retelling, the speaker is refusing the position of dominated colonial subject and is instead staking a claim to membership and rights in an idiom that invokes duties, obligations, and care. Being linked to the most eminent global power of the twentieth century has indeed provided material benefit and bestowed "a sense of respect and integrity" upon the islands and its inhabitants in the eyes of many. While some people choose to live in another's empire,[45] it is this hegemonic narrative of choice that represents the foundational circumstances under which Tutuila and Manu'a were drawn into the U.S. imperial orbit, and continuously recasts the present relationship as noncolonial.[46]

IMPERIAL FUTURES?

The case of American Samoa questions our tacit understandings of empire, how it works, and how we understand dynamics of power and agency. The archipelago has always been part (however small) of U.S. imperial ambitions, from fueling American trade with the East, to supporting military strategic interests and offensives, to demonstrating the fitness of the United States as a colonial power, to providing labor to different sectors of the U.S. economy. Football is rooted in American developmentalism in Samoa: the extension of the state apparatus, American plenary power and military governance, and creation of expendable pools of labor for the American neoliberal capitalist system.[47] In the context of contemporary global capitalism the prestige and material rewards associated with sporting success position football as an important opportunity for Samoans, but it also obscures the islands' peripheral economic positioning, asymmetrical integration into the United States and the global economy, racism against Samoans and other Pacific Islanders in the U.S. context, and realities of U.S. plenary power over the entities it claims as territories.

In this analysis I have drawn on Michel Foucault's theorization of disciplinary practices and modern institutions to examine how imperial formations as macrorelations of power are not simply repressive or oppressive, but productive in reshaping docile bodies. I have also used Loïc Wacquant's work on bodily capital to theorize how actors, through embodied action and performance, produce themselves as empowered subjects even in contexts over which they have little control. In the Foucauldian conception, protracted transformation of the body through the disciplinary regimes of sport paradoxically reshapes young Samoan men's bodies as docile. The further they submit to team hierarchy, coaching authority, and the contingency of recruiting processes, the more valued they are as team members. At the same time, their value is built through the same productive disciplinary transformations of the body to render skill, strength, and ferocity in its dominant performance on the field. Contrary to popular media depictions, successfully navigating the intense demands of sporting performance—becoming a star player, winning the game, making the key tackle or final touchdown—does not just happen naturally for Samoan athletes. These performances are made possible by submission to bodily regimens and agents of authority toward empowerment through correct training. While the lens of docile bodies helps bring into focus the workings of power, and whether the "link between increased aptitude and increased domination"[48] holds, it ignores actors' embodied action, rewards, and meaning important in a more nuanced understanding of social life. This is where ethnography helps us tease out the tension of football players as both docile bodies and empowered subjects, and how sporting prowess is turned to serious games of status, prestige, and capital. In this case, disciplinary mechanisms of sport and spectacular, highly visible performance in valued arenas are part of a fractured, incomplete, and unstable apparatus of empire in constant formation.

The intertwined logic of discipline, submission, and empowerment of the football industry is not alien to Samoan cultural contexts, although—importantly—the mechanisms, performances, and goals may be different. Samoan customary social relations are fundamentally structured by hierarchy, where performing deference to rank is often a path of empowerment (in terms of both demonstrating one's understanding of cultural protocol and garnering respect for that knowledge/performance). Learning how to perform protocol is also a process of molding subjectivity and retraining the body, learned through submission to intense discipline in appropriate contexts.[49] This articulation of intertwined logics is part of why the football sporting endeavor has been successful, and serves both the desires of some Samoan families and communities and the aims of sustaining U.S. empire.

Examining both discipline and empowerment helps us understand how imperial formations are lived and in this case, why a game quintessentially American in its nationalist imagery and performance is appropriated as a Samoan game. This claiming articulates an expanded and inclusive belonging that demands recognition. When families and communities celebrate sporting success of Samoan players, it is often in proportion to their positioning in the structure of the football industry—the higher, the more widely celebrated. These eruptions of collective joy as the cheer goes up enact recognition in multiple registers: of the individual's accomplishment, of fan loyalty, of family pride, of real or potential payoff. But the recognition is also of the tremendous amount of effort invested and the willingness of the player to submit to disciplinary processes that have worked to his, his family's, and his community's benefit. His gridiron capital is shared—like much else—through Samoan cultural logics of connection and the primacy of the social (family, church, village, etc.) over the individual.

At the same time, the success of Samoans and other Pacific Islanders in American football illuminates sport as a beacon proclaiming the possibility of social mobility in a time of seemingly diminishing prospects. This illumination blinds us to the very real structural dilemmas of poverty, debt, and inequality that plague Samoan communities in the islands and the continental United States and instead reinvigorates an attachment to U.S. empire. Football, as a highly visible path of geographic and social mobility that is structurally routed to and through the instructional and social worlds of American universities, reproduces a commonsense vision wherein the possibility of imagining a future without the United States is more than difficult—it is nearly impossible.

NOTES

1 This is a ritual ceremony performed for a variety of events, including welcoming guests of high status. It typically involves elaborate oration and ava (or kava, as it is more widely known), drinking among ranking chiefs, honored guests, and in some cases government officials.

2 "Gov. Togiola welcomes Secretary of State Hillary Clinton."

3 See, for example, Adams, "Sons and Lavas," 390–97, 445; Miller, "American Football, Samoan Style"; Saslow, "Island Hoping"; Spear and Pennington (dirs.), "Polynesian Power"; and Syken, "Football in Paradise." On "Sunday Samoans," see Pelley, "American Samoa: Football Island." "Gridiron" refers to the form of football played in North America, derived from the unique field markings.

4 Up until the tsunami of fall 2009, the two major employers of the working population had been the local government and two American canneries (Star-Kist and Van Camp), while a smaller proportion of workers were employed by the private sector. Van Camp ceased operations in the territory in 2009; its assets were acquired by Tri Marine International, which opened a cannery in 2014. As of 2013, the government employed 38.5 percent of the labor force, while the cannery share had dropped to 13.1 percent (from 28.6 percent in 2008) and the private sector absorbed the rest of the working population, an increase to 48.4 percent in 2013 over 35.9 percent in 2008 (*American Samoa Statistical Yearbook* 2013, 118).

5 See, for example Aina et al., "A Community of Contrasts"; and Mayeda et al., "'You Gotta Do So Much to Actually Make It.'"

6 The U.S. Census in 2010 reported average household incomes of $23,892. Currently in 2015 the minimum wage varies by industry from $4.18 to $5.59 per hour; it is set to increase periodically until it meets the federal minimum wage, but there is strong opposition from the local government and most notably the canneries to this wage increase. Unemployment is difficult to estimate; however, according to the U.S. Census in 2012, 47.1 per cent of residents sixteen and older are not in the labor force. While there are a number of critiques made about the accuracy of the census, it gives some basic descriptors of economic realities in the islands.

7 Here I draw on Ortner's use of crystallization in *Making Gender*.

8 Uperesa, "Fabled Futures."

9 Stoler, "On Degrees of Imperial Sovereignty"; Stoler and McGranahan, "Introduction."

10 Gems, *The Athletic Crusade*.

11 According to the American Samoa Under-19's website: "The independent non-profit is the official youth football development partner of the NFL, its 32 teams and the NFL Players Association. USA Football manages U.S. national teams within the sport for international competitions and provides $1 million annually in equipment grants and youth league volunteer background check subsidies. [It was] endowed by the NFL and NFLPA in 2002 through the NFL Youth Football Fund." For more on the organization, see http://u19championship.com/, accessed on May 15, 2014.

12 See for example, Kwauk, "'No Longer Just a Pastime,'" 1.

13 Uperesa, "Seeking New Fields of Labor."

14 See Adas, "Improving on the Civilizing Mission?"; Negrón de Montilla, *Americanization in Puerto Rico and the Public School System 1900–1930*; del Moral, *Negotiating Empire*.

15 Foucault, *Discipline and Punish*.

16 Guttman, *From Ritual to Record*.

17 Foucault, *Discipline and Punish*, 136.

18 Foucault, *Discipline and Punish*, 136.

19 Foucault, *Discipline and Punish*, 137.

20 Foucault, *Discipline and Punish*, 137.

21 Foucault, *Discipline and Punish*, 138.

22 Foucault, *Discipline and Punish*, 138.

23 The combine is an event designed to measure bodies and abilities according to set standard activities. Typical measurements include height, weight, hand span, "wingspan" (from fingertip to fingertip, arms outstretched to either side), forty-yard dash timing, vertical jump, and number of pounds one can bench-press.

24 Wacquant, "Pugs at Work," 67.

25 Here gridiron capital is a specific set of bodily practices, abilities, and orientations that can be converted profitably in gridiron football. Distinct from economic, cultural, and social capital players may accrue with football success, gridiron capital accrues in the very process of training one's body.

26 On New Zealand, Hokowhitu, "'Physical Beings'" and "Tackling Maori Masculinity." On Hawai'i, Tengan, "(En)Gendering Colonialism," *Native Men Remade*, and "Re-Membering Panala'au." On Guam, Diaz, "'Fight Boys, 'Til the Last.'"

27 Besnier and Brownell, "Sport, Modernity, and the Body."

28 Allison, *The Global Politics of Sport*; Brownell, *Training the Body for China*; Maguire and Falcous, *Sport and Migration*.

29 Scholarly works on the British empire and sport are the main exception. See Appadurai, "Playing with Modernity"; Baker and Mangan, *Sport in Africa*; James, *Beyond a Boundary*; Majumdar, "Tom Brown Goes Global"; and Mangan, *The Games Ethic and Imperialism*.

30 The notable exceptions are Gems, *The Athletic Crusade*; Guttman, *Games and Empires*; Keys, *Globalizing Sport*; and Klein, *Sugarball*. The special issue of the *International Journal of the History of Sport* 23 (2) also addressed issues of exchange, diaspora, and globalization as linked to but distinct from colonial histories of the Pacific. Ethnographic studies of sport and U.S. empire are an area yet to be developed.

31 For a more detailed history of football in the United States, see, for example, Danzig, *The History of American Football*; Dumas, *Integrating the Gridiron*; and Watterson, *College Football*.

32 Mangan, *Athleticism in the Victorian and Edwardian Public School*.

33 Gems, *The Athletic Crusade*, 9.

34 Stoler, "Intimations of Empire." On the legal tensions, see the citizenship challenge brought by *Tuaua v. United States* (2015) discussed in Uperesa and Garriga-López, "Contested Sovereignties."

35 Samoan translation of "wheelbarrow." This was a two-day fundraiser that traveled the eastern and western districts of the island, starting in the early morning hours collecting cash donations in a wheelbarrow to support the national team's upcoming trip to the IFAF Under-19 Championship in Texas.

36 Length of cloth wrapped around the waist, with a hemline that hits between the knees and ankle, depending on the formality of the occasion.

37 In one of the breaks the announcers pointed out that what USAF is trying to do is to grow football from the grassroots. In the United States and internationally these activities bring in kids as well as their communities, thereby stimulating wider interest in other countries. Essentially, the federation is globalizing the game of American football by cultivating a new market share: younger players and their communities. This globalization model has been a driving force in other sporting institutions such as Major League Baseball for some time now; see Klein, *Growing the Game.*

38 United Nations Charter, Chapter XI: Declaration Regarding Non-Self-Governing Territories. Under UN terms, non-self-governing territories must achieve independence, opt for statehood, or establish a relationship of "free association" as part of the decolonization process. See http://www.un.org/en/sections/un-charter/chapter-xi/index.html, accessed November 11, 2017.

39 At the request of the territory's congressional delegate Faleomavaega Eni Hunkin, the U.S. State Department issued an official stand in 2006, claiming the relationship between American Samoa and the federal government to be an internal issue and not one subject to the authority of the UN Decolonization committee. See Sagapolutele, "Clinton rejects U.N. label 'colony' for American Samoa."

40 See Uperesa and Garriga-López, "Contested Sovereignties."

41 "Gov. Togiola Welcomes Secretary of State Hillary Clinton."

42 McGranahan, "Empire Out-of-Bounds."

43 "Gov. Togiola Welcomes Secretary of State Hillary Clinton."

44 The political arrangement of United States' sovereignty and de facto local rule over the islands is rooted in the Berlin Act of 1899, an agreement that delineated competing colonial claims between the three imperial powers (Germany, Great Britain, and the United States) agitating in Samoa at the end of the nineteenth century. The political relationship between the United States and what became known as American Samoa evolved under the U.S. naval administration of the islands until 1951 and was further configured under the oversight of the Department of the Interior. Eventually top government posts were taken over by locally elected leaders beginning in the 1970s, claiming power over the local state government within parameters set by the United States.

45 Stoler and McGranahan, "Introduction," 26.

46 While this remains the hegemonic narrative, it is not the only one. Public critique of political status, financial dependence on the United States, and local corruption erupt in gossip, informal conversation, letters to the editor, and anonymous postings on online news articles. There is also humor, such as the article run by a mainstream newspaper published in independent Samoa, *The Samoa Observer*: "Hillary Clinton Shares US Money and Samoan Smiles."

47 Uperesa, "Seeking New Fields of Labor."

48 Foucault, *Discipline and Punish*, 138.

49 This is different from Bourdieu's discussion of body *hexis* in *Outline of a Theory of Practice*: in this context the social-political mythology is not inscribed in a

permanent disposition on the body, but rather one's dynamic social location (in terms of rank, age, gender, recognized accomplishments) is constantly calibrated, and expected behavior and appropriate protocol are learned through observation, direct instruction, physical repetition, and physical and verbal disciplining—all of which changes over the life course.

07 Exceptionalism as a Way of Life

U.S. Empire, Filipino Subjectivity, and the Global Call Center Industry

JAN M. PADIOS

In October 2013, the Philippine Board of Investments, in conjunction with the Philippine consulate in Washington, DC, held a small breakfast forum to market the Philippines as a top-notch site for outsourcing back-office medical work such as processing insurance claims and providing human resource services. Speaking to about thirty health-care administrators interested in moving some of their work offshore, Philippine government officials enthusiastically highlighted the country's robust economic growth and its recent investment-grade sovereign credit rating. While the latter information was meant to convey the promise of foreign capital's security in the Philippine economy, other components of the marketing presentations emphasized the more intangible forms of safety offered by Filipino workers who might be tasked with handling not only private information about health-care recipients in the United States but, in the case of actual phone contact with ill and vulnerable patients, sensitive interpersonal interactions. To this end, an American doctor and businessman who had successfully outsourced his clinic's health-care management to the Philippines testified to Filipinos' "passion to engage" patients, as well as their ability to motivate them to manage their own wellness. Citing Filipinos' ostensibly natural "compassionate ways," the speaker echoed earlier comments by a Filipino advocate of the Philippines Business Process Outsourcing industry, who claimed that Filipino call center agents "know how to smile when talking to you on the phone" and that such hospitable qualities define what Filipinos are "as a race."

This chapter takes these ethnographic observations as starting points for tracing articulations of Philippine nationalism and Filipino subjectivity as they are entangled within the discourses and practices of the nation's booming Business Process Outsourcing (BPO) industry, known colloquially as *the call center industry*.[1] Arguably one of the most important economic, social, and cultural developments in the country in several decades, the growth of the

Philippine call center industry raises important questions about how Filipinos in the twenty-first century grapple with identity, power, and value vis-à-vis the United States, its former colonizer and a primary source of call center jobs. As I demonstrate throughout the chapter, the call center industry constitutes a touchstone of Philippine postcolonial cultural politics, in which Filipino workers struggle to assert the symbolic autonomy and sovereignty of the postcolonial nation-state while still operating in the shadow of empire.

Drawing on ethnographic fieldwork conducted in the Philippines between 2008 and 2013, this chapter makes three primary arguments. First is that call center industry leaders and workers, along with state actors, utilize the industry's growth, marketing, and internal changes to make claims about the racial and affective qualities of Filipino subjectivity and the economic autonomy of the postcolonial nation-state. Thus a relatively routine marketing meeting between Global North actors in search of cost savings and those in the Global South eager to provide "flexible" labor doubles as an occasion to define the boundaries of "Filipino" as a particularly racialized and affective subject. Second, I argue that such articulations of subjectivity and nationalism are fraught and contradictory processes, insofar as they rely on a narrative of Filipino subjectivity as emerging from the Philippines' "exceptional" colonial history that is said to have bestowed upon Filipinos special affective attributes that make them ostensibly ideal for interactive service work. Building on critical race scholar Dylan Rodríguez's analysis and critique of "Filipino" as naming an ontologically secure "post-conquest" identity that seeks congruence with the history of U.S. imperialism, I demonstrate how industry discourses of Filipino identity reproduce narratives of Filipino/Philippine exceptionalism that have provided ideological support for U.S. imperialism.[2] Third, I argue, however, that these attempts to perform proximity to the United States exist alongside call center industry workers' and leaders' strong critiques of U.S. global hegemony—critiques that have emerged in the Philippines, as well as elsewhere in the region, as part of "the Asian century."[3] For many of my informants, for example, Filipino call center workers are not serving a U.S. customer base, but providing compassionate assistance to a United States in economic crisis. What I am calling "Philippine exceptionalism" thus revises colonial and neocolonial narratives of the Philippines as a source of "cheap labor" for the United States, while reproducing the underlying ideologies that justified U.S. imperialism. Together, these dynamics reveal that Philippine call centers are more than just sites of corporate communication about mundane matters such as printers and mobile phones but also spaces where workers actively construct Filipino identity and the Philippine nation-state through an engagement with, and disavowal of, the United States as both a material entity and an imaginary location.

By coupling ethnographic evidence with postcolonial analysis, the chapter analyzes and critiques nested ideologies of empire, identity, and nationalism within neoliberal globalization.[4] As American studies scholars have argued, U.S. exceptionalism has long underwritten U.S. imperialism, either in the form of denial (the United States has no empire) or through a claim to singularity (the United States has an empire but it is unique).[5] The latter, referred to by Julian Go as a form of "liberal exceptionalism," has held canonical sway amongst a faction of historians of U.S.-Philippines relations for decades.[6] Such scholars argue that throughout the twentieth century the two countries have maintained a "special relationship" that began with the United States bestowing the gift of American democratic institutions and education upon the Philippines as a colony, and culminated with Filipino and American troops joining forces against a common enemy in World War II. Within this narrative, the Philippines is cast as an exceptional colony, and thus Filipino subjectivity—which is said to emerge from this exceptional colonial history—as especially unique. Yet these claims to Philippine exceptionalism in particular have often been overlooked within contemporary scholarship on the Philippines, except when framed as a superstructural outcome of competition in the global labor market, rather than a process of subject formation bound up with colonialism and capitalism. In contrast, this chapter analyzes the rhetoric of exceptionalism as both a material strategy for selling Filipino labor and an articulation of Filipino postcolonial subjectivity. I ask: In what ways do exceptionalism and U.S. empire continue to operate in the Philippines today? And if, as Go asserts, "exceptionalism obscures more than it enlightens," how can ethnographic inquiry illuminate what lies in its shadows?[7]

To answer this question, I draw on interviews with members of the Business Process Outsourcing Association of the Philippines—an umbrella organization that represents the interests of the Philippine call center industry and U.S. corporations—as well as participant observation of the new employee training processes at Vox Elite, a leading global call center where I applied for and gained employment as a technical support call center agent, and where I subsequently conducted over a hundred hours of fieldwork. The training process for new employees included one week of training in "U.S. Cultural Competency" (cc), which orients new call center agents to features of American culture and society, thus preparing them to serve a U.S. customer base. Through this fieldwork, I uncovered ways individuals produce meaning and normative practices in relation to the everyday social and cultural processes in which they are embedded. I trace how working within the transnational call center industry seems to compel Filipinos to articulate notions of nation and identity in ways that reproduce colonial power relations through the production of subjectivity. In so doing, I demonstrate how, following Aihwa Ong, culture and subjectivity emerges from practices that are always embedded in and thus shaped by the social structures and political orders of capitalist accumulation.[8] Therefore, just as I bring an American Studies analysis of U.S. imperialism to bear on anthropological discussions of U.S. empire, so too do I highlight the efficacy of ethnography and anthropological critique for understanding the rearticulation and reconfiguration of U.S. imperial ideology in the twenty-first century. Finally, the convergence of American Studies and anthropology represented by this chapter underscores the importance of decolonized ethnographic practice, in which investigations of U.S. imperialism lead to an incisive critique of the nationalist and capitalist forces that underwrite it.[9]

Postcolonial nationalism and Filipino subject formation are two cultural processes intimately bound to the history of U.S. empire in the Philippines and the Philippine state's attempts to achieve the always elusive state of modernity. Analysis of the Philippine call center industry thus constitutes a crucial component of a discussion on U.S. empire—not only because of the political economic continuities between U.S. colonization and neoliberal globalization in which Filipino labor is exploited by U.S. capital, but also because of the ways in which Filipinos working in the industry reproduce narratives of U.S. exceptionalism via the notion of a uniquely Filipino, and uniquely affective, race. In the conclusion of this essay, I bring the materialist and rhetorical repercussions of this discursive account of power to bear on the contemporary moment by looking specifically at how the call center industry articulates with the U.S.-led War on Terror in the southern Philippines.

FROM INDUSTRY TO IDENTITY: REPRODUCING NARRATIVES OF EXCEPTIONALISM

Since the late twentieth century, massive transformations in the production and consumption of goods and information along neoliberal lines have led to the restructuring of customer service on a global scale. Toll-free "1-800" numbers dialed in the United States now reach offshore customer service and technical support call centers in South, East, and Southeast Asia, where agents answer customers' calls twenty-four hours a day, seven days a week. By 2011 the Philippines had surpassed India to become the call center capital of the world. By the end of 2015 the Philippine industry had generated just over U.S. $22 billion dollars. In 2015 it employed upwards of 1.1 million people.[10] By and large, Philippine call center industry leaders, state actors, and workers alike attribute the country's meteoric rise within the global services labor market to cultural factors, especially Filipinos' ability to speak

American English with light or "neutral" accents, their intimate familiarity with American media and ways of life, and their abundant affective capacity. This intense focus and articulation of Filipino difference illustrate what Anna Tsing has called a "niche-segregating performance"[11]—the process through which management and workers alike embrace difference and project cultural particularity in order to create or maintain a unique position in a supply chain.

In the ethnographic observation described above, the racial boundaries of Filipino identity are circumscribed around particular *affective* capacities, especially those related to compassion and human engagement. Indeed, the notion that Filipinos are naturally hospitable, caring, and empathic—and therefore ideally suited for interactive service work that requires emotional and other types of affective labor—has risen to the level of what Anna Guevarra, citing Melissa Wright, refers to as a "trope" regarding identity and productivity.[12] I encountered this trope most memorably when, in 2009, I visited the offices of the Business Process Outsourcing Association of the Philippines (BPAP), an umbrella organization that provides support to call center companies in the Philippines. There, I met with Melvin Legarda and Joseph Santiago, two of the organization's most highly ranked executives. Within minutes of the start of our conversation, it seemed rather clear that Legarda and Santiago approached our interview as yet another opportunity to demonstrate the readiness and success of the Philippines at providing quality service labor to the world; for Legarda and Santiago, even an academic researcher constituted a marketing audience.[13] When the conversation turned toward competition between countries within the global market for back-office work, Santiago began to speak about the cultural traits that allow Filipinos to be far better suited for customer service work than Indians.

JP What makes Filipinos more suitable to doing customer service [than Indians]?

JS There's an exact set of rules to service in India. They are more utilitarian. Filipinos are compassionate.

ML We are good at working with the heart.

JS It also has to do with our deep immersion at the bottom of the ladder for so many years. We were a colony of Spain, and then the United States, the Japanese invaded us during the war, and then the poverty really pushed us under.

JP What do you think is the effect of these experiences?

JS Benevolence. The Philippines is the only place that you can see a Japanese, American, and Filipino war memorial in the same place.

ML Also our religion.

JS We are for loyalty and equality. There are actually people within this industry who tell me that I should be more Western. I say to them, "Look, you are the ones who came here for our help, and you are telling me I should be more Western?" I think it's clear that the best programs are the ones in which agents are taught to be themselves. Just go back to basic nature and you have your answers. I even told someone from an Australian collections account that the Philippine psyche is perfect for helping them collect on debts from customers. We know what it means to be in debt. We present ourselves as part of the solution, as someone who can help manage their money. We are not targeting customers, attacking them [as scary debt collectors]. Our greatest strength is also sometimes our greatest weakness. Sometimes we are too obedient. We overdo things. If the manager of a company here is an American, no one will contradict him. That company would crumble.

JP Do you talk to investors this way, about these kinds of details, like the Philippine psyche?

JS Yes, we are very detailed. We talk about history.

Santiago and Legarda's responses illustrate a discourse that casts Filipinos as modern subjects who have passed through the crucible of colonialism, war, and debt to develop affective expertise that makes them ideal for serving Anglo-American clientele. Legarda and Santiago thus interpret the Philippines' rise to BPO prominence in nationalist and identity-based terms that speak to historian Renato Constantino's Fanonian critique of how "'the Filipino mind has come to regard centuries of colonial status as a grace from above rather than a scourge.'"[14]

Scholars analyzing state and market actors' mutual investments in Filipino labor migration have argued that the production and packaging of Filipino identity for sale on the global labor market is precisely the point of such discourse. As Anna Guevarra argues, labor-brokering agencies that match Filipina nurses and domestic workers with employers around the world work hard to make Filipino workers synonymous with "TLC"—tender loving care—in turn producing Filipino identity as an "added export value."[15] Similarly, analyzing a state-produced brochure that markets Filipinos as ideal for work in the shipping industry by virtue of Filipinos' long history with seafaring in the Spanish colonial era, Robyn Rodriguez writes that "histories of imperial violence and coerced labor are revisioned and sanitized" in efforts to export Filipino migrants.[16]

Although such conclusions highlight the significant ways that social constructions of culture and identity are constitutive rather than arbitrary inputs within the global economy, these acts of essentialization are built on a deeper assumption that there is indeed a collective identity to essentialize. In other words, the notion that Filipino subjectivity is an exceptional outcome of colonial history is troubling not only for its reinterpretation of the past and its use of what Dylan Rodríguez describes as "vulgar notions of cultural artifact and commodity" that reduce ethnic identity to a "product" of history and culture.[17] In the case of call center workers specifically, by tying subjectivity to colonial history, such claims reproduce the notion of "Filipino" as an ontologically secure "post-conquest" racial and national identity that "fixes" the Filipino condition "in a relation of political continuity . . . with the animus of U.S. nation building"—a process defined by "white supremacist institutionalities" of racial chattel slavery, frontier capitalism, and racial colonial domination.[18] Such continuity and fixity are achieved by casting Filipino subjects as products of a progressive historical trajectory, that is enabled by the dominant narratives of U.S.-Philippines relations described earlier.

Santiago's words are particularly striking for just how closely they mirror this exceptionalist rhetoric. Using the term *benevolence* to describe the outcome of the Philippines' unique colonial history, Santiago evokes the keyword and sentiment by which President William McKinley described the American colonial project in the islands in 1898. Following the precoordinated defeat of the Spanish fleet by Admiral Dewey's naval forces, McKinley proclaimed that while the U.S. military remained supreme in the islands, "it should be the earnest wish and paramount aim of the military administration to win the confidence, respect, and affection of the inhabitants of the Philippines by assuring them in every possible way that full measure of individual rights and liberties which is the heritage of free peoples, and by proving to them that the mission of the United States is one of benevolent assimilation substituting the mild sway of justice and right for arbitrary rule."[19]

The U.S. military would then move on to organize multiple campaigns of extermination of Filipino "insurgents" fighting for independence. Yet Santiago does not focus on this component of the historical narrative of "U.S.-Philippines relations." Instead, he refers to the coexistence of memorials that mark Filipino and American joint forces against the Japanese military in World War II (when the Philippines was still a colony of the United States), one of which—the Manila American Cemetery and Memorial—constitutes the Pacific's largest gravesite for *American* personnel killed during the war. Establishing a "historical congruence" between Filipino subjectivity and the

United States as an exceptional nation whose benevolence compels and deserves the allegiance of the colonized, Santiago thus rearticulates a dominant narrative about World War II as "another genesis moment of political union and nationalist coalescence" between Filipinos and the United States.[20] To suggest that native peoples inherited the supposed benevolence of their colonizers invisibilizes the genocidal nature of U.S. occupation, allowing Philippine modernity to be framed as an outcome of colonial history.[21]

Industry advocates mobilize these complex narratives of history and identity within marketing materials and meetings, as well as in relation to changes within the industry. Santiago drew one of the most striking illustrations of such nested imaginaries when discussing an important policy shift within the BPO industry in the Philippines, if not at large—that is, a shift *away* from training call center employees to mimic the national accents of the customer base (and use "neutral" accents instead), to mask their locations in the Global South, and to Anglicize or Westernize their names. According to some of my research participants, training in neutral accents was a response to customers angered and annoyed by the perceived insincerity and foolishness of these attempts. As the instructor of CC warned my training class, "Americans can always detect a foreign accent so don't bother trying to fake one"—the implication being that Americans not only police racial difference but also punish agents for attempts to transgress racial boundaries (all the while implicitly demanding that agents "relate" to their problems and concerns). According to others, this policy was also compelled by the American consumers' increasing *tolerance* for hearing foreign voices on the other end of the line. Thus Loren Ramos, a call center quality assurance manager, informed me that "most customers know that his or her service calls will be thrown somewhere in the Third World." Moreover, according to Andrew Ross, the economic motivation for accent neutralization policies lies in the fact that such programs cut the cost of training and allow staff to move easily amongst accounts that are linked to different parts of the world.[22]

However, the policy shift also created an opening by which people within the industry could reimagine Filipinos as "no longer needing" to prove their proximity to either whiteness or the Global North. In another portion of our interview, Santiago described a commercial that BPAP had developed in order to market the Philippine BPO industry to corporations with a U.S. customer base. According to Santiago, in the commercial, a white male customer service agent smiles and speaks fluent American English to a customer over the phone. At the end of the call, the white agent peels off a mask to reveal that he is really Filipino—clearly suggesting that Filipinos are so adept at sounding like native English speakers with American accents, that the usual disruptions in communication that come with difference in language and accent would not be a problem with Filipino agents on the line. Customers and corporations, the commercial implied, would never know—or hear—the difference.

Importantly, however, Santiago recalled that BPAP decided to drop the commercial after the organization realized it no longer needed to convince potential U.S. corporate clients that Filipino agents could affect the sound of an American accent in order to service a U.S. customer base. "At a certain point," Santiago explained, BPAP executives came to believe that "agents could simply be themselves" while on the phone with customers. For Santiago, the abandonment of national accent training signaled the arrival of the modern Filipino, one who discards aspirations for congruity with the colonizer, to reveal a single, integrated, racial, and national subject—a Filipino who can be himself or herself. Industry changes thus became what Kimberly Hoang, writing about Vietnam, describes as "a platform to articulate new national ideals that challenge common representations of poverty in the Global South and the latter's oppressed relation to the West."[23]

In this way, repetitive accounts of the links between Filipino identity, colonial history, and skill constitute tropes not only because they are ubiquitous, but also because—as the definition of the term *trope* suggests—they direct our attention toward other meanings. Indeed, the notion of Filipino cultural affinity with America or that Filipinos are particularly adept at affective labor are meant to imply, if not highlight, that the Filipino people had and maintain a unique intimacy with the United States. Thus to locate the success of the Philippine call center industry within what is imagined to be proximity between the two countries is to already reproduce the narrative of a special relationship.[24] And yet, as the example of BPAP's discarded commercial suggests, Filipinos struggle between the necessity to perform proximity to the United States—and thereby legitimize their ability to do call center work—and the postcolonial desire to assert the Philippine nation's symbolic sovereignty. I look more closely at this struggle in the following section.

THE CULTURAL POLITICS OF CAPITULATION AND CRITIQUE

As suggested in the opening of this chapter, when Philippine call center industry leaders, state actors, and workers represent Filipino call center workers as exceptionally compassionate and competent people, they do so within a context of dizzying economic growth rates of the early to mid-2010s. Coupled with the U.S. financial crisis of 2008, such remarkable economic developments in the Philippines and Asia more broadly have strengthened the narrative of Asian economic ascendency or what the Asian Development

Bank has referred to as the potential promise of "the Asian century."[25] As Kimberly Hoang writes, the decade between 2005 and 2014 "witnessed dramatic changes in global financial flows that have shifted the economic center of gravity more toward East Asia, raising important questions about the waning dominance of the West."[26]

Returning now to my interview with Legarda and Santiago, we can see how the latter's disavowal of the need "to be more Western" and indeed to cast off the proverbial mask of American whiteness participates in this shifting economic and cultural terrain. Indeed, the idea of Asian capitalism supplanting American capitalism was integral to Joseph Santiago's understanding of why Western companies were drawn to the Philippine call center industry in the first place. In another portion of our interview, Santiago explicitly argued that Americans fundamentally misunderstand capitalist enterprise. "Jan, you're from New York, right? Well, don't mind me saying so, but the way Americans think about capitalism is all screwed up," Santiago told me. "The beauty of capitalism is in innovation, not blowing the competition out of the water. The Americans forgot that when they went to India." This denouncement of American capitalism reinforces Santiago's earlier insistence that when Filipino employees fail to challenge American managers, they are doomed to "crumble."

For Santiago—as for the industry advocates described at the beginning of this chapter—the innovation that the Philippines offers the United States is tied to workers *being* Filipino, and all this is meant to imply about their talents for emotional and affective labor. In this way, national and racial differences are reinforced, even as they are ostensibly overcome, through the call center labor process.[27] Furthermore, however, this Filipino *being* to which Santiago attests ostensibly emerges from a progressive history in which the United States, and Western powers more broadly, take leave of global capitalism's center stage to make room for ascending or emerging Asian nations. As if to hammer home his point about the rise of Asian countries in the wake of U.S. decline, Santiago noted that many American families began living in extended households as a response to the global economic downturn, which he interpreted as "Americans beginning to see the beauty of the Filipino and Asian concept" of sharing families' spaces and resources.

Resistance to narratives of Western economic superiority in general and U.S. decline in particular animated U.S. Cultural Competency (CC), the training course for new employees that I participated in and observed as part of my fieldwork at the company Vox Elite. On the first day of class, our instructor—a Filipina in her late twenties named Bella—showed a PowerPoint slide detailing cultural differences between Americans and Filipinos. Americans, we were told, are "task-oriented," "individualistic," and "egalitarian," while Filipinos are "relationship-oriented," "collectivist," and "hierarchical." The bifurcated list clearly expressed an Orientalist epistemology that posits essentialized and immutable differences between Asian and Western peoples. Yet there were many moments in which Bella critically digressed from the thick training manual from which she read. For example, just before revealing the list to the class, Bella asked if anyone in the class knew the definition of "ethnocentrism," to which someone responded, "it means seeing things from your own perspective." Bella then uttered the following imperative: "Correct! So, remember this: on the [production] floor, it will always be the perspective of the Americans that you should be adopting [*Pause*] but this does not mean upholding Americans as the best!" Similarly, during an exercise meant to convey the idea of the U.S. as a melting pot of immigrant culture and upward mobility, Bella stopped to ask if people in the room "still believe that America is the land of milk and honey," to which someone emphatically replied "No, because now we have their [Americans'] jobs!"

Although the latter comment contributes to the misguided characterization of U.S. outsourcing as solely a competition between workers of advanced industrial nations and newly industrialized or developing ones—rather than the machinations of global capital against labor writ large—it also suggests that the United States was no longer a place where people, especially those in the middle class, could find and maintain stable, decent-paying jobs. This notion was further underscored by the U.S. financial crash, which occurred just prior to the time that I had started my research at Vox Elite in early 2009.

The official training script employed by CC clearly reflected the ways that call center employees were being trained in both national identity management[28]—including how to "play down" their Filipino identity so as not to distract callers—and authenticity work, in which agents strive to seem Western but also "themselves."[29] Yet the employees' responses demonstrated how Filipino workers struggle with the demands of cultural engagement in a postcolonial context in which Filipino identity and the nation-state are valorized precisely because of their distance from former colonial powers. Thus as we were getting further into the lesson on American culture, Bella implored the class to "Remember, we are not Americans! We are Filipinos!"—an exhortation that reinforces Filipinoness in contradistinction to American identity but also refutes the possibility that Filipinos *were ever* Americans. The necessity for such clarification only makes sense when placed alongside the colonial rhetoric that casts Filipinos as part of the American family, such as in the inclusionary racist mode that characterized Filipinos as America's "little brown brothers."[30] Together, these resistive postures—while intended for different purposes at the moment of their utterance—suggest the potential for anticolonial and decolonial subjectivities forming within and through the industry. Yet such efforts tend to collapse under the weight of the ideologies nested within. As Rodríguez (evoking Fanon) argues, it is entirely possible "for Filipino subjectivities to articulate *through* white supremacist institutionalities and epistemologics—for example, the university, the nation-state, the English language—even as they periodically represent political positions that purport to resist or oppose the vestiges of racial colonialism."[31]

The articulation of Filipino subjectivity through a colonial institution is perhaps best illustrated in relation to the middle-class cultural politics of English. Like call centers in India, Philippine call centers train employees to use the national English that corresponds to their customer base. Thus, from day one of U.S. Cultural Competency, Vox Elite instructed agents to speak American English with U.S.-based callers. To this end, Bella presented us with another bifurcated list—this time one that paired Filipino English phrases with their American English "translations"[32]—and were told to memorize the list. "I'll go ahead" would be substituted with "goodbye," and "Please hold for a while" would have to be rephrased as "Please hold for a minute." The lesson on avoiding "Filipinoisms" clearly alerted the class to the fact that Philippine English vocabulary would prove inadequate for customer service delivery to a U.S. customer base, thereby casting Filipino workers as always already deficient and in need of remediation.[33] Yet understanding the Vox Elite lesson as only a top-down construction of Filipino inadequacy fails to account for how Filipinos understand the development of Philippine English alongside the prioritization of American English represented by the call center industry.[34] It is significant, for example, that Philippine English was described as such, that is, an autonomous version of English rather than a derivative of American or British English. As language studies scholars have shown, the postcolonial proliferation of people who do not speak standard American or British English has engendered a politics of recognition that promotes the idea that non-native English speakers can "own" their type of English.[35] Furthermore, by accounting for Englishes at the periphery, the process of recognizing postcolonial Englishes constitutes an attempt to transcend the colonial past. Indeed, proponents of what has been called "global English" claim that "the racist attitudes prevalent during the colonial period have mostly given way to more rational approaches to cultural diversity."[36] In other words, stripped of its imperial roots, English can ostensibly function as a universal language that all people can speak in their unique, yet equally respectable way.

This project of what I call *liberal linguistic inclusion*—which effaces the hierarchy of national Englishes—articulates with middle-class Filipinos' attempts to decolonize English as part of a cultural nationalist project. Furthermore, as Vicente Rafael argues, English has undergone an important transformation amongst Filipino people since the late 1980s: "Unlike generations past, the post-EDSA middle classes no longer seek to affect the sound and sensibility of American English. In an era that has seen the closure of two large U.S. military bases, Clark Air Base and U.S. Naval Base Subic Bay, English has been reclaimed not as a sign of colonial dependency but as part of the national culture. In this sense, the Filipino bourgeoisie has sought to vernacularize English in the same way that the *ilustrado* generations of the late nineteenth and early twentieth centuries attempted to nationalize Spanish."[37] The historical markers that Rafael describes in the passage are instructive. The People Power revolution (or EDSA) that deposed Philippine president and U.S.-backed dictator Ferdinand Marcos—coupled with the end of ninety-some-odd years of U.S. military presence via base agreements—created postcolonial conditions of possibility in which the Philippine middle class aspires to command the English language without the imperialist trappings that the language has historically entailed.

The development and reproduction of Philippine English is thus crucial to this middle-class and elite cultural nationalist project as a kind of linguistic "third way" in which Filipinos can have English as a national language and speak it, too. Yet this project is continuously disrupted, I would argue, by both the imperative to train call center workers in American English and the effect the industry on the whole is having on both secondary school and higher education in the country. Indeed, at the beginning of the twenty-first century, there are two opposing views on English-language teaching and use in the Philippines: one focused on Filipinos' already proven success as speakers of English as an additional language, or what linguists call an "L2," and another focused on native-like mastery and fluency in American English, specifically.[38] The call center industry thus becomes an important flashpoint in this debate. As linguist Eric Friginal explains: "With the boom of employment in outsourcing . . . it is clear that fluency, accent reduction, and the acquisition of high-level English have gained the upper hand in setting the direction of language planning and shaping of popular opinion. As a key growth industry currently providing jobs and revenues to the country, the government and the education sectors are ready to respond to the language needs of call centers. . . . Highlighting the importance of fluency in English following the typical American variety could define the nature of macro and micro language policies in the Philippines."[39] Friginal's foreshadowing of how the offshore outsourcing may affect language policy in the Philippines is important here, as is his acknowledgment of the alternative approach to English-language teaching and policy in the country. According to the former, Filipinos have *already* achieved success in speaking internationally intelligible English, as measured by Filipinos' high rates of transnational labor migration. According to this argument, Philippine English already satisfies "the minimum requirement of corporations, hospitals, and private homes overseas."[40]

If call center language training poses a challenge to cultural nationalist politics centered on the recuperation of the English language from its colonial origin, then industry actors respond by claiming that shifts within the industry are manifestations of the arrival of the modern Filipino national and racial subject, as I have been arguing. The proposition that English-language teaching in the Philippines does not need to aim for native-like fluency in American English echoes and supports the kind of claims that BPAP executive Joseph Santiago and Vox Elite quality assurance manager Loren Ramos made about the importance of English proficiency, rather than perfecting an American accent. Indeed, in the absence of a clean break with American English, both Philippine English and neutral accents become objects of fetishization around which Filipinos can claim freedom from the coloniality of power.

In this way, processes of identity formation can assume anticolonial or resistive postures even as they reproduce the hegemony of global capital. Indeed, the middle-class investment in the English language in the Philippines fits squarely within what Neferti Tadiar has called the Philippine state's "fantasy" of global integration,[41] which emerged in the early 1990s. Through this fantasy, the Philippines has been increasingly imagined as an economic *partner* to the United States rather than its supplicant. "Equal, democratic partnership" constitutes "the new conceit" of this geopolitical discourse, as nations are cast as "models of the rational, free, self-interested political-economic man, seeking mergers rather than marriages."[42] Indeed, Santiago's framing of U.S. outsourcing as defined primarily by needs that Filipinos can fulfill—"you are the ones who came here for our help"—exemplifies this rhetoric of partnership. Through the call center industry, Filipinos are seen as entering a symbiotic relationship with the U.S. corporations, once again reinforcing the notion of the "special relationship" between the countries.

As a member of the Philippine elite, Santiago's rewriting of the Philippines' past and present in service of a highly profitable and growing industry reflects what Dylan Rodríguez describes as "the political animus of the Philippine national bourgeoisie" who are in part responsible for reproducing the large-scale fantasies of integration.[43] Yet Santiago and his counterparts in the marketing forum are not alone in harboring these predilections for progressive narratives. Many workers I interviewed also spoke of their aspirations for Philippine economic development in ways that echoed the framework Tadiar describes. One such person was Bryan Belarmino, the assistant director of communications for W3G, an "in-house" call center of a major European bank. After we talked about his ambition to "climb the corporate ladder" from his starting position as customer service representative, Bryan and I began talking about the persistent tension in the Philippines between those who struggle against foreign financial incursion in the country and for the development of national industries and those, like Bryan, who believe that the Philippine government ought to court investment from other countries as much and as often as possible. As Bryan explained, the Philippines "can no longer afford to be insular." "We live in a global society," he elaborated. "The world is so small. Being too patriotic doesn't suit us as a growing nation. Even China had to open up—it's the largest country in the world but it realized that it is not the world."

Bryan's comparison of the Philippines (a country of 90 million people and a GDP hovering around US$250 billion) and China (with 1.4 billion people and a GDP of $12.4 trillion) reveals how the post–Cold War rhetoric of partnership invites people to think about countries as occupying similar ethical terrain even as they inhabit radically different economic territories. By using the term *ethical* I mean to highlight how individuals such as Bryan not only see global integration as imperative for national development but also subscribe to the neoliberal idea that nations are engaged in businesslike social relations organized around responsible investment in one another. As Illana Gershon and Allison Alexy argue, neoliberal subjectivity—and neoliberal possessive individualism in particular—is characterized by the conception of the self as a business. In contrast to the core metaphor of the liberal self as property, "to say that the neoliberal self owns itself as a business means that the neoliberal self is a conglomeration of skills and traits that can be brought into alliance with other conglomerations, but is not rented or leased."[44]

Extending the neoliberal model of possessive individualism to the international arena, such relations are ideally organized in ways that "distribute responsibility and risk in such a manner that each participant can maintain their own autonomy as market actors."[45] The ethical imperatives of what are imagined to be business relations between two nation-states thus come down to distributing risk equitably but also to checking ethnocentric demands—such as the demand that Filipinos be more Western. This resistance to a kind of cultural imperialism emerges not from a critical examination of the global distribution of power but from an ostensible weighing of the "added value" of the traits and skills that nations bring to a transnational economic alliance. In other words, within this logic, one should not ask Filipinos to be more Western because of the ethnocentrism underlining the request, but because one recognizes the valuable skills that Filipinos bring to the global marketplace and thus the legitimacy of a possessive Filipino individualism.

Returning now to my opening ethnographic moment, it is rather significant that representatives of the Philippine state and call center industry court U.S. capital by flashing—quite literally, through a fast-paced video—indicators of its economic status and *sovereign* credit rating. In this way, uneven relations of production that exploit Filipino labor—represented by Philippine state support for low-wage labor, tax-free holidays, low rates ot unionization, and relaxed labor laws—are reconfigured as relations of exchange between willing *investors* and an exceptional nation. That this process took place in the U.S. national capital—the source of imperial imprimatur—is particularly telling in relation to the transnational circuits of empire.

THE POLITICS OF EXCEPTIONAL PARTNERSHIP: CALL CENTERS AND THE WAR ON TERROR

In the twelfth and final book of his career, controversial revisionist historian William Appleman Williams argues that imperial designs are so integral to the fabric of America that they created "a combination of patterns of thought and action that, as it becomes habitual and institutionalized, defines the thrust and character of . . . culture and society"—that is, a way of life.[46] Somewhat of a last polemical hurrah, *Empire as a Way of Life* rearticulates Williams's long-standing argument that the aim of U.S. foreign policy was to construct an American empire. Thoroughly cataloguing U.S. imperial statecraft from the origins of the republic to the oil crisis of the 1970s, Williams declares that "the empire as a territory and as activities dominated economically, politically, and psychologically by a superior power is the *result* of empire as a way of life," rather than the cause of it.[47]

Drawing inspiration from Williams's career-long incisive critique of U.S. exceptionalism, this chapter has argued that the discursive construction of Filipinos as historically primed for affective labor and thus ideal objects of investment reproduces the idea of Filipino subjectivity as enabled by the exceptionalism of U.S. imperialism and U.S.-Philippine relations. According to such narratives, Filipinos are incomparable workers because the United States is an extraordinary superpower, which gifted colonial subjects with the ability to speak English and then released them from benevolent bondage into a state of self-determination. Thus the compassion of the Filipino subject is born of both empathy with those "at the bottom of the ladder," as Santiago described it, and a unique experience of colonialism. In this way, Filipino exceptionalism is not an epiphenomenal result of a global competition for jobs but is instead imbricated within the very processes that produce Filipino national and racial identity, and thus a feature of everyday life. As I have also argued, the Philippines' global call center industry is an important contemporary site through which narratives of exceptionalism are rearticulated. That colonial ideologies of identity, modernity, and progress are nestled within the industry is no surprise, given Anibal Quijano's definition of globalization as "the culmination of a process that began with the constitution of America and colonial/modern Eurocentered capitalism as a new global power."[48] To speak of the Philippines as an emerging player on the global capitalist stage, as many of my research participants did, thus reinforces the coloniality of power at the level of subject formation.

By way of conclusion, I want to point to the large-scale material and political implications of these narratives of U.S. and Philippine exceptionalism. More specifically, I want to outline how my analysis speaks to the ways that U.S.-Philippine "partnership" in the realm of neoliberal capitalist enterprise provides both ideological and material support for partnership between the United States and the Philippines in the War on Terror. The articulations of U.S. exceptionalism that justify and render invisible the War on Terror as it operates in the Philippines are, I argue, part and parcel of the exceptionalist rhetoric underwriting the country's call center industry—a conclusion that makes sense if we consider the historical relationship between war (including wars of expansion, as well as genocide and slavery) and capitalism.

At the start of my research on the Philippine call center industry, it became clear rather quickly that advocates of industry growth found themselves beleaguered by "security concerns" in southern portions of the Philippines.[49] Largely populated by Muslim Filipinos, islands of the southern Philippines are said to be hotbeds of secessionist violence perpetrated by armed factions fighting for a province independent from the Philippine nation-state. For example, discussions of the lack of security in the South punctuated my interview with a human resource manager at a call center in the central Philippines who mentioned the unwillingness of corporate insurance companies to issue policies to American managers working in call centers in the region. Yet challenges to the expansion of call centers in the southern Philippines are only part of a larger story about economic and social development of the area as a way to subvert Islamic extremism. With illiteracy and poverty rates that exceed the national average, Mindanao has been targeted by development organizations such as the United States Agency for International Development (USAID), which spent millions of U.S. tax dollars on a program to train Filipino students in English and thereby increase their chances of finding employment in call centers. Known as "JEEP" (Job Enabling English Proficiency), the program was originally conceived during the Bush administration and was "intended to divert young people from the path of militancy" by enhancing their employability in various industries, including tourism and call centers.[50] Given the fact that jeeps, or jeepneys, are the Philippines' ubiquitous public transportation vehicles that were originally used by the American military during World War II, the name of the program and its purpose are striking.

As the literature on neoliberalism has made abundantly clear, the economic imperative to make countries "safe" for foreign investment, and the political imperative to quell any opposition to the extraction of value through capitalist production, has made neoliberal globalization "compatible with, and sometimes even productive of, authoritarian, despotic, paramilitaristic, and/or corrupt state forms and agents within civil society."[51] The aforementioned development efforts are thought to play a crucial role in preventing the growth of Islamic extremism, the logic being that global capitalism is strengthened if Filipinos are trained in call center work rather than militancy and if existing militants are exterminated. The inroads by the call center industry in the southern Philippines thus help to illustrate the ways in which U.S. imperialism, global capitalism, and a rhetoric of exceptionalism produce and reproduce the kind of violent conditions from which call center industry advocates and workers claim to be free. Indeed, the number of human rights abuses and extrajudicial killings that have come to light as part of the War on Terror—through operations aimed at ridding the country of violent revolutionary forces but which cause the disappearance of peaceful democratic actors[52]—constitute the genocidal underside to an industry that appears to run on benevolence and the voice of an exceptional modern Filipino.[53] Dylan Rodríguez describes this type of persistent imperial violence as instances of "incessant postindependence juridical codifications of US hegemony in the archipelago" which are "most conspicuously marked by the changing territorial occupations of the U.S. military and overbearing presence of American corporate and financial capital."[54]

In the effort to decolonize knowledge production about the contemporary Philippines—a motivation compelled by both anthropological critique and the critical positionalities of American and Filipino American studies—it is therefore important to remember that Filipino raciality and subjectivity is still "suspended" within the discursive and material enactment of U.S. imperialism, even as Filipinos assert the autonomy, sovereignty, and affective capabilities of Filipino workers. By suggesting that Filipino subjectivity emerges from an imaginary congruence with U.S. imperialism, my goal has not been to contest the materialization of U.S. colonization in the form of American school systems, English-language instruction, and cultural imposition. It has been to contest ideologies of identitarian and subjective autonomy that allegedly arise from these conditions and to underscore the ways that the narratives underwriting the power of colonialism shape Filipinos' ways of understanding and being in the neoliberal present.

NOTES

1 "Business process outsourcing" refers to the general process by which companies contract with third-party firms who provide a range of back-office services, such as data entry and medical transcription. Although the term *call center* refers primarily to sites where employees take inbound and make outbound customer service and technical support calls, the term has become metonymic of the BPO industry as a whole.

2 D. Rodríguez, *Suspended Apocalypse*, 4–5.

3 Asian Development Bank, "Asia 2050." See also Hoang, *Dealing in Desire.*

4 The language of "nested ideologies" was shared with me by Sumanth Gopinath, who heard and commented on a portion of this essay at the American Studies Association's annual meeting in 2013.

5 Kaplan and Pease, *Cultures of United States Imperialism*; Maira, *Missing.*

6 Go, "Introduction," 75.

7 Go, *Patterns of Empire*, 236.

8 Ong, *Flexible Citizenship*, 5.

9 De Genova, *Working the Boundaries*, 13–55.

10 Bajaj, "A New Capital of Call Centers"; Chrisee Dela Paz, "Philippines' Back Office Shines in 2015, Exceeds Target."

11 Tsing, "Supply Chains and the Human Condition," 157.

12 Guevarra, *Marketing Dreams, Manufacturing Heroes.*

13 Studying the operation of power at a national and global scale at times entails what anthropologists have called "studying up"—that is, observing and engaging with social actors with investments in the forms of power and profit creation that may also be the object of analysis and critique. See Nader, "Up the Anthropologist."

14 Constantino, quoted in Rodríguez, *Suspended Apocalypse*, 26.

15 Guevarra, *Marketing Dreams, Manufacturing Heroes*, 123.

16 R. Rodriguez, *Migrants for Export*, 63.

17 D. Rodríguez, *Suspended Apocalypse*, 104.

18 D. Rodríguez, *Suspended Apocalypse*, 103.

19 McKinley, "Benevolent Assimilation Proclamation," accessed November 11, 2017, http://www.humanitiesweb.org/spa/hcp/ID/23008.

20 D. Rodríguez, *Suspended Apocalypse*, 104.

21 The idea that colonial power operates in and through benevolence and other affective forms—a foundational concept in the study of colonialism—has been

theorized by, among others, Stoler, *Race and the Education of Desire* and *Carnal Knowledge and Imperial Power*, and elaborated in anthropology by Rutherford, "Sympathy, State Building, and the Experience of Empire"; settler colonialism studies by Cahill, *Federal Fathers and Mothers*; and Woolford, *The Benevolent Experiment*; and Philippine studies by Rafael, *White Love and Other Events in Filipino History*.

22 Ross, *Fast Boat to China*, 144.

23 Hoang, *Dealing in Desire*, 7.

24 Other scholarship that examines the way individuals naturalize and essentialize the demands of their labor as integral aspects of their identity make clear that Filipinos are not at all unique in this regard. However, the prevalence of productive tropes of identity begs the question of why this essentializing process seems, for some, not only unavoidable but also necessary. Once again, my sense is that these moves cannot be fully explained as epiphenomenal responses to capitalism's demands, but must reflect a particular understanding of subjectivity as "produced" through history. See Jones, "Better Women" and "Whose Stress?"

25 "Asia 2050."

26 Hoang, *Dealing in Desire*, 6.

27 Mirchandani, *Phone Clones*.

28 Poster, "Who's On the Line?"

29 Mirchandani, *Phone Clones*.

30 The term *inclusionary racism* comes from Kramer, "Race, Empire, and Transnational History." See also Shaw and Francia, *Vestiges of War*.

31 D. Rodríguez, *Suspended Apocalypse*, 160.

32 Although Vox Elite's lesson plans used the word *Filipino* to modify *English*, for the remainder of this article I use the word *Philippine* to do the same.

33 Mirchandani, *Phone Clones*, 36.

34 It also fails to account for my fellow trainees' palpable *delight* with the comparative list. Indeed, I observed that the class was most alert and interested in this part of U.S. Cultural Competency more than any other moment in the training; many broke out into laughter, as if the list revealed an uncanny likeness between Filipino and American English.

35 Erling, "The Many Names of English," 42.

36 Smith, "Global English," 57.

37 Rafael, *White Love and Other Events in Filipino History*, 199.

38 Friginal, *The Language of Outsourced Call Centers*, 32.

39 Friginal, *The Language of Outsourced Call Centers*, 32.

40 Friginal, *The Language of Outsourced Call Centers*, 31.

41 Tadiar, *Fantasy-Production*.

42 Tadiar, *Fantasy-Production*, 69–72.

43 D. Rodríguez, *Suspended Apocalypse*, 156.

44 Gershon and Alexy, "Introduction," 800.

45 Gershon and Alexy, "Introduction," 800–801.

46 Williams, *Empire as a Way of Life*, 12.

47 Williams, *Empire as a Way of Life*, 13, emphasis in original.

48 Quijano, "Coloniality of Power, Eurocentrism, and Latin America," 533.

49 McIndoe, "Call Centres Spring Up in Troubled Philippines South."

50 Following uproar from U.S. politicians seeking to protect American workers from further job loss from offshoring, the USAID program has since been suspended. Chanda, "Outsourcing fears nix US aid to teach English"; McDougal, "U.S. Suspends Controversial Outsourcing Program"; de Lotbinière, "'Threat to U.S. Jobs' Shuts USAID Training."

51 Brown, "Neo-Liberalism and the End of Liberal Democracy," 2; Harvey, *A Brief History of Neoliberalism*; Klein, *The Shock Doctrine*.

52 Examples of such operations include Oplan Bantay Laya (Freedom Watch) 1 and 2.

53 As scholars have argued, the conception of the Philippines as split between a majority-Christian and a minority-Muslim population is itself a colonial construction. Rafael, "White Love," 196; Kramer, "Race, Empire, and Transnational History," 179.

54 D. Rodríguez, *Suspended Apocalypse*, 162.

III

Temporality, Proximity, Dispersion

08

In Their Places

Cottica Ndyuka in Moengo

OLÍVIA MARIA GOMES DA CUNHA

Sa Mari lives in Bursideweg, a town that twenty years earlier was but a roadside settlement inhabited by Javanese families and a few Maroon Cottica Ndyuka drawn to a rather special place called Moengo.[1] Sa Mari's modest house is built on her father's land (*peesi*), close to the spot where, in 1916, the Dutch colonial state authorized ore extraction on 118 hectares of public land. This led to the installation of a subsidiary of ALCOA (Aluminum Company of America). Numerous Ndyuka families now live on lands occupied before and during the company's expansion. The Cottica Ndyuka Maroon kin group thus witnessed and took part in the transformations, accompanying the rise and slow decline of ore extraction and associated worker settlements.

After laboring to grow food in her garden (*goon*) and sell the produce in the streets of Paramaribo, Sa Mari has little time for her grandchildren.[2] She spends her afternoons transporting and preparing food, and collecting *pemba doti* (a type of clay) from the limestone pits left over from extraction. After being mixed with water and shaped into balls, the clay is dried to be sold as the sought-after *Moengo pemba*, used for cures and protection. During her daily journey to Moengo, Sa Mari passes through a mosaic of landscapes. Like the clay, images and entities from the colonial era of industrial opulence and discipline mix with destroyed buildings and spaces redolent with memories of the 1986–92 "Interior War" that pitted Maroons against the government forces backing further resource extraction efforts.

In the houses occupied by Maroons—recognizable from washlines draped with women's clothes like wraparound skirts (*pangie*), yards with small gardens, booths for selling food, and calabash trees—older women sometimes walk around with their breasts exposed as though living in a village in a different space or time. These areas thus offer a sharp contrast to neighborhoods divided into blocks, streets named after places and figures from the imperial era at the start of the twentieth century, and lined with the town's oldest buildings, such as the Catholic and Moravian churches. But these visible landscapes conceal only partially other space-times, or histories related to the occupation of the Cottica villages before SURALCO's arrival and the war. Instead of a now-decadent bauxite town, a monument to the aluminum empire built by "modern" Americans, my Cottica Ndyuka interlocutors thus conceive of Moengo as an overlapping of peesi: landscapes, inhabited and animated by memories, agencies, and other spiritual forces. This chapter is thus an attempt to get at those landscapes from a Maroon perspective, or an attempt at producing a "symmetrical," or decolonizing, exploration of this Moengo-oriented space/time.

Although I heard non-Maroon residents argue that after the civil war Moengo had been transformed into *een dorp van de Boslandcreolen* (a Maroon village), town life for my interlocutors bears little resemblance to the relations and etiquette of *lespeki* (respect) that guide life in the villages. Living in Moengo—and thus (re)approaching and moving away from those kin, growing crops for market, and the "difficult life" experienced by many in the refugee camps in French Guiana—generates among Maroons sensations of dislocation even as they recognize the importance of the relations that link them to the villages of their kin. In fact, Moengo is a place to live and work that permits interactions between people from different villages in the Cottica as well as a connection point, a territory of Cottica Ndyuka kin networks. Although these relations are associated with the arrival of bauxite extraction, they cannot be explained solely by either the exodus provoked by the 1986–92 Interior War or the histories of spatial control that punctuate the SURALCO period.

Cottica Ndyuka arriving in Moengo from refugee camps in French Guiana during the first half of the 1990s transformed the landscape constructed by a colonial, modern, urban U.S.-factory-based bauxite extraction project. By exploring movements between diverse Moengo landscapes, this chapter examines the Ndyuka presence within distinct existential spaces and times marked by empire. A key point is that the relations explored here are not reducible to imperial formations or to the histories evoked by the traces left of the territorialization process. The chapter thus opens by surveying literature produced by SURALCO and journalists about the arrival of the U.S. bauxite interests and their depiction of Maroons as primitives in a pristine wilderness. These contrasting images illustrate an interplay between two supposedly irreconcilable worlds. They are in a sense artifacts that reveal the presence of what are typically glossed as the modern—machines, electrical lighting, and other forms of enchantment conjured amid the vast green emptiness—and the primitive: seminaked men and women, almost grotesque figures, who watch with wonder the boats cruising the Cottica River. The existing literature on the bauxite industry in Suriname has reinforced these contrasts, keeping Maroon perspectives invisible or, at best, limiting them to the spatial, temporal, and "epistemological" margins of the processes often dubbed *modernization*. Such absences and misrepresentations underscore the importance of new approaches to the historical ethnography of empire.

In what follows I describe the overlapping and sometimes diverse levels and depths of spatial and temporal references with which my interlocutors describe the presence of Ndyuka Maroons. This helps reveal how people and nonhuman beings inhabit Moengo. It also highlights some of their effects on the space-time of the villages, colonial experience, and local industry, including the way the "existential forms of symbolic process," experienced by Maroons and their ancestors, intervene and dialogue with capitalist modes of capture in order to reveal other powers that occupy and act in places.[3] In fact, Moengo is marked by multiple inscriptions and spatiotemporal references involving the Maroon population that arrives, leaves, and returns there. Near this chapter's conclusion, I analyze the space-times of Ndyuka modes of existence and highlight the need to explore the effects of imperial reterritorializations from a Maroon experiential viewpoint. This pushes for a truly ethnographic understanding of how empire and its capitalist forces operate: As Collins and McGranahan emphasize in their introduction to this volume, such an approach promotes an encounter with empire "in the field." In this case, Maroons—traditionally studied in terms of their resistance to colonial and plantation forces—not only voice their own views about how the arrival of "specters of the empire" affected their lives and kin, and thus their own and "our" fields; they also experience these effects through their knowledge and bodies.

This chapter contributes to what the editors identify as a flourishing anthropological interest in "carrying ethnographic sensibility to imperial history." In fact, my approach has been inspired by a speculative question: What would a history of Moengo be like if told through some of the key concepts of Maroon modes of existence? This would not be a history that presumes the participation of other people—workers, staff, and foreigners who lived in the bauxite town—but instead a *toli*, a history told by elders, Ndyuka authorities, or those who know and can tell *Fositen* (First Time histories).[4] Thus the speculative nature of my question lies in the very impossibility of, in Maroon terms, telling old stories as a form of knowledge that encompasses non-Maroon perspectives. This is because all toli are successions of facts related to clans, matriclan conflicts, and the role of spirits and gods. Toli rarely include Bakaa (non-Maroon people) but when they do, the latter appear as secondary characters, often violent or stupid creatures. Toli contrast with Western historical genres that depict the occupation of the Cottica as an imperial venture carried out by modern forces. As a result, I want to suggest that these are histories of the Maroon themselves—their ancestors, the division of rights and duties within the villages—that foreground the potential of fissions and conflict.

Put simply, there is no "Ndyuka viewpoint" on the history of Moengo as an industrial experiment that stands as part of a larger U.S. imperial adventure in Suriname. As a result, I do not intend to translate or provide concepts analogous to "native" terms: Ndyuka are not highlighting different "events" (their native history or ethnohistory) within the "history" that we all think we know.[5] Nonetheless, Ndyuka histories are also knowable through a set of events marking what we might call the Ndyuka "deterritorialization" of the region. This deterritorialization emphasizes movements that impel a cosmopolitics, or the existential, ecological, and nonhuman forces that mobilize Maroon socialities and enable them to exist on distinct levels and in different places from those conceived by state, colonial, and capitalist governmentalities.[6] These forces are directly associated with the places in which the Maroons have lived and circulated. By focusing on Cottica Ndyuka conceptions of the place occupied by these forces, and their relations with the Bakaa (non-Maroons), I distance myself from attempts to encompass, include, and refer to different voices, subjects, and experiences marked by imperial formations but left out of official narratives. As Ann Stoler and Frederick Cooper put it, "In attending to dissonant voices rather than assuming coherence, we may see beyond an omniscient colonial apparatus to one shot through with conflicts between plantation entrepreneurs and the state . . . between colonial state agents who struggled—and often failed—to coordinate their efforts from top to bottom . . . such a perspective should allow us to explore how limited and decidedly non-hegemonic [colonial authority [may have been] . . . to those who . . . pushed it aside."[7]

The fact that Ndyuka see their own as well as the Bakaa presence in Moengo from another angle does not mean that they offer a particularly Maroon perspective on the history of Moengo. It means that their understandings of the forces operating in the space-time of Moengo challenge anthropologists' attempts to depict the making of "empire" as a dispute between social actors—be they indigenous or foreign—over the same territory. Hence I seek to understand the space-time created by the Ndyuka as knowledge that not only guides their own understanding, but may come also to inform anthropological apprehensions of the Ndyuka experiences. In Maroon ontology, what we call "U.S. Empire" is a force that may be personalized through the Bakaa's clothes and their money, and especially the Bakaa excavation and violation of sacred rivers and shrines. While academics typically conceive of empire as a powerful structure with multiple tentacles, Maroons strive to negotiate with humans, forest spirits, and gods. As a result, power is felt and conceived as an effect of multiple presences. It does not exist as or around an isolated entity, but as an outcome of "flows" of forces.[8]

In analyzing life in Kourou, French Guiana, Richard and Sally Price compare the relationship between the forces attracting and dehumanizing Maroons as they were transformed into unskilled laborers for the French empire in the tropics to argue that, though well aware of his subordinate position in the local labour market, "a man can maintain his dignity even when doing degrading and servile labor as long as he never accepts the Other's definition of the situation."[9] I am thus interested not simply in what changes actors' perspective on the situation, but in the very terms through which it is understood.

MODERN PLANTS, PRIMITIVE MEN

> "Moengo, is a romance . . . modern history and a monument to the power and perseverance of Americans [. . .] between the Suriname and Maroni rivers, lies the village of Moengo or Mongo, a former Aucaner Bushnegro village, since it has been abandoned, due the difficulty of building houses in the hard ground. Moengo signifies hill. The Djoekas call it 'Kondre Uman' [country woman] in contrast to Paramaribo, which they call 'Soeman Kondre' [country man]."
>
> [The incorrectly attributed terms appeared in Sranantongo, the language spoken by Creole and people from the city.] [—]Oudschans Dentz, "De Bauxietnijverheid en de Stichting van een Nieuwe Stad in Suriname," 485

On a map showing the urban layout of Moengo, Oudschans Dentz highlights the modern style of the buildings, streets, and avenues adopted by ALCOA's subsidiary in Suriname. A former employee, Walther E. Burside—whose surname now graces Bursideweg, the road on which Sa Mari's father and his kin eventually settled—was a company bookkeeper between 1917 and 1957.[10] In 1929 he described prospecting for and discovering bauxite deposits as part of an account that provides a historical record of the first mining activities on the slope close to the Moengo industrial plant. This prospecting would lead to a second initiative, undertaken in 1917 and 1918 in the Adjumakondee region and on Wana Kreek, sacred territories of indigenous and Maroon villages. In a memoir lauding the venture's success, Burside defines Moengo as a joint venture and lists the number of workers recruited in Paramaribo (Creoles) and Indonesia (known locally as Javanese), as well as the arrival of the first U.S. technicians and French refugees from the French penal cologne and forced labor regime known as the *bagne*, in neighboring French Guiana. Lengthy negotiations with local authorities led to the creation, on December 19, 1916, of the Surinamese Bauxite Maatshapij (SBM), renamed SURALCO in 1957.[11] In 1919 a journalist from the *De West* newspaper, invited by the company's U.S. staff, describes how the Moengo plant already had a large contingent of Creole and Javanese workers, along with an unspecified number of Maroons supplying timber for construction.[12] In 1921, already Dutch Guyana's fourth largest settlement in terms of number of buildings and population, Moengo accommodated miners and workers who loaded the bauxite ships that navigated the deep waters of the Cottica River to the port of Paramaribo. Under SBM's control, a public land concession had been transformed into an industrial settlement.

Oudschans Dentz's account of the grandiosity and impact of the U.S. project, an emblem of the Dutch colony's modern history, acquires another connotation when contrasted with the reports made by travelers, colonial military forces, and explorers who had ventured into the region's swamps and forests over preceding centuries, usually in search of fugitives from the numerous plantations lining the coast. References to this inhospitable nature were now combined by Dentz with the description of an almost improbable event: the appearance of a modern industrial town organized around services, powerful machines, and the construction and mining technology needed to produce a lightweight metal of extremely high wartime value.

Over the twentieth century, Moengo was transformed by diverse presences, colonial landscapes, and transnational agencies into a *bauxite town*. Its architecture and layout testify to occupation by hired workers, their Dutch superiors, and a small contingent of U.S. technicians. Between the arrival of the company in 1916 and the 1970s, when management of the concession was transferred fully to Surinamese staff, the bauxite town was tightly controlled in terms of the use of houses; circulation through the streets and neighborhoods; and membership in clubs, churches, and schools.[13] Technicians and managers—or the Dutch and U.S. employees—enjoyed privileges and beautiful houses. Although the American families were a minority, the installation of their tennis club and pool was observed with curiosity and fascination by the press and Surinamese and Dutch travelers. Despite most of the U.S. employees being technical staff, their habits and lifestyle, dwellings, leisure habits, and use of English would become irremediably associated with the history of SURALCO and Moengo. A symbol of the isolated Dutch colony's opening to the outside world, a pearl of modernity, the "Americans'" presence and their hygiene standards and habits and interests led Moengo to be admired by travelers, chroniclers, and hygienists who contrasted its exuberant modernity with the region's somewhat inhospitable isolation.

"Modern history"—which Oudschans Dentz contrasts with Dutch colonial policy and the declining production from sugar plantations, food crops, and timber during the workforce shortages and resurgence of indentured labor—might be represented as just another chapter in U.S. imperial expansion.[14] This reading, however, seems to have been less common among contemporary observers, journalists, and employees of the colonial government who visited Moengo during the first three decades after its implantation. In their travel reports, the empire's presence on the coast is depicted as the victory of modern culture and mentality over the erratic policy of local authorities. Descriptions of the plant's creation all emphasize the introduction of modern traits into a context of colonial inefficiency and an impenetrable natural environment—an empty landscape of forests and swamps with fleeting human presence. Yet the connection between modernity and the demographic vacuum acquires new connotations in the notes, anecdotes, and official reports about the curious presence in the region of *boschnegers*, as the Maroons were then called.

Ndyuka from villages along the Cottica River and close to Moengo were not entirely absent from the concession. The work of clearing large tracts of forest and marshland was undertaken via agreements and occasional formal contracts with Ndyuka, albeit almost always in difficult interaction with the region's wild and inhospitable nature and the Maroons living in villages and temporary camps located near agricultural plots (*kampu)* close to the rivers. Meanwhile, a lack of employees with sufficient experience working in the forest meant that some prospecting support services involved the assistance of Maroon men. The latter were generally seen to come "from the forest" as occasional and exotic daytime visitors. However as Bonne notes in his observation of Moengo's health conditions between 1920 and 1923, the plant was also linked to the villages and the Maroon presence. Indeed he blamed the latter for the outbreak of malaria in Moengo: "The places where malaria is found is the villages of Bush Negroes. Moengo itself was originally a Bush Negro camp. Upstream and downstream of Moengo are several Bush Negro villages and there is not one day when numerous Bush Negroes fail to come to Moengo to visit or do business. They often stay overnight."[15]

The arrival of the bauxite industry had a profound impact on the histories of villages and the Ndyuka people. These effects also included Catholic and Protestant missions in villages such as Wanhatti (Agitiondo), Tamarin, Adjumakondee, and Moengotapu. The work of the missions benefited from the absence of disciplined and skilled workers for the new mining ventures. By providing education to men living in the villages, missions were able to create new opportunities for Cottica Ndyuka people to work in the bauxite and timber industries. Simultaneously, and sometimes inadvertently, missionary work facilitated the mining company's access to villages, sacred gardens, and Christian Maroons. Imperial access to bauxite was facilitated by the support of these auxiliary forces active in the villages and promoting migratory movements into the bauxite town and the forest, thus transforming Maroon men and women into suppliers of food and labor. By the late 1950s, a small number of Maroons had come to live in peripheral regions of the concession. These included Wonoredjo—a neighborhood designated for occupation by Javanese immigrants and controlled by the local community—and Bursideweg, where Sa Mari's father opened his kampu. These populations gave rise to residents descended from temporary workers who were allowed to settle provisionally while working for the company so as to alleviate transportation difficulties.

Along with journalists, company staff, and the occasional traveler, the bauxite experiment was visited by specialists researching the impact of U.S. industry in Suriname and its complex relationship with Dutch colonial rule. In a report to the Institute of Geography and Planning (Geografisch en Planologisch Instituut) published in 1974, the Dutch sociologist G. Hesselink was among the first scholars to analyze the social and economic complexities of the American bauxite town.[16] Seeing the plant as an entity directly dependent on its Pittsburgh office, an "area of expansion" of U.S. capitalism into a virtually independent nation, Hesselink emphasized the spatial, social, and ethnic segmentations that oversaw Moengo's economic interactions. Maroons—confined always to the concession's periphery—enabled the company's expansion into the forest. Ten years later Carlo Lamur offered an analysis of the impact of "the American takeover" of the Dutch colony. Among the accounts of contracts, official and unofficial negotiations, the low price of public lands, and the effects of two World Wars on bauxite production, the region's Maroon population appears merely as a cheap temporary workforce. More recently, however, historians have produced accounts of Moengo. Relying on oral histories and interviews, they depict a kaleidoscope of perspectives on the history of Moengo, as seen by staff and workers.[17]

Despite—or perhaps due to—the attention paid to the spatial and social effects of the bauxite industry by earlier sociologists of colonial expansion in Moengo, recent works remain oriented by the spatiotemporal references produced by U.S. empire. The landscape in which Moengo emerges as a unique industrial project is composed of lines, buildings, machines, technological tools, and other physical marks. Sectors were demarcated and named after imperial figures, generating a mosaic of lopsided references in the heart of a flooded forest. It is in this space that capitalism conjured up a very light metallic material able to transform, and be transformed into, powerful machines. And space provided a crucial primary framework for this operation.

As many authors concur, spatial ordering has created specific relationships between Moengo's residents and workers, defining patterns of consumption and circulation, granting access to land and residential rights, and providing leisure and educational benefits. As a corollary, these spatial references are also temporally marked. Not coincidentally, the "changes" in Moengo's histories are signaled by political economic transformations that affect other places: ore prices on the international market, aluminum shortages during the two World Wars, the expansion of mining to other colonial areas.

Unlike the sorts of historical analyses described above—analyses that describe the implantation of an industrial project in a colonial territory and depict empty landscape traversed by the mobilization of transnational routes involving diverse populations and their histories, limited by ethnic reference points, and emphasizing the introduction of technologies, rules, and norms concerning labor relations and spatial discipline—I move now deeper into other understandings of life in Moengo. I thus challenge the idea of unity that seems to result from adding up the different historical perspectives on Moengo as a colonial experiment. And I limit the plurality of viewpoints to the different generations of Ndyuka men and women as Moengo takes form as a sequence of overlapping memory-places produced and occupied after the Interior War. These frames destabilize histories of Moengo's foundation as an imperial venture and they retell them through bodies of knowledge in which categories like peesi (place) and *ten* (time) never stand alone.[18] They always and necessarily "act with" or mobilize other forces that can transform, explain, or even cancel Maroon or Bakaa (white, non-Maroon) modes of existence.

Although European observers emphasized that Ndyuka movements around Moengo illustrated the rights of "natives" to live in the bauxite town and thus form part of the history of the imperial project, from the Maroon perspective "finding a place" (*fende wan peesi*) means being accepted by forces that animate a landscape. These forces include the Bakaa, their drilling machines, modern garments, habits and languages—all of which circulate outside the concession area. Building on Timothy Ingold's discussion of the links between "place" and "movement," it would thus appear that Ndyuka do not exactly *occupy* the Cottica region: since their ancestors moved through paths in the forest, they inhabited peesi everywhere.[19] Such "inhabiting" involves constant negotiations with various beings that participate in this movement, or dwell in forests.

Peesi refers not only to unique landscape inhabited by spirits, ancestors, and other beings but also defines behavior, commitments, and relationships between the living and dead. It hosts a convergence of relationships involving other living beings in which Cottica Ndyuka ancestors and their descendants participate. Peesi includes trees, fruits, rivers, birds, sounds, the ground, and everything that these elements may potentially create, affect, and make. The key question is not what a place or an event is, but what it does. Learning about the experiences of women such as Sa Mari reveals the existence of much more complex relationships between places and things, and thus between life inside and outside the villages.

BAKA FÉTI

From the viewpoint of the Maroon families who make up most of Moengo's population, the territory of the former concession can be described as a connection point in which histories of the town and Suralco converge with the many memories of life in villages along the Cottica River. These are histories of the period when Maroon workers began to be hired. They are also spatiotemporal inscriptions utilized to locate modes of existence in the time and space of the territory prior to Suralco's arrival, as well as to engage experientially the impact of the *féti*, as the Maroons call the Interior War. The expression *baka féti* (after the war) used by my interlocutors signals both a transformative moment and the suspension of the visible and invisible boundaries that once limited their access to Moengo and the spaces within the concession area. The expression thus does more than mark an event: it signals a new mode of existence, one never experienced previously, either in the villages or in Moengo.

The féti erupted in 1986 as an armed conflict between the Surinamese Army led by Dési Bouterse, a military officer who seized power after a coup d'état in the recently independent Republic of Suriname, and a Maroon guerrilla force led by Ronnie Brunswijk, a Ndyuka man from the Cottica River and a former military officer and Bouterse's head of security. Loss of power on the part of a group of military officers of Maroon descent, together with the political volatility of the Bouterse government and centuries of anti-Maroon prejudices and hostilities, all led to this war. And in the wake of attacks directed at seizing guns and supplies conducted by a small group led by Brunswijk, Bouterse's National Army (Het Nationaal Leger) retaliated with searches, imprisonment, and persecution of Maroons on the road from Moengo to Albina. The National Army also invaded Maroon villages, sanctuaries, and territories on the Cottica. Within a few months, Brunswijk's group had recruited young Maroons,who they organized into an armed force called the Jungle Commando.[20] Persecution of members culminated with army soldiers linked to local paramilitary indigenous groups invading houses and villages. In November 1986, soldiers invaded the village of Moiwana, throwing people from helicopters and setting buildings alight. Among the forty-one killed were children, youths, and the elderly.[21] Next to the Suralco installations lie the remains of a morgue, the setting for the incineration of the bodies of dozens of Maroon victims buried without identification or appropriate ritual treatment. Sequelae from these killings include spiritual effects on victims' relatives, who were denied the chance to perform the necessary funeral ceremonies and thus care properly for dead kin.

The suspected association of all Maroons with the guerrillas and the invasion of their villages drove thousands of families to take flight, leading to the arrival of around six thousand refugees in French Guiana. There they were concentrated and controlled in "refugee camps." Sa Mari and her five children managed to reach the Charvein refugee camp with the support of relatives and close friends in the Jungle Commando. Moengo experienced the effects of this destructive war directly, occupied first by the Maroon forces in 1986 and later, toward the end of the conflict, by the Surinamese Army. The marks of modernity and the presence of the U.S. empire in the Dutch colony quickly began to fade. Suralco buildings and installations were destroyed. Bauxite production was interrupted and the concession abandoned. Javanese, Creole, and Hindustani workers with ties to localities little affected or untouched by the conflict migrated, leaving behind their residences in Moengo. By the end of the war, both the condition of the plant and the demographic situation in Moengo had changed radically. Creole and Javanese families did not return, and the Maroons were reluctant to leave French Guiana. This depopulation was aggravated by the discovery of new bauxite ores elsewhere, and the slow process of deactivating the Suralco plant in Moengo began in 1992.

Among the motivations for the Peace Agreement signed between the army and the guerrilla forces in 1992 were compensation and resettlement of refugees in Surinamese territory. The territory chosen was Moengo, which after the cease-fire received some of its former residents and a contingent of Maroon refugees with no history of local residence. These people had moved from the villages to live in refugee camps in French Guiana and they soon took possession of the abandoned houses, workers' accommodations, and other buildings owned by Suralco.

The end of the war transformed Moengo, but the changes described above are not expressed in the same way by the Maroons, who prefer to differentiate the space-time in which they live from the memories of "Suralco times" recalled by some retired non-Maroon company employees—the latter punctuated by stories of abundant services and benefits and rigid demarcation of spatial, racial, and social boundaries. From the Maroon point of view, a reference point for marking differences in the relations between people, in the use of houses and yards, and in ways of dressing and speaking—important examples of which are, respectively, the use of pangie wraparound skirts and the proliferation of Ndyuka as a language spoken not only in the streets but at official events—is the war. The expressions *fosi féti* and *baka féti*, "before the war" and "after the war," are essential to understanding the meaning of *tan* and *libi* ("staying" and "living") in Moengo. As many Maroons recognize, the war brought huge transformations, many of which are visible in the landscape and everyday relations in Moengo. From Bakaa peesi, Moengo was transformed after the war into *Cottica Ndyuka peesi*. For some Cottica Ndyuka, though, like Binaa, Sa Mari's daughter, the war also comprises a landmark analogous to the 1760 Treaty with the Dutch colonial crown, an agreement that granted freedom and autonomy to the Ndyuka people. Due precisely to the ways it enables the association of diverse spatiotemporal references, the war must be distinguished from a landmark of decline, destruction and ruination of an existing empire or imperial world order, and understood instead as a process of profound transformation.

FOSI FOSI: MUNGO LIBA

During the 1992 hearings of the Inter-American Court of Human Rights in which participants assessed the violence perpetrated by the Surinamese State against Maroon peoples during the *féti*, many histories were expressed in relation to the Ndyuka presence in the Cottica prior to the bauxite industry's arrival in 1916. These differed radically from the imagery of an uninhabited landscape discovered by Americans and their modern machines, or the situation described by the Dutch observers cited above. An important aspect of this difference emanates from the fact that, when their forefathers left behind the violence of the plantations, or when Ndyuka men migrated from Tapanahoni to work on timber and balata extraction in the coastal area from the nineteenth century onward, these groups settling in the Cottica encountered nonhuman agencies animating their pathways.[22]

Between the seventeenth and nineteenth centuries, slaves fleeing plantations experimented with different forms of village settlement. In the process, they transformed the forest landscapes and dialogued with the beings inhabiting them. The alliances formed during flights from slavery signaled different ways of living in the forest, establishing affinities and organizing spaces of life and death, and above all distinct ways of making kin. The time of flight, the "domestication" of space and the instruments of communication—negotiations with spirits, forces, and languages brought from the plantation experiences—and the beings encountered in the forest, along with the affinal relations formed by the first fugitives, all orient contemporary modes of existence of the Ndyuka.

Collecting data and statements from the region's residents on the civil war turned into a unique set of narratives on the occupation of the Cottica and the emergence of the first Ndyuka villages in the later nineteenth century. *Kabiten* [Captain] Bron from Moengotapu, for instance, recounted how Ndyuka coming from the Tapanahoni River to extract and sell timber established the first *kampu* and villages close to the indigenous villages already existing in the region.[23] Like other villages along the Cottica, the history of the occupation and settlement of the first Ndyuka families in Moiwana was associated with employment opportunities along the coast and, in the twentieth century, with work in logging and bauxite mining. Although the work usually involved men, local modes of territorialization were directly associated with the villages and the matrilines from which migrants originated. Consequently, occupied lands, kampus, and villages maintained direct relations with the gods and spirits worshipped by the matriline and became subject to the rules and authority of villages on the Tapanahoni River.[24]

Ndyuka relations with forests, water courses, clearings, falls, and savannahs continue to be animated by diverse forces. These relations always include the possibility of negotiation, yet this does not preclude new events from being linked to, or even explained by, the whim of the gods. Nor does this prevent spirits from regulating the relations between affines in village spaces. A key example is the libation (*towe wataa*) proffered by Maroon men when working for mining companies in the forest. Kaolin and bauxite deposits are the territory of the *goonmama* spirit, which may be consulted before extraction and thanked after the toil is completed.[25] Another key example is the action of the *kunus,* vengeful spirits, recognized whenever a relative dies or suffers misfortune. Kunus perpetuate and avenge memory of dead kin, while fear of their presence and action regulates marriages. Families and people inherit kunus. Their actions, objects, and spaces are therefore subject to the unpredictable effects of the latter. The kunus act in time and space and bring to memory both an event—such as a death, illness, or a case of incest—and the vulnerability of a place.

In his research on the flourishing of the Na Ogii cult in the Cottica region, Thoden van Velzen describes the impact of colonial forces' 1910 imprisonment of the prophet Akule. The event was recorded by colonial administrators a few years prior to installation of the bauxite mine. Its effects extended to all those who entered into contact with or benefited from the abundance of work and resources in the region after the SMB's arrival. The first impact was felt by those responsible for banishing Akule from the Cottica River: the Bakaa and their descendants. Maroons blamed the outbreak of the First World War on the actions of kunus controlled by Akule. According to Akule's oracles, soldiers killed in the conflict claimed for revenge. This time their fury was directed at the Ndyuka and the presence of spirit mediums known as *sudatis*, recognized as dangerous forces and suspected to be the agents behind events like the Moiwana massacre in 1986.[26]

During his research on the Cottica River in the early 1960s, Köbben also collected histories concerning the arrival of specific lineages from the Tapanahoni River, thus revealing how events and spaces in the two places were mutually affected.[27] A structural relationship between villages, produced through kinship and connections between people, places, and times, is present in the myths relating to *Mungo*—the Ndyuka name for the hill where the Americans established the first facilities of the company in 1916—and the reasons for the abandonment cited by the elders.

My fieldwork in Moengo included various conversations about *Fosi Fosi*, or the time before Suralco's arrival. Rather than an empty space, there was a village that absorbed Maroons migrating to the area to work in felling and selling timber. Situated close to where the dead were buried, the village was divided in two by the river and populated with sacred buildings. Above all, it was a place (peesi) occupied by relatives from different matrisegments (*bees*). As a Ndyuka village, Mungo grew up on the shores of Mungo Liba—the name given to the Cottica River by the ancestors and elders (*gaansama*). Moreover, the central part of the old village was located where Suralco was first established: the Moengodorp neighborhood. Da Asowo, a seventy-five-year-old Ndyuka man from Peetondo village and a retired Suralco employee, tells how Moengodorp's streets retain signs of its existence prior to arrival of the bauxite industry. These include a *Manja boon* (mango tree) and other sacred trees behind the school and the oldest local Catholic church—a spot avoided at night. In fact, new constructions built by Suralco and the residents who returned to Moengo after the féti have all avoided this space, leaving a clearing, a forsaken terrain in a valorized area of town. Sa Mari's grandchildren never approach the spot and became terrified when I asked why the area is avoided. Other Ndyuka people recount versions similar to Da Asowo's explication for the "abandonment" of the locale. These histories, however, establish other connections to the company's "master narrative."

The first version links the initial presence of Ndyuka in Mungo to the arrival of the Americans and Dutch—the Bakaa. However the place was not a village but a kampu. One Ndyuka, Da Badjoe accepted that a Ndyuka presence prior to Suralco was plausible, albeit in the form of temporary encampments of women and men working in agriculture and logging. As pointed out by yet another interlocutor, Da Asowo, "It was a kampu. There were two or three families . . . the place where there was a market and there is a Manja [mango tree] . . . when the Americans came here to look after bauxite, they saw a man and his wife, they also gave them a job, he [the Ndyuka man] lived there until he died."

The second version describes how Mungo's villagers failed to observe a *kina peesi*—a taboo. In this case associated with the locale and the matrisegments, or bees, that resided there, the taboo prohibited work after nightfall. After using a pestle to pound rice, an explosion ripped open a hole in the earth. In some versions earth spirits (*goonmama*) provoked the noise. In others, the rice is replaced by the pemba clay mentioned at this chapter's outset and commonly found in abandoned bauxite pits. In all versions, the failure to observe taboos associated with nighttime occasioned a "large noise" that caused residents' flight.

A third version associates temporal and spatial taboos with the presence of the *gaansama*—the ancestors—after the arrival of the Bakaa. This version was told to me by the *kabiten* (captain) from Tukopi village: the toli in question recounts how the Bakaa were unaware that the area was once a Maroon village with *ala sani*—"everything" that a village contains, including prohibited spots inhabited by the dead. "It was a beautiful village and they [Ndyuka villagers] buried their people on both sides of the river." Members of the bees living there had spread along both shores of the river long ago. The problem occurred when Javanese workers hired by the Bakaa began to excavate and found bodies of gaansama behind the church—precisely the site of Mungo. The "Bakaa were scared," the Ndyuka (who worked for them) fled in terror to other places, *opo* and *bilo liba* (upriver and downriver on the Cottica). Here Mungo preceded not only Moengo, but all nearby present-day Ndyuka villages. Mungo's abandonment prompted the emergence of other villages founded by different clans: the *Pinasi-lo* founded Peetondo village, while the *Dju-lo* founded Ovia Ollo. An abandoned village is not empty, but is rather a peesi close to where ancestors are buried. Because Moengo is a spatiotemporal intersection between villages with their clans, matrisegments, spirits, and gods, it is also a space where vengeful spirits may wander.

PEESI, KIN, AND TIME

Beyond its multidimensional configurations and the possibility of comparing native and nonnative concepts, one of the most significant aspects of any ethnographic treatment of time and space involves the subordination of space/time to experience, and thus the attempt to keep time and space in dialogue with specific sociocultural planes. As observed by critics of the use of traditional notions such as "context" in ethnographic descriptions, the transformation of an analytical reference point—one created by the observer—into a geographical, political, sociological, and historical plane that explains actions may produce distortions on the types of theoretical elaborations possible.[28] In this way, "local" or native appropriations of lived space may come to be presented as minor or particular versions of more general patterns, and thus culturally limited inscriptions and cosmological references to the world that "natives" inhabit. This may leave unaffected the geography and topology of the world that "we," the modern producers of ethnographic accounts, claim to know so well.[29] My response is to concentrate instead on articulations of space and time in the construction of regional worlds of experience so as to expand analysis of the meanings of these notions in the fashioning of the memories and histories of particular events.[30] In other words, when a happening is transformed into an event, conceived not merely as a narrative of what happened in the past, but a creation, it works like an artifact that reaffirms and potentializes actions, lives, and present-day decisions.

Differences between concepts such as "space" and "place" allow us to explore the specificity of Cottica Ndyuka meanings. And we are able to perceive them not as isolated from, but as connected differently to imperial historical inscriptions, in part because "there is a tension evident in the relationship between the subject-position of place and the non-subject-position of space in the way landscape has been taken up as an analytical concept."[31] When the *kabiten* of Tikopie described the existence of a *kiina peesi* in Mungo, his reference to the interdiction on work was consistent with the definition of place: Peesi is a spatial category commonly associated with certain practices permitted to certain people and their kin. Hence treating a peesi as merely a geographic or spatial register is incorrect. Each and every peesi is not only occupied by human and nonhuman forces, limited by rules and subject to serious sanctions, but it is also an agency. What Ndyuka see when they look at a peesi is kinship. Time and space are recognizable insofar as their effects ("actions") are perceptible. Just as a place is a manifestation of the memory of a certain event, so is time the reiteration of the owners of these forces. When Ndyuka families occupy territories, networks of relatives and nonkin are activated and reconfigured around negotiations related to housing, the acquisition of goods, and labor. This arrangement allows new alliances with people who are close (but not affines) to the *bee sama* (matrilineal kin) to be incorporated into the Ndyuka part of what Köbben describes simply as the "kinship system."[32]

Having been born in Moengo does not preclude people from identifying the villages—generally those belonging to a matrilineage—as the place from which they came and where they go, or return, to attend funerals, resolve a family conflict, or obtain spiritual treatment. The suffering, tribulations, child-related problems, and marital conflicts all directly or indirectly connect people to the villages. From this viewpoint, every person reflects a relation with her matrilineage village, a relation between body and place. Every Ndyuka person results from the relations that her matrilineage—the bee—has established collectively over numerous generations. At least two types of relations exist with the bee: with affines living in the villages where one's closest living kin reside, and with the *gaansaman*—the dead ancestors buried or ritually prepared there. Living and dead ancestors participate in the simultaneously individual and collective composition of the person. In addition to their relation with the bee, every person possesses a spirit—a *bon gadu*—that occupies the same place as the vital principle, the *akaa*. But while the akaa is transformed following the demise of the physical body, *bon gadu* is an "interiorized" and indissociable part of the latter. Spirits participate in making the body and the person. They may act as a malevolence aroused by entering prohibited areas of the forest, the killing of sacred animals, or the consumption of sacred foods and plants. "Genitor" spirits are activated by following certain alimentary prescriptions during gestation, affecting the mother-child (bee-person) relation.[33]

The Ndyuka person results from the association of human and nonhuman agencies in the cosmic domains of forest and village. These act at different moments during the making of the person—or, in the words of Diane Vernon, in the "indissociability of the *paansu*," or the convergence of matrilineal bee and the person. The circularity of these agencies and their work of producing relations at cosmic and physical levels do not annul the creation (or fabrication) of a new existence. Singularity is not located in the body, or in the multiple associations that compose the akaa, or indeed in the constitution of specific social relations. It is instead fabricated over the course of relations, distancings, and approximations between different modalities of being and the places and times that these inhabit.[34] Richard Price described this imbrication of time and person in *First Time*, his analysis of *Saamaka* regimes of historicity. For Price, creating *Saamaka* histories or the "special Saramaka vision of their own period of formation" as essentially an art of transforming a generic past into a "significant" one.[35] Price thus affirms that "Events are history," in relation to acts performed at a particular moment against a certain person or persons. These mobilize eternal vengeance from the matrilineal kin of the dead. Spirits and ancestors participate in two different temporal registers, mobilizing different forces: the *First Time*—the time of warfare, flight, and encounter with and control of the forest that, as Price observes, are documented in colonial sources until approximately 1800—and the recent past, when ancestors and spirits intervened directly in the world of the living.

EMPIRE, RUINS, AND PEMBA: A CONCLUSION

The landscape of U.S. empire persists in the road layout, at the plant, among the partially ruined buildings, and—potentially—among analyses of empire as a historical formation. However, the landscape of exploitation in the forests of Suriname was continually altered after the Interior War of 1986–92 due to the ways Ndyukas conceive space, time, and their bodies since this civil war not only displaced villages, people, places, and sacred objects, but it altered the dynamics between matrilineal kin. As I have illustrated, the Cottica Ndyuka affected by the conflict have experienced transformations through modes of existence that the younger Ndyuka recognize as typical of the villages, and that elders know as antedating the installation of the bauxite infrastructure. They are thus producing marks in the peesi where Cottica Ndyuka live. These marks are visible in the re-creation of yards and houses with their pangies hung up to dry on the clotheslines and the calabash trees planted in front of the houses along with the cassava, herbs, and fruits.

The inscriptions of the bauxite histories and the Cottica Ndyuka's existential conceptions of space and time are incommensurable since they rely on distinct ontologies. As Marisol de la Cadena points out for the Andes, however, the latter is "not necessarily incompatible with extractive industries."[36] The contrast seems to be between descriptions of the landscape that claim the representational status of an event—the arrival of the bauxite empire in a supposed vacuum—and modes of occupation shared by workers: spaces as parts of experiences lived and produced, or in the words of Peter Gow, "in the sense of 'what' is going on."[37] Marks of events are not limited to physical evidence and its localization in a space-time coordinate. Among the Cottica Ndyuka, they more directly affect bodies. But while bodies are also events in Ndyuka ontology, since they articulate the agency of ancestors and spirits as well as their relations and effects on the paansu and the matriline, no happening exists separately from its effect. A happening is, by definition, an effect of an action or preexisting force.

As I remarked above, some of Sa Mari's activities revolve around the extraction of clay in prospecting areas abandoned by Suralco. However, the manufacture, sale, and use of Moengo pemba evokes other effects connected to the body and spatiotemporal dimensions. First, there is the association between Moengo, its surroundings, and the earth—the soil and the nonhuman forces that control them—and the healing powers of pemba, its ritual properties and its regenerative effects on the body. These are not limited to the soil's transformation into pemba doti. Ndyuka often speak of the relative tolerance of Suralco and its contractors, especially as concerned rituals involving libations and prayers when pits were opened as part of exploration and excavation activity. As a retired Ndyuka worker told me, "peesi have owners and permission and protection must be sought before any digging work." Second, producers and vendors of pemba are generally women from the Cottica. That region, and Moengo in particular, are key reference points in religious and ritual prestige. This is due to the worshipping of important oracles such as Na Ogii, introduced to villages following the arrival of Ndyuka workers involved in timber and gold, and subsequently in mining. Third, the Internal War meant that Moengo was a space of resistance for the guerrilla Maroon forces.

Satellite images of deforestation produced by imperial agents and the bauxite industry, the manufacture and sale of pemba, the journeys of Sa Mari and her children through Moengodorp and surrounding areas, the traces of the war marking many buildings, and the activities carried out in the Suralco installations are but a few of the inscriptions of what we might refer to as the (re)creation of existential territories in Moengo. Molded from remains, and located close to the near ruins of what was once emblematic of the opulence and aspirations of American empire, the lumps of *pemba doti* prepared and sold by Sa Mari are more than metaphors of the ambiguous effects of the modern forms of colonial domination and environmental degradation now visibly associated with aluminum contamination. This clay is certainly evidence of a reconfiguration of space through predatory logics of empire. It is a part of a landscape of intervention, reordering, and destruction, "exerting material and social forces in the present."[38] No radical opposition exists between the geometric, disciplinary, and colonial model of Moengo and the spatiotemporal configurations of place in which spirits, kin, non-kin, and other agents dialogue with each other. Indeed the myths on the existence of the village or a kampu occupied by a nuclear family mobilize, rather than ignore, the presence of the Bakaa and their machines. In this way they work as a force of attraction that is subject also, and simultaneously, to the sanctions of the place's spirits.

NOTES

1 I make free use of the ethnonym *Cottica Ndyuka* to differentiate my interlocutors and their kin from other Maroon people and groups. When transcribing Ndyuka, I shall favor the language spoken by my interlocutors—*Okanisi* (also *Ndyuka* and *Aucaner*)—over the equivalents in Sranantongo and Dutch. These terms generally appear in italics at their first appearance in the chapter. I have used the grammars produced by George Huttar and Mary L. Huttar, *Ndyuka*; and Goury and Migge, *Grammaire du Nengee*. All Okanisi, Sranantongo, and Dutch are my translation.

My thanks to Brazil's CNPq and FAPERJ for funding the research informing this article. For their generous comments and suggestions, I express my gratitude to H. U. E. Bonno Thoden van Velzen, John Collins, and Carole McGranahan. For his editing, I thank David Rodgers.

2 In order to protect the anonymity of my interlocutors I have decided to use pseudonyms, to conflate situations that involved different people, as well as to employ other narrative devices that help prevent identification of their names.

3 Gow, "Land, People, and Paper in Western Amazonia," 44. See also Munn, "The Cultural Anthropology of Time," 94.

4 In Pakosi's definition, *Fositen* (first time stories) or *Gaansaman toli* (elder's stories) are "matrisegment, clan, or lineage stories." With one exception, all other genres are related to kinship ties. Pakosi, "Oral Traditie bij de Bosneger," 159. On *Fositen Toli*, Thoden van Velzen writes: "A sheer repetition of 'facts' serves as a rhetorical device to evoke an underlying personal drama." Thoden van Velzen and Wetering, *In the Shadow of the Oracle*, 271.

5 Strathern, "I. Artifacts of history," 160–61.

6 Viveiros de Castro, "Exchanging Perspectives"; Cadena, "Indigenous Cosmopolitics in the Andes."

7 Cooper and Stoler, *Tensions of Empire*, 21.

8 Ingold, *Being Alive*; Viveiros de Castro, "Exchanging Perspectives," 466. For a discussion of Maroon personhood, see Vernon, "Les représentations du corps"; and R. Price, *Travels with Tooy*.

9 R. Price and S. Price, "Working for the Man," 201.

10 Burside, "The Early Years of the Suriname Bauxite Company."

11 Hesselink, *De Maatschappijstad Moengo*; Hoefte, *Suriname in the Long Twentieth Century*; Lamur, *The American Take-Over*; Koning, "Shadows of the Plantation?"; Koning, "Moengo on Strike."

12 "Naar Moengo II," 1.

13 Hesselink, *De Maatschappijstad Moengo*; Koning, "Shadows of the Plantation?," 33.

14 Oudschans Dentz, "De Bauxietnijverheid en de Stichting van een Nieuwe Stad in Suriname."

15 Bonne, "Hygiannische Ervaring te Moengo," 396; "Moengo" [1].

16 Hesselink, *De Maatschappijstad Moengo.*

17 Hesselink, *De Maatschappijstad Moengo*; Hoefte, *Suriname in the Long Twentieth Century*; Koning, "Shadows of the Plantation?"; Koning, "Moengo on Strike"; Lamur, *The American Take-Over.*

18 As Bilby puts it, the word *ten* "refers both to abstract time and to specific periods or moments. Like its English equivalent, it sometimes occurs in expressions that make it seem as if it had an independent existence of its own" (Bilby, "Time and History among a Maroon People," 144).

19 Ingold, *Being Alive*, 149.

20 Bilby, *The Remaking of the Aluku*; MacKay, *Moiwana Zoekt Gerechtigheid*; Polimé and Thoden van Velzen, *Vluchtelingen, opstandelingen en andere Bosnegers.*

21 Price, *Rainforest Warriors*, 83. This resulted in a judgment against the Surinamese state mandating that it restore the houses and territory and provide compensation to relatives of those killed.

22 Nonhuman agencies can be "animals, spirits, the dead, denizens of other cosmic layers, plants, occasionally even objects and artifacts." Viveiros de Castro, "Exchanging Perspectives," 466.
23 Polimé, Stefano Ajintoena et al., *Petitioners*, 15.
24 Köbben, "Unity and Disunity."
25 Vernon, *Les représentations du corps*, 25.
26 Thoden van Velzen, "The Maroon Insurgency," 173; Thoden van Velzen and Wetering, *The Great Father and the Danger*, 160–67. The arrival of Wensi, a Ndyuka from Tapanahoni, in the Cottica had a substantial impact in the region at the start of the twentieth century. The presence of his spirit was felt by Jungle Commando members, or Maroons fighting the national army, during the late 1980s. See Thoden van Velzen and Wetering, *In the Shadow of the Oracle*, 176–80.
27 Köbben, "Continuity in Change."
28 Foucault and Miskoweic, "Of Other Spaces"; Gell, *The Anthropology of Time*; Humphrey, "Reassembling Individual Subjects"; Strathern, "On Space and Depth."
29 Strathern, "On Space and Depth," 95–96.
30 Munn, "Excluded Spaces."
31 Hirsch, "Introduction: Landscape between Place and Space," 9.
32 Köbben, "Unity and Disunity."
33 Vernon, *Les représentations du corps*, 25.
34 Vernon, *Les représentations du corps*, 73.
35 Price, *First Time*, 5.
36 Cadena, "Cosmopolitanism."
37 Gow, "Land, People, and Paper in Western Amazonia," 44.
38 Stoler, "Imperial Debris," 165; Collins, "Ruins, Redemption, and Brazil's Imperial Exception."

Shifting Geographies of Proximity 09

Korean-led Evangelical Christian Missions and the U.S. Empire

JU HUI JUDY HAN

MISSIONARIES IN PERIL

In July 2007, twenty-three short-term missionaries from South Korea were captured by the Taliban and held captive in Afghanistan for nearly six weeks. The media release of the dimly lit video footage showing visibly frightened hostages held at gunpoint—seven men, sixteen women, nearly all of them in their twenties and thirties—captured headlines across Korea, and news outlets worldwide took interest in the "Korean missionaries under fire," as *Time* put it.[1] On the surface, the stated purpose of the nine-day trip seemed to be a fairly routine humanitarian mission; the missionaries were on their way to Kandahar to bring supplies and a helping hand to ill-equipped schools, medical clinics, and orphanages. The destination of Afghanistan was certainly uncommon, perhaps even considered exotic by the participants, but short-term overseas mission trips organized by churches and missionary agencies, especially in the summertime, are hardly unusual. This form of religious travel in fact has become for many Korean and American Christians as commonplace as Vacation Bible School.

The geopolitics of this particular mission trip to Afghanistan, however, posed extraordinary problems—the hostages were part of an evangelical Christian church group from Korea on a proselytizing mission in a Muslim-majority country in the midst of U.S.-led war and occupation. In the six years since the first U.S. airstrikes in Afghanistan in October 2001, the Coalition Forces' troop deployment had steadily increased with a surge in troop levels in January 2007, and 3,500 additional U.S. troops had arrived on the ground in March 2007.[2] South Korean troop deployment to Afghanistan that began in 2002 gave rise to the first Korean fatality just a few months earlier in February 2007, when a twenty-seven-year-old soldier with an engineering unit was killed in a suicide bombing attack against Vice President Dick Cheney at the

Bagram Air Base.[3] The Korean church's decision to send an untrained group of volunteers in July 2007 thus seemed absurdly imprudent and, as it turned out, the group had even defied explicit travel advisories by undertaking this mission trip. In a photograph that circulated widely in media coverage, the ill-fated church group was shown posing for a souvenir photo next to a large standing poster display at the Incheon International Airport terminals. The poster advisory clearly warned in large, bold print: "[The Korean government] has received information that the Taliban in Afghanistan are seeking to kidnap Koreans in order to exchange them for the release of Taliban prisoners. We urge you to refrain from traveling to Afghanistan."[4] But traveling to Afghanistan is precisely what the group did. In the airport photograph, one young woman even playfully mimicked the iconic pose by the child actor Macaulay Culkin from the film *Home Alone*, holding her face in both hands and feigning fear at the travel advisory. Whether the short-term missionaries were emboldened by their faith and a sense of purpose or misled by leaders who downplayed the risks involved, they certainly appeared in the photograph as though they were unconcerned about the trip.

On July 26, 2007, seven days after the hostage taking, the missionary group's leader, Pastor Bae Hyeong-kyu, was found dead. A second body was found by the roadside several days later and identified as Shim Seong-min, a young man who had so recently converted to Christianity that his own Buddhist family was not aware of his new religious faith. They reportedly did not even know that Shim was in Afghanistan as a Christian missionary until it was reported that he was among the hostages. Shim's and other desperate family members sought attention and help from the embassies of Pakistan, Uzbekistan, and Kazakhstan in Seoul. Their primary focus, however, was on the U.S. government, and the families held candlelight vigils outside the U.S. embassy to plead for U.S. intervention. This was not only because they deemed American influence and capacity for intervention to be greater than others' in Afghanistan, but also because a key condition in the Taliban's list of demands for the release of the Korean missionaries was that the hostages be exchanged with Taliban prisoners in U.S. custody. To the families' disappointment, the U.S. government reiterated its policy of not negotiating with terrorists, and public opinion soon began to turn against the church group. According to a survey conducted in Korea on August 9, 2007, over a week after the start of the hostage crisis, 56.6 percent of survey respondents felt the church that organized the ill-advised mission trip to Afghanistan must be held responsible for creating the crisis. While 26.1 percent thought the United States was ultimately responsible for instigating South Korean troop deployment, only 9.1 percent responded that the South Korean government was to blame for its decision to send troops to Afghanistan. On the question concerning the root cause of the hostage crisis, an overwhelming 67.5 percent of survey respondents said "aggressive and unreasonable proselytizing missions" were at fault, followed by "US attack on Afghanistan" (22.6 percent) and "Korean troop deployment to Afghanistan" (6.4 percent).[5]

The missionary hostage crisis renewed debates concerning Korea's military presence in Afghanistan and elsewhere. Antiwar and peace activists who had opposed from the start the deployment of Korean troops to Iraq and Afghanistan suddenly found unexpected allies in conservative Christians who now voiced criticism of U.S. foreign policy and called for an immediate withdrawal of troops to secure the release of the missionary hostages. Progressive and anticolonial theologians who have long been critical of proselytizing on the coattails of imperial war and colonial occupation were now joined by advocates of world evangelization in calling for swift action to secure the release of the hostages and to reform mission practice.[6] In the meantime, bomb threats received at mosques in Seoul raised concerns that new anti-Muslim violence may rise against the estimated thirty-five thousand Muslims in Korea, and interfaith religious leaders held prayer rallies urging the public to remain calm and refrain from stirring up Islamophobia and xenophobia. On the other end of the ideological spectrum, camouflage-clad right-wing war veterans held counterprotests to accuse left-wing activists of using the hostage crisis to enflame anti-Americanism and jeopardizing Korea's national security in order to save the lives of a few wayward civilians. For them, national security—fortified through geopolitical military alliance and imperial proximity—was of far greater concern.

The twenty-one surviving hostages were eventually released on August 29, 2007, but only after several significant conditions were met. In a significant military concession, the South Korean government negotiated for the release of the hostages by reaffirming its pledge to withdraw its two hundred noncombat troops stationed in Afghanistan by the end of 2007, a plan that was already under way. Also crucial was the second condition for the release of the hostages: the Korean government agreed to ban all further proselytizing activities by Korean Christians in Afghanistan. All nonessential Korean nationals were subsequently evacuated from Afghanistan—though many have returned since then to resume their work—and this included the personnel of several NGOs, many of them humanitarian and some of them Christian NGOs, who had previously worked for years in the region without major incident. In addition to the publicly disclosed terms of these negotiations, the Korean government was rumored to have paid the Taliban as much as US$950,000 (approximately US$50,000 per hostage) in ransom. Observers including mission theologian Dana Roberts stated as a fact that "the Korean government paid $4 million in ransom," but such claim remains speculative.[7]

The suburban church group of volunteers may not have anticipated the trouble of such magnitude when they set out on their summer mission trip, but the hostage crisis became a complex affair involving religious freedom, geopolitical agendas, and political economic interests, with the American empire serving as the stage and the catalyst for both Korean military and missionary activity overseas. The hostage crisis was widely considered as a setback in the Korean-led project of world evangelization. At home, the missionaries earned scant sympathies, as their endeavor was widely perceived as not only precarious but also terribly unwise. Critics denounced the missionaries for their imprudence and political naïveté, and characterized the hostage event as a symptom of "the danger of the new popularity of short-term missions."[8] The *Washington Post* focused on the religious devotion of the ill-fated missionaries as "Asia's apostles."[9] An editorial in the *Globe and Mail* derisively described them as zealous and "out of their minds for God," even while acknowledging that the missionaries were not simply irrational but motivated to move "from being a bunch of blessed Koreans into being a blessing" to the world.[10] Both in the American and South Korean Christian media, few rushed to defend the missionaries' purpose or strategy. Reaction among my evangelical contacts in Korea ranged from restrained sympathy to angry resentment for the negative publicity generated. "I've expected for a long time that something like this might happen," one mission strategist told me with a sigh. "This will make our work so much more difficult from now on." Postcolonial feminist theologians such as Nami Kim urged "collective self-reflection" and advised that "Christian missions in the global South will not escape the ignominy of reinscribing neocolonial realities, but only maintain, if not worsen, the already bleak living conditions of the majority of people living in the global South and on the margins of the empire."[11]

While the overall criticism directed at the hostage case tended to focus on the collusion between evangelical Christianity and U.S. imperialism, several other significant questions were also posed in the process: What in the world were Korean missionaries doing in Afghanistan? Who exactly were these missionaries—variously characterized as devoted church volunteers, intrepid humanitarian aid workers, and foolhardy zealots—and what propelled them to embrace the risks and dangers of foreign missions?[12] Arguably all evangelical missionaries seek to transform the world in one way or another by spreading the Christian Gospel, but how does the pursuit of world evangelization by this particular group of missionaries challenge or fortify the power relations of domination and subordination that underpin the project of U.S. empire? To what extent do Korean missionaries operate as proxies of the U.S. empire or assert their own neocolonial or subimperial ambitions? How do we theorize the deep linkages between the ethics of humanitarian service, imperative of religious expansion, mandate for geopolitical security, and logic of neoliberal capitalism?

I contend that the Korean-led missionary movement responded to these critical questions by reiterating evangelical missions as a secular and cosmopolitan project, and significantly, by conjuring the specter of Islam as geopolitical threat and global competitor. The hostage taking in Afghanistan thus served as a pivotal moment in religious geopolitics in the Korean context. But this story is impossible to narrate without a broader historical account of United States–Korea proximity; Korea's evangelical vigor arguably lies in its history of indebted engagement with the American empire. Politically and theologically conservative Korean Protestantism—which constitutes the dominant mainstream and political leadership of Korean Christianity, and is especially prominent among immigrant Korean Americans in the United States—is inextricable from its Cold War collusion with religious and geopolitical-economic reaches of the American empire. This discussion of history—not as a bygone past but as an enduring present—gestures toward my contention that Korean evangelicals are producing Islamophobia as a geopolitical-religious and world orientation project. By aligning Korea with the "Free World" even as Korea reaches out to the developing world, world evangelical missions not only consolidate and reinforce existing affinities and alliances, but also engage in an ongoing calibration of distance and proximity in relation to the empire.

This chapter draws from a larger research on the spatial politics of world evangelization. I have previously written about clandestine safe houses in China where vulnerable North Korean migrants were confined in oppressive missionary custody.[13] I have also discussed humanitarian and development projects in Uganda and Tanzania where capitalist work ethic and Christian family values were imparted as part of the Koreanized Christian gospel.[14] I have taken part in worship services and prayer revivals where hundreds of immigrant Korean Americans blessed George W. Bush's war in Iraq as a righteous Christian endeavor that Koreans were obliged to support, owing to the military and geopolitical alliances between South Korea and the United States.[15] I have sat through all-night prayer rallies for the salvation of homosexuals in Satan's clutches in San Francisco, and I have held my breath while such values as tolerance and equality were routinely denigrated as the work of immoral, Satanic, Communist, and secularist forces. More directly relevant to this chapter are the world evangelization strategy conferences and meetings I attended in South Korea, the United States, and Canada, where the so-called Islam missions—proselytizing activities designed to mobilize Christians to make a concerted effort to reach and convert Muslims—were touted as both a religious necessity and a geopolitical priority. Inspired by Anna Tsing's "ethnography of global connection" that refers to a portfolio of methods employed to pursue theories of the global, this chapter discusses how global connections move, align, and fall apart, involving a fluctuating dynamic of distance and proximity.[16] By showing how evangelical Christian missionaries grapple with politics of distance from each other and the rest of the world, I suggest that we locate Korea not only in terms of its subservience to the American empire, but also in terms of its proximity to empire.

LEGACY OF DEBT AND GRATITUDE

> "If it weren't for the American military ending the war and saving Korea, we would be praying to Kim Il Sung right now."
>
> —A middle-aged Korean deacon and missionary

Christian missionaries have long occupied a key place in historical record and religious life. Typically portrayed as spiritual giants, hardy explorers, heroic doctors, or intrepid travelers, missionaries such as David Livingstone (1813–73) and Albert Schweitzer (1875–1965) remain to this day venerated embodiments of Western benevolence and selfless service in evangelical discourse. In early nineteenth-century Korea, Western proselytizing missions brought "universal winds of civilization" and Enlightenment ideals, and appealed especially to elite Korean nationalists who embraced the new idioms of empowerment based on reason, liberty, and equality.[17] In line with classic colonial narratives of civilizing missions, this history of Western Christian influence in Korea is nearly always narrated in terms of missionaries' contribution to Korean modernity. Presbyterian and Methodist missionaries from the United States, for example, are said to have prioritized modern technology, medicine, and education, establishing Korea's first modern hospital and Western-style schools. The missionaries are often credited for promoting literacy and women's education in Korea and for contributing to the formation of empowered and modern womanhood.[18] Suffice it to say, mission history has long emphasized a litany of Christian contributions to Korean modernity—a predominantly favorable assessment of missionaries as modernizers, educators, and allies. Especially because it was Japan that colonized Korea (1910–45), Western missionaries in Korea were not primarily perceived as a colonial force but instead became identified as an anticolonial resource against the Japanese empire. Although there is perhaps a grain of truth in this historiography, the claims of Western missionaries' impartiality—politically neutral between Japanese colonialism, U.S. imperialism, and Korean nationalism—and

Korean Christians' role in anticolonial resistance have been the subject of increased critical inquiry in recent years. Some scholars have reassessed the role of American missionaries during the colonial era, for instance, as having largely acquiesced to Japan's rule over Korea rather than supporting anticolonial resistance. Many so-called impartial missionaries had in fact played a political role in mollifying nationalist stirrings through theological articulations of compliance and accommodation.

If the nineteenth-century wave of American missionaries claim to have liberated Koreans from premodern barbarism and Japanese colonialism, later waves of missionaries brought "liberation" in the form of the U.S. military involvement in the Korean War (1950–53). The war and the subsequent division of Korea between the U.S.-dominated South and Soviet-dominated North not only intensified ideological differences and sharpened theological divides, but also transformed the geography of Christian status quo in Korea.[19] Much of the intellectual leadership and demographic base of Christianity prior to 1945 had been concentrated in the northern part of the peninsula, particularly in Pyongyang and the surrounding area, so much so that Pyongyang was once known as the "Jerusalem of Asia." Many Christians in northern Korea belonged to the emerging middle class and landowning gentry, which meant that they suffered relatively more devastating financial and property loss as a result of land reforms led by the North Korean Workers' Party in 1946—"one of the most rapid and thoroughgoing land redistribution efforts in history."[20] Newly dispossessed and displaced, Christian landowners from the North fled to the South in large numbers, carrying with them intense bitterness and personal animosity against North Korea and Communism. Stories of Communist-led destruction of churches and persecution of Christians continue to circulate widely today, cementing the equation of Communism as the enemy of Christianity.

It is thus not surprising that, to this day, some of the most virulently anti–North Korean sentiments can be found in Protestant churches founded by those who fled their homes in what is now North Korea. They formed "the core of the fiercely anticommunist strand of South Korean Protestantism."[21] They clashed bitterly with progressive Christians and other leftists in the south, and denounced class-based struggles as proxies for Communism. Their anti-Communist theological-political formation was successfully reinforced by the South Korean state with President Syngman Rhee at the helm (1948–60), a Princeton-educated Methodist elder who had lived in the United States for nearly four decades before being elected the first president of the Republic of Korea.[22] Rhee favored in his appointments U.S.-educated Christians and anti-Communist expatriates from the North, and they in turn formed an important support base for Rhee's ruthless antidemocratic rule that ensued. With the U.S. military government "coming to the rescue" during the turbulent postliberation years (1945–48) and again "rescuing" South Korea from Communists during the three devastating years of the Korean War (1950–53), America's place in the Korean evangelical imagination was secured as a messianic figure. With the century-long history of missionary contact, the Protestant church in South Korea became the most "Americanized" and conservative segment of society, "a stronghold of pro-Americanism and the source of pro-American rhetoric that seeped into every sphere of civil society."[23]

To repeat the epigraph for this section, a middle-aged deacon and missionary once said to me, "if it weren't for the American military ending the war and saving Korea, we would be praying to Kim Il Sung right now."[24] To fervently anti-Communist Christians like him, the continued existence of North Korea serves as an alternate course of undesirable history, a continuing reminder of a nightmare averted. Organized around the idea of an historical affinity and strategic alliance between the United States and South Korea, his comment also contains a sentiment of indebtedness to the United States—both the missionaries and the military. A missionary involved in helping North Koreans escape to South Korea told me that Communists had killed more than half of her extended family during the Korean War. "[North Korean Communists] started the [Korean] War, and killed thousands of their own brothers and sisters. What else could it be but the work of Satan," she shuddered. "It's no wonder nothing grows there anymore. The soil is soaked in blood."[25] Her statement encapsulates the territorialized blending of "theological anti-Communism" with firsthand "experiential anti-Communism."[26]

While Korean evangelicals are grateful to the American missionaries who brought the Gospel and gifts of capitalist modernity, they are also ready to pay back—or pay forward—their debt by sharing the gift with the world. This was evident at an international mission strategy conference in Seoul in 2007, where a nationally prominent pastor led a prayer as follows:

> From 1884 and on, American missionaries arrived in Korea to devote themselves for the glory of the Lord and made enormous sacrifices to *plant the seeds* for all of us. Not only did they build churches, but they also trained and cultivated the next generation of Christian leaders. They built modern schools and modern hospitals that produced God's faithful servants who served this nation time and time again, withstanding crisis after crisis. The precious sweat and blood the American missionaries once shed in Korea, a nation that used to receive missionaries, have transformed Korea into a nation that can now send missionaries to the world's frontiers.[27]

In striking contrast to the blood-soaked and infertile soil of poverty-stricken North Korea, the "seeds" of the Christian Gospel are portrayed as having yielded a fruitful harvest in South Korea. In this portrayal, mission schools and hospitals are credited unequivocally for training and cultivating Christian leaders, and furthermore, there is rhetorical continuity that connects nineteenth-century missionaries directly with present-day Korean missionaries. The "precious sweat and blood" of American missionaries are depicted as the predecessors for the Korean missionaries working in "the world's frontiers." This sentiment of historical debt figures centrally in Korean mission theologies and practices, and serves as an incontrovertible tenet in the contemporary project of Korean-led world missions.

POSTCOLONIAL MISSIONS AND MISSIONARY GEOSCIENCE

The contentious history of proselytizing missions, of course, has been subjected to sustained criticism especially from postcolonial theologians and scholars. Even diehard evangelicals today begrudgingly admit that the "romance of missions"—adventure, danger, exotic locale—has all but faded away amidst considerations of power and pleas for pluralism and tolerance. It is by now a common contention that missionaries played a key role within the workings of colonial domination. Proselytizing missions have equipped colonial projects with an enabling moral pretext, carried out colonial agendas as de facto agents of empire, and pacified the colonized populations with teachings that stressed submission and acquiescence.[28] Such critical assessments help us reconsider the role of foreign missions in Korea as a "moral equivalent for imperialism."[29] They also point to how the American Protestant missionaries' "spirit of white supremacy, religious triumphalism, and cultural imperialism" sought to eradicate Korean traditions, religions, and customs by designating them as antithetical to modernity.[30] Aware of such criticisms to a certain extent, present-day evangelicals vow to change missions to be less paternalistic and more equitable. As a result, idioms of humanitarian volunteerism and internationalism, rather than imperialism and colonial conquest, figure prominently in contemporary missionary discourse that ostensibly emphasizes compassion, empathy, and "heart" as Melani McAlister aptly put it.[31]

Overtly racialized expressions such as "heathen regions" have been replaced by "unreached people groups," and the flagrantly imperialist depictions of "civilizing missions" have been reframed as "cross-cultural endeavors."[32] Mission training curricula draw from cultural anthropology for "in-depth knowledge of cultural differences" which in turn promises "cross-cultural understanding."[33] But still prevalent are comparable ideas that downplay the power-laden and historically contingent character of race and ethnicity, reproducing variations on the so-called objectivism of race and producing racial definitions and profiles in technocratic, pseudoscientific terms. The evangelical reliance on cultural anthropology, statistics, demography, and cartography together constitutes a "missionary geoscience."[34] One popular pledge among missionary geoscientists is that in addition to the cross-cultural missions, proselytizing missions must now be led by "cultural neighbors" who are supposed to be better suited for evangelizing those "unreached" by the Gospel. While the idea of "unreached people groups" conjures the image of forsaken frontiers, the notion of a "cultural neighbor" is based on environmentally deterministic ideas around ethnicity and language. According to this logic, touted as a postcolonial missionary innovation, an ethnic Korean missionary would perform better in China than a white German missionary with neither linguistic nor ethnic proximity to China.

Such logic can be seen throughout Perspectives on the World Christian Movement, or simply Perspectives in short, one of the most widely used mission curricula today and a large-scale international training program operating out of the U.S. Center for World Mission in Southern California. At the core of Perspectives is an unsophisticated but elaborate typology of "ethnolinguistic people groups" and a claim that in-group coherence allows a "natural flow" of Christianity. Its claim that "the gospel flourishes *amidst* a people group, and moves with more difficulty *between* people groups" supports the idea that missionaries can use shared heritage, cultural customs, and language to reach those considered to be "cultural neighbors." The evangelical conception of the "cultural neighbor" and how it interacts with notions of difference thus shapes the landscape of what has been dubbed "postcolonial missions," with an emphasis on South-to-South flows and an articulation of humanitarian aid and cultural exchange as the preferred mode of mission encounter. It is precisely in this context that some contend that the emergent Korean missionary movement, with its newfangled economic power and religious fervor, will eclipse centuries of Western-dominated Protestant missions, alter the global landscape of Christianity, and herald a new era of South-to-South missionary flows.[35] Consider this buoyant declaration by religious historian Andrew Walls, who describes the Western, especially European, missionary enterprise as "crumbling": "The missionary movement from the West is only an episode in African, Asian and Pacific Christian history—a vital episode, but for many churches an episode long closed. Missionary enterprise continues, but its Western, and especially its original European, component is crumbling. The great missionary nation is now Korea; in every continent there are Korean missionaries by the hundreds, in coming years we can expect hundreds more, preaching from Tashkent to Timbuktu, and reaching where Westerners have long been unable to tread."[36]

On the one hand, such assessment draws from the phenomenal growth of Korean Christianity in recent decades, applauded in evangelical circles as nothing short of a miracle. Though nearly half of the population (46.5 percent) reported no religious affiliation in the Korean Census of 2005, and the other half are split almost evenly between Buddhists on the one hand (22.8 percent) and Protestants and Catholics on the other (29.3 percent), Christians are overrepresented in top government and business posts, and Christianity remains a major social and political force in contemporary Korean society. Ten of the eleven largest megachurches in the world are said to be located in the city of Seoul, including the largest Pentecostal congregation, the largest Presbyterian congregation, the largest Methodist congregation, and the second-largest Southern Baptist congregation in the world.[37] Whereas the term *megachurch* generally refers to a congregation with an average weekly attendance of two thousand or more persons, several megachurches in Korea claim membership in the hundreds of thousands. Yoido Full Gospel Church in Seoul is reputedly the world's largest church, with nearly 800,000 members and 136,600 cell leaders, and claims 250,000 in worship attendance every Sunday.[38] If the megachurches attest to the growth-oriented—and export-oriented—feature of Korean Christianity, South Korea's rising status as the world's second-largest "mission-sending" country purportedly reflects a commitment to generosity toward the developing world. As of January 2010, it was estimated that over twenty thousand long-term, residential missionaries were sent by denominations and mission agencies to 169 countries. Add to this the thousands of participants who join short-term missions every month of the year, and South Korea easily emerges as "the great missionary nation."

But that passage by Walls also points to something beyond the spectacular rise of Korea. It also follows a supposed end of the Western missionary enterprise and the substitution of Korean missionaries in its place. Korean missionaries are expected to reach "where Westerners have long been unable to tread"—but where, and how come? If decolonization and postcolonial criticism were responsible for the demise of imperial geography and crippling of the traditional Western missionary enterprise, how do we understand the emergent Korean missionary movement and its place in the contemporary geography of Pax Americana and perpetual war? Key here is the dual strategy of denial. Just as the U.S. empire is notable as an "empire in denial," the claim that Korean missionaries present a "less imperial" model of evangelism while following the well-trodden path of imperial missions reflects a resolute denial of its own association with and proximity to the geography of empire.

I have written elsewhere about the political theology of neoliberal capitalist development that undergirds Korean-led missionary projects, and how missions corroborate the missionaries' faith in progress and achievement.[39] In preaching and proselytizing a distinctly Korean model of developmentalism and millennial capitalism, the missionaries reify and reinscribe an uneven geography of privilege and generosity in which the world is divided neatly between mission-sending and mission-receiving nations, and between aid-sending donor nations and aid-receiving nations in the developing world. In this geographical imaginary and praxis, destination mission fields are prefigured as lacking in work ethic and lagging behind in developmental aspirations. By contrast, South Korea as the mission-sending "donor nation" is put on display as an exemplary model of effort and achievement. This was especially evident in Uganda and Tanzania, where I observed how Korean missionaries thought of their contribution as paving the road to personal and national salvation through free labor, commerce, and moral and material improvement through Christianity.

One of the most common refrains I heard during the monthlong mission trip to Uganda and Tanzania was that Africa was "far"—not far from any place in particular, like from South Korea or from North American West Coast, but objectively and simply "far" in temporal and spatial distance from *everything*. Given the ways in which Africa is popularly imagined as a primordial and remote frontier, it was not surprising to hear that the missionaries thought they had traveled a long distance to arrive at a far-flung mission field. What was intriguing, however, was that the missionaries thought the very ground they were standing on, the very air they were breathing in, and the very people they were interacting with were all still *far*. The missionaries repeatedly claimed, even while they were physically present in Africa, that "Africa" was still simply "far"—far from Korea, far from the trappings of capitalist development, and far from what they considered to be familiar and comfortable. It was of little consequence that the missionaries had traveled from various points of departure, coming from not only the Far East Asia, but also the United States and Canada. Always seen through the lens of "farness," the "there-ness" of the mission destinations could never become "here-ness" through travel and encounter. Also missing in this articulation of perpetual distance was the grammatically required preposition, *from*, the signpost that marks the relative and felt distance between points of comparison. Africa was "far," not from any place in particular but from everywhere.

Distance thus functioned akin to difference. A place is usually discussed as far *from* someplace else, similar to how a thing is different *from* something else. Difference is measured by its divergence or distance *from* the norm. Africa's distance—or "farness"—was considered to be an objective condition, not relative, a location where Korean missionaries could utilize neither cultural nor linguistic proximity. Importantly, the "farness" of foreign mission destinations was imagined to be a shared feeling for Koreans and Americans.

There is also another key notion of evangelical distance and difference in operation here. Echoing the earlier passage by Walls in which the Western missionary enterprise is depicted as crumbling, Paul Choi, a controversial leader of a Korean mission agency called InterCP and the author of numerous books on world evangelization particularly in Muslim-majority countries, wrote as follows:

> The final curtains have closed on the age of world mission led by the Western Christian Church, including the American Church. In other words, the age of our White brothers managing the world in the name of Christ has come to an end. Today, the non-Western church, especially the Korean church, is more important than ever. The West and the non-West will long suffer from the conflict between Isaac and Ishmael, and the Korean Church, since we are pro-West yet Asian, will play an important role as the peace maker . . . The "Global Christian Leadership" has been passed on to the Korean church.[40]

In this commentary, Choi articulates three commonplace propositions about Koreans and world missions. The first proposition posits that the "final curtains" have closed on the age of empire, and a new chapter of history has begun. Implied is a belief that the Christian world is undergoing significant change, a sentiment echoed by many theologians and religious historians who describe that a "great transformation" or a major "paradigm shift" is at work.[41] Secondly, Choi's commentary explicitly acknowledges the colonial legacy of Christianity and the "old" world order. Yet the language of "managing the world" and exercising global leadership depoliticizes the imperial domination simply as a type of corporate management. In fact, the subtitle of his book from 2004, *Segye Yŏnjŏk Dohae* (Global Spiritual Mapping), is *Hananimŭi Segye Kyŏngyŏng* (God's Global Management). The theological rhetoric here is that God is the sovereign, and as His subjects, Christians are managers of God's Kingdom. Thirdly, Choi's phrase "our White brothers" unmistakably aligns Korea with the West, even as he claims that Korea maintains a neutral "peace maker" position between "the West and the non-West." An affinity with the "White brothers" and condescension toward the "non-Western" people are indicated in his choice of words, which are even more clearly marked in the intrinsically hierarchical structure of the Korean language in which this passage was originally written. Especially in oral presentations, Choi uses a deferential and honorific language to refer to the white missionaries (*kŭpundŭl*), but speaks condescendingly toward the non-Christian others—*kŭaidul*, which literally means "those kids," or even the much more pejorative *kŭnomdŭl.*

Mission strategists such as Choi insist that Korea occupies a liminal position neither in the West nor the rest, an in-between geopolitical position that serves both as a strategic advantage and a kind of divine destiny, whereby Koreans are urged to mediate as "peace makers in the continuing conflict between the Old Testament's Isaac and Ishmael"—Abraham's warring sons, who are said to be the respective progenitors of Judeo-Christianity and Islam. In his controversial book on Zionist mission eschatology, *Back to Jerusalem: God's Final Project*, Choi illustrates this point with a map that shows South Korea at the center of the world, a focal point between a giant rightward red arrow marked "The Rest" and a leftward blue arrow marked "the West."[42] Korea's geopolitical location is represented literally as where the Western imperial trajectory meets the Rest's countertrajectory. In extending the metaphor of "clash of civilizations" and "seismic shifts," Korea is mapped as located at the epicenter of tectonic shifts between opposing forces. In this illustration, Korea is imagined as literally occupying the intermediary space between the West and the Rest. Emphasizing Korea's emergence from a "missionary-receiving" country to a major "missionary-sending" country, evangelical strategists such as Paul Choi highlight Korea's role as an intermediary by divine design, forged between gratitude toward the West and a sense of indebtedness toward the Rest. It is a political-theological variant of American exceptionalism in which Korea emerges as an exceptional actor in evangelical geopolitics.

Are Korean missionaries differently located in their suitability and ability to proselytize in the developing world? Perhaps. Are Korean missionaries better positioned because of an intrinsically greater capacity for compassion and empathy based on their own firsthand experiences of colonization, war, and poverty? This is an impossible question to answer, yet it is precisely this claim that animates and justifies contemporary Korean world evangelization projects. On the one hand, Korean-led mission strategies do not simply mimic imperial hostilities or unquestioningly endorse American unilateralism. On the other hand, Korean-led missions rely on a wholesale faith in capitalist development, geographical imaginations that valorize the inherent virtues of the benevolent donor, the heroic aid provider, and the devoted volunteer. Korea's role and destiny as an imminent global mission leader rest on its proximity to empire and its self-perception as a preordained successor to the U.S. empire.

I met Paul Choi several years ago in Seoul when I visited the headquarters of his mission agency International Cooperation, referred to as "InterCP." InterCP is a thirty-year-old transdenominational mission agency boasting an impressive scale of organization and scope of work, with nearly a thousand paid and voluntary staff in over forty offices in Korea as well as forty offices outside of Korea according to its website. The majority of InterCP's overseas offices are located in the United States, but the website also lists offices in Mongolia, Australia (Sydney), Latin America, Germany, London, Ireland, New Zealand, and Japan.[43] The agency and its activities are enormously controversial even among evangelical Christians. Their bold and brazen tactics have been the subject of both scorn and concern, described by many of my informants as the missionary equivalent to "guerrilla warfare." The agency was expelled in late 2007 from Mission Korea, a national association of over thirty-five mission agencies, and in March 2011, an international committee of prominent pastors published an open letter urging Paul Choi and InterCP to transform the course of their mission programs and rework their heretical mission theology.

InterCP nonetheless continues to provide mission education, research, recruitment, and support services to the transnational evangelical community, offering curriculum materials and dispatching guest lecturers for their popular "vision school" program. Their bustling headquarter office in Seoul is slick and corporate, full of glistening promotional materials and laminated full-color maps and banners posted throughout the building. InterCP is best known for specializing in the most unforgiving mission fields in the so-called 10/40 Window, defined as a rectangular cartographic demarcation that stretches from ten to forty degrees latitude north of the equator in the Eastern Hemisphere, covering nearly four billion people and sixty-two countries in North Africa, the Middle East, West to Central Asia and East Asia.[44] The 10/40 Window is considered a priority evangelical destination, within which "the majority of those enslaved by Islam, Hinduism, and Buddhism live," according to Luis Bush, a mission strategist who coined and popularized the term in the 1990s at a mission conference in Seoul, Korea.[45] Although other Korean missionaries likewise invoke the concept of the 10/40 Window in their strategy, it has been InterCP that has consistently advocated prioritizing sending evangelical missions to Muslim-majority countries.

In the summer of 2010, a paid advertisement in a Vancouver-based Korean-language Christian newspaper announced a special two-day seminar featuring none other than Paul Choi himself as the special guest lecturer. The recurring ad grew larger from quarter-page to full-page over the course of several weeks, urging readers to come find out "how to view Islam," and to learn more about *Isŭlam kukjeundongkwa kŭllobŏl jihadŭ*, or the "international Islamic movement and the global jihad." With multicity North American tour with pit stops in Atlanta, Boston, Chicago, Los Angeles, and New York, Choi at the helm of this "Islam seminar" drew thousands of immigrant, Korean-speaking church-going evangelical Christians to learn about the growth of Islam. The newspaper advertisement was clear about the seminar's purpose. For instance, an email advert sent to subscribers of KCMUSA.org, a Korean American Christian news portal, for Choi's seminar in Boston on May 11, 2010, contained the following provocation:

> Muslim Population in the United States:
> 700,000 in 1970
> 9,000,000 in 2008
> Please come to Islam seminar to learn about growing Muslim population and how to bring them to Christ.

The Vancouver seminar, held at an immigrant congregation appropriately named the Frontier Church, featured gorgeously printed canvas banners along the aisles of the chapel, colorfully illustrated by names of countries, brightly smiling and pitiful faces, photos, and maps—always maps—associated with each country: Turkey, Iran, Chechnya, Tajikistan, India, Iraq, Saudi Arabia, Uzbekistan, and Afghanistan. As in his writings and other lectures, Choi offered his particular brand of geopolitical-theological interpretations of current world events, beginning the seminar by claiming that no credible books on Islam are currently in existence. He explained this dearth as the result of two factors. First, he claimed that the few books on Islam that exist are limited to formulaic and overly intellectualized books penned by Western researchers who possess no in-depth field experience. Unlike missionaries with firsthand field experience, he argued, academics can offer very little practical information or lessons applicable on the subject of "Islam missions." The second reason that books on Islam are not readily available, Choi laughed out loud, was that nobody desires a premature death. "If you insult Islam," he said with a hand gesture suggesting decapitation, "Muslims will kill you. Have we not already seen many meet an untimely death?" He was referring to both the beheading in 2004 of Korean missionary Sun Il Kim in Iraq and the deaths in 2007 of missionaries taken hostage in Afghanistan. According to Choi, authoring an irreverent exposé on the "truth of Islam" was tantamount to inviting murder and assassination. The only way ordinary Christians can glean truthful information about Islam, he said, was to attend seminars such as his, not by reading academic or popular tomes full of concessions to appease the Muslim censors.

His public persona presents an unusual mix of commitment and savvy: a scholarly theologian and a straight-talking politician, a seasoned field missionary and a fast-talking businessman, all the while displaying a somewhat gruff mannerism and crass humor of a performer on stage. Choi's rambling but engaging sermons and lectures are typically interspersed with sexist anecdotes and sexual innuendos. In the Vancouver seminar as well as other reported seminars, for example, Choi warned of Islam's spread in South Korea, facilitated by Muslim migrant workers from Muslim-majority countries such as Indonesia and Pakistan. Particularly worrisome are Muslim men from Pakistan, he claimed, as they are known to "target our women." Drawing a link to the fact that women constitute the majority of churchgoers in Korea, Choi claimed that Muslim men from Pakistan deceive impressionable Korean women with their English proficiency and physical height, towering over the "small-eyed, short-legged Korean men who simply cannot compete."[46] While unmarried Korean men languish in the rural countryside, Choi sighed, "these Pakistani men are coming to Korea and snatching up our sisters in marriage and converting them to Islam." If Islam was once imagined as a distant threat and an enemy of the "Free World," sensationalist and racialized evangelical discourses such as Choi's bring Islam closer to home for Korean Christians in the form of migrant workers represented as sexually depraved and devious foreign men.

EVANGELICAL GEOGRAPHIES IN PROXIMITY TO EMPIRE

Proponents of "Islam missions" believe that Christianity is a universal good and that Christian conversion of Muslims is an unequivocally desirable outcome. While the 2007 hostage taking of Korean missionaries in Afghanistan was unprecedented in terms of the number of hostages taken and the amount of international attention it generated, it was certainly not the first time that Korean missionaries found themselves in peril. Korean—and immigrant Korean American and Korean Canadian—missionaries involved in illegal proselytizing are routinely imprisoned or deported from China for their work with undocumented North Koreans in China. In 2004, eight Korean evangelists and pastors on their way from Jordan to Baghdad to lead a missionary event narrowly escaped from their kidnappers after pretending to be doctors and nurse.[47] In the summer of 2006, Paul Choi's InterCP reportedly gathered an astounding 1,600 Korean Christians for an evangelical "Peace Festival" in Kabul, Afghanistan, and all were subsequently deported for engaging in illegal proselytizing activities.[48] In the summer of 2009 alone, nearly a hundred Korean missionaries were reported to have been deported from Jordan, Yemen, and Iran, including twelve who were deported for allegedly proselytizing door-to-door in the city of Tabriz in southeastern Iran and four missionaries who were arrested on proselytizing charges in Madaba, Jordan.[49]

In 2004 thirty-three-year-old Sun-il Kim, who described his purpose in Iraq as "half business and half missionary," was abducted. Kim's employer, Cana General Trading Company, was a South Korean Christian firm charged with supplying goods and services to the U.S. military since the first Gulf War in 1991. Owned and operated by an entirely Christian staff, the company had been donating a sizable percentage of its profit to Islam missions. Even the company's name Cana was a shortened version of Canaan, the famed "land of milk and honey" and the biblical territorial basis for Christian Zionism. Kim himself had studied Arabic in school in Korea to prepare for proselytizing to Muslims. He was held hostage for weeks by members of the Islamist group Jama'at al-Tawhid wal-Jihad, who demanded that South Korea withdraw its several hundred troops from Iraq and cancel its plans to deploy three thousand additional troops. Their statement said, "Korean citizens, you were warned, your hands were the ones who killed him. Enough lies, enough cheatings. Your soldiers are here not for the sake of Iraqis, but for cursed America."[50] A few weeks after the gruesome videotape of his beheading aired on Al Jazeera, South Korea nonetheless proceeded with the troop deployment to Iraq, becoming the largest member of the Coalition of the Willing in Iraq after the United States and Britain. It is worth noting that both in Sun-il Kim's case and in the Afghanistan hostage case, it was the Korean troop deployment that put the missionaries in danger, not the other way around.

Contemporary Korean-led world missions must be understood in the interconnected contexts of empire, capitalist development, and humanitarianism, requiring careful and nuanced approaches to the idioms of location, distance, and difference. Religious power works not only as a force of domination, but also as an intensity of persuasion, a sense of obligation, and worldly orientation. If the United States is an empire in denial, Korean-led evangelical missions riding on the coattails of empire help enable the project of erasure through another instance of exceptionalism. In the meantime, Korean evangelical missionaries grapple with the politics of location and positionality and the fluctuating dynamics of distance and proximity of their association with the United States. The difficulty perhaps lies in analyzing the nuances of comparison and continuity without resorting to a simplistic argument of mimicry, and in theorizing without dismissing non-Western, non-American actors in pursuit of power and influence on the world stage as though they can at best aspire to emulate their Western counterparts, not surpass them. Korean/American evangelical missionaries may be following the trail of American footsteps, but they are also calibrating their strategic proximity to the U.S. empire. And they have their eyes set beyond the empire's horizon.

NOTES

Unless otherwise noted, translations are my own.

1 Veale, "Korean Missionaries under Fire."
2 Belasco, *Troop Levels in the Afghan and Iraq Wars,* FY2001–FY2012.
3 A. Wafa, "Cheney Unhurt after Bombing in Afghanistan."
4 K. Hwang, "Ŏsŏlp'ŭn 'Han'guksik Sŏnkyo.'"
5 H. Kim, "Ap'ŭgan P'irap, 'Miguk Chŏngbu Much'aegim.'"
6 N. Kim, "A Mission to the 'Graveyard of Empires'?"; S.-G. Kim, "Korean Christian Zionism."
7 Robert, *Christian Mission,* 73; Shim, "God's Work for the Taleban."
8 Robert, *Christian Mission,* 132.
9 Suki Kim, "Asia's Apostles."
10 Dueck, "Out of Their Minds for God."
11 N. Kim, "A Mission to the 'Graveyard of Empires'?," 20–21.
12 J. Chan, "South Korean Hostage Crisis in Afghanistan Ends"; K. Kim, "S Koreans Rethink Missionary Work"; Pulliam, "In the Aftermath of a Kidnapping."
13 Han, "Beyond Safe Haven."
14 Han, "'If You Don't Work, You Don't Eat'"; Han, "Our Past, Your Future."
15 Han, "Neither Friends nor Foes."
16 Tsing, *Friction.*
17 Schmid, *Korea between Empires, 1895–1919.*
18 H. Choi, "Women's Work for 'Heathen Sisters'"; H. Choi, *Gender and Mission Encounters in Korea.*
19 Chong, *Deliverance and Submission*; Kang, *Han'gukŭi Kaesinkyowa Pan'gongjuŭi*; M.-Y. Yi, "Haebang 50 Nyŏn, Han'guk Kyohŏisarŭl Ŏttŏke Pol Kŏssin'ga."
20 Armstrong, *The North Korean Revolution, 1945–1950,* 77.
21 Armstrong, *The North Korean Revolution, 1945–1950,* 118.
22 Cumings, *Korea's Place in the Sun.*
23 Kang, *Han'gukŭi Kaesinkyowa Pan'gongjuŭi,* 273.
24 Interview with anonymous missionary, Seoul, 2007.
25 Interview with anonymous missionary, Seoul, 2007.
26 C. Yu, "Han'guk Chŏnjaengkwa Pan'gong Ideologiŭi Chŏngch'ak," 144.
27 Pastor H., prayer at an international mission strategy conference, Seoul, 2007. My italics.
28 Comaroff and Comaroff, "Christianity and Colonialism in South Africa"; Comaroff and Comaroff, *Of Revelation and Revolution*; McClintock, *Imperial Leather*; Stoler, *Carnal Knowledge and Imperial Power*; Stoler, *Haunted by Empire.*

29 Hutchison, *Errand to the World*, 91.
30 Oak, "The Indigenization of Christianity in Korea," 3.
31 McAlister, "What Is Your Heart For?" See also Brickell, "Geographies of Contemporary Christian Mission(aries)."
32 Han, "Reaching the Unreached in the 10/40 Window."
33 The work of anthropologist-theologian Paul G. Hiebert has been particularly influential in this regard, and at least three of his books have been translated into Korean and distributed by a leading missionary research agency. Hiebert was a well-known theologian who taught missiology and anthropology at Trinity Evangelical Divinity School, Kansas State University, and Fuller Theological Seminary, where he had ample opportunity to work with and train Korean and Korean American seminary students.
34 Han, "Reaching the Unreached."
35 Jenkins, *The Next Christendom*.
36 Walls, *The Cross-Cultural Process in Christian History*, 45, quoted in S.-K. Kim, "Sheer Numbers Do Not Tell the Entire Story."
37 Johnstone, Mandryk, and Johnstone, *Operation World*.
38 Han, "Urban Megachurches and Contentious Religious Politics in Seoul."
39 Han, "'If You Don't Work" and "Our Past, Your Future."
40 P. Choi, *Segye Yŏngjŏk Dohae*.
41 See Walls, *The Cross-Cultural Process*; Wickeri, *Scripture, Community, and Mission*.
42 P. Choi, *Paekt'u Yerusalem*.
43 Information updated on April 3, 2011, from the InterCP website at http://www.intercp.net.
44 Bush, "Getting to the Core of the Core." Also see Han, "Reaching the Unreached."
45 Han, "Reaching the Unreached."
46 Paul Choi, at the Islam seminar, Vancouver, 2010.
47 K.-M. Yu, "Irak'ŭsŏ han'gukin 8 myŏng hanttae p'irap."
48 S.-G. Kim, "Korean Christian Zionism"; Pak, "'Chaknyŏn p'yŏnghwach'ukje yŏllyŏtsŭmyŏn t'alleban sarajyŏtsŭlgŏt.'"
49 Chŏng, "Wihŏm suwi nŏmŏsŏn kaesinkyo haewŏi sŏnkyo"; Pak, "Yupyŏlnan'gŏn 'chŏngpu'in'ga 'int'ŏk'ŏp'in'ga."
50 Sohn, "Pentagon."

Sites of the Postcolonial Cold War 10

HEONIK KWON

This way of narrating cold war history reflects the same provincialism. John Lewis Gaddis has written a history of America's cold war . . . As a result, this is a book whose silences are especially suggestive. The "third world" in particular comes up short.

—TONY JUDT, "Whose Story Is It?"

I was in Berlin a short while ago. It was my very first visit to the city, though I had long wished to see it, especially the Berlin Wall or what remains of it. The reason for my trip there was to join a gathering of historians and members of the interested public in the public forum called The Cold War: History, Memory and Representation. The event brought together a number of scholars specializing in German and European history, as well as others studying the international history of the Cold War. Our conversations focused on both the divided city and the divided world during the Cold War. Participants shared their opinions about how to preserve memories of the Cold War in Berlin, including the idea of opening a public museum at the former Checkpoint Charlie. They also discussed how to represent the city's past division within the broader historical context of the bipolar era. The event was about both Berlin in the world and the world in Berlin, with a third component being Europe as a region.

I was the only anthropologist at the gathering, and also the only speaker who addressed the Cold War outside of Europe. I talked about the bipolar political history experienced in decolonizing nations, particularly those in Northeast and Southeast Asia, and discussed the differences between this bipolar history and the Cold War as it was experienced in Europe and in the Transatlantic. I found the discussion that ensued to be encouraging, in spite of my relatively marginal role in both disciplinary and thematic terms, since it showed that the disparities between the postcolonial Cold War and the Transatlantic Cold War are important. It also showed that an understanding of these disparities is vital for a genuinely global Cold War history—a global history that is attentive to the locally diverse Cold War historical experience rather than one that encompasses this reality of plurality in favor of some unifying scheme of ideas.

In pursuing a more reasoned global understanding of the Cold War that is inclusive of regional and local diversity, I believe it is necessary first to confront the very conceptual contradiction embedded in the idea of the Cold War. Grasping this contradiction is crucial for coming to terms with the differences between the two types of the Cold War noted above: one waged in the decolonizing world, and the other experienced in the form of an "imaginary war," as the eminent historian of Europe, Mary Kaldor, writes of Europe's experience of the second half of the twentieth century, or even as the "long peace," as John Lewis Gaddis says with reference to the experience in Europe and North America of the same period.[1] This pluralist approach to Cold War history is important for ethnographic renderings of U.S. empire, the subject of this volume.

Cold War global politics is sometimes referred to as a contest between two separate imperial orders—the Soviet-led empire of equality versus the U.S.-centered empire of liberty.[2] Ethnographic studies of the sites of the U.S. empire within the polarized global political structure of the twentieth century aim to tease out the relations of domination found within the specific imperial system as well as to illustrate local forces of resistance within and against the systemic hierarchical order—that is, something other than the contest of power between the two contending global forces, which has been the main subject of investigation in conventional Cold War studies. The ethnographic approach to the U.S. empire also tends to focus on issues in local or subnational communities (or transnational connections) within the given international order. Ethnographic studies thus differ in terms of scales of analysis from conventional Cold War studies, which, although exceptions do exist, take the state and interstate relations as their primary focus.

Although the ethnography of U.S. empire focuses on relations of domination within a specific international order that existed as part of the larger bipolar global political order, this does not mean, however, that the ethnographic effort can ignore the contest of power dimension of the Cold War and, in particular, the local ramifications of this global power struggle. What is prominent in the Cold War era (in comparison to the earlier Europe-dominated colonial age) is the fact that in Cold War conflicts, the two aspects of this era's imperial formations—the relations of domination between the metropolis and peripheral locales, on the one hand, and, on the other, the contest of power between separate (structurally and ideologically) imperial forces—were closely intertwined in their unfolding. It follows that the distinct contribution of the ethnography of U.S. empire to the existing historiography of modern American power may, in part, consist of revealing both the hierarchical (relations of domination) and the reciprocal (contest of power) nature of this power in concrete contexts of local experience. As noted earlier, moreover, this empirical effort requires a reasoned, comparative, pluralistic understanding of the Cold War globally. This chapter explores these two interrelated issues: on the one hand, a dialogue between the ethnography of U.S. empire and a comparative approach to Cold War history and, on the other hand, two faces of America's Cold War–era power mentioned earlier. Before going further, however, let me first introduce a few stories from places where people experienced the era of the global bipolar political conflict in ways that contradict the idea of an imaginary war or the long peace.

XOI DAU

In the southeastern region of the Korean peninsula, there is a village that was once known as the region's *moskba* (Moscow)—the wartime reference for a communist stronghold. Each year, people originally from this village return to their homeland in order to join the ceremony held on behalf of the family and village ancestors. On these periodic occasions, the relatives from distant places are pleased to meet each other and exchange news—but not always so.

When, recently, a man cautiously suggested to his lineage elders that the family might consider repairing a neglected ancestral tomb, his suggestion broke the harmony of the family meal held after the ancestral rite. One elder left the room in fury, and others remained silent throughout the ceremonial meal. The man who proposed the idea was the adopted son of the person buried in the neglected tomb, having been selected as such by the family elders for a ritual purpose. The elder whom he had offended happened to be a close relative of the deceased. The ancestor had been a prominent anticolonial communist activist before he died at a young age without a male descendent; the elder's siblings and cousins were among the several dozen village youths who left the village together with the retreating communist army in the chaos of the Korean War (1950–53). The elder believes that this catastrophe in village history and family continuity could have been avoided if the ancestor buried in the neglected tomb had not brought the seeds of "red ideology" to the village in the first place. Beautifying the ancestral tomb was unacceptable to this elder, who believed that some of his close kinsmen had lost, because of the ancestor, the social basis on which they could be properly remembered as family ancestors after his death.

The morality of ancestor worship is as strong in Vietnamese cultural tradition as in a Korean context. These two countries also share the common historical experience of being important sites and symbols in Asia for United

States leadership in the global struggle against the threat of communism. Since the end of the 1980s, when the Vietnamese political leadership initiated a general economic reform and regulated political liberalization in the country, there has been a strong revival of ancestral rituals in Vietnamese villages—such rituals that were previously discouraged by the state hierarchy, who regarded them as backward customs incompatible with the modern secular, revolutionary society. In the communities of southern and central regions (i.e., what was South Vietnam during the Vietnam War, 1961–75), a notable aspect of this social development has been the introduction to the ancestral ritual realm of the identities previously excluded from public memory. The memorabilia of the former "counterrevolutionary" South Vietnamese soldiers and other hitherto socially stigmatized historical identities became increasingly visible in domestic and communal ritual space.[3]

In the home of a stonemason south of Danang, the family's ancestral altar displayed two framed pictures of young men. One man wore a military uniform, and his name was inscribed on the state-issued death certificate hanging above the family's ancestral altar. The other man, dressed in his high school uniform, had also fought and died in the war, and his death certificate, issued by the former South Vietnamese authority, was carefully hidden in the closet. In 1996, the matron of this family decided to put the two soldiers together. She took down the Hero Death Certificate from the wall and placed it on the newly refurbished ancestral altar. She laid him on the right-hand side of the altar, usually reserved for seniors. She had enlarged a small picture of her younger son that she had kept in her bedroom. She invited some friends, her surviving children, and their children for a meal. Before the meal, she held a modest ceremony, in which she said she had dreamed many times about moving the schoolboy from her room next to his elder brother. She addressed her grandchildren:

> Uncle Kan admired Uncle Tan. Uncle Tan adored the Little Kan. And the two were sick of the thought that they might meet in a battle. I prayed to the sprits of Marble Mountains that my two boys should never meet. The goddess listened. The boys never met. The goddess carried them away to different directions so that they cannot meet. The gracious goddess carried them too far. She took my prayer and was worried. To be absolutely sure that the boys don't meet in this world, the goddess took them to her world, both of them. We can't blame the goddess. So, here we are. My two children met finally. I won't be around for much longer. You, my children, should look after your uncles. They don't have children, but they have many nephews and nieces. Remember this, my children. Respect your uncles.

Another family living near Danang has a similar yet deeper and broader history of displacement and reconciliation. The family's grandfather is a former labor-soldier of the French colonial army and was part of a group of people who lived through the time of the Vichy regime, albeit somewhat differently from most of their neighbors. In 1937–38, the French colonial authority in Indochina conscripted numerous laborers from the central region of Vietnam and shipped them to the Mediterranean port city of Marseilles. There, the two thousand Vietnamese were brought to the notorious poudrerie—the powdery of Marseilles. The conscripts manufactured gunpowder for the French Army and, under the Vichy regime, for the German Army under French management. A number of these Vietnamese laborer-soldiers objected to their situation and joined the French résistance, whereas others continued to endure the appalling working conditions in the powdery. After sharing with the French citizens the humiliating experience of German occupation, these foreign conscripts found themselves in a highly precarious situation after their return home in 1948: the cadres in the Vietnamese revolutionary movement distrusted them, indeed looked upon them as collaborators with the colonial regime; the French took no interest in their past service to their national economy or their contribution to the resistance movement against the German occupiers. Many of these returnees perished in the ensuing chaos of war, and many of their children joined the revolutionary resistance movement in the following era, which the Vietnamese call the War against America.

The family's grandfather is one of the few returnees who survived the carnage and has an extraordinary story of survival to tell: how he rescued his family in 1953 from the imminent threat of summary execution by pleading to French soldiers in their language, and again in 1967 thanks to the presence of an American officer in the pacification team who understood a few words of French as a result of having fought in Europe during World War II. The man's youngest brother died unmarried and without a descendent, and so the man's eldest son now performs periodic death-anniversary rites on behalf of the deceased. His brother was killed in action during the Vietnam War as a soldier of the South Vietnamese army, and his eldest son is a decorated former partisan fighter belonging to the national liberation front. The eldest son, together with his father, also performs a periodic rite of commemoration for his great-grandmother who died in a tragic incident in 1948 shortly before her only surviving grandchild returned from France.

At that time, the woman was living alone in her bamboo house. She had lost her husband in 1936, her children shortly after, and her orphaned grandchildren had left the village for an urban ghetto or farther away. She survived on a small plot of land, where she grew vegetables; the neighbors regularly helped the lonely woman with rice and fish sauce. On the fifth day of the eleventh lunar month of 1948, she spotted a group of French soldiers conducting a house-to-house search. She was ill at the time and waved at the soldiers for help. The soldiers came, pushed her back into the house, closed the shutters, and set fire to the bamboo house. In the following era, the spirit of this woman came to assert her vitality through various apparitions, which eventually led the villagers to erect a small shrine in her memory on the site of her destroyed home. The locals then started calling her Ba Ba Linh, powerful grandmother. Throughout the chaos of the Vietnam War, her humble shrine attracted steady visits by local women who came to pray to the old woman for their family's safety. During the day, some Saigon solders saw the village women kowtowing to the shrine, heard the story, and prayed for their own wishes at the site. At night, the peasant militiamen, coming to survey the area, heard the same story. The village women saw that some of these partisan fighters were praying to the shrine before they hurriedly joined their group to move to the next hamlet. When people returned to the village after evacuation during the critical period of the Vietnam War at the end of the 1960s, they recall that there was nothing standing in the hamlet except the humble wooden shrine dedicated to Ba Ba Linh. Today, the old woman's shrine continues to attract prayers for other aspirations and desires.

Locals often refer to the precarious condition of life that confronted this family and many other people in the village for many years as *xoi dau*. Xoi dau refers to a ceremonial Vietnamese delicacy made of white rice flour and black beans. Used also as a metaphor, the term conveys how people of these regions experienced the Vietnam War. In this latter context, xoi dau refers to the turbulent conditions of communal life during the war, when the rural inhabitants were confronted with successive occupations by conflicting political and military forces: at night the village was under the control of the revolutionary forces, and in daytime the opposing forces took control. Life in these villages oscillated between two different political worlds governed by the two hostile armed forces. The people had to cope with their separate yet equally absolute demands of loyalty, and with the world changing politically from day to night, over many days and nights, to the extent that sometimes this anomalous world almost appeared to be normal. Xoi dau conveys the simple truth that when you eat this sweet, you must swallow both the white and black parts. This is how xoi dau is supposed to be eaten, and this is what it was like living a tumultuous life seized by the brutally dynamic reality of Vietnam's civil and international war.

I heard many painful episodes from living in "harmony" with thundering bipolarity, and equally many creative stories about subverting the zero-sum logic of the situation. One very common episode is about brotherly disunity:

how one brother joined "this side" (*ben ta,* the revolutionary side) and another brother (usually the younger one) was dragged to "that side" (*ben kia,* the Saigon or American side). The situation is tragic, and the result often painful: neither of them returns home alive, and the younger one has a problem in returning home even in memory. Yet it also has a creative side: how, for instance, the family hoped to have at least one of them survive the war by having them on different sides of the battlefield and also that the brother on the winner's side might be able to help his brother on the loser's side to rebuild his life in the case of the family having the extraordinary luck of seeing them both return home alive.

The meaning of xoi dau, of course, is quite incongruent with the meaning of the Cold War, as we usually understand it; yet, the extreme conditions of human life this Vietnamese idiom refers to, nevertheless, are very much part of global Cold War history as this was experienced by people in central Vietnam and many other communities in the decolonizing world. The experience of xoi dau by the two Vietnamese families introduced above, moreover, is hardly a thing of past but rather very much part of contemporary history, involving vigorous communal efforts to come to terms with the ruins and enduring wounds of the past destruction existing in communal life. The same is true with the community in South Korea mentioned earlier.

In these places, kinship rarely constitutes a politically homogenous entity since genealogical unity is crowded with the remains of wartime political bifurcation and related human displacement. In the customary practices of ancestral commemoration, people face not only the legacies of meritorious ancestors who contributed to the nation's revolutionary, or anticommunist, march to independence but also the stigmatizing genealogical background of working against the defined forward march. As in Sophocles's epic tragedy of *Antigone,* which inspired Hegel in his philosophy of the modern state, many individuals and families in these regions were torn between the familial obligation to attend to the memory of the war dead related in kinship and the political obligation not to do so for those who fought against the anticommunist or the revolutionary state. It is very common in these places for a family to have a few heroic fallen soldiers from the war to commemorate, and also siblings and other close relations killed in action on the opposite side of the war's frontier, to somehow be accounted for. The commemoration of the former group had been a legitimate and in fact highly encouraged, organized activity by the state hierarchy; that of the latter group had not. The memories of the dead in these communities are, at once, united in kinship memory and bipolarized in political history. The initiatives taken by people such as the stonemason's family or the man in Andong arise out of this long, turbulent political history, and, today, they continue to evolve and expand.

THE CONTRADICTION OF THE COLD WAR

The violence of the Cold War, such as that which brought deep and enduring wounds and crisis to the above families, was typically intertwined with the process of decolonization. In this sense, we may start thinking about the Cold War's globally encompassing, yet locally variant histories in terms of two broad realities: on the one hand, the imaginary war in Europe and North America and, on the other, the postcolonial experience of the bipolar era in which the very concept of Cold War becomes problematic and contradictory. This experience certainly varies across regions, in intensity as well as in temporality. The most violent manifestation of the global Cold War took its earliest tolls in Northeast Asia and Southeast Asia, represented by the outbreak of the Korean War and the First Indochina war (1945–54). In the following decades, while a new total war was being waged in Vietnam and its neighboring counties, the Cold War's political violence became much more transnational and generalized, engulfing other communities in Asia (such as Indonesia) and many nations in Africa, the Middle East, and Latin America. It is against this historical background that the celebrated Colombian writer Gabriel García Márquez once said that nations in Central and South America had not had a moment's rest from the threat and reality of mass death during the so-called Cold War.[4] The reality of mass violence endured in Latin America may be different in intensity and in character from that suffered by the Koreans in the 1950s and by the Vietnamese in the 1960s, which incorporated a total war as well as, as in places in Central and South America, systematic state political violence. Moreover, not all postcolonial states and communities experienced the Cold War in terms of armed conflicts or in other exceptional forms of political violence. South Asia is notable on this matter. Despite these exceptions, however, it is reasonable to conclude that for a great majority of decolonizing nations, the Cold War was scarcely an imaginary war, not to mention a period of a long peace. Quite the contrary, as Greg Grandin says with reference to the Cold War–era Latin America including the experience of the Q'eqchi'-Mayan communities in Guatemala, political terror and routine killings were "emblematic of the power of the Cold War."[5]

Saying that the Cold War was a global conflict, therefore, should not mean that the conflict was experienced on the same terms all over the world. Cold

War politics permeated developed and underdeveloped societies, Western and non-Western states, and colonial powers and colonized nations: it was a truly global reality in this sense. However, the historical experience and the collective memory of the Cold War have aspects of radical divergence between the West and the postcolonial world. Speaking of the decolonizing world's distinct experience of the Cold War, however, it is remarkable to notice that the specifics of this experience have long been ignored by scholars of Cold War history. It is even astonishing that the postcolonial Cold War experience continues to be largely a nonissue among scholars who specialize in postcolonial histories and theories. As I argue elsewhere, contemporary studies of postcolonial history have a strong tendency to disengage with the Cold War, relegating it to a business among powerful states of the twentieth century and thereby considering it of little importance for research agendas focused on decolonizing nations.[6] This regrettable situation, as Odd Arne Westad rightly observes, results from a view of the Cold War order merely according to the scheme of a balance of power and to the related, mistaken assumption that "the Cold War conceptually and analytically does not belong in the south."[7] This view disregards the fact that "the most important aspects of the Cold War were neither military nor strategic, nor Europe-centered, but connected to political and social development in the Third World," and that the Cold War order progressed in the way as we now know it did precisely because there were sustained, forceful challenges to it from the decolonizing world.[8] This is a serious problem in contemporary historical scholarship, a problem that we should confront head-on if we wish to advance a more grounded, comparatively rigorous understanding of the second half of the twentieth century and the place of American power in it.

Gaps such as these in postcolonial studies are, of course, quite different from gaps in conventional Cold War studies. The former are about the absence of Cold War global history in postcolonial history; the latter are mainly about the lack of attention to the postcolonial experience in the international history of the Cold War centered on Europe and the Transatlantic historical horizon. In my understanding, however, these two forms of absences are not unrelated and each reflects, following Tony Judt, a certain provincialism.[9] I believe that, in order to deepen and broaden our understanding of twentieth-century history and the place of U.S.-led empire of liberty in it, we must think carefully about these gaps and find ways to close them.[10]

The term *Third World* used to be a popular reference for the decolonizing and postcolonial world, much used during the forty-odd-year period of the Cold War. Indeed, as Westad explains, the aspirations and frustrations of the nations and communities that made up this world were very much part of the way in which the bipolar global political order took shape and evolved at that time. Conventional Cold War historiography, however, tends to treat these voices as a relatively marginal element in the constitution of the Cold War's dyadic structure, concentrating instead on the power struggles between the dominating state entities and the international alliances they led. This was hardly surprising given that the very reference of the Third World was a child to the Cold War's organization of a worldwide political duality, just as was that of the other two worlds from whose dyadic relationship it was created. In recent years, however, students of Cold War history have begun to pay more focused attention to the voices and agencies of the decolonizing world in the making of the Cold War's political structure, though these voices are still less than authentic. Much of the existing Cold War history literature discusses the Third World in terms of what this world meant for the power politics in and between the First and the Second Worlds. Little space exists in these premises for efforts to unravel what the Cold War meant for the Third World, or how decolonization helped to shape the process of political bipolarization. Those who claim to represent an authentic voice—such as scholars of contemporary postcolonial historical scholarship, writing primarily after the end of the Cold War geopolitical order in the early 1990s—tend to be oblivious to the various roles of the Third World in the Cold War, not to mention the Cold War's impact on the Third World, being intent instead on highlighting the decolonizing world's arguably uninterrupted struggle for self-determination and self-respect stretching from the time of institutionalized colonialism to the postcolonial era during and after the Cold War. In this somewhat impoverished state of contemporary historical scholarship of the Cold War and the Third World, therefore, there is either a failure to appreciate the conceptual relationship between the Third World and the Cold War—even though it was precisely when the Cold War progressed that the Third World became the "developing world," "the South," and variations thereof.

In conventional knowledge, the term *Cold War* refers to the prevailing condition of the world in the second half of the twentieth century, divided along two separate conceptions of political modernity and paths of economic development. In a narrower sense, it also means the contest of power and will between the two dominant states—the United States and USSR—that set out to rule the world and thereby, neither being able to overcome the other, divided it between them in an undeclared state of war. As such, the Cold War was a highly unconventional war, having no clear distinction between war and peace. Its ending was similarly unusual, failing to benefit from any ceremonial cessation of violence. The Cold War was neither a real war nor a genuine peace, an ambiguity that explains why some consider it an imaginary war, whereas others associate it with what in modern history was an exceptionally long period of peace. It is probably fair to say that—in the first two Worlds at least, and certainly in the West—the dominant image of the Cold War is of its having been fought mainly with political, economic, ideological, and polemical means; of the nations that waged this war as being engaged in building and stockpiling arsenals of weapons of mass destruction in the belief that they would never have to use them; and of the threats of mutually assured total destruction as assuring a prolonged duration of international peace. These strange features that constitute our collective memory of the Cold War make it difficult to come to terms with its history according to the conventional antinomy of war and peace.

As Walter LaFeber argues, however, this view of the Cold War speaks a half-truth of bipolar political history.[11] The Cold War era resulted in forty million human casualties of war in different parts of the world, as LaFeber mentions; the major "proxy"—i.e., Third World—conflicts of Korea, Vietnam, and Afghanistan between them spanned almost the entire duration of the period. How to reconcile this exceptionally violent historical reality with the predominant Western perception of an exceptionally long peace is crucial when it comes to grasping the meaning of the global Cold War.[12] According to Bruce Cumings, it is necessary to balance the dominant "balance of power" conception of the Cold War, on which the idea of the long peace view is based, with the reality of the "balance of terror" experienced in the wider world, which comes close to the meaning of xoi dau.[13]

If the various territories of the world did not experience the Cold War in the same way, it is reasonable to think that today they do not all remember the bipolar political era in the same way either, and that the end of this era did not mean the same to all peoples in all regions. The stories of the Danang and Andong families clearly show that the end of the Cold War as a geopolitical order is not the same thing as the end of the Cold War as a social order. This simple yet important recognition about the Cold War's complex spatiality and temporality is vital for an understanding of the postcolonial experience of the global bipolar politics. It is also important for any rigorous comparative understanding of the Cold War and grounded understanding of the place of American power in it.

These questions ought to be taken seriously—not least because they have much to offer for a better understanding of contemporary global realities—

and they should bring about further innovative questions related to the deep plurality of Cold War historical experience. One hopes, however, that the diversification of Cold War history is not to be mistaken for a fragmentation of Cold War global history and a denial of its basic unity. A global history is a history that is attentive to locally variant historical realities and to the fundamental diversity of human existence. It follows that the more we become familiar with the Cold War's diverse realities, the closer we will be to an understanding of the Cold War as a genuinely global history.

Another equally important issue is the need to tell Cold War history as public history, and this is what I learned in Berlin recently. In this sphere, it is important to be able to tell stories of the Cold War as both intimate social experiences and high politics, so that the public can feel the issues more tangibly. It is also important to remember that the public needs to hear not only stories that are familiar to them but also those from places that are farther away. For instance, the partitioned city of Berlin was undoubtedly the most powerful emblem of the Cold War political order in Europe.[14] Likewise, it is understandable that the fall of the wall that once divided the city became a signifier of the end of this order. Looking more broadly, however, the Berlin Wall may be one of many different instruments and symbols of containment that existed in the world. The politics of containment in other regions may have taken, as the concept of xoi dau entails, less materially tangible, more violent, and much more socially diffused and historically enduring forms than the wall.[15] The history of the two empires in the past century—the empire of liberty and the empire of equality—whether this is told in the context of Hanoi or Ho Chi Minh City, Berlin or Seoul, Beijing or Lhasa, Bombay or Harare, always has another, less familiar history. In bringing this history to public history, therefore, it is necessary to bring in the other's experience of the Cold War imperial powers as well.

NOTES

1 Kaldor, *The Imaginary War*; Gaddis, *The Long Peace*.
2 Westad, *The Global Cold War*.
3 Kwon, *After the Massacre*, 161–64.
4 Grandin, *The Last Colonial Massacre*, 170.
5 Grandin, *The Last Colonial Massacre*, 3.
6 Kwon, *The Other Cold War*.
7 Westad, *The Global Cold War*, 3.
8 Westad, *The Global Cold War*, 396.

9 Judt, *Reappraisals*, 371.
10 See Chari and Verdery, "Thinking between the Posts."
11 LaFeber, "An End to Which Cold War?," 13–14.
12 See LaFeber, "An End to Which Cold War?," 13.
13 Cumings, *Parallax Visions*, 51.
14 Borneman, *After the Wall.*
15 See McGranahan, *Arrested Histories.*

11 Time Standards and Rhizomatic Imperialism

KEVIN K. BIRTH

WHAT TIME IS IT?

The time on one's watch or clock is a product of a peculiar sort of supranational system—what Michael Hardt and Antonio Negri would describe as a component of empire.[1] The global importance of international time standards and the significant role of the United States in defining and distributing those standards are an example of what Prasenjit Duara describes as the new imperialism—an imperialism that maintains influence over dependencies and clients in part through cultivating the resemblance of the dependencies to the imperial power.[2] On the surface, it appears as if time standards belong to everyone—that they are a democratizing force that gives the entire world access to reliable, precision timekeeping. Yet, the precision time that is available to the world is set to the prime meridian that runs through the United Kingdom, the determination of the correct time is heavily shaped by American atomic clocks, and for much of the world, the availability of this time is mediated by GPS—a system of American satellites. As a result, while global time standards are available to all, many people depend on the United States, and the extent to which time standards have been woven into modern technology creates a broad and ubiquitous dependence that even entangles critics of American influence.

The reach of this system is broad; it is woven into the fabric of daily life for many across the globe. For instance, everything that a computer does gets a time stamp. Every transaction of a credit card, debit card, or ATM card, or even of a cash transaction at most stores, gets a time stamp. Telephone calls get time stamps, as do emails and text messages. The water meter on my house sends time stamps with its readings. The more computerized and electronically integrated one's life is, the more it is meticulously documented by time stamps. *All* of these time stamps are synchronized in order to be meaningful, and they all lead back to clocks such as those managed by the United States Naval Observatory (USNO) and the National Institute of Standards and Technology (NIST).

If you travel with your smartphone, you'll notice that it determines the local time for you. It may also determine your position. But that, too, is a function of time. Global Positioning System satellites are orbiting clocks, and GPS receivers determine position based on synchronizing themselves with the satellite system and then calculating distance from at least three satellites based on the time it takes for a signal to travel from the satellite to the receiver.[3] The Global Positioning System is set to the USNO's clocks.

The ubiquity of standardized clock time in daily life is part of a heritage of close ties between the representation of time and imperialism.[4] This heritage is indicated by the names of the dominant systems of time. The Julian calendar is named after the Roman emperor Julius Caesar; our month of July is also named after him, and August after his successor, Augustus Caesar. The Gregorian calendar is named after Pope Gregory XIII, who, after centuries of the church's recognizing the flaws of the Julian calendar, was prompted by astronomers to reform the calendar. Its implementation depended on the Spanish, Portuguese, French, and Holy Roman empires, and its hegemony over European colonial empires become complete when the United Kingdom adopted it in 1752. In 1884, when the British empire was at its most powerful, the prime meridian was defined as running through Greenwich, England—as if a suburb of London was an ideal location for the astronomical observations necessary to chart Earth's rotation. Greenwich Mean Time was the global standard of time until 1967, when it was replaced by Coordinated Universal Time (UTC). But this "universal" time is, itself, set to the prime meridian. While the sun now sets on the British empire, no sun in the universe sets on the United Kingdom's time zone.

In *Objects of Time*, I made the argument that clocks involve a special form of commodity fetishism in which not only does the focus on the commodity obscure the production process, but also the knowledge that is made available through the commodity.[5] As cognitive tools by means of which we "know" the time, clocks are devices with representations so simple that young children can use them, but with hidden algorithms that embody millennia of accumulated knowledge and decisions backed by governmental power. Clocks mediate the representation of time for the masses and the production of time by the specialized time metrologists. Through the design of clocks and the distribution of time signals that allow for the synchronization of clocks, the producers of time are able to think for the users of clocks.

Empires engage in the differentiation of their subjects, but empires also rely on uniformity and standardization. Loconto and Busch argue that standards are a form of governmentality that promote "a strategy of self-governance that pre-empts state-led regulation of markets."[6] This governmentality is not about a specific nation-state, but about the world, and it is a power that seeps into and governs practice. The governmentality of standards are much more far-reaching than how empire is normally imagined. On the Thirty-Eighth World Standards Day, in 2007, the International Organization for Standardization (ISO) issued a news release that stated: "A world without standards would soon grind to a halt. Transport and trade would seize up. The Internet would simply not function. Hundreds of thousands of systems dependent on information and communication technologies would falter or fail—from government and banking to healthcare and air traffic control, emergency services, disaster relief and even international diplomacy."[7] If standards and empire go together, then one of the features of modernity is that, without empire, the technologies on which many depend would disintegrate into chaos. The argument that empire keeps chaos at bay is an ancient one, but now it seems to have seeped into the very habitus of even those who are critical of empire.

This seems to indicate that standards are a source of immense power, and that those who set the standards have great power.[8] Yet, there are differences between the power to define a standard, the power to maintain it, the power to develop the technology to meet it, and the power to regulate it. Ronald Beard describes the current complicated division of labor that goes into developing, regulating, and disseminating time standards.[9] This consists of the cooperation between three different types of institutions—scientific associations, regulatory institutions, and those who manage the standards. The USNO and NIST maintain standards and engage in discussions to define standards. Nonetheless, as I discuss later with regard to the debate about the leap second policy, having immense power over the management of the global time system has not translated into unquestioned power over the ability to define the standards on which that system operates. Terry Quinn, the former director of the International Bureau of Weights and Measures (BIPM), writes of the Radiocommunication Sector of the International Telecommunications Union (ITU-R), a UN institution that sets policy for the global timescale, that "matters concerning the definition of world's civil time scale come under a Working Party of a Study Group of one of the Sections of the ITU. This is a ponderous decision-making process, and it makes the response time very long and leads to difficulties in coordination with the work of the national metrology institutes that actually establish the world's time scale."[10] Quinn's observation indicates not only the inability of any single nation-state to determine time policy, but a divide between those who determine policy and those who maintain and distribute global time. Moreover, Quinn's frustration indicates that policy making does not keep up with metrological science. Instead, from his perspective, the ITU acts as a brake on progress.

Coordinated Universal Time is the global time standard. Those who administer this standard seek global uniformity. Since time stamps are such an intrinsic component of computers and telecommunications, nonstandard timescales or deviations from the standard timescale are deemed a threat. This recognition crept into public view in 2000 with the concern about the Y2K bug. This bug was result of old time stamps saving bits by representing years with only two digits and assuming all dates were twentieth-century dates. The result was that these systems would roll over to the year 1900 rather than to the year 2000, and such divergence of time stamps threatened widespread computer crashes if not rectified. But this public view of the threat of computers running on different timescales is a persistent concern among those managing time on a daily basis. Discussions of the future of UTC policies commonly express concern about the proliferation of multiple timescales.[11]

Even underneath practices of temporal differentiation is the uniformity of UTC. For instance, both Jews and Muslims have available to them numerous software applications to tell them prayer times for their particular location. These applications often use data from the *Astronomical Almanac* generated by the USNO and the British Nautical Almanac Office. This almanac contains ephemerides, including various types of twilight, throughout the year for Greenwich, Jewish, and Islamic software applications to convert this information to apply to specific locations on the planet. As a result, a specific religious prayer time for a specific location is calculated based on celestial events as predicted by the *Astronomical Almanac.* These calculated times of religious significance then get converted into religious time terms that are then represented in the local time. Even representing the local time is a challenge for the software developers, since nation-states have the ability to define their own time zones and daylight saving time policies. For the applications to work directly, information from a time zone database must be used, such as the TZ Database maintained by the Internet Assigned Numbers Authority—the institution that manages Internet protocol globally. Last, some applications, like MyZmanim (Jewish) or Moonsighting (Islamic), modify the calculations based on ephemerides such as those published in the *Astronomical Almanac* with their own algorithms and information from their networks of observers.

If the religious time application is on a smartphone, it likely uses a GPS feature to determine the phone's location for purposes of the calculations. While the *Mishnah* and *Hadith* give abundant instructions for determining the times to pray based on direct observation, many Jews and Muslims prefer to rely on smartphone applications rather than master the traditional observational techniques.

The use of time standards for maintaining different traditions of religious timing is not the only way in which standardization and uniformity contribute to differentiation. Contrary to Castells's claims that the network society has erased time, or to David Harvey's claims that time-space compression has erased space, the distribution of standardized time over space creates experiences of differences between local time and UTC, and this can have biological consequences.[12] Time zones define the relationship of particular locations to UTC, and many social practices additionally define relationships between locales and the global cities.[13] As a result, it is common for the daily routines of many to be tied to daylight cycles many time zones away. Since light cycles are the primary determinant of human circadian rhythms, the disjunction between local time and global time can cause desynchronization between one's biology and social demands—a sort of perpetual experience of jetlag that gets labeled as normal. The degree to which somebody suffers from this is dependent on the time difference between that person and whatever global centers of power shape their lives. This is not a matter of "the West" versus "the rest," however. International traders working in Wall Street firms are among those who suffer most, since they may time their daily routines to be awake at the opening and closing of every major global exchange.

Standardization as a facet of empire is underappreciated, yet the history of the relationship of time standards and empire demonstrates that the two are closely connected. As a matter of empire, however, since time standards are about science—specifically the science of metrology—they cross the divide between politics and science that Bruno Latour documents in *We Have Never Been Modern*.[14] Imperial policies and practices reflect the attempt to maintain the divide between the social and scientific and yet require that certain scientific dimensions of empire—standards and measures—infuse social life. Because there is an attempt to keep science and politics separate, those who maintain the standards and measures are devoted to a scientific agenda of producing the most robust, stabile, accurate, and precise standards possible; those who engage in political discourse tend to forget about the science and technologies on which the implementation of policies and management of people and information depend. This separation is spatially manifest at the USNO, which is also the official residence of the vice president of the United States. With the exception of Vice President Gore, vice presidents have shown little interest in what goes on in the building next to their helipad and not too far from their front door. Congress and the rest of the upper levels of the administration show even less interest.

So the Latourian paradox, if one wishes to call it that, is that the science and technology developed by empires for empires and necessary for implementing global policies and managing global information seem disconnected from the most public manifestations of empire, such as the use of military power and diplomatic manipulation. In contrast to these public manifestations of empire, the technical infrastructure of empire is rhizomatic in the sense that it involves the proliferation of connections and associations in which ideas developed for one purpose become harnessed for other purposes.[15] European timekeeping is a history of rhizomatic technologies, with the clock, being an invention by monks to manage liturgical practices, becoming a means of organizing social life, disciplining labor, scientifically measuring phenomena, structuring datasets, coordinating actions of humans and machines, and building the architecture of computer systems. It is so rhizomatic that it spreads in ways that one might not expect by simply observing politics. Jihadists are reliant on technologies developed for the U.S. military, such as the Internet and GPS.[16]

Despite the desire for uniformity, those involved in precision timekeeping are not a group of institutions or people in full agreement with each other, and their debates reflect competing interests about how time should be managed. Yet, they have a culture—a shared discourse and knowledge base. Part of this shared culture is a belief in progress in time metrology. This shapes the narratives of the history of horology they tell, as well as providing motivations for improvement upon present technologies. Diversity challenges uniformity, however. Competing interests for competing uses of time allow for politics to enter into a domain where scientific and technical arguments are dominant. When this happens, political positions get couched in scientific and technical terms.

WHERE DOES TIME COME FROM?

For most electronic devices, time synchronization involves a service provider that periodically sets the clock on the device. Most devices have cheap quartz oscillators in them that do not keep time very well, so reliable timekeeping depends on synchronization. The service provider will often synchronize its server using Network Time Protocol (NTP). This protocol developed for clock synchronization over local computer networks in the 1970s has grown as the Internet has grown. In it, a time server will seek time signals from several other, more reliable, servers. It then compares these time signals with each other, discards the signals that are outliers (these are called "false tickers"), and keeps the most reliable signals, the "true chimers," from which an average is calculated.[17] The local time server then synchronizes its clock to this average and sends out this time across its network.

Network Time Protocol has a hierarchy of servers, with high-quality servers, such as the NIST's and USNO's NTP servers, that stand at the top of the hierarchy. But the USNO's and NIST's time servers are not the source of time. They are synchronized to a master clock.

The master clock is a computer, but it is not really the source of time. At the United States Naval Observatory, the master clock is located in a different building from many of the atomic clocks that report their time to it. The job of the master clock is to receive the times measured by a suite of atomic clocks and then to calculate a weighted average of these times with the best-performing clocks from the previous calculation being given the greatest weight. Not too far from the USNO's master clock is a museum piece: an old cesium beam clock. While the transition period of cesium-133 is still the global standard for the definition of the second, cesium clocks are no longer the state of the art. Hydrogen masers and Rubidium fountains are far better timekeepers than cesium beam clocks. So the master clock receives signals from a suite of hydrogen masers and rubidium fountains that are used to calculate the duration of a second equivalent to 9,192,631,770 transitions of cesium-133 atoms. This time is then a reliable source of time for purposes of NTP and GPS.

Originally, the second was treated as a fraction of a minute, which was a fraction of an hour, which was a fraction of a day. But the Earth's rotation varies throughout the year, giving rise to mean time and the equation of time for relating mean time to apparent solar time on a particular day. As the precision of clocks improved, it was noted that the Earth's rotation was slowing. This led Simon Newcomb of the USNO to calculate the ephemeris second—1/86400 of a day that would become the standard.[18] Newcomb used data from the eighteenth and nineteenth centuries for his calculation, which was published in 1895. The day he chose was January 1, 1900—so the length day he adopted was from a day that had not yet occurred when he published his results. But with corrections later made to his calculations, 86,400 seconds on January 1, 1900, is viewed as most likely representing a day sometime around 1820.

A second is not a fraction of this day, however. By the 1950s, the foibles of the rotational day were culturally discarded in favor of defining the second in terms of a fraction of the tropical year.[19] The tropical year varies far less than the Earth's rotation, so it seemed like a more reliable standard to which to peg the second than the day. In 1956, the International Committee on Weights and Measures (CIPM) adopted this definition. This new definition of the second came be known as the Système International second (SI second).

The adoption of this definition of the second is a story of shared and learned knowledge. The idea was first proposed in A. Danjon in 1929.[20] However, the formal proposal came from Clemence first in a paper offered in 1948, and then at the International Colloquium on the Fundamental Constants of

Astronomy in 1950.[21] When Clemence made his proposal, he did not realize that it had been made previously by somebody he knew and respected. When he came to this recognition, he published a confession of "inadvertent plagiarism."[22]

Historians of time standards would view this as the actions of individual scientists, but the anthropological view is a bit different. By emphasizing distribution and sharing of knowledge, the anthropological view is less about who came up with an idea first than how it gets distributed through social networks. The emergence of the idea to define the second in relationship to the tropical year and the enthusiastic response with which the proposal was greeted was a cultural phenomenon—to put it colloquially, "great minds think alike."

In 1955, L. Essen and J. V. L. Parry announced that they had calibrated a cesium beam oscillator to a second as measured at the Royal Greenwich Observatory. In *Nature* they announced that cesium-133 had a frequency of 9,192,631,830 transitions of plus or minus 10 cycles per second.[23] Because of the potential of this oscillator to be a tool for measuring precise time and defining a global standard, Essen and Parry worked with William Markowitz of the United States Naval Observatory to calibrate the atomic clock to the ephemeris second. The result was that 9,192,631,770 plus or minus 20 cycles of cesium-133 was deemed equivalent to a second.[24] In 1967, the Thirteenth General Conference on Weights and Measures adopted this as the definition for the SI second—dropping the plus or minus 20 component.[25] So a second is no longer related to a fraction of the Earth's rotation or a fraction of the year. Instead, a day is defined as 86,400 seconds.

The great minds thinking alike was part of a growing cultural shift in metrology away from using single objects, such as the meter rod housed in Paris, as a standard, and toward using standardized and replicable procedures to define standards, such as defining the meter as the distance light travels in a vacuum in 1/299792458 of a second. The new standards are not tied to a specific place that houses the standard-giving artifacts, but instead are tied to scientific protocols that could, in theory, be carried out anywhere, but which, in practice, are only carried out in facilities with the sufficient resources to participate in the global system of standards. This cultural shift in metrology from privileging a single location to the dissemination of protocols is a shift from a privileged imperial core to a rhizomatic empire.

Because time standards are not tied to a single time-giving observatory or laboratory, they allow for the participation by any nation-state that cares to do so. The global timescale is not determined by one clock—it takes a group of specialists managing multiple clocks to determine it. At first glance, this may seem like a rather diffuse system to manage global time, but in contrast to the nineteenth century, it is highly coordinated. In the nineteenth century, observatories would compete with each other and sell their time signals.[26] Railroad companies would often keep their own times that differed from those of their competitors. The seeming proliferation of organizations and agencies overseeing time standards was, in fact, a concentration of experts from formerly competing institutions. The proceedings of their meetings indicate an agenda of forging a stable, uniform, accurate and precise timescale, not an agenda of controlling global time. By creating a scientific community that concentrated all the experts on the same committees and in the same organizations, de facto coordination was achieved. But this was a mixture of politics and science. Participation in these conferences often involved government sponsorship, so the concentration of control was an outcome of political support for centralization even as the participants viewed their work through the lens of scientific progress. It is also important to note the subtle difference between a system that is coordinated and a system that is controlled. The global timescale is a product of coordination not centralized control.

The scientists at the USNO are among those specialists, but the seconds and time ticked (in a metaphorical sense) and computed by the master clock of the USNO is not the official global time. This time is a simulacrum of UTC, or to use the standard convention, it is UTC (USNO). Coordinated Universal Time is calculated by the BIPM, located near Paris. This agency receives time signals from time laboratories distributed across the world. It then uses its own weighted average, which also takes into account the Doppler effect of the movement of the signals and relativity, to create International Atomic Time (TAI). International Atomic Time is not globally distributed, however. The BIPM converts TAI into UTC by adding the number of leap seconds that have occurred since the beginning of the current time epoch, which is January 1, 1972. Coordinated Universal Time, along with the difference from UTC of all reporting time laboratories, is published once a month in *Circular T*. So one can only know what UTC really was the previous month, but not in real time. The BIPM has recently launched UTCr, which is a weekly reporting of a form of UTC based on a calculation from a subset of reporting time laboratories.

Why January 1, 1972? When the CGPM originally adopted the atomic standard for the second in 1967, it was known that with the Earth's slowing rotation, 86400 SI seconds would slowly drift away from the mean rotational day represented in Universal Time (UT). In fact, in 1966, the International Radio Consultative Committee (CCIR) had adopted a practice known as the "stepped atomic second" and colloquially dubbed the "rubber second" in order to keep UTC within 0.1 second of the earth's rotation. In this policy, 200-millisecond additions were made to UTC when necessary.[27] By the late 1960s, as computer technology became more widespread, such rubber seconds were an annoyance. They were also an overly centralized intervention in an increasingly diffuse, yet coordinated, system. In 1970, the CCIR approved a new practice called the leap second in which a second would be added to UTC when the divergence between UTC and UT was predicted to be 0.7 seconds. This system was implemented on January 1, 1972. In 1973 the International Astronomical Union (IAU) modified the CCIR resolution by recommending that leap second adjustments occur whenever a 0.9 second difference between UT and UTC was anticipated. The CCIR accepted this proposal in 1974, and the CGPM in 1975. With the exception of an occasional intervention to keep UTC close to Earth's mean rotation, the new protocol with leap seconds allowed the system to run based on ongoing coordinated synchronization rather than centralized determination of time.

It is not nation-states that create these policies, but international gatherings of institutions, such as the CCIR, CGPM, IAU, and ITU-R. These extragovernmental institutions make decisions that are not dictated by the state, but make recommendations to the state, and the resolutions they approve determine global practice even if nation-states do not formally adopt them. This has been the state of affairs since the Conference of 1884, and seems to be an example of Carnoy and Castells's argument that "globalization has eroded the nation state's monopoly of scientific knowledge."[28] Yet Carnoy and Castells's conclusion that the state's ability to enforce rules and regulations is still important for global finance capital does not hold.[29] Standardization is outside of state control, and in the case of Wall Street, the primary regulatory agency is FINRA (Financial Industry Regulatory Authority)—not a government agency, but an institution created by the financial institutions to monitor themselves. Standards foster self-regulation and often serve as a precondition for participation in global movement of information and capital.[30] Standards also foster the ability to audit such movements.

The time on one's computer, then, is received from a time server that synchronizes to another time server, which ultimately leads to a server at a time laboratory, which reports its time to the BIPM, which calculates the true time—a time that nobody knows until a month after the fact. At any given moment, the empire of time is an empire of managing the simulacra that produce the official time, but this empire is not under the control of any single nation-state. Indeed, the leaders of nation-states often exhibit ignorance of the existence of the global time system.

This is just how time is produced, not how the policies that govern its production are generated. The current situation is that the Radiocommunciation Sector of the International Telecommunications Union (ITU-R) thinks of itself as creating time policy. It gets this idea because it governs telecommunications and time signals that were originally sent by telegraph, then radio, and most recently over the Internet. The ITU-R does not have a supervisory role over the BIPM, however. Instead, the BIPM chooses to recognize ITU-R decisions. Whereas the ITU-R is a UN agency with delegates who are not specialists in time and frequency, the BIPM has experts in these areas. The ITU-R system does involve creating working parties of experts to generate resolutions, and there is often considerable overlap between the BIPM and time metrologists involved in national time laboratories and the participants in the ITU-R working party system.

The BIPM is in France; the ITU-R is in Geneva; the atomic clocks used to calculate time are distributed across the globe. Yet, in this system the United States has incredible influence and meets strong resistance. The United States controls the plurality of atomic clocks that contribute to the global timescale. It also has many of the highest-quality atomic clocks, so the time the NIST and USNO produce are often among those closest to the weighted average calculated by the BIPM and consequently should get the greatest weight in the next calculation of the TAI and UTC. Yet, there is concern over the clocks of the United States steering global time, so I have heard rumors that I cannot confirm that the weight given to the United States' clocks is capped in BIPM calculations. Even if the rumors are not true, they indicate a sentiment that the United States has too much influence over the global timescale. That said, resistance to American influence is different from the personal relationships of those who work on precise timekeeping. Those who shape time policies are typically not those in elected office or even directly appointed by elected officials. At times, it seems that their power to get things done is based, in part, on elected officials not having any knowledge of time metrology and not directly participating in debates about time policies.

THE LEAP SECOND DEBATE: POLITICS AND SCIENCE

In the late 1990s, American scientists, many associated with the U.S. Department of Defense and its contractors, started to point out problems with the existing leap second policy.[31] By 2001, the United States was able to get a resolution passed by the ITU-R calling for the investigation as to whether the leap second policy should be continued or not. Since then, the United States' Study Group 7A, which prepares the U.S. position for the ITU-R WP 7A, has been active in advocating the elimination of the leap second, and there has been a wave of publications by American scientists advocating this position. This wave has been met by a counterwave of publications and a Listserv arguing that the leap second should be kept, with many of these scientists being American, as well.

What changed the landscape of precise timing in the late 1990s and early 2000s was a combination of factors: the availability of GPS for civilian use and developments in computer science.

GPS was designed as a military application for purposes of navigation. It consists of clocks in orbit. While GPS was designed as a military navigational technology, soon after its availability to civilians, its utility as a time signal became clear.[32] Here were clocks in space, steered to be synchronized with UTC, that could provide high-quality sources of time anywhere on the planet one could receive a GPS signal. No longer did one need to be connected by a cable to a network to receive time, nor did one need to rely on radio signals of varying quality (largely because of the foibles of shortwave radio).

Then, in 1997, the Institute of Electrical and Electronic Engineers (IEEE) issued specifications for a new time protocol that would achieve levels of precision unheard of at the time for NTP. This new protocol, dubbed IEEE 1588/PTP, with PTP standing for "Precision Time Protocol," would be less reliant on hierarchies of time sources such as those found in NTP, and more reliant on high-precision clocks within local networks that would be synchronized with GPS signals. The original specification suggested that local networks could achieve a precision of one nanosecond, and that PTP time stamps of such precision would be accepted as legitimate. At this time, NTP could only achieve a precision of a microsecond, and most financial markets worked (and still work) at the level of milliseconds.

The IEEE was a relative newcomer and outsider to the process of defining global time standards. Its PTP standard could be viewed as a threat to the empire of time that had been built ever since the International Meridian Conference of 1884. After all, it set up locally controlled simulacra of UTC that did not report to the BIPM but instead received time from GPS systems steered by time information from the USNO and NIST. Yet, POSIX, the overarching set of standards defined by the IEEE, still maintained UTC as the global standard for time stamps. Precision Time Protocol is in a peculiar position, then. Its standard is managed by the BIPM, but the ability of PTP systems to have a time that matches the standard is reliant on GPS and ultimately, on the USNO. On the surface, this seems to enhance the power of the USNO.

The benefits of PTP are twofold. First, PTP is useful in any local network in which precision timing of automation is crucial. Second, PTP is also useful in managing large data sets. The use of "big data" has swept business, government, and intelligence services. Precision Time Protocol gives a substantial edge in effectively managing and mining big data sets. It must be remembered that every datum in such sets has a time stamp. The more precise the time stamps, the more fine-tuned the analysis can be. For instance, currently the NASDAQ stock exchange offers subscriptions to a service called NASDAQ-ITCH, which is real-time data with nanosecond time stamps.[33] The users of this service are high-frequency traders who rely on such hyperfine precision to hone their algorithms.

The problem with PTP is that it does not handle leap seconds well locally. In an NTP system, a local server will synchronize with multiple time sources, and such synchronization readily corrects the system. In contrast, PTP systems are insulated from other systems with a "boundary clock" mediating between the precise timekeeping in the system and the time kept by the rest of the world. Moreover, PTP systems use a simulacrum of TAI rather than UTC as their timescale. It is not actually TAI, because the BIPM does not broadcast TAI. Instead, it is GPS time, which is itself a simulacrum of UTC, minus the current number of leap seconds. If a leap second occurs and a PTP system does not correct its software that converts TAI into UTC, it issues UTC time stamps that are deemed a second off of what they should be. When communicating with other systems, a second off of the expected time sets off alarms, and if computer commands are being sent, it will typically result in the command received being blocked, and this generates an endless loop that causes a system crash.

The problem with PTP differs from that of NTP systems in which time providers face the difficulty of handling leap seconds. In the NTP hierarchy high-quality time sources like NIST servers have a standard time format of moving from 11:59:59 to 00:00:00. But when a leap second is implemented, they must move from 11:59:59 to 11:59:59 a second time before ticking 00:00:00.[34] As a result, time stamps are ambiguous—there is no way to discern the first 11:59:59 from the second. This ambiguity is particularly troublesome in the Pacific Rim, where leap seconds can occur at the beginning (in Asia) or the end (in Western North America) of the business day.

The leap second problem, then, is one of either ambiguity of time stamps or system crashes. Crashes have occurred with previous leap seconds. In 2012, Qantas Airways experienced a catastrophic computer crash due to a leap second problem in its reservation system. Because the reservation system crashed, and since that system contained all passenger information along with security checks of that information, Qantas's planes could not take off. This produced a four-hour delay.

In effect, PTP is vulnerable to leap seconds, yet PTP is an extremely powerful tool for data mining. Financial markets and intelligence services have come to rely on this technology. Moreover, the ambiguity generated by NTP's handling of leap seconds diminishes the value of time stamps during a leap second. Because of these two factors, it is no surprise that the United States government has taken a position that maintaining the stability and precision of such computer systems is more important than keeping UTC tethered to the mean solar day. The implicit threat of PTP systems abandoning UTC, a timescale for which the USNO and NIST disseminate a simulacrum, for a local PTP system's simulacrum of TAI, a timescale that the USNO and NIST do not distribute, is also a concern. Yet, as soon as the United States made its position clear through documents produced by its Study Group 7A, there emerged trenchant resistance to decoupling UTC from the Earth's rotation.

WHY THE LEAP SECOND STILL EXISTS

Despite years of effort on behalf of many time metrologists, the leap second persists. After a dozen years, the technical arguments for and against the leap second are well rehearsed, and they display two competing interests. Empires face the conundrum of seeking scientific and uniform standards for multiple and sometimes competing goals. A standard that is well suited to achieving one goal can be detrimental to achieving another. The leap second debate within the United States demonstrates this. Those who want to get rid of the leap second recognize it as a threat to the stability of computer systems; those who want to keep the leap second see it as ensuring an ongoing ability to track things in space from the rotating platform that we call Earth. It is clear that if UTC is decoupled from Earth's rotation, then it is more difficult to write and maintain software that astronomers use to target their telescopes to precise points in the sky. Similarly, it would create problems for satellite-tracking and satellite-surveillance systems.[35] While it is a gross oversimplification, the arguments for and against the leap second boil down to which function is more important: data management or celestial tracking.

On the surface, it would seem that this is a conflict between those involved in different technologies, and this is how the debate has played out within the United States, but globally other less technical and more political issues have become involved. Some of them involve patrimony. If the leap second is eliminated, then the UTC day will no longer be tied to the prime meridian, and the prime meridian is of great national significance in the United Kingdom. As a result, Great Britain has come out strongly in favor of keeping the leap second, with its former minister for Universities and Science,

David Willets, using rhetoric insinuating Great Britain's need to defend itself against U.S. influence, stating "Greenwich Mean Time would slowly move west towards America. I want to keep it in Britain."[36] Truthfully, however, GMT would not even reach the House of Parliament in Willet's lifetime.

Russia and China have both expressed concerns about the problems the leap second causes. The Russian equivalent of GPS, GLONASS, is reported to have problems with leap seconds.[37] China is adversely affected in a different way. Since the leap second policy is to implement the second at midnight UTC, that means implementing it at midnight at the prime meridian, which is the beginning of the business day in China. This problem has persuaded Japan to join with the United States to advocate for the elimination of the leap second, but China does not accept the U.S. position. China's lead scientist on the issue, Han Chunhao of the Beijing Satellite Navigation Center, agrees that the leap second poses a problem, but advocates a solution different from the one offered by the United States. At a workshop on the leap second organized by the ITU and BIPM, he argued in favor of a once a century adjustment.[38] More recently, at an early 2015 conference about the leap second, Dr. Han argued in favor of eliminating the leap second, but also maintaining a system to distribute Earth orientation data in order to maintain the traditional Chinese system of time reckoning that emphasizes astronomical rather than atomic cycles.

The decision to keep or eliminate the leap second is not in the hands of the United States, Great Britain, Japan, China, and Russia, however. It is in the hands of the World Radio Congress—the quadrennial general assembly of the ITU-R. The resolution to eliminate the leap second was on the agenda in 2012. At the last minute, it was withdrawn, and a resolution calling for further study was introduced and passed.

This curious substitution was the result of members of WP 7A polling delegates beforehand. What they discovered was that a large number of delegates were not intending on voting one way or the other on the resolution. Some of these delegates said they wanted more information, but it also seemed to be the case that many delegates were unwilling to pick a side not because they lacked technical knowledge, but because picking a side meant aligning themselves either for or against the United States and an initiative associated with the Department of Defense.

Indeed, there is anecdotal evidence that many nations did not need more technical information about the debate, but more information on the political consequences of choosing a position. The distribution of time laboratories contributing to UTC combined with the distribution of global expertise on such issues suggest that many nations could easily develop informed positions. Or, to put it more bluntly, if an anthropologist could learn the various positions, then the technical advisors available to many nations could, as well. The rhizomatic nature of this empire of time emphasizes international coordination even as it diminishes the ability of any one interest to control the empire. Yet, what is given up in terms of control is gained in the ability to move information and capital quickly and audit such movements precisely.

THE APPEARANCE OF DIMINISHED HEGEMONY

The inability of the official U.S. position to win out so far seems attributable to the dynamics of postcolonial politics and the difficulty of creating a uniform standard for competing interests. An empire without colonialism finds it difficult to manage such uniformity and to maintain standards for rhizomatic technologies, particularly when uniformity is in the hands of an institution such as the ITU-R that seems set up to curtail the ability of any one superpower to impose its will on such standards. Indeed, elements of the debate seem reminiscent of the nonaligned movement with passionate arguments coupled with much of the world refusing to take a side. At the same time, the global distribution of PTP is probably pushing much of the world toward a resolution of some sort—whether that resolution will be through the ITU-R or through the rhizomes steering practices through opting to use local simulacra of TAI for time stamps rather than UTC time stamps is hard to say.

At the same time, the greatest weakness of the United States' official position is the United States itself. The halls of the United States Time Service at the USNO do not leave the impression of being the seat of a great empire of time or even a place of great influence. The offices are modest, the displays are unkempt, the coffee is terrible, and the cleaning services are no longer funded for the guest house for visiting scientists. There is clearly investment in the atomic timekeepers, but that is constrained and channeled by byzantine rules cooked up by the U.S. Congress. A tour of the facility leaves one with an impression of Spartan quarters and immense creativity in finding ways to get things done. It does not feel like a seat of power or prestige—it feels like a university setting. The so-called time lords are not lords at all, but colleagues with stated motivations related to research and scholarship. Their position is structurally awkward. On the one hand, they are funded by those involved in the politics and policies of nation-states that are often shaped by those who have little interest in the technology. On the other hand, they are part of supranational cooperative and often collegial networks that manage the rhizomatic technologies and standards that make the global reach of nation-states possible.

So, on the one hand, tracing time from one's clocks to the source leaves an impression of a dystopic world in which one's every move is charted; seeing one of the sources of time leaves the impression of a dystopic world in which science is seen as an inconvenient but necessary expense. The current importance of GPS to global timekeeping is a result of the United States eclipsing the United Kingdom and France—though the European Union is striving to get its own satellite navigational system, Galileo, up and running in order to compete with GPS. But the United States, as reliant as it is on computer technology and big data management, cannot control the IEEE nor the ITU-R, and the ITU-R seems set up to delay if not prevent change. The next set of standards in the empire of time might not be from a nation-state or a UN agency, but from a dominant information technology company, such as Google or Apple, or a global company with strengths in application programming interfaces that allow data to move between different systems such as Oracle or Booz Allen Hamilton. As Stoler and McGranahan point out, in modern imperial formations, the "policies, personnel, and practices of multinational corporations and globalization technologies" become "entangled and embedded" with nation-state projects.[39] The work of the USNO is critical to the functioning of a military satellite system that is now used by civilian institutions such as the IEEE to create standards that business rely upon. As a result of this mixture of business, politics, and technology of both the private and public sector, nobody is completely in charge of determining the policies that govern time. With regard to managing time technology, synchronizing clocks, and distributing time, the technical expertise goes largely unnoticed by government leaders, and it is probably more reliable and stable because of this lack of attention.

The tendency in social science is to challenge and criticize imperialism. For instance, Catherine Lutz argues for "more explicit attention to and potentially revelatory insights into how the US empire operates and how lives might be different if imperialism were identified and challenged more effectively."[40] To do this, one must avoid the common trap of essentializing global institutions and eliding the material conditions on which these institutions rely. Avoiding the technological and material infrastructure that imperial practices create and on which they rely maintains the artificial divide between politics and science. Criticisms of the politics are made easier if one ignores the extent to which the ability to criticize depends on the same technological infrastructure developed by imperial practices. When empire is approached from a starting position of the science it supports and needs, rather than the military and diplomatic agendas it pursues, the picture is far messier. In this domain, scientific practice elides the politics at work and on which the scientific practice depends for funding and support. Instead, the science engages in a democratizing discourse of uniformity, access, and availability. This democratizing impulse fosters the rhizomatic aspects of the technology even as it generates stratification based on the cost of participation in the coordinated standard and the cost of access to precision timekeeping. Life without this rhizomatic empire is life without the Internet, networked computing, smartphones, and GPS. The new form of empire makes it much more difficult to imagine life without that empire, and instead of being subject to imperial control, the nature of imperial influence is more about complicity in being coordinated.

NOTES

1 Hardt and Negri, *Empire.*

2 Duara, "The Imperialism of 'Free Nations.'"

3 NAVSTAR GPS Joint Program Office, NAVSTAR GPS *User Equipment Introduction,* 1996, accessed August 25, 2014, http://www.navcen.uscg.gov/pubs/gps/gpsuser/gpsuser.pdf.

4 S. Stern, *Calendars in Antiquity.*

5 Birth, *Objects of Time.*

6 Allison Loconto and Lawrence Busch, "Standards, Techno-Economic Networks, and Playing Fields," 509.

7 Frost, "Standards and the Citizen."

8 Busch and Bingen, "Introduction."

9 Beard, "The Role of the ITU-R in Time Scale Definition and Dissemination."

10 Quinn, *From Artefacts to Atoms,* 316.

11 See Chadsey and McCarthy, "Relating Time to the Earth's Variable Rotation," 241.

12 Castells, *The Rise of the Network Society*; Harvey, *The Condition of Postmodernity* and "Between Space and Time"; Birth, "Time and the Biological Consequences of Globalization."

13 See Sassen, *Globalization and Its Discontents.*

14 Latour, *We Have Never Been Modern.*

15 See Deleuze and Guattari, *A Thousand Plateaus.*

16 Prucha, "Online Territories of Terror."

17 Mills, *Computer Network Time Synchronization,* 37–72.

18 Newcomb, *Astronomical Papers Prepared for the Use of the American Ephemeris and Nautical Almanac.*

19 CIPM, *Procès-verbaux des séances,* 77.

20 Danjon, "Le temps, sa definition pratique, sa mesure."

21 Clemence, "On the System of Astronomical Constants" and "On Revising the Official System of Astronomical Constants."

22 Clemence, "The Concept of Ephemeris Time."

23 Essen and Parry, "An Atomic Standard of Frequency and Time Interval."
24 Markowitz et al., "Frequency of Cesium in Terms of Ephemeris Time."
25 CGPM, "Resolution 1."
26 Bartky, *Selling the True Time.*
27 McCarthy and Seidelmann, *Time*, 227.
28 Carnoy and Castells, "Globalization, the Knowledge Society, and the Network State," 11.
29 Carnoy and Castells, "Globalization, the Knowledge Society, and the Network State," 17.
30 Loconto and Busch, *Standards.*
31 Chadsey and McCarthy, *Relating Time*; McCarthy and Klepczynski, "GPS and Leap Seconds"; Nelson et al., "The Leap Second."
32 Parker and Matsakis, "Time and Frequency Dissemination."
33 Nasdaq TotalView-ITCH 4.1, 2014, accessed August 27, 2014, http://www.nasdaqtrader.com/content/technicalsupport/specifications/dataproducts/NQTV-ITCH-V4_1.pdf.
34 H. Stern, "Time, Timestamps, and Timescales," 262.
35 Seago and Storz, "UTC Redefinition and Space and Satellite-Tracking Systems."
36 Swinford, "Greenwich Mean Time Could Drift to the US, Minister Warns."
37 Finkleman, Seago, and Seidelmann, "The Debate over UTC and Leap Seconds."
38 Chunhao, "Space Odyssey."
39 Stoler and McGranahan, "Introduction," 16.
40 Lutz, "Empire Is in the Details," 598.

IV Military Promises

12 Islands of Imperialism

Military Bases and the Ethnography of U.S. Empire

DAVID VINE

In the late 1950s, officials in the U.S. national security bureaucracy started growing increasingly concerned that they were losing control of the world. Despite the unparalleled power of the United States at the end of World War II, the country's relative supremacy had started to decline. The Soviet Union had acquired its own nuclear arsenal and become another global superpower. China was emerging as a regional competitor. With the decolonization movement gaining momentum, Britain, France, and other Western nations were giving up their colonial possessions. In the East-West confrontation of the Cold War, the alignment of newly independent nations was up for grabs. With the United States allied with most of the former colonial rulers, a perception was building that many of the new nations—and the world—were tilting toward the East. Although the erosion of U.S. power and influence was less significant in reality than it was in perception (U.S. military and economic power remained unparalleled), this made little difference to U.S. officials.

"Virtually all of Africa, and certain Middle Eastern and Far Eastern territories presently under Western control," navy planner Stuart Barber predicted, would soon "drift from Western influence." The inevitable result, Barber told his superiors in 1958, would be "the withdrawal . . . denial or restriction" of U.S. and Western military forces across a wide swath of an increasingly unstable globe. The ability of the United States to use its military to influence global events would decline accordingly.[1]

Barber's response to such fears was what he called the "Strategic Island Concept." A naval intelligence officer during World War II, "Stu" Barber had seen the critical role hundreds of small Pacific island military bases played in defeating Japan. The U.S. Navy ought to have more such island bases, Barber told navy admirals. Island bases near hotspots in the so-called Third World, he argued, would increase the nation's ability to rapidly deploy military force wherever and whenever officials pleased. Island bases would help maintain U.S. dominance for decades to come. But to ensure the military had access to such bases, it would have to gain control over as many islands as possible as quickly as possible before they were lost to decolonization forever.

Barber started to "scan all the charts to see what useful islands there might be," he later recounted. After considering hundreds of possibilities from the Galapagos in the Atlantic to the Marshalls in the Pacific, Barber looked to the Indian Ocean, where he found "that beautiful atoll of Diego Garcia, right in the middle of the ocean."[2]

The only problem, Barber believed, was that any targeted island would have to be "free of impingement on any significant indigenous population or economic interest." Barber was pleased to note that Diego Garcia's population was "measured only in the hundreds."[3]

More than half a century after Barber drafted his Strategic Island Concept, Diego Garcia is a multibillion-dollar U.S. air and naval base and one of the most significant bases in the world. Located nearly 6,000 miles closer to the Persian Gulf than the east coast of the United States, British-controlled Diego Garcia has been a major, if little known, launchpad for the wars in Iraq and Afghanistan. Long off limits to nonmilitary personnel, the island has been a secret CIA "black site," part of the CIA's "extraordinary rendition" program that has involved the extrajudicial transportation, interrogation, and torture of captured terrorist suspects. Prior to the establishment of the prison at Guantánamo, U.S. officials considered Diego Garcia as an alternate location. And for more than three decades, the base has been a centerpiece of U.S. attempts to control Middle Eastern oil and natural gas supplies.

Meanwhile, the people Barber described as numbering "only in the hundreds" (in fact, they numbered 1,500 to 2,000) have been living in exile for more than forty years. Between 1968 and 1973, the U.S. and British governments forcibly removed Diego Garcia's indigenous people—the Chagossians—and dumped them in impoverished exile in the western Indian Ocean islands of Mauritius and the Seychelles. Today, the military calls Diego Garcia the "Footprint of Freedom"—with no sense of the irony the name entails for the Chagossians.

Elsewhere, I have detailed the history of Chagossians' expulsion, their experiences in exile, and the people's struggle to return home and win proper compensation. While, I think it critical to explore and document the effects of empire at the same time as one explores how empires exert their power, for reasons of space, this chapter will focus on the latter.

Examining the history of Diego Garcia, this chapter aims to offer insights into the nature of the United States as an empire and the role of overseas bases in that empire.[4] U.S. Americans have long had trouble seeing their nation as an empire of any kind, given its powerful founding ideologies of democracy and freedom.[5] Many have thought that if the country was ever an empire, it was only briefly, and perhaps absentmindedly, around the Spanish-American War of 1898 and the acquisition of the Philippines, Puerto Rico, and Guam. (Many of the founders had little trouble reconciling imperial and democratic visions of the nation: George Washington referred to the United States as a "rising Empire.")[6]

For decades, revisionist historians and other leftist scholars have generally held that the United States has long been an empire. According to these scholars, following the conquests of 1898, the United States largely became a new kind of empire, an empire of economics, symbolized by "Open Door" trade policies initiated in China after the Boxer Rebellion.[7] Such scholars argue that the nation largely avoided the colonialism of the European powers based on territorial expansion and direct rule over subject peoples in favor of a more discreet, nonterritorial kind of economic imperialism. Economic control and exploitation, they say, have largely emanated from policies such as the "Open Door" in China and, later, the IMF and the World Bank. "The best-preferred strategy," says Neil Smith, "was to organize resource and commodity extraction through the market rather than through military or political occupation."[8] The use of state power to open up markets became the basis for continued imperialism.[9]

While I agree with the revisionists that the postwar period has been defined to a significant degree by economic forms of imperialism, I contend that the history of Diego Garcia shows how this understanding of U.S. empire is incomplete.[10] Here I follow a smaller group of scholars who emphasize military not economic might as the defining element of U.S. empire.[11] Several focus on the role of military bases, such as Diego Garcia. They argue that the United States has become an "empire of bases"—now numbering around 1,000—deploying military facilities globally, rather than colonizing foreign lands, to exert imperial control over weaker nations.[12] Today the United States controls around 95 percent of the world's foreign bases, thus possessing more bases than any nation, empire, or people in world history.[13]

The history of Diego Garcia and the "Strategic Island Concept" help demonstrate the importance of overseas bases to post–World War II U.S. power strategies and U.S. attempts to exert imperial control over much of the rest of the world. Overseas bases have long been a critical, but often overlooked, tool to launch wars and interventions, maintain systems of alliances, keep other nations in subordinate relationships, and maintain a global political-economic-military order to the perceived benefit of the United States and its elites.

Contrary to those who hold that the United States became an empire of economics in the twentieth century, Diego Garcia and island bases more broadly help demonstrate the U.S. empire's ongoing and underestimated reliance on conventional imperial tools of military bases and military force to maintain global dominance. This chapter does not seek to refute the empire of economics thesis but instead to rebalance perspectives on U.S. empire, showing how bases and military force have worked in tandem with economic and political tools of empire.

A TWO-PRONGED ETHNOGRAPHY OF EMPIRE

My work about Diego Garcia began in August 2001, when lawyers representing the Chagossians in lawsuits against the U.S. and U.K. governments invited me to conduct research about the people and the effects of the expulsion on their lives.[14] Concerned about focusing on the Chagossians' suffering alone,[15] I expanded my work to ask why and how the U.S. government created the base and exiled the people.

These kinds of questions quickly led me to a consideration of the United States as an empire, despite the general inattention to the issue among anthropologists.[16] I sought to contribute to Catherine Lutz's call for producing "ethnographies of empire" as a way to ethnographically explore the particularities, practices, shifts, and contradictions in empire, as well as its costs.[17] This chapter (and other work) is an attempt to use an ethnographic investigation of empire to build theory about the phenomenon. In so doing, I follow Lutz in challenging the false opposition of *theory* and *ethnography*, recognizing "their joint construction and application to the shifting complexities of empire's shifting forms."[18] I pursue this strategy echoing Lutz's concern about the white male domination of theorizing empire (and theory more broadly), especially given my unfortunate perpetuation of this raced and gendered phenomenon and my relative inattention here to race/ethnicity and gender (though not in my other work).[19]

Many anthropological analyses have long tended to treat large-scale forces and entities that shape and structure people's lives—the state, empire, the U.S. government—as abstract givens, without subjecting them to detailed analysis.[20] To say, as many do, that structural forces shape lives, constrain agency, or create suffering is one thing, but to demonstrate how these things happen is another. This chapter attempts then to subject extralocal forces to ethnographic investigation.[21] It also seeks to realize and expand upon a model for understanding widespread suffering developed by Paul Farmer.[22] Farmer's model argues that suffering is "structured by historically given (and often economically driven) processes and forces that conspire . . . to constrain agency" for those upon whom suffering is inflicted.[23] The task then is to detail what the historically given, economically (and politically) driven processes and forces are, how they operate, and how they shape people's lives. As Michael Burawoy suggests, "forces"—in this case, U.S. imperialism—"become the topic of investigation."[24]

To start, it helps to acknowledge that forces are people too. That is to say, forces are not merely abstract entities larger than any individual; forces are composed of and shaped by specific and identifiable actors—often powerful corporate, government, and military elites. Thus, Farmer's model demands an analysis that is "geographically broad," investigating how "the actions of the powerful" often shape the suffering of those far away.[25] Convinced about the importance of studying the powerful,[26] I sought to pursue an ethnography of empire that would devote the same anthropological attention to the U.S. government officials responsible for the Chagossians' expulsion and the development of the base on Diego Garcia as to the lives of the Chagossians whose lives U.S. officials shaped. I thus coupled my ethnographic research with the Chagossians (seven months in 2001–4, follow-up research in 2008–9) with ethnographic research focused on mostly former government officials (seven months in 2004–5, follow-up research in 2005–8). In total, I conducted more than thirty in-depth semistructured interviews with former and current U.S. government officials from the U.S. Navy, the U.S. departments of Defense and State, and the U.S. Congress, as well as with journalists, academics, and military analysts, among others. Unfortunately, I was unable to speak with some of the highest-ranking officials involved. Some were dead. Some did not respond to repeated interview requests. Some, such as former secretary of defense Robert McNamara, said they had no memory of the events involved.

Given these limitations, I balanced my interviews with an analysis of thousands of pages of government documents uncovered in the U.S. National Archives, the U.S. Navy archives, the Kennedy and Johnson presidential libraries, the British Public Records Office, and the files of the U.S. and British lawyers representing the Chagossians.

The aim with U.S. government officials in particular was not to demonize or blame those responsible for the base and the expulsion. Instead, the aim was to empathetically understand actors' involvement within the context in which they were living, while identifying processes and practices that shaped their actions. Although forces are people too, the people who shape such forces are themselves, of course, shaped by forces beyond their control.

At the same time, this kind of corrective would go too far to focus, like many traditional foreign policy scholars, on the actors and structural dynamics of imperialism while ignoring empire's costs. So too, it would be a mistake to focus on how the actors and forces of imperialism have shaped the Chagossians' lives without accounting for the people's resistance to empire and their individual and collective agency, however constrained. Indeed, Chagossians' more than forty-year struggle against the U.S. and British governments to return to Chagos forces us to see that the relationship between the U.S. empire and a tiny group of islanders is more of a two-way relationship than one might expect.

Inspired by similarly structured work,[27] I pursued a bifocal ethnography offering roughly equal ethnographic study of the Chagossians and U.S. empire and grounded in structural political-economic, historical analysis. My work attempts to do justice anthropologically to both sides of Diego Garcia, both sides of U.S. empire. Ultimately, the aim is to bring the two sides "into the same frame of study," and "posit their relationships on the basis of first-hand ethnographic research,"[28] though in this chapter my focus is firmly on the U.S. government side of the relationship.

AN "EMPIRE OF BASES"

Ever since the United States gained its independence from Britain, bases abroad have played a key, if forgotten, role in the country's history. From the late eighteenth to the end of the nineteenth century, more than 250 Army forts located in Indian lands—which was then *abroad*—helped enable the seizure of Indian territory and the expansion of the original thirteen states into foreign territory across North America.[29] After defeating what remained of the Spanish empire in 1898, the rising "American Empire" began building bases in the Philippines, Puerto Rico, Guam, and Guantánamo Bay. During the first three decades of the twentieth century, the military created new bases during repeated invasions and occupations of Latin American countries such as Nicaragua, Panama, and the Dominican Republic, as well as in Europe during World War I. Almost without exception, however, the military closed these bases at war's end.

The vast majority of today's collection of bases was built or occupied during World War II. First, President Roosevelt's "destroyers for bases" deal provided U.S. access to installations in British colonies such as Jamaica, Trinidad, and the Bahamas. Later in the war, the military had bases on every continent except Antarctica (after the war, there would be a base there too). They were found in places such as Mexico and Brazil, Burma and India, Portugal, Iceland, and Greenland, and on a string of small islands in the Pacific Ocean that were critical to the war against Japan. By war's end, the U.S. military was building base facilities at a rate of 112 a month.[30] The global total topped 30,000 installations at over 2,000 sites.[31] In only five years, the United States developed history's first truly global network of bases, vastly outstretching that of the British empire.

After the war, the military returned about half these bases but maintained what a former Pentagon base expert calls a "permanent institution" of bases abroad. During the Cold War, the number of bases fluctuated, spiking during the wars in Korea and Vietnam and declining in their wake.[32] By the Cold War's end, around 300,000 U.S. troops were permanently stationed in Europe alone.[33] Although the military vacated around 60 percent of its foreign bases following the Soviet Union's collapse,[34] the base infrastructure stayed relatively intact: Around 60,000 troops remain in Europe despite the absence of a superpower adversary. Globally, the United States now possesses around 800 military bases outside the fifty states and Washington, DC.[35] According to Department of Defense statistics, the United States still maintains 174 base sites in Germany, 113 in Japan, and 83 in South Korea well over half a century since the end of World War II and the Korean War.[36] Other bases are scattered around the globe in places such as Ascension and Australia, Bahrain and Bulgaria, Colombia, Kyrgyzstan, and Qatar—just to name a few. In Afghanistan and Iraq, bases in the two countries once totaled 550 and 505 respectively.[37] While there have been reductions in the number of overseas bases since the end of the Cold War, especially in Germany and elsewhere in Europe, new base construction continues around the globe (including in Germany).

In total, the U.S. military now has bases in approximately 80 countries and territories and troops in about 160 foreign countries and territories, not to mention its collection of aircraft carriers—floating bases—and a significant, and growing, military presence in space. Elsewhere, I have conservatively estimated that the United States spends $156 billion every year maintaining bases and military personnel overseas.[38]

"EXCLUSIVE CONTROL (WITHOUT LOCAL INHABITANTS)"

The fear of losing overseas bases was a significant source of anxiety for officials such as Stuart Barber in the late 1950s and early 1960s. Amid post–World War II decolonization, opposition to the occupation of land by foreign military facilities grew. Facing the loss of U.S. bases abroad and access to British and French bases in their former colonies, U.S. officials grew concerned about waning U.S. influence over regions bounding the Indian Ocean, from Southern Africa through the Middle East, South Asia, and Southeast Asia. Part of the concern, but only part at the time, stemmed from a growing interest in ensuring the flow of Persian Gulf oil to the U.S. and global economies.

The Strategic Island Concept's search for strategically located, remote island bases was Barber's answer to these perceived threats.[39] The United States would ensure unfettered base access by avoiding a reliance on mainland bases that likely would face protest, restricted use, and possible eviction. "Only relatively small, lightly populated islands, separated from major population masses, could be safely held under full control of the West," Barber said.[40]

If the United States was going to protect its "future freedom of military action," officials would have to act quickly to "stockpile" island basing rights. Just as any sensible investor would "stockpile any material commodity which foreseeably will become unavailable in the future," the United States would have to buy up small colonial islands around the world or otherwise ensure its Western allies maintained sovereignty over them. Otherwise the islands would be lost to decolonization forever.[41]

Others in the national security bureaucracy quickly embraced Barber's idea. In 1960, the navy settled on Diego Garcia as its most important island acquisition target. As Barber had seen, the small V-shaped island was blessed with a central location within striking distance of potential conflict zones, one of the world's great natural harbors in its protected lagoon, and enough land to build a large airstrip.

The U.S. Navy's highest-ranking officer, Chief of Naval Operations Admiral Arleigh Burke, initiated secret conversations with the British government about the island. British officials were immediately receptive to the idea. By 1963, the proposal to create a base on Diego Garcia had gained support among powerful officials in the Kennedy administration, including the Joint Chiefs of Staff, the Pentagon of Robert McNamara and Paul Nitze, Dean Rusk's State Department, and the National Security Council (NSC) of McGeorge Bundy.

Prodded in particular by the NSC's Robert Komer, the administration initiated formal negotiations with the British and, led by the State Department's Jeffery Kitchen, convinced the United Kingdom to detach the Chagos Archipelago from colonial Mauritius and other islands from colonial Seychelles to create a new colony solely for military use. They called it the British Indian Ocean Territory (BIOT). During secret 1964 talks in London, Kitchen and other State and Defense Department representatives insisted on an additional condition for the islands (embedded within a parenthetical phrase): That the United States would get "exclusive control (without local inhabitants)."[42] British officials agreed to the condition and to carry out the necessary deportations.

When the *Washington Post* and the *Economist* threatened to break news about the plans, the State Department pressured them to hold the story. The articles eventually ran months delayed. One day before publication, the author of the *Washington Post*'s story was called to the U.S. embassy in London.

His article would describe the population of Diego Garcia as consisting "largely of transient laborers," most of whom were "understood to have left."[43]

In 1965, in contravention of international agreements forbidding the division of colonies during decolonization, the British government paid Mauritius three million pounds to detach Chagos (a dependency of Mauritius since its settlement in the eighteenth century) and agreed to build an international airport for colonial Seychelles in exchange for its islands. A British official described the compensation as "bribes" to ensure both colonies would quietly acquiesce to the plan.[44]

A year later, the U.S. and British governments confirmed the arrangements with a little-noticed "Exchange of Notes." The Notes effectively constituted a treaty, but unlike a treaty, they required no congressional or parliamentary approval—allowing both governments to keep the plans hidden from their legislatures. Representatives for the two governments signed the agreement, as one State Department negotiator told me, "under the cover of darkness," the day before New Year's Eve, 1966.

According to the Notes, the United States would gain use of the new colony "without charge."[45] In confidential agreements accompanying the Notes, however, the United States agreed to secretly transfer U.S. $14 million dollars to Britain. Secretary of Defense Robert McNamara had approved the transfer of funds a year earlier, which circumvented the congressional appropriations process. The money was, as other secret documents show, to be used to establish the territory, to pay off Mauritius and the Seychelles "generously" to avoid "agitation in the colonies."[46] It would also serve to take those "administrative measures" necessary to remove the islands' inhabitants.[47]

"ABSOLUTELY MUST GO"

The islands' inhabitants, the Chagossians, and their ancestors had lived in Diego Garcia and the rest of the previously uninhabited Chagos Archipelago since the late eighteenth century, when Franco-Mauritians created coconut plantations on the islands and imported enslaved and, later, indentured laborers from Africa and India. Over the next two centuries, this diverse workforce developed into a distinct, emancipated society and a people known initially as the Ilois (the Islanders). By the 1960s, Chagossians lived in what remained a plantation society, which was far from luxurious but provided a secure life, generally free of want, and featuring universal employment and numerous social benefits, including regular if small salaries, land, free housing, education, pensions, burial services, and basic health care in islands described by many as "idyllic."

The Chagossians' expulsion unfolded in stages beginning in 1968. First, any Chagossians who left Chagos for medical treatment or for regular vacations in Mauritius were told that they could not return. Often they were marooned without family members and almost all their possessions. Next, the British began restricting supplies to Chagos, and by the turn of the decade more Chagossians were leaving as food and medicines dwindled. British authorities meanwhile designed a public relations plan that would, as Foreign Office legal adviser Anthony Aust proposed, "maintain the fiction that the inhabitants of Chagos are not a permanent or semi-permanent population."[48]

"We are able to make up the rules as we go along," Aust wrote. Anglo-American officials would simply represent the Chagossians as "transient contract workers" with no connection to the islands (continuing the line likely fed to the *Washington Post*).[49] Another Foreign Office official, D. A. Greenhill, was even more blunt in internal documents, when he called the Chagossians "some few Tarzans or Men Fridays."[50]

In November 1970, after facing some resistance to the plan within the Pentagon and on Capitol Hill (almost entirely on financial grounds), the navy, backed by its former secretary and then deputy secretary of defense Paul Nitze, won its first (classified) construction funds from Congress. In briefing chapters delivered to Congress, the navy described Diego Garcia's population as "negligible. . . . For all practical purposes . . . uninhabited."[51]

In early 1971, the navy began construction on Diego Garcia and ordered the British to complete the removals. When some U.S. Navy officers raised concerns about removing the people, the navy's highest-ranking admiral, Elmo Zumwalt, sent a three-word reply: "Absolutely must go."[52]

And so, British agents, with the help of U.S. Navy personnel, herded the Chagossians' pet dogs into sealed sheds and gassed and burned them in front of their traumatized owners awaiting deportation. Between 1971 and 1973, British agents forced the remaining islanders to board overcrowded cargo ships and left them on the docks in Mauritius and the Seychelles. In the Seychelles, the refugees initially had to sleep in a former prison.

In exile, the Chagossians received no resettlement assistance and quickly became impoverished. In 1975, the *Washington Post* exposed the story of the Chagossians' expulsion for the first time in the Western press, describing the people as living in "abject poverty."[53] Five and ten years after the last deportations, the people received small amounts of British compensation. It totaled less than six thousand dollars per recipient. Some Chagossians, including all those in the Seychelles, received nothing. Numbering between five and ten thousand today, including those born in exile, most Chagossians remain impoverished. Most live as marginalized outsiders, still struggling to win proper compensation and the right of return.[54]

The Strategic Island Concept revolved around a dream of strategically located, *people-less* bases. At the Concept's core was a realization that despite overseas bases' advantages, they involve significant risks in the form of protest, the imposition of operational restrictions by host governments, and, ultimately, eviction from strategic locations where large sums of money have been invested.

The Strategic Island Concept proposed avoiding these risks and protecting the United States' dominant position in the world by removing local peoples and postcolonial governments from the base equation. This meant finding remote and, in officials' eyes, insignificant islands where, with little attention, a small group of locals could be removed and where the United States could retain territorial sovereignty in perpetuity, either by purchase or by ensuring the maintenance of sovereignty by its closest Western allies. Officials would prepare the islands for base construction as future needs required.[55]

With the Chagossians removed, military planners were thrilled at the idea of a base with no civilian population within almost five hundred miles. The U.S. officials and their British counterparts wanted total, permanent control over Diego Garcia and the entire Chagos Archipelago without the possibility of outside interference or eviction by either foreign politicians or a population claiming rights to self-determination. Diego Garcia was attractive precisely because it was not subject to, as one navy officer explained, "political restrictions of the type that had shackled or even terminated flexibility at foreign bases elsewhere."[56]

A Foreign Office brief emphasized the importance of being able "to clear [Diego Garcia] of its current population. The Americans in particular attached great importance to this freedom of manoeuvre, divorced from the normal considerations applying to a populated dependent territory." The Foreign Office explained that U.S. officials "implied . . . we could not accept that the interests of the inhabitants were paramount and that we should develop self-government there."[57] The priorities of the U.S. and U.K. governments were clear: (1) Maintenance of complete political and military control over the islands, (2) the unfettered ability to remove any island populations by force, and (3) disregard for local inhabitants' international rights.

Given the "special relationship" between the United States and the United Kingdom, the U.S. military would have near *carte blanche* (pun intended given the racism underlying the plan) on the island. With any British role reduced to a few token functionaries and the right to be consulted before major U.S. deployment shifts, Diego Garcia is definitively a U.S. base and practically a U.S. territory (today, cars drive on the right side of the road).

Diego Garcia thus had all the advantages and almost none of the disadvantages of an overseas military base in the eyes of military and diplomatic officials. It had all the advantages as a relatively surreptitious way to exercise U.S. power and was controlled, as one naval officer explained, by "a longstanding ally (the United Kingdom) unlikely to toss [the United States] out for governmental changes or US foreign policy initiatives."[58] Even more, in the British government, the U.S. government had a partner willing to ignore international law and human rights guarantees by removing an indigenous population from their homes.[59] The British would do the dirty work of the expulsion. They would dispose of the population. For just fourteen million dollars, the United States would always have the legal and political alibi that Great Britain is the sovereign and is thus ultimately responsible for any island inhabitants.

With the population successfully exiled, the U.S. government had (and still has) what is almost the perfect base: strategically located, free of any potentially troublesome population, under de facto U.S. control yet with its closest ally as sovereign to take any political heat, and almost no restrictions on use of the island, save periodically consulting with the British. Free reign over an idyllic and strategically located atoll in the Indian Ocean—it's no wonder navy personnel call it "Fantasy Island."[60]

DIEGO GARCIA EXPANDS

The history of Diego Garcia shows that much of the national security bureaucracy adopted the navy's concept as an important strategic framework. At the request of the Joint Chiefs of Staff, the navy made plans for scores of strategic island bases around the globe. In the Indian Ocean, the idea was the basis for the creation of the BIOT and an initially planned "strategic triangle" of bases on Diego Garcia, the Seychelles' island Aldabra, and Australia's Cocos/Keeling Islands. Although the costs of the Vietnam War reined in the most far-reaching plans and left Diego Garcia as the only major base formally created under the Strategic Island Concept, the strategy became an important argument for the retention and expansion of major preexisting island bases, including those in Guam, Micronesia, Hawai'i, Ascension, Bahrain, the Azores, Okinawa, and Japan's Ogasawara Islands.[61]

In the Indian Ocean, U.S. officials coupled Diego Garcia with the first-ever buildup of U.S. naval forces in the region. Over time, the base and naval deployments increasingly enabled the insertion of military power into a large and unstable portion of the world. Fearing an unknowable and threatening future in the "Third World," and increasingly in the Persian Gulf and Southwest

Asia, officials crafted a plan for Diego Garcia to control the future through military force.

Far from being a geopolitical strategy alone, however, the intent was always political, military, and economic: Diego Garcia allowed what strategists euphemistically call "intervention" and the threat of intervention in the affairs of other nations but also helped protect U.S. business interests in the region. Initially, protecting U.S. access to Middle Eastern oil was just one of several motivations behind the military buildup. Within just a few years of the base becoming operational, however, oil was at the heart of Diego Garcia's raison d'être.

After the Iranian revolution and the Soviet invasion of Afghanistan in 1979, the base was at the center of the first large-scale thrust of U.S. military strength into the region. To respond to any future threats to the oil supply, Presidents Carter and Reagan developed a "Rapid Deployment Force" at bases in the region, including a rapidly enlarging Diego Garcia.[62] The base enjoyed the "most dramatic build-up of any location since the Vietnam War," with more than $500 million invested by 1986.[63] By now the total runs into the billions. The Rapid Deployment Force later became known as the U.S. Central Command, which has led the wars in Iraq and Afghanistan. In this evolution of Diego Garcia's role, the base's significance grows as one of the first steps by the United States to use overt military power in and around Southwest Asia to defend U.S. oil supplies (the establishment of a small naval force in Bahrain in 1949 was an important, though largely symbolic, forerunner).

Diego Garcia saw its first significant wartime use only during the first Gulf War, after the Cold War's end. Since the fall of the Soviet Union, the base has become a pivot point of U.S. strategy for the control of areas from the Southwest to East Asia. Prior to September 11, 2001, and the subsequent wars in Afghanistan and Iraq, the U.S. military was in the process of turning Diego into one of four major "forward operating locations" for "expeditionary" air force operations and a recipient of an eastward shift of materiel and weaponry from Cold War European bases. "It's the single most important military facility we've got," respected Washington-area military expert John Pike told me in an interview in 2004. Pike, who runs the website GlobalSecurity.org, explained, "It's the base from which we control half of Africa and the southern side of Asia, the southern side of Eurasia." It's "the facility that at the end of the day gives us some say-so in the Persian Gulf region." The dream for many in the military is, as Pike explained, "to run the planet from Guam and Diego Garcia by 2015, even if the entire Eastern Hemisphere has dropped kicked us" from bases on their territory.

Diego Garcia shows how the wars in Iraq and Afghanistan are, in important ways, the fulfillment of a strategic vision for controlling a large swath of Asia and, with it, the global economy. This dates from at least World War II, and has been advanced significantly by the establishment of the Indian Ocean base. As others have shown, the wars have significantly advanced the pursuit (if not the reality) of U.S. control over Persian Gulf and Central Asian oil and natural gas supplies—and with them, the global economy—through the presence of hundreds of thousands of U.S. troops and private military contractors and the creation or expansion of bases in at least Afghanistan, Iraq, Bahrain, Qatar, Kuwait, Oman, the United Arab Emirates, Jordan, Djibouti, Pakistan, and, until their closure, in Kyrgyzstan and Uzbekistan.[64]

The strategic logic of Diego Garcia, of using bases to control resource-rich regions, becomes even clearer when one considers reports that the United States has explored plans to develop a new base off the oil-rich west coast of Africa, in the Gulf of Guinea, on one of the islands of São Tomé and Príncipe.[65] Without the freedom to create new large bases in Africa given the opposition they would likely generate, the Pentagon is using a growing collection of small, often surreptitious bases on the continent in an attempt to control another crucial oil-rich region amid growing competition, in Africa and globally, from China, Russia, and the European Union. At least one U.S. official has described the proposed base on São Tomé as "another Diego Garcia." Much as with Diego Garcia, U.S. officials have denied having any interest in a base on São Tomé.[66]

A NEW FORM OF EMPIRE

Contrary to those who stress U.S. empire's reliance on economic tools, Diego Garcia and the Strategic Island Concept represent a reliance on traditional imperial tools of overseas bases and military power to maintain U.S. dominance. Clearly, Diego Garcia and the Strategic Island Concept were not the only reactions to the relative decline in U.S. power during the Cold War—there were economic, political, and other military reactions as well. But they provided part of a solution to perceived threats while simultaneously answering the challenges posed by decolonization to the exercise of power through overseas bases.

In the nineteenth century, Britain and other European powers tied their expansionist success to the direct control of foreign lands. Given the U.S.'s framing of World War II as an anticolonial struggle and its pledge to assist with decolonization upon war's end, large-scale control of foreign lands was no longer an option for the United States. After the war, the creation of the United Nations enshrined the decolonization process and the right of nations and peoples to self-determination and self-government.

"Decolonization did not mean that empires went away," writes Carole McGranahan, "but that they went underground, surfacing in guises ranging from socialist empire in the Soviet Union to various forms of neo-imperialist aggressive democracy as in the case of the United States. Yet each of these polities," she explains, "fiercely guarded itself against any accusations of empire or imperialism."[67]

Diego Garcia and the Strategic Island Concept were part of the invention of a new, more discreet form of empire, relying heavily on overseas bases and increasingly on isolated, often island bases to exert power. Responding to decolonization in particular, Diego Garcia helped usher in an ongoing shift of bases from locations near population centers to isolated locations insulated from potentially antagonistic locals. This model is now most clearly visible in the current "lily pad" basing strategy. Under the strategy, the Pentagon has been creating small, often-secretive bases that are isolated from population centers and potentially antagonistic locals, and that have as few political constraints as possible. Much as Barber initially envisioned a large stockpile of island bases, the military's aim has been to acquire as many bases as possible, in as many nations as possible, from Singapore and Poland to Honduras and Kenya.[68]

Alongside U.S. postwar economic and political power, the overseas base network became a major mechanism of U.S. imperial control that allows the control of territory vastly disproportionate to the land actually occupied. Without a collection of colonies, the United States has used what is likely the greatest collection of bases ever as well as periodic displays of military might to keep wayward nations within the rules of an economic and political system favorable to U.S. elites.[69] Indeed, it was the nation's unchallenged military superiority at the end of World War II that left it in a position to dictate much of the postwar international economic system upon which U.S. geoeconomic power is based.[70] While the total acreage occupied by bases has been relatively slight (especially compared to prior European empires), in the ability to rapidly deploy the U.S. military nearly anywhere on the globe, the basing system represents a dramatic expansion of U.S. power and a significant way in which the United States came to maintain its postwar dominance.

Specifically, bases and troops abroad have been "used to influence and limit the political, diplomatic, and economic initiatives of host nations," explains Joseph Gerson.[71] In the Philippines, for example, the United States used military and economic aid and defense promises to extract not only decades' worth of base access but favorable terms of trade and political influence as well.[72] With "a chain of military bases and staging areas around the globe," the United States developed "a means of deploying air and naval forces to be used on a moment's notice—all in the interest of maintaining . . . its political and economic hegemony."[73] "Global economic access without colonies" was the postwar strategy, explains geographer Neil Smith, "matched by a strategic vision of necessary bases around the globe both to protect global economic interests and to restrain any future military belligerence."[74]

To be clear, I agree with those who say that since the twentieth century, the U.S. empire has been characterized to a significant degree by economic forms of imperialism, such as the use of the World Bank, IMF, and World Trade Organization, to open and dominate markets and maintain other countries in subordinated relationships. The history of Diego Garcia illustrates how the U.S. empire has relied in important ways on the continued use of military force and on increasingly discreet overseas bases in particular to maintain its dominance. This is not to deny the significance of economics to U.S. empire, only to shift the balance toward the relatively underexplored military dimensions. In sum, Diego Garcia suggests a more balanced perspective on U.S. empire, highlighting how overseas bases, along with other military tools, have worked in tandem with and undergirded economic forms of power.

OF OCEANS AND EMPIRE: RETHINKING TERRITORIAL CONTROL

Viewed geographically, one sees how the small-scale acquisition of territory for island bases has allowed the United States to dominate large swaths of *ocean territory* upon which global trade and the nation's economy rely. Coupled with a powerful navy, island bases provide the force to effectively rule areas of ocean and any military or commercial traffic that might cross the seas (just as the Spanish, French, and British empires once did). At the turn of the twentieth century, the base at Guantánamo Bay, for example, owed its creation largely to U.S. leaders' interest in controlling the Caribbean and the major commercial trade route between the East Coast and the Central American isthmus, which was soon to provide passage to the Pacific. Since World War II, bases in the Pacific, from Okinawa and Japan's main islands to Guam and Pearl Harbor, have long allowed the U.S. Navy to make the ocean an "American lake." In the Atlantic, the navy enjoys unrivaled control from bases on the east coast, the naval station in Rota, Spain, and widespread access to other Atlantic port facilities. In the Mediterranean, the United States is again dominant with the help of extensive base and port facilities in Italy, Greece, and elsewhere around the sea. And in the Indian Ocean, maintaining a base on Diego Garcia—in addition to the Fifth Fleet's headquarters in Bahrain, other Persian Gulf facilities, and Camp Lemonnier in Djibouti—has helped the United States exert similar control, particularly over Middle Eastern oil traffic.

In the role that island bases and navies (including those floating bases, aircraft carriers) play in patrolling sea-lanes and protecting oceangoing commerce (including, but well beyond, oil), one sees a near literal way in which overseas bases undergird the economics of U.S. empire. Indeed, the ability of the U.S. Navy to provide unchallenged control of the Earth's major bodies of water since World War II, and thus to govern a significant proportion of global trade, has been another underappreciated pillar of U.S. empire.

The significance of the sea extends further if we begin to think of *territory* not just as the surface of the Earth covered by land but also as the surface of the Earth covered by water. Seeing the significant degree of de facto sovereignty that the United States enjoys over the world's oceans points to the further similarity (albeit a more subtle one) between the U.S. empire and the European *territorial* empires of centuries past. The same applies to U.S. dominance in the skies given the U.S. Air Force's supremacy over other air forces and the ability of U.S. intercontinental ballistic and shorter-range missiles to threaten any location on the planet with a nuclear or conventional strike. Here, technological changes have allowed the U.S. empire to exert power and influence over the entire globe in ways that were impossible prior to the jet and missile age.

Even if one disagrees that the control of oceanic or aerial territory constitutes a functional equivalent to the control exercised by prior territorial empires, it is worth remembering that the United States was in the nineteenth century, and remains today, a land-based territorial empire. Although the westward expansion of the thirteen original states and their conquest of Native American lands and peoples have long been naturalized and concealed by narratives of manifest destiny and Euro-Americans' "right" to the continent, there was obviously nothing natural about the displacement, dispossession, and death of Native Americans at the hands of the U.S. military and settlers protected by that military. These were the first stages of an empire whose territorial possessions quickly rivaled that of the largest European powers.

CONCLUSION: IMPERIAL SHIFTS, IMPERIAL CONTINUITIES

The history of Diego Garcia and of the Strategic Island Concept points to both shifts and continuities in the evolution of the U.S. empire and empire more broadly.[75] On the one hand, the extent to which imperial control has been exercised through the base network and not through colonies represents a break with previous empires. On the other hand, Diego Garcia and the base network represent several long-standing imperial trends including the persistence of territorial acquisition and displacement, the growing development of modes of informal and indirect rule, and the continued importance of a handful of remaining colonies and neocolonies hosting bases to exert dominance (e.g., Diego Garcia, Guam, Puerto Rico, Okinawa, Ascension, the Marshall Islands, and Thule, Greenland).

Other overseas bases likewise exist largely because of relationships between former European powers and their colonies. Bases acquired through lend-lease are a prime example, where the U.S. government negotiated continued occupation deals after World War II with the help of the still-ruling colonial power, Britain. The same is true for postwar French bases in Morocco (since closed). Until the 1990s (and perhaps increasingly once more), in Panama and the Philippines, the United States benefited from its own neocolonial relationships to maintain important bases near the Panama Canal and in East Asia. The maintenance of U.S. bases in these nations often represents a continuation of colonial relationships in a different form. That the existence of the base on Diego Garcia rests on the creation of Britain's last created colony, the BIOT, which was only possible with the dismemberment of the colonies of Mauritius and the Seychelles, also suggests that there is more continuity between the U.S. empire and previous versions than has been acknowledged.

Perhaps then Diego Garcia and much of the U.S. global basing network are in some ways best understood as a return to an earlier form of imperialism. The initial settlement of Diego Garcia was the result of Anglo-French imperial competition in the Indian Ocean two centuries earlier. In the eighteenth century, Britain and France competed to claim Indian Ocean islands as strategic bases to secure the lucrative spice trade with India and later to subdue the subcontinent,[76] in much the way that the United States has used Diego Garcia as a strategic hub from which to dominate the flow of global oil and gas supplies from the Persian Gulf and Central Asia.

From this perspective, the history of Diego Garcia comes full circle: the settlement of the island was the result of two European empires' efforts to claim strategic island bases as a means to dominate global trade and defeat imperial competitors; the transformation of the island into a major naval and air base was the result of a similar search by a new empire two centuries later.

NOTES

1 Stuart B. Barber, letter to Paul B. Ryan, April 26, 1982, 3. My thanks to Richard Barber for his help with many important details about his father's life and for providing this and other invaluable documents.

2 Barber, letter to Ryan.
3 Johnson, Memorandum for Deputy Chief of Naval Operations, 2–3.
4 The analysis in this chapter builds on Vine, *Island of Shame*, "Perspectives for a Secure World: Alternatives to NATO," and "The Lily-Pad Strategy."
5 I define *imperialism* as the creation and maintenance of hierarchical relationships of formal or informal rule, domination, or control by one people or sociopolitical entity over a significant part of the life of other peoples or sociopolitical entities such that the stronger shapes or has the ability to shape significant aspects of the ways of living (political, economic, social, or cultural) of the weaker. Empire is then the designation reserved for states and other entities practicing imperialism.
6 Lens, *Permanent War*, 18.
7 For example, Ferguson, *Colossus*; Gardner, La Feber, and McCormick, *Creation*; N. Smith, *American Empire*; Williams, *The Tragedy of American Diplomacy*.
8 N. Smith, *American Empire*, 360.
9 Harvey, *The New Imperialism*; Johnson, *The Sorrows of Empire*.
10 I use the term *U.S. empire* rather than *American empire*. Although U.S. empire may appear and sound awkward at first, it is more linguistically and geographically accurate than American empire and represents an effort to reverse the erasure of the rest of the Americas entailed in U.S. citizens' frequent substitution of *America* for the *United States of America*. My current employer's name, American University, is just one example of this pattern. The switch to U.S. empire also represents an attempt to make visible the nature of the United States as an empire and its consequences.
11 Engelhardt, "Baseless Considerations"; Johnson, *The Sorrows of Empire*; Lens, *Permanent War*; Sherry, *In the Shadows of War*; Lutz, *The Bases of Empire*.
12 See, especially, Johnson, *The Sorrows of Empire*.
13 Engelhardt, "Baseless Considerations."
14 I have never been employed by the lawyers nor paid for my work. The U.S. legal team reimbursed some of my expenses from 2001 to 2004 for research related to the Chagossians' exile.
15 See, e.g., Nader, "Up the Anthropologist."
16 For example, Asad, "Introduction"; Caulfield, "Culture and Imperialism"; Gough, "New Proposals for Anthropologists," 403, 405; Lutz, "Making War at Home in the United States," 732.
17 Lutz, "Making War at Home in the United States," 732.
18 Lutz, "Empire Is in the Details," 594.
19 For example, Vine, *Island of Shame* and "Taking on Empires," 171–91.
20 Burawoy, "Introduction."
21 Burawoy, "Introduction"; Farmer, "On Suffering and Structural Violence"; Lutz, "Making War at Home in the United States" and "Empire Is in the Details"; Roseberry, "Understanding Capitalism"; Trouillot, "The Anthropology of the State in the Age of Globalization"; Wolf, *Europe and the People without History*.
22 Farmer, "On Suffering and Structural Violence."
23 Farmer, "On Suffering and Structural Violence," 263.
24 Burawoy, "Introduction," 27–29.
25 Farmer, "On Suffering and Structural Violence," 274.

26 Despite exhortations to study imperialism and the powerful (Caulfield, "Culture and Imperialism"; Nader, "Up the Anthropologist"), most anthropologists continue to study those whose lives have suffered the impact of large-scale forces such as imperialism.

27 For example, Gill, *The School of the Americas*; Gusterson, *Nuclear Rites*; Lutz, *Homefront*. For more on my approach to the ethnography of empire and additional citations, see Vine, *Island of Shame*.

28 Marcus, *Ethnography through Thick and Thin*, 84.

29 Lutz, *The Bases of Empire*, 10.

30 Blaker, *United States Overseas Basing*, 23, 9.

31 *Monthly Review* editors, *Monthly Review*, "U.S. Military Bases and Empire," March 2002, accessed August 11, 2017, http://www.monthlyreview.org/0302editr.htm.

32 Blaker, *United States Overseas Basing*, 32; Stambuk, *American Military Forces Abroad*, 9.

33 Nelson, *Defenders or Intruders?*, 10.

34 Department of Defense, "Strengthening U.S. Global Defense Posture," 5.

35 What one counts as a "base" is complicated. I generally use the term *base*, which I take to mean a place regularly used for military purposes of any kind. The Pentagon uses the term *base site*. The estimate of 800 bases comes from the Pentagon's count of base sites in its annual "Base Structure Report" coupled with bases excluded from the list. For a fuller discussion, see Vine, *Base Nation*.

36 Department of Defense, "Base Structure Report Fiscal Year 2014 Baseline (A Summary of DoD's Real Property Inventory)," report, Washington, DC, 2014.

37 Turse, "Afghanistan's Base Bonanza: Total Tops Iraq at That War's Height."

38 See Vine, *Base Nation*.

39 I stress *perceive* because threats are a matter of subjective rather than objective assessment.

40 Rivero, "Enclosure to memorandum to Chief of Naval Operations, July 11, 1960." See also Rivero, "Enclosure to memorandum to Chief of Naval Operations, May 21, 1960."

41 Rivero, "Enclosure to memorandum to Chief of Naval Operations, July 11."

42 U.S. Embassy London, "Telegram to Secretary of State, February 27, 1964," 1–2.

43 Estabrook, "U.S., Britain Consider Indian Ocean Bases."

44 U.S. Embassy London, "Telegram to RUEHCR/Secretary of State, May 10, 1965."

45 United Kingdom of Great Britain and Northern Ireland, "Availability of Certain Indian Ocean Islands for Defense Purposes," 1–2.

46 Peck, "Defence Facilities in the Indian Ocean."

47 Chalfont, "Letter to David K. E. Bruce."

48 Aust, "Immigration Legislation for BIOT."

49 Aust, "Immigration Legislation for BIOT."

50 *Regina (on the application of Bancoult) v. Secretary of State for the Foreign and Commonwealth Office* [2006], EWHC 1038, para. 27.

51 Leddick, "Memorandum for the Record, November 11, 1969."

52 Cochrane, Jr., "Attachment to memorandum for Deputy Chief of Naval Operations," 2.

53 Ottaway, "Islanders Were Evicted for U.S. Base." See also *Washington Post*, "The Diego Garcians."
54 See, e.g., Madeley, *Diego Garcia*; Vine, *Island of Shame*. As a result of their legal and political struggle, in 2002, most Chagossians received full British citizenship, having previously been eligible for a kind of second-class citizenship along with residents of Bermuda, the Falklands (Malvinas) Islands, and other remaining British colonies.
55 See Vine, *Island of Shame*.
56 Ryan, "Diego Garcia," 133.
57 U.K. Foreign Office, "Steering Committee," para. 10–11.
58 Dunn, "Shore up the Indian Ocean," 131.
59 Expulsions and forced relocations are clearly prohibited by customary international law and a range of international and regional agreements. See Aceves, et al., "Declaration of International Law Scholars on Forced Relocation," 1, 31–32.
60 Dunn, "Shore Up the Indian Ocean."
61 U.S. officials eventually returned the Ogasawara Islands to Japanese sovereignty.
62 Bandjunis, *Diego Garcia*.
63 "Diego Garcia 'Camp Justice' 7°20'S 72°25'E," Globalsecurity.org, accessed October 15, 2017, https://www.globalsecurity.org/military/facility/diego-garcia.htm.
64 See Vine, *Base Nation*, 41–42.
65 *Monthly Review* editors, "U.S. Military Bases and Empire."
66 VOAnews.com, "São Tomé Sparks American Military Interest."
67 McGranahan, *Imperial Formations*, 180.
68 See Vine, *Base Nation*, chap. 16.
69 Johnson, "America's Empire of Bases"; Editors, "U.S. Military Bases"; Johnson, *Blowback*; N. Smith, *American Empire*.
70 Editors, "U.S. Military Bases."
71 Gerson, "The Sun Never Sets," 14; see also Editors, "U.S. Military Bases."
72 Lutz, "Empire Is in the Details."
73 Editors, "US Military Bases," 13–14; see also n11.
74 N. Smith, *American Empire*, 349, 360.
75 See also Vine, "War and Forced Migration."
76 Scott, *Limuria*.

Domesticating the U.S. Air Force 13

The Challenges of Anti-Military Activism in Manta, Ecuador

ERIN FITZ-HENRY

BECOMING "DOMESTIC IN A FOREIGN SENSE"

Between 1999 and 2009, the U.S. Air Force operated the largest forward operating location (FOL)[1] in the Western hemisphere in the bustling tuna-fishing port of Manta, Ecuador. Used principally for the monitoring of narco-trafficking along the corridors that stretch from Bolivia to the United States, for just under ten years the facility housed some two hundred U.S. military personnel and nearly twice as many civilian private military contractors employed by DynCorp. Comprising fewer than a dozen buildings and a renovated runway nestled unobtrusively within the confines of a preexisting Ecuadorian Air Force base, it served as the main hub in the southern theater for the aerial monitoring of cocaine trafficking throughout the hemisphere. However, this minimal physical infrastructure belied the facility's extensive surveillance capacities. After repeated allegations that the U.S. Air Force was using these capacities to violate Ecuadorian sovereignty by illegally sinking eight fishing vessels in territorial waters between 2000 and 2004, the facility was spectacularly evicted by the leftist-populist administration of Rafael Correa in 2009.

It is not, however, this well-documented and oft-celebrated eviction that most interests me here. By dwelling instead on the struggles among antimilitary activists, local supporters of the facility, and U.S. military personnel—struggles that both preceded and followed this eviction—my aim in this chapter is to shed light on an intensifying set of challenges faced by leftist movements in Latin America more broadly. In fact, at a time when the framing devices that have historically proven so successful in mobilizing grassroots communities are losing much of their potency to persuade, the struggles of the antimilitary movement in Ecuador are particularly illuminating. From the followers of Emiliano Zapata at the turn of the twentieth century to the adherents of the Bolivarian Revolution at the turn of the twenty-first, leftist movements in

Latin America have long articulated their struggles for social justice, agrarian reform, and demilitarization in terms of an opposition to an undeniably *foreign* influence—and most frequently, that of the United States. However, as Michael Hardt, Antonio Negri, David Graeber, and growing numbers of international relations scholars concerned with what John Ruggie has termed the *new medievalism* have recently pointed out,[2] the contemporary moment might be described as an era of intensifying global accountability gaps, unevenly scaled alliances between local NGOs and multilateral banks, a proliferating development rhetoric of multistakeholder participation, and novel forms of public-private collaboration between such hitherto antagonistic actors as conservation groups and chemical companies. It is therefore becoming exceedingly difficult to "locate the production of oppression" in the clearly bounded terms of the *foreign* and the *domestic*.[3] "We suffer exploitation, alienation, and command as enemies," Hardt and Negri observe, "but we do not know where to locate the production of oppression."[4]

Confusion about where the foreign ends and the domestic begins is not, however, as I argue in this chapter, simply an inevitable product of shifts on the global political-economic stage. Nor is it as novel as some theorists have suggested. Instead, it is an ambiguity strategically nurtured by powerful institutions such as the U.S. military that, hoping to avoid the hypervisibility and overextension of the World War II era, increasingly resorts to unmanned aircraft, drone attacks, tiny landing strips within host nation airfields, a predominantly civilian workforce, and perhaps most fundamentally, a recurrent insistence that resultant imperial practices are in fact fundamentally domestic to the countries in which they operate.

Attention to processes of strategic "domestication" on the part of the U.S. military is particularly urgent for the social movements that must contend with that domestication. Despite the region's turn to the Left, which has brought radical populist leaders such as Hugo Chavez and Rafael Correa to political power after more than a decade of neoliberal rule, in the years since the facility's eviction from Manta, the U.S. military has dramatically extended its reach into Latin America. Since 2008, and despite growing opposition to the militarization of the region, especially by transnational groups such as Fuera Bases (themselves composed of dozens of national organizations in Argentina, Brazil, Chile, and elsewhere), the U.S. Southern Command has created two new naval bases in Honduras; negotiated talks with the Paraguayan government about amplifying its presence in that country; established two additional naval bases for the control of narco-trafficking in Panama; and further expanded Mexico's heavily militarized response to the growing cartel violence, Plan Mérida. While this extension has often taken the form of humanitarian outreach programs and joint military training exercises, it continues to be most frequently defended by asserting that the U.S. military is little more than an unobtrusive part of a host country's domestic military architecture.

Drawing on sixteen months of ethnographic fieldwork on and around the United States FOL in Manta between 2006 and 2008, during which I conducted dozens of interviews with U.S. military personnel, antimilitary activists, and local civilians, I trace in this chapter the oft-repeated claim that the U.S. military in Ecuador was essentially domestic. Paying close attention to when, how, why, and by whom that domesticity was mobilized, exaggerated, and inverted, I show how ambivalences surrounding the facility were embraced by the antimilitary movement, but in ways that ultimately weakened the power of the movement at the local level.

At a time when U.S. military bases and locations are mushrooming throughout the region and national-level organizing has already faltered or failed in many parts of the continent, it is increasingly important to explore what sociologists call the "framing strategies" by which American military facilities are constructed by both supporters and opponents as either "foreign" or "domestic."[5] Scholars convinced that a genuinely transnational grassroots movement against U.S. military overreach can be achieved only by broadening the oppositional consensus at all levels would do well, it seems to me, to explore more sensitively the strategic deployment of these categories in ways that too often result in a dampening of resistance at subnational levels. In the face of an intensifying U.S. military strategy of "invisibility through domestication," and at a moment when the old tactics of the anti-imperialist Left are beginning to run aground as leftist regimes throughout the region enact draconian security measures in some ways more brutal than those of their rightist predecessors, it is urgent that we better conceptualize the ongoing contestations around U.S. military bases in Latin America.[6]

THE TERMS OF THE DISAGREEMENT

"We get so tired of the activists calling us a 'foreign base,'" the U.S. Air Force commander of the facility at Manta complained to me one March morning in 2007 in his office in the Military Operations Area, a long narrow corridor of offices located directly adjacent to the runway built by the North Americans. "The activists just don't get it . . . We're not an American base. We occupy less than 10% of this facility." Frequently bolstered by before-and-after aerial photographs of the runway renovated by a North Brunswick, New Jersey, contractor that invariably indicated no extension beyond the previously existing Ecuadorian Air Force perimeter, this negligible percentage of physical area was repeatedly invoked by U.S. Air Force and embassy personnel as proof that what both the Americans and their Ecuadorian military counterparts called the *puesto de operaciones de avanzada* (or "forward operating location") was simply not a base. This was the view reiterated—time and again—in State Department publications. There was simply no U.S. military base in Manta. What there was—and if activists couldn't understand the difference, "to hell with them!," the commander of the Quito-based U.S. Military Group exclaimed in March 2007—was an outpost within an army base fully controlled by the Ecuadorians. "The FOL is not an American base," begins the first line of the information packet given by the U.S. embassy to all journalists inquiring about the facility. "It is located fully inside the Base Aérea Ecuatoriana Eloy Alfaro and it occupies less than 10% of the physical territory of the Eloy Alfaro base." And then again, some pages later: "The FOL uses 66.5 of the total 1425 acres of the FAE [Fuerzas Armadas Ecuatorianas, or Ecuadorian Armed Forces] base, which to say, less than 5%." And again, a page later: "Is it true that the United States has dozens of bases in Latin America? The government of the United States has only one base in Latin America, and it is located in Guantánamo, Cuba. The three FOLs that are located in Central America and Ecuador can't and shouldn't be considered 'bases' since they are limited *presences* located inside host nation installations."

These protestations notwithstanding, no amount of minimalization of the physical could convince the predominantly Quito-based antibase activists led by prominent human rights groups that what they had in their midst was little more than an "operating location" under the oversight of the Ecuadorian armed forces. "It's an occupation!," local activists often reiterated. "It may be a low-level occupation, but it's an occupation." Drawing parallels with significantly larger and more environmentally destructive military facilities in Vieques, Puerto Rico, and Okinawa, Japan, local activists from the only antibase group in the city of Manta, the Movimiento Tohalli, routinely called attention to the fact that the Americans were constantly extending their presence in ways that were more than a little jurisdictionally dubious. Perhaps they were technically located fully within an Ecuadorian military base. Perhaps they even answered to the Ecuadorian armed forces, at least most of the time. But, like old-fashioned imperialists with perhaps just a bit more media savvy than in years past, they had repeatedly violated the terms of their lease agreement by intercepting boats ostensibly carrying both drugs and migrants within Ecuadorian territorial waters. They also allegedly used information obtained from their radar planes (AWACS) to participate in the counterinsurgency efforts of Plan Colombia. Just as controversially, they had refused to investigate renegade private military contractors from DynCorp who, in 2004–5, established a training camp under the name of EPI Security on the outskirts of Manta for the training of Colombian and Ecuadorian mercenaries for the Iraq War. Thus, operationally, from the perspective of these activists, not only was there nothing fundamentally Ecuadorian about the facility, but it was, on the contrary, a near-frontal assault on Ecuadorian sovereignty.

It is this interpretive gap between an obviously domestic and a blatantly foreign military presence around which the following pages pivot. How was this gap differently exploited by both military personnel and antimilitary activists? What were the changing stakes in seeing the facility as either Ecuadorian or American? And what lessons might those shifting stakes hold for the building of more successful movements in opposition to the U.S. military? Both anthropologists of the U.S. military and antimilitary activists have been quick to point to what Catherine Lutz has rightly called this "time-honored practice of renaming" whereby "clusters of soldiers, buildings, and equipment become 'defense staging posts' or 'forward operating locations' rather than military bases."[7] While this work of demystifying military categories remains critically important in an era in which the "political trajectories of words" have become dangerously murky, the suggestion of this chapter is that in addition to critically engaging military classifications along these lines, anthropologists are also particularly well situated to explore how such classifications, emergent from the highest defense policy circles in the United States, are being exploited, inverted, and redirected toward divergent agendas by the residents of military host communities throughout the world.[8] It is toward this work that I now turn.

"EVERYTHING IS GOING TO MOVE EVERYWHERE . . ."

In August 2004, George W. Bush announced the "Integrated Global Presence and Basing Strategy," which the Government Accountability Office called, with little exaggeration, "the most comprehensive restructuring of US military forces overseas since the end of the Korean War." This view was echoed by then-Pentagon Undersecretary for Defense Douglas Feith, who similarly called it "the most thorough restructuring of US military forces overseas since the major elements . . . were set in 1953."[9] As part of this restructuring, the Pentagon transferred some seventy thousand troops back to the United States, shuttered bases in Germany and South Korea that were prepositioned for Soviet tank invasions, fortified a multitude of minor locations in the "arc of instability,"[10] and, most dramatically, accelerated what they termed "strategic theater transformation." As one anonymous Department of Defense official explained in 2004, strategic theater transformation entails a shift away from heavily fortified "garrison forces" toward austere, "bare-boned," relatively soldier-less "forward operating sites" (FOSS), forward operating locations (FOLS), or "cooperative security locations" (CSLS),[11] many of which include little more than renovated runways or lone control towers tucked away on host nation airfields. Unlike the main operating bases of the Cold War, which depended upon elaborate command and control infrastructures, permanent troop numbers in the thousands, and robust family support facilities, these minimalist sites (known colloquially in idioms both organic and electrical as "lily pads" or "light switches") are "cold" spaces in which "there [are] little or no permanent parties, *certainly on our part,* but areas where . . . we . . . have agreement with a government that, for purposes of training, . . . we could use a facility or for purposes of operation, depending on what the circumstances were."[12] As these lily pads continue to proliferate, making for a military that is capable of increasingly rapid mobility, the Department of Defense anticipates that it will be able to reduce the number of main operating bases around the world. As Douglas Feith further summarized this transformation, "Everything is going to move everywhere. . . . *There isn't going to be any place in the world where things are the same.*"[13]

This end-of-history formulation of thoroughgoing structural transformation, however, is rarely the vision that is offered to the host nations where new facilities are located. On the contrary, negotiations surrounding the agreements for such installations have often been accompanied by pointed efforts on the part of U.S. State and Defense Department personnel to foster the impression among recipient nations that the world *is* precisely the same as it used to be, at least in terms of the capacity on the part of local officials to maintain oversight over national military facilities. Because the American presence, they suggest, is intimately connected to, embedded within, and monitored by host nation operations, and because it is increasingly made up of a heavily U.S. civilian workforce in the form of private military contractors, Coast Guard officials, and Homeland Security representatives (many of whom are technically "civilian"), it is never exactly foreign, never exactly permanent, and increasingly, never exactly military.

This metamorphosis of bases into amorphously domestic and civilian locations began with particular intensity in Latin America in the late 1990s, when it first became clear that negotiations with Panama for a multinational counternarcotics center were faltering for lack of a consensus about whether such a facility might be used by the United States for nonnarcotics missions. In 1997, when the United States was finally forced to withdraw from Howard Air Force base in Panama as stipulated by the Carter-Torrijos Treaty of 1977, the U.S. Southern Command (SOUTHCOM)—responsible for all combatant operations in Central and South America and the Caribbean—moved swiftly to negotiate the establishment of four new FOLS in the Western Hemisphere.

They hoped these locations would fill the void in surveillance operations left by the loss of Howard. The smallest of the new FOLs, which continue to operate today, are in the Caribbean and Central American transit zones of Curaçao, Aruba, and El Salvador, where they remain nearly invisible to the outside observer and have attracted little domestic opposition. But by far the largest and most operationally central was, for just under ten years, located in the Andean source zone of Ecuador.

From the very beginning, the negotiations between Ecuador and the United States for the base at Manta were characterized by ambiguities about the precise lines between a "forward operating location" within an operationally Ecuadorian facility and a very clearly military U.S. Air Force base. All throughout 1998–99, negotiators for the U.S. embassy repeatedly asserted that there were no U.S. military bases in (or planned for) Ecuador. Some ten years later, following the eviction of the base in August 2009, it was precisely this same sort of argument that was still being invoked. As Ambassador William Brownfield explained, defending the proposed establishment of seven U.S. military sites in Colombia against charges that they represented an assault on national sovereignty, these facilities were merely extensions of preexisting agreements between Colombia and the United States about joint narcotics policing, training, and aid. They were not formal military bases. Successive U.S. embassy and defense representatives in Quito likewise held steadfastly to this claim across the duration of the military operations out of Manta, even in the face of the fact that, according to criteria set forth by the U.S. Department of Defense's own *Base Commission Report*'s (2005) Glossary of Terms, "forward operating locations" are defined as both rapidly "expandable" and "scalable" to main military operating bases.

Ecuadorian and international social justice activists from SERPAJ (Servicio de Paz and Justicia) and the Quito-based INREDH (the Human Rights Foundation) were among the first to suggest that these ambiguities were little more than sleights of hand intended to disguise what might more properly be considered a straightforward foreign military occupation. As early as 2000, when a number of local and national NGOs first came together in Manta to begin to articulate a strategy to end the American military presence in Ecuador, this fledgling network of antimilitary activists pointed out that regardless of the FOL's designation as a mere "location," the articles of the bilateral agreement of 1999 actually granted U.S. personnel significant powers of potential extension over the territories adjacent to the Ecuadorian Air Force base. According to Article II, for example, "The Republic of Ecuador will grant all US military personnel, their dependents, and military contractors, access to and use of the Ecuadorian base at Manta, as well as the port of Manta and all installations related to the base or in its vicinity."[14] And again, in a subsection of the same article: "The Republic of Ecuador will allow all planes, boats, and vehicles operated by or for the United States access to the FAE base, the ports, and the installations related to the base or in its vicinity."[15] Such wording, activists routinely pointed out, essentially provided legal permission for the potential co-optation of all areas "related to" or "in the vicinity of the base." This represented an area that could conceivably extend the entire length of the country and beyond, depending on the expansiveness of the definitions of *vicinity*, *related to*, and even *installations*. Thus, the signing of this agreement was, they insisted, dangerously expansive in ways that made the protection of Ecuadorian national sovereignty unlikely, and in some of the strongest formulations, even "transformed all of Ecuador into a US military base."[16] This activist perspective, however, was not one that was widely shared in Manta, least of all among the U.S. servicemen, who often rotated in from deployments in Iraq and Afghanistan where American occupation looked significantly more pronounced.

"YOU SHOULD SEE SOME OF THE SHIT WE'VE GOT IN SAUDI ARABIA!": THE U.S. MILITARY

For most American lieutenants, sergeants, and airmen working on the ground at the facility at Manta, the U.S. embassy's public relations emphasis on occupying only the tiniest percentage of land within an Ecuadorian Air Force base seemed not like a whitewashing of an "American occupation," but if anything, more or less unnecessary. To them, as I discovered in focus groups on the base and at late-night bars in the city, it was simply common sense that what existed in Manta was little more than an operating location, and any accusation that such terminology was some sort of ideologically driven euphemism intended to disguise an American imperial outpost on Ecuadorian soil could easily be refuted by recourse to personal experience. For Lieutenant Colonel Javier Delucca, the head of the Manta FOL in 2006–7 and a lifetime air force officer, this flimsily guarded, barbed-wire corner of an Ecuadorian training camp simply could not be considered a base when compared to the sprawling complexes in Okinawa on which he had previously been stationed. Four or five small buildings staffed by fewer than two hundred Americans, but home to hundreds of Ecuadorian soldiers, their families, and faux-towns complete with banks and supermarkets, simply did not constitute an American base in his eyes. Walking together across the grassy quad that separates the barracks from the cafeteria on the nonmilitary operations side of the base one afternoon in April 2007, he explained: "The problem in Okinawa, and we all knew it, is that the military occupies too much space. Nobody's disputing that. But that's not just the case here. Like I told you, we're not a base."

Okinawa has long served as a lightning rod for anti-American protest in the Asia-Pacific region. Even before the well-publicized rape in 1995 of a young Okinawan girl by a U.S. Marine, the American presence was, Delucca acknowledged, understandably contentious. Some sixty years after the conclusion of World War II, somewhere in the neighborhood of forty thousand U.S. military personnel are still housed on bases across the island, of which the U.S. Marine Corps facility at Futenma—located in the very center of Ginowan City—remains the most politically problematic.[17] With a runway that spans some nine thousand feet and revelations that Agent Orange has been seeping into groundwater supplies since at least the 1980s, locals have been agitating for eviction on environmental grounds while U.S. negotiators continue to push for relocation within Okinawa. It is precisely to avoid such a scenario in the future that the Department of Defense (DoD) increasingly opts for "lily pads" like that in Manta.

Echoing a similar sentiment one afternoon at Gag's Lockdown Bar—the FOL's improvised recreation room replete with flat-screen television, pool table, and convenience store—was an experienced airman in his mid-forties. A volunteer at the local language school in Manta, he was fond of citing those "bullshit studies done by guys from Yale" or reminding me of the work of sociologists who too often feigned sympathy for military culture only to turn around and produce scathingly inaccurate portraits of life in the armed forces. "Look," he pointed out when I asked him why he thought that anti-base activists might worry over the distinction between a base and a FOL, "If you think this is anything, you should see some of the shit we've got in Saudi Arabia! This is *absolutely* nothing."

When once I suggested hesitantly to Lt. Col. Delucca that as the activists had often pointed out to me, regardless of both limited spatial extension and stripped-down living facilities, FOLs might nevertheless maintain an enormous military reach (essentially akin to that of "main operating bases"), he tried another tactic to make the distinction clearer, obviously amused by what he took to be my activist-shaped inability to understand a reality so glaringly self-evident. "Look, for you to get here," he got right down to business, "you had to go through the FAE [the Ecuadorian Air Force], right? They're the ones that make the access decisions. We send all our paperwork through the FAE. That's because it's their base, not ours." This was precisely the same response I received on my very first visit to the facility in early 2007 from Gloria Parraga, the secretary of the American private military contractor DynCorp. Gloria worked in the large office just outside the American base commander's, alongside the head of Community Relations, a young reservist from the northeastern United States. In response to questions about how her compatriots thought about her employment with DynCorp at a time when the company was being increasingly indicted in the national press for its coca-crop spraying just over the border in Colombia, Gloria explained, "People sometimes call it the 'North American base,' but I tell them, 'It's just a little, little place; it doesn't belong to the United States.' And they say, 'But how can you be there as an Ecuadorian?' And I tell them again, 'Because it's an Ecuadorian base.'" She continued: "Sometimes people I know [Ecuadorians] even get angry because they call and want to tour the base. But what I always tell them is that they have to go through the FAE . . . that access has nothing to do with the Americans." Although there were obvious material benefits to be reaped by such a characterization of the facility as unequivocally Ecuadorian (since Gloria's monthly salary at DynCorp was more than three times the average local salary), the fact that a significant part of her daily routine was taken up with processing access requests over which her Ecuadorian compatriots at the FAE had final oversight viscerally confirmed for her that the FOL was, as one American airman put it, "just a guest on an Ecuadorian airfield."

In a certain technical sense, both Gloria Parraga and Lt. Col. Javier Delucca were right—access *was* primarily controlled by the Ecuadorian armed forces. In January 2007, when I first put in my request to visit the facility with the U.S. Military Group in Quito, I was told by the mission chief and the head of public relations that I was tentatively approved, but that final security clearance would need to come from the Ecuadorian Armed Forces. They could not promise me anything, they said, because they simply did not control the access. They could not imagine there would be a problem (there never was), but the visit could not be guaranteed until the FAE commander signed off on it. Arriving at the facility some three weeks later, permission and passport in hand, I was again permitted entry only after passing through a FAE checkpoint staffed by two members of the national armed forces who, with automatic rifles slung over their backs, purple-tinted sunglasses, and the air of dubious cordiality that was to be their trademark through the months, checked and rechecked that my name appeared on their list of approved visitors. Time and again, week after week, we repeated this routine at the checkpoints, and always, the message was clear: It was they, the Twenty-Third Combat Wing of the Ecuadorian Air Force, who controlled entry to the Eloy Alfaro base. It was their name inscribed over the Roman arches at the entrance, a statue of their early twentieth-century liberal reformer just outside the gates, and this was undoubtedly an Ecuadorian aviation camp. Thus, from the perspectives of those who lived and worked on the facility, the language of the "forward operating location" was not some sinister euphemism designed by the Department of Defense to disguise or downplay American occupation. On the contrary, it named quite precisely the institutional structures that American military personnel were asked to navigate on a daily basis—from Ecuadorian checkpoint to Ecuadorian checkpoint.

"UNA BASE, SÍ, . . . PERO DE LOS GRINGOS?": THE LOCALS

For some time, civilian variations on the assertion that in Manta there was little more than an Ecuadorian base had been one of the most recurrent refrains in my fieldwork. When I had first begun to ask around about *la base* without specifying its nationality, I was so regularly offered litanies of complaints about the Ecuadorian Air Force or the adjacent Naval Base of Jaramijó that I quickly realized the need to add, "la de los gringos," the gringo base. One example should suffice. I first met Pablo Ríos, a barrio leader from the *parroquia* of La Florita, in January 2007. La Florita is a small community of some three hundred families who make their lives directly alongside the barbed-wire fence that surrounds the base, some hundred meters or so from the world-class runway that the U.S. Southern Command revamped and expanded. The parroquia remains one of the poorest and most dangerous barrios in Manta—a place where locals worried constantly about my safety even as they accompanied me on the street and forbade me from carrying the most rudimentary of personal items. I had been cautiously spending time there whenever I could to get a sense of the kinds of health problems that antibase activists told me were such persistent problems given the noise and exhaust of the FOL's radar planes. One of the nurses who worked at the small, understaffed clinic at the edge of the barrio introduced me to Pablo, explaining excitedly that he was always eager to talk about "la base."

At our first meeting, however, in a steaming back room at the clinic, it took more than an hour to convince Pablo that my interest was not primarily the Ecuadorian military, but the U.S. Air Force. While, as he admitted later, there was some hesitation on his part to complain to a *gringa* about the Americans, for Pablo, if there could be said to be an enemy worth investigating in Manta, that enemy was the Ecuadorian armed forces. "They just took all these properties," he complained one afternoon some time later, as we sat watching three newly hatched chicks squabble over seed just outside the small thatched house that is home to the clinic's overseer. "The Naval Base robbed them. They took these properties as 'protected areas' because there was a danger that the base might be attacked. They cleared all the land around it, all the way up the coast to Jaramijó. There were even demonstrations back then [in the 1970s], but not many, because if you resisted, they would either pay you off to be quiet or kill you." Throughout the months, and despite his occasional worry about the loss of fishermen's boats to the activities of the U.S. military, his overarching concern remained the maneuverings of the Ecuadorian armed forces, with their ever-increasing co-optation of good beach property and their transformation of inland farms into "restricted zones."

Given the minimal amount of space occupied by the FOL, the degree to which the Ecuadorian armed forces appeared to maintain control over access-related paperwork, and the fact that the most vivid and objectionable presence on the local scene remained the Ecuadorian armed forces, it was not difficult for city officials to argue that the facility remained essentially Ecuadorian. Their interests in doing so, however, were rarely aligned. When asked by media reporters about the base, the conservative Social Christian Party (PSC) mayor, Jorge Zambrano, often responded, as he famously did one afternoon while taking a break from playing baseball with American airmen just outside the city's only mall, "What base? I get so tired of that question. There's only an Ecuadorian base here in Manta." Although his position vis-à-vis the FOL was notoriously mutable—determined more, I was frequently told by activists, by construction projects and his own Right-leaning political aspirations as a member of the Social Christian Party than by any a priori appreciation of its benefits—he regularly emphasized its Ecuadorian-ness. "What is happening here, Doctor," he addressed one of the most vociferous local antibase activists at a municipal council meeting in March 2007, "is that we are speaking about the same thing with two different discourses—All of us present here love this city and want to defend it, but I don't want to debate with you about this now because you have talked about a military base. And yes, there is a military base here in Manta, but it's Ecuadorian—There is not a North American military base [of the sort that] exists in other places."

This assertion was widely shared among local residents in Manta. Raúl Cevallos was a middle-aged proofreader at the Right-leaning local newspaper, *El Mercurio*, who schooled me in the ins and outs of coastal Spanish at the only language school in the city and generously accompanied me to some of the most dangerous barrios of the city. Although his views at times wavered, he most often described his support for the facility by noting that "if the Ecuadorian armed forces are supposed to accompany the Americans on all their flights and they don't, that's not the fault of the United States and that doesn't mean they're an American base. That makes the Ecuadorian armed forces complicit since they're the ones who have the obligation to the *pueblo*." If the United States Air Force was not as embedded within the domestic military as it presented itself, he and numerous other local men argued—that is, if the Ecuadorian military did not have effective control over the Americans—then that was an Ecuadorian problem, not the result of strategic obfuscations on the part of the United States.

Of course, in this Raúl was only partly right. As recently leaked Wikicables demonstrate, all throughout this time the United States actively fostered confusion about the nature, aims, and jurisdictional location of the FOL. According to a cable dated September 28, 2004, that aimed to assess the threat posed by the mayoral election in Manta that returned Jorge Zambrano to power:

> Quiñónez [a local official with whom the Embassy consulted] said the FOL was not an electoral issue in Manabí and suggested that the *current air of mystery* surrounding the FOL works in USG [U.S. government] interests.
>
> Local people do not have direct access to the FOL, and assume that FOL personnel and vehicles may be monitoring *local narco-activity.* This uncertainty acts as a brake on criminal activity in the area, he suggested.
>
> For that reason, Quiñónez recommended that the FOL not take actions to demystify its presence by opening the FOL to public events.

As the cable suggests, the USG was well aware that there was uncertainty about the nature of the facility in Manta and, in fact, explicitly believed that if it could continue to be portrayed as involved in the fighting of local narcotrafficking (rather than the Pacific flights as far north as Guatemala, in which it was actually engaged), it would more likely continue to be experienced as "local" or "domestic."

In no small part because of these strategic obfuscations, a range of local civilians—from desperately poor tuna factory workers in La Florita to comparatively affluent teachers and journalists—came to believe that there was nothing like an American military base in the city. For antibase activists, this lack of belief proved enormously difficult to dislodge. But the ways in which they attempted to do so—by reversing the ambiguities so carefully nurtured by the U.S. military to hold the United States accountable for violations of the Ecuadorian military—did little to aid the antimilitary cause.

"AL CARAJO IMPERIO!": THE ACTIVISTS

It was against this widespread commitment to seeing the forward operating location as essentially embedded within the Ecuadorian military that anti-FOL activists had doggedly worked since as early as 2000. The leader of the only explicitly antibase movement in the city, the Movimiento Tohalli, was a constitutional lawyer, professor of law at the local university, and longtime champion of *campesino* rights. Having been repeatedly forced to move his downtown firm to get away from CIA agents (or so he repeatedly told me—I have no proof beyond his frequent relocations and tales of being followed at night), he was understandably suspicious of U.S. Americans. Nevertheless, he regularly agreed to meet with me in his second-floor office in Manta's central business district. Shortly after we first met in March 2007, he explained that twenty-five thousand hectares of land had been expropriated by the Americans, who had evicted more than three thousand campesinos from their homes without so much as a gesture toward compensation. "¡Imagínate! [Just imagine that!]," he exclaimed, leaning back outraged in his office chair one morning. "They even created a *polígono de tiroteo* [a firing range] in Jaramijó, just like what they had in Puerto Rico." For more than sixty years prior to its 2003 departure, the U.S. Navy's University at Sea had operated on the small island of Vieques, Puerto Rico. It served as the central Caribbean hub for "integrated training scenarios," live-fire exercises, amphibious landing exercises, parachute drops, and submarine maneuvers later used in interventions in the Balkans, Haiti, Iraq, and Somalia. Almost ten years after its removal, residents of the community continue to deal with the effects of depleted uranium, vast tracts of unusable land, and beaches too polluted for human use.[18] "The Americans practice on this range just like they did in Puerto Rico," the leader of the Movimiento Tohalli went on to point out that March morning. "They use it as a training ground. They even cleared fifty additional kilometers around the base for this, *just the amount of space needed for a missile launch.* You really think they'd go somewhere they couldn't protect themselves?"

By drawing a parallel between the infamous training ground at Vieques and the firing ranges in Manta, whose depleted shells were routinely photographed by antibase activists as evidence of the American-led militarization of the city, this lone, self-identified anti-imperialist vigorously rejected the notion that the facility was not an American base and even went as far as to suggest that it might house an American missile launcher—a possibility expressly forbidden by the agreement signed in 1999. Insisting that the gringos were engaging in precisely the sorts of dislocations and expropriations for which they had finally been evicted from Puerto Rico, he continued, "It may be a low-level occupation, but it's an occupation. . . . The fishermen call it 'low-intensity warfare.' And that's what it is." While such language felt extreme to many local residents who identified such anti-imperialism with far-Left parties who had too often achieved too little, this activist and his allies had good reason to be suspicious about the efforts of the United States to construe the facility as little more than a phenomenologically ambiguous "presence." While occupying a mere 5–10 percent of the physical space of the Ecuadorian base, the Americans had, in fact, and on numerous occasions, extended themselves considerably beyond the confines of the Ecuadorian base, though in ways that principally affected small-scale fishermen and unlucky migrants from the Sierra hoping to escape to the United States via boats so unseaworthy that they were often picked up by the U.S. Coast Guard.

Luis Arteaga was a journalist in his mid-forties who worked at an international whitefish association, a regular blogger on all issues related to the FOL, and one of my closest interlocutors in Manta. Sitting one spring afternoon in his fifth-floor downtown office, he explained that activist fears about a possible takeover of the port had actually materialized, albeit briefly, for a number of months in early 2005. At the request of the FOL, and partly because of George Bush's rhetorical escalations that had transformed "narcotraffickers" into "narco-terrorists," the port authority sealed the main dock in the city to all Ecuadorian-flagged fishing vessels after it was discovered that small groups of Ecuadorian fishermen were engaging in "retaliations" against the U.S. Coast Guard for the alleged sinking of Ecuadorian-flagged ships in territorial waters. As has been well documented in numerous human rights reports and testimonials from survivors, these destructions resulted in the disappearances of at least eighteen young fishermen and the capture of some two hundred migrants caught fleeing the country. "The US, of course, took the threat very seriously," he continued, "and started even further militarizing the port. They hired their own private security companies, put up 'No Cross' barriers all over the place, and prevented the boats from docking where they used to be able to dock." Although none of the feared reprisals on the part of narco-terrorists ever materialized, and the only real consequence of the measure was that the U.S. Navy boats that regularly pass through the city eventually stopped docking at the port altogether because the risk of terrorist activity was simply too great, artisanal fishermen were inconvenienced by the measure for a number of months.

Such violations of the terms of the bilateral agreement, however, went largely unrecognized by a sizeable portion of the community in Manta. This was in part because the municipal hall, the mayor, and the Chamber of Commerce were actively engaged in supporting the FOL. But equally important was the fact that the antibase movement had, by that time, already lost significant credibility among locals by playing on the ambiguities between an Ecuadorian "location" and an American "base" in ways that seemed, at least to many in this politically conservative city, disingenuous. Some of the reasons for this growing feeling of disingenuousness were made particularly vivid in a publication put out by a coalition of local, national, and international antimilitary NGOs formally inaugurated in Quito as the No-Bases coalition in March 2007. After more than seven years of local and national networking on the part of the Movimiento Tohalli, the Association of Christian Youth (ACJ), and a number of prominent Quito-based human rights organizations, the No-Bases Coalition came into being as the first formal international coalition explicitly opposed to the U.S. military base at Manta. To celebrate its inauguration, more than four hundred antiwar, antimilitary, and environmental activists from Okinawa, Guam, Quito, the United States, Peru, and Colombia came to Ecuador to attend a four-day conference that culminated in a protest march to the FOL. It was during this march through the streets of Manta on March 9, 2007, that a publication authored by the No Bases Coalition and titled simply Base de Manta, was widely distributed to local onlookers. In it, there appears the following paragraph, some version of which was repeated to me by nearly every activist working on the Manta base issue, regardless of whether they were based in Quito or local to Manta:

> Since the installation of the Base at Manta, there have been various conflicts affecting the local population, including: the exploitation of quarries [*canteras*] in Chorrillo in order to provide the material necessary for the construction of the runway; the increase of sex workers in 1999 and 2000; the displacement 30 years ago of more than 800 *campesino* families to consolidate the actual territory of the Naval Base of Jaramijó (also involved in the lease agreement for the Manta Base); the sinking of fishing boats; the interdiction of migrant boats; the limitations placed on fishing activities for "security reasons" and the risk for populations living near the firing ranges.[19]

In this narrative and many others like it, the Ecuadorian Naval Base at Jaramijó is seamlessly merged with the American FOL. The expropriations of thirty years ago are treated as the work of the same entity that now interdicts migrant boats. And references to the "firing ranges," which many locals knew to have been the work of the Ecuadorian military, are placed directly alongside references to the "sinking of fishing boats," for which the American military was widely accepted to have been responsible.

"Go talk to the lady that sells coconut water along the Manta-Jaramijó," one activist from the neighboring city of Rocafuerte advised me in late 2007, when I gently expressed my concern about the veracity of this narrative. "She lives by the ranges set up by the Americans. She'll tell you about them." This coconut stand turned out to be a windowless bamboo house, nestled between a brick wall, six sun-bleached hammocks, a laundry line, and a dry grove a mile out of town. As we pulled up in a taxi, a heavyset woman in a yellow T-shirt emerged from behind the beads that separated porch from kitchen, swatting away flies and pressing her hair back as she moved hurriedly toward us. After downing the requisite coconut juice out of a small plastic bag, I asked her about these *polígonos de tiroteo* (firing ranges) about which the activists had so often spoken. "No, no," she shook her head emphatically, "that was a lie [*eso es mentira*]. There used to be one out back that the FAE ran . . . but that ended years ago, at least three or four. . . . They haven't been here for a long time. . . . Now I only hear the shots coming from further off." This was an opinion reiterated by everyone who lived in any proximity to the allegedly "American" ranges. While I cannot, of course, definitively rule out the possibility that these ranges were used at some point by the U.S. Air Force, I never met anyone who could confirm the American-ness of these facilities and, some six years later (I have returned to Manta four times since), I still have not. It is now generally accepted that the Americans did not, in fact, maintain such ranges, though they may, on occasion, have participated in joint training exercises on them.

By moving, then, erratically backward and forward in time in this way, from the "increase in sex workers" in 1999 to the displacements of "30 years ago," the No-Bases narrative participates in a sort of temporal blurring of the two facilities, which mirrors the spatial blurring strategically encouraged by the American forces in their insistence that they were little more than a corner of an Ecuadorian base. This tactic of using temporal ambiguity to suggest U.S. Air Force responsibility for what were widely remembered to be the excesses and expropriations of the Ecuadorian armed forces ultimately alienated large numbers of city residents. Such conflations on the part of activists were, for Mayor Zambrano and other members of the Municipal Hall, not just irksome, but unconscionable. After all, he pointed out, student and journalist activists in Manta regularly collected depleted shells from these alleged "firing ranges" and routinely published them as evidence that the FOL was, in fact, a facility with such weapons. One montage that regularly made the rounds on the international No-Bases circuit, after first appearing in the *Coalición No Bases* publication of 2007 referred to above, displayed four black-and-white photos—the first, of two pairs of hands holding depleted shells; the second, of a weather-beaten sign that read, "Armada del Ecuador, Prohibido El Paso"; the third, of what appear to be somewhat rusted, Soviet-style rocket launchers; and the fourth, of an Airborne Warning and Control System (AWACS) plane being serviced by American personnel—the implication being that all four were the work of the Americans. Upon seeing this montage of photos at a city council meeting in late 2007, Mayor Zambrano reacted as diplomatically as he could, directing his comments at a young councilmember opposed to the FOL:

> It's good to bring these photos. . . . You know, I see this book, but you'll have to excuse me because when I see these photos. . . . I don't know if they are a montage or what . . . but here is a photo of missiles, it looks like, made of very old iron, but the text insinuates . . . well, I would not like to say whether there are North American missiles here in Manta or not, I don't know, but to put a photo like that and then a commentary about 1,500 *campesinos* being removed from their land—that is not right. We all have to defend our concepts, our ideological positions, but by describing things as they actually *are*.

Given his long-standing support for the Americans on the grounds that they would provide much-needed visibility to the struggling city, the right-of-center mayor undoubtedly had an investment in a particular slant on "how things actually *are*." However, he was far from alone in expressing frustration over efforts to fundamentally misrepresent the U.S. Air Force as decisively more "foreign," more weaponized, and more involved in the expropriation of campesino lands than they actually were.

Just as in other parts of the world, activists have been met with hostility when they produced information that clearly contradicted local memory and chronology. In Manta, the ambiguity of the temporal referents deployed by activists angered, frustrated, and fatigued many local residents, whose memories rejected the retrospective Americanization of a facility that was experienced as clearly Ecuadorian. Local activists recognized in the arrival of the FOL an opportunity to draw international attention to the plight of farmers who had historically remained unrecognized even by the Ecuadorian government, having routinely had their land expropriated by national military forces. Nevertheless, the strategy of presenting temporally ambiguous claims about the chronology of these alleged expropriations appeared to the majority of locals as not only profoundly misleading, but even a falsification of the real history of their city. Because Manta is a city that since the late 1970s has been profoundly entangled with the Ecuadorian military, against which complaints are still regularly made in court about land seizures, people's attention remained squarely focused on the national armed forces as responsible for their plight. As a result, the efforts on the part of activists to suggest the culpability of the Americans were read as blatant falsifications of local history and memory. From the perspective of many local civilians, it was the Ecuadorian Armed Forces who had built the firing ranges and confiscated large tracts of land on either side of the facility. The arrival of the Americans had done little to change that, and they most certainly did not constitute an "occupation."

Legally ambiguous spatial enclaves have been characteristic of American overseas unincorporated territories ever since their legal formalization in a series of turn-of-the-last-century U.S. Supreme Court rulings known as the Insular Cases.[20] The first of these cases (*Downes v. Bidwell*—1901) settled the status of Puerto Rico shortly after the close of the Spanish-American War, when a U.S. orange importer sued the port of New York for levying taxes on goods coming from Puerto Rico. Drawing implicitly on the precedent of the "domestic dependent nation" first worked out in relation to the Cherokee Nation (*Cherokee Nation v. State of Georgia* 1831), Justice Edward Douglas White rendered the still-remarkable verdict that "whilst in an international sense Puerto Rico was not a foreign country, since it was subject to the sovereignty of and was owned by the United States, it was foreign to the United States in a domestic sense, because the island had not been incorporated into the United States, but was merely appurtenant thereto as a possession."[21] It was this legal ambiguity that allowed the United States to first make peace with its interim government on the island, while denying Puerto Ricans the full citizenship rights that domestic status would have necessitated. Some hundred years later, related ambiguities, while no longer recognized by the federal courts in the same way, remain in force within the sorts of public relations campaigns run by the U.S. military. As part of these campaigns, we see a similarly strategic invocation of the ambivalent status of the United States armed forces as both "foreign" and "domestic." As historians of the Insular Cases, Christina Duffy Burnett and Burke Marshall, point out: "No one today defends the colonial status sanctioned by these cases, yet the idea of a relationship to the United States that is somewhere 'in between' that of statehood and independence—somehow both 'foreign' and 'domestic' (or neither)—has not only survived but enjoys substantial support."[22]

Ecuador is not legally "foreign in a domestic sense" in the way that Puerto Rico (and Guantánamo) remain to this day, since Ecuadorian sovereignty is at least nominally recognized by the United States. Nonetheless, the FOL in Manta was constructed as both foreign and domestic at different moments, and in the service of different ends, in ways not entirely dissimilar from other U.S. extraterritorial locales. Despite the fact that this jurisdictional ambivalence is in large part a reflection of shifts in a global political-economic order in which it has become increasingly difficult to disentangle the foreign from the domestic (whether that be in the form of corporate subsidiaries or forward operating locations), these confusions also have long precedents in the history of U.S.-led empire. At the turn of the twentieth century, the category of the unincorporated territory was used principally to legalize in the eyes of the American public the foreignness of those "alien races" who threatened to "turn the United States into a monstrous hybrid creature." Not dissimilarly at the turn of the twenty-first century, the category of the mostly civilian, mostly domestic "forward operating location" was used to dilute in the eyes of the Ecuadorian public the foreignness of the United States that threatened to fundamentally compromise Ecuadorian national integrity.[23] However, more interesting still is the fact that it was precisely these ambiguities around the "blurred borderland between the domestic and the foreign"[24] upon which antibase activists also seized, subsequently redeploying them, but in ways that inadvertently undermined their efforts to build a broad-based local opposition campaign.

It is only, I think, when we begin to really wrestle with these ongoing spatial and technical ambiguities—often multiply and differently deployed by officers and activists alike—that we can more subtly theorize the processes by which U.S. military bases come to be accepted by many of those who live in their shadows. They are accepted not just because of the economic benefits they provide, and not just because they hold out promises of development or political prestige. Both of these claims may be true, but they are not the only reasons. At a time when the U.S. military presence continues to grow throughout much of Latin America by means of proliferating agreements about ostensibly domestic "sites" and "locations," and when the lines between the domestic and the foreign are as difficult to discern in Department of Defense manuals as they are in the agreements routinely made between multinational corporations and their "domestic" subsidiaries, the task of more subtly understanding the range of local responses to U.S.-led militarization remains urgent. Without an ethnographic appreciation of how these processes of ambivalent domestication come to be enacted, internalized, and transformed by those who live in closest proximity to these facilities, the transnational movement against U.S. military bases is unlikely to command sustained sympathy or even understanding.

NOTES

Unless otherwise noted, all translations are my own.

1 Forward operating location, or FOL, is a relatively small military site that provides tactical support operations and is rapidly "scalable" to a main operating base. Unlike a main operating base, however, it generally houses a limited number of military personnel and does not provide full support facilities.

2 Ruggie, "Territoriality and Beyond."
3 Hardt and Negri, *Empire.*
4 Hardt and Negri, *Empire*, 211.
5 Benford and Snow, "Framing Processes and Social Movements."
6 Goodale and Postero, *Neoliberalism Interrupted.*
7 Lutz, "Empire Is in the Details."
8 For more on the "political trajectories of words," see especially Eekelen et al., *Shock and Awe*, 1.
9 Campbell and Ward, "New Battle Stations?," 95.
10 The "arc of instability" refers to the zone of politically unstable states that stretches from North Africa to parts of Southeast Asia and includes large parts of the Middle East, the Balkans, and Central Asia.
11 FOLs, FOSs, and CSLs all refer to U.S. military facilities used primarily for regional training in counterterrorism or interdiction of drug trafficking. They are usually located within host nation military installations and lack the full operational capacities of main operating bases. For all practical purposes, the terms are interchangeable.
12 Global Posture Review 2004, 5; Cooley, *Base Politics*, 237; Vine, "The Lily-Pad Strategy."
13 Campbell and Ward, "New Battle Stations?"
14 Coalición No Bases, *Base de Manta*, 43.
15 Coalición No Bases, *Base de Manta*, 43.
16 Salgado-Tamayo, "La base de Manta."
17 Inoue, *Okinawa and the U.S. Military.*
18 McCaffrey, *Military Power and Popular Protest.*
19 Coalición No Bases, *Base de Manta*, 24.
20 Kaplan, *The Anarchy of Empire in the Making of U.S. Culture.*
21 Kaplan, *The Anarchy of Empire in the Making of U.S. Culture*, 2.
22 Burnett and Marshall, *Foreign in a Domestic Sense*, 2.
23 Kaplan, *The Anarchy of Empire*, 67.
24 Kaplan, *The Anarchy of Empire*, 15.

14 The Empire of Choice and the Emergence of Military Dissent

MATTHEW GUTMANN AND CATHERINE LUTZ

The problem we address in this chapter is fairly simple: what would cause enlisted soldiers who have willingly signed enlistment papers to work for the U.S. military to abandon a volunteer military force that they themselves have chosen to join? Because this is a job they chose and because it comes with economic and social rewards, shouldn't we assume they joined with some ideological commitments and enthusiasm, or at least a vested interest in staying the course, doing their time, and exiting the service with an unblemished record? This question is important because it allows us to explore the motivations and situations of the lowest-level agents of the imperial military missions of the United States in the current, still imperial, era; because it suggests what the vulnerabilities or assurances of success are for that mission; and because it allows us to explore the severe limits that the concept of choice places on our ability to understand military recruitment.

There are numerous studies on the All-Volunteer Force;[1] civilian-military relationships; citizen-soldiers; and recruitment priorities, successes, and challenges. Generally, though, the questions asked about how the military fills its ranks concern how low the bar should be set on intelligence tests, police records, or psychiatric conditions. That volunteer troops are reliable politically and ideologically is so taken for granted by the U.S. military and the rest of the U.S. government that when enlisted soldiers, sailors, and marines do question their own roles in wars of intervention and occupation, it may appear that the only explanation, at least for their officers or other officials, is individual pathology or cowardice.

This chapter extends arguments we developed in a book about six antiwar veterans of the Iraq War in which we explore, in good part through our conversations with them, how workers in the military institutions that are at the heart of the U.S. empire have experienced, judged, and rethought their role.[2] We found that they had one or more in a series of political and moral epiphanies that began during the recruitment process and continued through training, deployment to Iraq, and return home. In this book, we sought to put into practice an earlier call for ethnographic work to play a key role in questioning "the singular thingness that the term *empire* suggests by identifying the many fissures, contradictions, historical particularities, and shifts in the imperial process," and "to make the human and material face and frailties of imperialism more visible, and in so doing, to make challenges to it more likely."[3]

Before elaborating on the particular fissures present in these soldiers' lives, it bears noting that their importance to empire stems in significant part from the fact that the U.S. empire is a military one, invested in the assertion of the right and responsibility of the United States to wield and threaten violence to protect the country, to protect allies, to protect the innocent, and to protect the collective good and most especially trade, in short, to safeguard the globe for all. The United States does not simply or even primarily assert its right to freedom of economic activity or the right to exert political power over others. So though the country's reach is obviously cultural, political, financial, and economic, the post-continental expansion of the United States is said to have developed a distinctively nonterritorial empire. This is excluding the not small exceptions of Hawaiʻi and its many military bases, as well as Guam, Puerto Rico, American Samoa, and the U.S. Virgin Islands. These territories include some of the vast collection of territorial fragments of empire that are constituted by the United States' more than one thousand foreign bases. These bases give the United States a historically unprecedented global reach and erosive effect on local sovereignties, though the scale is so vast and the politics so sensitive that the official count varies.[4] These bases are the nodes of a 24/7 attempt at global surveillance and power projection, and they help construct strategic doctrine based in that global military readiness and presence.[5]

That the United States is a military empire is evident first in the federal budget: its military elements totaled $1.1 trillion in 2017, and that spending has had profound impact on everyday life in the United States. The state both makes places with these bases and money, and it erases its presence and its abuses from public view and memory. Diego Garcia is one such place where local residents were forcibly removed from their island in the early 1970s and a secretive, if mammoth, U.S. naval base laid over their homes.[6] As Ann Stoler notes, "US empire, in a familiar imperial mode, has historically constructed places exempt from scrutiny and peoples partially excluded from rights."[7]

U.S. militarism entails a particular belief system that supports the idea of using military violence to pursue American values and interests. While these beliefs, of course, are both emergent and contested, U.S. militarism is most commonly framed as security "gifts" to others. These gifts take the form of military interventions, arms sales, military training, or basing: they can come in the form of the sale of Tomahawk missiles for British use against a Libyan dictator, military bases for Okinawa in the shadow of a surging Chinese military power, or training for the Philippine military in counterinsurgency techniques in Mindanao.

In this chapter, we focus on the rhetoric of choice that is central to recruitment into the U.S. military, to public discourse about the U.S. armed forces and about war, and to how the U.S. government represents its military actions and presence around the world. That rhetoric itself has powerful effects in shaping how the four soldiers we profile here approached the military and in shaping if and how dissent is possible within military institutions and the social order at large.

What is that rhetoric? In the first instance, it is a rhetoric of choice. A young man or woman is said to *choose* to join the military, even though it is often the case that he or she has no or few other routes to either wide social approval or a paycheck. The Congress is said to *opt* to budget for a particular type and size military, even though the systematic construction of a political economy in which military contractors' success in garnering multibillion dollar contracts for weapons they themselves have invented or retooled each year is overdetermined.[8] The United States posts troops in Okinawa on the claim that both the United States and the Japanese governments and people chose to put them there, even though those bases have been there since the accident of the island's having been a last landing area used in preparation for the invasion of Japan at the end of World War II; and even though most Americans cannot find Okinawa on a map, and the overwhelming majority of Okinawans do not want the bases there.[9]

It should not be surprising that choice, that central concept of an individualized self, appears as an important engine of every U.S. institution and practice. Nonetheless, it is worth exploring the effects of this rhetoric in the contemporary military because it is an institution most associated with hierarchy, coercion, and obedience, concepts often seen as the antithesis of choice. Moreover, rhetorics within an institution whose activities have such epic-scale effects bear close examination. Drawing on interviews with these veterans and with a larger group of forty self-identifying dissenting veterans as well as on long-term work around U.S. military bases and on questions of masculinity and conscription,[10] this chapter examines three related issues.

First, notions of electoral choice and civilian control of the military are assumed to make of the U.S. state, people, and military a unified "we" that chooses to build and wield an imperial military at each of the thousand-plus bases and through each of the dozens of military operations conducted by the United States in the late twentieth and early twenty-first centuries.

Second, morale and esprit de corps/unit cohesion among the troops are contingent on several beliefs. These include the idea that they have chosen to enlist in a military very explicitly, even ostentatiously called the All-Volunteer Force: they are the "select few" who have, without exception, offered their full support. Also crucial to morale is the belief that recruits have enlisted for worthy causes, from the generic "defense of our American freedoms" to a specific threat, such as routing a tyrant in Iraq or protecting Afghan women and providing for the education of their girls. Choosing to do something noble through soldiering is strongly evident in most of our transcripts, and they are especially apparent in the language of the men in uniform, for whom serving is most often linked to protecting and thus takes on its distinctly male-gendered hue.

Third, the rhetoric of choice in the All-Volunteer Force makes dissent especially risky, particularly when the peculiar labor contract of the military suggests that there is but one choice point and that is in the recruiter's office. Even if soldiers have subsequent qualms or wish to withdraw altogether from their military contract, they are routinely informed by recruiters and other military officials that they no longer have the option of quitting and must serve out their full term. The people we interviewed frequently observed deceitful or abusive treatment in recruitment and training. Those observations often contradicted some of the more righteous claims and desires on which their choices had hinged. The fact of being lied to about their contracts in turn contributed to their anger and dissent.

THE AMERICAN "WE" OF WAR MAKING

Notions of choice centrally frame how Americans think about the relationship between themselves, the nation, the state, and the military. Democratic elections and militaries that answer to an elected civilian commander-in-chief are the mechanisms by which it is commonly argued that "we," the nation and government and military service members, in essence, choose to go to war. Citizen armies, and, in the United States, the All-Volunteer Force (AVF), are the central institutional embodiment not simply of acquiescence but of unforced participation in military projections of U.S. empire around the world. Americans, in other words, vote for empire, vote to give the commander-in-chief the right to establish bases, wage war, and otherwise have their "will" expressed through their government's foreign policy. This makes the state and the people as one. A rhetoric of "we" quite commonly expresses this notion: "*We* invaded Iraq"; "*We* should not have invaded Iraq";

"*We* have troops in Japan and Germany sixty-five years after the war ended"; "Should *we* withdraw from Afghanistan sooner or later?"

This set of assumptions has also informed the debate within anthropology about the controversial Human Terrain System that is designed to embed anthropologists and other social scientists in Afghanistan. A common rhetoric around that program aimed at U.S. civilians, including potentially recruitable scholars, is that it allows *us* to help ease the burden of the occupation of the country on local civilians and help U.S. soldiers avoid mistakes in interacting with them.[11] Its proponents argue that since elected civilians choose war and send soldiers to the war zones, it is the citizens' obligation to assist those soldiers in the counterinsurgency project until such time as they elect someone who brings the troops home.

This sense of "we" does not emerge simply and naturally from either experiential affinities or particular cultural formations of nationalism. There have been intense investments made, and work done, to develop and retain the sense of "we," particularly by the Pentagon and other corporate and government affiliates. Those investments are made in several ways, including the employment of personnel. The 22 million U.S. veterans and 2.1 million active duty and reserve service members constitute fully 10 percent of U.S. adults.[12] Nonetheless, as many politicians and commentators have pointed out, the U.S. population as a whole has become less involved with the volunteer military than it was with the draft army into which, in theory, anyone's son or husband or brother of the right age could, at any moment, be made to join. Class makes a difference in who knows people at war, who is affected by someone's absence in war, and who is considering joining the military, just as it has made a vital difference in who has died in U.S. wars.[13]

On the other hand, many more people today are exposed to the idea and attractions of choosing to join the military than was true during the Vietnam draft era. Before the AVF, viewers of U.S. media in the 1960s and 1970s rarely saw military ads (or of course military video games and websites). In 1973, with the initiation of the AVF, Congress tripled the Pentagon recruiting budget, doubled enlisted pay, offered bonuses to those who signed up for combat units, and opened most military positions to women. The military also began, for the first time, to advertise widely across media venue for its jobs. Since the 1970s, billions of dollars have been spent each year to convince people that the military is a good way to start life after high school.

Given attrition and retirements, the volunteer force in recent nonrecessionary conditions must recruit over 300,000 new workers each year (this figure includes active duty and reserves), and a huge military recruiting and advertising budget is used to promote that work. This investment exploded even further during the 2000s: the military's recruiting and advertising budget, already $4 billion in 2003, mushroomed to $20.5 billion in 2009. This figure includes payments to Madison Avenue firms and "outreach" activities directed at the people, such as parents and football coaches, called "influencers" in military marketese, as well as bonus payments to new recruits and reenlisters.[14]

In addition, the science of military public relations has advanced and expanded on the ever more entrenched notion that modern warfare is fought on what is called human terrain. This is not only the terrain of counterinsurgency battlefields but of domestic public opinion, which affects the public's willingness to serve and pay war taxes. So the Pentagon has invested much effort in coordinating and briefing; they created a group of ex-generals to conduct White Ops by disseminating the official version of military events and goals through the mainstream media. This is, in other words, counterinsurgency in plain view and aimed at the U.S. public.[15] And it has invested in military journalism proper, with legions involved in producing content for the military and informing the mainstream media. By one accounting, the Pentagon directly employs twenty-seven thousand people in recruitment, public relations, and advertising, and many more by subcontract.[16]

In part as a result of all of this public relations work, Americans over time have increasingly positive views of the U.S. military and its workers, and the media increasingly avoid critique and actively celebrate military workers. Gallup's Confidence in Institutions poll reported the military on top of its list in 2016 (above the medical system, the police, the president, Congress, journalism or small business, and, even, above religious institutions and public schools).[17] The military has risen to the top of that poll every year since 1998, and was first or second in almost each year since 1975, when the poll began. Via this public support, U.S. recruits and soldiers receive a cultural wage, that is, they are given cultural valuation as more exemplary, selfless, disciplined, professional, and efficacious than others. They have become, in a sense, supercitizens. As a billboard from 2013 for the Marines phrases it, "a commitment to something greater than themselves." So even evidence of systematic atrocity in Iraq and Afghanistan, thousands of civilian deaths each year, and repeated news about epidemic sexual assault in the military could be ignored or treated as exceptions.

As an additional result of the advertising, PR, and media collaboration, and the moral responsibility entailed by the "we" of national military activity, many Americans hold more strongly than in the past to a historiography in which the military is not imperial but defensive,[18] responding only to attack rather than pursuing national or sectoral interests through violence. The belief has grown over time that the military is competent, professional, and apolitical (evidence of its political narrowing and evangelization notwithstanding), and more civilized and demographically inclusive/representative.[19]

In the United States, military enlistment provides young people, especially men and the working and middle class, with financial incentives in the form of jobs and, often overlooked by antiwar activists, idealistic incentives and cultural rewards. Military service is touted as an escape route from unemployment or poverty and crucially as an opportunity to "give back" to their country. Any analysis that dismisses the AVF as simply a poverty draft in disguise captures only certain motivations for enlisting and in this way can too easily overlook the potential for disappointment, disillusionment, and even outrage when ideals of service to others prove more elusive than many young recruits had imagined.

VOLUNTARY AND NOBLE SERVICE

Ricky Clousing had been a missionary in Thailand and Mexico, experiences he looked back on with a mixture of pride for trying to help others and with excitement for learning about other peoples and cultures. He was living in Germany after 9/11, when the first waves of U.S. soldiers going to and returning from Afghanistan were pouring through in early 2002. "I talked to all these guys before and after Afghanistan, and I heard their perspective on things. That was the first time I actually contemplated joining the military."

Debating whether to enlist or return home to Washington State and finish college, Ricky was concerned not to jump into a pile of school debt, though he did want to finish college. He explained to the recruiter that he did not want to be a frontline combat fighter. Ricky's father suggested that if he enlisted, he should try to get into intelligence as he himself had done. The job of interrogator sounded appealing, so Ricky took the qualification tests, passed, and two weeks later, in July 2002, was on a plane back to the United States for basic training.

Ricky's life had renewed purpose, pride, and excitement: "Not many people get to be trained as an interrogator and learn a foreign language. And meanwhile I would be serving my country and doing something with the patriotism that came with 9/11. I would also have funds for college later. It would be paid for."

During his time in Iraq, however, he saw things that violated his sense of what he and his peers would and should be doing as soldiers. Riding to and from the prisons where he worked interrogating prisoners, or out on any interrogation assignment, the men who drove him around sometimes shot randomly at objects on the side of the road: abandoned cars, trash, sometimes even people's animals, "just popping off rounds at some guy's sheep for fun." "When I was in Iraq," Ricky reported, "I brought up each individual incident that happened to the respective commander," whether it was about the kill ing of civilians or farm animals or arbitrary detention of prisoners by U.S. troops. "I went to my chief every single time, which was probably ten or fifteen times, and I said I was not okay with certain things, or asked him about certain things. And then I went to the commander, even the colonel, a few times. Probably three times to Lieutenant Colonel Gibson, commander of the Second Brigade of the Eighty-second Airborne." By the time he returned home, with no uptake from commanders and no satisfaction from multiple conversations with his chaplain and a conviction that he did not object to all war and so did not have a valid claim to CO status, Ricky went AWOL and eventually ended up in the brig.

Tina Garnanez joined the army shortly after finishing high school, where she rose through the ranks of the Junior Reserve Officer Training Corps (JROTC) in the northwest corner of New Mexico, where she lived on and off the Navajo reservation. She was not looking for war, she insists, just some money for college and an experience that would continue to test her physical and mental abilities as JROTC had. A long-distance runner, she had always liked a good challenge. Then came 9/11 and eventual deployment to Iraq, where she served as a medic.

By the time she returned home a year later, Tina was filled with anger, shame, and confusion about what she had seen, heard, and done in Iraq. She told one of her brothers, Miles, that she wished she had not gone to war. She told him she had learned a new word, *pacifist*, and that it completely characterized who she was. Tina became active in the antiwar movement, sometimes traveling across the country to speak at rallies, organize other veterans, and conduct counterrecruitment in high schools. Most of her family supported her, but her brother was unhappy. The way he saw it, "You choose, you lose."

> My brothers really don't know what I'm doing. My brother Miles told me, "Well, you did sign up." And I said, "Well, yeah, I did." I told him if the war were really truly for terrorism I wouldn't be protesting. I would just shut my little mouth and go about my life. But it wasn't about terrorism. It was about one man's agenda and his greed. He and his wonderful buddies, just making money while poor kids are sent off to be cannon fodder. I disagreed with that, so I spoke out when I got home. It's very sad. He told me, "You do have a point. You didn't volunteer for *this* cause."

Despite Miles's coda, the rhetoric of choice in the All-Volunteer Force exists alongside the notion that one will need to obey orders, whatever one's political views. You don't get to choose wars. The president chooses wars, and the president is chosen by citizens, including soldiers. Dissent makes little sense in this context.

Tina agreed that no one made her volunteer for the army. Nor does she feel that going to Iraq was all wrong; she in fact reinterpreted the experience as one that developed or enhanced her prosocial emotional skills:

> At times I am really grateful for the experience of being in Iraq, because it opened my eyes to so much. Not only are we all connected, but we have to work together. We have to love one another. There's no way one of us or a small group of us is going to make it alone. It's just not possible. Compassion and love were things I learned in Iraq. Because of the war. Without the war, I don't think I would feel it so much. I mean, I always thought we should work together, but not until that experience did it really fully hit me.

One critical aspect of the widespread belief that soldiers and volunteering revolves around widely shared, sometimes unspoken, notions of masculinity. Of particular salience is the warrior ethos that provides the rationale for fighting and dying for noble causes, buttressed by the idea that real men provide, serve, sacrifice, and protect no matter what the personal costs. Yet if participation in war represents for so many men and women the most sanctified modern male experience, it is worth considering how antiwar feelings and activities challenge or exploit such foundational beliefs about what it means to be a true man. With the men we interviewed, it was not simply the act of putting on a military uniform that made them feel like men. It was their later acts of dissent, too, that they explained and justified as requiring the courage that men must demonstrate, even in the face of public ridicule and even if it meant risking retaliation, for example, by a vengeful military or Veterans Affairs. Only the unmanly or cowardly, many suggested, obey rules they know are wrong.

This phenomenon has been noted before. Historian George Mosse writes of the antiwar classic from an earlier war, *All Quiet on the Western Front*: "Here the ideal of masculinity so closely linked to war even informed the attitudes of those who asserted their hatred of the military conflict."[20] In both pro- and antiwar stances, men can see themselves through a prism of manhood that serves higher purposes and aims. Dissent from war can propel a soldier to question social injustice more broadly. Nonetheless, this never happens automatically.

A masculine calling to voluntarily serve and protect is evident throughout the multiple and contradictory masculinities both inside the military and among its antiwar veterans. The choice to contribute to the well-being of the nation and its people, if more secondarily to the needs of others around the world, is crucial to the sense of personal loyalty and manly commitment to causes greater than oneself. The armed forces have historically drawn commitment for the mission on the basis of allegiance by young men to the code of disciplined military masculinity.[21] Nonetheless, such military restraint is in marked contradiction to the violent spontaneity required in actual combat,[22] and is but one aspect of the inconsistencies soldiers are expected to live with.

Of great importance, and in contrast to the tribal male-bonding framing of many Hollywood war movies, military masculinities come in a far wider array, with multiple patterns corresponding to different services and units of the armed forces, with varying specializations, regional backgrounds, and more. From the autonomy of "fly boys" to the camaraderie of the infantry, from the elite academic training of generals to the 4 AM drills of boot camp, military masculinities utilize qualities that run the gamut from individualist to collective impulses, disciplined to spontaneous reactions, immediate to long-range ambitions.[23] And of course it is crucial never to conflate the ideas of masculinities of those sent to war with those of the people who send them.

The manly attributes required to face death compared to those required to send others to die are distinct, as reflected in the very different training programs for officers versus those in enlisted ranks. Risking one's own life and limb requires a choice centered on a willingness to endure pain and suffering, even if it leads to the "ultimate sacrifice." To order others into such circumstances requires a morally and manly superior ability that enables true leaders to place socially necessary goals above individual desire and to accept with sadness but never remorse the consequences of losing one's own troops.

The fact remains that choice (e.g., with respect to training, promotion, and deployment) is for most troops severely restricted after enlistment, while the fact that they were not forced to the military is invoked repeatedly during their service. This assumes an especially gendered quality when one of the most frequent charges against male soldiers who are disgruntled for one reason or another is that they must not be manly enough to "take it" and are trying to shirk their duties because they have come up against their own limitations as men. With female soldiers the charge is similar: they are proving themselves incapable of the tasks *because* they are women.

As Aaron Belkin notes, "Military masculinity becomes the model of the ideal American," and men who wish to be ideal Americans therefore can choose enlistment to best achieve this aim.[24] More broadly we can say that constructions of masculinity in the United States have themselves long been based on the fact that it is primarily male citizens who participate in the military (they make up 85 percent of the total) and through this directly in the maintenance of empire.[25] Although the draft has existed periodically to help compel men to join the armed forces, even more in the last hundred years in the United States, the military has represented the essence of American manliness precisely because so many young men have, whether drafted or not, joined, and, in so doing, they have implicitly announced that they have what it takes to survive and pass manhood's most vigorous test. The voluntary nature of the All Volunteer Army should not be understood in merely negative terms—something that has emerged only because the draft cannot be reinstated for political reasons. It can also be understood as a powerful engine for the production of a democratic empire—of empire, freely chosen and altruistic and of a particular form of masculinity that produces and is produced by it.

The Iraq War veterans we interviewed, and the young men in particular, explained their antiwar activity within familiar frameworks of protection of a population, self-sacrifice, idealism, and duty. In discussing Iraq (and Afghanistan), many soldiers make reference to the Vietnam War and to the notion that history has repeated itself in the two recent wars.[26] As in Vietnam, many young men shipped out to Iraq expecting they would be embraced as liberating heroes.[27] And as in Vietnam, the pride and idealism of young men and women sent to fight in Iraq overpowered initial doubts and sustained many of them.[28] An enormous difference between the two eras, of course, is that there is no draft to supply troops for the wars in Iraq and Afghanistan. The antiwar movement has tended to minimize the significance of the absence of a draft, pointing to the fact that the troops are predictably drawn in all these wars less from the middle class and more from the poorest in U.S. society. But this perspective remains a macrosociological one. Noneconomic factors also motivate enlistment, including idealistic aspirations that are couched in a masculine language combining the desire to protect others and to take responsibility for one's own decisions.

When progress in the war in Iraq became ephemeral and atrocities were committed by their colleagues, some service members began to lose faith in their own and their leaders' moral authority. Some began to believe that the military had been betrayed and undercut by the U.S. government and politicians. Others began to believe that American citizens were, at best, ill-educated about the realities of the Iraq War and ignoring its costs and consequences and at worst hypocritical and criminally implicated. Still others argued that if they did not choose to speak out against the war, they would become the true enemies of all those ideals that led them to enlist and deploy.

It is extremely difficult for dissent to emerge within the ranks of the U.S. military today. A number of things, we have suggested, make this so. They include the rhetoric of choice; the normalization of militarism or the marketed idea that this is the way the world should be and that the world is better on account of the U.S. military and its wars; and the assumption of a "we" of the military and society, more common now than in the Vietnam era, which suggests that it is possible and necessary to support people in uniform even when one disagrees with the policy that sent them to war, since policy is ultimately an electoral matter. Even more than this, perhaps, an increasingly militarized U.S. electorate has come to take the president as the commander-in-chief not only of the military but of themselves as well, making assent to war always and in every case necessary.

Dissent, on the other hand, has become more of a possibility in some ways than it might have been in earlier wars because of the porousness of the battlefield to other sources of information. Many of the soldiers we spoke with had read critiques of the war on the Internet or even web-chatted with Iraqis experiencing the war from the other end of the rifle. Many were able to order books online by Noam Chomsky and Howard Zinn and learn alternative ways of thinking about the war and about the United States.

Most crucially, however, they came to their major epiphanies about the war as a problem when the mission they *thought* they were on confronted the mission they *were* on. They began with a sense that they were in Iraq on a noble mission, as part of the most respected and respectable institution in the society from which they come. In basic training, the military instructed them not only in the technical aspects of war, such as marksmanship and map reading, but also the Rules of Engagement, including how to treat civilians and prisoners according to the Geneva Conventions and other laws of war. Along with every other soldier in Iraq, Garett Reppenhagen discovered that the Rules of Engagement are so much paper. He and other soldiers found themselves or their fellows raiding home after home in which no insurgent activity or evidence was found, terrorizing the families inside, kicking, butt-stroking and clothes-lining Iraqi prisoners of war, spraying machine-gun fire into homes after hearing a single shot from somewhere in a village, throwing urine-filled bottles and feces-packed food packets at people walking along the side of the road, shooting farmers working in their fields at night (who were taking advantage of erratic electricity to run their irrigation systems) simply because they were out after a U.S.-mandated curfew, and being commanded not to stop for pedestrians and instead to run over anyone or anything as their convoys roared down highways.

In addition to training Iraqi soldiers and police, Garett had contact with Iraqi civilians at checkpoints. These were well-established inspection sites or more often "surprise" checkpoints to catch imprudent Iraqi insurgents carrying explosives or ammunition. If drivers and passengers were lucky, they simply got waved through and were allowed to continue. The less fortunate had their vehicle meticulously examined for hours in the hot sun. The inability to communicate except through pantomime compounded problems. At checkpoints throughout Iraq, U.S. soldiers reported deadly shootings of civilians because their car approached too quickly or because the driver did not stop in time.[29]

One particular night, Garett found himself once again flagging down a quickly approaching vehicle. His unit was in the town of Al Khalis, around the end of April 2004. A search of some houses was planned, and Garett and about fifteen other soldiers were to provide the protective cordon. "We set up a hasty checkpoint—we tried to be unpredictable—with our Humvees blocking the road. Two rolls of concertina wire and traffic cones." It was about midnight, and there was little traffic. Garett was in front waving cars down to stop them for searches. "And here came a guy probably driving home in the middle of the night, who drove this way all his life. And normally there were no checkpoints in this spot. Until that day."

"And he saw the checkpoint too late. He was coming up too fast. You're thinking there could be a car bomb. You got your heart pumping and your adrenaline flowing because you think you're just going to get bombed," Garett said, his words coming faster and faster.

> You're thinking about the time when somebody didn't fire and he got in trouble for not firing because they said he was endangering his unit. You're thinking about the guy that did fire another time and killed an innocent, but he didn't get in trouble for firing. A few of us in the middle of the road were trying to wave this guy down, and he hit the brakes and the car screeched to a stop. My adrenaline was through the roof. So I rushed this guy. I was on the driver's side. I rushed the car door and I tried to open it. I was yelling at the guy in the car, 'Get the fuck out of the car! Get the fuck out of the car!' Only he didn't speak English, so he was not getting out of his car, you know? His hands were in the air and he was trying to explain something.
>
> I was trying to open the door, but the door was jammed because his car sucked. It was junk. And I was frustrated because you couldn't open the door. I was embarrassed that I was trying to open a door that didn't open. So I just grabbed the guy by the shirt and kind of under his armpit. I pulled him out the window and I threw him on the ground, rolled him

over, and I zip-stripped him.[30] And then I realized, out of the corner of my eye, that his wife and kids were staring at me with this intense hatred in their eye, like, "My god, what are you doing to my father?" And it was a look of hatred, is what it was. It was this angry look of, "I do not like you. I don't like Americans. I don't like what you're doing and I'll probably never like you." I just realized I was part of the problem. And I didn't mean to be, and I didn't want to be, but I was there, you know? And that was the crime. The crime was that I was there.

Especially noteworthy here, Garett couches his agonized portrayal of the events at the checkpoint that day both in the language of epiphany, and of horrified realization, and he also invokes choice, or rather the absolute, categorical *lack* of choice that he experienced. He hated himself and the situation—but that, at least at the time, neither absolved him of his complicity in this crime against Iraqi civilians, nor allowed him escape from the situation.

> I felt like if we weren't there in Iraq, my soldiers and myself would not be in danger, so we felt justified to use oppressive and abusive tactics against Iraqis to ensure that we live. We didn't have to be there. That didn't have to be going on. It just really made me question the whole thing. It made me question myself because I always saw myself as doing the right thing, that would take the proper course of action, that thought about ethics and morality. And here I was, the one with my hands on this dude feeling justified to rip him out of his car and throw him on the ground and put him in handcuffs.

They searched the car, found nothing. Eventually they cut the zip-strips off the man's wrists and freed him and his family.

"It made me feel like an asshole. It was like, Here I am, I'm the guy acting like a Nazi."

Of his moral choices in some other situations of this kind, Garett said, "Once you get into the situation and you're surrounded by people that have been there for a year, that have been dealing with that for a year, those slip away, you know? You're like—you're like just one gear in this huge, churning machine, and you can't not choose to spin, you know? You just spin with the whole thing."

Garett's words here highlight how the rhetoric of choice ignores structural constraints and the power of the group. Recruits also enter, as Garett and others note, with preexisting selves and imperfect knowledge about what they will be engaged in once they join the military, particularly how gigantic the institution is and how much effort goes into constructing a mythic view of the American Project. There are, quite literally, recruits who believe they will not be required to carry a gun if they wish not to, or believe that it is a jobs-training program as much as a military one. Although recruiters entice some youths to enlist through promises of combat adventure, many more young men and women join the military seeking stable employment and future educational opportunities.

BECOMING AND STAYING A GOOD MARINE IS COMPLICATED

Chris Magaoay is a young Filipino from Hawai'i. He grew up literally in the shadow of military warships and surrounded by men and women in uniform, in one of the most heavily militarized states in the country. Like Tina, he had been active in JROTC in high school, though in his case he also ran into some trouble with the law, and only after strenuous efforts on his part was he finally allowed to join the Marines. After barely making it through a turbulent basic training and, somewhat to his surprise, graduating, Chris felt a tremendous sense of pride and accomplishment. He was sent for further training to Twentynine Palms, in California, for training, and he seemed to find a good sync between his interests and abilities and what was required to be a competent marine.

But it is one thing to drive a truck around in the sand in California and another to go to war. For Chris, too, there was no excitement at the news that he and his unit should prepare for deployment to Iraq. He remembers asking their sergeant, who had already been to Iraq, what it would be like. The sergeant decided on a visual shock approach, handing him and the other members of his platoon a photograph of a smoldering body, with this same sergeant leaning over lighting his cigarette off a small, human flame. "It was the most horrible thing I've ever seen." Chris had looked at this man as a leader. "I knew his wife. He had always seemed very honorable. But the disgrace he wanted to make out of someone's death was beyond my understanding." After already sliding into serious doubts about the mission in Iraq, and more than a little ambivalent about the Marines—he hated basic training, but, after all, he'd proved himself capable there—Chris began to have serious thoughts of not deploying with his unit.

He was not thinking that war in some abstract sense was wrong. He was thinking this man, and this kind of excitement, was wrong. "You're not supposed to take pictures in combat. You're a warrior. It's not your job to flaunt around what you do. You fight, you come home, and you forget about the things you've done, 'cause you have to do bad things, and you're not supposed to be proud of the bad things you did. He was obviously proud of the bad things he's done."

"I tried to get my wife to break my leg with a baseball bat" to get out of training operations in preparation for deployment. She tried but could not do it. That's when Chris "stomped down" on a barbeque brush lying on the ground. "It sliced through the cartilage of my heel. I had to go to the hospital to get stitched up." He was put on light-duty assignments.

He was sliding into a darker place, fearing the thought of killing civilians, or acquiescing to war crimes committed by other troops. "I thought it would be an honorable career to protect and defend the Constitution. That was my thing. I was there to do honorable service. I was an American who didn't just kill for his country, but really fights deep down in his heart for his country and won't do anything wrong." He told his wife, "I don't want to be here."

> I broke. I lost my belief in everything. I had taken an oath to be a Marine, and no one is going to take that title away from me. I'm proud that I went through the training that many people could never do. I'm proud of the oath I took and that I was ready to give my life up for my country. But the mission they put me on was wrong. I believe I didn't betray the Marine Corps. The Marine Corps betrayed me as a Marine, and betrayed the American people.
>
> Leaving the Marine Corps wasn't a choice. It was my responsibility not to be involved in any part of it. Guilty by association. Literally. I know what's happening there and I can't keep my mouth shut. As a Marine it's my responsibility to say something about it. So, to be a good Marine, I could not be involved with the war. To be a good person, I could not be involved with the war. I could not be involved with taking people's lives for oil, covering up collateral damage or intentional killing of civilians. I could not. No.

It seemed like a sudden decision, but clearly it had been a long time coming. He and his wife made a desperate escape across most of the United States, driving over the border into Canada, where his wife was from, by pretending he was being stationed at the U.S. embassy in Ottawa.

Did he feel like a coward? Did he feel as if he was leaving his friends and colleagues to fight in his place, to risk their lives so he would not have to risk his? Did he feel like this, too, was a voluntary decision?

"For me it took more courage to resist against the government, and resist against your friends, your family, and the political beliefs of your entire nation. Well, at least what they portray as the political beliefs of the entire nation. A coward is the one who just follows direction and gets pushed around.

It takes courage to make your own decisions and say, 'No, forget it.' That's my personal opinion."

Many U.S. military personnel go to war with high ideals: helping others, liberating people from the bullies in their country or region, making their parents proud of how they can accomplish difficult tasks. They feel they are making a choice, and that choice is usually heavily validated by others. The military tells them they have but one choice point, in the recruiter's office, and that after that they are in their officers' hands, and God's. Some of those who entered the military with the aim of self-sacrifice for a greater good, in this war as in previous ones, have the hardest time dealing with the violence and injustices they see. The most idealistic, those who believe they will be greeted as liberators and welcomed as saviors from oppression, and instead find rejection, hatred, and opposition to U.S. invasions and occupations—among such ranks may be found those who, traumatized as they might be through the experience, come to question and contest the entire military project of empire.

CONCLUSION

Although the preenlistment life choices facing young men and women in the United States are far from limitless, it is still reasonable to ask why the military is consistently seen by so many young men and women as offering more favorable odds for their future than the alternatives. Why do so many young people see in the military an opportunity to be their best selves in the sense of service to others, including to nation and to humanity itself? Liberalism's insistence on voluntary association, on the ability to think and act independently, is not lost altogether in a regimented military, but on the contrary, this independence can be seen by recruits as entailing both their choice to join and their choices while in the military. They can also see the military as harnessing the best in themselves for a higher purpose than themselves.

The Achilles heel of modern, mass citizen armies has long been that their lowest-ranking volunteers are drawn disproportionately from the most dispossessed men and women in society.[31] It is also true, however, that to some extent these young people join of their own will and see themselves in that way. That choice carries with it a sense of obligation to finish what they committed to. The rhetoric of choice—from voting for political candidates to enlisting in the military—is ubiquitous in the enculturated discourses of citizenship and empire in the United States: children learn early on that Americans make themselves as individuals and they select their government and so decide what their country will be and do. No one is forced to join the armed forces, but when they do, they both protect the country, its allies, and, sometimes, the world's weakest populations and they choose to instantiate a highly valorized masculinity. This ideological complex of choice and manliness is central to producing the sense of a unified "we" of contemporary U.S. empire; if they have in some meaningful sense chosen to be warriors, then they share both the "we" of armed forces personnel compared to the broader civilian population, and they constitute a "we" who have individually and collectively and freely opted to do the work of empire, whatever that may entail.

Ricky Clousing chose to be a Christian missionary in Thailand and Mexico, and then an army interrogator in Iraq. In both cases, he says, he chose to do good in and for the world. In both cases he was also doing what a man is supposed to do: to protect others even if this entails great personal risk. Garett Reppenhagen, like Ricky, was appalled by the treatment of civilians at the hands of the U.S. military in Iraq. For him, just as he chose to enlist (in his case more for economic than any other reasons), he also chose his response to the atrocities carried out against Iraqis. But he knows that some of his peers chose instead to behave more brutally during their time in Iraq.

The military emerges from the larger social order of the United States. Despite the increasing political emphasis on the distinction between the military and society or the soldier and the civilian, it is precisely the "civilian" life histories, civilian approbation, and encounters with Iraqi civilians of these young men and women in American uniforms that provide insight into the contradictions of empire. They demonstrate what can happen when people in uniform personally experience the shock of discovering the realities of invasion and occupation and the sharp contrast between this knowledge and what they have been led to believe is the American way and goal of war. They can undergo a series of moral and political epiphanies, and come to see themselves not as liberators and protectors as promised, and not as they hoped to see themselves when they voluntarily joined the military.

Emerging from the crucible of Iraq, they start to use the rhetoric of choice, not to explain and excuse their participation in invasion and occupation, but instead to profoundly reframe what they will do next. Just as they sometimes blame themselves for joining—and sometimes wonder what might have happened to them if they had chosen a different course—they take righteous pride in describing the choices they have made with their new understanding of empire. And then, in some cases, they wonder if they in fact had much of a choice at all, if they wanted employment and education, or if they were simply a gear in a machine whose forward motion they had little hope of stopping. And, finally, neither could some choose the route of staying silent about the war and its injustices.

ACKNOWLEDGMENTS

Thanks to Carole McGranahan and John Collins for inviting us to participate in this project, to Betsy Brinson for contacting us years ago to write a book about antiwar Iraq War veterans, to Louie Montoya for assistance in preparing the manuscript, to Anna Christensen, Lindsay Cunningham, Spencer Amdur, Lindsay Mollineaux, and Jenna Williams who helped transcribe the interviews, to Brown University veterans of the Iraq War Eric Rodriguez and Scott Ewing who provided editorial assistance, and especially to the veterans who shared their lives and experiences with us.

NOTES

1 It began, and the draft ended, in 1973, necessitating an increasingly large Pentagon recruiting budget. See Burk, "Theories of Democratic Civil-Military Relations"; and Krebs, "The Citizen-Soldier Tradition in the United States."
2 Gutmann and Lutz, *Breaking Ranks.*
3 Lutz, "Empire Is in the Details."
4 Turse, "The Pentagon's Planet of Bases."
5 Lutz, *The Bases of Empire.* The notion of choice also structures many of the narratives about how empire's reach has come to be what it is (see Stoler and McGranahan, "Introduction") with Guam, for example, said to have chosen to be affiliated with the United States, or the Republic of Korea to have chosen to give the United States land for bases and to give U.S. generals wartime command of Korean forces.
6 Vine, *Island of Shame.*
7 Stoler and Bond, "Refractions off Empire," 95.
8 Hartung, *Prophets of War.*
9 Inoue, *Okinawa and the US Military.*
10 Lutz, *Homefront*; *The Bases of Empire*; Gutmann, "Military Conscription, Conscientious Objection and Democratic Citizenship in the Americas."
11 Price, "Human Terrain Systems, Anthropologists and the War in Afghanistan."
12 US Department of Veterans Affairs, "Population Tables, Table 1L."
13 Kriner and Shen, *The Casualty Gap.*
14 Stiglitz and Bilmes, *The Three Trillion Dollar War.*
15 Barstow, "Behind TV Analysts, Pentagon's Hidden Hand."
16 Associated Press, "Pentagon sets sights on public opinion."
17 Gallup, "Confidence in Institutions."
18 Engelhardt, *The End of Victory Culture.*
19 This is notwithstanding the existence of a rigid quota system of no more than 15 percent women in the armed forces, and testing and recruitment techniques

that ensure that the military does not become racially more black than the population at large.

20 Mosse, *The Image of Man*, 108.

21 Snyder, "The Citizen-Soldier Tradition and Gender Integration of the US Military."

22 Higate and Hopton, "War, Militarism, and Masculinities."

23 Barrett, "The Organizational Construction of Hegemonic Masculinity."

24 Belkin, *Bring Me Men*, 182.

25 Connell, "Globalization, Imperialism, and Masculinities." In fact it is also and ever more important to extend our discussions of military masculinities to those sometimes not counted as fully in the ranks, such as reservists and "civilian" contractors (Higate and Hopton, "War, Militarism, and Masculinities").

26 Mariscal, *Aztlán and Vietnam.*

27 Caputo, *A Rumor of War*; Herr, *Dispatches.*

28 Moser, *The New Winter Soldiers*; Stacewicz, *Winter Soldiers*; Terry, *Bloods.*

29 Iraq Veterans Against the War, Glantz, and Swofford, *Winter Soldier, Iraq and Afghanistan*; Wood, *What Was Asked of Us*; Hedges and al-Arian, *Collateral Damage.*

30 Plastic strips used as handcuffs by U.S. soldiers because they are cheaper than metal handcuffs and do not need a key.

31 Kimmel, *Manhood in America.*

V

Residue, Rumors, Remnants

15 Locating Landmines in the Korean Demilitarized Zone

ELEANA KIM

> Japan became a signatory [to the 1997 Mine Ban Treaty]. And if you sign the treaty, you have to destroy the mines. Japan was ordered to destroy them, and I heard that it took them fifteen days to destroy however many tons of mines and TNT. But in our country [South Korea], not only are the mines not destroyed, they continue being buried. And this has to do with what we were talking about before. Our fellow villagers were just going about their business, and three people died—on a road that they frequented every day. There—right in the place where they eat and fetch water. One day, three people go there, two people get killed, and one of them is too scared to say anything. As it turned out, one of them was able to crawl away a bit. So, the first one died right away—the one who stepped on the mine. The person behind him was hit with shrapnel and was able to crawl away, and crawl away, and then died. What could the husband do, knowing this? If only he had been faster—perhaps, we can't know—she might have lived. But since he hid himself and didn't get help, she died. This person [the husband] killed himself. He committed suicide, and their children—where could they go? They were sent for adoption overseas. What can you say about this? What you can say is that, however you look at it, these are all war victims. As I said before, this is an extension of the war [*chŏnjaeng'ŭi yŏnjangsŏn*].
>
> —MR. LEE, mayor of Cheongjeon-ri, Cheolwon County, Gangwon Province, South Korea, May 2012

This story emerged out of a conversation with four longtime residents of Cheongjeon-ri, in Cheolwon County, South Korea, located five kilometers from the border with North Korea. What had started as an interview about local views on plans to designate the Demilitarized Zone (DMZ) as a United Nations Educational, Scientific, and Cultural Organization (UNESCO) Biosphere Reserve very quickly turned to stories of landmines and civilian deaths. For these residents, recent framings of the DMZ by the state and NGOs as a zone of ecological preservation and as a source of ecotourism income coexisted uneasily with their personal and collective histories of fear and restriction. After reminding me that the United States used Agent Orange not only in Vietnam but also in the Korean DMZ, my interlocutors concluded, "So if you ask the local people, they'll say, 'what nature?'" "Everything's been ruined, frankly. America has ruined everything."

Since the late 1990s, with the documentation of rare and endangered species living in the DMZ area, various state and regional projects have endeavored to capture the "natural capital" of the "no-man's land" between North and South Korea. Ecological surveys have found that the DMZ and adjacent areas host more than 13 percent of the total species on the Korean Peninsula, including 106 rare and endangered species. Given these findings, efforts to preserve the DMZ area's environment and to capitalize on its associations with nature and biodiversity have intensified on the southern side of the border. Under the banner of the "Peace and Life Zone," or PLZ, a branding mechanism invented by the Ministry of Culture, Sports and Tourism in 2007, the DMZ's pristine ecology is presented as a vehicle for cooperation and exchange through the promotion of the DMZ as a greenbelt of peace and understanding.[1]

Despite the widely accepted fact that the Korean Demilitarized Zone is the most heavily militarized border in the world and is littered with one million landmines, during my fieldwork on the ecological value of the DMZ, landmines—if they appeared at all—were in the margins of the frame, a persistent problem that was only briefly mentioned as a "stumbling block" by policymakers in their Arcadian models for the "peaceful utilization" of the DMZ. As it would take an estimated 489 years to clear all landmines from the DMZ and South Korea, no one could deny that they presented a primary challenge to converting the DMZ into a peace park or biosphere reserve. Yet only one person I met outside of the NGO world seemed to have an interest in directly addressing the problem of landmines, by setting up a rehabilitation center for mine amputees, but his plans for slow food tours and ecotouristic experiences more often than not took center stage.

If landmines themselves were hard to discern in discussions of the DMZ, landmine *signs* and barbed wire were ubiquitous in the visual production of government documents, reports, touristic pamphlets, and marketing. And popular representations of the DMZ invariably describe it as crisscrossed by barbed wire and littered with landmines. With promotion of the DMZ as an accidental ecological sanctuary, images of birds perched on barbed wire or flowers blooming next to landmine signs have become commonplace in South Korea. Thus, the DMZ as a "forbidden zone" is frequently highlighted in order to create a jolting juxtaposition between wildlife and militarization, and to foreground the irony that landmines are what protect endangered species from the ravages of human development and pollution. These images tell a story of nature's resilience and indifference to human politics and militarized violence. Yet the widespread fetishization of mine signs has another effect of displacing the actuality of landmines and their deadliness, especially in what I refer to as the "inter-Korean borderlands": the Civilian Control Zone (CCZ)—a five- to ten-kilometer wide area that buffers the DMZ from the rest of South Korea—and the "border area," an underpopulated, economically stagnant region adjacent to the CCZ.

The Korean War (1950–53) has technically been over for more than six decades, but the signing of the armistice agreement in July 1953 merely brought an end to overt hostilities, and sixty years on, although outright war seems unlikely, military skirmishes and saber rattling between north and south are frequent reminders that a peace treaty has yet to be signed. In South Korea, the ambiguous and contradictory temporalities of war/postwar, conflict/postconflict, and ongoing war/future peace are nowhere more present than in the inter-Korean borderlands. Landmines highlight the heterotopic nature of the DMZ, and bring these multiple temporalities into simultaneous focus, along with the perduring effects of the Cold War on "post–Cold War" environments. When it comes to landmines, Rob Nixon's notion of "afterdeaths" is apropos. As he writes, "in such societies, where landmines continue to inflict belated maimings and what I call afterdeaths, the *post* in post–Cold War has never fully arrived. Instead, whole provinces inhabit a twilight realm in which everyday life remains semimilitarized and in which the earth itself must be treated with permanent suspicion, as armed and dangerous."[2]

The post–Cold War era is also, however, an epoch in which "armed and dangerous" environments have become "ecologically preserved" environments. With the closure or decommissioning of more than four hundred military bases in the United States alone, these sites of toxicity and military pollution are being converted into spaces for biodiversity protection and wildlife management through "M2W" (military to wildlife) conversions.[3] Moreover, the U.S. Department of Defense has been particularly attuned to how to use environmental exception at times to evade responsibility for remediating military pollution, and at other times to expand territorial control in the name of national security and military readiness.[4] As Katherine McCaffrey writes, regarding the former U.S. bombing site in Vieques, Puerto Rico, the U.S. military's response to environmentalists in the early 2000s was to "[turn] environmentalism on its head."[5] In congressional hearings, military leaders presented bases as "national assets," akin to national parks, to argue against the "encroachment" of civilians who threaten national security by infringing on the proper training and military readiness of the troops.[6]

My research on the ecological turn in the DMZ and the inter-Korean borderlands reveals similar patterns, in which a notion of pure nature discursively depollutes, decommissions, and depoliticizes heavily militarized spaces. Unlike decommissioned Cold War bases, however, the DMZ and its contiguous borderlands are sites of ongoing war and its ruinations. The anomalous status of landmines in South Korea highlights the complex temporality of the DMZ, where peace is anticipated in landscapes marked by material, social, and ecological extensions of war. For the United States and South Korea, mines are not considered to be "military waste" as they would be in postconflict zones; rather, they are viewed as crucial to "keeping the peace." Therefore, figuring the DMZ as a "peace and life zone" requires grappling with the actuality of landmines in civilian areas, their existence, their deadly agency, and discourses about them.

In this chapter, I track landmines and their material and affective traces in the landscapes of the inter-Korean borderlands as techniques for rendering U.S. empire analytically apprehensible as an imperial formation.[7] This is especially important as, in the ambiguous spatiotemporalities of the DMZ as "peace and life zone," landmines and their victims too often disappear into the landscape, replaced with military kitsch or state-sanctioned "peace and life" narratives that metaphorically decommission landmines as elements of a distant past.

MILITARIZED ECOLOGIES AS IMPERIAL FORMATIONS

In the very sparse ethnographic research on explosive remnants of war, anthropologists have discussed the social effects of landmines and explosive remnants of war (ERW) in "postconflict" settings.[8] I consider landmines through the lens of "imperial debris,"[9] viewing them as constitutive elements of the human/nonhuman landscapes of South Korea and as organic actants or cyborgian live munitions that are both the ruins and active remains of imperial power. Ann Laura Stoler and David Bond write evocatively of the importance of identifying imperial formations "by tracing them through the durabilities of duress in the subsoil of affective landscapes, in the weight of memory, in the maneuvers around the intimate management of people's lives."[10] Landmines are, if nothing else, such "durabilities of duress." They materially embody and are embedded in histories of power and domination that suggest "how imperial formations persist in their material debris, in ruined landscapes and through the social ruination of people's lives."[11] Thus, following landmines in South Korea is not just about the environmental effects of war.[12] Nor is it only about "militarized landscapes."[13] It also about how landmine-infested landscapes are both metaphors and models of imperial power, its slow violence, and unspectacular time.[14]

Rob Nixon writes, "In the long arc between the emergence of slow violence and its delayed effects, both the causes and the memory of catastrophe readily fade from view as the casualties incurred typically pass untallied and unremembered. Such discounting in turn makes it far more difficult to secure effective legal measures for prevention, restitution, and redress."[15] This is especially true of landmine victims in South Korea, where the state expressly absolves itself of responsibility for landmine accidents and where victims rarely sue the government for compensation. There are no comprehensive records of casualties or deaths related to landmines in South Korea, and legislation to "support" (not "compensate") landmine victims and their families was approved after eleven years of lobbying, in late 2014. As a form of environmental racism, globally speaking, landmine contamination often affects the most politically, economically, or racially marginalized groups.[16] This is no more true than in Korea, where a survey of 228 survivors found that the majority lived below the poverty line and had no more than a primary school education.[17] Even as accountability is of key concern for victims and their advocates, however, landmines evade clear origins or teleologies, especially in "postconflict" settings. I do not seek to trace landmines "back" to an American "source" that justifies claims for compensation, but instead suggest how the indiscriminate and slow violence of landmines and their forensic ambiguity materially and affectively reveal and constitute relations of imperial power and sovereign exception.

Journalist and DMZ chronicler Hahm Gwang Bok calls landmines "living creatures, intelligent, higher forms of life [*chiroenŭn saengmul, chinŭng'ŭl katch'un kodŭngsaengmul*]."[18] Landmines are laid into the ground and become, like the mine signs that both repel and fascinate, naturalized elements of militarized landscapes, and take on a life of their own. Like the ruins of Yael Navaro-Yashin's ethnography of northern Cyprus,[19] landmines suggest the less than romantic appeal of some nonhuman actants over others. They are spatiotemporal, socioenvironmental, material-affective, lively and deadly, and can be "smart" or "dumb." M14 antipersonnel landmines, for instance, are smaller than a hockey puck, made out of lightweight plastic, and are easily dislodged during floods or heavy rains. They can remain active for decades, and "because their [original army green] color fades to gray after a long period of burial, they are difficult to distinguish from fallen leaves."[20]

As natural-cultural elements of the inter-Korean borderlands, whether scattered randomly or laid deliberately, they create indelible effects on the humans and nonhumans that inhabit these landscapes, securing and proliferating borders. Their deadly liveliness and slow violence make them horrible to contemplate yet good to think with, offering a vantage point on U.S. empire, which, like landmines, can be random, indiscriminate, self-destructive, and, as I learned, may even be a source of unexpected transcendence.

LANDMINES IN THE DMZ AND BEYOND

In postconflict settings, landmines restrict not only land use, but also, due to the cost of demining procedures (between $300–$1,000 per mine), which is often viewed as "prohibitive," lead to thousands of deaths and casualties every year.[21] Since 1997, 161 countries have become party to the Mine Ban Treaty, spearheaded by the International Campaign to Ban Landmines (ICBL).[22] Today, antipersonnel landmines are widely seen as a humanitarian issue, given the fact that 70–85 percent of mine casualties are civilians in countries no longer at war. As stated on the International Campaign to Ban Landmines website, "Landmines don't obey peace agreements or ceasefires."[23] South Korea has the dubious distinction of being a country with one of the highest concentration of landmines in the world.[24] According to South Korean government figures, 970,000 mines are in the southern part of the DMZ, and another 38,000 mines in other parts of the border area. South Korean NGOs, however, assert that there are an estimated 600,000 mines in the CCZ and border areas. Based on defectors' testimonies, it is believed that North Korea has also buried at least as many landmines on their side of the border as has South Korea.[25]

The U.S. and UN forces used landmines extensively during the Korean War. According to an account from a lieutenant in the U.S. Corps of Engineers, 120,000 mines were sent to Korea, but "only 20,000 were recorded or on hand. The remaining 100,000 were either abandoned or buried unrecorded!"[26] Antipersonnel mines included the M14 "toe-popper" and the M16 "Bouncing Betty" fragmentation mine. M6 antitank mines were also laid widely. North Korean and Chinese troops did not initially use mine technology, but began to deploy mines captured from the other side against U.S. and UN forces. Eventually, Soviet-made wooden box "Schu" mines became part of their arsenal. Large numbers of U.S. casualties were attributable to mine incidents. Lt. Sam D. Starobin of the Sixty-Fifth Engineer Combat Battalion stated: "Failure to record minefields was a serious problem in Korea. It is not until you return to a mined area that you appreciate accurate minefield reports. We should lay mines indiscriminately only if we never intend to return and do not value the friendship of the population. Yet we had repeated instances of units laying minefields which they did not record. Under the pressure of hasty withdrawal, mine-laying sometimes degenerated to pitching armed mines from the back of a moving truck."[27]

What this testimony does not indicate is that the indiscriminate laying of minefields was not just due to "the pressure of hasty withdrawal," but was also part of approved U.S. military strategy. According to the 1952 army training guide, *Land Mine Warfare*, "nuisance minefields" are those in which "all types of mines, booby traps, dirty trick devices, and firing devices are used. The desired effects of demoralization, confusion, and fear are quickly gained by such use of mines. . . . Nuisance minefields may be laid to standard patterns or may be scattered. Scattered mining is preferable because of added difficulty in removal by the enemy."[28]

U.S. battalions that withdrew from Korea after the war left an estimated thirty thousand mines in unmarked mine fields. And in response to the Cuban Missile Crisis in 1960 and the attack on the South Korean presidential mansion by North Korean spies in 1968, mines were laid in the southern half of the DMZ and in areas throughout the CCZ. The Asian Games of 1986 and the Seoul Olympic Games of 1988 were additional occasions for heightened national security, which also entailed the laying of mines around sensitive military bases, and other strategic sites, including Umyeon Mountain in southern Seoul.[29] Most recently, the South Korean Ministry of Defense has reported 1,100 "planned" mine fields, and 208 unconfirmed ones.[30] The Status of Forces Agreement (SOFA, or Mutual Defense Treaty) between the United States and South Korea shields the United States from accountability for any number of violations, including environmental pollution and landmine casualties due to U.S.-laid mines.

With the softening of tensions between the two Koreas during years of the "Sunshine Policy" (1998–2008), the South Korean Joint Chiefs of Staff began a process of mine clearance, especially in areas flooded by heavy rains and in certain areas deemed militarily appropriate in the CCZ. Landmines are frequently dislodged in mudslides and flooding during the summer rainy season, and both South Korean and North Korean mines have led to civilian deaths in the border areas as well as the islands off the west coast as recently as April 2013.

The International Campaign to Ban Landmines has been one of the most successful civil society movements in recent history, transforming landmines into a global humanitarian issue, which led to the historic signing of the Mine Ban Treaty in 1997. The reluctance of the United States to become a signatory, despite its stated commitment to "humanitarian mine action,"[31] has been premised on the "Korea exception," which rationalizes the United States' stockpiling of mines as necessary to ensure military readiness on the

Korean peninsula. Although the U.S. reports that it no longer stockpiles "dumb" mines on American soil, it continues to store remote self-neutralizing or self-detonating "smart" antipersonnel mines in South Korea.[32]

The "Korea exception" is premised on the distinction between the ongoing war in Korea and postwar settings such as Bosnia, where landmines are categorized as "military waste." In South Korea, mines are not simply unexploded ordnance, but active parts of national security strategy, even as their antihumanitarian image has forced the U.S. and South Korean governments to deny or dissimulate when asked about the laying and/or stockpiling of landmines.[33] Whereas some observers question the necessity of landmines as a deterrent given the revolution in military affairs, in which tanks themselves are being retired as dinosaurs of a previous generation's military arsenal, in the case of the two Koreas, landmines are still considered to be the most effective deterrent, and crucial for maintaining peace. In response to the Mine Ban Treaty in 1997, the position of the South Korean security state was quoted in the *New York Times*: "'Many people talk about the humanitarian aspects of land mines,' said Lieut. Gen. Park Yong Ok, the Deputy Defense Minister and a fervent defender of the mines. 'Deterrence of war is more humanitarian than anything. If we fail to deter war, a tremendous number of civilians will be killed. And the use of land mines is a very effective way of deterring war.'"[34]

The Orwellian attempt to harmonize "humanitarianism" with landmines is no longer part of state rhetoric, but the principle that landmines constitute an essential part of national defense strategy continues to be upheld. The South Korean state spends approximately US$1 million on mine removal but risk education and security of minefields is lax, if not nonexistent. In the border area in particular, many minefields are unmarked or poorly maintained, presenting an ongoing threat to civilians and soldiers, and in clear violation of the law on the Use and Regulation of Landmines and Certain Conventional Weapons.[35] Because antipersonnel mines like the M14 are plastic, and contain only a small amount of metal, they are very difficult to locate with a metal detector. The safest and most effective way to clear antipersonnel and antitank mines is to use a specialized tractor that overturns the top layers of the earth, which either explodes the mines or exposes them for easy removal. Another challenge is the mountainous terrain of much of the country. Clearing mines on steep terrain is very difficult, and these are the areas from which mines are often swept away during the summer rainy season.

South Korean activists and NGOs associated with the Peace Sharing Association (PSA; formerly the Korean Campaign to Ban Landmines) and the Korea Research Institute for Mine Clearance have brought increasing attention to landmine victims, who have, as the PSA argues, "suffered in silence" for too long. Official data on landmine casualties do not exist in South Korea, but the PSA estimates at least 1,000 civilian casualties, and 2,000 to 3,000 military casualties.[36]

THE INTER-KOREAN BORDERLANDS

Because of the inaccessibility of the DMZ, ecological knowledge production and the development of tourism based upon the DMZ's natural renaissance take place in the Civilian Control Zone (CCZ), immediately south of the DMZ. The CCZ was established in February 1954 as a militarized area to secure the border with North Korea and to house the heavy artillery and armed troops disallowed in the DMZ. Training grounds, barracks, and military facilities are scattered throughout this area. The majority of the 600,000 South Korean troops and roughly 30,000 U.S. troops are stationed in the CCZ, and, combined with the one million soldiers on the North Korean side, they are what justify the DMZ's reputation as the most heavily militarized border in the world.

In the late 1950s, the South Korean state began moving civilians into the CCZ for both economic and political purposes, allowing some to return to extant villages and assigning others to reclaim land in new settlements. Cheongjeon-ri was one of 111 such "strategic villages" established by the state to repopulate the CCZ between 1959 and 1973, to counteract propaganda villages in the North, and to reestablish agricultural production, particularly in the Cheolwon plain, the historic rice bowl of the peninsula. These postwar settlers of the border area were either formerly enlisted men or poor urbanites who were lured with promises of land and secure livelihoods. Yet this was also a biopolitical, anti-Communist nation-building project, and civilians were subject to a strict screening process to ensure their patriotism and ideological commitments. That the farms established in the CCZ took the form of "Israeli kibbutz-style" collectives is a fact that is celebrated today, though residents in Cheongjeon-ri explained that it was necessitated by the fact that the land was owned by the state and because few of the settlers had any prior experience with rice farming or agriculture. At a time when South Korea was less economically developed than the North, these farms were meant to be visual displays of South Korean prosperity and wealth for the workers in the North Korean collective farms that were visible across the border.

The farmland was eventually divided up into privately owned parcels, yet life in these villages remained difficult, and residents, especially at the height of the Cold War, were subject to onerous military restrictions, including curfews, checkpoints, and limitations on development and land use. In addition, because the North Korean spies who attacked the presidential mansion in 1968 had come through the DMZ, minefields were reinforced and new ones were laid throughout the CCZ. In the 1980s, villages began petitioning to be removed from the CCZ, and today only eight remain inside the restricted zone. In essence, the border checkpoints have moved northward, around the village peripheries, such that the villages are now part of the "border area," which was designated in 2010 as a special development zone characterized by low population growth, economic stagnation, and high unemployment, among other indicators.[37] All of these shifting boundaries mean that parts of the border area, formerly in the CCZ, are also full of minefields, oftentimes poorly maintained or unmarked.

The DMZ may be an accidental sanctuary, but access to it is strictly prohibited. Therefore, attempting to leverage its associations with "pure nature" has meant that the CCZ and border area are the primary sites for tourism development, despite the fact that these environments are radically different from what exists in the DMZ itself. Extensive agricultural activity characterizes the western and central parts of the CCZ and border area, and, culturally, the residents have long been viewed as internal primitives, communities left behind by the nation's rapid modernization. Now that these rural landscapes are being resignified as extensions of the DMZ's pristine nature and associated with "peace and life," an oppositional discourse of ruination has emerged in which residents identify the despoliation of their ecologies with both the conservation movement and the South Korea state's subordination to U.S. empire.

DURABILITIES OF DURESS

When I visited Cheongjeon-ri in 2012, after a two-hour bus ride heading northeast from Seoul to the plains of Cheolwon County, my trip coincided with an ecotourism-training program spearheaded by a professor at the provincial university. This professor of geology was seeking to integrate local communities into a touristic and conservation project that would link the border area to a future UNESCO Geopark.[38] With major support from the provincial and county governments, his project was focused on "sustainable development" and the participation of "local residents" (*chiyŏk chumin*) in keeping with global mandates in conservation and ecotourism that frame "local" or "indigenous" people as important "stakeholders" in biodiversity preservation projects. The Geopark founder viewed locals as important assets to the region's cultural diversity and biodiversity, and enrolled them as tour guides who could objectify signature activities or practices as "local culture" while educating domestic tourists in geological features of the landscape as touristic attractions.

Mrs. Kim, who had been trained as one of these resident experts, was eager to play this role, and became my personal guide for the day. She herself had married into Cheongjeon-ri in the 1970s, and, when she was not working as a tour guide, managed a rice farm with her husband. Cheolwon County, where Cheongjeon-ri is located, is renowned as a rice-growing area, particularly for its local brand, Odae-ssal. For farmers like Mrs. Kim, who make a comfortable living from rice growing and other crops, becoming a tour guide was less about economic incentives than about connecting to broader networks of power, whether through initiatives like the Geopark, or via international scholars like myself.

Following a tour of White Horse Hill, which was the site of the most numerous and brutal battles between South Korean and Chinese forces during the Korean War, we convened at the community center, named the "Red-Crowned Crane Peace Hall," after the highly endangered red-crowned crane, which winters in the Cheolwon plain and has become iconic of the DMZ's ecological renaissance. Posters outside the hall featured dramatic images of the endangered cranes, with statements such as "Cheolwon, the Land of Life [*saengmyŏng*]! Red-Crowned Cranes, Eternal Life! We are all Life." *Saengmyŏng* refers to biological, or vital, life, and the posters outside of the Red-Crowned Crane Peace Hall brought together the symbolic meanings of nature, ecology, and place in a typical display of PLZ values, creating equivalences among land, human and nonhuman life, and peace. Inside, community volunteers had prepared a huge vat of steaming hot sticky rice that each of us took turns pummeling with a comically large mallet, in order to mush it and soften it into the handmade rice cake delicacy, *injŏlmi.*

After this participation in "local slow food culture" we nibbled on the freshly made rice cakes, while listening to a presentation by a representative of the Korea Rural and Territorial Development Institute. He showed photographs from a model village elsewhere in South Korea that created a welcoming environment for tourists, where the mayor of the village had mastered the art of hosting. He greeted visitors personally and never bored guests by speaking about the village history for more than fifteen minutes. Activities for tourists were structured as games or competitions, and food was prepared and presented in an ecofriendly way. The presentation ended with recommendations for Cheongjeon-ri, such as expanding the bathroom facilities, streamlining the composting system in the cafeteria, and, instead of serving coffee, providing a locally produced organic tea. In conclusion, he addressed the mayor of Cheongjeon-ri, Mr. Lee, an energetic man in his early fifties, instructing him to create a "concept" that would be immediately recognizable to visitors upon entering the village—in other words, a brand—that would function as a refrain across different activities and sites along the tour.

In response to this display of state paternalism, Mayor Lee simply left the hall. When Mrs. Kim and I sat down with him, he didn't try to hide his resentment toward "PhDs and experts" who come with "their research materials and tell us to keep in mind the 'originality' of our village." As he said, "if you were to believe them, we are going to hell [*manghae*]."

He lodged a familiar complaint about the onerous restrictions and unwarranted penalties imposed by the state and supported by environmentalists in the name of environmental protection, stating, "If I never had to hear the word preservation again, I'd be happy. That's what I think. Now it's DMZ this, DMZ that, DMZ has become known worldwide, so tourists will come. If that's so, realistically speaking, what benefit will there be for local people? We need to think about that. Now it's DMZ, Geopark, it's all the same. In the end, for these people, it's a theme."

Mrs. Kim, who was still invested in her role as a well-trained tour guide, heartily agreed, "It's a theme, it's about building content, content-ification" [*kŏnt'ench'ŭ hwa*]. Contentification, for the mayors of Cheongjeon-ri, however, merely represented the latest efforts to engage local residents in a neoliberal version of "rural development"—an antipolitics machine,[39] in which "preservation" was its immediate point of entry, but its longer-term effects were to extend state power through the technical solution of thematizing the village as a touristic site, while depoliticizing the state and the immediate concerns of the local community. Those immediate concerns became apparent during the course of my interview, when what I thought was to be a conversation about ecological preservation turned into a discursive mapping of landscapes of ruination.

Among the three residents I spoke with, each had lost a close relative to landmines—for Mrs. Kim, it was her father-in-law in 1998. He had gone to pay respects to at his own father's tomb. According to her, when he went every year, he would collect firewood along the same route, but didn't know that the previous autumn the local military battalion had laid more mines. Mrs. Kim described how they had to search for his bodily remains, "one foot, one leg hanging off a tree, but that's all we could find. . . . And three hours later it started raining and it rained until his funeral." The problem was that the newly laid mines were made of plastic, so even had he used a rifle to poke the ground, he wouldn't have been able to detect them. An explosive powerful enough to scatter his remains across the landscape meant, they reasoned, that it couldn't have been a regular antipersonnel mine or even a North Korean wood-box mine that might have been dislodged in the summer rainy season, but a high-explosive antitank mine that killed him. Carrying a load of firewood must have given him enough weight to set it off.

Mr. Lee then added that his father, one of the first settlers of the village, had died from a landmine in 1970, when Mr. Lee was eight years old, right before his youngest sibling's one-hundredth-day birthday celebration. As these residents recounted tragic stories of kinship loss, they cracked jokes about their traumas in a way that suggested that landmine casualties and deaths are a part of their everyday lives, and an integral aspect of their situated knowledges of landscape and nature. As Mr. Lee told Mrs. Kim, "Oh, you should have asked me—I would have been able to find all of his body parts!" In fact, in the first decade, before people learned where the landmines were concentrated, it was common for one or two people to die every year, as after each death, women who collected wild herbs and mountain vegetables for the funerary banquets also perished from landmines while foraging.

Even as black humor was a source of momentary levity, as our conversation continued, deep resentments surfaced. For Mr. Lee, the sudden death of his father left his mother a widow with two children and no government support or compensation.[40] Instead, soldiers showed up at their house to interrogate his mother about her husband's whereabouts and activities at the time of his death. The indifference of the state was still a sore spot for Mr. Lee: "They didn't send us anything, not even a bottle of rice wine for the funeral." Mr. Lee wanted state recognition of the sacrifices of mine victims as honorable war heroes of an enduring war, more than he desired financial compensation. As he said, the government will send support to Angola for the victims of mine injuries even as it ignores the unknown numbers of landmine victims in its own country. Mr. Lee described his case as even more pitiful, since, with the death of his father and the extreme poverty of his family, he was left to clearing minefields in order to survive. As in other postwar areas, military waste and landmine pollution became economic resources in the form of scrap metal. As another resident explained,

> We had cultivated the land, but there were no big rains. One only had to look at the sky. The rice wasn't coming up. People had to put their thinking caps on [*saramdŭli mŏrirŭl ttan tero kullin kŏya*]. President Park [Chung-hee] came up with the project modeled on Israeli kibbutz-style collective farms, and we tried it. But they should have given us food; there was nothing to eat. So, then, [we decided,] let's sell scrap metal, meaning steel, artillery shells, *sintchu. Sintchu* is what goes into making artillery shells. Spent cartridges. If you sold those things, like spent shells, barbed wire, you could bring in a lot more than from farming. And if you cleared mines, there was explosives inside, and *sintchu.* If you took it all apart,

then you could go somewhere and sell it and that was more than you could get from farming. So farming took a back seat.

There are many ruins one can point to in the DMZ and CCZ, from the demolished ruins of the Labor Party Headquarters in the former Cheolwon town center to the remnants of the Japanese colonial era or the infiltration tunnels built by North Korea and discovered by the South. Or even the new ruins of hypercapitalism and utopian visions such as the underutilized Peace and Life complex with a huge parking lot, built in a nearby village but already a material sign of the provisional nature of utopias. But to think of landmines is to acknowledge that the political economy of the inter-Korean borderlands has been built on ruins of another kind—ERW and military waste, the very ruins that have no purchase in the new economy of "content-ification," except as distant histories of heroic nation-building.

But the pathetic conditions that led to Mr. Lee risking his life by clearing mines was also connected to more surprising modes of existence. One day, while sharpening his farm tools, he heard an explosion nearby. Instinctively, he entered the minefield where two people had been thrown. They were scrap metal scavengers who were miraculously unhurt. He was suddenly struck with astonishment by his ability to trespass into an active minefield without consequence, marking for him a transformative a moment when his "overwhelming fear turned into ecstatic joy [*hwanhŭi*]." From this point forward, Mr. Lee became an active mine clearer, whose activities led to three citations for the "destruction of military property." Whereas residents view mines as deadly military waste, the state categorizes them as military property, and requires residents to report mines to local military battalions. Instead, the desperately poor people living in the CCZ, especially in the 1960s and '70s, scavenged scrap metal, from mines to copper from telecommunications wires, activities that created persistent tensions with military authorities.

It is undeniable that the losses of Mr. Lee's father and other members of the community were devastating, yet there was something more than economic desperation that drew him to become such an active mine clearer. Whereas utopian visions of policy makers and state projects portray the DMZ as an ecological treasure by repressing the existence of landmines, or minimizing them as "stumbling blocks," their durability is an unavoidable fact for residents of the inter-Korean borderlands. For Mr. Lee, the affective charge, from overwhelming fear to ecstatic joy—a momentary sense of transcendence over a highly restricted, militarized space—empowered him to transform a forbidding landscape into one that was life bestowing, providing a source of supplemental income for a family that had lost its primary breadwinner, and, however counterintuitively, a sense of life-affirming agency.

Yet this exhilaration and vindication cannot be understood solely through the framework of "resistance," in which landmines represent the power of the state, which is overcome through a valorization of illicit mine removal. Mr. Lee, in fact, viewed his mine-clearing activities as an expression of patriotic citizenship and unacknowledged contribution to the national building project. Moreover, as our conversation continued, it became clear that for Mr. Lee and the other residents, the landmine-infested border is also tied to geopolitical duress—South Korea's subordinate relationship to the United States.

Mr. Lee recalled that at a press conference in Japan that then–President Bill Clinton had claimed that there were no mines in South Korea. After a Japanese antimine activist corrected him, he replied that he would need to examine the issue more closely. I was unable to verify this exchange, but in an official statement regarding the United States' decision not to sign the 1997 Mine Ban Treaty, Clinton attempted to explain the justification for the Korea exception: "Anybody who's ever been to the DMZ and who has ever driven from Seoul to the DMZ and seen how short it is and has seen a million—you know, the numbers of troops there, and you see our people up there in those outposts and how few they are—and again I say, these mines are put along the DMZ in clearly marked areas to make sure that no children will walk across them. There is no place like it in the world."[41]

The U.S. position rests on a conjunction of "humanitarian mine action" and the "Korea exception" that, in effect, disavows the existence of South Korean mine victims, tacitly underwriting the South Korean state's antihumanitarian stance toward mine victims, and underscoring Stoler and Bond's assertion that "modern empires thrive on such plasticities and reproduce their resilience through the production of exceptions."[42] Yet even as actually existing landmines may disappear from view under the shadow of the Korea exception, they now reappear in the economically liberalized landscapes of the inter-Korean borderlands, where the branding of the DMZ continues apace.

LANDMINES AS GOLD MINES

In the western part of the CCZ, close to the Joint Security Area, where North and South Korean soldiers face off across the actual border, DMZ-related security tourism is being supplemented with ecotourism and the branding of "local culture." In commemoration of the sixtieth anniversary of the armistice treaty, T'ongil Village (Unification Village), located within the CCZ, unveiled its updated image as "Unification Brand Village" (*T'ongilch'on pŭraendŭ maŭl*) at their "Branding Event" occurring in July 2013. Following speeches by local government leaders and military officials, the T'ongilch'on Village Museum was opened to visitors. Developed in conjunction with an ethnographic researcher at the Kyeonggi Province Cultural Institute and the "T'ongilch'on Brand Village Development of DMZ Global Brand Business," it also received funding from the municipal and provincial governments as well as the Ministry of Security and Public Administration. In keeping with recent developments in the South Korean tourism industry, a key methodology employed in the museum was that of "storytelling" (*sŭt'ori t'elling*). Following this "storytelling" mandate, the museum exhibitions foregrounded the voices and experiences of the villagers themselves, with artifacts from their personal effects, as well as video interviews with the aging residents in their sixties and seventies who comprise the majority of the eighty households who have lived in T'ongil Village since its founding in 1973.

A placard featured quotes from villagers who described the entire area around their homes as "an unidentified minefield," especially following the reinforcement of forward positions after the attack in 1968 on the presidential mansion. Although the original Korean states, "Even today, minefields and farmland coexist in the village surroundings," the English-language translation is ambiguous: "Mines and farmland existed together around this village until the present." This indistinct use of the past tense in the English translation reflects a broader indistinction in representations of landmines and mine victims, especially in the past-present spatiotemporality of the museum, located in the very village that may be surrounded by unidentified mine fields.

Actual landmines and *sintchu* were displayed as part of the material culture of the village, but victims were noticeably absent in the museum's master narrative and in the accompanying text, "Research Report on Unification Village: Unification Village People, Stories of their Lives."[43] The oral histories of the elderly villagers were consistently told in the past tense, conforming to a narrative of progress and development: "It was scary. It was impossible to live. People died from stepping on mines as they worked. Hurt their legs. Back then, this was an impossible place to live. Things have gotten much better."[44] Not surprisingly, the most recent mine accident in May 2012 was not mentioned, nor were the more recent conflicts between locals and the South Korean military over rights to farm unidentified minefields and the dispossession of farm land by the U.S. military when it unilaterally expanded a firing range in the western CCZ.

The landmines included in the exhibition were presented as if they were historical relics of the past (they were U.S. military-issue mines, not South Korean ones), and displayed innocuously in glass vitrines, surrounded by slogans of future unification and peace. These displays recalled other ones I had seen, which exist at the entrance of the checkpoints one must pass through to gain entry into the CCZ. At these checkpoints, landmines are not framed as relics, but as samples, intended to act as informational warnings for visitors. Nevertheless, in the dozen times I have passed through CCZ checkpoints, the soldiers allowing us passage have never pointed out or explained the landmines to me or my traveling companions. Thus even the samples had a relic-like quality, but unlike the mines in the museum, were displayed in the open air, neglected, and unremarkable. They existed as part of the military's mandate to provide "risk education," but, like other aspects of their stated programs, have not been implemented.[45]

Between the Korea exception and the folklorization of border village cultures, landmines as imperial debris and their persistent potentiality may be disappearing from view, but the branding of the DMZ demands more iconography, and mine signs have thus proliferated in DMZ-related promotional materials. The telltale red sign appeared as the final image in a state-produced video about the DMZ's ecological renaissance, with a message inscribed on it: "The DMZ is the gold mine of nature." The Korean word *pogo* (repository or treasure trove), was translated as "gold mine," creating a pun out of "landmine" and "gold mine" that renders momentarily apprehensible the violence that neoliberal captures of "natural capital" depend upon. This slippery and perverse sign suggests that, in a moment when the state is seeking sources of surplus value in the DMZ, its landmines are being symbolically neutralized and abstracted from deadly ordnance into natural resources that can be exploited and commodified.

Development of the border area has followed typical neoliberal patterns in South Korea, which, since the shift to local self-governance in the 1990s, has led to the build up of tourism and branding of "local cultures" across the nation. The DMZ's Geopark and the Unification Brand Village are just two examples of such attempts to conform to the demands of global capital. In addition, border area agricultural products are marketed with the DMZ name, creating associations between rice and other produce with the DMZ's purportedly pristine air and water. Indeed, when I was conducting fieldwork in the border areas in 2012, as the United States and South Korea negotiated their free trade agreement, there was more insecurity regarding South Korea's economic subordination and fears among farmers about the domestic rice market than there was regarding North Korea's aggressions toward the South.

The narrative of the DMZ's natural restoration is a utopian one that represents the present as if it were past history. Landmines are presented as artifacts of a past overcome even as they continue to inhabit landscapes of ruination in zones of indeterminacy. That the mine sign, which functions to index the existence of actual mines, can be mobilized to brand the DMZ as a zone of "peace and life" intimates that the interpenetrating processes of militarization and naturalization at the border may have reached a new level of convergence with capital. Landmines mediate and embody the multiple registers and scales of U.S. empire, as military and economic hegemon, but the affective engagements and incommensurable narratives of border denizens such as Mr. Lee exceed the folkorized versions of "branded" villages, and state-funded "storytelling," leaving the future of landmines as natural-cultural elements of the DMZ's militarized ecology and their relationship to "peace" and "life" as yet indeterminate. Landmines, in their ambiguous and frightening spatial and temporal materiality, are proving to be at once "stumbling blocks" and "content" that may yet bring the relations of imperial power into critical visibility.

NOTES

Unless otherwise noted, translations are my own. Cheongjeon-ri is a pseudonym.

1 Some policy makers anticipate the DMZ functioning like the German Grünes Band, which was converted into a greenbelt following the end of the Cold War. Others imagine "politically neutral" projects that could bring North and South Koreans together around a new Sunshine policy focused on "biodiversity" and "science." North Korea, meanwhile, has maintained its position that any "peaceful" use of the DMZ would have to follow an actual peace treaty, which has yet to be signed.
2 Nixon, "Of Land Mines and Cluster Bombs," 169.
3 Havlick, "Logics of Change"; see also Coates et al., "Defending Nation, Defending Nature?," and Masco, "Mutant Ecologies."
4 Lachman, Wong, and Reseter, *The Thin Green Line.*
5 McCaffrey, "Environmental Struggle after the Cold War," 231.
6 See also Lachman, Wong, and Reseter, *The Thin Green Line.* The transfer of Vieques from the Department of Defense to the Fish and Wildlife Administration means that this toxic-waste-dump-turned-nature-preserve is off-limits to civilians, and also that the Department of Defense is absolved from its obligation to conduct a thorough cleanup. Cf. McCaffrey, "Environmental Struggle after the Cold War," 218–42.
7 Stoler and McGranahan, "Imperial Formations."
8 See Henig, "Iron in the Soil"; Schwenkel, "War Debris in Postwar Society."
9 Stoler, "Imperial Debris."
10 Stoler and Bond, "Refractions Off Empire," 95.
11 Stoler, "Imperial Debris," 194.
12 McNeill and Unger, *Environmental Histories of the Cold War.*

13 Pearson, Coates, and Cole, *Militarized Landscapes.*

14 Nixon, *Slow Violence and the Environmentalism of the Poor.*

15 Nixon, *Slow Violence and the Environmentalism of the Poor.*

16 Nixon, *Slow Violence and the Environmentalism of the Poor.*

17 International Campaign to Ban Landmines, *Landmine and Cluster.*

18 Hahm, *30 Years of Journeys in the DMZ*, 161.

19 Navaro-Yashin, *The Make-Believe Space*, 19.

20 D. Kim, "Floods Prompt Concerns over Buried Mines."

21 Nixon, "Of Landmines," 163. Although there can be no exact accounting of mines buried around the world, humanitarian mine clearance efforts have led to a reduction of ICBL's estimate in 1996 of 100 million.

22 The Mine Ban Treaty (or "Ottawa Treaty") refers to the 1997 Convention on the Prohibition of the Use, Stockpiling, Production and Transfer of Anti-Personnel Mines and on their Destruction.

23 See http://www.icbl.org/en-gb/problem/arguments-for-the-ban.aspx, accessed November 11, 2017.

24 Yoo, "Unending War."

25 K. Kim, "The DMZ as Ecological Repository."

26 Starobin, quoted in Westover, *Combat Support in Korea*, 23.

27 Starobin, quoted in Westover, *Combat Support in Korea*, 24.

28 Department of the Army, *Training Circular No. 34, Land Mine Warfare*, 11; reprinted in Smith, *Landmine and Countermine Warfare: Korea 1950–1954*, 64.

29 Im and Kwon, "Before Reunification Comes . . . Tasks to Be Completed."

30 K. Kim, "The DMZ as Ecological Repository."

31 U.S. Department of State, *US Landmine Policy.*

32 International Campaign to Ban Landmines, "Landmine and Cluster." According to the *Landmine and Cluster Monitor*, a South Korean official stated in 2011 that the country "safeguards a stockpile of antipersonnel mines that belongs to the US military on its territory" (http://the-monitor.org/en-gb/reports/2014/korea,-republic-of/mine-ban-policy.aspx, accessed November 11, 2017).

33 International Campaign to Ban Landmines, "Landmine and Cluster."

34 Kristof, "South Korea Extols Some Benefits of Land Mines."

35 Green Korea United, *Fact-Finding Report on 47 Mine Fields in the Border Area.*

36 The ministry of defense reported in August 2010 that thirty-two mines exploded between 2001 and 2008, with six deaths and thirty-five casualties; see D. Kim, "Floods Prompt Concerns."

37 Proposals to boost local economies feature the PLZ in a central role. Border tourism has followed a typical template for regional development—leisure sports (biking, hiking, marathoning, and fishing), local cuisine, and celebrity events tied to K-Pop or television dramas.

38 Although this venture ultimately failed, guide training programs and implementation of tourism infrastructure and services continue.

39 Ferguson, *The Anti-Politics Machine.*

40 The majority of landmine deaths and casualties are heads of their households and the primary breadwinners of the family (K. Kim, "The DMZ as Ecological Repository").

41 Public Papers of the Presidents of the United States, *William J. Clinton, Book II*, 1185. Clinton's statements were most likely based on the claims made by the South Korean state, which, until 1998, attempted to obscure the existence of landmines in the CCZ and the fact of civilian deaths and casualties (Cho, "Legacy of US Military Intervention," 8).

42 Stoler and Bond, "Refractions Off Empire," 95.

43 Kyeonggi Province Cultural Foundation, "Research Report on Unification Village."

44 Kyeonggi Province Cultural Foundation, "Research Report on Unification Village," 108.

45 International Campaign to Ban Landmines, "Landmine and Cluster."

16

Love and Empire

The CIA, Tibet, and Covert Humanitarianism

CAROLE McGRANAHAN

What does love have to do with empire? The *Oxford English Dictionary* defines love as "a feeling or disposition of deep affection or fondness for someone, typically arising from a recognition of attractive qualities, from natural affinity, or from sympathy and manifesting itself in concern for the other's welfare and pleasure in his or her presence; great liking, strong emotional attachment; a feeling or disposition of benevolent attachment experienced toward a group or category of people, and (by extension) towards one's country or another impersonal object of affection."[1] As nonromantic affection and attachment, love draws on ideas of sympathy and benevolence and on building a connection with another that feels important. This is the sort of relationship and sentiment retired CIA officers and Tibetan army veterans both repeatedly narrated to me during my research on joint U.S.-Tibet military and intelligence operations in the 1950s and 1960s. Love in the service of empire and nation certainly, but also love as something more than that, as ethnographic love that anthropologist Catherine Besteman describes as a relationship "defined by the experience of mutuality, solidarity, collaboration, and self-transformation."[2] In this chapter, my goal is an analysis of imperial affect in two CIA-Tibet operations that took place during the Cold War. I argue that an ethnographic analysis of the CIA, rather than only a political or historic critique, requires asking new questions about love as well as about spies and empire. To begin with, it requires taking spies seriously as not only imperial subjects, but also ethnographic ones.

Ethnographic subjects are human. Since its beginnings in the mid-nineteenth century, the discipline of anthropology has worked to humanize societies, to make them intelligible and meaningful, to place people on the same analytical scale, be it an evolutionary one or a comparative one or a relative one, and to offer and defend a system that reckons certain forms of life as equally human. This requires the turning of humans into the humane, transforming human life from "physiological fact" to "ethical subject" such that compassion, sympathy, and ethics become the ground upon which human connections rests.[3] For Tibetans in the 1950s, such human connections to the CIA and the U.S. Department of State led to relations and repercussions that continue today.[4] Both the CIA and State Department were integral components of U.S. empire from the Cold War on through to the current political moment, working to make the world safe for U.S. business and political interests.

The Tibetan involvement with U.S. empire came at a very specific moment in world history—the Cold War and period of decolonization, that historical moment when empires necessarily appeared in the world as anticolonial and anti-imperial. In the case of the United States this manifested as anticommunism, whereas for the Soviet Union and People's Republic of China, it was expressed as anticapitalism. One shared feature of Cold War imperial formations was invisibility.[5] Empires have always had secrets, but not all empires have been covert. What changes when empires go underground? Covert empire includes the concentration of power in the hands of intelligence officers, an informal and invisible imperial rule that runs parallel to official foreign policy, that is, an apparatus that "barely" exists on paper, specifically conceived for an anti-imperialist world, and that involves the cultivation of certain types of domestic sentiment and participation. The covert is a space that is deeply human and yet, how the covert is conceptualized and practiced is not always the same; it moves with and through different logics, different systems, and different bodies. Divergent structures of feeling grounded, animated, and arose from the varied CIA-Tibet operations, including practices of concealment and deception as well as the sharing and generating of secrets. My goal is thus to move toward an ethnographic analysis of the CIA that is critical but that is neither celebratory nor contemptuous. I do this alongside a discussion of Tibetan political agency in light of readily available, and sometimes deployed accusations of co-optation and compromise for any peoples connected to the CIA.[6]

Histories of two CIA-Tibet operations will ground my arguments.[7] The first is about the American Emergency Committee for Tibetan Refugees (AECTR). The AECTR was a CIA "front" that presented itself publicly as a legitimate nongovernmental humanitarian organization. It was privately organized for the CIA by a group of well-connected, wealthy conservative businessmen, doctors, and politicians in the United States. From 1959 through 1967, the AECTR provided conventional humanitarian aid to Tibetan refugees in India: foodstuffs, clothing, medicine, skill-based training, and education. Now as then, the AECTR has flown very low under everyone's radar. There are no histories of this group, just occasional suspicions of CIA links or comments of their "mysterious" disappearance from India in 1967.

The second history is of the grassroots Tibetan army called Chushi Gangdrug, which fought against the Chinese People's Liberation Army from 1956 through 1974.[8] Their military defense of their families, communities, country, and political and religious leaders, including the Dalai Lama, was partially funded by the CIA. For example, the CIA flew several thousand Tibetan soldiers from Asia to Colorado, where they trained them at Camp Hale from 1958 through 1964. Located at 11,000 feet in elevation, Camp Hale was the former military training site for the Army's Tenth Mountain Division ski corps during World War II and was as close as the CIA could get to the Himalayas in the continental United States. This operation was top secret in both the United States and Asia. I've written extensively about the Chushi Gangdrug Army from a Tibetan perspective, emphasizing Tibetan experiences and interpretations of the war, rather than subsume this history into one of U.S. Cold War politics as is so often the case. In this chapter, I now seek to explore another side of this history by focusing on the questions of imperial sentiment and covert humanitarianism.

HUMANITARIANISM, EMPIRE, AND SYMPATHY

What makes something humanitarian? According to Michael Barnett and Thomas G. Weiss, to be humanitarian "is to respond to the suffering of others regardless of their identity, to act selflessly, to do what can be done to save lives, and to place humanity above all other considerations."[9] Anthropologists Ilana Feldman and Miriam Ticktin further explain that genealogies of humanity as a universal category posit the commonality of human beings as a "starting point for elaborating the political and social obligations that humans have to each other—the humanitarian connection."[10] Humanitarianism thus ostensibly involves selfless obligation, human connection, and cooperative governing, traversing possibilities of the political, from the politically neutral to the politically grounded. However, humanitarianism rarely, if ever, exists in a domain of pure altruism outside of politics.[11] Additionally, humanitarianism's narratives of rescue and rehabilitation, of benevolence and transformation, are not new. These are the same narratives that underlie empire, discourses that legitimate imperial as well as humanitarian interventions and practices.

In the period between the end of the Cold War and 9/11, most U.S. military interventions were not operations of war, but claimed to be in response to humanitarian crises.[12] One such project was Operation Continuing Promise, the U.S. Navy's "seagoing medical treatment facility" which provided free health care in countries throughout Latin America and the Caribbean from 2007–11 on a ship named *Comfort*.[13] In September 2017, the *Comfort* was deployed to Puerto Rico in the aftermath of Hurricane Maria. Such military humanitarianism "provides cover for the raw power ambitions" of empire in "a kind of partially arrested dialectic, whereby the transnational humanitarian identity becomes an important articulation point of imperialism" albeit one that is "never fully contained or exhausted in the imperial project."[14] This is how humanitarianism shields empire, via projects and sentiments that articulate but also precede and exceed imperial expectations.

In an interview in 1993 with the *New York Times*, the Dalai Lama stated that unlike earlier U.S. support for Tibet, which was motivated by anticommunist politics, current U.S. support is "truly out of sympathy and human compassion" and thus is something "really precious [and] genuine."[15] Genuine or not, sympathy was long part of the European civilizing mission.[16] Following the work of scholar Amit Rai, we might approach sympathy in two, related ways: first as a paradoxical mode of power in that in order "to sympathize with another, one must identify with that other," which requires bridging the very cultural or racial differences that enable the ground of sympathy in the first place.[17] Second, it is a form of subjectivity "instrumental in . . . marking off populations in need of benevolence, and thus of normalizing subjects into better citizens."[18] This is sympathy as a "principle of sociality and cohesion . . . as a mechanism of differentiation and normalization . . . [and as] a way of establishing affinities as relations of power."[19]

This productive, interested aspect of sympathy is clearly a technology at work across empires. Sympathy is rooted in inference, in apprehending and responding to the sentiments of another, and thus relies on notions of familiarity, recognition, and habit, all components of knowing another person or people. Anthropologist Danilyn Rutherford argues that imperial sympathy is neither "proof of the colonizers' good intentions" nor "a fleeting sign of imperialism subverting itself from within."[20] In the space of empire, it is easy to consider sympathy as insincere, as a form of privilege enabled by power, but it is always? What degrees of sincerity are possible, including in relationships of and with CIA officers? Following Rutherford's charge to avoid presumptions about the character, tenor, or direction of sympathy in imperial relationships recalls Michel Foucault's reminder that all sentiments, even "the noblest and most disinterested," have a history. These are histories we need to learn and write, rather than presume we already know.

In 1950 President Truman authorized a new type of political action and propaganda via the top secret National Security Council Report 68. Supporting anticommunist regimes was specifically advocated by NSC-68, including constructing a private sphere to support explicit as well as covert ideology and policies. Thus enabled, the U.S. government created a network of supposedly citizen-led organizations that would promote what we now know as "the American way of life."[21] Such organizations' CIA funding was kept secret, including to their members, the overwhelming majority of whom had no idea about their group's connections to the CIA.

Some of the groups and projects produced after NSC-68 were the following: Air America during the Vietnam War, propaganda efforts such as Radio Free Europe and Radio Liberty, the covert backing of supposedly neutral international organizations such as the International Commission of Jurists, citizen groups the CIA either created or supported such as the National Student Association and the Congress for Cultural Freedom, Cold War publications on both the Right and the Left such as the *Partisan Review* and the *Kenyon Review*, philanthropic organizations such as the Ford and Rockefeller Foundations, the National Endowment for Democracy, cultural institutions such as the Boston Symphony Orchestra and the Museum of Modern Art in New York City, student diplomacy initiatives such as the Fulbright Program (the first agreement for which was with Chiang Kai-shek's nationalist China in 1947) and the Foreign Student Leader project, which was billed as a Department of State endeavor, but which was really run by the CIA and in which Cold War maven Margaret Thatcher participated in 1967. Although these connections were made public over fifty years ago through the *Ramparts* magazine exposé in 1967, and despite more recent revelations about NSA spying on U.S. citizens, the American public remains mostly unaware of former or current CIA penetration into domestic U.S. society.[22] One such CIA front group that worked at home and abroad was the American Emergency Committee for Tibetan Refugees.

THE AMERICAN EMERGENCY COMMITTEE FOR TIBETAN REFUGEES

In March 1959, the Dalai Lama escaped from Tibet to India. One month later, an elite group of men met in New York City to form the AECTR for the CIA. The head was the five-term Minnesota congressman Dr. Walter H. Judd, who had been a medical missionary in China and who was the leader of the pro-Nationalist, anticommunist China Lobby, a governmental private-sector group that strongly advocated on behalf of Chiang Kai Shek's Republican China. Other members included Suydam Cutting, the extremely wealthy explorer who was one of the first westerners to enter Lhasa; Angier Biddle Duke, of the aristocratic Duke family who is noted for having had a long career as a "gentleman diplomat"; Lowell Thomas, the writer, broadcast journalist, media personality, and explorer who had traveled to Tibet in the 1940s; B. A. Garside, a former Protestant missionary to China and anticommunist relief executive; Harold Oram, a public relations and fundraising legend long associated with social justice causes; and Marvin Liebman, a conservative activist, fundraiser, and key private-sector member of the China lobby who would later go on to be a founder of the Log Cabin Republicans and, with his friend William Buckley, founder of *National Review.* This powerful group immediately began to privately raise funds, secure massive donations of medicines from pharmaceutical companies, make official arrangements with the Government of India for the AECTR to conduct aid work there, and find the appropriate person to serve as the AECTR's field director in India. The man they recruited had several decades of experience working in U.S. government security and intelligence and was at the time involved in a Hong Kong–based CIA front organization called Aid Refugee Chinese Intellectuals.[23] His name was Travis L. Fletcher.

Fletcher was a skillful undercover agent. He played his part well, fastidiously avoiding any connection of the AECTR with the U.S. government, instead presenting it as a privately funded organization. Over the years he hired a staff composed of both American and Indian citizens who all thought they were working for an "independent, private organization."[24] In his work, Fletcher strove to be "scrupulously humanitarian" so as to leave no openings for criticism from "communists and critics of America." Being scrupulously humanitarian meant actively coordinating and delivering a wide range of aid programs in various Tibetan refugee settlements throughout India. Publicly and privately, Fletcher performed the sympathy expected of a humanitarian while simultaneously secretly monitoring the refugee situation and relations between Nehru and the Dalai Lama. He worked closely with his Government of India counterparts on the Central Relief Committee for Tibetan Refugees that coordinated and led aid efforts. He sparred with European aid providers and wrote proudly, gloatingly even about the AECTR being the first to deliver medicine and aid to Tibetans when other organizations had only been able to promise but not deliver. To his compatriots back in New York and DC, he delivered report after report about aid operations, and letter after letter of behind-the-scenes political commentary.

Fletcher's correspondence is also full of complaints about Tibetans. Ironically perhaps, he was perturbed that the Dalai Lama's brothers Gyalo Thondup and Thubten Jigme Norbu Rinpoche were more interested in Tibetan political independence than in helping Tibetan refugees. As he wrote to the AECTR founders, the Dalai Lama's brothers' political concerns got in the way of his spy cover of providing humanitarian aid. In addition, he frequently criticized wealthy Tibetans in his letters, advising the AECTR group not to provide any financial assistance to such Tibetans. Like any society, Tibet was one stratified by class, and the refugee community included Tibetans from all class positions from rich to poor. Fletcher's style of humanitarianism had a well-developed sense of righteousness, applied here to the audacity of some Tibetans to not be poor. In response, how does a recognition of class or of Tibetan political desires disrupt the narratives of rescue and aid that necessarily ground humanitarianism even when it is merely a front for spying?

In public, Fletcher played the role of paternalistic humanitarian, an expected combination of selflessness and service. He spoke of Tibetans as if they were children, writing about how his disgust with Tibetan aristocrats dissipated when he saw "the faces of the kids and the poverty stricken people." His concern was with the Tibetans who he considered to be true refugees, of whom he publicly proclaimed: "Surely no group of refugees were ever more deserving, none more courageous—none more grateful."[25] For their part, as individuals and as a community in response to groups such as the AECTR, Tibetans learned to perform their gratitude to their donors. This was a requirement embedded in the humanitarian project that Tibetans recoded in their own cultural terms around the concept of *sbyin bdag*, or sponsor.

The AECTR encouraged private U.S. citizen support for Tibetan refugees. The involvement of Lowell Thomas, a popular media figure, was instrumental in soliciting support over the radio and TV. There was a local branch of AECTR in Seattle composed of what we would today call "Tibet supporters," and other groups more or less active, more or less formal throughout the United States. One was the Women's Club of Westfield, New Jersey. The members of this club, who as far as I can tell were mostly homemakers, held dessert and bridge parties and fashion shows to raise funds for Tibetan refugees, which were all routed through AECTR. In 1964, for example, the club sold crystal bracelets to raise money to furnish a home with the name "Woman's Club of Westfield" in the Lowell Thomas Hospital complex for Tibetan refugee children in Mysore, India. At Travis Fletcher's suggestion, the Woman's Club also sponsored a young boy named Thupden for three years, as well as a young girl named Deke Dolkar for twelve years. The head of the club, Mrs. George W. Mann, corresponded frequently with both Fletcher and Deke Dolkar. As reported April 6, 1978, in the *Westfield* (N.J.) *Leader* newspaper, "Deke . . . [is] an outstanding student, [who] has always been at the top of her class." The article also states that Deke calls Mrs. George W. Mann

"Auntie" and "deeply appreciates the friendly interest and substantial assistance" given to her by the international relations department of the Woman's Club. The Woman's Club sponsored Deke until her graduation from college in 1979, and marked the graduation of this "Tibetan protégé" with a fundraising party—homemade dessert at 1:00 with bridge playing through 4:00.

Such sponsorship of Tibetan students remains an important part of the Tibetan exile community to this day, and has links to the covert humanitarian efforts of the CIA and more broadly to the reinforcement of U.S. imperial hegemony through domestic citizen support of democracy abroad. Such citizen initiatives were an important classed and gendered part of U.S. politics of this period. For example, U.S. housewives' participation was important in the calculated emergence of the modern Japanese woman during the reconstruction of Japan after World War II.[26] The construction of an international network of citizens to support Tibet, to build person-to-person ties, relied on a specific sort of imperial model of benevolence, volunteerism, progress, and humanity. It depended also on the figure of the refugee as a readily available humanitarian subject.[27]

In 1965, Congressman Judd made a trip to India to observe AECTR operations. In his official report of the trip, he praised Fletcher's "humanitarian and totally important work" with these "needy people," helping them move toward "freedom," and providing them with an "image of the American Way." One of Fletcher's efforts was to improve the Tibetan diet. Perhaps the greatest nonpolitical excitement in his papers is when he proclaims that Tibetans are "taking to noodles like hot cakes." He had bought a noodle-making machine for experimenting with donated American surplus wheat and, as he told an AP reporter, the experiment was such a success that he intended to buy more machines.[28] Among the AECTR group back in New York the noodle excitement is contagious, but the applause of Fletcher's humanitarian genius misses something very telling: Tibetans were already noodle eaters. All sorts of homemade noodles—*thukpa, tenthuk,* and so on—were then (and remain today) staples of the Tibetan diet. For Fletcher, and in ways distributed throughout AECTR efforts, Tibetans were not individuals who potentially possessed a cuisine, but were instead a category of people—refugees—who had been converted into a project that sustained, legitimated, and burnished the AECTR's self-congratulatory imperial humanitarianism. The cover of refugee aid enabled a covert American presence in India at a politically charged global moment when nonaligned India was friendly with both the United States and the Soviet Union. If, for example, the Soviets approached the Dalai Lama, Fletcher was determined to find out. Monitoring this situation via humanitarian action was one part of the U.S. project of winning both Indian and Tibetan "hearts and minds" in the 1960s.

In contrast to the AECTR, for which my research was entirely archival, my research on the CIA and the Tibetan resistance army was ethnographic, involving interviews, conversation, shared meals, and relationships with retired CIA officers, including relationships that continue to this day. Since 1999, I've met with them in their homes, in California, Florida, Maryland, and Massachusetts, and spoken with others on the phone. I've also spent time with many of these men and their families at two group events—one at CIA headquarters in Virginia in 2009, and one at Camp Hale in Colorado in 2010. As a result, my research with this second group involves family members and personal relationships, and feels ethnographically deep in comparison.

In conducting this research, I would think often of Antonius C. G. Robben's writings on ethnographic seduction, on his visiting with an Argentine general in his home, and on what happens when historical figures are humanized, when violence is softened.[29] One of the CIA officers from Camp Hale whom I interviewed was a hardened, infamous man who was widely, albeit wrongly considered to be the model for the heinous Colonel Kurtz in *Apocalypse Now*. He is now deceased, but his name was Anthony Poshepny, though he went by Tony Poe. I met with him in his home in San Francisco, and he told me stories of war in his living room. He shared with me memories of how hard-core the Tibetans were, stories of their physical bravado and ability to subsist anywhere. He narrated stories of his time later in Laos, of his penchant for women and for ears cut off of dead enemy bodies, and his inability to suffer either fools or bullshit. Both, he told me, were reasons why he liked the Tibetans: they also had a low tolerance for these things. As Roger McCarthy, his former boss at Camp Hale, would later say, Tony was "a rebel with a cause," and he appreciated others who fought with purpose and passion.[30]

As we spoke one day, we sat in side-by-side chairs facing a TV that was on and his narrations competed with a steady stream of infomercials—Richard Simmons's diet products, Pokémon products, and the like—until his Lao wife switched the channel to ballet. Earlier, on the phone, he told me that the problem with the CIA was "we sell out everyone we work with. They'd thank me, and I'd say, no, you made me. They didn't understand. Those Tibetans killed a hell of a lot of Chinese. We trained them and improved their resistance abilities. But it was an impossible situation. There was no hope." He told me about his health, which was failing and his triple bypass surgery the year before, saying he had maybe only two years left, a sobering reflection on the very real bodies involved in the making and telling of this history. His job, he said, had been military training at Camp Hale as well as escorting the soldiers back to East Pakistan [now Bangladesh] from where they would secretly transit into India and on to their base in Nepal.

"I wasn't involved in the politics after, but went back to Laos [where he spent the bulk of his career]. I jumped around a lot. I spent over thirty-five years in Asia. It was like the British, build relationships. We took care of local people, of families. The British do this well with MI6." In person, Poe was loquacious though clearly in ill health. As he told me his story, he fleshed it out with people from his past, names of friends I should contact, folks to whom I should mention his name, a genealogy of the making of a CIA guerrilla warfare expert. His first CIA assignment was in Korea, where he was introduced to guerrilla warfare. He stayed for three years and "got a reputation for being an idiot" after which, he said, "the directors always sent me wherever interesting things were going on: Tibet, Indonesia, the Thailand border. They would send materials to read up on for background. I already knew some of the Tibet material from Kipling. He's one of my favorites. *Kim* is one of the Agency training manuals." Of his time in Camp Hale he explained, "There were as many as two hundred men per group. Every five to six months we would graduate them. Then drop them in East Pakistan. It was a big operation. We'd give them medals, awards, and they'd have their whole life's treasures around their neck. It was difficult, though. Food was tough. In the beginning there was no cook. I was the cook, cooking out of the Army Manual. All of them gained weight."

Tony Poe was not only the cook, but also the on-the-ground guerrilla ops instructor. He taught Tibetans about demolitions, picking locks, burning dead bodies, getting information through collecting wallets and IDs, and sniper training. "On Sundays, I would take them on field trips. Divide the group in half. One group would ambush the other, then we'd do the reverse the next week." One time, he told me, "I got two mules for them. The mules hated me. But those Tibetans? They'd say something in the mule's ears. They loved the mules and the mules loved them." Sinking back into his chair, ballerinas twirling on the TV in front of us, he concluded our conversation with "We learned a lot from the Tibetans. Man, they knew how to go in the snow. They put sticks in their hands. They'd work the snow down to a path, and then the horses and troops would follow." He narrated this technique with a voice and demeanor appreciative of its brilliance, some forty years later still clearly impressed.

I gathered my things to leave, and he told me it was just about time for the TV show *Baywatch*. As I left he said to me, "I used to be somewhat of a rounder. But not all written about me is true. I used to drink a lot in Laos. It was to be able to shoot a machine gun. It was necessary." The literature on Tony Poe is colorful; he was a character foreign correspondents loved.

He wasn't a sailor but he swore like one, and he lived in the field as a larger-than-life caricature of who he was. He did so, however, in his own often repeated words: while taking care of his people. He also often repeated his sentiments about the Tibetans, or more specifically about the Khampas or eastern Tibetans who comprised the bulk of the Tibetan resistance army. In our conversations, he spoke several times about how central Tibetans were worthless, and it was the Khampas and Amdowas who were the real fighters.[31] Earlier, in an interview with a journalist about the CIA in Laos, Poe was asked about the Tibet operation: "We don't talk about that. No comment, no comment. . . . No fucking comment, but those Khampas are the best people I ever worked with."[32]

If the AECTR was the paternal side of empire, then the Camp Hale operation was the fraternal one. Officers of the CIA and Tibetan soldiers lived together in a small, secret military camp. In their downtime the CIA officers played Monopoly and Scrabble, drank Schlitz beer, drove to nearby Glenwood Springs to meet girls, and hung out with the Tibetans on site: shooting slingshots, playing practical jokes on each other, learning to take snuff Tibetan-style. Theirs was a shared experience in ways that the AECTR's aid work never was. As such, it was generative of different performative registers of sympathy, sincerity, and human connection that remain personally activated and felt today. In the military operation, the covert was a shared space; in the humanitarian operation, it was solely American.

THE MAN-TEARS OF EMPIRE

On September 10, 2010, an unusual event took place in Colorado. In a ceremony at Camp Hale, the U.S. government publicly acknowledged the CIA's secret training of Tibetan resistance soldiers during the years 1958–64. Hosted by U.S. senator Mark Udall, the ceremony included the installation of a plaque acknowledging the operation, and speeches both prepared and impromptu by the former CIA officers and Tibetan veterans who were able to make it to Camp Hale for the ceremony. Most of these men had not seen each other for fifty years. Also present were many of their descendants, especially on behalf of those American and Tibetan participants who could not be there in person or who were deceased. It was a glorious day, one filled with intense high-altitude sun and deep emotion. Publicly evident were the sentiments both Tibetan veterans and retired CIA officers had privately shared with me about each other over the years. Again and again, each would tell me of the mutual admiration and respect they had for each other, about how for the Tibetans the CIA teachers were *mi yag po red*, or "good people," and for the CIA officers how the Tibetan operation was one unmatched in the rest of their career in terms of how well they got along with the Tibetans and developed relations of true commitment. On both sides, these stereotypical tough guys narrated their relationship to me with great sentimentality.

"We cried." Thinking back to the moment of departing Camp Hale, Tibetan veteran Lobsang Jampa told me of how the American teachers and Tibetan soldiers both shed tears despite their best efforts not to for different cultural reasons. The plaque installed at Camp Hale used this very theme to memorialize their relationship. It reads:

> CAMP HALE
>
> From 1958 to 1964, Camp Hale played an important role as a training site for Tibetan Freedom Fighters. Trained by the CIA, many of these brave men lost their lives in the struggle for freedom.
>
> "They were the best and bravest of their generation, and we wept together when they were killed fighting alongside their countrymen."
>
> *Orphans of the Cold War*, by John Kenneth Knaus
>
> This plaque is dedicated to their memory.

Speeches at the ceremony were deeply emotional. One Tibetan veteran spoke poignantly about the closeness between the Tibetans and Americans: "We would cry when we left here, so would the instructors." Several speakers, Americans and Tibetans both, had to pause in their talks, overcome with emotion. The daughter of one of the Tibetans trained there thanked all of the unsung Tibetan heroes, and explained that the covert nature of the operation was on the Tibetan side as well as the American side. When she was a young girl, she said, "We thought our father had an American accent from watching movies. We didn't know what he did. . . . [We didn't know why] he was really good at reading maps." The son of Roger McCarthy, the late head of the Camp Hale operation, gave an especially moving tribute. In a prepared speech, delivered with great emotion and humility, he read a list of all the CIA officers involved in the project and also spoke directly to the Tibetan veterans: "For all the Tibetans involved in the program, my father deeply admired your courage, character, determination, and desire to excel in any challenge. He couldn't help but to fall in love with each of you."

Love is not a sentiment often associated with the CIA. This love was homosocial, grounded in respect and shared experience, and part of a social relationship narrated by both parties as a form of solidarity. As with sincerity, solidarity is a sentiment linked to sympathy. Tibetans were sincerely committed to their mission, and thus sincerely engaged in their training. The CIA officers were sincerely impressed with the Tibetans. For Tibetans, sincerity of their American counterparts, that is, of men who they knew personally, did not necessarily translate into a presumption of similar sincerity at higher levels in the U.S. government. As time went on, it became clear to (at least) some Tibetans that American interest in Tibet was really self-interest in antagonizing, not defeating, communism in China. Differentiating between the government and its representatives, however, was not a problem for those Tibetans who trained in Colorado. For those CIA men who lived and worked with the Tibetans, and with those Tibetans who lived and worked with the Americans, a sense of solidarity grounds interpretations of Tibet-U.S. relations as collaborative and cooperative rather than as coercive or compromised.

The September 10 ceremony at Camp Hale started with a speech by CIA officer Ken Knaus and his statement that the "US promise to Tibet remains unfulfilled." Both Tibetans and Americans felt this sense of commitment, an obligation and responsibility born of shared experience. As a Tibetan veteran put it: "The word America is magic in Tibet. . . . We are still hopeful America will do something for Tibet." This hope that Tibetan veterans have resides in a different emotional genre from either expectation or entitlement. This hope continues to be borne patiently, albeit with a new engagement in the last two decades, as more Tibetans migrate to the United States from South Asia.

In his speech at the Camp Hale ceremony, a Tibetan veteran emotionally declared, "I am very happy to be here. This is like coming to my own home." His words were preceded by those of Senator Udall, who shared that he and others were working to turn Camp Hale into a national park. The national parks belong to all Americans, they are "home" for all citizens, and in the case of Camp Hale, for those foreigners for whom geography, politics, and sympathy convert to honorary "brother" status. While fraternity is a familiar military theme, such conversions are composed of multiple cultural logics. Tibetan practices of reincarnation provide a different, but related framework for Tibetan brotherly love. As Doma Norbu explained, speaking in tribute to her late father, Athar Norbu, one of the first Tibetan CIA trainees, "He talked about the teachers as Khampas reborn as Americans." This is a different sort of kinship from the paternalism of the AECTR. In important ways, the constituent parts of the CIA military and refugee aid operations look the same—the people involved, the imperial sympathy underlying the operations, the requisite performances of gratitude, and the importance of sincerity and solidarity in grounding or claiming to ground "real" human connection. But sentimental experiences vary wildly between the two operations such that while AECTR reveals the CIA performance of humanitarian sincerity, Camp Hale shows the sincere performance of CIA humanitarianism. But what do these differences mean, and how do they matter?

What I see here is sentimental imperialism embedded in realpolitik, such that sentiment is substantive of experience and action rather than just embellishment to them.[33] And yet, just because sentiment is sincerely felt does not mean it is void of the violence of empire. The major difference between the AECTR and the Camp Hale operation was the ways CIA officers interacted with the Tibetans in these two different projects. The AECTR provided charity to Tibetans in a classic hierarchical fashion, whereas the CIA officers at Camp Hale lived together with the Tibetan soldiers for months, even years at a time, working collaboratively with them; theirs was a shared project in ways that the AECTR never was. Both operations were covert, both were designed top-down to gain intelligence against China and India more than anything else, and both involved thousands of ordinary Tibetans. Given the comradeship that so often develops in military situations,[34] it is perhaps not surprising that close bonds developed between Tibetans and Americans in that shared space of a secret military camp. And yet what history do we write for these noble but interested sentiments? In so doing, we need to get at the violence endorsed by imperial sympathy, at the violence that can constitute both sincerity and solidarity in unexpected directions, toward not only Tibetans but also perhaps to American CIA officers.

CONCLUSION

State assessments of the contents and distributions of rogue CIA sentiments of love and sympathy in the 1960s and present day are, as with many things related to the CIA, not easy to access. There are clear continuities and disjunctures in how the CIA theorized humanitarianism and conceptualized humanity as a part of its operations in the 1960s and now, and between the many individuals within the CIA from the very highest levels at Langley on down to the "seasonal" workers such as the mostly college-aged group of smokejumpers from Montana who flew CIA planes over Tibet in the off-season. As with any imperial formation, the CIA is composed of agents, officers, and contract employees who participate in imperial ventures in ways that are not always regular or predictable.[35]

Taking the Central Intelligence Agency and other covert institutions and actors seriously as ethnographic subjects is needed as part of the continuing anthropological project of studying power, or as Laura Nader put it, "studying up."[36] For a range of reasons—political, methodological, ethical—it is much easier and less fraught with tension to engage the CIA as either a historical or political subject than it is to situate its members within a domain in which the ethnographic is foregrounded. To foreground an ethnographic subjectivity for the CIA is to bring questions of sympathy and humanity to an institution and actors who are often considered to be devoid of both. To humanize the CIA is to reject internal and external efforts to place the CIA outside of ethnographically knowable domains. It is to reject its claims to exist outside the norm, in the shadows, in domains where rules may be suspended, and to instead argue that the covert is deeply human and must be engaged with as such. This is not to romanticize the CIA or to privilege the CIA over those they co-opted or lied to or killed, or, in those rare cases such as the one I discuss here, over those with whom they collaborated. Tibetans fought against the Chinese independent of both the CIA and anticommunist rhetoric. The Tibetan struggle was driven by other issues, and yet, because their struggle was with the People's Republic of China, the CIA supported it in a complicated, covert stretch of empire.

In the case of Tibet, covert empire rested on a politics of sympathy that simultaneously legitimated and masked violence—representational violence, structural violence, and physical violence. Travis L. Fletcher and Company provided humanitarian aid to Tibetan refugees in covert exchange for spy access to India and the Dalai Lama's exile government. Tony Poe and the CIA Camp Hale teachers provided military support and emotional solidarity to Tibetan resistance soldiers in exchange for Tibetan intelligence gathering in and warfare against the People's Republic of China. Sympathy is a key part of each of these imperial humanitarian missions. Sympathy works to establish affinity and sincerity as a relation of power, to forge sociality and trust, to differentiate between and to normalize suffering and deserving subjects. But this is only one of the registers in which one might experience or receive empire, covert or not. Heonik Kwon has critiqued Cold War history as "fundamentally an anthropological problem" in that we need to uncover and understand "the human dimension of the geopolitical order" rather than resting at the level of a political-historical engagement of the central players and their truths.[37] The human dimension exists at the grounded, experiential level of those individuals, both American and Tibetan, who participated in this covert empire.

Imperial love, ethnographic love, homosocial love are all forms of action; these are sentiments that are in motion. If, as Talal Asad argues, a "doctrine of action has become essential to our recognition of other people's humanity,"[38] and if we can locate such action and humanity within the CIA, then how does this reorient discussions of sentiment, political participation, and the always-compromised nature of agency? Answering this question in the case of Tibet is to write with and against particular politics and literatures. It is to write in between celebration and castigation, but is not necessarily to walk some sort of middle ground. It is to refuse guilt by association, to reject blunt force analysis, while operating within a critical and imperial framework. It is to acknowledge that a self-proclaimed anti-imperialist China drew Tibet into the

United States' anticommunist orbit. It is to recognize that to dwell squarely in the U.S. imperial sphere is a position circumscribed in various ways, none of which close down all possible options or strategic needs for thinking, for being, or for sharing relationships of sympathy, sincerity, or solidarity, including love with CIA officers.

NOTES

1 "Love, n.1," *Oxford English Dictionary,* accessed April 15, 2014, http://www.oed.com/view/Entry/110566?rskey=041uZb&result=1#eid.

2 Besteman, "On Ethnographic Love."

3 Thomas Laqueur in Feldman and Ticktin, "Introduction," 4.

4 On Tibet and the U.S. imperial domain, see McGranahan, "Empire out-of-Bounds."

5 Ho, "Empire through Diasporic Eyes."

6 Yeh, "Tibet and the Problem of Radical Reductionism."

7 A third operation was the Cornell University Tibet program (1964–67), in which several groups of Tibetan students were enrolled at Cornell for one-year study programs.

8 McGranahan, *Arrested Histories.*

9 Barnett and Weiss, "Humanitarianism," 6.

10 Feldman and Ticktin, "Introduction: Government and Humanity," 3.

11 Peter Redfield, *Life in Crisis.*

12 DiPrizio, *Armed Humanitarians,* 2.

13 On military humanitarianism, see Nosheen Ali, "Books vs. Bombs."

14 Gott, "Imperial Humanitarianism," 30.

15 Quoted in Knaus, *Orphans of the Cold War,* 313.

16 Rai, *The Rule of Sympathy.* See also Stoler, "On Degrees of Imperial Sovereignty."

17 Rai, *The Rule of Sympathy,* xviii.

18 Rai, *The Rule of Sympathy,* xix.

19 Rai, *The Rule of Sympathy,* xix.

20 Rutherford, "Sympathy, State Building, and the Experience of Empire," 21.

21 See Helen Laville's "The Importance of Being (In)Earnest."

22 Laville and Wilford, *The US Government, Citizen Groups and the Cold War.*

23 On this group, see Hsu, "Aid Refugee Chinese Intellectuals, Inc., and the Political Uses of Humanitarian Relief, 1952–1962."

24 All direct quotes are from Fletcher's correspondence in the AECTR files, Hoover Institution Archives, Stanford University.

25 "The Role of the Voluntary Agencies in the Tibetan Refugee Relief and Rehabilitation Programme," by Travis Fletcher, Field Director, American Emergency Committee for Tibetan Refugees, posted April 18, 1961, to B. A. Garside, Hoover Institution Archives.

26 Yoneyama, "Liberation under Siege."

27 Malkki, "Speechless Emissaries."
28 "Noodles Solve a Tibetan Problem."
29 Robben, "Ethnographic Seduction."
30 Waldman, "A Cold War Coda."
31 Khampas are Tibetans from the eastern region of Kham. Amdowas are Tibetans from the northeastern region of Amdo.
32 Warner, *Backfire*, 93.
33 Stoler, "Affective States," 5–6.
34 See also MacLeish, *Making War at Fort Hood.*
35 Stoler and Cooper, "Between Metropole and Colony," 7.
36 Nader, "Up the Anthropologist."
37 Kwon, *The Other Cold War*, 8–9.
38 Talal, "Comments on Conversion," 272, as quoted in Keane, *Christian Moderns*, 3.

Trust Us

17

Nicaragua, Iran-Contra, and the Discursive Economy of Empire

JOE BRYAN

A PROPOSITION

One by one, the vultures flew in imperfect arcs, their heavy bodies falling against a steady onshore breeze blowing off of the Caribbean before coming to rest in half dead tree. Across the dirt street, I sat down in front of a locked, white painted door to take stock of my disappointment at being stood up once again.

It was April 2004, and I had been coming to the house off and on for months in search of an interview. The house served as the regional headquarters of the Miskito-led YATAMA political party in Bilwi, the capital of the North Caribbean Coast Autonomous Region (RACCN) in eastern Nicaragua. Formed with U.S. support in 1987 during the Contra War, YATAMA's stated political objective was the defense of indigenous right to land and territory. Since the group had now gained the status of a political party, I was keen to hear from YATAMA representatives themselves how they perceived massive state-led efforts to title and demarcate indigenous and black community lands throughout eastern Nicaragua. The week before, I'd managed to catch one of the party's top officials enjoying the quiet of the building while completing his econometrics homework for a distance-learning course offered by a Spanish university. He asked me to come back the following week at the same time, for an interview. One week later, I returned to find the office once again vacant, save for a woman raking leaves and trash into a burn pile in one corner of the yard.

Sitting in front of the locked doors, a man in a sweat-stained T-shirt and tattered jeans approached and greeted me in in Miskito.[1] He was not the official I had hoped to meet. "Do you have a project here?" he asked, in halting Spanish. "No," I replied. I was just a student doing research. Undeterred by my answer or perhaps prompted by it, he sat down next to me and launched into a story of how he'd been to the United States once. It was during the 1980s, at the height of the Contra War. He'd traveled there with a group of other Miskito combatants aboard an American military transport plane that picked them up at an airstrip in Honduras. My ears perked up.

What had he done there? I asked. He began with a description of life on an anonymous military base in a setting that looked "just like" the pine savannah that dominates northeastern Nicaragua. During the day, he received training in a litany of "low-intensity" warfare techniques that other Miskito war veterans had told me about: blowing up bridges, ambushes, field communications, and map skills. At night, he recalled sharing the occasional shot of whiskey with a cook who spoke Spanish. Through the cook, he learned that he was in North Carolina.

Turning the conversation back to me, he asked what kind of work I was doing. After describing my research on the role of mapping in recognizing indigenous land claims, I inquired further about his map skills. "I can read maps really well," he assured me, sensing that he might have a marketable skill. Again he asked me if I could give him a job. "No," I countered, repeating that I was just a student doing research and had nothing to offer. Refusing my answer, his voice switched to a more urgent tone. "Look," he said, "I haven't had a job since the end of the war. I can do lots of things, anything you want. I'll find bin Laden. I'll find Saddam Hussein. Give me a job."

Sensing my incredulousness, he pushed on. "I can give you the coordinates of a place in the *llano*," he said, referring to the pine savannah that stretched inland from edge of town. "You tell me when you want to come, and I will have three hundred men waiting for you there. You can take us away in helicopters. We'll go anywhere—Iraq, Afghanistan, anywhere—it doesn't matter. We'll go there and no one will have to know. Think about it, *boss.*"

His last word, spoken in English, hung in the air. He got up, and walked away. At the far edge of the yard, a woman finished sweeping leaves and trash into a pile on top of concrete slab. She set fire to it, the plastic sending an acrid plume of smoke into the air. I got up from my seat on the concrete steps, and turned to walk home in the dark.

CONSPIRACY

The man's proposition lingered with me for a long time afterward, alternately inviting understanding and eluding it. The most immediate way to grasp its meaning was through the history of U.S. imperialism in eastern Nicaragua. During the Contra War in the 1980s, the United States had in fact armed Miskito forces to fight against the Left-nationalist Sandinista party. After the group came to power in a 1979 revolution, the United States had moved swiftly to contain any threat that the Sandinistas' project would spread. Toward that goal, the Ronald Reagan administration backed a litany of counterrevolutionary (*contra*) proxy forces that included a number of Miskito-led armed groups. In 1987 YATAMA itself was founded with U.S. support. In this fight Sandinista officials and their allies cast Miskito fighters as hapless dupes of U.S. Cold War policy.[2] Miskito forces' insistence on fighting for their indigenous rights to territory and autonomy struck many in Nicaragua and beyond as delusional, playing into the hands of U.S. imperialism at the expense of their advancing their objective interests in overcoming their marginalization.

At the same time, the man's proposition captured the political and economic abandonment that permeates postwar life in northeastern Nicaragua. The region routinely ranks among the poorest in Nicaragua, a country often regarded as the second-poorest country in the Americas after Haiti. Unemployment hovers around 80 percent in Bilwi, the economic and political center of the region. Contra war veterans make up a prominent part of the unemployed, congregating in public spaces to pass the time. If war had previously brought U.S. attention to an isolated corner of Central America, valuing its people within Cold War geopolitics, then perhaps war could also be a means of restoring economic value to its inhabitants. The ex-combatant's proposition immersed me within his understanding of imperialism, rather than the other way around. Instead of seeing its historical legacy, his proposition positioned me actively within a decidedly imperial present. What if I were to take his proposition at face value, thus joining in his conspiracy and resisting the temptation to historicize his plea?

The authors of scholarly accounts of U.S. imperialism are often quite wary of joining in such conspiracy. Perhaps this is a function of attempts to avoid a penchant for unverifiable details and events in order to fashion a truer understanding of its political economic rationale and geopolitical interests. And through such efforts to parse and establish a scholarly vantage point, U.S. imperialism becomes a geohistorical category that is legible as an object of scholarly inquiry.[3] This may also mean that whatever is gained in terms of an understanding of empire as a totalizing abstraction comes also to obscure, at least partially, the fractured and disjunctive ways in which it is materially experienced.[4] But conspiracy interrupts that process, shifting the emphasis to the present through reinterpretation of events and objects, repurposing them for new ends through the imposition of an order delivered by rhetorical force. All the same, gaps remain in the form of missing evidence, faulty logic, or alternative explanations refused. Perhaps this is why Walter Benjamin was so enamored with conspiracy as a method. Unable to impose order on chaos, conspiracy "rendered tribute to chance," shifting emphasis from narrative to narration.[5] For Benjamin, chance forced a consideration of the contingency of knowledge and its uncertain connection to material objects. A monument to progress could also be a ruin, depending on the relationship between the viewer and the object described.[6]

This shift toward acts of interpretation draws attention to the workings of what Charles Briggs terms a *discursive economy* used to organize and assign value to knowledge in order to craft an authoritative account.[7] Conspiracy, Briggs contends, draws our attention to the practices of exclusion associated with that effort, reflecting both the position from which an account is told and the workings of the object it describes. No wonder that conspiracies flourish when their subject is imperialism, their proliferation scarcely diminished by more authoritative accounts. Part of this has to do with the ways in which imperialism relies on a notion of conspiracy as deceit, of fabricating a rationale or truth that creates the cover for something else to occur. To discover the real truth, that deceit must be discarded in order to reveal its destructive tendencies. Where scholarly accounts often go wrong is in their rush to a kind of empirical historicism that joins a judicious display of the facts with the reasoning of a discursive economy. That action requires disqualifying knowledge as false or immaterial to an understanding of the object at hand. To the extent that there was anything to the man's proposition to me in Bilwi, its value could be derived only by dismissing most of what was shocking and unsettling about it. Why would anyone in eastern Nicaragua want to go to Iraq to fight in a war?

Any viable attempt to answer that question could not simply resort to imperialism as an explanation. It had to first reckon with the force of imperialism as an ongoing process, one equally capable of degrading peoples' lives and conjuring spectacular force. Such processes capture the "fragility of power and the force of destruction" through which imperialism is actively constituted and experienced.[8] Ann Laura Stoler refers to this process as one of "ruination," a force that persists in the present, shaping the materiality and mental activity of peoples' lives long after the withdrawal of troops and the ends of wars. Ruination further sustains imperialism in the present, fashioning the conditions for its reproduction from the debris that it has created. Conspiracy adds to that approach through its efforts to repurpose and reinterpret the signs and symbols of imperialism's destructive force. The effects can often be unsettling for hegemonic understandings of imperialism, confounding its categories of analysis and objects of inquiry. To the extent that the effects deviate from efforts to discern the truth of imperialism, they force a consideration of how people live with that formation. The difficulty of making sense of events such as the man's proposition to me captures the possibilities that come with this shift, creating new aesthetic sensibilities that are alive to inadvertent effects.[9] Such an approach can make new associations possible, connecting Nicaragua and Afghanistan, and scholars and ex-combatants, in ways that illuminate the meshes of power that bind them together. This also brings imperialism's reality-altering qualities into view.

TRUST US

In 2002, two years before my exchange with the ex-combatant in Bilwi, journalist Ron Suskind interviewed a senior aide in the administration of George W. Bush, pressing him on the administration's rationale for invading Iraq. Unable or unwilling to answer Suskind's questions directly, the aide deflected. "We're an empire now and when we act, we create our own reality." Chiding Suskind and critics of the Bush administration, the aide continued on, "And while you're studying that reality—judiciously as you will—we'll act again, creating other new realities. We're history's actors . . . and you, all of you, will be left to just study what we do."[10] Later attributed to Karl Rove, the quote was widely read as capturing the imperial hubris of the Bush administration.

Rove's quote did not so much describe a reality as it proposed one. Like the Bush administration's use of aerial photographs to document weapons of mass destruction in Iraq, it conjured an image of a reality by way of asserting its existence. Unburdened by history, Rove and his co-conspirators in the Bush administration claimed the ability to command new realities into existence. Their claim was imperial in the most literal sense of the term derived from the Latin *imperium*, meaning to command with absolute power or sovereignty. The word's etymology suggests a performative approach to power, implying that the ability to command does more than simply affirm sovereignty. It is also constitutive of it.[11] Spectacular displays of force like the "shock and awe" campaign that launched the invasion of Iraq in 2003 demonstrate this capacity, and shore up claims to sovereignty by bringing a reality into existence through brute force. As Rove's comment suggests, the key to exercising imperial power is much more than a matter of "judiciously" using the historical facts. Instead, it may be a matter of winning people's trust in the image of power projected. In this approach, what people believed to be reality trumped historical, after-the-fact accounts every time. Or at least so Rove claimed.

The problem was that by 2002, to take Rove's quote and others like it at face value risked complicity with the imperial project invoked. One did not need a conspiracy theory to find reason to be skeptical of such claims. In the run-up to the U.S. invasion of Iraq in 2003, it was precisely that skepticism that had helped make imperialism a subject of popular debate. Scholarly accounts of imperialism followed suit, describing it as a particular form of economy and mode of power. Much of that work sought initially to explain the geostrategic rationale of U.S. imperialism after the fact, typically in terms of control over global oil supplies and the threat that Islamist movements posed to U.S. hegemony.[12] Subsequent analysis added much needed detail to these understandings, adding historical context and shifting attention to the central role that war itself plays in capitalist political economy.[13] For all the analytical insight that work has generated, much of it reinforces the solidity of imperialism as a geohistorical category. As noted in the introduction to this volume, the qualities and characteristics of the empire described transforms scholarship on imperialism in ways that risk affirming its power as a totalizing force. Imperialism's ability to make other people's geographies and histories is thus reflected in the term's influence on making sense of the world itself.[14] Much like reading the ex-combatant's proposition as conspiracy theory, the authority of their accounts of U.S. imperialism affirms its all-encompassing power while overwriting its materiality as a lived reality. Too often, their descriptions of imperialism as a form of economy and mode of power provided all the cover needed for its reality-making plots to proliferate.[15]

One of Rove's co-conspirators in the Bush administration was Vice President Dick Cheney. Cheney's insistence on executive power is well known, and is itself the object of popular conspiracy theories on everything from his role in colluding with oil companies to plan the invasion in 2003 of Iraq to his direct involvement in the attacks in 2001 on the World Trade Center.[16] Regardless of their validity, such theories draw out Cheney's insistence on the authority of the president to define and pursue national security interests on his or her own terms, constituting a hallmark of sovereign authority. On Cheney's read, that authority suffered immensely in the wake of scandals such as Watergate and Iran-Contra. Both scandals corroded the value of trust as a political commodity along the lines indicated by Rove by introducing a permanent skepticism toward presidential power.[17] Against that trend—or perhaps to spite it—Cheney continued to champion executive power. Aboard Air Force Two en route to Oman in 2005, Cheney fended off reporters questioning his views on executive power with a reference to a minority report he wrote as a Wyoming representative disputing the findings of the congressional inquiry into the Iran-Contra affair. "Nobody has ever read them," Cheney quipped before continuing on. "I think that they are very good in laying out a robust view of the President's prerogatives with respect to the conduct of especially foreign policy and national security matters."[18]

Cheney's remark drew an arc connecting Iran-Contra to the everywhere-expanding War on Terror. The reference was only weakly historical. Instead, the arc relied on Cheney's assertion of executive power. Often formally understood as the authority of the president to shield cabinet debates and decisions from the public, Cheney's approach extends that power to the ability to define reality. His invocation of executive power reduced the voting public to a role of trust, turning the latter into a political commodity whose circulation obscured the improvised and unseemly means through which reality was commanded into existence. Cheney's minority report said as much, arguing that the full disclosure of the facts called for by the inquiries into Iran-Contra undermined the president's ability to maintain the public's trust. Judicious accountings of facts were antithetical to executive power. Instead, the only thing left to believe or study was the rhetorical force of its own narrative. To the extent strategy was involved, it was a matter of continuous improvisation.

A reconsideration of the details of Iran-Contra reinforces Cheney's point. They also bring to light the scandal's improvised qualities, which are often overshadowed by attempts to explain the U.S. efforts in terms of criminal intent. Iran-Contra did not in fact begin with a coherent scheme to fund the Contras. It arguably didn't even start in Central America. Instead, its genesis lay with events in the Middle East, beginning with the Iranian military's dependence on spare parts for the U.S.-made weapons acquired prior to the revolution of 1979. Iran first purchased these arms through Israeli intermediaries, later acquiring them directly from the United States in exchange for help freeing American hostages held by Iranian-backed Hezbollah forces in Lebanon. Profits from the sale were then laundered into Contra bank accounts, helping the Reagan administration pursue objectives in Central America and circumvent congressional bans. The sale circumvented congressional bans on selling weapons to "state sponsors of terrorism," to say nothing of the United States' ongoing support for Iraq in its war with Iran. That was 1985. But by then the Contras were no strangers to Israeli assistance. At the request of U.S. officials, in 1983 the Israeli military transferred over three hundred tons of Soviet-bloc weapons captured from the Palestinian Liberation Organization during the Lebanon War of 1982.[19] Through it all, Iran was arguably the more important geopolitical focus, with the United States using continued arms sales to build ties with "moderate" elements there. Rather than a coherent strategy, such efforts involved an enterprising opportunism that relied on a mix of secrecy and improvisation. U.S. national security advisor Robert McFarlane's secret trip to Tehran in May 1986 captured this approach anecdotally. Traveling aboard private planes with fake Irish passports, MacFarlane and a group of advisors, who (possibly?) included Oliver North, arrived in Tehran to meet with moderates within the Iranian government. To demonstrate their hopes, McFarlane brought a Bible and a "key-shaped cake to symbolize the anticipated 'opening' to Iran."[20] Arriving during Ramadan, MacFarlane found few takers for his cake. Nor did he build the hoped-for political ties among Iranian moderates, who remained skeptical of his efforts. Instead he found himself locked in an argument with Iranian officials angry at having been overcharged for the weapons.

Not that any of those details deterred MacFarlane. Shortly after the failed trip, McFarlane and fellow National Security Council staffer Oliver North pushed to continue the sales to Iran, redirecting the profits to fund proxy forces in Nicaragua in spite of a congressional ban barring aid to the Contras. Allegedly dubbed "the Enterprise" by some of the arms dealers involved in the network, the arrangements associated with Iran-Contra were but one of several equally improvised efforts to aid the Contras. Those efforts ran the gamut from relying on proxy support from U.S. allies such as Israel and Argentina, to enlisting the help of drug traffickers, mercenaries, and private entities from the anticommunist Christian Right. In another time and place, any number of these entities might have been branded as terrorists.[21] These networks flourished in the shadows of the Reagan Doctrine, their messy materiality overwritten by the administration's marriage of anticommunist rhetoric with U.S. claims to be fighting a virtuous war defending freedom from tyranny.[22] Iran-Contra was scarcely exceptional. Instead, it captured what had come to be the norm for such efforts characterized by their improvised and contingent tactics. Against that setting, the public furor directed at the scandalous aspects of Iran-Contra provided the cover for other plots "to go underground, to spawn and skein."[23]

Cheney's remarks in 2005 on executive privilege hinted at the degree to which Iran-Contra's improvised approach to building secret networks remained the norm, rather than the exception, when it came to matters of foreign policy and national security. According to the journalist Seymour Hersh, that same year officials in the Bush administration convened a "lessons-learned" meeting among officials with direct knowledge of Iran-Contra.[24] The goal of the meeting was to generate ideas for using proxy forces to neutralize Iranian influence in postwar Iraq. The meeting was led by Elliot Abrams, Reagan's assistant secretary of state who later plea-bargained his way out of an indictment for his involvement in Iran-Contra. Abrams returned to the White House with the George W. Bush administration as a member of the National Security Council. Officials who attended the meeting later told Hersh that the lessons of Iran-Contra were clear. Any covert operations had to be run out of the vice president's office under the cloak of executive privilege. That way they could be run entirely outside the legal regulations that other government agencies, including the CIA, are subject to.[25] Hersh's article went on to describe a new round of proxy wars orchestrated by Cheney's office to fund Sunni militant groups for the purpose of undermining Iran's Shiite influence in the Middle East. According to Hersh's sources, among the groups supported were a number of militias sympathetic to al-Qaeda. Just as occurred during Iran-Contra, the enemy of the United States' enemy was once again poised to become its ally.

Arrangements such as these have served to reinforce readings of Iran-Contra as paradigmatic of U.S. imperialism, building an image of American power as smoothly operating machine. In this machine, sovereign power is wielded strategically by a secret cabal of "history's actors," to recycle Rove's term, whose hands rest on the levers of power. Indeed historian Greg Grandin has gone so far as to write that "Reagan's Central American wars can best be understood as a dress rehearsal for what is going on now in the Middle East."[26] In this configuration, Latin America served as the nothing more (or less) than the "Empire's workshop," to borrow the title of Grandin's book. His suggestion raises an important point about the historical mobility of American imperialism and its ability to draw on knowledge produced by past experiences to forge new strategies.

As much as Grandin's account (and others like it) have sought to expose the inner workings of empire by revealing its secrets, their judicious histories cannot help but affirm imperialism's power through revelation of its interests and intent. No one in the "insurgent New Right coalition" forged in Central America in the 1980s could have imagined the wars of the future, much less realized that they were involved in "dress rehearsal." At best, such characterizations represent a careful study of the reality created by American imperialism, judiciously done. At worst, they ascribe to those efforts a strategic and rhetorical coherence that obscures the material practices through which they are created and maintained.[27] The phantasmagoria, to use Benjamin's phrase, remains undiminished, its spectacular qualities overwriting the materiality of its workings.

DEBRIS

Efforts to make a life under imperial conditions demonstrate a similar degree of improvisation. The man's proposition to recast his experience in the Contra War as an employable skill for work in Iraq captured this point. Instead of being fashioned from arms deals and secret alliances, his proposition was fashioned from the remnants of wars past aligning the familiar symbols of U.S. imperialism, myself included. This allowed him to revive the geopolitical connections associated with Iran-Contra. Yet that alignment was not born out of any specific political objective or allegiance to U.S. imperialism. It grew out of his effort to secure a job. If the overarching rationale for my interlocutor's claim seemed conspiratorial, the elements from which it was crafted begged a closer consideration of how the material remnants of wars past indelibly shaped possibilities in the present. Often regarded as fragments of a past that is no longer present, those remnants are often cast aside as debris or refuse, deemed too mundane or inconsequential to be worthy of a second thought. And yet it is this *debris*, to use Ann Stoler's term, that provides a material reminder of how imperialism shapes the present long after the last soldier has been demobilized and the last refugee returned.[28]

Eastern Nicaragua is littered with this kind of debris. The physical form and location of Bilwi furnishes an immediate example. Alternately known by its Spanish name of Puerto Cabezas, the city was founded as a logging camp in the 1920s by the New Orleans–based Standard Fruit Company.[29] The city was named for the Nicaraguan military hero, Rigoberto Cabezas, who had led the "reincorporation" of the British-backed Miskito Reserve in 1894. The camp grew quickly, subsuming the nearby Miskito community of Bilwi with its expanding gridwork of houses and streets created to accommodate the influx of labor tied to the mill. Over time, the camp became a city that served as the center of an enclave economy controlled by U.S.-based companies on up through the 1960s. During the height of the enclave, its decimation of the region's forests was obscured by the jobs, consumer goods, and other symbols of progress it brought to an otherwise isolated corner of the Caribbean. Memories of that progress persist in nostalgic accounts of "Company Time" made all the more apparent by the deteriorating infrastructure that remains. Rusting fire hydrants on street corners in the residential zone reserved for company management have long since been disconnected. Railroad beds furnish paths through town, their rails long since removed for scrap. The Contra War added another layer of debris to the city. Residents of indigenous Miskito and Mayangna communities fleeing violence in the surrounding region found shelter in Puerto Cabezas, building informal neighborhoods that surrounded the grid built during the enclave era. Their presence, coupled with the claims of the Miskito armed struggle to defend indigenous rights, helped return the name Bilwi. So too did the Sandinistas' official recognition of Bilwi as the official name of Puerto Cabezas as a part of their designation of the region's autonomous status in 1987.

The debris accumulated by these changes is not only nonhuman material. It is human too. Ex-combatants dominate regional politics through parties such as YATAMA founded on wartime alliances. Underemployed ex-combatants are also prominently visible in public space, often congregating conspicuously. They are prominently visible in public spaces, often in Bilwi's central park. Their presence speaks volumes to the difficulties that many have faced returning to civilian life following the end of the war.

War stories are deployed against these conditions, claiming ex-combatant status as a means to add value and authority to voices otherwise unheard. The man's proposition to me mirrored this logic. Abandoned by U.S. allies and the Nicaraguan state, claiming ex-combatant status to a gringo like me was a means of resuscitating a forgotten alliance. My claims of being just a student were not only inconsequential to that narrative. They also reflected how much I had to learn from ex-combatants such as the man who had approached me at the YATAMA offices. How else could one make sense of a gringo with no apparent ties to a development agency or nongovernmental organization? Indeed as I would later learn, his proposition was not even that far-fetched. At the time of our conversation, private security companies had indeed been combing Central and South America for men with military experience willing to go work in Iraq and Afghanistan.[30] Seen from that perspective, conspiracy's capacity to shed light on imperialism in the present seemed infinitely more useful than judicious accounts of imperialism.

PARANOIA

Or was it?

That was the question that struck me six years later, in 2010, as I sat in the cinder block office of the former Miskito "Head of State" who had commanded YATAMA's armed forces in the late 1980s during the final years of Contra War. Now a lawyer, his office was located in a building he shared with a Miskito-language radio station just off one of the main streets of Bilwi. The radio station itself was a relic of the war. First set up with U.S. support in Honduras, the station broadcast Voice of America news programs prepared by the U.S. government along with Miskito-language programs to refugees and Miskito fighters on patrol in Nicaragua during the Contra War. After the war ended, the station was relocated to Bilwi, where it continues to broadcast Voice of America reports along with music and news programs in Miskito. The radio studio was separated from the comandante's office by a third room that was almost always empty during my visits. Its one remarkable feature was an engraved blue vinyl sign that hung above the door identifying it as the "William J. Casey Memorial Room." Casey headed up the CIA under the Reagan administration in the 1980s and was by most accounts the architect of the networks exposed by Iran-Contra. Casey's testimony before the congressional panel investigating the affair was cut short by a sudden stroke that left him unable to speak, ultimately leading to his death. His demise made him a key target for conspiratorial accounts of Iran-Contra. The sign over the empty conference room used by former Miskito fighters only added to the intrigue.

Although I had been to the comandante's office several times before, I was surprised this time by four photographs that hung on the walls. On all my previous visits, the walls had been bare save for a coat of paint colored a distinct shade of Caribbean turquoise blue. Two of the photos showed the comandante shaking hands with George H. W. Bush and Dan Quayle, respectively, each signed with a dedication to the comandante. A third photo captured the comandante in fatigues, posing with a group of Miskito fighters holding an array of assault rifles and submachine guns. Yet another photo showed the comandante at a much later date, dressed in a coat and tie and posed with a group of men and women in formal attire all wearing medals that hung from red, white, and blue ribbons around their necks. I immediately recognized the faces of several people in that photo. Contra leader and Reagan ally Adolfo Calero's shock of white hair and smile stood out in the back row. The comandante stood off to the side, somewhat awkwardly. And there, in the middle of the group, was the unmistakable gap-toothed smile of Oliver North.

Taken aback by the images, I started asking the comandante about his experiences during the war. He replied with a narrative that I'd heard versions of before. Fleeing the Sandinistas' increasingly militarized efforts to curb Miskito political demands, the comandante had gone to Honduras in 1981 with a group of other young men. Once there, they had received military training from Argentine instructors supported by people the comandante took to be CIA operatives.[31] The Argentines abruptly left within a year of his arrival, after their brief war with the British over the Falkland Islands strained their relationship with Washington, DC. The Argentines' departure forced the Americans to take a more direct role, all the while working around congressional bans on Contra aid. What aid did make it through went overwhelmingly to the better-known Contra groups such as the Fuerzas Democráticas Nicaragüenses (FDN), with only limited supplies ever making it to Miskito hands.[32]

The situation changed drastically in late 1986. While media coverage of Iran-Contra dominated headlines in the United States, providing a prism through which the intricate improvisations of the Reagan Doctrine could be glimpsed, other plots proliferated. To begin with, Republicans in Congress finally managed to soften the ban on Contra aid, allowing the United States to solicit support from other countries so long as it did not include supplying weapons. There were also renewed rumors of an impending U.S. invasion of Nicaragua. Those rumors were fueled by a growing awareness among the Sandinistas, Contra forces, and U.S. policy makers that the war had been fought to a military stalemate. To resolve the stalemate, U.S. officials began making the rounds of the various Contra groups fractured as much by political differences as by the personalities of those leading them. U.S. officials' intention was to unify the various groups into a single force, and thus strengthen the military pressure on the Sandinistas. Their efforts included the various Miskito forces, some of which were beginning to negotiate with the Sandinistas. In exchange for the Miskito forces unifying in their opposition to the Sandinistas, U.S. officials promised military aid and training.

Efforts on the part of the United States coincided with debates among the armed Miskito groups themselves at a time when Sandinista promises of limited political autonomy were gaining appeal. Sandinista promises drove a wedge in the various Miskito groups, dividing those who favored a negotiated recognition of indigenous rights and those who remained committed to driving the Sandinistas from office. U.S. military aid added to that polarization, at long last promising to deliver the weapons that would allow the Miskito forces to drive the Sandinistas from eastern Nicaragua, if not from power altogether.[33] In June 1987, these Miskito factions unified under the banner of YATAMA, merging their goals of defending indigenous rights to land and territory with defeat of the Sandinistas. In exchange for their effort, the comandante claimed that U.S. representatives offered him the chance to send troops to the United States for advanced military training. The comandante accepted, boarding 250 Miskito fighters under his command onto a C-130 Hercules transport plane at an airstrip in Honduras during the middle of the night. Once in the United States, the fighters received training in "parachuting, urban warfare, explosives, and amphibious assault." The skills were all consistent with the commando tactics favored by U.S. military advisors working with proxy forces under the guise of "low intensity warfare."[34] Meanwhile, back in Honduras, rumors began to circulate about an impending U.S. invasion of Nicaragua in response to a buildup of Sandinista forces on the border. The covert phase of the war seemed poised to give way to open conflict. Or so it seemed.

At the height of the buildup, the comandante flew to the United States to attend the graduation ceremony for the men he'd sent there for training. He recalled that the CIA took charge of his travel plans, flying him on a private jet to Miami. There he boarded another plane. According to the comandante, no one would tell him where he was going next. Once he was on the ground again, however, he was able to piece together his location. He'd been taken to Fort Bragg, North Carolina, the home base for the U.S. Army's Special Operations Forces set in the pine forests along the state's coastal plain. It looked surprisingly similar to the pine savannah of eastern Honduras and Nicaragua. That was not the only surprise. During the graduation ceremony, the comandante was startled to see that his Miskito fighters had not undergone the training alone. Among the other graduates from the course were mujahidin from Afghanistan and members of Jonas Savimbi's UNITA forces from

Angola. In the shadow cast by Iran-Contra, the Reagan Doctrine's support for proxy forces of "freedom fighters" was in full swing.

The comandante paused, as if to allow time for me to respond, knowing that what he had said was not exactly common knowledge. The memory of the ex-combatant's proposal flashed in front of me, though I could not quite think of what to say next. Instead, I turned to the photos on the wall, asking in particular about the image of the comandante with Oliver North. The comandante explained that the photo had been taken in 2006 during a ceremony in Washington, DC, hosted by Duane Clarridge. Clarridge directed CIA operations in Latin America during the 1980s before being indicted for his role in the Iran-Contra affair. He was later pardoned by George H. W. Bush, freeing him up to launch a lucrative private intelligence consulting firm that works almost exclusively under contract with the U.S. government. He had also found the time to establish the "Honorable Company of Freedom Fighters" as a means of honoring the role that proxy forces had played in defeating communism.[35] The first inductees into Clarridge's order were the thirty-one leaders of the Contra organizations he'd helped organize and supply during the 1980s. The comandante was included among them for his role in leading YATAMA.

Not that the ceremony made much of a difference to the comandante. As his tone turned bitter, he said that he'd told North during the ceremony that he would have been much happier to receive the cash spent on his travel, lodging, food, and medal than to have attended the event. Now suffering the effects of chronic back injury inflicted during the war, the comandante shifted awkwardly in his plastic chair. "At times, I think that they were very bad allies," he said, gesturing to the photos of Bush, Quayle, and North. The gringos had given them training and arms, even paraded them around as "freedom fighters," but in the end had left them nothing in return. But then again, he offered, they never really understood what the Miskito were fighting for.

He paused, picking up the story again with an account of another trip he'd made to the United States during the height of the Contra war. That trip had been coordinated by the U.S. State Department, and sent him around to college campuses to describe the real war in Nicaragua. Everywhere they went, he noted, the number of people listening to their account were outnumbered by protestors. "People who say that the U.S. intervened in Nicaragua are wrong," he offered. "We were 100 percent volunteers fighting for our rights. We needed help, but people in the United States didn't understand that. They were manipulated into thinking otherwise."

His parsing of the Miskito struggle picked up the pieces of what had been a vitriolic debate in the 1980s over Miskito involvement in the Contra War. Over and against the Left-Right polarity of that debate, a small group of Miskito and their supporters had insisted that theirs was a fight to defend their indigenous rights to autonomy and territory.[36] Their efforts to pry the Miskito struggle out of the grip of the Reagan Doctrine's anticommunism was met with considerable skepticism, particularly from Sandinista supporters in the United States.[37] It also drove a wedge between the Miskito armed groups themselves, separating those fighting for territory and autonomy from those whose saw their primary objective as the defeat of Sandinismo.[38] The distinction was routinely blurred, played up at times by competing Miskito efforts to secure U.S. support and eventually covered over by the unification as YATAMA. The transition by YATAMA itself into a political party following the war had been driven in large part by its emphasis on indigenous rights, a focus that had estranged many ex-combatants from the party's base. The comandante was among them, making no secret of his anti-Sandinista stance well after YATAMA as a party had begun entering into political alliances with their former foes. The formal decision by YATAMA to campaign on the same electoral ticket with the Sandinistas in the national elections of 2007 only made the terms of this estrangement all the more pronounced. The comandante himself had run for governor of the North Caribbean Coast Autonomous Region, on the staunchly anti-Sandinista Liberal Constitutional Party ticket. He lost, and now here he was telling me that the Americans had been duped all along.

The comandante's account of his involvement in the Contra War described a space that allowed for Miskito demands for autonomy and territory to align, however contingently, with the broader framework of U.S. imperialism. During the administration of Jimmy Carter, U.S. policy had shifted its attention to defending human rights while, at the same time, increasing reliance on proxies to carry out and support counterinsurgency campaigns against Leftist groups.[39] The approach allowed Carter to cut aid to key U.S. allies such as Somoza by way of demonstrating U.S. commitment to human rights, while relying on proxies such as Argentina and Israel to continue to supply military aid. Ronald Reagan perfected this approach under his "Reagan Doctrine" of providing support for groups struggling to defend their freedom from totalitarian threats.

The approach sketched out a remarkable set of geopolitical connections, captured by Reagan himself in his address in 1985 at the Bitburg Air Base in Germany. Standing before the graves of more than 2,000 German soldiers, Reagan proclaimed: "I am a Jew in a world still threatened by anti-Semitism. I am an Afghan, and I am a prisoner of the Gulag. I am a refugee in a crowded boat foundering off the coast of Vietnam. I am a Laotian, a Cambodian, a Cuban, and a Miskito Indian in Nicaragua. I, too, am a potential victim of totalitarianism."[40] Reagan used the speech to invoke a virtuous understanding of American military power framed in terms of defending freedom.[41] The effort was nearly undone by the graves of forty-nine members of Hitler's SS visible from the podium.[42] Against Reagan's forced historicism, his opponents charged him with overlooking the materiality of the struggles he invoked, playing their participants for dupes or worse.

As legible as the comandante's account of his involvement in the war was within the broader context of the Reagan Doctrine, it also appeared to confirm the suspicions about the Miskito held by Sandinista sympathizers in the United States. From their perspective, the Miskito were the dupes for fighting against their own political interests, interests that had a better chance with the Sandinistas than under any other U.S.-backed regime. If the comandante's reversal of the charge of being duped sounded conspiratorial, it was a less a function of its details than a matter of his position. Ensconced within the workings of U.S. imperialism, he was too enmeshed in its discursive economy to do much more than add detail to a history already well known. And yet, as his current location reminds, he was undeniably at the margins even of those historical accounts of U.S. imperialism, a sentiment measured by his feelings of betrayal. The sacrifices he had made, both for the Miskito people and the United States could never be rewarded. All they could do was force submission to a geopolitical order constituted by ruination and marginalization.

AFTERMATHS

Backlit by the sun, all birds look black. The particularities of their feathered bodies are reduced to shape and trajectories of flight, made visible by a sun that illuminates them and erases their singularity. So it is too for lives lived under imperial conditions. For all that the idea of imperialism as geohistorical category makes those lives visible, it creates a means of understanding and an image of reality that quickly come to stand in for engagement with its particulars. The image of imperialism, however judiciously wrought, can all too easily write off the lives of those marked by imperial power. Writing them off as dupes only affirms the power of imperialism and perpetuates its ruinous force. Conspiracy affords an imperfect method for disrupting this account, taking stock of active processes of ruination. The particulars expose conditions rife with questions about the purpose and effects of struggles, fueling doubts that can be debilitating. Anticolonial struggles such as those fought by the Sandinistas *and* the Miskito have too often failed to find true liberation from imperialism. In place of the revolutionary force of total war, they have given way to the improvised and often individualizing tactics of managing doubts and fears. Conspiracy attempts to deflect those concerns, fashioning orderly accounts of the fragmentary and chaotic qualities of postconflict life.[43] What they lack in form or reason, they make up for with the force with which they force consideration of ruinous conditions of the present. Authoritative accounts of imperial history are no antidote to the failure to create the hoped-for revolution, and no hoped-for future can promise redemption from its atrocities. What is left is a view of the present as a catastrophe without logic or form.[44] What kind of life is possible under such conditions?

The comandante's account and the ex-combatant's proposition offer examples of what such life might look like, fashioned from the debris of imperialism. It is hard to resist the temptation to rework them into something more akin to a systematic historical account. That effort, however, all but requires overwriting the materiality of individual questions in order to maintain focus on the "big picture" of imperialism as a globe-spanning geohistorical project. As analytically insightful as that approach may be, it enforces a set of exclusions. That effort pushes people such as the Miskito ex-combatants to the margins of a discursive economy that organizes understandings of U.S. imperialism, treating them either as dupes or damaged goods, or both. Their exclusion overwrites the materiality of their experiences. It also demonstrates how imperialism works through the continued exclusion of certain kinds of experience and knowledge. As is so often the case with the social sciences, their knowledge—and with it their lives—only counts if it can describe something larger than themselves.

Conspiracy disrupts this discursive economy. It does not explain imperialism so much as provide pause for reflection on how knowledge of it adheres to a discursive economy that sets limits on whose knowledge counts. Such accounts do not tell the truth of empire so much as they invite consideration of it otherwise. The ex-combatant's plea for employment thus marks an antidote to isolation and abandonment through a return to war. But it also hints at a deeper struggle that, as the comandante suggests, Americans would never understand so long as they remained caught up in their own ideological understandings of power. Neither approach offers redemption, much less hope. Instead they offer up material reminders of the struggle against abandonment and marginalization, experienced in highly individualized ways that are the signature of U.S. imperialism as well as the raw material from which it is made.

NOTES

Unless otherwise noted, translations are my own.

1 For this and other conversations presented here, the use of quotation marks reflects phrases directly noted in field notes. Phrases without quotation marks para-

phrase portions of conversations. This exchange has been previously described by Paglen in *Blank Spots on the Map*, 209–12.

2 Hale, *Resistance and Contradiction.*

3 Coronil, "Beyond Occidentalism."

4 Fluri, "Geopolitics of Gender and Violence from Below"; Sharp, "Geopolitics at the Margins."

5 Taussig, *My Cocaine Museum*, xii; see also Martel, *Textual Conspiracies.*

6 Benjamin, "Unpacking My Library."

7 Briggs, "Theorizing Modernity Conspiratorially."

8 Stoler, "Imperial Debris."

9 Spivak, *An Aesthetic Education in the Era of Globalization.*

10 Suskind, "Faith, Certainty and the Presidency of George W. Bush," 51.

11 On this point, see in particular Butler, *Precarious Life.*

12 This debate is well known and summarized extensively elsewhere. In particular, see Harvey, *A Brief History of Neoliberalism*; N. Smith, *American Empire*; and Sparke, *In the Space of Theory.*

13 Gregory, *The Colonial Present*; Retort, *Afflicted Powers.*

14 Coronil, "Beyond Occidentalism"; see also Hart, "Denaturalising Dispossession"; Lutz, "Empire Is in the Details"; and Stoler and Bond, "Refractions Off Empire."

15 Masco, " 'Sensitive but Unclassified.' "

16 Among the more high-profile proponents of Cheney's involvement in the 9/11 attacks was former Minnesota governor and professional wrestler Jesse Ventura. See "Jesse Ventura's 9/11 theory: Dick Cheney 'allowed it to happen to further their agenda,' " accessed online, and, in print, Ventura, *63 Documents the Government Doesn't Want You to Read.*

17 Fenster, *Conspiracy Theories*, 71.

18 Cheney, "Vice President's Remarks to the Traveling Press." See also Paglen, *Blank Spots on the Map*, 238–39.

19 Kornbluh and Byrne, *The Iran-Contra Scandal.*

20 Gwertzman, "McFarlane Took Cake and Bible to Tehran, Ex-C.I.A. Man Says."

21 Mamdani, *Good Muslim, Bad Muslim.* One of oft-repeated slogans of opponents of the Reagan Doctrine was "Can you tell the difference between a freedom fighter and a terrorist?"

22 See the introduction to this volume as well as McGranahan, *Arrested Histories.* On virtuous war, see Der Derian, *Virtuous War.*

23 DeLillo, *Underworld*, 51.

24 Hersh, "Annals of National Security."

25 Hersh, "Annals of National Security"; see also Paglen, *Blank Spots on the Map.*

26 Grandin, *Empire's Workshop*, 5.

27 A similar critique of Grandin is raised, in passing, in the introduction to this volume.

28 Stoler, "Imperial Debris."

29 Pineda, *Shipwrecked Identities*; Vilas, *Del colonialismo a la autonomía*; Molieri, *El desafío indígena en Nicaragua.*

30 Paglen, *Blank Spots on the Map.* See also "Rara forma de buscar Nicas para ir a Irak"; "Mil hondureños a Irak y Afganistán"; Bermúdez, "Pistoleros a sueldo

(mínimo)." For an overview, see Scahill, *Blackwater: The Rise of the World's Most Powerful Mercenary Army.*

31 Argentine involvement in training anticommunist paramilitary groups was organized by the Carter administration under the aegis of "Operation Charly." See Honey, *Hostile Acts*; Mamdani, *Good Muslim, Bad Muslim*; and McClintock, *Instruments of Statecraft.*

32 Bataillon, "Yugo"; Comandante Coyote/Benjamin, "Reseña histórica de la lucha indígena en Nicaragua"; Nietschmann, "Bruno Gabriel."

33 Hale, *Resistance and Contradiction*; Comandante Coyote/Benjamin, "Reseña histórica de la lucha indígena En Nicaragua."

34 As a variation on counterinsurgency, this approach was outlined by both the CIA and the U.S. military during the 1980s. See, for example, U.S. Army Command and General Staff College, *Field Circular 100–20.*

35 Lake, "Secret Honors for Cold War Spies."

36 Bataillon, "Cambios culturales y sociopolíticos en las comunidades mayangnas y miskitus del Río Bocay y del Alto Río Coco, Nicaragua (1979–2000)"; Morris and Churchill, "Between a Rock and a Hard Place"; Nietschmann, *The Unknown War.*

37 Hale, *Resistance and Contradiction.*

38 Bataillon, "Yugo"; Nietschmann, "Bruno Gabriel."

39 Mamdani, *Good Muslim, Bad Muslim.*

40 Reagan, "Remarks at a Joint German-American Military Ceremony at Bitburg Air Base in the Federal Republic of Germany," accessed October 19, 2017, http://www.vlib.us/amdocs/texts/reagan051985.html.

41 Der Derian, *Virtuous War.* For a close reading of Reagan's speech, see Jensen, *Reagan at Bergen-Belsen and Bitburg*; and Olson, "The Controversy over President Reagan's Visit to Bitburg."

42 Weinraub, "Reagan Joins Kohl in Brief Memorial at Bitburg Graves."

43 Nelson, *Reckoning.*

44 Clark, "For a Left with No Future."

18

Empire as Accusation, Denial, and Structure

The Social Life of U.S. Power at Brazil's Spaceport

SEAN T. MITCHELL

INTRODUCTION: CONSPIRACY, DENIAL, AND THE ETHNOGRAPHY OF POSTIMPERIAL EMPIRE

A few years ago, I had a long conversation with a Brazilian diplomat stationed at his nation's New York consulate. We discovered a mutual interest in Brazil's space program, about which he hopes to write a book. When I told him about my ethnographic research on the conflicts around Brazil's main spaceport—a flashpoint of national controversy, international intrigue, launch failure, land dispute, Afro-Brazilian political mobilization, and conspiracy theory—he asked me pointedly: "So, who planted the bomb?"

The diplomat's question and accusatory stare were (unhappily) a sharp reminder of the suspicions that I (a U.S. anthropologist) often navigated during years of ethnographic research around the spaceport and (happily) a reminder of the importance of the topic I was then writing about. This allegation of U.S. sabotage is one of several claims of hidden interference by foreign powers—most frequently, the United States—that permeate the fraught politics of the spaceport. These claims often call forth vociferous rebuttals, such as my own: "There was no bomb!" But was there?

In this chapter, I draw on my ethnographic work around the spaceport to analyze how transnational forces—most often U.S. empire—are invoked in a dialectic of accusation and denial, and the relationships between this dialectic and the functioning of U.S. power in an era in which extranational power projection is usually legitimated in anti-imperial terms.[1] The corollary of the United States' often invisible and frequently disavowed power is suspicion of omnipresence; if something is visible nowhere then it might be everywhere. The basic shape of my conversation with the diplomat is frequently replicated worldwide: suspicion of imperial conspiracy, countered with blanket denial.

The resulting global epistemic condition—one of imperial imaginaries, suspicion, doubt, and fear—is a structural feature of the contemporary world system, though it is seldom treated as such. To understand the contradictory nature of seemingly imperial U.S. power in an ostensibly postimperial age, we need to understand its relation to the stories that people tell about it—stories that are shaped by interested actors, with their own histories and worldviews, a task that ethnography is well positioned to perform.

Another surprising claim about imperial power at the spaceport is that its racial politics have been shaped by U.S. empire. Some context is called for. Brazil's Air Force built the spaceport on the equatorial peninsula of Alcântara in the 1980s, in a region inhabited by the descendants of enslaved Africans, some of whom escaped slavery as the regional cotton economy declined beginning in the 1820s. They and their neighbors then built free communities on the margins of a slave society that persisted until the abolition of Brazilian slavery in 1888. Many of these villagers had their lands expropriated during the base's original construction. The remaining independent villagers surrounding the existing base are still threatened with expropriation. Nonetheless, aided by a wide network of allies in Brazil and abroad, they have so far been able to retain their land in the face of plans for the spaceport's expansion. Their claims to their land hinge on mobilization around a recently forged ethnoracial category, with land rights guaranteed by Brazil's Constitution of 1988: *remanescentes das comunidades dos quilombos*—literally, "remainders" or "descendants" of escaped-slave communities. *Quilombola*, as it is generally shortened, has become an identity crucial to black consciousness movements and to land struggles throughout Brazil.[2]

For some proponents of Brazil's space program, the United States has deliberately fostered quilombola identity and Afro-Brazilian mobilization in a bid to undermine Brazil's space program and sovereignty, another of the claims of an imperial presence haunting the spaceport I frequently encountered. In this conceptualization of empire, villagers, by politicizing Afro-Brazilian identity and history, are acting as pawns in an imperial plot to undermine national power. In surprising ways, this accusation resembles accusations made in longstanding academic debates about relationships between U.S. power and Afro-Brazilian mobilization.[3] Below, I detail the logic of this claim. Here, I want to make clear that although this accusation is false, and draws some of its content from local histories and contingencies, it also points to opaque aspects of the global conjuncture: (a) U.S. cultural and political institutions have had a large influence on the recent politics of racial identification in Brazil, and (b) the U.S. government has long opposed Brazil's space program, often secretively.[4]

Although I am re-creating the structure of accusation and denial here, it is important to debunk the accusation that the quilombolas are somehow

U.S. dupes, both because it is false and because it aims to undermine the hard-won rights of long-marginalized and exploited communities. I also show how the histories of villager political mobilization and space program development have been impacted by the United States' "structural power" in Susan Strange's sense: power that shapes, often invisibly, the contours of possibility for groups pursuing their own goals.[5] My argument is that conspiracy theory, denial, and structural power are linked, and are crucial aspects of what we might call the "postimperial empire" of the U.S.-dominated world system.

As Collins and McGranahan argue in the introduction to this volume, the projection of U.S. power has been legitimated in anti-imperial terms since the nation's founding. Moreover, and unlike more conventional empires, current U.S. global hegemony is not founded principally on territorial conquest.[6] Rather, it is founded on stealth punctuated by displays of overpowering violence, on governance through far-flung institutions and corporations, and on disavowal.[7] Although U.S. power is ubiquitous in the twenty-first century, its contradictory, perpetually self-denying character gives it a strange social life. It exists at once as material fact and shadowy suspicion, as disavowal and political accusation, and as a structuring force in the lives of people and institutions.[8]

Consider again the diplomat's "bomb." He was alleging that the United States had sabotaged Brazil's VLS-1 (*Veículo Lançador de Satélites*) satellite launch rocket in August 2003. The explosion of the rocket was a major setback for Brazil's fledgling program. It carbonized twenty-one engineers and technicians and the cause has never been explained to the satisfaction of most observers. This chapter is not about that explosion.[9] However, widespread suspicions in Brazil about U.S. sabotage are closely linked to the matters I discuss here. U.S. empire is not a clear material presence in my ethnographic data; I describe no U.S. bombs. But in the year leading up to the Brazilian explosion, the United States continued to wage a major war in Afghanistan; expanded its involvement in a counterinsurgency across Brazil's Amazonian border in Colombia, funded partially by a secret budget; covertly supported a failed coup d'état against Venezuelan president, Hugo Chavez; pre-emptively dropped some 2.4 million pounds of explosives on Iraq in two days, in a campaign dubbed "Shock and Awe"; released a national military doctrine affirming the need to permanently maintain the capacity and right to carry out such actions everywhere, anywhere, and forever; and undoubtedly carried out other covert military actions that never appeared in newspapers.[10] Given that the style and strategies of twenty-first-century U.S. global hegemony were honed in Latin America, residents might reasonably be expected to worry about U.S. bombs.[11]

This seemingly omnipresent capacity for violence, surveillance, and control—as well as wide-ranging influence through media, corporations, foundations, multilateral institutions, and NGOs—is coupled with a self-denying and opaque character. Thus, U.S. power in the twenty-first century tends to generate discussions that oscillate between wild conspiracy theories, on the one hand, and denials that U.S. power could have any effect at all, on the other. This dialectic of conspiracy theory and denial not only helps keep the subtler aspects of U.S. global power invisible but it has its own effects in shaping the global system, though in ways that are neither predictable nor uniform.

A BRAZILIAN EMPIRE?

In 1944, a few months after the countries that would win World War II established in Bretton Woods, New Hampshire, the financial architecture for the United States' then emerging global hegemony, Brazilian sociologist Gilberto Freyre gave a series of lectures at Indiana University, prepared "especially for an Anglo-American" public.[12] Freyre, arguably the twentieth century's most influential interpreter of Brazilian history and society, is generally credited with adding scholarly heft to a still influential but thoroughly debunked vision of Brazilian society as a harmonious (if unequal) mixture of ethnoracial groups—often glossed as "racial democracy."[13] Imagining Brazil's possible influence in the decolonizing postwar world, Freyre predicted that "the Soviet Union and Brazil, though fundamentally different in their conceptions of social and economic organization, will probably join in the near future as leaders of a movement towards making of racial equality an international issue."[14]

But in that period of U.S. global ascendancy, the movement toward racial equality that would gain the most international reach was not Brazilian (or Soviet), as Freyre predicted, but the U.S. Civil Rights Movement.[15] During the second half of the twentieth century, the influence of Brazilian models of race relations declined in the United States.[16] In early twenty-first-century Brazil, it is a supposed U.S. Americanization of Brazilian race relations that causes controversy.[17] The twenty-first century may still realize parts of Freyre's prediction if Brazil's international influence again grows as it did during the century's first decade, when some envisioned the specter of a twenty-first-century Brazilian "sub-imperialism," particularly in Lusophone Africa and in Latin America.[18] But the twentieth century brought almost the opposite of Freyre's prediction.

I mention Freyre's predictions for three reasons. First, an ostensible U.S. influence on Brazilian race relations is a fundamental aspect of the ethnographic situation I describe here, and the inheritors of Freyre's "Lusotropical" nationalism are important defenders of what they see as a Brazilian racial order undermined by an imperial United States, thus pointing us to some of the surprising ways in which U.S. power is imagined. Second, attentiveness to these dynamics shifts our focus in thinking about power in international relations from macropolitics to micropolitics, from *hegemony* as used in international relations to the *hegemony* of Gramsci,[19] from the formation of states to the formation of subjectivities. It is in these intimate, everyday aspects of domination that ethnographers have especially good data to bring to bear on discussions of global politics. Finally, the recognition that something as unambiguously liberatory as civil rights might ride to global influence, at least partially, on an imperial wave, should help us recognize that the world of Pax Americana has less coherence and fixity than we might think, undermining the too-tidy conceptions of imperial agency and purpose that cloud understanding of global power.

THE ETHNOGRAPHIC SETTING

Villagers surrounding Brazil's spaceport in Alcântara have lived in constant danger about their right to their ancestral lands and livelihood for more than three decades.[20] In building the spaceport from 1983 to 1990 the Brazilian Air Force forcibly relocated some fifteen hundred residents from coastal fishing and swidden-agriculture communities to new inland communities, *agrovilas*. In the agrovilas, land-tenure was transformed from a rotating communal system to one based on small fixed individual plots, quickly resulting in overuse and depleted soil. Located far from the ocean, residents of the agrovilas were no longer easily able to supplement farming and gathering with fishing. Unlike relatives in Alcântara's historical villages, people in the agrovilas were transformed into contingent wage laborers, dependent on irregular and meager work at the spaceport.[21]

Since 1987, many of the still existing historical villages have been slated for expropriation for spaceport expansion. But surprisingly, these cash-poor swidden horticulturalists, who fish, gather, and build their houses from wattle and daub; who live in villages formed by people who escaped and left slavery on the fringes of the region's faltering cotton economy in the nineteenth century, as well as other villages formed after slavery's abolition;[22] and who, until 2006, had no electricity, much less serious representation in national politics, have managed to hold onto their land legally in the face of pressure from the space program.

The Brazilian space program in Alcântara, which has yet to successfully launch a satellite, is divided between military (Air Force) and civilian wings that disagree about the program's direction.[23] In 2008, a court decision ended a villager blockade, ceding to their demands that civilian launching sites in a proposed Ukrainian-Brazilian collaboration should be built within the existing base, which is controlled by the air force, instead of on villager land.[24] Military resistance to civilian and foreign projects within the existing area, not technical considerations, had pushed these plans onto villager land prior to the court order.

The most important reason for the (still tenuous) success of villagers in holding their land has been the organizing of the widespread quilombo movement, which became active in Alcântara via a seminar in 1999 put forth by NGOs, anthropologists, and lawyers. The local quilombo movement has since found allies throughout Brazil and beyond, helping villagers mobilize around a clause in Brazil's Constitution of 1988 that requires the state to grant inalienable land rights to quilombos, or escaped slave-descended communities.[25]

Perhaps more stunning than its success in protecting villager land has been Alcântara's quilombo movement's success in transforming people's sense of their ethnic identities and political horizons. In conversations and interviews, villagers born before 1980 often refer to representatives of the spaceport as *gente grande* (big people), describing their relation to the people from the spaceport principally in terms of their own relative marginalization and low status. But younger people generally speak very differently about themselves and their relation to Brazilian society. They refer to themselves confidently as quilombolas—a term mostly absent in the lexicon of older villagers, except for the most politicized—secure that this status grounds their rights as citizens and as holders of their land. And while their parents tend to refer to themselves with a variety of color- and context-specific ethnoracial terms (e.g., *roxo, moreno, caboclo*), young people usually refer to themselves as *negro,* or black, aggregating and building ethnoracial solidarity among people of widely varying appearance—as does the United States' "one drop rule."[26] These important transformations in ethnoracial and political subjectivity have been crucial to the ability of locals to build alliances and to make constitutional claims to protect their land in the face of Brazilian government efforts to expand its strategic outpost on the eastern coastal perimeter of the Amazon forest.

Critics and skeptics of quilombo identity and land claims sometimes identify an imperial presence fostering the growth of politicized subnational identities in order to undermine Brazil's territorial sovereignty—particularly in the Amazon—and its technological progress—particularly in military or dual-use fields such as aerospace. This suspicion crosses otherwise sharp ideological and material divides between proponents of a military-nationalist space program and proponents of a civilian, profit-seeking one, as well as Left-Right political divides in Brazil.

Consider a conversation a friend from one of Alcântara's villages and I had in 2006 when we ran into a group of civilian workers from the space program in a bar in the state capital, São Luís. When the brief conversation turned to the conflicts around the spaceport, one young space program technician touched the arm of my friend, a light-skinned young man, and said drunkenly: "Look at me. My skin is darker than this *caboclo* [a term that, locally, is generally used to describe rural people without marked African ancestry].[27] How is he a quilombola? All this talk about quilombos is just a strategy against the space program. You know there are a lot of Americans around Alcântara. I'm not military, but those military guys are right that some countries don't want us to advance."

Flustered, neither of us had a ready response, and the conversation quickly dissipated with the arrival of other acquaintances in the bustle of the bohemian downtown nightlife of the old city center. Later that night, my friend rehashed rebuttals he could have used: "The quilombos have been in Alcântara for hundreds of years!"

I have often encountered similar assertions, from widely varied sectors of Brazilian society, that quilombo identity and rights exist to benefit empire. I have also frequently encountered blanket denials like those of my friend. In 2006, Sergio Gaudenzi, the socialist then president of the Brazilian Space Agency claimed that the "lobby" against the base (which could only mean the quilombolas and their allies) was the product of "direct and indirect maneuvers" of international competition.[28] In 2009, Brazil's conservative defense minister, Nelson Jobim, made a similar suggestion.[29]

The vision of "racial equality" that Freyre thought might spread from Brazil during the second half of the twentieth century was one of supposedly cordial relations and blurred ethnoracial lines. Instead, the increasingly agonistic and sharpening ethnoracial lines in early twenty-first-century Alcântara (and Brazil) appear to some to be the result of an outsized U.S. influence. This assertion of U.S. influence on Brazil's changing race politics is particularly prominent in Brazilian critiques of the nation's twenty-first-century affirmative action programs.[30] This claim had its greatest international repercussions in the debate over Pierre Bourdieu and Loïc Wacquant's argument that an imperial imposition of the "U.S. folk concept" and folk categories of race have been imposed on Brazil by U.S. scholars and foundations blind to their own imperial hubris and power.[31] "Undoubtedly," they write, this is "one of the most striking proofs of the symbolic domination and influence exercised by the USA."[32]

But the accusation that these transformations may be part of a *deliberate* bid for U.S. political domination has not, as far as I know, made it into the scholarly literature. This lapse is surprising because I found this idea to be common in discussions of the politics of the spaceport. The assertion has continuities with a broader claim—one with origins in the military, but present outside it,[33] that world powers, especially the United States, are deliberately fostering indigenous identity and environmental concerns to undermine Brazilian sovereignty in the Amazon. In this imaginary, imperial control takes on the paradoxical appearance of liberatory, subaltern struggles, fomenting subnational identities under the pretense of human rights and environmentalism, with the real intent of weakening elite Brazilian projects that might compete with empire. These include the space program and development of the Amazon.

These claims are false in most particulars. The United States has indeed tried to block the advancement of Brazil's space program, as has been revealed by diplomatic cables released by Wikileaks.[34] Yet there is no evidence that such strategies involve the quilombo movement. Careful scholarly work has shown how quilombola identities have emerged instead due to the organizing of Brazilian social movements that cannot be characterized as following some imperial script.[35] Moreover, I have analyzed elsewhere the fantastical character of nationalist narratives about the Amazon, which have spread partially due to fraud and luck.[36] Also, covert U.S. interventions into Brazilian politics have certainly not been uniformly opposed to Brazilian military power—notably, U.S. sponsorship of the coup d'état in 1964 that installed a right-wing military government that lasted for twenty-one years. The idea of an imperial plot to empower ethnically splintered subalterns is a clear fantasy, though it is widespread.

Nonetheless, the idea of such an imperial plot is a fantasy that draws on real aspects of global politics that we need to think about in any serious analysis of twenty-first-century empire. The emergence of governance in the Global South by foreign-supported NGOs and the neoliberal privileging of ethnic politics above all are clearly part of the reason that Alcântara's politics have taken the form that they have, and thus this politics arises in indirect form from the policy and outsized power of the United States.[37] Even social movements that have patently emerged in response to local conditions—such as those in Alcântara—do so in the context of broader forces. This post–Cold War world of neoliberalism, multinational institutions, transnational corporations, and proliferating NGOs is the world that the United States created.

The diffuse, self-denying, omnipresent, and opaque power that the contemporary United States wields is hard to conceptualize, and harder still to trace throughout the world. It is no wonder that U.S. power is the subject of such outrageous conspiracy theories, which dialectically call forth their denials. For ethnographers to put together a better understanding of life under the twenty-first-century Pax Americana, we need to rise above this dialectic of conspiracy and denial, and instead make it an object of study.

Conspiracy theories—like official narratives—may be true or may be false, and they are always interpreted and deployed by culturally embedded and interested actors. There is no a priori reason to assume that any given conspiracy theory, denial, or official narrative illuminates anything in particular about the global system. But in systems of extraction in which relationships of domination are often hidden and disavowed, even as they are combined with violence, it is inevitable that some conspiracy theories should illuminate structural power—and ethnographers interested in global power need to write about them.

Consider that the late anthropologist Michel-Rolph Trouillot, hardly a conspiracy theorist, made observations similar to the claims described above: "International organizations, private or state-sponsored, now help to fashion throughout the periphery an incipient public sphere that expands beyond national confines. For better and for worse, this new arena incorporates North Atlantic dominant tropes from the language of the ecological movement and the discourse on individual human rights to the rhetoric of ethnic or racial preferences. The knowledge necessary for the management of local populations in the postcolony increasingly accumulates in foreign hands, both private and state-sponsored."[38] The circulation of human rights and environmental discourses, the emergence of ethnoracial rights discourses—but where critics of Alcântara's quilombos see design, Trouillot sees broader structures of influence. Where the president of Brazil's Space Agency asserts imperial deception, Trouillot focuses on the structural forces that shape the actions of people and groups worldwide—though in differing ways and degrees.

The perspectives on U.S. power I have so far discussed sometimes do a better job of identifying the vast reach and effects of that power than do most U.S. commentators, but those perspectives also misrecognize that power in significant ways. They assume a too straightforward purpose and uniformity for power that is harnessed by many differing groups—in many cases, groups unaware of the power they are wielding. They are guilty of what Walton has called a "nostalgia for an obvious, black-and white geopolitical topography of power," that arguably existed in a self-avowedly imperial era, but that is much more confusing in an era of ostensibly self-determining nation-states.[39]

Most anthropologists are now careful about too easily reifying the state as though it were an agent with clear intentions and purpose.[40] Yet about this still more confusing and contradictory entity, empire, we too often forget these lessons—witness the debate during the twenty-first century's first decade about whether the United States should be called an empire. This debate is structurally similar to the dialectical interplay of conspiracy and denial: either empire is deliberate, omnipresent, and visible, or it is nothing.

The heading of this section, "Global Monroe Doctrine," is intended to direct our attention, instead, to the similarities between contemporary United States power and its nineteenth-century hegemony in the Western Hemisphere. The phrase, Global Monroe Doctrine, is owed to Neil Smith, who cites Woodrow Wilson's advocacy of expanding the Monroe Doctrine of U.S. supremacy to the world.[41] This vision of indirect control, sporadic invasions and occupations, and the equality of nation-states "on paper" has largely come to fruition. The Monroe Doctrine provides a different model for contemporary U.S. power than do pre-twentieth-century empires, which—despite many differences among them—were usually founded on the territorial conquest and control of *formally unequal* territories from a single metropole.[42] In writing of the "globalization of the banana republic," John Kelly provides a metaphor similar to the Global Monroe Doctrine.[43] This metaphor points to the importance of corporations, finance, and multinational institutions in the wielding of contemporary global power.[44] It also hints at the complex character of that power. Unlike earlier imperial systems premised on the *formal inequality* of metropole and colony, today's global system is premised on the *nominal equality* of self-determining nation-states—Washington and Windhoek in the twenty-first century are formally symmetrical national capitals in ways that Lisbon and Luanda never were in the eighteenth century. Nonetheless, that nominal equality can always be undermined and unmasked by material inequality.

Whether we describe this hegemony as empire is not so important. The United States is equipped to act imperially when necessary, even if done under the rubric of "democracy," "human rights," or "security." People around the world are aware of U.S. bombs and drones sent over national borders in mostly undeclared wars, and, with the disclosures of the reach of the U.S. surveillance apparatus made by Edward Snowden in 2013, people worldwide are also generally aware of the global reach of U.S. surveillance. As Brazilian security scholar Geraldo Lesbat Cavagnari Filho has argued, and Collins and McGranahan suggest in this volume's introduction, the United States is an empire everywhere in potential.[45] That constant potential for violence and control, always ready to hop from the United States' expanding global network of "lily pad bases," shapes politics and generates anxieties worldwide in unpredictable ways.[46] Empire exists as a force, as an imaginary, as a project, as an enemy, as a logic, even in places where it isn't materially present. Ethnographers may not gain frequent access to those who wield imperial military, economic, and political power.[47] But we often gain unique access to more subtle, unexpected, intimate, and everyday aspects of the world system. In this light, ethnographers of something as far-flung, confusing, and powerful as U.S. power need to analyze that power as both an imaginary and a material presence.

EMPIRE AND STRUCTURAL POWER

U.S. power also functions in a third way. It is a structuring agent, shaping the reality to which institutions and people must conform. The story of the Technology Safeguards Accord between Brazil and the United States for the use of the Alcântara spaceport is a case in point.

In 2000, the Brazilian and U.S. governments negotiated a Technology Safeguards Accord for the use of the Alcântara spaceport by the United States. The accord directly curtailed certain aspects of Brazilian sovereignty on its own spaceport, something hard to imagine the U.S. allowing on its own national territory. For example, the accord (1) restricted Brazilian access to those areas of the base assigned to the United States, as well as to U.S. materials there; (2) prohibited Brazil from using the money gained from the accord to support the Brazilian space program; and (3) prohibited Brazil from negotiating with other countries to allow them to use the spaceport. Although signed by Brazilian president Fernando Henrique Cardoso, the highly restrictive document provoked enormous controversy in Brazil and the nation's Congress never ratified it. By May 2003, the new administration of Luiz Inácio Lula da Silva had rejected it. In the years since, there were frequent reports that the accord would be reopened or renegotiated, and a petition was circulated by supporters of the civilian program that included a demand for the renegotiation of the accord.[48] In 2017, there were reports that the Michel Temer government, installed in 2016 by a legislative coup d'état, was renegotiating the agreement with the United States. This generated opposition on the Brazilian Left and Right and left the accord's status uncertain as this book goes to press.[49]

The accord has also been important in Alcântara's local politics. Although often at odds about the space program's direction, supporters of the civilian and military space programs often find common ground opposing quilombo land-rights, sometimes claiming that quilombola identity is an imperial imposition. Similarly, accusation of an imperial U.S. influence has sometimes facilitated a contingent alliance between the air force and quilombo movement activists,[50] despite their enmity in other matters. Machado (a pseudonym), one of my closest friends and informants in Alcântara, is a well-known and militant quilombo movement activist. Yet, when he publicly opposed the Technology Safeguards Accord in 2002–3, he was openly thanked by air force officers, themselves strongly opposed to the accord, despite their disdain for the quilombo movement. For Machado, the key concern was the threat to villagers by the expansion of the spaceport. For the officers, on the other hand, the foreign threat was not to villagers, but to Brazilian sovereignty and to military control of the spaceport. The existence of a perceived imperial threat to all these valued goals was enough to produce a temporary and tenuous alliance.

Such sentiments became wildly popular in Brazil at the time. During September 2002, the Comissão Contra a ALCA (The Commission Against the FTAA, the Free Trade Area of the Americas) held a plebiscite that reportedly reached 70 percent of Brazil's (then) 5,561 municipalities.[51] Some 150,000 volunteers; more than one hundred movements, NGOs, and organizations of various types and a few political parties worked to mobilize popular opinion and spread forty-two thousand voting booths across Brazil.[52] Although the deck was stacked by the partisan character of the plebiscite, the results cannot simply be discounted and remain impressive. To the first question—"Should the Brazilian Government Sign the FTAA?"—a resounding 98.33 percent of the more than ten million voters voted "no." To the second question—"Should the Brazilian Government continue participation in the FTAA negotiations?"—95.94 percent voted "no." The third question was an add-on, not the main topic of the plebiscite, but closely linked to nationalist concerns over the FTAA: "Should the Brazilian government surrender part of our territory—the Alcântara base—to the military control of the United

States?" Unsurprisingly, the votes on this question were the most univocal of all. A reported 98.59 percent voted "no."

The dispute over the accord and the massive public campaign opposed to it have had a major impact on Brazilian perceptions of Alcântara. Frequently, when I tell people in other parts of Brazil that I lived in Alcântara, they ask: "In the American base there?" My usual response is to explain that there is no U.S. base there (a suspect claim from a U.S. citizen, I imagine). But, as in the case of Alcântara's quilombos, this dialectic of conspiracy and denial hides a knottier relation.

Although the accord is typically presented as something the United States demanded of Brazil, the reality is more complex. At least in part, the accord resulted as part of a process initiated by Brazilians in order to develop a commercial spaceport—a field dominated by the United States and by unofficial U.S. rules.[53] One official in the space program, for example, told me under conditions of anonymity that Brazil had initiated the contact with the United States in order to facilitate the commercialization of Alcântara: "it's almost impossible to have a viable space program without U.S. approval," the official said in 2005.

This official's statement is corroborated by the public testimony of José Monserrat Filho, an important proponent of Brazil's civilian space program and then president of the Brazilian Society for Scientific Progress. According to Monserrat, an early plan to commercialize the base in 1996 involved setting up a consortium with an Italian company. In his telling, the U.S. government pressured the Italian government to block the deal. The United States presented its demands in a *nonpaper*—an unofficial, off-the-record, policy statement—claiming that Brazil, in Montserrat's paraphrase: "was not a country that met all of the requirements of security and trust"[54] Brazil, however, had already taken steps to demilitarize its space program to assuage the United States.[55]

The Italian government blocked the deal in response to this unofficial U.S. pressure. Supporters of the Brazilian space program then realized that the Brazilian government needed to strike a deal with the United States for Brazil to enter the lucrative international launch market. Ronaldo Sardenberg, who would soon become the minister of science and technology, sought the deal with the United States. But according to my interviewee and Monserrat, the U.S. government initially refused these negotiations and demanded that Brazil stop work on Brazil's satellite launch program.[56]

Brazil was forced to accept the United States' hard conditions to get a deal that the Brazilian space program sorely wanted. For Monserrat, the Accord was negotiated between two unequal parties: "two parties in unequal situations; the Americans with the upper hand, in principle not interested in the deal, and the Brazilians wanting the accord, fundamental to make Alcântara politically viable in the universe of commercialization of Space activity."[57] The accord is usually publicly framed in one of two ways: either as an imperial U.S. imposition, or as a free choice of the Brazilian government, seeking the benefits of U.S. technology and support. It was not either of those things. The accord and the discussion around it are best understood as result of what Susan Strange called "structural power," or "the power to shape and determine the structures of the global political economy within which other states, their political institutions, their economic enterprises and (not least) their scientists and other professional people have to operate."[58] This conceptualization provides another angle on how contemporary power functions internationally. Certainly, a worldwide network of military bases is a particularly obvious manifestation of U.S. power,[59] and, undoubtedly, a necessary condition of more diffuse and ambiguous forms of U.S. power. But, whatever the intention of U.S. military planners in Alcântara, it is U.S. domination of the satellite launch industry and of the politics that regulate it that shape the logic of Brazil's attempt to reach space. This is not imperial power in the conventional sense, but it might as well be. Structural power shapes the logic of inevitability, so that groups, in pursuit of their own interests, must conform to a set of rules established elsewhere, and often established secretly.

CONCLUSION: THE PARANOID STRUCTURE OF EMPIRE

In this chapter, I have described and analyzed some of the surprising, contradictory, imaginary, and structural forms that U.S. power took around Brazil's spaceport in the first decade of the twenty-first century. The materiality and reach of that power, coupled with its opaque and disavowed implementation, generates an often-repeated dialectic of accusation and denial. The belief that the VLS-1 explosion was part of a U.S. plot to deny Brazil's access to space, for example, or the belief that the quilombo movement and the changing nature of Brazilian racial subjectivity are U.S. imperial impositions, are both widespread theories about U.S. power in Alcântara. They are most often met with blanket denials like my own. There is no clear evidence indicating a deliberate role of the United States in either phenomenon, but the United States has shaped the histories of Brazil's space program and its race politics in complex structural ways, ways that are not always intentional. Moreover, these narratives themselves form part of a set of global imaginaries about power, the existence of which is an important part of the global system.

It is this last claim—that the dialectic of conspiracy and denial has a structural role in the global system—that is hardest to substantiate. Although the form of this dialectic is ubiquitous, its contents and its effects are highly contingent and dependent on the specificities of sociohistorical contexts. Yet the global epistemic condition of suspicion, fear, and awareness of the opacity and force of imperial power could not help but have profound global effects.

While considering how to write about the suspicion, power, and forms taken by empire, I read through some of the long and contentious discussions about David Graeber's *Debt: the First 5,000 Years* carried out in 2012–13 on the popular academic blogs *Crooked Timber*, *Savage Minds*, and elsewhere. At one point in those discussions, Graeber makes precisely this point: "The actual connections between military force, currency regimes, and economic power are impossible to pin down . . . it's therefore inevitable that paranoid conspiracy theories abound. Yet, speaking as an anthropologist, I cannot help but find these myths and rumors significant—in fact, I see them as themselves playing a key role in the system."[60]

Those discussions, like the content of Graeber's book, are beyond the scope of this chapter. But the crux of contention, as I saw it, hinged on Graeber's reading of Michael Hudson's analysis of the United States' global political and economic hegemony.[61] Hudson describes a post–World War II order in which the United States exports dollars and imports goods and, through this extractive process, underwrites its military imperialism. Although most pundits conceive of this relation as one of growing *U.S. indebtedness to external creditors*, Graeber argues that it is more accurately described as *imperial tribute to the United States from external subjects*—all made possible by violence and threat of violence.

Overwhelmingly, as blogosphere commentators rejected Graeber's argument that the international credit and exchange system is characterized by tribute to the United States and held together by fear of U.S. violence, the discussion itself took on the form of the dialectic of conspiracy theory and denial. I have not seen evidence that such disparate governments as those of Japan, China, Switzerland, India, Russia, and Brazil—to pick a handful of the top foreign holders of U.S. treasury securities—understand their relation to the United States as one of tribute, though international opposition to dollar hegemony exists and seems to be mounting.[62] So tribute—in which subjects are well aware that that is what they are paying—is not a perfect analogue for the globally unequal system of dollar hegemony. But it is also hard to imagine the system of dollar hegemony being maintained without U.S. military hegemony.

Graeber's account, like others I described earlier, assumes too much deliberate awareness of those playing their parts in an imperial system, but it points clearly to the structural relationship between paranoid conspiracy theory and global power. The paranoid theories he describes are inevitable given the opacity and violence of global power politics, and, as he suggests, they help fuel the global fear of violence that holds the system together. Paranoia is both a consequence and necessary condition of a set of exploitative relations.

Of course, how conspiracy theories are imagined, crafted, and manipulated by interested actors in particular locations is as variable as those locations themselves. There is no easy trick for deducing the nature of the contemporary global imperial system from a simple formula. So, ethnography is crucial for our understanding. But particular ethnographies will not give us a complete picture of the global postimperial/imperial system. Far from it. In our studies of the local, intimate, and everyday, we can do our best to describe some fragment of the elephant, like the blind people in the familiar parable. But as Trouillot argued just before the start of the era of unending "war on terror," it is through such fragmentary ethnographic approaches that we might piece together the global system's effects, and from its effects, its structure.[63]

NOTES

Unless otherwise noted, translations are my own.

1 The United States is not the only subject of conspiracy narratives. For example, fears of Russian influence in the United States produce a similar dialectic (Gessen, "Russia"). But U.S. power's vast scale make narratives about the United States central to global power relations. However, the example of Russia does suggest that under Donald Trump, conspiracy and U.S. empire may both be shifting in ways too new to fully understand.

2 Mitchell, "American Dreams and Brazilian Racial Democracy."

3 Bourdieu and Wacquant, "On the Cunning of Imperialist Reason"; for a critique of the claim, see, Hanchard, *Orpheus and Power* and "Acts of Misrecognition."

4 U.S. Secretary of State, "Responding to Ukrainian Questions."

5 Strange, *States and Markets.*

6 The United States does have a clearly imperial relation with Puerto Rico, American Samoa, and a few other twenty-first-century colonies. This only underscores the difference between these conventionally imperial relations and the less straightforward relations of hegemony between the United States and much of the rest of the world.

7 Gindin and Panitch, *The Making of Global Capitalism*; Kaplan, "Violent Belongings and the Question of Empire Today"; Lutz, "Empire Is in the Details."

8 I should note that the strange epistemic character of U.S. power extends even to those who wield it. As security scholar Richard K. Betts, who has held numerous positions inside and outside the U.S. security apparatus, notes: "The United States

is not a nation where norms of realpolitik are consciously respected among political elites; so the logic of power politics does not serve very well to explain how aggressive primacy is rationalized in the policy-making process" (Betts, "The Political Support System for American Primacy," 1).

9 As I make clear (Mitchell, "Space, Sovereignty, Inequality"), I do not know and have not been able to determine what caused the explosion, although there is no evidence that a bomb was involved. The event's indeterminacy is one of the reasons it has generated a wide range of interpretations.

10 On covert actions by the United States in the Amazonian borderlands of Colombia and Brazil, see Priest, "Covert Action in Colombia"; and, for particular attention to the budgets, see Sweig, "What Kind of War for Colombia." On "Shock and Awe" see Sanders, *The Green Zone*. And on military doctrine, see U.S. National Security Council, *The National Security Strategy of the United States of America*.

11 Grandin, *Empire's Workshop*.

12 Regarding the title of this section, there was an actual nineteenth-century Brazilian empire (and there still exists a Brazilian imperial family). On the lectures, see Freyre, *Brazil*.

13 Freyre's most influential statement of this is in *Casa grande e senzala*, which—partially because of its contrast with a United States characterized by the "one drop rule" and a sharp "color line" (Du Bois, *The Souls of Black Folk*)—is a foundational text for Brazilian nationalism (cf. Andrews, "Brazilian Racial Democracy, 1900–90"; and Collins, "Melted Gold and National Bodies"). Although Freyre is usually associated with the term *racial democracy*, it doesn't appear in his most famous works and was likely first used by Brazilian anthropologist Arthur Ramos in 1943 (Campos, "Arthur Ramos"; Guimarães, "Racial Democracy").

14 Freyre, *Brazil*, 127.

15 Spence, "Cultural Globalization and the US Civil Rights Movement." It is worth noting that during the height of the Civil Rights Movement, U.S. groups on the political right and many Southern Democrats decried what they saw as Soviet influence in the U.S. civil rights movement, c.f. Anderson, *Eyes off the Prize*. A comparison between those groups and those who decry U.S. influence in contemporary Brazilian racial politics would be fascinating, but is beyond the scope of this paper.

16 Hellwig, *African-American Reflections on Brazil's Racial Paradise*; Sansone, *Blackness without Ethnicity*.

17 "U.S. Americanization" is not a pretty phrasing. But writing about Latin America, in a book about empire, I am left without decent alternatives, since I want to resist the familiar imperial gesture, "American." In South America, "North American" is often the preferred adjective for "United States-ian—a gesture with anti-imperial intentions that I can only imagine are lost on Mexicans and Canadians. Spanish and Portuguese variants of the tongue-twisting *estadosunidense* exist and are seldom used.

18 Bond, "The Rise of 'Sub-Imperialism.'"

19 To gloss this distinction: *hegemony* in international relations generally refers to the control of one state by another. In the Gramscian sense, hegemony describes the way domination and inequality shape the consciousness of the dominated. As the Comaroffs point out, however, Gramsci never clearly defined the term, which has

allowed it to serve varied analytical purposes, including my own (cf. Comaroff and Comaroff, *Of Revelation and Revolution*, 19).

20 I first conducted preliminary fieldwork in Alcântara as a beginning graduate student in 2001. I engaged in intensive fieldwork there from 2004–6, and in many subsequent visits, and I maintain personal and research relationships there today.

21 See the extensive documentation in Almeida, *Os quilombos e a base de lançamento de foguetes de Alcântara*; Andrade and Souza Filho, *Fome de farinha*; Mitchell, *Constellations of Inequality*; and Pereira Junior, *Quilombolas de Alcântara*.

22 Almeida, *Os quilombos*, vol. 1.

23 Mitchell, "Space, Sovereignty, Inequality."

24 Alcântara-Cyclone Space was a Brazilian-Ukrainian partnership to launch commercial satellites from Alcântara. The Ukrainian space program (unlike, so far, Brazil's) developed successful launching technology and was interested in the gravitational advantages of Brazil's equatorial base, but the company was dissolved in 2015.

25 How this identity should be assigned has been the topic of continuing debate. Since a decree in 2003 during the presidency of Luiz Inácio "Lula" da Silva, the main criterion has been autoaffirmation.

26 Hanchard (*Orpheus and Power*) provides an influential analysis of some of the consequences of the relative historical weakness of such solidarities in Brazil, an analysis that has faced accusations of U.S. imperialism.

27 In other areas of Brazil, particularly in the Amazon region, *caboclo* usually describes people of mixed European and Amerindian origins.

28 Melo, "Brasil quer entrar no mercado de lançadores de satélites, afirma presidente da AEB."

29 Peduzzi, "Jobim defende que comunidades quilombolas de Alcântara sejam transferidas."

30 Fry et al., *Divisões perigosas*; Risério, *A utopia brasileira os movimentos negros*; on this, see, Mitchell, *Whitening and Racial Ambiguity*.

31 Bourdieu and Wacquant, "On the Cunning of Imperialist Reason," 48.

32 Bourdieu and Wacquant, "On the Cunning of Imperialist Reason," 46. See also Hanchard, *Orpheus and Power* and "Acts of Misrecognition."

33 Mitchell, "Paranoid Styles of Nationalism."

34 U.S. Secretary of State, "Responding to Ukrainian Questions."

35 Almeida, "Os quilombos e as novas etnias"; Arruti, *Mocambo*; French, *Legalizing Identities*; O'Dwyer, "Os quilombos e a prática profissional dos antropólogos."

36 Mitchell, "Paranoid Styles of Nationalism."

37 On the support of NGOs, see Kamat, "The Privatization of Public Interest"; on ethnic politics, Comaroff and Comaroff, *Ethnicity, Inc.*

38 Trouillot, *Global Transformations*, 94.

39 Walton, "Hungry Wolves, Inclement Storms," 106.

40 Abrams, "Notes on the Difficulty of Studying the State"; see also Coronil, *The Magical State*; Ferguson, "Introduction"; and Trouillot, "The Anthropology of the State in the Age of Globalization."

41 Smith, *The Endgame of Globalization*, 73.

42 I qualify this claim with *usually*, because, as Gindin and Panitch argue, the disaggregation of territorial, political, and economic control, so fully realized under

the twentieth-century hegemony of the United States, began under the British empire in the nineteenth century (Gindin and Panitch, *The Making of Global Capitalism*, 5).

43 Kelly, "Seeking What," 57; see also Grandin, *Empire's Workshop*; Kelly, "U.S. Power, after 9/11 and before It"; and Kelly et al., *Anthropology and Global Counterinsurgency*.

44 Hardt and Negri's influential attempt to give a biopolitical and deterritorialized reading of empire tries to get at this contradictory, not-quite-national character of contemporary power. While there is much to like about their attempt to describe power and resistance in an era when power can't simply be traced to the actions of states, and resistance to familiar categories of political identity, their analysis of a diffuse and underspecified empire confronting a diffuse and underspecified multitude provides limited analytical purchase on the world's changing forms of power and resistance (Hardt and Negri, *Empire*).

45 Cavagnari Filho, "O argumento do império," 1.

46 Vine, "The Lily-Pad Strategy."

47 Although see recent counterexamples: Gill, *The School of the Americas*; Ho, *Liquidated*; Lutz, "Military Bases and Ethnographies of the New Militarization"; and Ouroussoff, *Wall Street at War*.

48 Petição Publica Brasil, "ACS—Mudanças já ou o destrato do acordo."

49 Barrocal, "Em segredo, Brasil volta a negociar Base de Alcântara com os EUA"; Mier, "Alcântara Spaceport."

50 Mitchell, "Space, Sovereignty, Inequality."

51 The FTAA (Free Trade Area of the Americas, or ALCA, its Portuguese acronym) was a U.S. plan to create a so-called free trade zone roughly akin to NAFTA (the North American Free Trade Agreement) but incorporating most of North, Central, and South America. The last round of discussions for the FTAA faltered in Miami in 2003. The FTAA met strong opposition in Brazil and, as of this writing, shows no signs that it will regain life.

52 Diário Vermelho, "Congresso recebe resultados do plebiscito da ALCA."

53 Because it is just south of the equator, the spaceport on the peninsula of Alcântara offers a savings in fuel costs over other spaceports. The presence of a deep-water port, a medium-sized city nearby, and stable weather patterns make it a potentially very lucrative site for commercial launches.

54 Monserrat Filho, "Testimony at a December 4th Public Hearing"; Monserrat Filho and Leister, "The Discussion in the Brazilian National Congress."

55 Mitchell, "Space, Sovereignty, Inequality."

56 Monserrat Filho, "Testimony at a December 4th Public Hearing"; Monserrat Filho and Leister, "The Discussion in the Brazilian National Congress."

57 Monserrat Filho, "Testimony at a December 4th Public Hearing."

58 Strange, *States and Markets*, 25.

59 Lutz, *The Bases of Empire*.

60 Graeber, "Seminar on Debt."

61 Graeber, *Debt*, 6, 364–67; Hudson, *Super Imperialism*.

62 Lin, *Against the Consensus*.

63 Trouillot, "The Anthropology of the State."

VI

9/11, the War on Terror, and the Return of Empire

19 Radicalizing Empire

Youth and Dissent in the War on Terror

SUNAINA MAIRA

COMING OF AGE IN A MOMENT OF EMPIRE

In the generation whose political subjectivity has been deeply shaped by the War on Terror, the so-called 9/11 Generation, what are emergent forms of politics that provide a critique of Islamophobia, racism, and imperial violence? How do young people whose communities are targeted in the War on Terror, within and beyond the United States, engage with the "political" at a moment when their politics are under constant scrutiny and, often, surveillance? Answering these questions requires ethnographic attention to current possibilities for political dissent by Muslim and Arab American youth who are targeted by the state as potential "homegrown" terrorists.

I view the War on Terror as a technology of nation-making that produces youth as subjects that must be preserved and protected, as well as monitored, contained, or removed, if necessary through violence. The specter of Muslim and Arab youth who are inherently anti-American has been used to justify policies of surveillance, incarceration, and deportation targeting youth who are seen as vulnerable to "radicalization." This is a particularly gendered and generational form of regulation as youth is a category viewed as liminal, hence unstable; young Muslim/Arab males are racialized as embodying "terrorist" or "jihadist" tendencies while young Muslim/Arab females are viewed as objects of rescue.

This chapter focuses on Arab, South Asian, and Afghan American youth in northern California and draws on a larger ethnographic project based in Silicon Valley that interrogates the meaning of political subjecthood for these youth and new alliances that have emerged in the decade since the attacks of 9/11.[1] The political movements and coalitions challenging the War on Terror and Islamophobia generally rely on a discourse of rights, particularly civil rights or human rights. I am interested in the possibilities, pitfalls, and contradictions of rights-talk when the vocabulary of rights and democracy, particularly of liberal humanitarianism, is frequently used to justify imperial interventions. What is the nature of political solidarity and cross-racial alliances at a moment when U.S. nationalism is understood as not just multicultural but also postracial, particularly after the election of Barack Obama?

Arab, South Asian, and Afghan American youth engage in a politics that is both identity- and rights-based, mobilizing around a notion of pan-Islamic identity as well as of civil rights and human rights. In doing so, they grapple with the tensions generated between and within these axes of mobilization, as I explore in the larger project. These two major approaches in their collective mobilization—pan-Islamic and rights-oriented—often overlap, with many youth becoming involved with civil rights and antiwar organizing while simultaneously being active in Muslim student and community groups. The various strands of this emergent politics bridge the national and the transnational: young Muslim American activists have made linkages to a domestic history and discourse of civil rights, sometimes on the basis of "Muslim rights," and also invoked the notion of human rights to express solidarity with and illuminate the suffering of Muslims elsewhere. (I want to note that not all the youth in my study were Muslim or identified as such, but there is a new "Muslim American" politics that many of them engage with, regardless of their religious or secularist affiliations.) In this chapter, I explore the turn to civil rights by young Muslim Americans after 9/11 as a political strategy and discourse in response to the War on Terror and briefly discuss the ways in which notions of "moderate" and "radical" politics regulate and repress youth activism.

ON U.S. EMPIRE AND IMPERIAL FEELINGS

My work explores the experiences of youth in relation to what I have described as the "imperial feeling" of the post-9/11 United States.[2] Imperial feelings are the everyday "structures of feeling" that undergird what William Appleman Williams incisively described as "empire as a way of life," or the "habits of heart and mind" that infuse and accompany structures of difference and domination.[3] Imperial feelings, or the complex of psychological and political belonging to empire, are often unspoken, but always present. But as Williams observed, "from the beginning the persuasiveness of empire as a way of life effectively closed off other ways of dealing with the reality that Americans encountered."[4] The historical amnesia and willed forgetting of empire have infused what Amy Kaplan and Donald Pease analyzed as the "cultures of U.S. imperialism," in their groundbreaking collection of the early 1990s.[5] My research builds on this work by excavating the cultural processes of imperialism that shape understandings of belonging and dissent for South

Asian, Arab, and Afghan American youth after 9/11. It explores the implications of living in/with imperial cultures for young people who are identified as opposing the American "way of life" constitutive of empire and the complex and conflicting politics this generates.

The definition and very existence of U.S. empire has been the focus of a global debate intensified since September 11, 2001, and subsequent U.S. military invasions and occupations. Historicizing this debate is important because the War on Terror and the assault on civil liberties unleashed by the national security state during the Bush-Cheney-Rumsfeld regime are embedded in a long history of U.S. expansionism and global political and economic domination. The War on Terror and PATRIOT Acts continued under Barack Obama, who ratcheted up the war in Afghanistan and drone warfare on the "Af-Pak" border, failed to close Guantánamo and end practices of torture, and authorized an increasingly extensive apparatus of surveillance and detention justified by counterterrorism policies. The U.S. state's military, political, and economic hegemony is rooted in its evolving imperial power and foundational genocidal violence; that is, the state of permanent war must be situated in relation to the very formation of the settler-colonial state, built on the conquest and cleansing of new frontiers and the control of territories through direct and indirect methods.[6] In other words, war is constitutive of the American imperium. Yet collective amnesia and suppression of this history have obscured the realities of U.S. empire for those who benefit from its spoils, as noted by John Collins and Carole McGranahan in their introduction to this volume, in part due to the discourse of humanitarian empire leading the "free world."

The "post-9/11" moment, then, is not a radical political rupture, but rather a moment of renewed contestation over the state's imperial power and the paradox of imperial democracy, what Alain Badiou calls the "long war against terrorism."[7] Much work has theorized this historical moment as indicative of the "state of exception," drawing on the work of Carl Schmitt and Walter Benjamin; this suggests that the expansion of executive power and suspension of democratic rights are not the exception but the rule—the constitutive paradigm of Western government and law since World War I—blurring the distinction between "peace and war."[8] The "state of emergency" is permanent for empire that exercises repressive, preventive, and military force and where the crisis of civil rights simply becomes more visible for certain groups at specific historical moments.[9]

The resuscitation of the term *empire* since 9/11 led in some cases to an obfuscation, rather than clarification, of U.S. imperialism. New languages and paradigms focused on "empire" that sprouted after 9/11, particularly in mainstream U.S. public discourse, were ambiguous and sometimes apologetic about the structural violence of U.S. political, economic, and military imperialism. Contrary to Michael Hardt and Antonio Negri's model of empire as primarily a decentered, deterritorialized network of power embedded in capitalist globalization, which evades the persistent and repressive apparatus of (U.S.) state power and military force, I argue that returning to the notion of "imperialism" is important to understand the nature of U.S. hegemony and the planetary War on Terror. Shifting to the rubric of empire for some presupposes an end to imperialism, and its territorialized force.[10] The shape of U.S. imperialism and settler colonialism has clearly shifted over time, from the genocide of Native Americans to the colonization of the Philippines, Hawai'i, and Puerto Rico; the annexation of parts of Mexico as well as Hawai'i, Guam, and other Pacific territories; the proxy wars in Latin America and Africa; the weapons of mass destruction used against Japan; the devastation of Southeast Asia; and the contemporary mix of covert and overt strategies of domination, including the bombing of Afghanistan, occupation of Iraq, drone attacks in Pakistan, and U.S.-backed client regimes, military bases, and wars in other countries.

An important feature of U.S. imperialism is that it is often marked by invisibility, secrecy, and flexibility in its operation of power, and by nebulous, nonterritorial forms of domination that do not resemble traditional forms of territorial "colonialism." Harry Magdoff has described this as "imperialism without colonies"—an assemblage that blurs the boundaries of "formal" and "informal" empire and relies on imperial strategies of both direct and indirect control.[11] The ambiguity and invisibility of U.S. imperialism obscure the workings of imperial power and aid in its collective denial. The United States created new designations of overseas territories, under varying degrees of U.S. control—such as Guantánamo—and new categories of persons and citizens, with gradated rights, which serve imperial interests while obscuring the nature of U.S. imperialism.[12] Ann Stoler argues that the inherent blurring of rights of colonized populations and "epistemic murk" of degraded and deferred sovereignty of colonized territories are constitutive of the very architecture of settler colonial states.[13] The exceptionalism of U.S. empire is underwritten by a rhetoric of democracy and freedom that has cloaked the U.S. imperial project in a discourse of "benevolent imperialism." U.S. imperial power shrouds itself in the language of human rights, women's rights, and gay rights but as Joanne Barker observes, in the settler colony, "Native humanity and human rights are made contingent on the empire's interests."[14] The logic of a "war for democracy" reworks Cold War logics and raises contradictions for dissent on the ground, for I found that young activists simultaneously deploy the concepts of "democracy" and "rights" and critique the slippages and exceptions of these paradigms.

A central premise of my analysis is that empire works on two fronts: the domestic and the foreign. U.S. foreign policy is linked to the "policing of domestic racial tensions" and disciplining of subordinated populations through gender and class hierarchies at home.[15] However, the link between the two fronts of imperial power are often obscured, effectively preventing marginalized groups in the United States from connecting their subjugation within the nation to dominance overseas, thus generating divisions and undermining solidarity.[16] Strikingly, in the case of Iraqi or Afghan Americans, the (neo) imperial relations of the United States to their home countries where the United States has created zones of occupation, warfare, and degraded sovereignty are generally not recognized as such—even in some cases within these communities. These are some of the paradoxes that I grapple with in my ethnography of college-age Arab, South Asian, and Afghan American youth in Silicon Valley.

Doing an ethnography of empire, and particularly of Muslim American youth after 9/11, raises tangled methodological and ethical questions about what I call *post-9/11 area studies*. This new area studies of the United States emerged quickly in the aftermath of the 9/11 attacks with the profusion of research that focused on Muslim American communities and that, in many instances, positioned youth within reified frames of religion, terrorism, national security, assimilation, and the trope of a "clash of civilizations." The nuanced stories of Muslim American youth—as students, workers, cultural consumers, or critical political subjects—are generally not explored. Nor is the very construction of the category *Muslim* sufficiently interrogated. Putting U.S. imperialism at the center of the story dislodges accounts ensuing from a narrow focus on faith-based identities or worn dichotomies of alienation/assimilation in favor of an analysis linking the domestic and global faces of empire.

DOING AN ETHNOGRAPHY OF EMPIRE AND YOUTH

Youth is a key site through which to understand imperial nation-making given the construction of youth as a "transitional" category in relation to the social order and civic personhood.[17] Youth is a liminal category symbolizing change or protest and so is often overdetermined within imperial knowledge formation. The notion that youth is an inherently unstable ontology means that young people's political commitments are often suspect and that they are portrayed as the objects of overtly nationalizing, disciplinary, and repressive practices. If the category *youth* has been viewed as a critical stage in the development of political and national identity, then immigrant or second-generation youth are perceived as doubly liminal and their national allegiances subjected to heightened scrutiny. For Muslim and Arab American youth, this perception is even more acute; they are constructed in mainstream U.S. discourse as culturally or religiously alien, vulnerable to indoctrination by "extremists," and potential threats to the nation. Furthermore, the very category of *Muslim youth* and buzzwords of counterterrorism-speak, such as *radicalization*, often stand in for a certain politics the imperial state opposes through domestic as well as global policing, securitization, and warfare.

The specter of Muslim American youth who are inherently anti-American has been used to justify regimes of surveillance, detention, deportation, and torture that have swept unknown numbers of minors into the dragnet of counterterrorism operations. A few years after 2001, and particularly after the 7/7 bombings in London, the focus of the War on Terror shifted to domestic terrorism and to ferreting out the fifth column of "terrorsymps" (terrorist sympathizers) within the United States. Such ferreting has included the use of FBI informants recruited to infiltrate mosqued communities and networks of Muslim American youth, as well as to entrap young Muslim American males in particular.[18] These forms of surveillance rest on expert knowledge that presumably explains the will to terrorism. They are enacted with the cooperation of cultural insiders, or "native informants."[19] Ethnographic knowledge production about Muslim youth thus becomes central to knowing empire and also to empire's ways of knowing. In the U.S.-led War on Terror that links London and Lackawanna to Lahore and Bagram, the "radicalization" of youth variously defined as Muslim, Middle Eastern, Arab, Afghan, or South Asian has come to embody a threat to Western, secular, liberal democracy and a "knowable" politics. In this globalized regime of biopolitics, what kinds of politics are permissible for young people who are profiled as potential "jihadists"?

A fraught question I grapple with in my research projects is how can we produce an ethnography of everyday life in empire that is not completely complicit with state profiling and surveillance of the targeted population after 9/11, given the ongoing state projects of data gathering and mapping focused on Muslim American communities? Are there methods, modes of interpretation, and strategies of dissemination that can allow our research to safeguard vulnerable individuals and groups, and the possibilities of dissent and resistance, while still offering a complex, critical analysis? To do so, we need to question the epistemology of categories deployed by state intelligence gathering—such as "moderate" and "radical" Muslims, and the reified concept of "Muslim youth"—while paying attention to what forms of subjecthood are targeted or domesticated.

My fieldwork in the Silicon Valley area between 2004 and 2011 focused on middle- to upper-middle-class, generally second-generation, South Asian, Arab, and Afghan college students at both community colleges and four-year institutions.[20] There are large communities of South Asians (generally Indians—mostly Hindu, Muslim, and Sikh—as well as Pakistanis) and Arab Americans (mostly Lebanese, Palestinians, Egyptians, Iraqis, and Yemenis, and including both Christians and Muslims) in the San Jose area, and the Fremont/Hayward area is home to the largest Afghan community outside Afghanistan.[21] Silicon Valley has a visible, relatively affluent, and organized Muslim American community that has grown since the 1980s. It has established businesses and major Muslim institutions, such as the MCA (Muslim Community Association) Sunni mosque in Santa Clara, which draws a large, ethnically diverse population from the region and has an Islamic school, as well as a Shia mosque. There is also a working-class and economically precarious lower-middle- and middle-class population in all these communities, which is less visible and has struggled with the impact of the economic recession and housing crisis, or what some call the realities hidden behind the Silicon Curtain.

Silicon Valley is an interesting context in which to explore questions of dissent and (disciplinary) inclusion because it is generally narrated as a site of entrepreneurial dynamism, self-reinvention, multicultural tolerance, and the California/Silicon Dream. South Asian, Afghan, and Arab American youth from this area grow up in a racially and ethnically diverse context with other youth of color—Latinos, Asian Americans, and to a much lesser extent, African Americans. Young South Asian, Afghan, Iranian, and Arab Americans have created and joined cross-racial campaigns and organizations in college, often through new coalitional rubrics, such as "MESA" (Middle Eastern and South Asian) or "AMEMSA" (Arab, Middle Eastern, Muslim, and South Asian), and participated in or produced alliances with other immigrant and minority communities through antiwar, immigrant rights, civil rights, and global solidarity movements. The intensified (re)codification of the racialization of Muslim-ness has generated new forms of solidarity, including pan-Islamic affiliations as well as anti-imperialist alliances, while fortifying other lines of division, religious or national. So the politics of cross-racial and interfaith coalition building is an interesting one to understand in this local context where Muslim Americans are well established and the discourse of liberal "tolerance" and diversity shapes, as well as contains, cross-racial and interfaith affiliations.

CIVIL-RIGHTS-BASED ACTIVISM

After 9/11, many national Muslim American political organizations, including groups based in Silicon Valley such as CAIR (Council of American Islamic Relations), launched or intensified civil rights programs in response to the heightened discrimination faced by Muslims, Arabs, South Asians, and "Muslim-looking" people in the United States. The Muslim institutional infrastructure in some cases morphed into a civil rights complex, which coproduced with juridical structures the notion of "racial profiling" or "religious profiling" as the proper paradigms for redress. A young Pakistani American woman from San Jose who was active in the Muslim Student Association (MSA) observed that after 9/11, "There were all those events set up for people to know their rights and stuff. . . . It was hard, people were being held up at the airports. Nobody even knew about the PATRIOT Act. So people had to be informed about that, like this is what is going on." Post-9/11 civil rights activism has been viewed by many Muslim American community activists as well as youth as an outgrowth of a tragic experience that led to an intensified mobilization of the community and the strengthening of a Muslim public sphere. September 11 was viewed as a catalyst for an increasingly public formation of a political Muslim American identity that could lead to national incorporation and recognition. However, as I argue here, civil rights campaigns are not always the basis of an oppositional counterpublic, for when emerging on the terrain of liberal rights they reinforce dominant mythologies of national regeneration through rights struggle and multicultural inclusion.

The language of civil rights generally resonates with the younger generation of Arab, South Asian, and Afghan Americans who find in it a framework for linking their critique of Islamophobia and racism to a larger history of struggles by racial minorities. For example, Aisha, a young Palestinian American from Fremont and student activist, observed, "African Americans had their struggle, they fought for their civil rights, and now Muslim Americans have to do the same. I think it's about democracy." The racial, religious, and political profiling of Muslim and Arab Americans thus becomes unexceptional, and provides a context in which these groups can become aligned with nonwhites and, in particular, with African Americans, who Angela Davis observes are viewed as the "representative subjects of 'civil rights.'"[22] This is a complex shift, given the ambiguous and contradictory racial classifications and self-categorizations of and by these racially diverse groups as variously white and nonwhite, and the reracialization of Muslims after 9/11 as the "new blacks" or enemy aliens.[23]

While networks of civil rights activists and lawyers sprang up to address what was often coded as "post-9/11" or "AMEMSA" issues, the backlash made most vulnerable those who were not privileged enough to adequately defend themselves. Immigrants working in the service sector, whether working as taxi drivers or gas station attendants, were easy targets in public spaces of the most violent assaults after 9/11. But even professionals and other more privileged Muslim, Arab, and South Asian Americans found themselves at risk of being harassed, losing their jobs, having their bank accounts frozen, being subjected to wiretapping and FBI interrogation, being profiled at airport security, or being taken off planes. In fact, discrimination faced by Muslim, Arab, and South Asian Americans in employment and travel have persisted across the decades after 2001, including incidents of Islamophobia and bullying in schools.[24]

In this context, educating targeted communities about civil and immigrant rights seemed an urgent task. Many organizations began hosting "Know Your Rights" workshops, often in coalition with civil and immigrant rights groups from other communities. This organizing was certainly a necessary and minimal line of defense for communities under siege and facing daily racism and is not to be easily dismissed; indeed, I participated in some of these Know Your Rights campaigns myself after 9/11. Free legal clinics and pamphlets translated into various languages instructed community members on what to do if an FBI agent came to their door to interview them, how to deal with the government interview program targeting Muslim males who were noncitizens ("Special Registration"), or how to respond to interrogations at airports. Many Muslim American groups developed programs for "civic engagement" and encouraged community members, including youth, to become more actively engaged in the public square and electoral politics or serve as "bridge builders," particularly through interfaith projects.

Several youth I spoke to entered the sphere of formal politics via this "new civil rights" movement. Malaika, a young Pakistani American woman who was born in Santa Clara and grew up in San Jose and Tracy, attended a Know Your Rights workshop conducted by CAIR at her mosque, while she was in high school; she went on to work with CAIR in its local civil rights and government relations programs. In fact, I first met her at a panel in the Bay Area on civil liberties where she spoke along with Japanese Americans and Italian Americans whose families had been interned during World War II—an example of interethnic alliances staged after 9/11 through a shared discourse of civil rights. Malaika described her work as part of a larger process of constituting a "community" through engagement with national electoral politics: "Part of CAIR's mission, in addition to protecting civil liberties and educating people of their rights, is empowering the community. Being politically active and engaged, and then also developing better relationships with public officials. . . . And then also, we go to [voter] registration drives, have workshops . . . reaching out to the mosque and making sure the community is active. You know, making sure that their voice is heard."

Civil liberties, in this view, are central to mobilizing and "empowering" the Muslim American community through rights education and giving it a "voice" in the political sphere through engagement with the structure of representative government. Other young people organized on the platform of civil rights using street protests and public rallies, often in alliance with larger immigrant and civil rights or antiwar movements and sometimes in coalition with Latinx and other Asian American groups. A focus on pressuring the nation-state to live up to its liberal-democratic promise of constitutionally mandated rights and racial and religious equality united these electoral and grassroots strands of civil rights activism. Drawing on David Eng's critique of queer citizen-subjects who petition the imperial state for rights, the question this organizing and rights-talk raises is: What are the implications of a politics that involves "an increasing inscription of individual lives within the state order" through struggles centered on winning rights?[25]

The surge in post-9/11 civil rights activism did to some extent expose the racialized distribution of rights by the state, but in its reformist variant, it also facilitated a process and discourse of nationalization. Commenting on the shift to greater "civic engagement" by Muslim Americans, Selcuk Sirin and Michelle Fine cite a remark by a young Muslim American man that illustrates the ways post-9/11 civil rights mobilization shores up a nationalist narrative: "Especially in this nation, when one strives to do something, anything is possible."[26] In this narrative predicated on liberal democracy, Muslim Americans are the latest group to fight for inclusion in the nation and—like African Americans, Latinx, and other Asian Americans before them—they will become part of the national community as deserving citizens and subjects by means of the crucible of civil rights activism. The "story of racial and ethnic inclusion," as Nikhil Pal Singh observes, is central to a redemptive national narrative based on notions of "America's exceptional universalism" and "religious tolerance."[27] The election in 2008 of Barack (Hussein) Obama, an African American from a partly Muslim family, was viewed by many as a vindication of a national history of civil rights activism centered on the sanitized icon of Martin Luther King Jr. It was used to affirm the ultimately inclusive and tolerant tenets of a nation that had come under global critique for its imperial policies and so provided a narrative of national redemption, for Muslim Americans as much as anyone else.

For some, the Obama moment signified the closure of this epoch of civil rights struggle, the beginning of a "postracial" era. And yet, the War on Terror continued globally, accompanied by expanding surveillance and racial, religious, and political profiling within the United States; ratcheted-up government plans to root out “homegrown” terrorists; increased deportations targeting immigrant communities—not to mention the rush to bail out the banks who had created the spiraling financial crisis. In the post-9/11 climate, the notion of civil rights became reinvested with a desire to suture it to the national mythology of racial equality and religious tolerance, and to provide an opportunity, yet again, to articulate the redemptive story of inclusion and democracy for the imperial state. The campaigns waged by Muslim Americans became a platform in which to enact the drama of Americanization for another group who could eventually be welcomed into the national fold (if they were “moderate,” peace-loving Muslims).

Post-9/11 civil rights activism by Muslim Americans was also framed as a break with antidemocratic traditions in repressive home countries. This narrative, including its Orientalist variant, is also evident in some studies of post-9/11 mobilization, which suggest that Muslim, Arab, and South Asian American community activists had to “convince immigrants to believe in the American way of activism, advocacy, and mobilization.”[28] Muslim civil rights activism has been framed by many of its proponents as a test of the true nature of “American democracy” and national tolerance but with a new group of canaries in the coal mine. Liberal civil rights politics draws anti-imperial dissent into a national consensus about liberal democracy built on the recuperation of black power and radical protest movements through a politics of legal egalitarianism in the Cold War era.[29] As Alain Badiou argues, the concept of “democracy” is ultimately for many political movements a form of the state, or of the “good State,” and a consensual norm that is extremely difficult to question.[30] The civilizing story of the “nation of immigrants” evades the history of dispossession of natives by settlers, the genocidal violence against indigenous peoples, slavery and Jim Crow, the colonial appropriation of other territories, and imperial interventions for “democracy promotion” overseas.

For some youth, however, political organizing is framed in part by the discourse of democracy and rights, but not circumscribed by it. Instead, they simultaneously critiqued U.S. imperialism and the limits of domestic civil rights discourse by challenging global regimes of militarism, incarceration, and occupation in the name of “democracy.” This dual critique links the two fronts of empire that the state conjoins in the domestic and global War on Terror. For example, Yasser, whose father was Pakistani and mother Mexican American, attended Ohlone College in Fremont; he commented: “Muslims need to start standing up for their opinion and start attacking the credibility of the CIA and the FBI and telling them they're full of shit. Stop being scared! Unite! Who cares if they kill you or you lose your jobs? Or they do all this funny stuff like they did with the Black people and their Civil Rights Movement? If you start standing up, other people will start standing up. If we start standing up, people will follow along."

Yasser links the targeting of Muslim Americans by technologies of surveillance and infiltration, locally and globally, to the repressive strategies used against African American civil rights activists in the COINTELPRO (Counter Intelligence Program) era, critiquing the exceptionalism of U.S. liberal democracy. In this view, interracial solidarity emerges from a radical genealogy of antistate struggle. Yasser argued vehemently that Muslim Americans should be willing to challenge the imperial state and risk the financial security of employment and class mobility, or even life itself. Yasser suggested that Muslim Americans could be a vanguard for resistance, but one at the forefront of a movement that would be willing to risk the financial security of employment and class mobility, or even life itself. Being a canary in the coal mine thus means rejecting fear, including fear of death and disappearance. This also means rejecting antiracist struggle based on a notion of racial inclusion, for as Yasser said incisively about Obama:

> He's a good guy but it's the same thing. . . . The only way I'll believe that Obama actually did something is if in ten years, I see that America's not being imperialistic to South America by putting interest on them and taking away their money . . . the leaders are puppets, people are starving and dying. . . . So I'll only acknowledge Obama's success when . . . the Third World is done suffering from the U.S. hand. . . . America's been interfering with Nicaragua, they went to El Salvador. . . . They attacked Panama in the Gulf War and killed many civilians, they dropped bombs on them. And these are poor people who have nothing. They did the same thing to Iraq, Afghanistan. . . . To me, Obama and Bush are on the same boat. No, it's still the government, still the people standing behind the curtain.

Yasser's critique emphasizes a systemic analysis of U.S. racism and global capitalism, challenging the notion that the election of one African American president would change the enduring structure of an imperial state and its "evil" military, economic, and political interventions inflicting violence on other countries. He was adamant that a politics of "change" based on racial representation, including African Americans or Muslim or Arab Americans at the highest levels of executive power, cannot end ongoing imperial statecraft. Yasser linked U.S. wars in Iraq and Afghanistan with historical interventions in Central and Latin America and critiqued the transnational apparatus of counterterrorism and counterinsurgency. He pointed to the ways in which U.S. imperial power has rested on proxy wars, covert operations, and client regimes and on neoliberal policies tied to the IMF and World Bank, imposing structural adjustment and onerous debts on the Global South. Yasser's framework shifts the premise of imperial interventions from "regime change" for democracy or the liberation of women (and gays) to the global war for economic and political hegemony.

Other youth I spoke to also engaged with a discourse about imperialism and sovereignty—often via recourse to human rights as a universalist or internationalist framework. Farid, whose family is from northwest Pakistan and who grew up in San Jose, was managing an auto body shop in San Jose where I spoke to him. He said: "The day that the Virginia Tech shooting happened [on April 16, 2007], the U.S. shot a missile into Afghanistan and it accidentally missed and hit an elementary school in Pakistan, and 148 kids five years and younger died. But nobody mentioned that because 32 people died here." Farid was frustrated that these civilian deaths were simply "collateral damage" in the Af-Pak war, which the U.S. administration claimed was precisely waged with drone missiles and "smart" weapons, and that they were eclipsed in the U.S. mainstream media by acts of violence targeting Americans. The racialized politics of imperial violence and terror defines who is expendable or worthy of saving and also, fundamentally, who is "human," and where.[31] As Barker observes, "some humans are not, or not enough, human to warrant the recognition, rights, and entitlements of the empire."[32]

REPRESSION AND RADICALISM

For Yasser, Farid, and other youth I spoke to, rather than simply seek inclusion on the terrain of civil rights, dissenting movements must challenge U.S. plans for global hegemony and link domestic to overseas repression. Several youth acknowledged, implicitly or explicitly, that the discourse of civil rights often failed to link U.S. policies of racial profiling, incarceration, deportation, or surveillance to an ongoing imperial structure of repression, containment, and annihilation, within and beyond the nation. The failure of a liberal model of civil rights to account for this structural racism and imperial violence drove many young people to express their dissent against the state through a language of human rights, linking their critique to transnational movements waged against imperial warfare, settler colonialism, and neoliberal globalization.

Some of the youth I spoke to were involved in such organizing in Silicon Valley, on their campuses or in the larger community, and were cutting their teeth in political mobilization with antiwar and Palestine solidarity movements that focused on issues of occupation, imperialism, and settler colonialism. They also engaged with rights-talk, often through the framework of human rights, with all its contradictions. These young activists were concerned about the implications that U.S. empire has for people in other places, in other nations and on other continents, and with expressing sentiments of global solidarity. In this, they are enacting continuities as well as discontinuities with the previous generation of Arab and Muslim American activists, whose political activism in the United States has historically focused on opposing U.S. imperialism in West Asia, supporting the Palestinian liberation struggle, and challenging U.S. support for Israel.[33] For many young people I spoke to, interestingly, the Israeli war on Lebanon in 2006 was a catalyst for their involvement in antiwar activism even more than the events of 9/11, given that they were older at the time of the devastation of Lebanon by the U.S.-backed Israeli military.

For example, many youth attended large demonstrations in Silicon Valley and Fremont to protest the Israeli massacre in Gaza in winter 2008–9. In fact, for many youth, it was this war that was a turning point in their political involvement in international human rights and Palestine solidarity campaigns.[34] On January 11, 2009, there was a rally in Santa Clara between a shopping mall and an upscale outdoor mall, Santana Row, attended by a diverse and multigenerational crowd of Arabs, Afghans, Iranians, South Asians, and white Americans. A young woman in hijab stood at the intersection in the middle of the street, waving a large Palestinian flag high in the air. Another woman in hijab, with a *kaffiyeh* (traditional Arabic scarf) wrapped around her shoulders, was shouting through a bullhorn: “Free, FREE Palestine! Stop bomb-ing Ga-za!” There were dozens of children and many youth standing on the sidewalks, several of whom were carrying posters denouncing the killing of Palestinian children. Of the at least fourteen hundred Palestinians who were killed in the massacre, four hundred were estimated to be children.[35] So the violence of the Israeli military, backed by the United States, deeply affected many young people I spoke to, making them feel emboldened to participate in public protest in the midst of a commercialized space of consumption.

I should note that in a climate of political repression and surveillance, some were (understandably) cautious about the political registers in which they shared their political views publicly. A few youth participating in the Gaza solidarity protest expressed unease about some young men whose faces were swathed in kaffiyehs and who resembled too closely the “terrorist” enemy for their comfort. Representations of terror and terrorists are both deeply racialized and gendered. Young Muslim American, particularly Arab or Afghan and increasingly Pakistani American, men are most likely to be labeled potential “extremists” or vulnerable to “radicalization.” Meanwhile, much of the dominant discourse reproduces an Orientalist portrait of Muslim

American girls as passive victims of inflexible, backward "traditions." In this context, it is interesting to note that there is a generation of young Muslim and Arab American women, including hijabi women, who are visibly at the forefront of student and community groups and engaged in leadership roles. The hypervisibility and intense scrutiny of Muslim Americans has created a self-consciousness about gendered performances, which are understood to always be performances on a public stage.[36] As a result, I found that political protest is often strategically and self-reflexively staged.

Muslim and Arab American youth who engage in protests of imperial violence or the U.S. state's support for settler colonial policies in the Middle East are often accused of violating the parameters of civility, and of being inherently anti-American or anti-Semitic, unlike those who engage in liberal civil rights or interfaith (Muslim-Jewish-Christian) programs. This underscores how certain forms of politics are defined as "properly" political. A liberal nationalist framework of "civil rights" colludes with imperial nationalism and emerges from a conjuncture with "civility" and with the larger question of civilization itself in the War on Terror. A racialized and also colonial logic defines what counts as "civil" disobedience and what is "uncivil" resistance, within and beyond the United States. This logic seeps into the post-9/11 culture wars and shapes what is considered possible and permissible political mobilization in the War on Terror, delineating "good" and "bad" Muslim subjects. In the nationalist narrative of civil rights struggle that has been consolidated since 9/11, groups that engage in peaceful struggles or interfaith dialogue shaped by liberal democratic politics are rewarded by integration into the political order.

There is also an acute self-awareness of the distinctions being made between Muslim American politics deemed "radical" (militant, "angry") versus "moderate" (peaceful, pro-U.S. liberal democracy) that underwrites the counterterrorism regime. The question of a moderate politics and "safe" Islam is key to the imperial regulation of political subjecthood through surveillance. Muslims must be made "safe" and acceptable/assimilable for Western modernity and U.S. liberal democracy. But the United States and many Western nation-states are no longer "safe" for Muslims. Given the surveillance and criminalization of Muslim Americans not just for their political activities, but for their political and also theological beliefs, at a moment when the United States has propagated the "correct" Islam compatible with its imperial multiculturalism, the assertion of "moderate" Muslimness is often a strategic and not just ideological question for Muslim American youth. There is a complex and charged tactical debate for the 9/11 generation about what forms politics should take given the panic about "radicalization" among Muslim

Americans. I engaged in countless discussions with students about the ways in which the regulation of moderate/radical politics has shaped politics of MSA and Students for Justice in Palestine groups and their protest strategies, particularly in the wake of the criminalization of the "Irvine 11" students who interrupted a speech by the Israeli ambassador at UC Irvine. These eleven Muslim and Arab American students were prosecuted by the Orange County district attorney on a felony charge for their civil disobedience and the university suspended the MSA for a protest that they did not even organize.[37] Subsequently, many students engaged in Palestine solidarity activism around the country began doing protests at talks by Israeli officials and soldiers with their mouths taped shut, dramatically highlighting the censorship and exceptional repression of Palestinian human rights campaigns.

Several youth involved in Palestine solidarity activism in Silicon Valley spoke of the disciplining and backlash they encountered in their political organizing, and the repressive tactics used by both campus administrators and off-campus groups to shut down their events. The acceptable framework for discussing Palestine on many campuses is the interfaith paradigm emphasizing Jewish-Muslim "dialogue" and religious "tolerance," a depoliticized approach that is firmly embedded in liberal "religious multifaithism."[38] In trying to frame the issue of Palestine through the discourse of human rights and especially of settler colonialism or apartheid, these youth ran up against a well-entrenched Arabophobia and also a well-established anti-Palestinian and Islamophobic apparatus that has silenced critique of Israel and reframed anti-Zionist critique as anti-Semitic.[39] As I argue in the larger project, the discourse of human rights fails in the case of Palestinian rights activism, which is a space of exception in human rights and unworthy of the protections of civil rights and academic freedom. The Palestine question thus becomes the charged boundary of "radical" politics and the fulcrum of censorship for student activism, as is apparent with growing attacks on campus groups for boycott and divestment campaigns against Israel. Yet many youth continue to challenge current manifestations of U.S. imperialism and oppose the extensions of empire, from Israel to Afghanistan or Pakistan, revealing the exceptionalisms that shroud these projects of Western imperial modernity.

What is at work is a process of defining what constitutes the "political" in the post-9/11 era and what the limits of "activism" are in the era of the Irvine 11—a process in which the state is actively engaged. Discussions with youth in Silicon Valley also brought home to me how deeply affective the experience of grappling with the "political" and with resisting imperial power is, for these conversations were infused with complex feelings of fear, anxiety, fantasy, desire, and empathy. The War on Terror has seeped into intimate and social relations and has also reconfigured structures of political feeling and sentiments of dissent and solidarity, defining which forms of outrage or compassion are acceptable.

CONCLUSION

The contradictions generated by civil rights for post-9/11 activism and by the regime of human rights, as I have briefly discussed here, are constitutive of U.S. imperial technologies of shaping and producing Muslim, Arab, Afghan, or South Asian political subjects. The containment of politics through rights claims is not new, certainly, and there is a much longer history of tensions in political subjecthood along the axes of civil and human rights organizing, in response to settler-colonialism and racial supremacy. For example, Black Power movements in the 1960s and 1970s departed from the domestic agenda of the liberal civil rights movements and internationalized the freedom struggles of African Americans during the era of anticolonial movements in the Global South, attempting to take it to the United Nations as a human rights issue, so that the "distinction between 'civil rights' and 'human rights'" became a "coded distinction between Cold War liberalism and internationalism" and anti-imperialism.[40] The post-9/11 debate about these two approaches, one focused on domestic civil rights and the other on global human rights, parallels the tensions that emerged in the earlier civil rights, antiwar, and Third Worldist movements: between a domestic "rights-equality framework" and a "nationalist-decolonization" movement.[41] The "civil rights-industrial complex" that has emerged from a nationalist framework for civil rights has been erected as a front in the U.S. ascendancy to global power.[42]

The current discourse about subjects of empire, including liberal critiques, generally defines them in relation to governmentalities of counterterrorism or racial policing instead of to an imperial present, evident in the general failure of the larger U.S. antiwar movement to become an anti-imperialist movement and the delayed opposition to the "just" war in Afghanistan and drone war in Pakistan. It is striking that even in progressive scholarship, there is little work that focuses on Iraqi, Afghan, or Pakistani Americans as imperial or neocolonial subjects living in the metropoles rather than primarily as ethnic and/or religious subjects. It is important to grapple with what it means to consider the relationship of these groups to the U.S. state as an ongoing imperial relationship, not simply a relationship of migration, exile, and exclusion, or belonging. This is an important intervention that critical scholarship on U.S. empire and imperialism, particularly in ethnic and American studies, needs to make. A great deal of intellectual, cultural, and psychic work is invested in reframing disappearing imperial subjects and the imperial present in plain view. This disjuncture underlies imperial feelings of domination, ambivalence, denial, guilt, or anxiety that are masked by the liberal discourse of civil liberties and democracy and by the right-wing language of annihilation and messianic regeneration. In both cases, there is a notion that U.S. policies need to be amended so as to achieve the essential liberatory promise of American nationhood, whether defined as individual or collective freedom, in a moment of imperial decline.

The narrative of exceptionalist U.S. democracy dissolved, somewhat, with the emergence of the Arab uprisings and the incredibly powerful popular revolts, including youth protests, which partly inspired the Occupy movement. Abed, an Egyptian American from San Jose who was very involved with the Students for Justice in Palestine (SJP) group on his campus and also with MCA, talked to me in February 2011 as I was finishing this research. He commented on the contradictions of U.S. media discourse about Tahrir Square:

> Nobody's taking a step back and saying, okay, well, the only reason they [the Mubarak regime] have been in power is because of the U.S. government [giving Mubarak] 1.3 billion dollars annually. . . . what bothers me is that the US is meddling in all of this, again . . . and it's not just Obama's administration, this is something the US has been doing since the 1800s, that whenever they see a country of interest . . . maybe there's political change and they are not sure where's it gonna go, they say . . . "Well, let us help you," and it's just . . . Keep your hands off other people's business! It's none of their business.

Abed situates U.S. military, financial, and political support for the Mubarak regime—and other repressive and colonialist regimes in the region—in a much longer imperial history of U.S. and Western intervention in the affairs of other, sovereign nations.

The fig leaf of imperial "democracy" has been ripped off, in many cases by Arab youth in the uprisings, and young Arab Americans such as Abed as well as others participated in solidarity demonstrations in U.S. cities, including in northern California, invoking a discourse not just of rights but of dignity, freedom, and justice. As revolutionary movements unfolded from Egypt and Tunisia to Yemen and Bahrain and demanded true democracy, overturning U.S.-backed dictatorships in some cases and challenging neoliberal capitalist regimes, the alibi for U.S. imperialism in the region and in the War on Terror has been overtly challenged, including by youth. These revolts and solidarity movements have erupted as cracks in the U.S. empire's global hegemony and economic viability deepen. The questions raised by these young people about the nature of dissent and the utility of rights raise in turn pressing questions for this next phase of empire, and its decline and possible defeat.

NOTES

1 Given Afghanistan's liminal location between South and Central/West Asia, it is often not included in South Asia, partly as a result of colonial and Cold War cartographies. In the larger project, I dwell on the (re)suturing of Afghanistan to Pakistan/South Asia through the violently enforced label *Af-Pak* in the U.S. war on the border region.
2 Maira, *Missing.*
3 Williams, *Empire as a Way of Life*; Stoler, *Haunted by Empire*, 2.
4 Williams, *Empire as a Way of Life*, 5; Pease, *The New American Exceptionalism.*
5 Kaplan and Pease, *Cultures of United States Imperialism.*
6 Pease, *The New American Exceptionalism.*
7 Badiou, *Polemics*, 20.
8 Agamben, *State of Exception*, 22.
9 Ganguly, *States of Exception*; Hardt and Negri, *Empire*, 17.
10 See an early analysis by Perlo, *American Imperialism.*
11 Magdoff, *Imperialism without Colonies*; Smith, *The Endgame of Globalization.*
12 Kaplan, "Where Is Guantánamo?"
13 Stoler, *Haunted by Empire*, 8–9.
14 Joanne Barker, "The Specters of Recognition," 34.
15 Pease, "New Perspectives on U.S. Culture and Imperialism," 31.
16 Young, *Postcolonialism*, 28.
17 Maira and Soep, "Introduction."
18 Maira, "'Good' and 'Bad' Muslim Citizens."
19 Maira, "Deporting Radicals, Deporting La Migra."
20 Maira, *Missing.*
21 The Arab American community has been present in the Bay Area for three generations. The South Asian community includes some descendants of early migrants who came to the United States in the early twentieth century but the vast majority are post-1965 immigrants. The Afghan American community consists largely of refugees who are less affluent than the other two groups and who came in two waves, one an early wave after the Soviet invasion of Afghanistan in 1979, and the other after the rise of the Taliban in the 1990s. The college students I interviewed in Silicon Valley were generally the children either of professionals who had mostly come to the United States in the 1960s and 1970s as graduate students or technical workers or of refugee parents who had fled Afghanistan or Afghan communities in Pakistan and India.
22 Davis, *The Meaning of Freedom*, 182.

23 Jamal and Naber, *Race and Arab Americans after 9/11.*

24 In 2013, CAIR reported that the largest number of civil rights complaints received in northern California were related to employment discrimination against Muslims, followed by complaints about interactions with law enforcement, including interrogations by the FBI and concerns about profiling and surveillance; the total number of complaints had actually increased since the previous year, and included incidents of bullying and harassment of Muslim students at schools. See *Standing Up for Your Rights, Preserving Our Freedom.*

25 Eng, *The Feeling of Kinship*, 28.

26 Sirin and Fine, *Muslim American Youth*, 110.

27 Singh, *Black Is a Country*, 19.

28 Bakalian and Bozorghmehr, *Backlash 9/11*, 178.

29 Reddy, *Freedom with Violence.*

30 Badiou, *Polemics*, 78–90.

31 Mbembe, "Necropolitics."

32 Barker, "The Specters of Recognition," 44.

33 Naber, *Arab America.*

34 Barrows-Friedman, *In Our Power*, 38.

35 "Amnesty."

36 Mir, *Muslim American Women on Campus.*

37 For more details about the Irvine 11 case, see www.irvine11.com; also see Salahi, "Behind the Scenes with Israel's Campus Lobby." A group of civil rights organizations (including the Center for Constitutional Rights, the Asian Law Caucus of San Francisco, and CAIR) submitted a report to UC president Mark Yudof in 2012, documenting the fear that Muslim and Arab, including Palestinian, students at UC campuses express about involvement with Palestinian rights activism and the worry that it will affect their educational and work opportunities. See Abunimah, "Climate of Fear Silencing Palestinian, Muslim Students at UC Campuses, Rights Groups Warn."

38 Kundnani, *The Muslims Are Coming.*

39 Salaita, *Israel's Dead Soul.*

40 Daulatzai, *Black Star, Crescent Moon*, 37.

41 Bruyneel, *The Third Space of Sovereignty*, 128.

42 Dudziak, "Desegregation as a Cold War Imperative"; Singh, *Black Is a Country*, 1–6.

20 Deporting Cambodian Refugees

Youth Activism, State Reform, and Imperial Statecraft

SOO AH KWON

Boran is a Cambodian refugee who as a very young child came to the United States with his family in the 1970s, having fled the brutal Khmer Rouge. After serving a sentence for a crime he committed as a young man, he was not released but instead transferred directly into an Immigration and Naturalization Service (INS) detention center and slated for deportation to Cambodia.[1] Boran was one of the thousands of Cambodian refugees whose life courses were radically altered by recent changes in federal law. The Illegal Immigration Reform and Immigrant Responsibility Act (IIRIRA) of 1996 in particular made significant changes facilitating the deportation of permanent residents and refugees to their home countries after serving out their prison sentences. Yet it was not until Cambodia and the United States signed a formal repatriation agreement, a memorandum of understanding (MOU), on March 22, 2002, that deportations began. According to Returnee Integration Support Center, 229 Cambodian refugees have been deported from the United States as of 2010.[2] Approximately two thousand more await deportation.[3] Boran is the older brother of Sammy, a member of Asian/Pacific Islander Youth Promoting Advocacy and Leadership (AYPAL), a youth activist group whose participants I came to know well as a volunteer staff member and ethnographer in the early 2000s.[4] The organization is a pan-ethnic Asian and Pacific Islander coalition of six ethnic nonprofit community-based organizations, formed in 1999 with the express mission to promote social justice, youth community involvement, and youth leadership. The organization drew the participation of some first- but mainly second- generation Asian and Pacific Islander youth (ages fourteen to eighteen) in Oakland, from Cambodian, Chinese, Filipino, Korean, Laotian, Mien, Samoan, Tongan, and Vietnamese immigrant and refugee families with diverse histories of migration and relocation.

In this chapter, I follow AYPAL youth and their campaign to put an end to these deportations—a campaign that spanned a period of two years (2002 to 2004) and culminated with their congressional representative's cosponsorship of a bill (H.R. 3309) to repeal the IIRIRA—in order to examine the relations of power, including geopolitical ones, that produce and limit young people as political actors. Each year the young members of AYPAL decide upon and lead a community-organizing campaign to produce concrete changes in their lives and communities. During my time with the group, the young people successfully led several youth-organizing campaigns, including instituting district-wide school reform policies, pressuring their city council members to increase programming and staff at neighborhood recreation centers, and stopping the expansion of the local juvenile hall. The deportation campaign was their first attempt at effecting national politics. First, I chronicle young people's direct engagement with the state and the political process—visiting with their congressional representative—and how the state engaged with them. This process revealed two things to AYPAL youth: first and foremost, the limitations of the "power of the youth" in the democratic process; and second, the limits of the liberal democratic state. They learned through repeated attempts to pressure their congressional representative to meet their demands that in a government regulated by a representative democracy, they held little sway in making her responsible to them as a nonvoting constituency. As young actors who were not of voting age, they confronted a state that encouraged them to be active but denied them the right to representation and "voice" in the laws of their governance. Relegated to the status of "not quite citizens," ineligible to vote and with no legible political power, these youth came face to face with circumscribed notions of politics and political action within a liberal democracy, which can for our purposes be understood as a "formal rational system of law, procedure, and administration that manages political possibility."[5] Members of AYPAL realized that as youth they were deemed an important category of care as future leaders and as subjects of state benevolence; but in exercising their political power, they held little sway. Rather, in challenging the state to act against deportation, they found common ground with refugee deportees as disenfranchised subjects of U.S. empire. This admittedly asymmetrical parallel between young people and refugee deportees underscores their contradictory relationship to the state. Both these groups have little actual power in affecting state power; their relationships to the state are defined more precisely as subjects of its governance.

Second, I critically examine how, in confronting the limits of their relationship to the state, AYPAL youth uncovered that the neoliberal state is an imperial state. As young people learned of and challenged the deportation cases of people around them, they came to understand that discourses and practices of democratic citizenship are produced by an imperial nation-state that enacts daily violence through the expulsion of its undesirable "others." As a diverse group whose members come from immigrant and refugee families, AYPAL youth readily identified deportation as an unjust law that, by its very nature, targeted immigrant communities. In addition, they were deeply troubled by the double injustice of deporting refugees, such as Boran, who not only served a sentence for his crime but also was forced to return to a country from which the United States presumably "rescued" him. In focusing on the plight of Cambodian refugees, AYPAL members forced a public dialogue about the social conditions of Cambodian "criminal aliens" as political refugees in order to reveal the practices of imperial statecraft.

In realizing their limited power in overturning the IIRIRA, AYPAL youth called attention to immigration policies as technologies of neoliberal governance, aimed at producing citizen-subjects who exercise "good" choices and personal responsibility, while rendering invisible state violence and power. Against this schema, in which people such as Boran are bad immigrants who *deserve* deportation, AYPAL's young people expressed a sophisticated transnational critique of the United States' imperial state and its geopolitical histories in Southeast Asia.

DEPORTING REFUGEES: NEOLIBERAL REGIME OF INCARCERATION, DETENTION, AND DEPORTATION

On September 30, 1996, President William Clinton signed into law the IIRIRA. The IIRIRA, along with the Anti-Terrorism and Effective Death Penalty Act (AEDPA) passed earlier in April the same year, have radically altered immigration policies. Specifically, these changes in immigration law accelerated and facilitated the removal of documented and undocumented immigrants, including legal residents such as refugees and permanent U.S. residents. Together these laws called for the removal of those documented residents classified as "criminal aliens" *after* they had served out a criminal conviction involving a prison or probation sentence. Key changes in the AEDPA and IIRIRA included the reduction of the prison sentence that triggers deportation from five or more years to one, the redefinition of *aggravated felony*, a retroactive "grandfathering" of these new prerequisites, and mandatory detention without bail or due process for all immigrant or refugee defendants facing deportation. The implications of these changes are immensely serious and far reaching. For instance, the redefinition of *aggravated felony* now includes nonserious crimes for which the sentence of incarceration or parole exceeds 365 days, lowering the threshold of crimes eligible for deportation. Violations such as urinating in public, bouncing a check, or failing to pay a subway fare became cause for deportation. The IIRIRA also denied individual cases the right to be reviewed by an immigration judge to take into consideration the defendant's family support, rehabilitation, or the severity of his or her crime.[6]

The legal changes made in 1996 are the confluence of several factors: increased vigilance against terrorism after the bombings of the World Trade Center in 1993 and Oklahoma City in 1995; anti-immigrant backlash in the 1990s, as evidenced by the passing of Proposition 187, the "Save Our State Initiative," in California that directly targeted undocumented citizens' right to publicly funded benefits; and Republican control of both houses of Congress in the elections of November 1994.[7] The IIRIRA was passed a month after the Personal Responsibility and Work Opportunity Reconciliation Act of 1996, also known as the Welfare Reform Act, which drastically cut welfare benefits and replaced them with workfare programs. These laws underscore the central tenets of neoliberalism: privatization and personal responsibility. In naming both *immigrant responsibility* and *personal responsibility* in the laws' titles, these acts denied individuals' claims to state resources in favor of privatizing both welfare and immigration rights as matters of personal responsibility and "good" self-governance. The IIRIRA further generated the "bad" "criminal alien" as a category of people deemed morally reprehensible and deserving of removal, regardless of the severity of his or her crime.

As recent scholarship argues, deportation, like immigration, is an economic policy that not only works to discipline labor and depress wages but also works as a political instrument of the neoliberal state.[8] The logic of neoliberal capitalism privatizes citizenship as a self-governing exercise that reproduces a moral political economy to distinguish between worthy and unworthy citizens. The immigration policies from 1996, based on discourses of immigrant responsibility and governmental efficiency in managing the immigration "problem," are key to neoliberal empire. The detention and removal of "irresponsible" immigrants and refugees highlight the sweeping regime of surveillance, criminalization, incarceration, and detention that defined United States' empire before the September attacks and have become undoubtedly pronounced in the attacks' aftermath. As Sunaina Maira notes, "A crucial point is that the 'post 9–11' moment is not a radical historical or political rupture, but rather a moment of renewed contestation over the state's imperial power and ongoing issues of war and repression, citizenship and nationalism, civil rights and immigrant rights."[9] This regime of deportation and detention of immigrants and refugees mandated in the IIRIRA of 1996 is found in the criminalization and targeting of "suspected terrorists" mandated in the USA PATRIOT Act of 2001. Both before and after 9/11, this regime of punishment and discipline is a racialized regime: just as the processes of criminalization and incarceration overwhelmingly target racial minority groups, deportation is a system of removal aimed at unwanted immigration populations.[10] The targeting of and subsequent spike in rates of deportation and detention of Arab, Arab American, Muslim, and South Asian immigrants as part of the United States' war on terror are a case in point.

The events of 9/11 definitively facilitated the removal of unwanted immigrants and refugees. The Bush administration stepped up its deportation efforts by pursuing repatriation agreements with countries that did not already have official contracts with the United States. Southeast Asian countries in particular posed a special interest to the United States, since by 2001, one-third of the detainees in INS detention centers were of Southeast Asian descent.[11] The MOU between Cambodia and the United States was the result of a strong-arm strategy by the United States, which threatened to deny foreign aid to Cambodia, in the form of International Monetary Fund and World Bank assistance, and U.S. visas to Cambodian officials.[12] Vietnam signed an MOU with the United States in January 2008 and a similar agreement is being sought with Laos. For Southeast Asian communities, it was not until the signing of the MOUs that the impact and consequences of the IIRIRA fully materialized in disappearances and deportations.

Moreover, although mandatory detention of "terror suspects" has come under increasing scrutiny since the passage of the USA PATRIOT Act in 2001, the indefinite detention of noncitizens such as legal residents and refugees, and challenges to this detention, were not uncommon before 9/11. For instance, legal residents whose countries of origin did not have formal repatriation agreements with the United States were held indefinitely in INS detention centers instead of being allowed to return to their homes after serving their prison sentences.[13] Kim Ho Ma, a Cambodian refugee who spent a year and a half in a detention center after being transferred directly from the prison where he had served his sentence, challenged the legality of indefinite detention in 2000.[14] The Supreme Court ruled on his behalf. But although Ma was eventually released from his indefinite detention, he was deported just seven months after the signing of the MOU with Cambodia.[15]

In 2003, the Supreme Court rejected a due process challenge to mandatory detention without bond made by Hyung Joon Kim. Kim, a permanent resident who immigrated with his parents when he was six years old from South Korea, had served a sentence for aggravated felony that involved shoplifting less than $100 in merchandise.[16] The fluid movement of deportees from incarceration and detention in facilities that also house U.S. citizens points to the interlocking mechanisms of incarceration and deportation. Deportation, in short, illuminates a racialized neoliberal regime of punishment (of detention, incarceration, and deportation) and governance (of shaping good and bad moral subjects).

None of the AYPAL youth I worked with had heard of the IIRIRA or the MOU with Cambodia until they undertook the campaign against deportation. But they knew of the pending removal of Boran, the brother of their fellow AYPAL member Sammy, and they directly challenged the state's right to do so. In the following section, I chronicle AYPAL youths' bold challenge to reveal how, in the process of engaging with policies and practices that make up the neoliberal state, they came face to face not only with the limits of an institutional and bureaucratic democracy, but also with this state's investment in transnational governance. As such, their actions illuminate the limits of a liberal democracy yoked to a model of demanding rights and resources from an imperial state, and gesture toward alternative political strategies and agendas for comprehending its violence.

YOUTH CONFRONT THE LIMITS OF A LIBERAL DEMOCRACY

With passionate energy, the young people of AYPAL took the task of overturning the IIRIRA to the one person they believed could meet their demands—their elected congressional representative and lawmaker. In doing so, they followed one of the fundamental principles of democracy—the right to fully and equally participate and partake in making decisions about their governance.[17] They spoke with a handful of Bay Area elected officials (or, more precisely, their aides), staged multiple community awareness actions including several "No Deportation Zone" block parties, held two press conferences, took to the streets in protest, disseminated a report about deportation, and built coalitions with local and national immigrant rights groups and labor unions. Through these activities that compose the core of liberal democratic politics, young people embodied in practice the understood characteristics of good U.S. citizens. They lived up to discourses of an active and engaged citizenry and reinforced idealistic notions of contemporary youth as future leaders. But the majority of AYPAL youth, most of whom were under eighteen, quickly came to realize that within a representative democracy, they had little clout. In working with their elected congressional representative, they came to view "the system" as an inefficient institutional bureaucracy that gave its nonvoting constituents little real political power.

Young people's first taste of the limits of a representative democracy came when AYPAL staged the first of two press conferences against deportation in May 2003, eight months into their campaigning. Approximately one hundred people gathered on a cold windy afternoon in front of the federal building outside the congresswoman's office. They huddled in small circles in the shadow of the building, with its distinctive twin towers joined by a bridge. The crowd—AYPAL members, associates from its ally organizations, and a few inquisitive bystanders—waited to hear the congresswoman announce to the media and to the public her plans to officially propose the repeal of the IIRIRA to Congress. Instead, they heard from her aide. He said,

> You should know that [the] congresswoman stands in solidarity with you. We absolutely support what you're trying to do. We are absolutely going to try to repeal the 1996 IIRIRA Act and we're going to try to fight these injustices. . . . We are here today and together we can make a change, we can make a difference. Together we will make a difference. Although sometimes the wheels of justice work slowly, they indeed do move forward and we will put this together to bring it back down. The congresswoman will certainly do everything she has in her power to support the bringing down of this act and will encourage her colleagues to bring down this 1996 IIRIRA Act.

Although the congresswoman's aide praised the young people's commitment to democracy while assuring them that she would be an important advocate on their behalf, it became clear that the representative had no concrete plan to repeal the IIRIRA. Rather, the aide warned the crowd of the difficulty of making *anything* happen in a timely fashion: "The wheels of justice work slowly." To make matters worse, hardly any press was present at the press conference. Besides two field reporters from local Korean newspapers, no mainstream television or newspaper reporters were in sight. Considering that AYPAL's major goal for the press conference was the congresswoman's public announcement to the press of her plans to repeal the IIRIRA, and to thus generate media attention about these deportations, the event was less than satisfactory. A strong youth base was not sufficient to make a congresswoman take notice, let alone change a national immigration policy.

Members of AYPAL concluded that the only way a group of youth could pressure their congresswoman was to garner the backing of the people she was most accountable to—her adult voting constituents. Hence AYPAL's strategy for the following year was twofold. First, they sought to exercise grassroots power by building a mass base of community support and awareness around the issue of deportation. Second, they planned to use the media to gain moral power by telling the personal stories of deportees and families destroyed by deportation.

To achieve these goals, AYPAL youth engaged in classic forms of grassroots organizing and built a wider coalitional base that went beyond the safety of familiar youth organizations. They took to their neighborhood businesses and community spaces on weekends, recruited people to antideportation block parties, and knocked door to door in order to collect over nineteen hundred signed postcards in support of their campaign. Additionally, they gathered over sixty endorsements from local and national organizational allies, including local chapters of labor unions, the Immigrant Freedom Network, and the California and Nevada United Methodist Church Coalition. They also became members of the Southeast Asian Freedom Network (SEAFN), a national coalition of grassroots organizations formed in 2002 in response to the sudden mandate of Cambodian deportation, put into devastating effect just months after the signing of the MOU. This group sought to provide aid to those facing deportation and to create a national network of activists working to stop deportations.

In another push to pressure their representative to commit to a bill that would repeal the IIRIRA, AYPAL youth staged a second press conference almost a year after their first attempt. Once again, the congresswoman was absent and her aide noncommittal in proposing an antideportation bill. Her aide sang the same song as he had the past year: yes, the lawmaker opposes the IIRIRA, and we applaud your efforts. But this time, his tone was different:

> I'm here today to tell you that the congresswoman fully supports what you are here for. We fully support the repeal of this terrible, terrible law and we will do everything we can to make sure that this law is repealed but we need your help. We need you to not be here in front of Congresswoman's [office]. She's with you. We need you to be in your communities where they don't understand this issue is on the ballot. We need you to go talk to your friends, your family, and continue to build grassroots coalitions, build the energy, build the momentum, we can get this law repealed. Once the Democrats take over Congress, once we get George Bush out of the White House, we can definitely make it happen and I want you to know I want to thank you on behalf of the congresswoman for your support, and thank you for your continued energy and passion.

Yet spreading the word to their friends, family, and community members and building grassroots coalitions was *exactly* what AYPAL youth had been up to for the past year. And who else had the power to help their cause of repealing a national law, if not their U.S. congressional lawmaker?

The youth and staff of AYPAL were frustrated by their inability to persuade their local representative or to otherwise affect the bureaucratic web of representational democracy. Her aide deflected the congresswoman's inaction to the larger political climate and more insidiously directed responsibility onto young people by suggesting they *work harder*. In this manner, he articulated the demands of a larger neoliberal system of governance that frames social problems as individual or "community" problems and views political change as hinging on individuals' responsibilities or, in this case, young people's "self-help."

Following the second press conference, AYPAL members stepped up their campaign to pressure their congresswoman while openly recognizing the limits of her support. In subsequent meetings, AYPAL youth and staff discussed their next steps. Ideas included holding a community town-hall meeting with the representative, increasing media exposure, and asking ally organizations to pressure her office. But one thing was clear—they needed to stage an escalating event to force the lawmaker to take action. They ultimately decided to return to their original demands: a meeting with the congresswoman *actually present* where she would commit to introducing a bill to Congress to repeal the IIRIRA and a public event to make her accountable to her plans. In this process, one of the AYPAL staff members made an unexpected discovery. He learned that H.R. 3309, or the proposed Keeping Families Together Act of 2003, had been introduced to Congress by a representative of San Diego in October 2003. H.R. 3309 sought to do exactly what AYPAL members demanded: "to amend the Immigration and Nationality Act to restore certain provisions relating to the definition of aggravated felony and other provisions as they were before the enactment of the Illegal Immigration Reform and Immigrant Responsibility Act of 1996."[18] The discovery brought the campaign to a halt. The AYPAL youth quickly changed their campaign demand for the upcoming scheduled meeting with the congresswoman and decided to ask her instead to cosponsor H.R. 3309, which she did four months later.

On one hand, AYPAL members viewed the end of the deportation campaign with a sense of accomplishment. A group of teenagers convinced their congresswoman to sponsor a bill that sought to amend a federal law, though in the end she merely cosponsored a bill that had already been drafted and introduced in the House. The congresswoman was the last of twelve representatives who cosponsored the bill. Not surprisingly, H.R. 3309 died in Congress, and no motion was made to have it progress further. Although it was not an easy task, and it took two years of grassroots community organizing, coalition building with adult organizations, and vigilant contact with her office, young people did bring to her attention an issue that was not on her agenda.

On the other hand, many youth and staff viewed the culmination of events with less enthusiasm. As one AYPAL youth voiced out loud during a meeting, "Was she even planning on proposing a bill at all?" Or rather, was her cosponsorship of H.R. 3309 a convenient way of pleasing the crowd and finally putting the pesky youth to rest? And why had her office not known about the bill in the first place? Moreover, the closest AYPAL members ever got to the congresswoman was in a video message she sent to the group in which she thanked them for their accomplishments. The Congresswoman's elusiveness and the young people's persistence underscore the reality of an institutional democracy. As young people discovered, democracy is not an open practice of "the people" but an entity comprising formal representation and bureaucratic channels geared especially for voters. They surmised that traditional political participation offers limited ways in which the "political" is legitimated. Although young people learned to engage politically on a national level, they also quickly realized that, as the lawmaker's aide said, "the wheels of justice work slowly." In the process, young people did not come face to face with democracy, but instead with the failures of liberalism. Their efforts highlight the contradiction of promoting youth as future political leaders, as the rhetoric of democracy so often does, when their activism is not authenticated by the state. Yet as one of the adult organizers reminded AYPAL staff at a post campaign "processing meeting," there were alternative goals that went beyond the material win of repealing the IIRIRA. These included "youth learning that the system needs to change, as opposed to the fact that all we need to do is express our voices and make demands." In the next section, I turn to how young people's voices and actions not only called attention to the shortcomings of the "system," as the institutional strictures of engaging in the democratic process, but also exposed the state's neoliberal governance, producing "good," morally responsible immigrant-subjects and rendering the violence of the United States' imperial regime both "at home" and abroad seemingly invisible. Their actions pointed to an alternative vision, in which "democracy signifies not merely elections, rights, or free enterprise but a way of constituting and thus distributing political power."[19]

"DEPORTATION IS A CRIME": U.S. IMPERIALISM AND THE "GOOD" IMMIGRANT

You wage war on my country,
Now I'm called a refugee.
We are here with our demands,
Join us now and take a stand.
Deportation is a crime,
When we already did our time.
Immigrants are not to blame,
George Bush should be ashamed!

So went the chant that AYPAL members sang out at their antideportation events. This chant underscores state power as a force of ruthless punishment and discipline and calls attention to past and present histories of the United States' empire. In their activism against deportation, AYPAL youth forced a public dialogue about the circumstances that facilitated Cambodian refugee deportees and their deportations, refusing to accept those arguments that these immigrants and deportees were "criminals" and deserved mandatory removal. They called attention to the transnational character of Asian American and, particularly, Southeast Asian American communities, and articulated the need to move beyond conceptions of politics and the political as bounded within the nation-state. Moreover, the chant exposes deportation as part of a regime of neoliberal governance that rewards "personally responsible" and "self-sufficient" immigrants and refugees and punishes the rest. The AYPAL youth flipped the question of blame from individual immigrants to the system.

As they worked on the campaign, AYPAL youth learned of more stories of Cambodian refugees deported or facing deportation. Probably the most familiar accounts are those of Loeun Lun, Many Uch, and Kim Ho Ma, featured in *Sentenced Home* (2006), a 2006 documentary produced by David Grabias and Nicole Newnham that followed these Cambodian refugees targeted for deportation, and in Deborah Sontag's spread in the *New York Times Magazine.*[20] Loeun Lun is a Cambodian refugee who fled the Khmer Rouge killing fields as a baby in his mother's arms and who grew up in an urban housing project in Tacoma, Washington. When he was a teenager, Lun shot a gun into the air at a shopping mall while fleeing from a group of armed boys. Fortunately, nobody was hurt. He pled guilty to assault charges and served an eleven-month sentence. After his release, he did his best to put his past behind him. He found gainful employment, married, and had two daughters. Upon the urging of his Cambodian American wife, who was born in the United States, he applied for citizenship. When he appeared for his naturalization interview, instead of being allowed to take his citizenship test, he was arrested. It did not matter that the incident at the mall occurred seven years earlier and that he had served his sentence. He was deported three months later, caught up in the retroactive clause of the IIRIRA and the repatriation agreement that mandated his removal to Cambodia.

What disturbed the young people of AYPAL most about the plight of deported refugees such as Lun and Boran was the state's disposal of them as "criminal aliens" without consideration for their histories, their situations. Missing foremost were the social and political contexts of these refugees' lives. For example, take Many Uch, a Cambodian refugee awaiting deportation after serving out his conviction for driving the getaway car at a robbery of a rival gang member's house. Of his experiences growing up in the housing projects in the Seattle area, he said, "We were a bunch of poor Cambodian, Vietnamese, and Laotian kids, hanging around without much adults."[21] He added, "We wanted to make a name for ourselves, we wanted to be the toughest ones in all of Seattle. The cops called it a gang but when we grew up we just think we had a bond."[22] Uch's words tell a familiar narrative of surveillance and criminalization heard in stories of other young men deported or awaiting deportation to Cambodia. The twin processes of criminalization and incarceration of youth of color were easily understood and relatable to many AYPAL youth, especially in light of their activism against the expansion of juvenile hall in their neighborhood that I describe elsewhere.[23] But with deportation as a possible consequence of such criminalization and incarceration, AYPAL youth now understood the transnational reach of United States' state power. This point was made clear to attendants at a conference in 2003 that AYPAL youth organized to raise community awareness around Cambodian deportation. As part of the conference, they heard from affected family members. One person said about her brother awaiting deportation, "He will be sent back to Cambodia, but he doesn't know Cambodian culture. He doesn't even know American culture, all he knows is American jails." Another woman at the conference described the inhumane conditions of filth and inadequate health care at the INS detention center where her brother was being held, awaiting deportation for a crime he committed ten years prior. She said, "A little package [of Tylenol] costs him three bucks . . . he gets sick all a time . . . and the phone calls it cost four bucks a minute, you know. *This system, they're not only detaining people, but they're making a profit off of them.* And it ain't right" (emphasis mine).

Also missing in "mainstream" stories of Cambodian deportees were their histories of migration, including the United States' interventions in Southeast Asia and its exercises of imperial statecraft as the necessary background for their arrival to the United States as refugees. Cindy, a Cambodian American, spoke to this point in a fiery speech at an antideportation rally:

> Deportation is not right! And what they are doing to us is that they are not giving us no free trials. And what they are doing to us is double jeopardy. It's like punishing us for a crime we already served, twice. And that is not fair. And they treat immigrants like animals and not humans, giving them no rights, no lawyers, no kind of respect. They treat us like we are unwanted people. But we were also here. We're the ones that made this place what it is. We lived here for most of our lives, half of our lives. And if were sent back, what the hell are we going to do? What kind of shit do we know there? Like, how are we going to survive? What kind of language

is there for us or stuff like that? If they send us back, we ain't got no rights there either.

Here Cindy points to the "double jeopardy" of deporting refugees. Although refugee deportation does not technically violate the Fifth Amendment's protection against double jeopardy (being tried and convicted for the same crime twice), for many deportees and their allies there is little difference in the double punishment of incarceration in the United States and lifetime banishment to Cambodia. Having spent almost the entirety of their lives in the United States, only to be exiled to a country whose government at one point committed one of the gravest genocides of the twentieth century against its own people, these deportees lack the language skills and cultural knowledge to create new lives for themselves in their foreign "homelands."

High rates of poverty and unemployment in Cambodia make reentry and adjustment extremely difficult. Deportees are also viewed as outsiders by Cambodian society, and little support exists for deportees there; an exception is a halfway house run by the Returnee Assistance Program (now Returnee Integration Support Center) in Phnom Penh. Many deportees suffer from depression as they confront the reality of never returning to their homes or families again. Their only hope of returning to their relatives in the United States under current law is in a casket.

Many of the Cambodian, Laotian, and Mien youth of AYPAL grew up hearing their parents' stories about the brutal consequences of war—rape, torture, murder, starvation, sickness, and suffering—ravaging their homelands and families during the wars in Southeast Asia. The atrocities of the Khmer Rouge are particularly harrowing. The forces of the Khmer Rogue, led by Pol Pot between 1979 and 1995, sought to turn Cambodia into an agrarian utopia, a goal that left an estimated two million people dead.[24] The regime persecuted many of the elite and educated classes while forcing thousands of others to work in brutal labor camps. Common stories that surfaced of this time include appalling descriptions of tortured and maimed bodies left for dead on stakes or buried alive in the infamous killing fields. It is no surprise that parents who lived through the Cambodian genocide find the removal orders of their sons unbearable and unfathomable. (As noted before, all Cambodian deportees have been male, except two.) Paularita Seng, president of the Cambodian Women's Association in Seattle, observed, "The deportations really rattle these mothers, more than Americans could possibly imagine. . . . During the Khmer Rouge time, the soldiers would take away their sons and their husbands for 'reeducation,' and they knew it was a death sentence. Now, once again, the authorities are at the door for their men."[25] Removal of Cambodian refugees who grew up as Americans to a country with such a volatile and violent past seemed more than unfair; refugees are not voluntary immigrants, after all—they are the displaced victims of war.

But the expulsion of Cambodian refugees as a rightful return of "criminals" to a country ravaged by internal civil war fails to recognize the direct role and impact of United States' policies on the plight of Cambodian refugees. First, U.S. bombings along the Cambodian border during the Vietnam War not only displaced thousands but also destroyed the country's economic infrastructure and agricultural productivity.[26] Second, the inadequacy of U.S. government policies to resettle the displaced Southeast Asian groups has shaped the welfare of these populations.[27] The temporary Interagency Task Force (IATF), created by President Gerald Ford in 1975 to deal with the sudden influx of Southeast Asian refugees, quickly proved unsuccessful. The IATF acknowledged its failure to quickly assimilate refugees and minimize economic impact upon local communities by dispersing them across the United States through family sponsorships.[28] As Lavinia Limon, the executive director of the U.S. Committee for Refugees, stated, "The Cambodians are manifestly the greatest failure of the refugee program in this country. Mistake No. 1 was that we didn't treat the Cambodians as different. The scope and breadth and depth of what they endured—the only thing you can compare it to, was the Jewish Holocaust."[29] Moreover, the majority of Cambodian refugees who survived the Khmer Rouge were from rural areas; being often poor and less educated, they were scantily equipped to undertake urban life. A recent survey in Los Angeles County, home to the largest Cambodian community in the United States, revealed that Cambodians rank the highest in most indicators of social poverty, including income and education levels.[30] In Oakland, almost half the Cambodian population lives below the poverty line.

The children of these refugees—such as Boran, Lun, Ma, and Uch—do not fit the bill of sensationalized news stories of successful middle-class Asian American students. The men featured in the film *Sentenced Home*, like Boran, left Cambodia as infants and grew up on the urban streets of Oakland and Seattle, where they were caught up in underground economies of extralegal activities as well as systems of criminalization that target youth of color. They were child refugees who fled because of war in their country, and the United States government had direct involvement in both their displacement and resettlement. The social, political, and economic contexts of Cambodian refugees paint a wider picture, situating the lives of these men and the impact of their deportations, than that recognized by a neoliberal regime that sees only "criminal aliens" who failed to exercise personal responsibility. As such, deportation stands as a ruthless attempt by the United States to control its unwanted immigrant populations that are the consequence of its imperial ambitions.

In their critique of deportation, the young people of AYPAL moved beyond a focus on the individual refugee "criminal" to point to the imperial state and its instruments of rule. Consider, for instance, a conversation I witnessed on a late afternoon in March 2003. About fifteen AYPAL youth—largely Cambodian and Mien—responsible for the logistics of the first press conference on deportation, were gathered around a large conference table to plan for the upcoming event. Marie, a staff member who was cofacilitating the session with me, reminded the group that this was a press event and that we should think of some powerful images or symbols to grab the media's attention. One of the youth, Johnny, suggested, "We should play on this theme about deportation hurting families." The others nodded their heads in response. Matt excitedly offered, "We could paint a family portrait and the father's face can be missing, and we'll put a large question mark where his face is supposed to be." "We could write over his face, 'Where is my daddy?'" said Annie. "And the child in the picture can have a real sad face on him," added Fay. Here the young people underscored the fact that deportation was also gendered. They also considered the theme of "keeping families together," a tactic also used among conservative groups to reinforce a claim to "family values" and other norms in their public appeals.

The excitement began to build as others in the room proposed more ideas. Suggestions included a reworking of old Uncle Sam military draft posters, with the saying "We want you!" replaced with "You're next!" Yet everyone was most enthusiastic about Matt's image of the Statue of Liberty. He explained to the group that the statue, instead of representing freedom and liberty for immigrants, should rather stand for "what is really going on with our government." Others jumped on his idea and suggested that boats filled with people being deported back to Asia should be drawn underneath her feet. And in the crook of her arm, she would hold a book titled "List of Deportees" with actual names of deportees written on it. Her other arm would be outstretched with a finger pointed toward a map of Asia. Another youth offered a variation on the Statue of Liberty idea, picturing the statue as pulling the Golden Gate Bridge like an elastic slingshot, loaded with deportees, across the span of a map of the United States, aimed at Asia.

Selected from the much longer list of ideas, the Statue of Liberty became the basis for a flyer for the press conference. This figure and the other images young people articulated at the meeting illustrate vividly the critical understanding of United States imperial statecraft put forth by the youth. Here, the Statue of Liberty is not the gleaming symbol of democracy and freedom, but rather one that deports "the huddled masses yearning to be free." Deportation takes form in this instance as a political instrument of state power, repression, and violence, and the youth's resulting image vividly captures the irony of U.S. exceptionalism, particularly the discourse of the United States' being *made by* immigrants and *made special* because of its immigrants. These youth argue that, contrary to this discourse, immigrants, refugees, and policies regarding their welfare, are—and have always been—an apparatus of state expansion and repression.

TRANSNATIONAL CONNECTIONS AND ACTIVISM

The deportation campaign and its implications for immigrants and refugees highlighted the lives of AYPAL youth as diasporic and transnational. It also underscored that the United States' racialized regime of criminalization and incarceration is not limited in its exercise to its borders, but that it is transnationally deployed and that our activism must respond to that fact. Through a focused campaign against Cambodian refugee deportation, AYPAL understood the issue as one that affects *all* immigrant and diasporic communities. For the diverse group of young people in AYPAL, whose families and histories encompassed the vastness of experiences and particular histories of the Asian and Pacific diasporas, their understanding of the impact of deportations were by no means uniform. But members of the group were for the most part unified in opposition. And, unlike their previous campaigns for school reform and juvenile justice that were youth centered, the campaign afforded many young people the opportunity to connect their parents and family members to their organizing work and form broader coalitions with immigrant rights groups and community members.

The most vocal group participating in the campaign was, unsurprisingly, Cambodian American youth who readily identified with the cause. For some of these young people, the campaign allowed them to translate the circumstances of their familial, "personal" histories into broader political action and meaningful critical and cultural theory. This was facilitated by AYPAL's program of cultural arts projects, offering young people opportunities to explore their cultural heritages, discover the political histories of their parents' homelands, and examine the other resonances of their racial identities and cultural experiences that departed from dominant discourses of liberal multiculturalism. For example, for the yearly AYPAL cultural arts project, the Cambodian youth produced and acted in a play about the Khmer Rouge, based on Loung Ung's memoir *First They Killed My Father: A Daughter of Cambodia Remembers*, which recounts her family's survival of the Khmer Rouge atrocities.[31] As they learned their lines in rehearsals and Cambodian political history in workshops, the hardships and violence of their parents' experiences slowly unfolded before them. In one rehearsal, Pim, a cast member, noted about her mother, "To learn about what she went through, how she survived, and how she worked so hard, and the sacrifices she made. I was born in a refugee camp and now I know what that means. So now, I have lot more respect for her."

The issue was by no means limited to the Cambodian youth of AYPAL. The Mien youth, whose parents were also refugees, and whose plight was a direct consequence of U.S. intervention in Laos, were also quite sympathetic to the cause. Other youth also recognized deportation as an issue that affects all immigrant communities and all noncitizens, regardless of how long a person has been here or whether that person considered himself or herself to be "American."

In addition to providing an occasion for some AYPAL youth to discuss their activism with their parents, the deportation campaign also offered young people opportunities to plan events that drew a wider audience of supporters and that sought a broader understanding of the scope of the United States' empire. On two different occasions, youth organized a block party to raise awareness of deportation not only in their own communities but also in connection to other immigrant communities. These events were held in two different Oakland neighborhoods that AYPAL youth marked with "No Deportation Zone" signs. These block parties were planned to draw as much support and attention from neighboring residents as possible. The first block party was held at the Fruitvale Village in what is known as the San Antonio–Fruitvale neighborhood of Oakland, highly populated by Southeast Asian and Latino residents. The event drew over a hundred people including AYPAL youth, their friends, families, allies from various nonprofit organizations, and Latino community members. It included festivities such as cultural arts performances, games, and arts and crafts booths for children. These social activities supplemented the educational outreach against deportation, which took the form of speeches by AYPAL youth and local community activists. Recognizing also the impact of deportation on Latino communities, AYPAL purposefully asked Leo, a Spanish bilingual youth activist they knew from an ally youth organization, to speak at the event. Mexico was the leading country of origin of persons deported by the United States, followed by Guatemala and Honduras, in 2004.[32] In addition to bringing together immigrant communities around the issue of deportation at these block parties, AYPAL sought and received formal sponsorship by national immigrant organizations and coalitions doing similar work, such as the Immigrant Freedom Network.

In their activism against deportation, AYPAL engaged in classic democratic processes for state reform and, in the process, built multiracial and intergenerational ties. Again, the youth also made clear that deportation is linked to a racialized regime of criminalization and incarceration that is not limited to U.S. borders, but transnationally deployed ("You wage war on my country, now I'm called a refugee"). I contend that their activism around deportation thus calls attention to the limits of political action wedded to national organizing identities or rights-based campaigns born of the post-civil-rights-era and U.S.-centered organizing. In an era of neoliberalism, Asian American political organizing must engage in analysis and activism that confront power at what Inderpal Grewal refers to as its "transnational connectivities."[33] Although squarely situated in its programming and structure as a youth development and youth organizing group, the deportation campaign extended young people's activism beyond a local youth-focused agenda.

In advocating against Cambodian refugee deportation, the youth were exposed to and worked with a larger network of activism led by Asian American activists that did not privilege traditional racial categories and nation-based borders of organizing among communities of color. As mentioned previously, AYPAL was a member of SEAFN, a national coalition of organizations working against Cambodian refugee deportation; SEAFN maintained an analysis that such removals were intricately tied to the United States' war on terror. More locally, AYPAL worked closer with Asians and Pacific Islanders for Community Empowerment (API ForCE), a community organization in Oakland that was deeply involved in the cause of Cambodian deportees.

In this chapter, I have examined the convergence of the state's failure to recognize young people as a nonvoting youth constituency and young people's growing consciousness of the state's incapability to identify them as political actors. In this process, AYPAL youth and their activism revealed that practices of imperial statecraft bear both "local" and transnational consequences, such that seemingly "domestic" practices for the criminalization and incarceration of youth of color are also geopolitical in their scope and that activism must respond to these facts. In doing so, the youth challenged discourses of United States' exceptionalism as a site and arbiter of democracy: first, by articulating the state's irresponsibility to refugees by pointing out that "deportation is a crime," especially when it strips away rights of due process and legal representation; and, second, by illuminating histories of imperial statecraft that had a hand in producing the contexts of violence from which Southeast Asian refugees fled in the first instance. They also called attention to the more subtle forms of governance that regulate immigrants and refugees as "good" moral neoliberal subjects. One of my favorite slogans that youth came up with during the deportation campaign was "Green Card. Accepted Everywhere but Here," a play on the popular Mastercard commercials that commented upon both the necessity of immigrant labor to the United States' economy as well as the state's refusal to fully accept them. Through their community outreach and educational events—such as the block parties, press conferences, youth conference, rallies, marches, and coalition building with other nonprofit organizations—AYPAL youth expressed an alternative vision of democracy and politics as open ended and informal. They embodied political action as a process in the making that challenged conventional notions of institutional and bureaucratic democracy. Young people's activism against Cambodian refugee deportation makes clear the contradictions of neoliberal discourses and practices, revealing that the neoliberal state and its hegemonic projects are never fully complete or totalizing.

NOTES

1 As of March 1, 2003, the INS agency transitioned its services and reinforcement functions to the Department of Homeland Security. Enforcement of immigration law, including deportation and detention, is now under the purview of the U.S. Immigration and Customs Enforcement (ICE). See U.S. Citizenship and Immigrations Services, "Our History."

2 Reported in email correspondence with Returnee Integration Support Center on July 20, 2010.

3 Chang, "Life after 9/11."

4 All names of AYPAL individuals are pseudonyms.

5 Castronovo and Nelson, "Introduction," 6.

6 The exclusionary provisions to deport aliens with criminal activity were actually put into place earlier, by the Immigration Act of 1990. However, amendments and changes in both the AEDPA and IIRIRA facilitated deportations. For information on the IIRIRA and AEDPA, see Capps, Hagan, and Rodriguez, "Border Residents Manage the U.S. Immigration and Welfare Reforms"; Dow, "Designed to Punish"; Farnam, *US Immigration Laws under the Threat of Terrorism*; Freeman, "Client Politics or Populism?," 712; Hing, "Deporting Cambodian Refugees"; Morawetz, "Rethinking Retroactive Deportation Laws and the Due Process Clause" and "Understanding the Impact of the 1996 Deportation Laws and the Limited Scope of Proposed Reforms"; Park and Park, *Probationary Americans*; and Shuck, *Citizens, Strangers, and In-Betweens.*

7 Farnam, *US Immigration Laws.*

8 Cole, *Enemy Aliens*; DeGenova, "Migrant 'Illegality' and Deportability in Everyday Life"; Maira, "Deporting Radicals, Deporting La Migra."

9 Maira, *Missing*, 23.

10 See DeGenova, "Migrant 'Illegality' "; and Maira, "Deporting Radicals," for excellent accounts of deportation as a racialized regime of state power.

11 Park and Park, *Probationary Americans*, 6.

12 Cochrane, "A Bitter Bon Voyage," 56.

13 If no formal forced removal agreements exist between a detainee's home country and the United States, the maximum time a person can be held in detention centers is nine months. Yet this is not always enforced. Members of AYPAL learned of people whose family members were moved directly from prison to detention centers for longer than nine months with no plan of release. Moreover, detainees are often moved across the country from one facility to another; the law does not require that family be notified of these moves. Also see Seng, "Cambodian Nationality Law."

14 Dow, *American Gulag*, 273; American Civil Liberties Union, "Brief of the American Civil Liberties Union."

15 Richard, "Banned for Life."

16 Taylor, "Demore v. Kim."

17 Mansbridge, *Beyond Adversary Democracy*; Pateman, *Participation and Democratic Theory*.

18 Keeping Families Together Act of 2003.

19 Brown, *States of Injury*, 52.

20 Grabias and Newnham, *Sentenced Home*; Sontag, "In a Homeland Far from Home."

21 Sontag, "In a Homeland Far from Home," 52.

22 Grabias and Newnham, *Sentenced Home*.

23 Kwon, *Uncivil Youth*.

24 For more information on the Khmer Rouge, see Chandler, *Voices from S-21*; Chandler, *A History of Cambodia*; Hein, *From Vietnam, Laos, and Cambodia*; and Hinton, *Why Did They Kill?*

25 Sontag, "In a Homeland Far from Home," 50.

26 Hein, *From Vietnam*; Hing, "Deporting Cambodian Refugees"; Loescher and Scanlan, *Calculated Kindness*.

27 Gordon, "Southeast Asian Refugee Migration to the United States"; Hing, "Deporting Cambodian Refugees"; Loescher and Scanlan, *Calculated Kindness*.

28 By 1980, about 45 percent of the first wave of Southeast Asian refugees had resettled to urban cities, seeking coethnic communities (Hing, "Deporting Cambodian Refugees," 272).

29 Sontag, "In a Homeland Far from Home," 51.

30 Sontag, "In a Homeland Far from Home," 51

31 Ung, *First They Killed My Father*.

32 Dougherty, Wilson, and Wu, "Immigration Enforcement Actions."

33 Grewal, *Transnational America*, 22.

21 Hunters of the Sourlands

Empire and Displacement in Highland New Jersey

JOHN F. COLLINS

Some years ago, on a January morning during New Jersey's winter bow hunting season, I sat with a fifty-one-year-old man above a bottomland that served as a peach orchard from soon after the American Revolutionary War until the Great Depression. Focused on the now-dense secondary growth opened up by our position, my companion cradled his weapon and struggled to make out his quarry. He would stare down, and then cock his head while listening for a crack of a twig or the rustle of leaves that might indicate that white-tailed deer (*Odocoileus virginianus*) were on the move. As we gazed across the leafless canopy, and the sun rose and no deer appeared, I listened as my burly interlocutor offered an account of "taking" his first deer.

Still a teenager, and following his grandfather's advice, "Moose" hid alongside a clearing cut by a pipeline as his elder went off to flush deer. When a doe appeared, he made sure that his sight lines were free of humans, took aim, and then shot. This produced not a sense of accomplishment, but a gush of tears and what he described to me as a sick feeling of "what have I done?" and "why have I destroyed such a beautiful thing?" Moose, who admitted that the experience "made me cry like a baby lamb," emphasized that the most immediate response to the doubts washing over him as the life ebbed from the animal he had shot, was his grandfather's knowing hug, and an assurance that "it'll be all right."

In this chapter, I follow my interlocutor's account of a doe's death, and a grandfather's hug that helped prepare a boy emotionally for the killing of deer across a lifetime, into an ecology of working-class men who kill deer, on one hand, and their more bourgeois neighbors who steward threatened landscapes and defend nonhuman animals in a rapidly gentrifying, exurban area of central New Jersey, on the other. But this ethnography of hunters, their critics, their ethics, and the circulation of their stories and kills is not directed at usual suspects such as the Anthropocene, interspecies companionship, or the suburban sprawl and deer-related ecological degradation that threatens to reduce forests to parking lots and grasslands. I focus instead on contemporary forms of U.S. empire as they relate to performances of class politics in order to argue that an ecosystem-bending rural gentrification taking place in a region of New Jersey, known as the "Sourlands" and located less than two hours from New York City, has provoked conflicts over hunting and access to land that configure and make more apparent the status of local hunters as a particular type of imperial subject. These white, working-class, male, and North American hunters-as-imperial-subjects are important to comprehending what empire does and how it does it since, just as Moose symbolically loses and then regains his humanity at the scene of his first kill, in an imperial United States making things "all right," or livable, rests on dislocations of violence.

One of the most basic contradictions running through *Ethnographies of U.S. Empire* as a collective project involves imperialism as a site, or sites, of complex displacement that also stand as nexuses of toxic interdependency. In fact, displacement surfaces repeatedly in descriptions of modern imperial power, or what Partha Chatterjee once tellingly defined as "the power to declare the exception."[1] This is true whether one understands dislocation in relation to the forced removal of Native Americans, the sequestering of the fruits of the labor of the colonized via everything from the clock and the overseer's whip to intellectual property legislation, or the political theologies brought to bear in redemptive attempts to disengage colonizer and colonized, as well as liberal democracy, from the rapacious exploitation that analysts typically seek to banish to the past. In short, as Robert Bickers asserted for post–World War II Britain, in the United States today empire "is within us, in our waking lives, and in our dreams and nightmares."[2] But in this haunting that refuses to be confined to just those institutions that might be evaluated as securely colonial rather than dangerously hybrid or even redemptive, the imperial takes form as a force capable of becoming productively confused with institutions, representational systems, and forms of everyday life that might at first glance appear to have little to do with extraction or exploitation.

Observers of U.S. policy in the Middle East may have noted how quickly during the Second Gulf War the administration of President George W. Bush became rather interested in the rights of Muslim women.[3] And scholars of hemispheric "cooperation" have noted how the U.S.-Mexico borderlands were "secured" via public health campaigns, and U.S. agencies and the Rockefeller Corporation worked to overcome insect-borne diseases at critical moments of twentieth-century U.S. intervention in Latin America.[4] Meanwhile, U.S. consulate-sponsored programs on black rights, multiculturalism, and citizens' empowerment have increased in Colombia and Brazil over the last two decades, or precisely at a moment marked by agribusiness expansion into lands held by black peasant communities whose members' everyday practices are increasingly celebrated as fungible "culture."[5] Empire and the good life, or at least claims about the improvement of both *zoë* and *bios*, might thus seem to go together handily—if also cynically and dangerously—in U.S. government and civil society initiatives.

It does not seem an exaggeration to see empire everywhere, and nowhere either entirely or chastely, as it forms as an untrustworthy elixir in which so many people find themselves as citizens, subjects, and objects. This is one reason my ethnography conducted at a moment of mounting rural gentrification in central New Jersey refuses "empire" as a thing that might be extracted so as to be contemplated or even expunged without regard for the tissues that connect us all, differentially. Instead, I treat dislocations and reformulations, and thus evasions of responsibilities and transformations in substance that may nonetheless continue violent or exploitative relations, as generative of everyday habits and techniques that open into an everyday or ordinary ethics. And I take such ethics as a means of struggling to live as more than the sum of one's parts.[6]

I am interested in the United States as a distributed, automobile-dependent, carbon-spewing, and often expansively destructive entity. I therefore work to avoid seizing upon a single institution or network of actors to trace ligaments I might then present neatly, or as emanating from an imperial state perceived as a centered entity—if institutions require identification in this chapter, then an institution writ large I follow is "sport hunting," a multibillion-dollar business critical to U.S. wildlife policy and the management of citizens. But hunting is not a naval base. Nor does it appear, at least at first glance among U.S. citizens concerned with animal rights who shop at supermarkets, to be much like a moralizing public health campaign. Might then my resistance to identifying and following diligently a single, coherently "colonial" institution in New Jersey, together with a focus on empire as a haunting, agentive medium that recomposes all it encounters, risk turning everything and anything into imperial murk?[7] Or, as Alyosha Goldstein, warns, does a concern with "multivalent informality" threaten to become detached in the process from "continental colonization and conquest"?[8] How, then, might we follow brute force and concentrated power alongside what Ann Stoler describes as "sliding scales of differential rights" and powerfully yet often ambiguously "gradated forms of sovereignty" so as to attend to the violence and rapaciousness of the imperial formations in which we live, even if our sites of inquiry are not clearly or habitually recognized as imperial?[9]

This chapter does not offer a definitive answer. But it does develop an ethnography around the displacements so much a part of both hunting and stewarding of deer in New Jersey. Perhaps curiously, these displacements—which, following my orientation to empire in this chapter, may also function as sites of agonistic connection—encourage a focus on the centrality of violence and the attempted "possession of another being" in hunting, as well as in empire.[10] They also foster a consideration of how such intensities infiltrate one another, institutions, and everyday life, to an extent that may remain unnoticed. This is one reason that I am interested not simply in hunting, but in its relationship in the Sourlands to transductions and attempted transductions of violence by hunters, hunters' neighbors, and community groups that stitch together the apparent banalities of everyday life in a region undergoing suburbanization.

Before describing further the people, historical processes, and section of New Jersey represented, I offer an important aside: At no point in this chapter do I defend or condemn the shooting of nonhuman animals. Or, put slightly differently, I never forget that hunting is predicated on capture, death, and certain forms of finitude that mitigate against certain types of transformation. I state this clearly at the outset because among the risks incurred in this ethnography of exurban New Jersey is the possibility that what follows might be read as a defense of killing animals or the instrumental rights of armed men traipsing through forests for fun, rather than an analysis of how the violent conditions of possibility of certain forms of ethical life reappear, in new and unhomely form, in spite of ourselves. That said, I invite my reader to the "Sourland Mountains."

"IT'S IN NEW JERSEY, BUT IT SCREAMS VERMONT"

Sourland Mountain, or "the Sourlands," encompasses just under eighty square miles of Appalachian foothills celebrated today for forests, scenic views, and high-elevation wetlands. Located forty miles east of Philadelphia and seventy miles southwest of New York City, and running north from Mercer, into Hunterdon, and on to Somerset Counties, the Sourlands make up the largest expanse of unbroken deciduous woodland in New Jersey, the nation's most densely populated state. This ridge called a "mountain" even as it never reaches six hundred feet above sea level also presents some of the highest concentrations of deer and fastest rates of exurban growth and automobile-dependent sprawl in the eastern United States. Overwhelmingly rural and still substantially dependent on farming until the 1970s, surrounding valleys house Princeton University, which has helped attract biotechnology, Wall Street "back office," and publishing operations. In part as a result, in 2014 nearby Hunterdon County posted the United States' fourth-highest median household income. The region's rapid transformation, alongside its centuries-long direct linkages to cities and a variety of scales in the global economy, is generating new spatial patterns associated with the congestion, infrastructural problems, gentrification, and ecological changes that accompany deindustrialization.

Although the Sourlands and surrounding valleys were essential to provisioning colonial and early republican New York and Philadelphia, Hunterdon languished and the population remained static from 1860 until about 1950. Home to a small gentry, whose inherited wealth and wooded landholdings meant they often played little role in local commerce and typically sent children to boarding schools while remaining outside the public eye, the region grew again after World War II as Eastern and Southern European arrivals left New York. These arrivals joined an existing working class and drew on family farms, skilled trades, and seasonal work in construction or agriculture in the surrounding Hopewell and Amwell Valleys in order to supplement the gardens, hunting, fishing, trapping, and forest product extraction at the core of household economies. Yet, by this point, the Dutch and English Sourlanders who had displaced indigenous people in the mid- and late eighteenth century had come to take on a special significance.

Stigmatized as "mountain people" and portrayed even in adjoining communities as backlanders akin to the Ramapo Mountain People, or the Ramapough Lenape Nation, a community to the north supposedly put together by indigenous people, escaped slaves, Hessian deserters, and prostitutes forced from New York following the Continental Army's defeat of the British, residents normally lived in one- or two-room houses heated by woodlots and served by an outhouse. Beginning in the 1960s, some secured union wages in expanding industry and in rural prisons and social services institutions that cared for unruly citizens sent by the state to "the country" from urban, northern New Jersey. A majority traded wood-heated homes and outhouses for "cape" and "ranch-style" tract houses that sprouted on nearby bottomlands and rocky hillsides. Today it is common to see older dwellings listing in the shadow of much larger homes.

Newer, ostentatious "McMansions" belong overwhelmingly to new arrivals from "the (New York) City" and northern New Jersey, as well as the minority of long-term residents able to serve new arrivals as tradespeople or hold onto land, as cash, credit, and a highly educated workforce displace the majority of the region's working class. Those dispossessed often seek to replicate former lifeways by moving to regions with low prices for large tracts of farm and woodland, including central Pennsylvania and Vermont's Northeast Kingdom. One consequence has been a fracturing of forested areas, typically between fifty and two hundred acres and often treated as communal resources by neighbors who had interacted for generations, into six- to twenty-acre plots. These usually include a driveway and, now by law, a septic field planted with grasses and covered with soils trucked in from elsewhere. These alter the composition of the forest floor, and thus the mix of species that flourish in forests that arose as peach orchards carved into the clay responsible for the term "Sourland" became economically unfeasible due to the opening of western lands via the Panama Canal and the challenges to mechanized agriculture posed by swamps, stone-walls, and ridges.

As Moose once put it, stands of majestic hardwoods strewn with glacier-tumbled boulders attract capital and highly educated workers "like moths to a porch light." Hunterdon County, which votes overwhelmingly Republican in presidential elections, is over 90 percent white and boasts some of the highest rates of formal marriage and high school completion together with the lowest rates of participation in federal food aid programs, children born into single-parent homes, and violent crime in the state of New Jersey. Interspersed in this affluent and almost symptomatically upper-middle-class, politically conservative landscape are a variety of households—usually families or divorced adults, since unmarried children of the working class tend to depart due to vagaries of inheritance and the sorts of disincentives to property ownership more typically associated with Latin American working classes—who fail to fit into communities in which bicycling, hiking, photography, college prep courses, and the preservation of fauna increasingly take precedence over the tracking and shooting of deer and squirrels or the collection of dewberries and hazelnuts on neighbors' land.

Each year, there are fewer residents who leave washing machines on porches, or who make a living with chain saws and well-drilling equipment that they tend to leave idle when presented with opportunities to escape to the woods and hunt. Those able to remain report that they feel there is no longer a place for them "on the Mountain" and that unlike in previous decades—when police, Fish and Wildlife agents, or "horse [gentleman] farmers" presented threats from outside—they feel dispossessed "from within" by land prices, property taxes, and neighbors who condemn their collection of timber or berries and distaste for property lines. Shifts in property relations and decreases in working-class numbers, practices, and landholdings, together with an increase in population density and average home size as well as depictions of the region such as an article in the *New York Times*' Sunday Real Estate Section in 2007 that promised, "It's in New Jersey, but it Screams 'Vermont,'" have made the area attractive to outsiders and encouraged patchwork environments.[11] As a consequence, sunlight and a proliferation of food sources that border sheltering forests have generated explosions in deer populations. This threatens other plant and animal species, whether oak trees or migrating birds and forest lilies, due to an overgrazing that has removed significant portions of the understory from forests. These will no longer be able to reproduce as forests if ungulate numbers are not reduced.

One result of the recognition that deer are parasitical upon humans' suburban, carbon-dependent lifeways has been an attempt to establish hunting as a solution to ecological crisis. In a reversal of earlier programs designed to increase numbers for the benefit of the state's "sport" hunters, experts from the Department of Natural Resources have established deer management zones. Depending on the unit, and thus the state's estimate of deer populations and damage, hunters must "take" or "harvest" a number of does that varies by zone before they may shoot a coveted, antlered buck. Management Zone 12, which includes most of the Sourlands discussed here, supports some of the most liberal bag limits in the United States—in a logic justified by, but by no means limited to, considerations of reproduction and population dynamics, hunters may take an unlimited number of does across the hunting season. They may also kill, and extract from the woods, two deer at once.

By participating in and following byzantine rules, hunters enroll in a management campaign made necessary by sprawl. This administration of environment through the encouragement of human lethality centers on the control and animation of humans who kill in the woods and, increasingly, in or near suburban subdivisions. Killing becomes a technique for dulling the environmental injury wrought by how people live today. In the process, the utility and the symbolic trappings of practices associated with that kill circulate widely across society, supporting the "good life" of people who tell me repeatedly that they move to the Sourlands because of its natural beauty, cultural heritage, and exceptional landscapes they commit to preserving. Palpable and yet typically unspoken, however, is the recognition that in order to preserve their properties they must take advantage of, or live alongside, approaches to the living world that they oppose. Increasingly, newly arrived residents who most identify as conservationists tend to recognize their painful reliance on hunting and hunters most clearly when complaining about damage to fruit trees, at-times fatal automobile collisions with animals, and the debilitating fevers of a Lyme Disease transmitted through ticks that attach to mice and deer attracted by suburbanization.

Another result of hunters' enlistment into the management of deer that reproduce too quickly due to lawns and "No Trespassing" signs is a valorization of a certain type of hunter. Landscapes checkered by roads lack large stands of difficult-to-traverse forest so they support extraordinary numbers of underfed animals, but relatively few mature bucks coveted by trophy hunters. This, alongside regulations that encourage killing does, encourages a special sort of "sport" hunter, one for whom meat is increasingly valuable.

Many of the men who hunt in the Sourlands keep one or more large freezers in basements, a corner of the kitchen, or upon a porch. They reserve the appliances for the results of hunting forays, which may include shooting from the porch. In light of shifting political economic relations and the unlimited number of female deer that Sourlanders may kill, these freezers are an important resource. As a consequence, not quite two hours from New York City and in a region where Land Cruisers with summer beach passes affixed to their bumpers increasingly replace tractors or battered pickup trucks on boulder-strewn, twisting mountain pathways paved only over the last three decades, meat provides an increasingly salient, economically justifiable, rationale to so-called sport hunters.

Attempts to colonize hunters as managers of deer alert us to the breadth, creativity, and genres of the displacements of violence put forth by various actors in the Sourlands today. I am not interested in this in relation to any defense or explanation of hunting as economically or ecologically sensible, but as a means of focusing attention on the form, or materiality, of displacements as they tie into imperial lifeways. Accounts like the hunting narratives so much a part of U.S. national imaginaries and stories of colonial expansion around the world disseminate affect and images in relation to situated viewpoints. Like recipes for skinning or eating game, the aesthetics and techniques of taxidermy, and definitions of "fairness" and "sport" essential to defining hunting as a chase, rather than a slaughter, tales of the hunt are semiotic vehicles that spiral out from the event to reinvigorate and resituate that death, often in another form. These activities, directed at symbolically bringing deer in from the outside, transform that animal into meat, a stuffed display, an actor in a yarn, or a challenge and "opponent" to a hunter locked in a deadly "game." I am therefore interested in the next section of this chapter in ways that a CNN account of philanthropy centers on the distribution of venison in the Sourlands as a form of charity—a rather cynical type of redistribution often linked tightly to the extractivism and intimacies of violence of colonialism by an array of commentators—both represents and participates in transformations and dislocations that conspire to permit empire to become instantiated, and perhaps more visible, as a part of ordinary life.

IDENTITY AND DISPERSION: ENROLLING HUNTERS

In a manner that augmented what seemed its bulging metaphysical unity produced around militaries, oil, cable news, heartfelt messages, and geopolitics, empire seemed to call out to Hunterdon Hunters, and U.S. publics, on

Christmas Eve, 2009. That night, "CNN Newsroom" aired a special segment about a New Jersey institution, with chapters in multiple states, linked tightly to the post-mortem circulation of deer and images of the Second Gulf War. Part of a "Giving in Focus" series, the segment looked at "creative and traditional ways people are giving of their time, their resources and their love, highlighting acts of generosity that can be found not only at the holidays, but throughout the year," and featured a report on a bit of vernacular philanthropy practiced by Hunterdon County-based members of Hunters Helping the Hungry (HHH), a volunteer association.[12] Affiliated with Catholic Charities and founded in 1998 by avowed hunter and master plumber Les Geise, HHH takes deer shot locally to a network of butchers who, for a reduced fee paid by the hunter, prepare the meat for donation to a central food bank. An additional rung of social services institutions then extracts the deer carcasses that have become food, and distributes them to the needy.

While I missed the programming when it first aired, I obtained a transcript from CNN's website after watching it once.[13] My multiple readings of the account bring to light a serialization of images closely related to the management of life itself, in this case in the form of an intense juxtaposition of textual fragments, discursive locations, and voices. The arrayal inserts HHH into a global network of relatively melodramatic, mediatized connections in which truth seems to turns on the production of absent objects. It does so through the circulation of powerful affect and the distribution of knowledge, as opposed to the clarification of analysis and the specification of the content of what is in play. Permit me to be more concrete.

Four modules make up the broadcast: (1) the story of a son and father separated when the boy's mother returned to her native Brazil; after she remarried and passed away, Brazilian courts gave custody of the boy to his stepfather and maternal grandparents, who barred contact with his North American genitor; (2) Hunters Helping the Hungry; (3) an account of the military deployment in Iraq of a father and son, and thus their absence from the Christmas dinner table, and; (4) the revelation that the video bars that made up supposedly coded messages from Al Qaeda, which a government contractor dreamed up to entice the CIA into spending hundreds of thousands of dollars on his decrypting software, were a hoax. In three of its four episodes, CNN constructs or remediates an imagined community by means of a circulation of emotion and animal and human bodies whose representations quite literally flow through the world. Then, in the fourth, CIA-centered vignette, viewers experience an unveiling presented as a truth-making operation. This journalistic truth produced in the wake of the first three accounts corrects the mistaken suspicions of CIA analysts in a way that reveals those experts were duped. On top of this, and peppered throughout the broadcast, are a series of "Merry Christmas" messages phoned in by men and women serving in U.S. forces in Iraq.

Over the course of but a few seconds, the viewer moves from an image of Hunterdon County HHH founder Les Geise in his tree stand or alongside his pickup and a dead deer to the voice of a Private First Class announcing, " 'Hello, I'm PFC Ronnie Lasley with Alpha Company 615, Camp Taji, Iraq. I'd like to say happy holidays to my family back home in Sherman, Texas. I love you. See you soon.' " The intrusion of the voice, as something disembodied and from afar, is especially poignant when read as part of the television transcript: The broadcast, when laid out as a transcript rather than incorporated on video, makes even clearer the extent to which U.S. empire building enters and even conjugates the everyday life of holidays and emotions "back home" in New Jersey.

The intrusions from soldiers in Iraq punctuate stories about the lives of the Americans depicted "back home" to juxtapose the violence of the Mideast conflict, and a boy's perhaps love-filled exile in Brazil far from his father in the United States, with a depiction of deer hunting as a form of philanthropy that brings together the more and less fortunate in the rolling hills of New Jersey. As a document peppered with emotional crises and nuggets of feeling both visual and aural, the transcript hides in plain sight a sense-making operation dependent on circulation or exchange and, finally, a rather hermeneutic unveiling of a con man's artifice aimed at the CIA. This architecture, with its focus on family, its thin development of detail and characters, the text's constant punctuation by soldiers' shout-outs, and an overt reliance on affect, conforms rather tightly to the conventions of melodrama, or an affective field filled with phenomena revealed as not quite what they appear to be. Melodramatic performances of revelation establish the broadcast as an allegory of "seeing beyond appearances, going past how things should be, to seeing how they actually are."[14] How, then, *are* things, in relation to the enrollment of hunters into an affective field that culminates in the realization that a field of bars that supposedly contains a master code is a hoax?

To recap, with a difference: I take CNN's program as roughly isomorphic with a broad U.S. military-industrial-entertainment complex, or as a part of an assemblage we permit to symbolize or conjure up empire in fixed form, so as to talk about a macropolity, and an imaginary, that makes its way across diverse institutions as what Ann Stoler and Carole McGranahan describe aptly as an often mutating, hard to pin down, and nonetheless densely impactful "imperial formation."[15] The message produced in the recruitment of HHH into the imperial broadcast is itself a performance of the practice of meaning making that reveals that there is no secure meaning down there, to be found in codelike form, once the audience considers the evidence. The bars that the con man showed the CIA were precisely that, a set of bars. Significance thus arises in the broadcast by means of the deflection, often affective, from one account, actor, or institution to another. The segment enacts the making of a form of meaning that, like empire, lies in—and is—the deflection or the passing on of affect and message, not in what the narrative or bars point to as a referent or conclusion.

This is a specific form of sense making. Yet its operation is not unknown among members of HHH—at certain points in the year the passing on of the results of a kill becomes a key form of sociality among working-class hunters on and around Sourland Mountain. And hunters and their friends spend many a cold winter night admiring photos showing hunters cradling their just-shot "game" in a technology whose images conform rather rigidly to shifting conventions for showing antlers, the deer's eyes, and the hunter's eyes. Like the CNN broadcast as redimensionalized on paper, and like the CNN broadcast as moving forward through a serialization of emotion punctured by those "serving" abroad, pieces of deer pass through networks and into freezers and onto walls in a process of making and remaking different sorts of meaning. But I am not primarily interested in meaning. I am more interested in the ethical habits that structure that field of dislocation, whether a CNN broadcast or the performance of a hunt.

DEVELOPING ETHICS: DISLOCATION AND MOURNING, OR "THE DAMNED THING WOULDN'T DIE"

Moose, a man who stands over six feet tall, weighs nearly three hundred pounds, and is someone I have feared at times due to his temper, initially surprised me on the day we engaged in rather frank discussion of empathy and fragility around his first kill. Since then, however, I have listened to repeated descriptions of overpowering affect and irrational behavior from Moose and his peers. These men point out that in spite of the shock and contradictory emotions surrounding their first kill, their quite reflexive and public reactions to the death of the animal were quickly papered over as they learned alternative, more appropriate means of commemorating nonhuman death—at least in relation to how they emerged from the woods and how their community of hunters defined appropriateness. Among the most salient, accepted means of commemorating the death of a deer are taxidermy, photography and record books, giftings of venison, recounting stories, caring for the biological well-being of a species so as to retain healthy individuals to be killed, and use of muzzle-loading guns or bows thought to tie the hunter to tradition, especially via Native American and colonial-era lore and figures. Adulthood, rationality, masculinity, insertion into tradition, and the very status of "hunter" and human claimed by Moose and his peers thus rest on learning to commemorate the taking of a life, and to do so via a specific example of provisioning, connection to nature and tradition, or participation in activities such as Hunters Helping the Hungry's philanthropic efforts to displace and remember the hunt. It is not simply the hunt, but its dissemination, that is integral to what makes and keeps the human human.

This is an insight explored in evolutionary theories and at length by anthropologists interested in demonstrating how everything from gendered social structures, to landed property, and on to kinships systems depend and even arise in relation to hunting techniques and manipulations of the fruits of hunting. In such accounts the nonhuman animal as bearer, or form, of a life taken becomes abstracted into food chains, natural orders, and hunting as a practice long marked as constitutive of the very sociality of, and thus the basket of exceptional qualities that characterize, the human species. The violence of the hunt becomes distributed across new affective registers of possession, heritage, and even participation in the renewal of landscapes molded by men who kill deer. Hence, as illustrated in this chapter's opening vignette, a learned failure to mourn in a sense marked as socially appropriate to recognizing other members of our species both separates and fuses the human and nonhuman animal. And if one focuses on hunting, deer, and their death and modes of consumption by hunters and their neighbors, this failure to mourn appropriately does so in manners that, as Judith Butler has put it in a rather different context, "authorize us to become senseless before those lives we have eradicated, and whose grievability is indefinitely postponed" as ostensibly sovereign hunters imagine themselves as higher order beings immune to, or warding off, injury.[16]

A satisfying or final account of a violent subject who wards off all entailments of an originary or even ongoing violence, and thus undergoes final redemption as ethically one with the world, is as uncommonly realized in dominant modern philosophy and religious and literary traditions as it is definitive of the end of history. Such an account is similarly far from representative of Moose's life, and experience. In 2011, sitting next to him at a local bar that will appear as an ethnographic site in subsequent sections of this chapter, I quizzed Moose about shooting deer, something I have never practiced in spite of my time spent in the highlands of New Jersey. Moose responded by returning to his "first time" and added morsels of information he had left out earlier. "I froze while I shivered. I was bleating like a little lamb with its tail flapping around while that thing bled out in the field," he admitted, chuckling wryly and repeating basically what he had told me before. But he continued, "The doe wouldn't die. The damned beautiful thing wouldn't die. It walked, with its guts hanging out, along the clearing. I chased after it. It looked at me with those big brown eyes. The damned thing wouldn't die. I remember my grandfather told me to talk to it."

Like his recourse to profanity in relation to an animal he often treats linguistically in an almost mystical sense, Moose's emphasis on a "thing" in telling how his grandfather instructed him to speak to the animal that gazed at him indexes the emotion of the moment, and his act of recollecting for me the act, of death. It also rehearses the borders of the human and animal, borders that he violated on the occasion of his first kill as the affective charge seized him, overwhelmed him, and yanked him from the category of proper, emotionally controlled, subject. Only his grandfather's hug—and that man's ensuing tutelage in how to clean, skin, and then divide up and preserve a deer and the moment of its kill—brought him back into humanity. Moose's experience, then, is part of a larger human and nonhuman interface around killability and ethical attention to the sufferings of proximate others. His emphasis on eyes, and faces and recognition, recalls not simply the ethics of Emmanuel Levinas, but his interpellation by the suffering animal and status as another animal. As biological anthropologist Matt Cartmill has put it, "hunting takes place at the boundary between the human domain and the wilderness, the hunter stands with one foot on each side of the boundary and swears no allegiance to either side. He is a liminal and ambiguous figure who can be seen as a fighter against wildness, or a half-animal participant in it."[17]

Wild or "vestigial" human populations associated with nonwhite or colonized peoples and with irrational appetites or a primitive susceptibility to moral infection have long helped secure modernity by serving as internal others within metropolitan projects. Symbolic primitives and children open to infection such as "rednecks" or such as Moose on the day he first shot a doe; hunters and their moral evaluation by neighbors, state agents, and the U.S. media and academia have girded not simply in the nation's westward expansion, but public norms and affective tableaux basic to the U.S. as a polity. Hunters are people almost always potentially out of place—and thus potential non- or quasi-humans, around whom congeal perceptions of injury, loss, and recuperative politics. But here Moose, in quiet confidence, speaks about internalization and attempts to deflect not simply what I will explore below as his tarring and feathering as a supporter of empire, but the violence of the kill that seems to attach most insistently to him in relation to practices that certain of his neighbors may take as signs of barbarity. Yet I will suggest that these practices are also a technology deeply imbricated with particular forms of ethics.

Moose makes clear that it is difficult to ignore that, however much it is mythologized, the actual practice of hunting is violent, often gory, and may present marked dangers for the hunter. Hunters face not simply the much-lampooned danger of being shot by a fellow hunter or injured by their quarry, but more quotidian injury. One in three of the over 80 percent of Midwestern hunters who hunt from a tree stand will fall, and about 3 percent of those will suffer permanent disability.[18] But Moose emphasizes his social and economic precarity, rather than the physical precariousness of the hunt.

As a resident of New York who spent summers in the Sourlands as a child, I have known Moose for decades. Each June when we would catch up as I returned to the "country," I would hear about progress and pitfalls experienced at the edges of a metropolitan area in which I also made a life. The child of an "old" Sourlands family in that his father was descended from settler families who arrived in the region from England in the nineteenth century and his mother's side arrived in the region with the eastern European immigrants of the early twentieth century., Moose tells me he has no place in the Sourlands today. A high school graduate and union carpenter, grinding days on his knees have produced forms of arthritis that make it difficult to put in a full day's work. Family and friends are increasingly distant, forced from the Sourlands by taxes and land prices. Divorced and the father of three boys who live with their college-educated mother in a subdivision funded by her work in the "Route 1 High-Tech Corridor" adjoining Princeton, Moose hangs on in his mother's basement. Meanwhile, in early 2017 the bar that serves as his most important site of sociality has been put up for sale.

"When I get into the woods, John, I come alive. When I sit there and figure out where I stand it's all a lot easier than before," Moose has repeated to me on multiple occasions in multiple ways. Claims about the restorative qualities of the natural world or the vitality that precedes a death, and especially one's own death, are common in my world. Yet a vehemence becomes apparent when Moose speaks of escape by means of hunting, from trying to survive in a region where he increasingly sees himself as a problem, or at very least a person out of place in relation to his more middle-class neighbors and their approaches to species, planetary, and individualized life: "You know me, I like frogs. I always did. A nice fat, bulging bullfrog. I used to like catching them, feeding them bugs, and letting them go. Sometimes I'd catch a bass with one. But I'm not going to go to some special event where they teach city people how to look at frogs and then claim they're saving the Sourlands. I mean, did you see the water gushing down that deep cut and stone channel into Stony Brook the . . . [well-off, suburban family] family have put in to keep their 'mansion' dry?"

Environmental engineers confirm Moose's assessments about a shared environment, pointing out that waterways now ricochet between peak and low flows. As water levels vary rapidly, turgidity increases, oxygen levels drop, and Sourlands streams that were once perennial go dry as moisture that once percolated through scree or between vernal pools floods down blacktop and gutters. These respond to people's desires for easy access to town, dry basements, and the efficient septic systems that have replaced packed dirt roads and dirt floors, linoleum, gray water sinks that discharged directly into gardens, and outhouses. Perhaps as a result, Moose's sojourns in the woods, and the joy he now takes in expert techniques he claims to have developed for skinning deer carcasses and draining them of blood in anticipation for butchery are tempered by the realization that his "escapes" are not discoveries of who he really is, but unresolved situations. "I don't know how long I'm going to be able to continue hunting," he has told me repeatedly. At times, the possibility of no longer hunting the Sourlands arises from the possibility that he will escape chronic underemployment, and join relatives in southern New England who promise well-paying jobs that might not wreck his body. Sometimes he worries that injuries incurred "on the job" will make it impossible to scramble across boulders and downed trees. At other moments he bewails the loss of "open" land, or the sorts of commons owned by neighbors who once permitted hunters and neighbors, and thus hunters treated as real neighbors, to hunt their lands. He also laments his own inability to ever earn, much less save, enough money to purchase land on Sourland Mountain.

Yet Moose is not looking to escape. "I hold on because my kids are here, my parents. But this is also where Jack Hellerich taught me to track a deer and Mrs. Manasek stopped feeding her geese and came across the road to show me a better way to skin it." It is also where, he tells me over and over, he'd like to do right for himself. Musing about doing right for oneself, on the part of a boy who told me he first realized he would indeed become a man when his grandfather told him "it's gonna be all right," is a rather active mode of attention to the self. "Jack had this contraption in his shed. Chains with these big butcher's hooks he got somewheres. He taught me how to hang the deer up on the chains. The hide peels right off."

Moose's worldview put forth across the years, in bits and pieces and often in relation to hunting or the woods, includes descriptions of the importance of his regular service as a youth counselor at a local Roman Catholic Church. His accounts also lead me toward an ordinary ethics that mitigates against universal principles of morality, even as many institutions with which he is involved seek to universalize a particular moral positioning, as well as overt concerns with care of the self via some supposedly agentive expertise in rational contemplation. Here attention to language, to gesture and corporeal disposition, and thus to mundane acts of setting aside, of forgiving, and of sharing the violence and efficacy of the hunt come together in Moose as a threatened, modern primitive who walks a bit too much like the animal. This assertion may shock those invested in particular forms of interspecies care such as animal rights projects or vegetarianism, or bounce up against some universalizing form of ethics when considered in relation to a relationship to self and the good that runs through the killing of deer. It is thus important to emphasize that I do not link ordinary ethics and hunting to deny or denigrate the perspectives of anyone who advocates nonviolent, interspecies care. Instead, I am interested in expanding not only on, as Bhrigupati Singh and Naisargi Dave have put it, "'How ought one to live,'" but also a darker question of "How do we kill?"[19] In turning to an ethics composed in relation to or contemplation of violence, I emphasize that the life that Moose leads has led him into a positioning "as a dimension of everyday life in which we are not aspiring to escape the ordinary but rather to descend into it as a way of becoming moral subjects."[20]

The ordinary into which Moose descends is an ordinary that defies cleanly linear time, and whose violence stops up, becoming thick and stigmatizing, as he comes to realize that he can no longer circulate effectively through networks of friends and neighbors. People who prepare and eat venison, or who exchange vegetables from large gardens, gather species of nuts increasingly unknown or exoticized by neighbors, or red raspberries in late July and blackberries in August, are increasingly absent. Many neighbors—even those willing to look beyond strip malls and online ordering for their provisioning—are no longer present in July. They prefer, and are able, to take seaside vacations not to the Jersey Shore, but to places like Martha's Vineyard or Miami, rather than tend gardens and fields or split firewood for the fall. Yet gathering raspberries, fishing, marking deer habits in the hope of returning to shoot the animals "in season," and tending to family gardens while working on farms, is precisely how Moose spent his summers while growing up. My description of this lifeway stares back at me, however, almost as if I have lifted it from a vintage Sears catalogue or a worn edition of *Huck Finn*. But it is as accurate a representation as I can muster of what Moose loves, what he finds ordinary and what establishes that ordinary, how for decades he contributed to his family and to making ends meet while eating morsels from the woods, and what he continues or expands upon in improving himself. Moose is an anachronism seemingly more at home in foundational American fictions than in his own home, and in the forests and "No Trespassing" signs that now surround it.

Moose kills, and given dominant contemporary configurations of this action in the Sourlands, he relates in an anachronistic vein to his environment, his community, and nonhumans for whom he lies in wait. Prominent local critics of hunting argue to me that this places him on the wrong side of history, or at very least, at an earlier, violent, node of historical development that defenders of hunting such as Moose nonetheless valorize. As in the colonial world, in which forms of expert knowledge arose as means of contrasting a supposed subaltern propensity for violence or infection by savage dispositions to metropolitan modernity and rationality, an organizing language for this detachment involves "tradition." For Moose, tradition is an umbrella under which preparation for the hunt, postkill rituals, manners of relating to deer outside hunting season, and techniques for dividing up meat all fit neatly and discursively. It is where he finds himself at even as many of his neighbors define that tradition as something violent and out of place.

By hitching themselves to traditions, hunters such as Moose wallow in practical activity to produce the human immanently, out of everyday struggle projected back in time. In invoking tradition, then, Moose does more than appeal to the past and an emotional structure reducible to strategic essentialism or invented positions: he positions himself as part of a broad ethics within which hunting stands as part of shared inheritances—and thus the very weave and weft of those ethics and associated technologies as performed, very ordinarily, across time. Moose, like many of his fellow hunters, justifies or renders sensible these actions by pointing to the practices' inherited status, and their putative role in making humans human by defining the bases or activity of connection, and thus of self-making. In fact, Marc Boglioli, in an ethnography of hunters in modern Vermont, refers to the cultural expressions that so comfort Moose when he prepares dead deer for their journey out into social networks, as "gestures of respect."[21] But how does one deal ethically with gestures of respect when, if, "what gives power to" these specific, historically developed versions of the subject "that gives all kinds of reasons for its killings while at the same time refusing to call those killings 'killings' at all," is a rendering "of the subject's own destructiveness righteous and its own destructibility unthinkable"?[22]

SHARED PRECARITY AND INTERIOR FRONTIERS

Ecological and social changes, like historically fluctuating idioms for expressing those changes and crafting selves, rose to the surface at a February 2016 event sponsored by the Sourland Conservancy. The conservancy is an active, sophisticated community preservation group, founded in 1986 and dedicated to Sourland habitats and residents' quality of life. Committed to maintaining "open space," challenging polluters and invasive species, and preserving farmland, the Conservancy boasts a seemingly well-chosen and active board that includes physicists, chemists, environmental engineers, educators, and financial and political leaders committed to preservation. Held in the Sourlands bar and restaurant called "Hillbilly Hall"—not an ethnographic moniker, but in fact the venue's real name—that, tellingly, was listed with its five-acre plot for sale for nearly two million dollars just a few months after the talk, the public Conservancy event featured a local historian who entitled his recounting of legends and mysterious tales of violence, lawlessness, and frontier-style bravery "Explore the Dark Side of the Sourlands—Missing Persons, Murders, Bootleggers, Bandits and Other Unsavory Characters." Hillbilly Hall is not far from Highfields, the seven-hundred-acre estate to which Charles Lindbergh moved to escape publicity after his transatlantic flight, and the site of the kidnapping followed by murder of his toddler son in 1932. Each hunting season, the bar and its roadside sign that advertises "Moonshine 'n Vittles" serve a rather different Sourlands constituency as a Department of Natural Resources deer-tagging and -weighing station.

A local news site reported that the public historian "told the crowd of about 85 that the remoteness and terrain of the Sourlands made it a refuge for desperate and impoverished people who bred indiscriminately, distilled bootleg liquor and murdered each other and intruders with impunity. 'There weren't many nice people who moved up here because it was scenic,' he said wryly."[23] The description put together by a community historian born in a nearby county seat, and who now lives in the rural area near Hillbilly Hall, drew on histories of a different sort of Sourlands "characters" whose actions have supposedly led to some sort of legacy that animates the Mountain today. Among the historical figures both celebrated and denigrated in the talk were moonshiners, slaves who regained their freedom, fiddlers, kidnappers, thieves, and murderers.

While I did not attend the discussions at Hillbilly Hall, on another occasion, at the bar and later in the parking lot, I learned about the event with two people who had been present. "Bill" and "Theresa," two graduate students from Princeton University, attended the talk after Hillbilly Hall's Yelp ratings as a "dive bar" alerted them to the possibility of alternative, seemingly salt-of-the-earth, experiences atop Sourland Mountain. They decided to attend the Sourlands Conservancy fundraiser. When we discussed it subsequently, after I bumped into them when they had returned to Hillbilly Hall for drinks one evening, they expressed disgust at, and generalized the identity of, one of the historical archetypes trundled out in the presentation. This man, Millard Whited, was a "lanky" Sourlander whose protruding ears, backwoods demeanor, and inability to conform confidently to a single narrative on the witness stand subjected him to derision as "the redneck witness" during his testimony at the trial in 1934 of the Lindbergh kidnapper.[24] "Whited was a redneck like the guy at the bar tonight," Bill told me some eighty years later. He spoke in relation to a man at the bar that evening who held forth, while making racist statements about other people to the couple, about his attachment to the Mountain and prowess in fisticuffs. Theresa noted, in recounting her version of the incident, that the green of the camouflage used by Hillbilly Hall patrons contrasted with the gray or tan fatigues that emerged after the Gulf Wars in ways that unnerved her since the fabric brought her back to images of a Vietnam War that ended before her birth. This is an important statement given my interest in the ways that hunting, and violence, make U.S. empire thinkable.

By associating hunters and the military within a familiar script marked aesthetically and epochally by a camouflage that makes it unhomely, Theresa historicized the offense at the bar and connected to a national imaginary and a moment she did not experience. For Theresa, a shift in colors and a connection of hunters and empire in postmemory made racism, as well as her own elaboration within that empire as a flawed but lived and remembered formation, palpable and sensical, in a comparative or expansive sense. Bill seemed to agree, telling me what I wrote down later as "They're a bunch of rednecks. Theresa's right. Just look at the camo. Look at them when they pull that plastic contour map out from behind the cigarette machines and lay it on the pool table to plot their deer killing. I'm not coming back here. Racist bar. Racist people. Next thing I know that guy's gonna be telling me he was at the battle of Fallujah, killing Muslims."

In pointing out how a white Sourlands identity might attach commonsensically and troublingly to racism and empire, neither I nor the two visitors appear guilty of misrepresenting U.S. history or social relations. There is little doubt, as made evident by the xenophobia, racism, and willingness in 2017 of the Trump administration to employ force or argue that Iraqi oil should have been sequestered by the United States, that racism, governance, the resentful politics of a white working class, and U.S. empire too often fit together in ways that have impacted the nation, and the world. Indeed, one reason I undertake ethnography in the Sourlands is to understand how violence, attachment to nation, and imperial vocations mesh, in the hope that such an understanding might be used to break up such correlations in the future.[25] But over the course of this research I have noted how often people come quickly to the conclusion that rural whiteness and an express racism, rarely attached to more cosmopolitan folk, go together with an imperialist vocation like peas in a pod.

Linda, a seventy-eight-year-old retired schoolteacher from New York City, who in 2001 moved with her husband, a former accountant, to a newly constructed, approximately three-thousand-square-foot home on a twenty-acre plot in Hunterdon County, told me: "The problem here is the hunters. They mess the woods up, putting up tree stands, throwing around their beer cans, planting stuff in clearings to attract animals, and killing deer instead of preserving nature and caring for native plants. I go out and at the edges of my property, along the brook, I find bullet casings [spent shotgun shells] and beer cans. They have no respect for nature. They just want to kill things and disturb these woodlands."

Most ecologists and wildlife biologists I have consulted in the Sourlands disagree. They argue that the woodlands have been disturbed more significantly by lawns, shrubbery, golf courses, shopping malls, subdivisions, and the type of long-drivewayed, multi-million-dollar home in a clearing owned by Linda. Nonetheless, in a fusion of phenomena and social formations common in discussions of empire whose scripts police what may be properly considered imperial or an imperial effect, Linda went on in her conversation with me to compare hunters' camouflage clothing to military garb. She suggested angrily that hunters sought to relive what she imagined as their experiences in Iraq, where, she told me, "they learn to kill. All these rednecks love guns. I don't know why they like shooting things in the woods so much! Messing up my woods."

Linda continues important themes brought up by Theresa. Their enunciations make sense in relation to a tradition apparent in a *New York Times* article from 1919, whose author worries that a decline in Eastern deer herds and changes in game laws represents "a serious phase to this hunting problem which has to do with national sociology. Students of social science the world around have always ascribed to the American a . . . superiority of manhood because of his early training and natural propensity for hunting. For sharpshooters and marksmen the American army has no equal."[26]

Linkage of hunting to prowess in war and manhood continues to inflect what may and may not be said in recounting an entwined natural and political history of the United States. In the hands of politicians such as Theodore Roosevelt, the linkage has long united, typically in relation to myths of the frontier and settler whiteness, the "Big Stick" of nascent twentieth-century U.S. imperialism, national landscapes, and the inculcation of manly virtue.[27] I will not excavate here the "why" and the "how" of Linda's, or Bill's or Theresa's, assumption that hunters are imperial agents. This has been undertaken in a variety of ways in relation to a larger story of U.S. expansion and environmental violence.[28] So too have studies of poachers and state control, "slob hunters" who litter woods with beer cans, and debates about "sport hunting," techniques, indigenous people's ostensibly unethical or "unsportsmanlike" hunting methods, and fairness that shifted across classes and regions as hunting became a staple in the national state's management of public opinion, wild animal populations, and rural people's calendars and practices.[29]

I am more interested in how Linda makes apparent her concerns and position as a defender of wildlife by means of a symbolic violence and denigration that draws upon, or draws into an imperial imaginary as actors, her neighbors who hunt. She positions them as savages, close to the very beasts hunters set themselves off against in their arguments about the economic roles, sociality, tradition, rationality, efficacy, and evolutionary importance of the hunt. Within such an emphasis on hunting as tradition and an engagement with nature, it functions much like Linda's garden, which concerns her year-round and keeps her supplied across the winter with sauces, canned vegetables, tubers, and dried spices.

Linda struggles against voracious deer, usually by means of an eight-foot-high "chicken wire" fence supported by stakes cut from the forest. She composts carefully, worries about tomato blight, and reads old almanacs and gardening books in concocting "natural" recipes to combat the disease. Linda says such "traditional" sources help her return to a moment before citizens in a "disposable society forgot how to take care of gardens, and themselves." They also put her in touch with a time she remembers mainly from photographs, or the times during World War II when as a child she would accompany her parents on trips from Manhattan to their Victory Garden set up in the Bronx. Linda ascribes her gardening skills to her attachment to an earlier moment in U.S. consumerism, a moment prior to the "disposable" society she condemns and still marked by the struggles of world war and the overcoming of the Depression.

Efforts to provision in the Sourlands continue to take place in a number of spheres, and not only through hunting. But as should also be clear from pronouns across this chapter, I know of no women who hunt Sourland Mountain. Yet I have talked at length with many, like Linda, whose declarations about their gardens recall rather closely the extent to which an emphasis on ordinary tasks and the production or exchange of everyday items leads to a discussion of tradition and production of the self in relation to what deer hunters also portray as nature. Gardens as renewal, and senses of self that emanate from productive activities, play a role for Linda and her neighbors that is remarkably consonant with hunting as represented by the few men who still hunt in the region. However, Linda's permanence on Sourland Mountain and version of tradition are not threatened by the forces that encircle Moose, and her circulation of vegetables does not touch upon accepted, or habitual, manners of recognizing violence.

Comfortably retired, Linda does not depend on gardening to make ends meet. While she is happy to save money, a major source of satisfaction arises from her creative ability to make things grow, and then to exchange or give them to friends and neighbors. At the same time, she spends thousands of dollars a month with local tradespeople like Moose so as to keep up and "improve" her large, newly built home planted atop an embankment intended to make a muddy hillside buildable. Linda sometimes offers proficient craftspeople some preserves when they complete jobs for which she pays an hourly or piecework wage. More than one man who has worked for Linda has remarked that if she would only permit him to pick the raspberries rotting on her bushes or hunt deer from atop her septic field, neighbors might share venison, clear snow without charge, or even prop up her mailbox the next time vandals knock it down.

Anthropologists are well known for bewailing losses associated with capitalist modernity. My goal in quickly comparing hunting and gardening in a nostalgic mode is to gesture at real change, but also to illustrate something of how the two practices separate out a man configured by many new neighbors as a violent figure and a woman who condemns hunting and sees herself as a steward of nature. Yet the two share a relationship to provisioning, and thus displacements of what has long been held apart in social and intellectual life as the natural world.

CONCLUSION

This chapter has followed displacements of killing, and the materiality of interaction between humans and deer, in order to take seriously some of the ways that dislocations, and even disavowal, may function as an agonistic type of connection. This gives rise to two principal arguments. First, techniques for dispersing and in effect expanding the range of the violence of the kill, so often represented as violent propensities or a lack of civilization by critics and "tradition" or sociality by practitioners, make up a contradictory form of mourning in the Sourlands. In circulating objects and cultural performances, this mourning entifies and brings into dialogue the violence of hunting and the violence of living a life in a United States seemingly dependent on inequalities and imperial connections. As a result, hunters' circulation of the results of their forays is not some neat, redemptive act that isolates violence or the hunt as a thing in itself. Nor is it simply some functional result of an adaptive strategy, which might be "explained" as an origin or source of the human. Instead, hunting spreads out symbolically to take on a hybrid, or blurred status reminiscent of, and useful for analyzing, the "messy, troubled spaces of colonial lineages" that are nonetheless tied intimately to life, death, and evaluations and gradations of humanity.[30]

Second, displacement reiterates a certain experience of living in, accepting, and engaging the ordinariness of, and yet comprehending the extent to which in the Sourlands survival involves—and has long involved—an attempt to flourish in the face of pain. Or, expressed differently, my ethnography of technologies that announce and memorialize the killing of deer by sending the hunt's corporeal and emotional tokens across community circuits suggest that this form of carnal mourning, and commemoration, produces hunting as an often unrecognized performance of working-class engagement with the bowels of a system whose violence toward multiple groups or constituencies is so often denied. This witnessing whose elisions mirror empire's elisions is a troubling responsibility borne in displacement and in working-class Sourlanders' recognition that the medium or practice in which they survive, love, enjoy, and gain identities is painful and perhaps even fleeting, even as it becomes configured as tradition. As such, it is an important road into interpreting empire and its varied forms of occlusion.

Building on his concerns with the extent to which humans are subject and object of knowledge, Michel Foucault described one of the tasks of genealogy as "to expose a body totally imprinted by history, and the process of history's destruction of that body."[31] The history of the Sourlands, and the stories and lifeways described in this chapter, are also a history of ongoing ruin, as well as the construction of an icon of that very process of destruction. One such "body in perpetual disintegration" is the deer, or the sign vehicle and material entity sent across networks it both nourishes and sets apart, and into which it becomes subsumed through consumption and display.[32] As a consummate symptom of ecological crisis that has nonetheless gathered around it an array of practices that respond to the necessity of surviving, and even thriving, in spite of the social marginalization faced by Sourlanders, the body of the deer calls up and bears the marks of the privations that have produced it. Another body in disintegration today is the body of a Sourlands community of working people, now undergoing political economic dispossession.

Eyal Weizman reminds us that, whether you are a "a territory, a photograph, a pixel, or a person, to sense is to be imprinted by the world around you, to internalize its force fields, and to transform. And to transform is to feel pain."[33] Indeed, as Michel Foucault argued so eloquently, interpretation is cutting and agonistic reversal. Sourlanders who labor, hunt, and live, feel pain. And their sensibility to the pain of a deer merges with, and makes apparent, a certain sensibility to the pain of life "on the mountain," as well as the pain of killing that deer as part of a human life. Hunting is not simply killing. Nor is it, when understood as a metonym for a broader, working-class way of

Sourlands life, exactly surviving. And that is why hunting as a practice being displaced in New Jersey provides not only a conceptual guide, but a practical path into how empire consistently assembles and reassembles in novel and deadly manners even in the most violently caring of North American communities.

NOTES

1 Chatterjee, "Empire and Nation Revisited," 487.

2 Bickers, *Empire Made Me*, 1. On blurrings of the violent and the redemptive in empire, see especially Ahuja, *Bioinsecurities*; Goldstein, "Introduction"; Shotwell, *Against Purity*; and Stoler, *Haunted by Empire*.

3 Stoler, *Duress*, 317–19.

4 Cueto, *Cold War, Deadly Fevers*; Hands, *Latin America's Cold War*; Mckiernan-González, *Fevered Measures*.

5 On multicultural initiatives, inequality, and racial politics in Brazil and Colombia in recent decades, see especially Collins, *Revolt of the Saints*; Dawson, *In Light of Africa*; Mitchell, *Constellations of Inequality*; Perry, *Black Women against the Land Grab*; and Wade, "*Mestizaje,* Multiculturalism, Liberalism and Violence."

6 For approaches to ordinary or everyday ethics on which this chapter draws, see especially Biondi, *Sharing This Walk*; Das, "Ordinary Ethics"; and Lambek, "Toward an Ethics of the Act."

7 I am influenced by Taussig's emphasis in "Culture of Terror—Space of Death" on murkiness, rather than clarity or neat taxonomies, as a basic modality of colonial rule and exploitation. On imperial formations as arising in relation to, or even depending on, such fuzziness, see especially Stoler, *Duress*; and Stoler and McGranahan, "Introduction."

8 Goldstein, "Introduction," 11.

9 Stoler, "Imperial Debris," 193.

10 Ortega y Gasset, *Meditations on Hunting*, 48.

11 Capuzzo, "It's in New Jersey, but It Screams Vermont."

12 "Giving in Focus: Twelve Days of Goodness," CNN.com, August 12, 2017, http://www.cnn.com/SPECIALS/2009/giving.in.focus/.

13 "American Dad Reunited with Son in Brazil," December 24, 2009, accessed August 13, 2017, http://www.cnn.com/TRANSCRIPTS/0912/24/cnr.05.html.

14 Benavides, *Drugs, Thugs and Divas*, 11.

15 Stoler and McGranahan, "Introduction: Refiguring Imperial Terrains." See Bickers, *Empire Made Me*, for a discussion of living under empire and working for a colonial elite to which one may never really belong in spite of ostensibly shared racial and European identities. Pérez, *Citizen, Student, Soldier*; and Frederickson, *Cold War Dixie*, provide rather different, yet complementary, optics on everyday life, North American modernity, and imperial formations. Grazia offers a related

examination of the everydayness of empire in constructing post–World War II Europe and its regimes of consumption in *Irresistible Empire*.

16 Butler, *Precarious Life*, xvii.

17 Cartmill, *A View to a Death in the Morning*, 31.

18 Clemons, "One in Three Hunters Will Fall."

19 Singh and Dave, "On the Killing and Killability of Animals," 233.

20 Das, "Ordinary Ethics," 134.

21 Boglioli, *A Matter of Life and Death*, 75–76.

22 Butler, *Frames of War*, 47.

23 Epstein, "'Barbarianism Ruled on Sourland Mountain,' Says Historian," tapinto.net, February 29, 2016, accessed August 13, 2017, https://www.tapinto.net/towns/flemington-slash-raritan/articles/barbarianism-ruled-on-sourland-mountain-histor.

24 Gardner, *The Case That Never Dies*, 201.

25 It is also to take seriously the extent to which talk of voting patterns on the part of a dispossessed and often maligned white working class may draw on scapegoating to cover up support today for conservative or exclusionary positions on the part of wealthier, college-educated whites.

26 Crawford, "Open Season Threatens the Extinction of Deer."

27 Chang, *The Color of the Land*; Kosek, *Understories*; Roosevelt, *Hunting Trips of a Ranchman and The Wilderness Hunter*.

28 Haraway, "Teddy Bear Patriarchy"; Kaplan, "Left Alone with America."

29 See Isenberg, *The Destruction of the Bison*. On masculinity, empire, and the development of "sport hunting" and ideas about fairness, see Reiger, *American Sportsmen*. Yet this "Americanist" literature on an expansive national imaginary associated with settler colonial practices across the present volume is rarely paired, for example, with work on British imperialism and hunting by colonizers and whites in India, Canada, or Kenya. On empire and such partibility, see especially Coronil, "Beyond Occidentalism"; and Stoler, "On Degrees of Imperial Sovereignty." On the widespread representation of hunters as civilizationally unfit in the United States, see Baker, "The Slob Hunter Argument."

30 Stoler, *Duress*, 21.

31 Foucault, "Nietzsche, Genealogy, History," 148. On ruin and ruination, see especially Collins, *Revolt of the Saints*, and Stoler, "Imperial Debris."

32 Eiss, "Hunting for the Virgin," presents a different, but complementary, analysis of meat, memory and the material semiotics of deer.

33 Weizman, *Forensic Architecture*, 129.

From Exception to Empire 22

Sovereignty, Carceral Circulation, and the "Global War on Terror"

DARRYL LI

Umar and Imad were deported from Bosnia-Herzegovina within months of one another, in the aftermath of the September 2001 attacks in New York and Washington. One morning in January 2002, after dispersing the protesters outside, the police took Umar and five other Algerians from Sarajevo's jail. The men, after settling in Bosnia during and after the war in the 1990s, mostly worked for Islamic charities. A local court had ordered charges against them for plotting to attack the U.S. and U.K. embassies dropped due to lack of evidence, so they were surprised to find themselves transported to the airport. Years later, Umar would recall the cold of that morning. "We were wearing thin coveralls, like the ones on gas station attendants. It felt like it was twenty degrees below zero." Several months earlier, Imad, an Egyptian who had come to Bosnia in the name of jihad before settling and marrying a local woman, had a similar experience. After two and a half months awaiting trial for using a false name, he was handed an order for his release. Policemen grabbed him from the courthouse, drove him to a new building, and left him shackled to a radiator overnight. In the morning, an officer came carrying a black hood and duct tape. "I understood what would come next," Imad said later. He would be bound, blindfolded, and put on a plane with another Egyptian veteran of the war. When the policeman apologized and said he was following orders, Imad replied understandingly, " 'Carry out your orders, just don't forget this day and what you have done.' "[1]

Umar and Imad were among several thousand Arabs who arrived in Bosnia during its 1992–95 war to serve in the predominantly Muslim army, work for Islamic charities, or both. They were among the few who stayed on after the war, married, and started families, taking on Bosnian citizenship. Both were swept up in the worldwide U.S.-driven hunt for "out-of-place Muslims"—immigrants and travelers who arouse suspicion for moving across the Global South.[2] Both were arrested and deported at the behest of the U.S., their Bosnian citizenships revoked. But their fates were different.

Umar and the other Algerians were sent to Guantánamo Bay, Cuba (GTMO). Their case became a global cause célèbre: because they were captured far from battlefields and deported in violation of local judicial processes, the "Algerian Six" dramatized the "Global War on Terror" (GWOT) as a campaign without clear geographical, temporal, or legal boundaries (using the national security state's terminology and acronyms, such as GTMO and GWOT, is here an attempt to jar the reader rather than demonstrate mastery of technocratic knowledge). The incident generated a trail of litigation in Bosnian, U.S., and European courts. *Boumediene v. Bush*, the U.S. Supreme Court decision permitting GTMO detainees to challenge in civilian courts their imprisonment, bears one of the men's names.[3] At long last, the men had a habeas corpus hearing in 2008: Umar and four others were exonerated and released.[4] Imad's case is not as well known, but no less disturbing: he was repatriated to Egypt, his birthplace. Reportedly tortured before his conviction by a military tribunal, Imad was finally released in 2009. Although a Bosnian court has found his deportation unlawful, Imad remains unable to return to his once-adopted country, a situation that has forced his Bosnia-born wife and children to uproot themselves and relocate to Egypt.[5]

In this chapter, I argue that notions of sovereignty—and specifically the logic of sovereign exception—prevalent in anthropology fail to capture crucial dimensions of the so-called GWOT insofar as they focus solely on the relationship between sovereign power and its *interior* without reference to all that remains outside, including other sovereigns. In contrast, a nuanced analysis of the circulation of bodies between the carceral spaces of U.S. empire emphasizes an understanding of sovereignty as multiple and disaggregated. The most visible aspects of this circulation are extraterritorial sites and extraordinary legal categories. But if the image of an island prison is meant to convey Guantánamo's allegedly special status outside the law, one must also bear in mind that archipelagos are only the above-water aspects of larger interlinked, submerged formations. For each extraterritorial and extraordinary prison like GTMO, there are many more "ordinary" prisons and detention sites run by other governments in their own territory. These act as sorting centers and dumping grounds for people detained at the behest of the United States.

Theorizing sovereignty as relational and multiple highlights a distinguishing feature of U.S. hegemony: the mediation of unequal relations in a world order based on nominally equal sovereign states. The juridical form of sovereignty is about more than the exercise of legal authority; it also entails formal responsibility, especially vis-à-vis other sovereigns. Much work of U.S. hegemony is about calibrating the relationship between authority and responsibility, with the goal of satisfying strategic goals while displacing burdens onto client regimes. Attention to sovereignty's multiplicities is thus central to approaching ethnographically an empire that is sustained through much of the world *without* formal U.S. rule. Kwame Nkrumah described this neocolonial dynamic as "the worst form of imperialism. For those who practise it, it means power without responsibility and for those who suffer from it, it means exploitation without redress."[6]

This dynamic is not particular to the GWOT, as the persistent problem of sovereign debt for postcolonial states makes painfully clear. But the GWOT presents an opportunity to retheorize forms of U.S. global power, especially in relation to the work of Giorgio Agamben: Despite the widespread appropriation and critique of Agamben's work in relation to the GWOT, his inattentiveness to empire and external dimensions of sovereignty have gone largely unnoticed.[7] Animated by older insights about the nature of U.S. global power—whether it is called imperialism, neocolonialism, informal empire, empire without colonies, or merely hegemony—this essay interrogates Agamben's work in order to develop a different approach. Such a reconsideration is especially relevant in light of how the discourse Agamben helped shape has spread beyond the academy: one day, while perusing a website started by some of my interlocutors—Arab war veterans in Bosnia who had settled in the country and started families there—I found an article by Syrian human rights activist Haytham Manna decrying the GWOT as a "globalization of the state of exception" (ʿawlamat al-ḥala al-istithnāʾiyya).[8]

I draw on thirteen months of fieldwork conducted in Bosnia-Herzegovina, mostly between 2009 and 2013, including multiple interviews in an immigration detention center outside Sarajevo. Over the course of fieldwork, many of my Arab interlocutors came under increasing pressure from the authorities through loss of legal status, detention, and in some cases deportation. Accordingly, my background in human rights organizations and training as an attorney became necessary for maintaining access. Visits to Egypt, France, GTMO, Israel/Palestine, and Yemen also inform these arguments.

Bosnia is a resonant site for the study of U.S. empire and two of its key modes of articulation: the GWOT and liberal humanitarianism. The transfer of the Algerians to GTMO was perhaps one of the earliest signs of the expansive scope of the new campaign. Yet U.S. concerns over armed transnational Islamist activists ("jihadists") in the Balkans, especially Arabs, existed before 2001. In September 1995, the CIA orchestrated the abduction in Croatia of Ṭalʿat Fuʾād Qāsim while en route to visiting the jihad in Bosnia. Qāsim, an Egyptian Islamist living as a refugee in Denmark, was sent home and "disappeared" shortly thereafter.[9] This was the first known case of what would become known as "extraordinary rendition," or the abduction and transfer of individuals to their home countries for interrogation.[10] When the United States decided to impose a solution to the Bosnian war, a key demand was the expulsion of "foreign fighters." Only a minority, like Imad, remained in the country as civilians, often marrying locally and taking Bosnian citizenship.[11]

Before Bosnia became part of the everywhere/nowhere battlefield of the GWOT, it was a node in the other dominant mode of U.S. imperial power in the post–Cold War era, humanitarian intervention. The Balkan crises, marked by large-scale expulsions and atrocities in the service of creating nationalistically pure territories ("ethnic cleansing"), were a test for Washington at the dawn of the age of U.S. unipolarity. The end of the armed conflict witnessed the emergence of a joint U.S.-EU protectorate over Bosnia, notwithstanding its official status as an independent nation-state. Bosnia's Constitution—literally an annex to the U.S.-brokered Dayton agreement—provided a labyrinthine structure that institutionalized political divisions along nationalist lines. This constitution recognizes three "constituent nationalities" (Bosniaks, Croats, and Serbs) and divides the country into two "entities" that retain governmental power at the expense of the central state: the Federation of Bosnia and Herzegovina—which covers 51 percent of the country's territory and is dominated by Bosniaks and Croats—and the Republika Srpska, reserved for Serbs. The country has a tripartite presidency, reserved exclusively for a Bosniak, Croat, and Serb, respectively. Those who reject or otherwise do not identify with these categories are barred by law from the office.[12] As a result, manifold forms of Euro-American management have been deemed necessary. The Office of the High Representative (OHR), always headed by a European diplomat, maintains the power to remove elected officials and impose legislation; the constitution requires that three of the nine judges on the highest court be foreigners appointed by the president of the European Court of Human Rights. These and other controls make the country a particularly useful site for the study of contemporary empire since scholars are often "less skilled at identifying the scope of empire when the contracts are not in written form, when policies are not signaled as classified, nor spelled out as confidential, secreted matters of state."[13] In Bosnia, however, foreign officials enjoy powers that would be incompatible with conventional notions of national sovereignty, making contemporary forms of empire more open than elsewhere and therefore more amenable to analysis. Yet informal and furtive forms of power continue to be extremely important. In this respect, I thus make use of State Department cables made available by Wikileaks. These identify in detail the extent to which the United States has shaped putatively local campaigns against Arabs in Bosnia. While these provide only a limited view of the post-Dayton protectorate, they nonetheless comprise valuable data until other archival resources become available.

In order to understand to understand the GWOT in relation to U.S. hegemony, let us return to the Algerian Six transferred to GTMO, and to Imad, who was sent directly to Egypt. The United States was intimately involved in both decisions, providing "intelligence" and orchestrating the deportations.[14] In the case of the Algerians, the United States exerted pressure on the Bosnian government to expel the men even after they had been cleared by a local court—notwithstanding Washington's avowed goal of promoting the "rule of law" as a framework for its management of the country. Deputy U.S. ambassador Christopher Hoh famously told Alija Behmen, then prime minister of the federation, that if United States demands were not met, the embassy would be closed and "may God protect Bosnia-Herzegovina."[15] The divergence here is telling: the Algerians were sent to an extraterritorial U.S. prison designed to keep them suspended between regimes of ordinary legal protection, a situation that attracted worldwide attention. But Imad was not held in a space between states. Instead, he was sent home in an official bilateral transfer—putatively an "ordinary" deportation from one country to another, without any U.S. responsibility—and allowed to fall into domestic, national space. The contrasts between the men's fates raise a question notably absent in the interminable debates around the War on Terror: how are decisions made about where to send detainees?

At one level, the explanation is simple: as equal sovereigns, governments make independent decisions about whether to accept the repatriation of nationals captured abroad. But the formal categories of sovereignty and citizenship need to be grounded in the concrete power relations fostered under U.S. hegemony. Egypt was not only ready to take Imad, but its diplomats (and their U.S. counterparts) met with senior Bosnian officials in Sarajevo on the day Imad was stripped of his Bosnian citizenship.[16] In contrast, Algeria refused two requests to accept its citizens. Only then did sending them to GTMO apparently become the favored option.[17] Here Egyptian and Algerian decisions should be understood in the context of the U.S. empire and its shifting modulations. Egypt and the United States enjoyed an extraordinarily close strategic relationship, inaugurated by the Camp David Accords in 1979 and based on billions of dollars of military aid. In the 1990s, collaboration between the two countries' intelligence agencies pioneered the extraordinary rendition program, which grew exponentially during the George W. Bush administration. The strength of this relationship likely explains why only seven Egyptians were known to have been transferred to GTMO, less than 1 percent of the prison's peak population, despite anecdotal evidence suggesting a strong presence of Egyptians among Islamist activists in Taliban-controlled

Afghanistan.[18] It is likely that captured Egyptians were sent directly home and "disappeared." While Algeria was also eager to take advantage of Washington's "War on Terror," it did not enjoy a similarly close working relationship as proxy jailer or torturer. Had U.S. officials not taken an independent interest in those men, the Algerian secret police would have had far less interest in jailing Umar and his compatriots.

Attention to the texture of U.S. relations with client states reveals a loose network of GWOT detention and transfer practices that goes far beyond GTMO to include facilities maintained by the Pentagon and CIA, both secret and semisecret, in Afghanistan, Djibouti, Iraq, Poland, Romania, and Thailand; and, perhaps most numerous and difficult to discern, prisons of U.S. client states such as Egypt, Jordan, Morocco, and Pakistan.[19] This is not a single program or plan, nor even a set of sites per se (since many of them, as we shall see, also perform functions not related to GWOT imperatives), but rather a capacious logic that can appropriate airplanes, hotel rooms, hangars, and other secret or public spaces, subject to civilian or military authority, whether run directly by the United States or other sovereigns. Bodies, data, and other things circulate through this field of relations in accordance with tempos and themes adumbrated by Washington.[20] The itineraries of "out of place Muslims" caught up in the GWOT reflect the heterogeneity of this network: they may be picked up by local police, interrogated by the CIA, sent to U.S. military prisons, then transferred home for imprisonment. Or they may be abducted by the CIA, sent home to be tortured, and then passed back to the United States before eventual repatriation. Multiple variations are possible, and indeed helpful, to preserving the flexibility and relative invisibility of this circulation.

The diffuse reality of U.S. power as seen through GWOT detention practices requires a significant revision to some prevailing theories of sovereignty and emergency, especially those of Giorgio Agamben. Drawing from Carl Schmitt's work on sovereignty, Agamben highlights the logic of exception, or the ability to suspend law without annulling its authoritative force, thereby sanctioning violence that is by definition unlimited yet legitimate. Like Schmitt, Agamben argues that the logic of sovereign exception characterizes modern states and he emphasizes the ultimate indeterminacy of the distinction between rule and exception. He cautions that attempts to limit exceptional powers through increasingly rational regulation miss the ultimately decisionist nature of sovereignty. Yet Agamben moves beyond Schmitt in exploring the subjection entailed by sovereignty: to do so, he turns to the Roman legal category of *homo sacer* (sacred man), or he who can be killed without such an act being considered sacrifice. Homo sacer is a status that exists at the limit of law, which is also sovereign power in its purest form.

Agamben identifies the camp, or a space that may exist anywhere, as the *spatial* expression of sovereign exception, or a generalization of the status of homo sacer. Here the camp is not merely the instantiation of exception, but a fundamental spatial paradigm for thinking modern politics.

Agamben's work resonated at a specific moment; in the decade before 2001, Michel Foucault was arguably the most influential social theorist in Anglophone anthropology. Yet one of the appeals of Foucault's work—that it enabled certain kinds of analytical attention to power outside a formalistic emphasis on the state apparatus and its juridical categories—was precisely what appeared unsatisfactory as scholars struggled to confront forms of state violence that appeared at once "classical" (i.e., shockingly coercive) and frighteningly new. Hence Agamben's *Homo Sacer: Sovereign Power and Bare Life* fortuitously drew attention, as an attempt to link Foucault to Hannah Arendt's work on totalitarianism via a revival of Carl Schmitt.[21] Agamben's arguments seemed to provide a critical lens on violence that spoke to the post-9/11 moment, avoiding typical liberal critiques of the state and self-serving typologies based on "democratic" versus "authoritarian" regimes.

Agamben's work on sovereignty and exception has not escaped critique, most effectively by those who point out that states of exception often look more like states of saturation of ordinary bureaucratic procedures, or a plenitude of law rather than its evacuation.[22] While I share these concerns, the GWOT presents another problem for engaging Agamben's framework: the need to understand sovereignty—and by extension citizenship—in plural rather than singular terms, especially in the context of a contemporary empire that relies on the preservation of *other* states' juridical sovereignty. As Anne Caldwell has argued, "The space of indeterminacy characterizing sovereign power must touch upon another community or the international space where different political groups interact. Those crossings open up a space in which sovereignty can no longer be anchored to the territory of the nation state, nor to one political community."[23] The analysis of sovereignty and law in anthropology too often acts as if what is at stake is a *single* sovereignty that operates according to a spectrum that has absolute direct violence on one end and total abandonment (which is of course another form of violence) on the other. Such an approach must be rethought when confronted with an empire that is premised on multiple sovereignties as a modality of operation and a form of justification. So if we recall the stories mentioned above of prisoners shipped from Bosnia to Cuba and Egypt for various forms of detention, let us turn to Agamben's discussion of Guantánamo:

> Not only do the Taliban captured in Afghanistan not enjoy the status of POWs as defined by the Geneva Convention, they do not even have the

status of persons charged with a crime according to American laws. Neither prisoners nor persons accused, but simply "detainees," they are the object of a pure de facto rule, of a detention that is indefinite not only in the temporal sense but in its very nature as well, since it is entirely removed from the law and from judicial oversight. The *only thing to which it could possibly be compared* is the legal situation of the Jews in the Nazi *Lager* [camps], *who, along with their citizenship, had lost every legal identity,* but at least retained their identity as Jews.[24]

While some may find the comparison between the legal status of denationalized Jews in Nazi camps and prisoners in GTMO hyperbolic, the real problem is that it is factually untrue. As Agamben notes elsewhere, the Nazis were scrupulous about rendering individuals (Jews and others) stateless before deporting them to the camps.[25] The United States, in contrast, depends on these detainees *retaining* their citizenship. This empirical error can be productive nonetheless for understanding something about the U.S. empire not captured by Agamben's domestic notion of sovereignty imagined within the boundaries of a single state.[26] Tellingly, Agamben accuses the United States of "ignoring international law externally and producing a permanent state of exception internally."[27] This dismissal of the United States as "ignoring," rather than appropriating, international law is surprising since the power of Agamben's contribution has derived largely from his attentiveness to the juridical *form* of sovereignty and his consequent refusal to take the state of exception as a solely empirical matter.

Theorizing sovereignty as multiple, rather than singular, through carceral circulation provides a way to approach empire in conceptually richer and historically grounded terms. As mentioned above, different citizenships were pivotal in the sorting of detainees, with repatriation as the default option and direct U.S. control a fallback when states are deemed unwilling or unable to follow Washington's directions. The principle of carceral circulation at work is that it is best to let client states do the dirty work of handling their own citizens. But, if they cannot, then the United States must act directly. In GTMO, the United States hosted delegations from the security services of many states to conduct interrogations of their own nationals.[28] This included even strategic rivals such as China, turning the camp into a sort of photographic negative of a UN, where states at odds with one another in the realm of great power politics may nevertheless cooperate against human rights. To equate statelessness with rightslessness, as Agamben does following Arendt ("lost every legal identity"), is to misunderstand the logic of a U.S. hegemony in which the sovereignty of client states enables the displacement of responsibility, and foreign citizenship provides a physical "address" for eventual deportation.

When Guantánamo is viewed not as an aberration, but as the most visible node of a global network of formal and informal incarceration arrangements, citizenship's importance in determining where detainees are sent and how they are disposed of becomes visible. Rather than debating whether "exceptional" sites are spaces for the absence of law or its excess, we can attend instead to how empire mobilizes multiple state sovereignties as a way of structuring and mediating unequal power relations. For example, the experiences of those captured in Afghanistan differed according to their citizenship. For Yaser Hamdi, U.S. citizenship meant rapid transfer from GTMO to a military brig in the continental U.S. and prompt review of his case by the Supreme Court.[29] For British Muslims, the result was a relatively early return home thanks to pressure from a key U.S. ally. However, for Yemenis, citizenship from a "weak state" condemned them to languish in prison, even when individually cleared for release, simply because their government was deemed incapable of controlling them.

The logic of sending out-of-place Muslims "home" was also at work in the worldwide hunt for alleged "jihadists," including those, like most of the Arabs who fought in the Bosnian war, not affiliated with al-Qa'ida. Imad was one such person. A key figure among Arab fighters in the Bosnian war, he was prominent in proselytizing Bosnians about "correct" (i.e., Salafi) Islam. Such stances drew critiques from the country's Islamic establishment, and few shed tears when he was deported. According to my interlocutors—many of them Imad's former comrades—around the world, other Egyptian veterans of the Bosnian jihad also found themselves captured and repatriated. Reda Seyam, an Egyptian-German national who produced media materials for the fighters, was arrested in Indonesia but had some good fortune; the Germans insisted on escorting him back to their country to keep him out of the CIA's hands.[30] No matter where these men were captured, their fates were generally the same: to be sent "home," either directly or via a detour in some extraterritorial prison.[31] A jarring example of the importance of citizenship in an imperial order based on national sovereignties is Marwan al-Jabur, whom I met in Gaza in 2007. Born in Jordan to Palestinian parents who had earlier lived in Gaza, al-Jabur was raised in Saudi Arabia but lived in Pakistan for most of his adult life. The CIA abducted him in 2004 and he spent the next two and one-half years in secret prisons in Afghanistan and elsewhere. Once the CIA concluded that he should be released, a problem arose: where should he go? Pakistan and Saudi Arabia refused him, so he was flown to Jordan. The Jordanians handed him over to the Israeli secret police, who sent him to Gaza, where he had never spent significant time. As a stateless Palestinian, there was no readily available proxy sovereign to take charge of him: al-Jabur was passed between and along as a kind of unclaimed parcel with no return address.[32]

However unusual or innovative, this broader worldwide formation of detention sites and practices nevertheless emerges from and is marked by a deeper history. Again, we can rethink Guantánamo in relation to a lacuna in Agamben's work: The only reference to colonialism in *Homo Sacer* is an aside locating the origins of the modern camp nearly simultaneously in early twentieth-century Cuba and South Africa, where "a state of emergency linked to a colonial war is extended to an entire civil population."[33] He then moves on to discuss Weimar-era Germany. The reference to Cuba is helpful for exploring the relationship between sovereign exception and imperial order. Cuba's nominal independence and its "voluntary" decision to allow an indefinite U.S. lease on the GTMO base were entwined: U.S. forces landed at Guantánamo Bay while taking the island from Spain in 1898 and have remained ever since, with the lease formalized by the 1903 Cuban-American treaty. Throughout its history in the western hemisphere, the United States has often preferred national independence as a formal framework for keeping smaller powers in line. While the British experimented with messier indirect rule in India, sub-Saharan Africa, Southeast Asia, and some of the Arab lands,[34] the United States, claiming an anticolonial tradition of its own, justified imperial ambitions through a looser relationship between responsibility and control. This would serve Washington well going forward.

As the club of nations expanded after World War I, European powers sought to maintain hegemony through the League of Nations.[35] Here, too, the U.S. approach to empire was useful: while Washington remained outside the organization, it could wield influence through the votes of Latin American client states.[36] After World War II, the United States took the lead in establishing the UN and its family of specialized agencies that mediated tensions between great powers and managed decolonization. In this system, international financial institutions were key in maintaining leverage over postcolonial states in a burden-sharing arrangement with other wealthy states. Against this backdrop, Guantánamo was never a zone of legal exception; it was an exemplary space of indirect rule taken to its limits, "voluntarily" leased out by a local sovereign who ceded all effective control over it at the moment of independence.

THE PLACE OF SOVEREIGNTY

Attention to the interaction between sovereignty's internal and external aspects can help us move away from a limited focus on exception and instead understand the GWOT in broader histories of U.S. empire. Whereas the expulsions mentioned at the beginning of this essay were blatantly extralegal, we can turn now to more "ordinary" cases as reflecting adaptations engendered under the U.S. empire. Let us start with Bosnia's first immigration detention center, the "Reception Centre for Irregular Migrants" in Lukavica, a neighborhood on the outskirts of Sarajevo. Unlike GTMO or the sites normally associated with extraordinary rendition, Lukavica operates under a duly created statutory scheme as a temporary holding facility for those the state wishes to deport.

Nonetheless, before my first visit to the prison in 2009, I received a letter describing it from the children of one of the detainees held there, Abu Hamza:

> You decide to take a taxi up there and every cabbie asks you where it is, because they DO NOT KNOW. And how would they know, when leading to the Center is a gravel path through a part of the forest, that one would never imagine ends at some state institution flying the flag of the European Union? There are actually three barracks, and the grounds [*prizemlje*] are enclosed by a five-meter-high steel structure. Even from outside you can tell that it is sooooo cold in there, since a shack [*baraka*] is a shack, and you can't catch any glimmer of warmth, or anything that tells you this is a place where human beings live.[37]

Abu Hamza's children were right: the taxi driver did not know the route to the center, which is located in a suburb once part of Sarajevo, but now located in Republika Srpska. Each time we stopped for directions, I thought of this letter and the sense it conveyed of heading into a strange land on the other side of a nationalist boundary. In the hills behind the Slavija football club stadium, there was an old Yugoslav army barracks housing Serb refugees from now predominantly Muslim areas of Bosnia, its walls adorned with a spray-painted cross surrounded by four *S*s in Cyrillic script, a popular Serb nationalist symbol.[38] Just up the path beyond the barracks stood the detention center, surrounded by metal fences. Two of the buildings were white-walled one-story structures, the third was the permanent facility, still unfinished and unoccupied. The fence, which also enclosed an exercise yard, was similarly incomplete. Uniformed guards milled about. Over the guard shack at the main gate flew the flags of both Bosnia and the EU, a reminder of the 1.2 million-Euro grant from Brussels that helped fund construction.[39] At that time, the prison held six Arabs. All were long-term residents with Bosnian wives and children, but had been labeled "threats to national security" on the basis of secret evidence. All had been on partial hunger strike for the past weeks; none faced criminal charges.

I arrived as a volunteer with the Helsinki Committee for Human Rights in Bosnia, a local NGO. I had proposed to the Committee that I monitor the conditions at the center and the detainees' cases in light of the hunger strike. I had with me a bag of pears and bottled water since Abu Hamza's children told me the strikers would accept food from visitors. After handing over my phone and passport, I was escorted into one of the prefabricated buildings. I sat in a sparsely furnished room near the entrance. Abu Hamza was escorted into the room a few moments later. His beard covered half of his chest, in accordance with the forms of piety he maintained since his days in the jihad. He wore an orange *jalabiyya* (a long, loose-fitting garment) and a baseball cap. Emblazoned on both was the word *BOSNATANAMO* in black letters, a portmanteau of "Bosnia" and "Guantánamo." Although tired and having lost weight from the hunger strike, he seemed in decent spirits, or at least happy to receive a visitor. The guard left us alone.

Abu Hamza's choice of dress is a barbed allusion to the orange jumpsuits seen on detainees from GTMO and references a common condition: In both Guantánamo and Lukavica Muslim travelers and immigrants—often those embracing visual markers of Islamic piety such as long beards—are detained outside of ordinary legal frameworks on the basis of evidence they cannot see.[40] Yet there are major differences: Lukavica is an "ordinary" immigration prison, a specialized facility that all civilized states are now expected to employ. Although first used to house people, such as Abu Hamza, who had lived in Bosnia and were declared a threat to national security, its nominal purpose is to hold recent migrants on a short-term basis, pending deportation. Authorities were explicit about its nonpunitive function, referring to the detainees as "users" (*korisnici*), allowing them to circulate inside the building, and not forcing them to wear uniforms or conform to kinds of bodily regulation typical in prisons. Management often stressed efforts to comply with "European" standards of efficiency and humaneness. Moreover, detainees declared as threats to "national security," such as Abu Hamza, were entitled to have their detention regularly reviewed by courts, albeit according to nonexistent standards that have amounted to rubber-stamping. The center was not used to interrogate and torture, and relations with the authorities were relatively positive in the first few years (though this would change). Perhaps most important, detainees could receive family visits, something never permitted at GTMO.

More important than comparing and contrasting the conditions in and legal frameworks for GTMO and Lukavica, however, is situating them in a broader framework of techniques and adaptations in U.S. empire. Lukavica's apparent adherence to legalism—as opposed to GTMO's reputation for "lawlessness"—was shaped in part by the fallout from the immediate post-9/11 deportations. The Algerian group and Imad were stripped of their citizenships in a summary manner and expelled with little or no legal process, producing a number of headaches for local authorities later on: the Algerian incident sparked a backlash among some Bosnian Muslims, as well as sharp criticism from European and UN officials. The Human Rights Chamber of Bosnia-Herzegovina, a hybrid local-international court, found violations of basic human rights in both cases—although tellingly, its jurisdiction did not allow it to rule on the actions of the United States and other external actors. Subsequent efforts to remove suspicious Arabs therefore had to proceed in a more legalistic fashion. This reflected a shift in the U.S. role, away from influencing individual deportation decisions and toward rewriting laws and helping to build an infrastructure for broader security agendas.

In late 2005 a special state commission was afforded powers to revoke naturalizations granted since independence in 1992. The review process was aimed ostensibly at cleaning up naturalization records in general. But officials made little secret that the priority was dealing with suspicious Arab ex-fighters. Notably, one of the few restrictions on its powers was that they could not be used to render anyone stateless—*pace* Agamben, foreign citizenship remained crucial.[41] This was not only important, but explicit: by law, the nine-member official state body reviewing naturalizations—often considered a core part of sovereign decision-making—included three foreigners. This quota was larger than those for any of the country's three constituent nationalities.

A U.S. Army officer and a British immigration official were appointed to the State Commission. The chairman, assistant security minister Vjekoslav Vuković, was close to the U.S. embassy and took calls from American officials several times when I interviewed him in 2006. In cables to Washington, the U.S. embassy in Sarajevo described the denationalizations as a "top USG counterterrorism priorit[y]" and assured superiors that "we are working with Bosnian law enforcement agencies to ensure they are making adequate preparations for an eventual deportation of Abu Hamza."[42] Unsurprisingly, the State Commission met behind closed doors and canceled some 660 Bosnian citizenships, mostly of Muslims. Although many of those denationalized were living abroad and may not have developed close ties with the country, the focus of the effort was on several dozen Arabs who had settled in Bosnia. Abu Hamza was the best known of this group.

As the State Commission produced newly "foreign" subjects, an infrastructure to dispose of them began to develop with the establishment of an immigration police in the fall of 2006 under the Ministry of Security, the Service for Foreigners' Affairs (Služba za poslove sa strancima, SPS), which manages the Lukavica facility. Although the detention center flies the EU flag, the bureaucracy that runs it was heavily U.S. influenced and oriented toward GWOT imperatives. The U.S. embassy boasted of its role in transforming SPS "from an idea on paper to an effective organization," with a special focus on "identifying foreign fighters who illegally obtained [Bosnian] citizenship . . . so that they can be detained and expelled."[43] A U.S. adviser seconded to SPS had input on everything from legislative initiatives to procedural rulebooks and budgeting. The U.S. government donated automobiles, office equipment, radios, night vision equipment, and even batons.[44] Additionally, the embassy decided to contribute $4.5 million for SPS to develop a biometric data program, including equipment and training for border crossings and overseas embassies.[45] It sponsored a training course for SPS officers on interviews and interrogations, including "how to read verbal and non-verbal indicators to determine whether an individual is being deceptive"—similar to the behavioral profiling employed in U.S. airports.[46]

While U.S.-backed efforts to create institutions intended to denationalize suspicious Arabs unfolded, Abu Hamza and a small group of Arabs sought to take their case to anyone who would listen. They formed a group called Ensarije (from the Arabic term for one group of the Prophet Muhammad's early supporters) to publicize their cause. Several rallies were organized in Sarajevo and Zenica in 2007 and 2008, attended by hundreds of Bosnian Muslims who expressed gratitude for Arab volunteers and their role in the war. The Arab veterans made direct appeals to Muslim politicians, especially wartime prime minister Haris Silajdžić and Bakir Izetbegović, the son of Bosnia's first president and later president himself.[47] Abu Hamza was litigious, contesting the efforts to strip him of Bosnian citizenship and deport him. Abu Hamza and his comrades also targeted international audiences, granting interviews to the BBC, *New York Times*, *Washington Post*, and *Der Spiegel.* He actively sought the help of rights groups. I began to meet and correspond with him during this time in late 2006. Upon learning of my background in human rights organizations, he would often seek my advice.

Here, the state of Bosnia-Herzegovina appears less as a sovereign triggering the ontological potential of pure yet self-legitimizing violence and more as a space of negotiation between an imperial power and individuals it wishes to put in their proper "place." The United States and its allies crafted Bosnian legislation and enmeshed themselves in state institutions. From their end, Abu Hamza and the Arabs made their appeals in Bosnian courts and to voters even while knowing that the real power lay elsewhere. By acting as a buffer, the Bosnian state permitted the United States to avoid direct responsibility for the removal of the Arabs. And the Arabs lacked any ability to petition directly an authority that might truly determine their fate.

The United States as sovereign power was not acting to place Abu Hamza at the threshold of "the law" (however defined or delimited) as a kind of homo sacer. Rather, by refracting its power *through* the sovereignty of the

Bosnian state it was treating him as an out-of-place Muslim. This rendered him transportable in a circuit of relations between sovereign states. It did so in a way that minimized or eliminated U.S. responsibility. Here, a monolithic notion of sovereignty, or of power in general, is unhelpful, since one state (Bosnia) was exercising authority in a way that allowed another state (the United States) to pursue its goals without assuming public responsibility.

Abu Hamza was forced to deal with the powers that mattered through the media or NGOs in lieu of (rather than in addition to) traditional avenues of direct appeal and interaction. Little did it matter: In October 2008, the Constitutional Court of Bosnia upheld the decision to strip Abu Hamza of his citizenship. Now rendered Syrian and nothing else, he had an unambiguous address for a deportation guided by the logic of the U.S. empire. He was arrested by SPS, who brought him to Lukavica. The U.S. embassy duly reported the arrest and monitored the case.[48]

Abu Hamza spent the next seven and one-half years in Lukavica. With Syria's ability to serve as a willing jailer in doubt because of the civil war that erupted in 2011, he could no longer be put back into his "proper" place. In February 2012, the European Court of Human Rights ruled that he faced an unacceptable risk of abuse in Syria and that being declared a threat to national security was insufficient for detention.[49] According to the ruling, Bosnia could seek to deport Abu Hamza or release him (the United States, of course, could not be party to the lawsuit). For the next four years, it did neither: with circulation disrupted, indefinite detention remained the next acceptable option. And because he was held in an ordinary Bosnian immigration jail rather than an extraterritorial prison such as GTMO, his case attracted virtually no international attention. Detained under the flags of Bosnia and Europe, he was in many ways a prisoner of U.S. empire until his eventual release in February 2016.

CONCLUSION: OTHER CIRCULATIONS

It is inadequate to think about sovereignty in terms of exception when facing an empire in which power is often refracted through the sovereignty of other states, independent in name but enmeshed in relations of dependency. The network of carceral practices organized under the GWOT rubric, however, entails only one—and highly regulated—form of mobility generated under the U.S. empire. Far more common, of course, have been forms of migration premised on ever greater "flexibility" (or rather precarity) demanded by evolving forms of capitalism.[50] Here, Guantánamo and Bosnia-Herzegovina again provide glimpses of the larger beast: At GTMO, there are two major kinds of so-called third-country nationals who are neither American nor Cuban. The first are the prisoners such as Umar and the other Algerians rendered from Bosnia. The second is a worker population, comprised mostly of Filipinos and Jamaicans, who became indispensable after the Cuban Revolution led to a near-total cutoff of the base's local labor supply.[51] Both third-country national prisoners and workers at GTMO share the predicament of dwelling in a space between the juridical protections of their governments, the local state, and the U.S. hegemon.

While the U.S. conditions different forms of coercive circulation of bodies, these are attempts at governing a far broader range of forces and peregrinations that exceed its power. After years in GTMO and after winning his case in the U.S. courts, in 2008 Umar returned a free man to his adopted country. But because of the accusations linked to terrorism, it was difficult to find work. So in 2010, Umar left again: he traveled to China to get into the import/export business. Although questioned by police on departure, for the first time in a long while he traveled internationally as an ordinary person. Umar came away disappointed, however. "There are so many barriers to foreigners doing business here," he complained, "so many taxes and regulations. They look for any excuse to . . . give you trouble, even if you are bringing in goods that are almost perfect." While unsuccessful in this venture and still struggling to support his family, Umar's peregrinations are a small victory in one sense: not only did he win his freedom from GTMO, but he resumed a life that straddles national categories. As an Algerian in Bosnia, Umar's trip to China is the latest foray in a life marked by movement, including a pilgrimage to Saudi Arabia in 1989, his study and work in Pakistan, and his fateful decision to travel to Bosnia and marry there. Between stereotypes of privileged jet-setting cosmopolitans and toiling migrants, Umar's restored mobility—as an Algerian with a Bosnian passport in China—illustrates the challenges he faces while gesturing also to a matter-of-fact attempt to get by in an imperial order based on sovereignty.

This chapter has focused on the logic of circulation rather than exception, through a focus on carceral practices. It takes seriously the suggestion that "empire is a moving target"—not so much a target in motion, but one that is moving in the *transitive* sense, causing the circulation of other things, such as imprisoned bodies. The stories recounted touch upon a few of many potential fates. Carceral circulation may be consummated in a way that effectively consigns detainees to invisibility, such as with Imad's deportation to Egypt. It may be interrupted and leave individuals stuck without clear legal basis or political responsibility, as with Abu Hamza in Lukavica. And it may be converted into a "freedom" tied to labor precarity, as shown by Umar and his search for business in China. Rebuilding the itineraries traced by those bodies, and recording ethnographically the juridical signposts noted along the way, provides one possible glimpse of U.S. empire and its many far-flung parts.

NOTES

Unless otherwise noted, translations are my own.

1 Beganović, "Islam je ponovo zasijao gradovima Egipta," 22–24.

2 See Li, "A Universal Enemy?" My use of the term *out of place* is intentionally ambivalent. Dirt is, famously "matter out of place" in the work of Mary Douglas, and hence a source of threat in the cultural systems that shape understandings of the world. Douglas, *Purity and Danger*. For Edward Said, to be "out of place" is also, of course, a constitutive state of separation from "home" (conceived as family or homeland) that can condition new forms of subjectivity (Said, *Out of Place*).

3 553 US 723 (2008).

4 See *Boumediene v. Bush*; *Bensayah v. Obama*, 610 F.3d 1102 (D.C. Cir. 2010). The sixth Algerian, Belkacem Bensayah, was repatriated in 2013.

5 See *Eslam Durmo v. Federation of Bosnia and Herzegovina.* Since the fall of the Mubarak regime, Imad has resumed his earlier work as proselytizing Islam to Bosnians according to the Salafi orientation, this time via videos posted on YouTube.

6 Nkrumah, *Neo-Colonialism*, xi.

7 For attempts at remedying this disconnect, see Gregory, "The Black Flag," and Svirsky and Bignall, *Agamben and Colonialism*. For an important critique of the role of race in Agamben's work, see Weheliye, *Habeas Viscus*.

8 See https://web.archive.org/web/20120401181005/http://www.ensarije.com/index.php?id=1132.

9 Kellogg and El-Hamalawy, *Black Hole*, 19–21; Ṣalāḥ, *Waqāʾiʿ Sanawāt al-Jihād*, 144–49.

10 To be sure, the United States has a long history of abducting individuals overseas, often to bring them to trial within the country. Extraordinary rendition is distinctive insofar as it involves moving individuals *between* multiple foreign countries without U.S. jailers (except in the transit phase), entailing more complex negotiations of sovereignty. The closest example I could locate was the CIA transfer in 1952 of Bulgarian activist Dimitre Dimitrov from Greece to a U.S. military hospital in the Panama Canal Zone, where he was labeled a psychiatric patient under false pretenses—cf. Albarelli and Kaye, "The Real Roots of the CIA's Rendition and Black Sites Program." Even here, official U.S. authority over Dimitrov renders that case more akin to GTMO than rendition per se.

11 Although Umar served in the Bosnian Army, he said he was providing only religious instruction and was not a combatant.

12 Bosnia's constitutionally recognized "constituent nations" are Serbs, Croats, and Bosniaks—in other words, Slavs of Orthodox, Catholic, or Muslim background,

respectively. Long-standing populations in the country excluded from these categories include Jews, Roma, and Albanians. The term *Bosniak* remains deeply contested from multiple perspectives and will be used interchangeably with the term *Bosnian Muslims* here without prejudice to the question as to whether Bosniaks are an "authentic" nation or not, or if Bosnians of Muslim background should primarily identify themselves as Bosniaks.

13 Stoler, "On Degrees of Imperial Sovereignty," 142.

14 The proceedings before the Human Rights Chamber of Bosnia-Herzegovina—a hybrid local-international court—clarified the U.S. and Egyptian roles: "On 22 May 2001 the US Embassy informed the Ministry of Interior of the Federation of Bosnia and Herzegovina that two citizens of Egypt who are connected to terrorism are residing within the territory of the Federation. After receiving additional information from the Egyptian authorities, it was clear to the Federation that the applicant was one of these persons" (*Durmo*, 121).

15 Declaration of Alija Behmen, *Boumediene v. Bush*, 04-cv-1166 Exhibit 11 to Petitioner's Traverse for Writ of Habeas Corpus (D.D.C., Oct. 17, 2008), 12.

16 *Durmo*, 58.

17 See *Hadž Boudellaa et al. v. Bosnia and Herzegovina and Federation of Bosnia and Herzegovina*, 51–52. Interestingly, the Bosnian government informed a senior Algerian intelligence officer of their suspicions about the men even before the arrests (50).

18 Gerges, *The Far Enemy*.

19 The prospect of GWOT detainees captured abroad brought to the United States for trial has sparked debates over whether such defendants "deserve" the procedural protections of the criminal justice system. This debate tends to overlook continuities between GTMO and prisons on the mainland, especially technologies of solitary confinement, and to reinforce the assumption that domestic U.S. carceral practices are categorically distinct from (and more benign than) those elsewhere.

20 Bruce O'Neill has remarked on the inadequacy of Agamben's concept of the camp for capturing the spatial contours of the U.S. GWOT detention network, preferring instead to rely on Deleuze and Guattari's metaphor of the rhizome: "rendition works not by being caught inside the walls of 'the camp,' but by being forced to pass through an ever-changing assemblage of transnational spaces" (O'Neill, "Of Camps, Gulags, and Extraordinary Renditions," 11).

21 Agamben, *Homo Sacer*.

22 Cf. Hussain, "Beyond Norm and Exception"; Johns, "Guantánamo Bay and the Annihilation of the Exception." Anthropologists employing the conceptual vocabulary developed in Agamben's work on sovereignty (*camp*, *homo sacer*, *biopower*, *ban*) have found that those actually enmeshed in such categories proactively engage, contest, and appropriate them for their own ends; see, e.g., Agier, *Managing the Undesirables*; Bryant and Hatay, "Guns and Guitars"; Farquhar and Zhang, "Biopolitical Beijing"; Fassin and Vasquez, "Humanitarian Exception as the Rule"; Rozakou, "The Biopolitics of Hospitality in Greece." This is not exactly a challenge to Agamben's concepts, insofar as he is engaged in an excavation of the conditions of possibility for certain phenomena, rather than purporting to provide a social theory for understanding what people actually do in the camp or when

reduced to homo sacer. Interestingly, Agamben's separate work on community—which seems more closely linked to core anthropological concerns—has generally received less attention from the discipline. See Stevenson, "The Psychic Life of Biopolitics."

23 Caldwell, "Bio-Sovereignty and the Emergence of Humanity," 16

24 Agamben, *State of Exception*, 3–4 (emphasis added).

25 Agamben, *Homo Sacer*, 132.

26 Gregory, "The Black Flag," 407–8.

27 Agamben, *State of Exception*, 85.

28 These included Bahrain, Canada, France, Germany, Italy, Jordan, Libya, Morocco, Pakistan, Saudi Arabia, Spain, Tajikistan, Tunisia, Turkey, the United Kingdom, Uzbekistan, and Yemen. See Center for Constitutional Rights, "Foreign Interrogators at Guantanamo Bay," May 21, 2008, accessed August 13, 2017, http://ccrjustice.org/learn-more/faqs/foreign-interrogators-guantanamo-bay.

29 See *Hamdi v. Rumsfeld*, 542 U.S. 507 (2004).

30 Marty, *Alleged Secret Detentions*, 32.

31 One important exception: Ṭāriq al-Sawāḥ, an Alexandrian working in Greece who joined the jihad, was caught in Afghanistan and handed over to the Americans, who then shipped him to GTMO, where he remained the last Egyptian detainee until his January 2016 release. It is possible that al-Sawāḥ was treated differently because he was a dual Bosnian-Egyptian citizen, leading to uncertainty over his disposition.

32 Li, "Hunting the 'Out-of-Place Muslim' "; Mariner, *Ghost Prisoner*.

33 Agamben, *Homo Sacer*, 166.

34 Benton, *A Search for Sovereignty*; Lugard, *The Dual Mandate in British Tropical Africa*; Mamdani, *Citizen and Subject*.

35 Anghie, *Imperialism, Sovereignty, and the Making of International Law*; Mazower, *No Enchanted Palace*; Rajagopal, *International Law from Below*; Wright, *Mandates under the League of Nations*.

36 In *The Wretched of the Earth*, Fanon repeatedly pointed to the example of Latin American states to dramatize to his Algerian comrades and others the potential dangers of independence when dominated by the national bourgeoisie (97, 153–54, 174, 201). Being Martiniquan and thus a resident of a French Caribbean colony (Alessandrini, "Fanon Now"), the Latin American example of "independence" under U.S. hegemony would have been close to hand.

37 "TO JE SVE ŠTO MI MOŽEMO—OSMJEHNUTI SE SA ZADOVOLJSTVOM JER SMO MU PORODICA," Statement from the Husin-Softić family, October 6, 2009.

38 The four Ss denote the slogan *Samo sloga Srbina spasava*—Only unity can save the Serbs.

39 Delegation of the European Union to Bosnia and Herzegovina, "Handover ceremony of the EU-funded Reception Centre for Irregular Migrants in BiH," accessed November 10, 2017, http://europa.ba/?cat=12658&paged=41. The center is Bosnia's first immigration prison. It is worth noting that Bosnia still lacks a prison for criminal convicts and continues to rely on prisons run at the entity level. Immigration and border enforcement have accordingly been one of the areas where Western donors have prioritized investment.

40 In this respect, the situation in Lukavica is somewhat worse. While Guantánamo detainees generally cannot see the evidence against them (and indeed in most settings any utterances they make to outsiders are presumptively classified, meaning that their attorneys cannot share their statements without permission of the government), their lawyers often can if they have obtained security clearances. In Lukavica, there is no provision for defense attorneys to access classified evidence.

41 See "Law on the Amendments to the Law on Citizenship of Bosnia-Herzegovina."

42 "Bosnia: Citizenship Review Underway as Negative Media Attention Grows," cable by Amb. Douglas McElhaney, 11; "Abu Hamza Supporters Rally to Oppose Deportation," cable by Amb. Charles English, 8.

43 "Bosnia: INL-Managed SEED-Funded Projects Update: Focus on the Foreigners Affairs Service," cable by Amb. Charles English.

44 Total aid to SPS amounted in its first two and one-half years of existence to around $700,000, the agency's annual budget being just over US$5 million. "Bosnia: INL-Managed SEED-Funded Projects."

45 See "Bosnia: INL-Funded Project Highlights and Rule of Law Round-up," cable by Amb. Charles English, 4.

46 "Bosnia: INL-Managed SEED-Funded Projects Advance Post's Rule of Law Agenda," cable by Amb. Charles English.

47 The reluctance of Security Minister Tarik Sadović to expeditiously deport the Arabs led to his expulsion from the main Bosniak nationalist party, the SDA; the party then turned to the U.S. embassy to help vet his replacement. See "Bosnia—Request for Information on Possible Nominees for Minister of Security," cable by Amb. Charles English.

48 "Bosnia: Foreigners Affairs Service Detains Imad al-Hussein (AKA Abu Hamza al-Suri)," cable by Amb. Charles English.

49 *Al Husin v. Bosnia and Herzegovina.*

50 De Genova, "The Deportation Regime"; Feldman, *The Migration Apparatus.*

51 Lipman, *Guantánamo.*

AFTERWORD

Disassemblage

Rethinking U.S. Imperial Formations

ANN LAURA STOLER IN CONVERSATION
WITH CAROLE McGRANAHAN

On October 29 and 30, 2015, Ann Laura Stoler and Carole McGranahan sat down together in New York City for a conversation about this volume, about empire now, and the conceptual and temporal moves from the colonial to the postcolonial and the decolonial, and more. In this afterword, we present an edited version of our much longer discussion, touching on points relevant to thinking about ethnography and empire in the twenty-first century.

CM: Let's get right to it: What constitutes U.S. empire has shifted over time. In this volume we bring together scholarship on settler colonialism and sovereignty in Native American communities; on U.S. colonies abroad linked by the 1898 Treaty of Paris: the Philippines, Puerto Rico, and U.S. Samoa; on the U.S. military overseas and on the many peoples in imperial relationships with U.S. businesses, missionaries, spies, and diplomats as well as the military; and on new communities of empire in the post-9/11 U.S. at home and abroad. One of our main goals is simply to connect all of these areas and these peoples. To show the sinew, the tissues of connection, and in so doing, we hope to bring together bodies of scholarship too often kept separate.

ALS: Calling these various political arrangements by their imperial name is important, but making available the tissue of their connections is no easy task. One approach is to ask what kinds of similar problematizations (as Foucault would have it) are called forth, what kinds of "uncertainties" have challenged our understanding of empire in these contexts and situations. All of these are parts of U.S. empire—from the Pine Ridge Reservation in South Dakota to Guam—and sites of ongoing political contest and interventions. Calling something by name can be a performative that interpellates. Obviously it doesn't produce empire, but it does call out empire and demands a response to that call.

I see this volume as an engagement with the very nature of imperial entailments, one you can see coherently across the chapters.

CM: This is part of the impulse behind the whole volume, to get at the conceptual edges of empire as much as the obvious, overt components, something your own work has insisted upon for some time. We want to call out the imperial as much as the colonial, and to think these together in part to see both anew.

ALS: The supposed peripheral zones or "quasi" imperial zones are not only the heart of empire, but are also exemplary sites to see and show how such relations of subsumption work. For example, if Palestine or Puerto Rico are construed as only marginal parts of the story, we buy into an imperial script itself, one that dictates what is and is not a subject of inquiry before the question is asked. Instead of categorizing these places as outside imperial formations, we need to ask what model of empire demands that exclusion. In *Duress*, I argue that we can take precisely those blockages as occasions, not obstacles but objects of inquiry in themselves, and thus see past the script imperial agents write for us.

Here is where I think the concept of *disassemblage* could be useful. First let me step back to Paul Rabinow's astute observation that Weber was not after the actual connection between things, but "the conceptual interconnections of problems."[1] And to Rabinow's own equally generative understanding of Michel Foucault's project to address how knowledge-things are assembled.[2] I see both of these as strikingly helpful formulations in identifying how relations of power work. Each provokes us to ask how social kinds are produced to become "problems" with security regimes installed to protect some fictive "us" from those "problems" and the "dangers" they are construed to represent. Beyond the actual connection of things, we need to look at the conceptual interconnection of problems and who and what are made into them. That is, we need to ask not only how things are assembled, but also how they are disassembled, conceptually and politically severed from the conditions that made them possible. At issue here is something that Fernando Coronil—a dear friend, colleague, interlocutor who was supposed to be with us as you know too well for this conference—and I both thought of as "relational histories" that are made into nonrelational ones. We see this so clearly in the U.S. imperial script: that Samoa is not related to the Philippines is not related to Nicaragua is not related to Iraq.

Assemblage is not always the issue. Sometimes the political task is to identify how things get cut off from one another in our conceptualizations. What prevents people, relations, and things from being seen as proximate, implicated, and dependent? How do we track the processes by which things cannot be assembled, the practices by which they are construed as noncontingent and made to be kept apart?

CM: This is your argument for working along the grain rather than just against it.

ALS: In part what it means to work along the grain versus against the grain is to understand how things are and come to be seen as self-evident—the logics and affective economies that allow them to be rendered as commonsense. This is not to take for granted what seems obvious or to avoid it, but to look at the range of logics that imperial formations call upon and the arrangements they call into play. I think this openness is key: it is not to decide and define what is an imperial formation once and for all; on the contrary, it is to retain the specificity and particularity of time and place and persons to ask what is reflected upon, made available, brought into the service of imperial pursuits as their supports and in what way.

One piece of this effort would be an attentiveness to concept-work, that to my mind entails an appreciation of the fragility of concepts, and a willingness to make conceptual incisions through the artifice of a concept's coherence. Foucault's choice of language informs my thought here. If history is for cutting, then one of our tasks is to cut into the "ready-made syntheses" out of which concepts emerge. What are the maneuvers that make disassembled, severed histories such common sense that we and our methodological conventions reproduce them? We do so through institutional structures—look at current U.S. congressional debates on Puerto Rico, for example—and we do so through academic conventions where disciplinary conversations are sometimes kept separate: American studies from anthropology from history from literature. Right now we are in a moment of productive convergence, of scholarships of empire coming together in conversations that had not taken place before.

CM: It seems different burdens were placed on these separate scholarships along the way. They had impulses and imperatives to answer different questions.

ALS: Disciplinary border crossings are no longer transgressive acts. In this volume those crossings are producing a new kind of space for calculating things differently, pushing things up against one another. My concern, however, remains that grounded historical work can get short-shrifted in that multidisciplinary pursuit—it needn't, but it does and often on the assumption that those histories are known quantities and not really subject to permeability and change.

CM: Our approach here to challenge what we think we know about imperial histories is ethnographic. Ethnography is at the center of our effort to understand contemporary U.S. imperial formations, to consider empire as lived and experienced, or as William Appleman Williams called it, "empire as a way of life." Collectively, I think we all see this as involving classic ethnographic fieldwork, and also the sort of sensibility you so carefully honed from early on with the ethnography in the archives approach. Your work to seek the ethnographic in the colonial past, by doing close readings in and of the archives, has opened up ways for us to read contemporary documents as well, to realize that the ethnographic archive is not just oral.

ALS: I find the French philosopher Gaston Bachelard's notion of the "epistemology of the detail" powerful to think conceptually. It is crucial to understanding how, where, on whom, and with what intensity imperial relations impose and thrive.

CM: This is one of the things we are working toward here, getting to the details ethnography enables us to see.[3] In the case of U.S. empire, an epistemology of the detail brings us to the cultural and political worlds that shape, sustain, inform, and contradict life. And does so across such varied fields. Doing ethnography in the archives has definitely sharpened my ethnographic sensibility of the contemporary world, and not just vice versa, as people sometimes seem to presume. But your work on ethnography in the archives is also a way of understanding histories of the present, or as you say in *Duress*, of a continuing colonial presence.

ALS: I work with the term *colonial presence* as a challenge, one that puts transparencies, recognizabilities, invisibilities, and co-temporalities into immediate question. It acknowledges that we still don't know all the ways colonial or imperial practices and dispositions shape the spaces we inhabit, and the "rifts" in time, as Palestinian writer Raja Shehadeh puts it, in which people so disparately live.

CM: Many of the chapters in the volume speak to this, an imperial presence, the presence of Americans or things American in so many places around the world. Ethnography gets at that presence in really crucial ways. An ethnographic approach alongside the historic and the political is possible in this current moment of U.S. empire as a coeval series of colonial and imperial formations in a way that wasn't possible for earlier eras.

ALS: This returns us again to something that Fernando [Coronil] and I often talked about, these histories that are relational but were pulled apart and made separate, and how we could bring them together. Think of his article "Beyond Occidentalism: Toward Non-Imperial Geohistorical Categories," which has this goal at its core. Bringing together histories that were meant to be separate, juxtaposing them, and imagining possibilities that were defended against. Innovative methodologies here are political acts in themselves: refusals to abide by the divisions as they are drawn. There has been an explosion in ethnographic scholarship that does just this, trying to get at the multiple logics and emotional economies at play. And yet, the concepts of empire and even colony are still difficult to think for the U.S. and of course are made difficult to think. Why is this? Some of this involves myths we know, that America was anticolonial, was anti-imperial, was unlike Europe.

CM: We seem to be in a discordant moment right now, where for some it is redundant to say the U.S. is an empire, and therefore critical to make connections such as those we make in this volume, and yet for others empire is an entirely absent or incorrect category for the U.S. I'm reminded of what you write in *Imperial Debris*, that the category of empire "disappears easily into other appellations and other, more available, contemporary terms."[4]

ALS: Identifying some of those substituted terms is important, but there may be a deeper problem with how we conceptualize the ways imperial formations operate and what they do. We tend to imagine discrete macropolities identified by name. However, it may be that imperial practices don't have a dedicated institutional structure but rather opportunistically work through other available political forms. Indeed there are other sites of blockage: sometimes it is a matter of what we *expect* the relationship between colonial past and present to look like and therefore don't see what is in front of us. And then there's a question that motivated much of my earlier work that went into *Along the Archival Grain*: How does one know and not know what it is to live the conditions produced by imperial pursuits, to know and not know at the same time?

CM: This brings to mind Barney Cohn's insistence on connection, that we consider colonized and colonizer in the same analytic frame or field. And your and Fred Cooper's argument in *Tensions of Empire* that we consider colony and metropole together. In this volume we look at Hawai'i, Bosnia-Herzegovina, and the Osage Nation, for example, in the same analytic framework. Yet there is still debate over what counts as U.S. empire, or if the U.S. even is an empire. In my work on Tibet and the CIA during the Cold War, I encounter scholars who tell me that the U.S. is not an empire but is instead a "dominant power," or perhaps who grant that Tibet's relationship with the U.S. is imperial, but then ask so what?

ALS: Right: *Dominant power* is not only a different sort of term; it confers a different status, demands a different comparison, and makes a different political claim. But there is also the retort: If the U.S. is an empire, and everything is empire, is there anything outside of it?

CM: This is empire as paralysis. But the idea that empire is all or nothing misses the point.

ALS: This is what these chapters do so well together: they ask what it means that empire is there, not that empire is everywhere. They ask what it means to be hugging its edges or squarely inside.

CM: And to not presume that space is singular or always disabling or even primary. I think Audra Simpson's work on refusal makes this point so well. She argues that refusal is not necessarily a response to the imperial, but something that insists on preceding it, that calls forth another ground of engagement and orientation.

ALS: One important move that follows is to see imperial formations not as consisting of discrete singular types such as settler colonialism or semicolonialism, for example, but to see even these as consisting of gradations rather than fixed forms. The volume is organized around these types, a loose sense of the types perhaps, but it is about making connections within as well as across them. U.S. empire has multiple forms, and it can be easy to think we know them. What this volume does so beautifully is open up a productive challenge to that, thinking different sorts of imperial experiences and histories up against each other in order to better understand the lack of fixity. This helps us see both inside and outside various imperial formations, and to recognize that the topography of U.S. variants is far vaster than many of us initially realized.

The nexus of history and ethnography is critical to the conversation. I think this unsettles the notion that settler colonialism is a "type" with a specific originary moment rather than the effect of multiple dissensions, failed visions, and political contests over what a colony should do, look like, and be. If we turn back to what Foucault argued about the art of governance in *The Birth of Biopolitics*,[5] that it's not about what administrations did but how they reflected upon what good, effective governance required, what have been construed as settler issues take on a wider valence in numbers of different colonial sites.

CM: We're back to colonial presence. You start *Duress* by asking how colonial histories matter in the world today. The ethnographic stories we tell in this volume about, say, Cambodian refugees or South Asian Muslim teens in California, need to be put in dialogue with histories of settlement and conquest and vice versa. Colonial histories undergird imperial actions in many places. This was some of the work we did together in *Imperial Formations*, in stepping out of thinking of empire as just colonial or only European, but considering places that are imperial but not colonial, and of thinking of U.S. empire from its inception as both colonial and imperial.

ALS: And thinking about territorial and deterritorial forms of possession and occupation and force not along an historical continuum but as alternatives that exist at the same time. Hardt and Negri's notion that earlier forms of empire were territorial, and that the nomos of the new Empire with a capital *E* is deterritorialized, was unhelpful in this regard, setting up a false dichotomy that was rarely operative. U.S. empire has always involved deterritorialization in some form. One of the prime examples of that is its investment in the Middle East and Israel. We might want to remember Scott Atran's important observation from 1989 that colonialism is sometimes a surrogate project.[6] While he was looking at Israel and Palestine in relation to Britain, we can draw on this insight to think about U.S. empire too. The essays in this volume go a long way to show that surrogacy is a constitutive feature of U.S. empire.

Turning to Israel in the context of this volume transfigures a conceptual map of U.S. empire. Israel is important to this story—and not because academic battle lines are being drawn around BDS [Boycott, Divestment, Sanctions] and against it—but because it raises crucial questions about how U.S. empire is implicated, how imperial forms are often unevenly sedimented and layered, here in the context of the Palestinian-Israeli situation. Your work on Tibet shows this too with the British and the Americans. Another very nondiscrete situation.

As a community of scholars of empire, the contemporary history of Palestine took a long time to register. In *Duress* I explicitly raise that question: why Edward Said's *Orientalism* could become a foundational text of colonial and imperial studies, but not *The Question of Palestine*, which came out in 1979, just a year later.

CM: Including in this volume, which when we conceptualized it in 2009 as a conference, we invited Sunaina Maira, a scholar who works on Palestine, but had her present her research on South Asian Muslim youth in the post-9/11 U.S.

ALS: A proliferation of "exceptions" you might say: Israel and the U.S. hailed by some as the quintessential ones. This is linked to what I call in *Along the Archival Grain*, "the politics of disregard." There is something about imperial denial, about disregard that endures so strongly. People are pressed into the service of not seeing, not knowing, of looking away. Sometimes there is no need to look away, because you can't see what is before you. A different category has been named: Israel is not a colonial power. The U.S. is not an empire. And so on. Naming those things we've been educated not to see allows us to get at the tensions of certain moments. Race figures here prominently. The history of slavery has been written as a national tragedy or as part of an international history of slavery, but not necessarily as part of the history of U.S. empire. It is somebody else's empire.

CM: Race and racism are both part of the story, and yet, you're right, racism is not always addressed in imperial terms. Sometimes the history goes back in a different direction to slavery, as you said, but not always to empire. What it means to be black in the U.S. right now, for instance, may or may not link up to empire as people experience or articulate it. Nor do racism and colonialism always link to slavery in Africa, as Jemima Pierre's work in Ghana shows.[7] In the time since we held our conference [in 2011] to right now, the political moment in the U.S. has shifted, and so have conversations about racism.

ALS: The work was being done, but perhaps in a more muted way, under the sign of disassemblage one could say. We can now, for example, read Michel-Rolph Trouillot's *Silencing the Past* as firmly about U.S. empire as about the French. I always read it that way and thus hardly noticed at the time, that U.S. empire was almost so obvious it wasn't named. We can now read it in a new way.

CM: You've written that colonial racism is imagined to be more fierce than racism today. The idea perhaps that somehow things were more blunt or overt in the past? Why is it that colonial racism is perceived as more fierce, and why are we staking out these differences? In some ways that is a moral stance, and in other ways it is a temporal stance that really doesn't work.

ALS: As a moral stance, it does specific kind of work: namely, to distance us all, albeit differently, from histories that make up the fabric of inequities today. Maybe "they" were far less self-conscious than "we" are about the structures of dominance as Stuart Hall so well put it, but we are caught in our own comforting regimes of truth as well. There are cultural forms that were inherent to colonial racism and that permeate the subjacent corners of our lives—how space is used, how one walks a street, what hails as proper conduct or comportment. These sorts of ways we are in the world, and can be in the world, have enormous effects in how our senses calibrate sound and smell and proximities that are then called on to mark differences of consequence.

I think the notion of the fierceness goes back to the idea that empire's agents and architects were racist and either they didn't acknowledge it or it was blatantly virulent; either way, "our" racism always comes out in the story as being more subtle and complex. We fool ourselves to imagine that the production and performance of moral virtue was less nuanced in the late nineteenth or early twentieth century than it is today.

When the criterion of race was erased from legal documents in the Netherlands Indies in the early twentieth century, racism was neither muted nor went away but rather fortified in other ways. Just over a decade later in the 1930s, Nazi clubs had become popular among both poor and prominent Dutch colonials in the major cities of Java. How do we understand that relationship between the legal inscription of race, its legal erasure, and its fortification? We need to know more about how such matrices of law, affect, politics, and civility produce their racial effects and assemble fictitious racial kinds and other "knowledge-things."

In the contemporary U.S., we are deft at making differential treatment and opportunities not about race—or for that matter about empire. Jury selection is now notorious for its veiled system of racialized selection, where the criteria for selection are explicitly called "nonracial." Potential black jurors are "excused" from juries for "speaking in monosyllables," "not making eye contact," or "slouching"—far more often than whites. This is systemic racism presented as objective assessment, racism with a deeply imperial lineage.

CM: This is that durability of cultural forms. Dutch empire, French empire, American empire all denying racism through the same sort of language.

And of course, this imperial availability to deny is still operative among whites in the contemporary U.S.—"I'm not racist, but . . ." It is chilling to see this continuity. Talk about a contemporary phrasing.

ALS: Did you say freezing?

CM: Phrasing. A contemporary phrasing.

ALS: Yes, you're right, but it is also a freeze, an arrest that says "no," we can't go there, because I am not that, so let's not even consider that comparison, not even go to that place. But we don't want this to devolve into an iteration of the privileges of whiteness. And yet those remain.

CM: Those remain. Maybe it is worth pausing and reflecting on the moment that we are in right now in the U.S., in one of the most racially charged moments since the 1960s. And at the same time, questions of U.S. empire are on the table in a new way.

ALS: So one way to parse this collective project would be to see it as an effort to capture how racism is folded through the contemporary history of the U.S. and unevenly recessed and then in relief in its relationships to empire. *Haunted by Empire* made an effort in that direction but only in partial ways. It didn't really make that organic bridge. *Tensions of Empire* never even got close. *Imperial Debris* again invites us to do so by asking what would it take to reposition white sharecropping, as James Agee wrote it so viscerally and described it as a condition of "slendering forms of freedom"[8] that was part of an imperial deprivation. How was "white trash" not just a national issue, not just a Civil War issue, not just about the North and the South, but a heavily racialized piece in the production of empire itself, about cotton and tobacco, about its rise, fall, and relocations? Sven Beckert's book on *The Empire of Cotton* crafts a powerful imperial history of cotton, but it is striking how white impoverishment in the South remained marginal to his story.

CM: This volume doesn't fully do it either. It is only on the cusp, on the cusp of decolonizing, of bringing together, of what you're calling disassemblage.

ALS: But work on these subjects is shifting and ever new interlocutors deploy the old terms, call on them differently, and turn to new ones.

One question to ask is what is American about all of this. What does America look and feel like in American Samoa, for example? What work is that adjective doing? As Fred Cooper might remind us, not everyone desires what they are programmed to desire. We see this in

Jan Padios's chapter here on the Philippines, which for me calls to mind Homi Bhabha's "Of Mimicry and Man" essay that mocks the assumption that everyone wants to be white. As my doctoral student Erick Howard so eloquently has put it, Bhabha "observes a stutter, a scene of perpetual audition for that which the colonized subject will never be cast."[9] But maybe sometimes there is no desire even for the audition. As Padios shows, and I've argued with respect to a "mixed" Indo population in Java, Filipinos might become "American," but not everyone desires that label or transformation. This is what ethnographic research helps with, showing us the languages and registers of critique and refusal in which people speak.

CM: This is where we are now, I think, in an ethnographic moment calling on histories to make sense of how the world is still imperial. We've been educated to think it isn't, to think that empire is past tense, that we are postcolonial, and so the acknowledgment of a colonial and imperial presence is both unsettling and urgent. And yet, of course, there are some for whom this acknowledgment has always been there, for whom it is not new.

In 2006, you and David Bond cowrote an article on U.S. empire. In it you wrote, "Historical literacy should disquiet and discomfort rather than reassure."[10] If history is to disquiet or discomfort, then what is ethnography? Is it to disrupt?

ALS: When I think about critique, I think that it is really about an ethics of discomfort. But what sort of discomfort? Discomfort that moves you away from what you were thinking, or discomfort that unsettles the very categories you thought you knew, or work that makes you act in a different way? Rather than thinking of history as disquiet and ethnography as disruption, it may be the way the two come together that is the most disruptive of all.

But, we are still left to ask what is being disrupted? Does our pedagogy do that? Does the academy endorse (and easily absorb) our slightly brazen moves that do little to disrupt the status quo? Is fearless speech even possible within academia? Probably not. Here I think of Foucault's question concerning the forms that *parrhesia*, or truth-telling, could take in Ancient Greece. Something else is at play here, not emanating from our scholarship, but from the urgency with which people call on these histories to make their claims. Critique and parrhesia come together here in a potent mix: critique as "reflective insolence" and a fearless speech that puts you at risk. Together these shape the outer edges of what we can, cannot, and need to say.

CM: To return to where we started, naming and pushing past such edges were our goals here, calling out the ways U.S. empire is best seen as a purposeful disassemblage of imperial formations. Insolence, risk, fearlessness comes in various degrees for the different contributors; we are all positioned differently in the communities with whom we work, in relation to U.S. empire as a thing, whether a knowledge-thing or a material, military, symbolic, intimate, intransigent, bureaucratic sort of thing to say out loud just a few of the ways empire appears in the chapters here. What is risky for some of us are everyday realities for others.

ALS: Yes, and such battles are going on all the time, over who gets the right to speak, who is disenfranchised, over where connectivities are being made and applauded. And, in this time of connectivity, the disconnections between people, and how people are so abjectly disconnected, is even more important. Inequalities have not receded. There are so many seemingly benign ways of occluding inequalities, of coding them, of calling them "benevolence" and opportunities for "development" and the like. Such ideas ride strong currents throughout the history of empire, for these relations depend on not challenging the entitlements those inequalities afford.

Critical scholarship in anthropology and (post)colonial studies over the last forty years questioned categories, speech, action, practice, knowledge production, and what counts as knowledge. If these are not new scholarly goals, there are some minor signs that new configurations of actors are practicing critique in a different way. Critique is not over as Latour would have it; the fact that it doesn't look as it once did, emanating from the same quarters, and the same sources, with the same locutions, is the good news—not a sign of its demise. Some of this has to do with changes in scholarly demographics, and some with appreciating what counts as politics.

CM: We're in a new moment of making claims and demands, and responding to them, thinking scholarly responsibility anew.

ALS: Maybe. Critique is increasingly launched not in the imposed categories we might use as anthropologists, but in the various idioms and vernacular forms in which people hold these concepts themselves. This is a defining element of the world now and should be of scholarship too.

CM: In addition to epistemology, it is perhaps the ontology of the detail as well as we suggest in the Introduction—the seeing, the being, and the productive discomfort of both.

Ann, thank you for this conversation, and for the rich detail and rigorous provocations of your decades of thinking about empire from the Dutch to the French to the American, from Indonesia to Vietnam to Israel. Your model of scholarship as reflective insolence resonates deeply with this project of mostly U.S.-based scholars engaging with U.S. empire. May our collective insolence move forward the project of not just thinking through, but also responding to disassemblage in the context of U.S. imperial formations.

Postscript, November 8, 2017. In the aftermath of the U.S. presidential election and the victory of Donald Trump, we find ourselves in a new but familiar place regarding empire and race. "I'm not racist, but . . ." repeated once more. Repeated again and again as it has been for so long across time and across imperial formations. We hear it in relation to Standing Rock and the Dakota Access pipeline. We hear it in discussions of aid to Puerto Rico in the aftermath of Hurricane Maria. We hear it in continuing debates about the Black Lives Matter movement. We hear it in nostalgia for a "white" America. In closing this volume on U.S. empire, we return to the introduction to reemphasize this racism is not merely a past problem or politics or something that is "post." Empire and the racism that undergirds it are vivid realities here and now.

NOTES

1 Rabinow, *Anthropos Today*, 36.
2 Rabinow, *Anthropos Today*, 85.
3 See Lutz, "Empire Is in the Details."
4 Stoler, "Introduction: 'The Rot Remains,'" 23.
5 Foucault, *The Birth of Biopolitics.*
6 Atran, "The Surrogate Colonization of Palestine 1917–1939."
7 Pierre, *The Predicament of Blackness.*
8 Agee and Evans, *Let Us Now Praise Famous Men*, 96.
9 Personal communication. New School for Social Research, New York, February 2014.
10 Stoler and Bond, "Refractions Off Empire," 97.

Bibliography

Abraham, Nabeel, Sally Howell, and Andrew Shryock, eds. *Arab Detroit 9/11: Life in the Terror Decade*. Detroit: Wayne State University Press, 2011.

Abrams, Philip. "Notes on the Difficulty of Studying the State." *Journal of Historical Sociology* 1, no. 1 (1988): 58–89.

"Abu Hamza Supporters Rally to Oppose Deportation." Cable by Amb. Charles English, 08SARAJEVO202, February 4, 2008.

Abunimah, Ali. "Climate of Fear Silencing Palestinian, Muslim Students at UC Campuses, Rights Groups Warn." *Electronic Intifada*, December 4, 2012. Accessed August 8, 2017. http://electronicintifada.net/blogs/ali-abunimah/climate-fear-silencing-palestinian-muslim-students-university-california-rights.

Aceves, W. J., et al. "Declaration of International Law Scholars on Forced Relocation." February 25, 2000. Originally written and submitted for *Doe v. Univocal Corp*. 110 F.Supp.2d 1294 (C.D. Cal 2000) litigation.

Adams, Mark. "Sons and Lavas." GQ, September 1999.

Adas, Michael. "Improving on the Civilizing Mission? Assumptions of United States Exceptionalism in the Colonisation of the Philippines." *Itinerario* 22, no. 4 (1998): 44–66.

Adelman, Jeremy. *Sovereignty and Revolution in the Iberian Atlantic*. Princeton, NJ: Princeton University Press, 2006.

Agamben, Giorgio. *Homo Sacer: Sovereign Power and Bare Life*. Translated by D. Heller-Roazen. Stanford, CA: Stanford University Press, [1995] 1998.

Agamben, Giorgio. *State of Exception*. Translated by Kevin Attell. Chicago: University of Chicago Press, 2005.

Agee, James, and Walker Evans. *Let Us Now Praise Famous Men: Three Tenant Families*. Boston: Houghton Mifflin, [1939] 2001.

Agier, Michel. *Managing the Undesirables: Refugee Camps and Humanitarian Government*. Cambridge: Polity, [2008] 2012.

Ahuja, Neel. *Bioinsecurities: Disease Interventions, Empire, and the Government of Species*. Durham, NC: Duke University Press, 2016.

Aina, Sefa, Nia Aitaoto, Keith Castro, Calvin Chang, Dan Ichinose, Josanna Lee, Tana Lepule, Natasha Saelua, Joanna Tsark, Alisi Tulua, Christopher Vaimili, and Kehaulani Vaughn. "A Community of Contrasts: Native Hawaiians and Pacific Islanders in the United States." Los Angeles: Empowering Pacific Islander Communities and Asian Americans Advancing Justice, 2014. Accessed October 20, 2015. http://empoweredpi.org/demographic-report/.

Albarelli, H. P., and Jeffrey Kaye. "The Real Roots of the CIA's Rendition and Black Sites Program." *Truthout*, February 17, 2010. Accessed June 8, 2017. http://truth

-out.org/archive/component/k2/item/88113:the-real-roots-of-the-cias-rendition-and-black-sites-program.

Alessandrini, Anthony. "Fanon Now: Singularity and Solidarity." *Journal of Pan-African Studies* 4, no. 7 (2010): 52–74.

Al Husin v. Bosnia and Herzegovina, application no. 3727/08 (Eur. Ct. Human Rights), February 7, 2012.

Ali, Nosheen. "Books vs. Bombs: Humanitarian Development and the Narrative of Terror in Northern Pakistan." *Third World Quarterly* 31, no. 4 (2010): 541–59.

Allison, Lincoln. *The Global Politics of Sport: The Role of Global Institutions in Sport.* New York: Taylor and Francis, 2005.

Almeida, Alfredo Wagner Berno de. *Os quilombos e a base de lançamento de foguetes de Alcântara: Laudo antropológico.* Vol. 1. Brasília: Ministério do Meio Ambiente, 2006a.

Almeida, Alfredo Wagner Berno de. *Os quilombos e a base de lançamento de foguetes de Alcântara: Laudo antropológico.* Vol. 2. Brasília: Ministério do Meio Ambiente, 2006b.

Almeida, Alfredo Wagner Berno de. "Os quilombos e as novas etnias." In *Quilombos: Identidade étnica e territorialidade*, edited by Eliane Cantarino O'Dwyer, 43–82. Rio de Janeiro: Editora FGV, 2002.

American Civil Liberties Union. "Brief of the American Civil Liberties Union and the American Civil Liberties Union of Washington as Amici Curiae in Support of Respondent, Janet Reno, Attorney General, et Al., v. Kim Ho Ma." 9th Cir. 2000.

American Samoa Department of Commerce, Statistics Department. *American Samoa Statistical Yearbook.* Pago Pago: American Samoa Government, 2015.

"Amnesty: U.S., Europe Shielding Israel over Gaza War Crimes." *Haaretz*, May 27, 2010. Accessed August 8, 2017. http://www.haaretz.com/news/diplomacy-defense/amnesty-u-s-europe-shielding-israelover-gaza-war-crimes-1.292505.

Anaya, Rudolfo A. and Francisco Lomeli. *Aztlán: Essays on the Chicano Homeland.* Albuquerque: University of New Mexico Press, 1991.

Anderson, Carol. *Eyes off the Prize: The United Nations and the African American Struggle for Human Rights, 1944–1955.* Cambridge: Cambridge University Press, 2003.

Anderson, Warwick. *Colonial Pathologies: American Tropical Medicine, Race, and Hygiene in the Philippines.* Durham, NC: Duke University Press, 2006.

Andía, Jonny F., Sherry Deren, Rafaela R. Robles, Sung-Yeon Kang, and Hector M. Colón. "Peer Norms and Sharing of Injection Paraphernalia among Puerto Rican Injection Drug Users in New York and Puerto Rico." *AIDS Education and Prevention* 20, no. 3 (2008): 249–57.

Andrade, Maristela de Paula, and Benedito Souza Filho, eds. *Fome de farinha: Deslocamento compulsório e insegurança alimentar em Alcântara.* São Luís: EDUFMA, 2006.

Andrews, George Reid. "Brazilian Racial Democracy, 1900–90: An American Counterpoint." *Journal of Contemporary History* 31, no. 3 (1996): 483–507.

Anghie, Antony. *Imperialism, Sovereignty, and the Making of International Law.* Cambridge: Cambridge University Press, 2004.

Appadurai, Arjun. "Playing with Modernity: The Decolonization of Indian Cricket." In *Consuming Modernity: Public Culture in a South Asian World*, edited by Carol Breckenridge, 23–48. Minneapolis: University of Minnesota Press, 1995.

Armstrong, Charles K. *The North Korean Revolution, 1945–1950*. Ithaca, NY: Cornell University Press, 2004.

Arruti, José Maurício. *Mocambo: Antropologia e história do processo de formação quilombola*. São Paulo: EDUSC, 2006.

Asad, Talal, ed. *Anthropology and the Colonial Encounter*. Ithaca, NY: Cornell University Press, 1973.

Asad, Talal. "Comments on Conversion." In *Conversion to Modernities*, edited by Peter van der Veer, 263–74. London: Routledge, 1996.

Asad, Talal. "Introduction." In *Anthropology and the Colonial Encounter*, edited by Talal Asad, 9–19. London: Ithaca Press, 1973.

"Asia 2050: Realizing the Asian Century." Asian Development Bank. August 2011.

Associated Press. "Pentagon Sets Sights on Public Opinion." *NBC News*, February 5, 2009. Accessed August 8, 2017. http://www.nbcnews.com/id/29040299/ns/us_news-military/t/pentagon-sets-sights-public-opinion/#.WTm6_hPyuRs.

Atran, Scott. "The Surrogate Colonization of Palestine, 1917–1939." *American Ethnologist* 16, no. 4 (1989): 719–44.

Aust, Anthony. "Immigration Legislation for BIOT." Memorandum, U.K. Lawyers for Chagossians Trial Bundle, January 16, 1970.

Ayala, César J., and José Bolívar. *Battleship Vieques: Puerto Rico from World War II to the Korean War*. Princeton, NJ: Markus Wiener, 2011.

Bachelard, Gaston. *La philosophie du non: Essai d'une philosophie du nouvel esprit scientifique*. Paris: Presses Universitaires de France, 1940, 12.

Badiou, Alain. *Polemics*. London: Verso, [2006] 2011.

Bajaj, Vikas. "A New Capital of Call Centers." *New York Times*, November 25, 2011.

Bakalian, Amy, and Mehdi Bozorghmehr. *Backlash 9/11: Middle Eastern and Muslim Americans Respond*. Berkeley: University of California Press, 2009.

Baker, Ron. "The Slob Hunter Argument." In *The American Hunting Myth*, edited by Ron Baker, 188–192. New York: Vantage, 1985.

Baker, William J., and J. A. Mangan. *Sport in Africa: Essays in Social History*. New York: Africana, 1987.

Bandjunis, Vytautas B. *Diego Garcia: Creation of the Indian Ocean Base*. San Jose, CA: Writer's Showcase, 2001.

Barker, Joanne Marie. "Recognition." *Indigenous Studies Today* 1 (2005–6): 133–62.

Barker, Joanne Marie. "The Specters of Recognition." In *Formations of United States Colonialism*, edited by Alyosha Goldstein, 33–56. Durham, NC: Duke University Press, 2014.

Barnett, Michael, and Thomas G. Weiss. "Humanitarianism: A Brief History of the Present." In *Humanitarianism in Question: Politics, Power, Ethics*, edited by Michael Barnett and Thomas G. Weiss, 1–48. Ithaca, NY: Cornell University Press, 2008.

Barrett, Frank. "The Organizational Construction of Hegemonic Masculinity: The Case of the US Navy." *Gender, Work and Organization* 3, no. 3 (1996): 129–42.

Barrocal, André. "Em segredo, Brasil volta a negociar base de Alcântara com os EUA." *CartaCapital*, January 21, 2017. Accessed August 8, 2017. https://www.cartacapital.com.br/politica/em-segredo-brasil-volta-a-negociar-base-de-alcantara-com-os-eua.

Barrows-Friedman, Nora. *In Our Power: U.S. Students Organize for Justice in Palestine*. Charlottesville, VA: Just World Books, 2014.

Barsh, Russel Lawrence. "Indigenous Peoples: An Emerging Object of International Law." *American Journal of International Law* 80, no. 2 (1986): 369–85.

Barstow, David. "Behind TV Analysts, Pentagon's Hidden Hand." *New York Times*, April 20, 2008.

Bartky, Ian R. *Selling the True Time: Nineteenth-Century Timekeeping in America*. Stanford, CA: Stanford University Press, 2000.

Bataillon, Gilles. "Cambios culturales y sociopolíticos en las comunidades mayangnas y miskitus del Río Bocay y del Alto Río Coco, Nicaragua (1979–2000)." *Journal de la société des américanistes* 87, no. 87 (2001): 376–92.

Bataillon, Gilles. "Yugo: Un comandante runguero." TRACE *(Travaux et Recherches dans les Amériques du Centre): Relatos de la Vida* 41 (2002): 65–96.

Beard, Ronald L. "The Role of the ITU-R in Time Scale Definition and Dissemination." *Metrologia* 48, no. 4 (2011): S125–S131.

Beckert, Sven. *The Empire of Cotton: A Global History*. New York: Knopf, 2014.

Beganović, Ezher. "Islam je ponovo zasijao gradovima Egipta." SAFF 290 (2011): 22–24.

Behrendt, Larissa. "Finding the Promise of Mabo" (Mabo Oration). ADCQ. 2007. Accessed November 22, 2015. http://www.adcq.qld.gov.au/resources/a-and-tsi/mabo-oration/2007-mabo-oration/Finding-the-promise-of-Mabo.

Belasco, Amy. *Troop Levels in the Afghan and Iraq Wars, FY2001–FY2012: Cost and Other Potential Issues*. Congressional Research Service, July 2, 2009. Accessed October 31, 2017. https://fas.org/sgp/crs/natsec/R40682.pdf.

Belkin, Aaron. *Bring Me Men: Military Masculinity and the Benign Façade of American Empire 1898–2001*. New York: Columbia University Press, 2012.

Benavides, O. Hugo. *Drugs, Thugs, and Divas: Telenovelas and Narco-Dramas in Latin America*. Austin: University of Texas Press, 2008.

Benford, Robert, and David Snow. "Framing Processes and Social Movements: An Overview." *Annual Review of Sociology* 26 (2000): 611–39.

Benjamin, Walter. "Unpacking My Library: A Talk About Book Collecting." In *Illuminations: Essays and Reflections*, edited by Hannah Arendt, translated by Harry Zohn. New York: Schocken Books, [1968] 2007.

Benton, Lauren. *A Search for Sovereignty: Law and Geography in European Empires, 1400–1900*. Cambridge: Cambridge University Press, 2010.

Bermúdez, Darío. "Pistoleros a sueldo (mínimo)." *La Nación*, September 25, 2005.

Berreman, Gerald. "Is Anthropology Alive?: Social Responsibility in Social Anthropology." *Current Anthropology* 9, no. 5 (1968): 391–96.

Besnier, Niko, and Susan Brownell. "Sport, Modernity, and the Body." *Annual Review of Anthropology* 41 (2012): 443–59.

Besteman, Catherine. "On Ethnographic Love." In *Mutuality: Anthropology's Changing Terms of Engagement*, edited by Roger Sanjek, 259–84. Philadelphia: University of Pennsylvania Press, 2014.

Betts, Richard K. "The Political Support System for American Primacy." *International Affairs* 81, no. 1 (2005): 1–14.

Bickers, Robert. *Empire Made Me: An Englishman Adrift in Shanghai*. New York: Penguin, 2003.

Bilby, Kenneth M. *The Remaking of the Aluku: Culture, Politics, and Maroon Ethnicity in French South America*. Baltimore: Johns Hopkins University Press, 1990.

Bilby, Kenneth M. "Time and History among a Maroon People: The Aluku." In *Time in the Black Experience*, edited by J. Adjaye, 141–60. Westport, CT: Greenwood, 1994.

Biondi, Karina. *Sharing This Walk: An Ethnography of the PCC in Brazil*, edited and translated by John F. Collins. Chapel Hill: University of North Carolina Press, 2016.

Birth, Kevin. *Objects of Time: How Things Shape Temporality*. New York: Palgrave Macmillan, 2012.

Birth, Kevin. "Time and the Biological Consequences of Globalization." *Current Anthropology* 48, no. 2 (2007): 215–36.

Blackwater v. Plint, [1998] BCSC.

Blackwater v Plint, [2001] BCSC 997.

Blackwater v. Plint, [2005] 3 S.C.R. 3, SCC.

Blaker, James R. *United States Overseas Basing: An Anatomy of the Dilemma*. New York: Praeger, 1990.

Boglioli, Marc. *A Matter of Life and Death: Hunting in Contemporary Vermont*. Amherst: University of Massachusetts Press, 2009.

Bond, Patrick. "The Rise of 'Sub-Imperialism.'" *Counterpunch*, November 23–25, 2012. Accessed August 8, 2017. http://www.counterpunch.org/2012/11/23/the-rise-of-sub-imperialism/.

Bonne, C. "Hygiënische Ervaring te Moengo." *Nieuwe West-Indische Gids* (1923): 395–404.

Borneman, John. *After the Wall: East Meets West in the New Berlin*. New York: Basic Books, 1992.

Borneman, John. "Responsibility after Military Intervention: What Is Regime Change?" *PoLAR: Political and Legal Anthropology Review* 26, no. 1 (2003): 29–42.

"Bosnia: Citizenship Review Underway as Negative Media Attention Grows." Cable by Amb. Douglas McElhaney, 06SARAJEVO1748, August 4, 2006.

"Bosnia: Foreigners Affairs Service Detains Imad al-Hussein (A.K.A. Abu Hamza al-Suri)." Cable by Amb. Douglas McElhaney, 06SARAJEVO1748, August 4, 2006.

"Bosnia: INL-funded Project Highlights and Rule of Law Round-Up." Cable by Amb. Charles English, 09SARAJEVO234, February 26, 2009.

"Bosnia: INL-Managed SEED-funded Projects Advance Post's Rule of Law Agenda." Cable by Amb. Charles English, 09SARAJEVO406, April 1, 2009.

"Bosnia: INL-Managed SEED-funded Projects Update: Focus on the Foreigners Affairs Service." Cable by Amb. Charles English, 09SARAJEVO563, May 5, 2009.

Boudella, Lakhdar, Nechle, and Lahmar v. Bosnia and Herzegovina, Federation of Bosnia and Herzegovina, CH/02/8679/ et al. Human Rights Chamber of Bosnia-Herzegovina, 2002.

Bourdieu, Pierre. "The Forms of Capital." In *The Forms of Economic Life*, edited by Mark Granovetter and Richard Swedbag, 241–58. Boulder, CO: Westview Press, 1986.

Bourdieu, Pierre. *Outline of a Theory of Practice*. Vol. 16: Cambridge: Cambridge University Press, 1977.

Bourdieu, Pierre, and Loïc Wacquant. "Confronting the Ethics of Anthropology: Lessons from Fieldwork in Central America." In *Decolonizing Anthropology*, edited by Faye Harrison, 110–26. Washington, DC: American Anthropological Association, 1991.

Bourdieu, Pierre, and Loïc Wacquant. "On the Cunning of Imperialist Reason." *Theory, Culture and Society* 16, no. 1 (1999): 41–58.

Bourgois, Philippe, and Jeff Schonberg. *Righteous Dopefiend*. Berkeley: University of California Press, 2009.

Brands, Hal. *Latin America's Cold War*. Cambridge, MA: Harvard University Press, 2010.

Brickell, Claire. "Geographies of Contemporary Christian Mission(aries)." *Geography Compass* 6, no. 12 (2012): 725–39.

Briggs, Charles L. "Theorizing Modernity Conspiratorially: Science, Scale, and the Political Economy of Public Discourse in Explanations of a Cholera Epidemic." *American Ethnologist* 31, no. 2 (2004): 164–87.

Briggs, Laura. *Reproducing Empire: Race, Sex, Science, and U.S. Imperialism in Puerto Rico*. Berkeley: University of California Press, 2002.

Brown, Wendy. "Neo-Liberalism and the End of Liberal Democracy." In *Theory and Event* 7, no. 1 (2003). doi:10.1353/tae.2003.0020.

Brown, Wendy. *States of Injury: Power and Freedom in Late Modernity*. Princeton, NJ: Princeton University Press, 1995.

Brownell, Susan. *Training the Body for China: Sports in the Moral Order of the People's Republic*. Chicago: University of Chicago Press, 1995.

Bruyneel, Kevin. *The Third Space of Sovereignty: The Postcolonial Politics of U.S.-Indigenous Relations*. Minneapolis: University of Minnesota Press, 2007.

Bryant, Rebecca, and Mete Hatay. "Guns and Guitars: Simulating Sovereignty in a State of Siege." *American Ethnologist* 38, no. 4 (2011): 631–49.

Burawoy, Michael. "Introduction: Reaching for the Global." In *Global Ethnography*, edited by Michael Burawoy, Joseph A. Blum, Sheba George, Zsuzsa Gille, and Millie Thayer, 1–40. Berkeley: University of California Press, 2000.

Burbank, Jane, and Frederick Cooper. *Empires in World History: Power and the Politics of Difference*. Princeton, NJ: Princeton University Press, 2010.

Burk, James. "Theories of Democratic Civil-Military Relations." *Armed Forces and Society* 29, no. 1 (2002): 7–29.

Burnett, Christina Duffy, and Burke Marshall. "Between the Foreign and the Domestic: The Doctrine of Territorial Incorporation, Invented and Reinvented." In *Foreign in a Domestic Sense: Puerto Rico, American Expansion, and the Constitution*, edited by Christina Duffy Burnett and Burke Marshall, 1–36. Durham, NC: Duke University Press, 2001.

Burnett, Christina Duffy, and Burke Marshall, eds. *Foreign in a Domestic Sense: Puerto Rico, American Expansion, and the Constitution*. Durham, NC: Duke University Press, 2001.

Burns, Louis. *A History of the Osage People*. Fallbrook, CA: Ciga, 1989.

Burside, Walter E. "The Early Years of the Suriname Bauxite Company." *Suralco Magazine*, 18, no. 2 (1986): 3–9.

Busch, L., and J. Bingen. "Introduction: A New World of Standards." In *Agricultural Standards: The Shape of the Global Food and Fiber System*, edited by L. Busch and J. Bingen, 3–28. Dordrecht: Springer, 2006.

Bush, Luis. "Getting to the Core of the Core: The 10/40 Window." Last modified October 22, 1996. Accessed October 29, 2017. http://www.ad2000.org/1040broc.htm.

Butler, Judith. *Frames of War: When Is Life Grievable?* New York: Verso, 2010.

Butler, Judith. *Precarious Life: The Powers of Mourning and Violence*. London: Verso, 2004.

Byrd, Jodi. *The Transit of Empire: Indigenous Critiques of Colonialism*. Minneapolis: University of Minnesota Press, 2011.

Cadena, Marisol de la. "Cosmopolitanism: Conversation with the Authors." *Cultural Anthropology Online*, November 20, 2012. Accessed October 8, 2015. http://www.culanth.org/curated_collections/13-cosmopolitanism/discussions/8-cosmopolitanism-conversation-with-the-authors.

Cadena, Marisol de la. "Indigenous Cosmopolitics in the Andes: Conceptual Reflections Beyond 'Politics.'" *Cultural Anthropology* 25, no. 2 (2010): 334–70.

Cahill, Catherine. *Federal Fathers and Mothers: A Social History of the United States Indian Service, 1869–1933*. Chapel Hill: University of North Carolina Press, 2011.

Caldwell, Anne. "Bio-Sovereignty and the Emergence of Humanity." *Theory and Event* 7, no. 2 (2004): 16.

Calhoun, Craig, Frederick Cooper, and Kevin W. Moore, eds. *Lessons of Empire: Imperial Histories and American Power*. London: New Press, 2006.

Campbell, Kurt, and Celeste Johnson Ward. "New Battle Stations?" *Foreign Affairs* 83, no. 5 (2003): 95–103.

Campomanes, Oscar V. "New Formations of Asian American Studies and the Question of U.S. Imperialism." *Positions: East Asia Cultures Critique* 5, no. 2 (1997): 523–50.

Campos, Maria José. "Arthur Ramos: Luz e sombra na antropologia brasileira: Uma versão da democracia racial no Brasil nas décadas de 1930 e 1940." MA dissertation, University of São Paulo, 2002.

Capps, Randy, Jacqueline Hagan, and Nestor Rodriguez. "Border Residents Manage the U.S. Immigration and Welfare Reforms." In *Immigrants, Welfare Reform, and the Poverty of Policy*, edited by Philip Kretsedemas and Ana Aparicio. Westport, CT: Praeger, 2004.

Capriccioso, Rob. "Native Apology Said Out Loud." In *Indian Country Today*, May 28, 2010. Accessed October 31, 2015. http://indiancountrytodaymedianetwork.com/2010/05/28/native-apology-said-out-loud-81350.

Caputo, Philip. *A Rumor of War*. New York: Ballantine, 1977.

Capuzzo, Jill. "It's in New Jersey, but It Screams Vermont." *New York Times*, November 18, 2007.

Carnoy, Martin, and Manuel Castells. "Globalization, the Knowledge Society, and the Network State: Poulantzas at the Millennium." *Global Networks* 1, no. 1 (2001): 1–18.

Carter, Sarah. *Lost Harvests: Prairie Indian Reserve Farmers and Government Policy.* Montreal: McGill Queen's Press, 1990.

Cartmill, Matt. *A View to a Death in the Morning: Hunting and Nature through History.* Cambridge, MA: Harvard University Press, 2006.

Castells, Manuel. *The Rise of the Network Society.* Oxford: Blackwell, 2000.

Castronovo, Russ, and Dana Nelson. "Introduction: Materializing Democracy and Other Political Fantasies." In *Materializing Democracy*, edited by Russ Castronovo and Dana Nelson, 1–21. Durham, NC: Duke University Press, 2002.

Cattelino, Jessica R. "Anthropologies of the United States." *Annual Review of Anthropology* 39 (2010): 275–92.

Cattelino, Jessica R. *High Stakes: Florida Seminole Gaming and Sovereignty.* Durham, NC: Duke University Press, 2008.

Caulfield, Mina Davis. "Culture and Imperialism: Proposing a New Dialectic." In *Reinventing Anthropology*, edited by Dell Hymes, 182–212. New York: Pantheon Books, 1969.

Cavagnari Filho, Geraldo Lesbat. "O argumento do império." *Política Externa* 12, no. 1 (2003): 75–83.

CGPM. "Resolution 1: SI Unit of Time (second)." The 13th Conférence Générale des Poids et Mesures, 1967–68. Accessed August 26, 2014. http://www.bipm.org/en/CGPM/db/13/1/.

Chadsey, H., and D. McCarthy. "Relating Time to the Earth's Variable Rotation." *Proc. 32nd Annual Precise Time and Time Interval (PTTI) Systems and Applications Meeting*, November 28–30, 2000.

Chalfont, Alun A. G. J. "Letter to David K. E. Bruce." December 30, 1966, National Archives and Records Administration, RG 59/150/64–65, Subject-Numeric Files 1964–66, Box 1552.

Chan, John. "South Korean Hostage Crisis in Afghanistan Ends." *World Socialist Web Site*, September 12, 2007. Accessed August 8, 2017. www.wsws.org/en/articles/2007/09/kore-s12.html.

Chanda, Nayan. "Outsourcing Fears Nix US Aid to Teach English." *The Straits Times*, May 1, 2012.

Chandler, David. *A History of Cambodia.* Boulder, CO: Westview, 2000.

Chandler, David. *Voices from S-21: Terror and History in Pol Pot's Secret Prison.* Berkeley: University of California Press, 1999.

Chang, David. *The Color of the Land: Race, Nation, and the Politics of Landownership in Oklahoma, 1832–1929.* Chapel Hill: University of North Carolina Press, 2010.

Chari, Sharad, and Katherine Verdery. "Thinking between the Posts: Postcolonialism, Postsocialism, and Ethnography after the Cold War." *Comparative Studies in Society and History* 51, no. 1 (2009): 6–34.

Chatterjee, Partha. "Empire and Nation Revisited: 50 Years after Bandung." *Inter-Asia Cultural Studies* 6, no. 4 (2005): 487–96.

Cheney, Richard B. "Vice President's Remarks to the Traveling Press," December 20, 2005. Accessed January 10, 2013. http://www.presidency.ucsb.edu/ws/index.php?pid=82325.

Cho, J. K. "Legacy of U.S. Military Intervention: Landmine Issue in South Korea." Paper presented at the Doshisha International Conference on Humanitarian Interventions in the 21st Century, Doshisha University, Kyoto, Japan, 2012.

Choi, Hyaeweol. *Gender and Mission Encounters in Korea: New Women, Old Ways.* Berkeley: University of California Press, 2009.

Choi, Hyaeweol. "Women's Work for 'Heathen Sisters': American Women Missionaries and Their Educational Work in Korea." *Acta Koreana* 2 (July 1999): 1–22.

Choi, Paul. *Paekt'u Yerusalem (Back to Jerusalem).* Seoul: Pyŏnaegi, 2007.

Choi, Paul. *Segye Yŏngjŏk Dohae: Hananimŭi Segye Kyŏng'yŏng (Global Spiritual Mapping: God's Global Management).* Seoul: Pyŏnaegi, 2004.

Chomsky, Aviva. *Linked Labor Histories: New England, Colombia, and the Making of a Global Working Class.* Durham, NC: Duke University Press, 2008.

Chong, Kelly H. *Deliverance and Submission: Evangelical Women and the Negotiation of Patriarchy in South Korea.* Cambridge, MA: Harvard University Press, 2008.

Chŏng, Nak-in. "Wihŏm Suwi Nŏmŏsŏn Kaesinkyo Haewŏi Sŏnkyo (Protestant Overseas Missions Exceed Danger Level)." *Sisa jŏnŏl*, September 16, 2009. Accessed August 8, 2017. www.sisapress.com/news/articleView.html?idxno=50134.

Choy, Catherine Ceniza. *Empire of Care: Nursing and Migration in Filipino American History.* Durham, NC: Duke University Press, 2003.

Chunhao, Han. "Space Odyssey: Time-scales and Global Navigation Satellite Systems." *ITU News* 7 (2013). Accessed December 11, 2014. https://itunews.itu.int/En/4273-Space-odyssey-BRTime-scales-and-global-navigation-satellite-systems.note.aspx.

CIPM. *Procès-verbaux des séances, deuxième série, v. XXV, session de 1956.* Paris: Gauthier-Villars, 1957.

Clark, T. J. "For a Left with No Future." *New Left Review* 74 (2012): 53–75.

Clemence, G. M. "The Concept of Ephemeris Time: A Case of Inadvertent Plagiarism." *Journal for the History of Astronomy* 2, no. 2 (1971): 73–79.

Clemons, Don. "One in Three Hunters Will Fall." *Deer and Deer Hunting.* February 25, 2008. Accessed August 8, 2017. http://www.deeranddeerhunting.com/deer-hunt/deer-hunting-tips/p3_one_in_three_hunters_will_fall.

Coalición No Bases. *Base de manta: Ojos y oídos del Plan Colombia.* Quito: No Bases, 2007.

Coates, Peter, Tim Cole, Marianna Dudley, and Chris Pearson. "Defending Nation, Defending Nature? Militarized Landscapes and Military Environmentalism in Britain, France, and the United States." *Environmental History* 16, no. 3 (2011): 456–91.

Cochrane, E. L., Jr. "Memorandum for the Deputy Chief of Naval Operations (Plans and Policy)." March 24, 1971. Naval Historical Center, 00 Files, 1971, Box 174, 11000.

Cochrane, Joe. "A Bitter Bon Voyage." *Newsweek*, August 5, 2002. Accessed August 8. 2017. http://www.newsweek.com/bitter-bon-voyage-144003.

Codlin, Lee. "Black Spot on the Hearts of Survivors Revealed." *Windspeaker* 30, no. 1 (2012). Accessed October 31, 2015. http://www.ammsa.com/publications/windspeaker/black-spot-hearts-survivors-revealed.

Coffman, Tom. *Nation Within: The History of the American Occupation of Hawaii.* 2nd ed. Kihei, HI: Koa Books, 2009.

Cohn, Bernard. *An Anthropologist among the Historians and Other Essays.* Delhi: Oxford University Press, [1980] 1987.

Cohn, Bernard. *Colonialism and Its Forms of Knowledge: The British in India*. Princeton, NJ: Princeton University Press, 1996.

Cole, David. *Enemy Aliens: Double Standards and Constitutional Freedoms in the War on Terrorism*. New York: New Press, 2003.

Coll, Steve. *Private Empire: ExxonMobil and American Power*. New York: Penguin, 2012.

Collins, John F. "'But What if I Should Need to Defecate in *Your* Neighborhood, Madame?': Empire, Redemption and the 'Tradition of the Oppressed' in a Brazilian Historical Center." *Cultural Anthropology* 23, no. 2 (2008): 279–328.

Collins, John F. "Melted Gold and National Bodies: The Hermeneutics of Depth and the Value of History in Brazilian Racial Politics." *American Ethnologist* 38, no. 4 (2011): 683–700.

Collins, John F. *Revolt of the Saints: Memory and Redemption in the Twilight of Brazilian Racial Democracy*. Durham, NC: Duke University Press, 2015.

Collins, John F. "Ruins, Redemption, and Brazil's Imperial Exception." In *Imperial Debris: On Ruins and Ruination*, edited by Ann Laura Stoler, 162–93. Durham, NC: Duke University Press, 2013.

Colón, Héctor M., Rafaela R. Robles, Sherry Derren, Hardeo Sahai, H. Ann Finlinson, Jonny Andía, Miguel A. Cruz, Sung-Yeon Kang, and Denise Oliver-Vélez. "Between-City Variation in Frequency of Injection among Puerto Rican Injection Drug Users: East Harlem, New York, and Bayamon, Puerto Rico." *Journal of Acquired Immune Deficiency Syndromes* 27, no. 4 (2001): 405–13.

Colón, Héctor M., Rafaela R. Robles, and C. A. Marrero. "Frequency of Drug Injection in Puerto Rico and among Puerto Rican Injection Drug Users Compared to Other Ethnic Groups and Geographical Regions." Paper presented at the American Public Health Association Annual Meeting and Exhibition, Washington, DC, October 30–November 3, 1994.

Comaroff, Jean, and John Comaroff. "Christianity and Colonialism in South Africa." *American Ethnologist* 13, no. 1 (1986): 1–22.

Comaroff, Jean, and John Comaroff. *Ethnicity, Inc.* Chicago: University of Chicago Press, 2009.

Comaroff, Jean, and John Comaroff. *Ethnography and the Historical Imagination*. Boulder, CO: Westview, 1992.

Comaroff, Jean, and John Comaroff. *Of Revelation and Revolution: Christianity Colonialism and Consciousness in South Africa*. Chicago: University of Chicago Press, 1991.

Conklin, Ken. *Hawaiian Apartheid: Racial Separatism and Ethnic Nationalism in the Aloha State*. Montgomery, AL: E-Booktime, 2007.

Connell, Raewyn. "Globalization, Imperialism, and Masculinities." In *Handbook of Studies on Men and Masculinities*, edited by Michael Kimmel, Jeff Hearn, and Raewyn Connell, 71–89. Thousand Oaks, CA: SAGE Publications, 2005.

Cook, Karen S., ed. *Trust in Society*. Russell Sage Foundation Series on Trust 2. New York: Russell Sage Foundation, 2001.

Cooley, Alexander. *Base Politics: Democratic Change and the U.S. Military Overseas*. Ithaca, NY: Cornell University Press, 2008.

Cooper, Frederick. *Colonialism in Question: Theory, Knowledge, History.* Berkeley: University of California Press, 2005.

Cooper, Frederick. "Empire Multiplied: A Review Essay." *Comparative Studies in Society and History* 46, no. 2 (2004): 247–72.

Cooper, Frederick, and Ann Laura Stoler, eds. *Tensions of Empire: Colonial Cultures in a Bourgeois World.* Berkeley: University of California Press, 1997.

Coronil, Fernando. "Beyond Occidentalism: Toward Nonimperial Geohistorical Categories." *Cultural Anthropology* 11, no. 1 (1996): 51–87.

Coronil, Fernando. *The Magical State: Nature, Money, and Modernity in Venezuela.* Chicago: University of Chicago Press, 1997.

Coronil, Fernando. "Towards a Critique of Globalcentrism: Speculations on Capitalism's Nature." *Public Culture* 12, no. 2 (2000): 351–74.

Coulthard, Glen. *Red Skin, White Masks: Rejecting the Colonial Politics of Recognition.* Minneapolis: University of Minnesota Press, 2014.

Coyote, Comandante/Santiago Benjamin. "Reseña histórica de la lucha indígena en Nicaragua: Los hechos más relevantes de la lucha indígena de 1973 a 1989, tanto en Nicaragua como en el exilio (Honduras y Costa Rica), compiled by Gilles Bataillon." TRACE *(Travaux et Recherches dans les Amériques du Centre): Relatos de la vida* 41 (2002): 50–64.

Crawford, Remsen. "Open Season Threatens the Extinction of Deer: Hunter Permitted by New Law to Kill Does as Well as Bucks—Quail Still Protected but Fight for End of Restrictions Is in Prospect." *New York Times*, November 16, 1919.

Crum, Galen. "Daily Oklahoman Editorial." *Osage Shareholders Association.* Last modified July 14, 2007. Accessed August 27, 2009. http://www.osageshareholders.org/disc50_frm.htm.

Cruz-Malavé, Arnaldo. "The Oxymoron of Sexual Sovereignty: Some Puerto Rican Literary Reflections." *Centro* 19, no. 1 (2007): 50–73.

Cueto, Marcos. *Cold War, Deadly Fevers: Malaria Eradication in Mexico, 1955–1975.* Baltimore: Johns Hopkins University Press, 2007.

Cumings, Bruce. *Korea's Place in the Sun: A Modern History.* New York: W. W. Norton, 1997.

Cumings, Bruce. *Parallax Visions: Making Sense of American–East Asian Relations at the End of the Century.* Durham, NC: Duke University Press, 1999.

Da Col, Giovanni, and David Graeber. "Foreword: The Return of Ethnographic Theory." *HAU: Journal of Ethnographic Theory* 1, no. 1 (2011): vi–xxxv.

Danjon, A. "Le temps, sa définition pratique, sa mesure." *l'Astronomie* 43 (1929): 13–22.

Danzig, Allison. *The History of American Football.* Englewood Cliffs, NJ: Prentice-Hall, 1955.

Das, Veena. "Ordinary Ethics." In *A Companion to Moral Anthropology*, edited by Didier Fassin, 133–49. Malden, MA: Wiley Blackwell, 2015.

Daschuk, James. *Clearing the Plains: Disease, Politics of Starvation and the Loss of Aboriginal Life.* Regina, Canada: University of Regina Press, 2013.

Da Silva, Ferreira Denise. *Toward a Global Idea of Race.* Minneapolis: University of Minnesota Press, 2007.

Daulatzai, Sohail. *Black Star, Crescent Moon: The Muslim International and Black Freedom beyond America.* Minneapolis: University of Minnesota Press, 2012.

David, Emmanuel. "The Sexual Fields of Empire." *Radical History Review* 123 (2015): 115–43.

Davis, Angela. *The Meaning of Freedom: And Other Difficult Dialogues*. San Francisco: City Lights Publishers, 2012.

Davis, Jeffrey Sasha, Jessica S. Hayes-Conroy, and Victoria M. Jones. "Military Pollution and Natural Purity: Seeing Nature, Knowing Contamination in Vieques, Puerto Rico." *GeoJournal* 69, no. 3 (2007): 165–79.

Dawson, Allan. *In Light of Africa: Globalizing Blackness in Northeast Brazil*. Toronto: University of Toronto Press, 2014.

de Genova, Nicholas. "The Deportation Regime: Sovereignty, Space, and the Freedom of Movement." In *The Deportation Regime: Sovereignty, Space, and the Freedom of Movement*, edited by Nicholas de Genova and Nathalie Peutz, 33–65. Durham, NC: Duke University Press, 2010.

de Genova, Nicholas. "Migrant 'Illegality' and Deportability in Everyday Life." *Annual Review of Anthropology* 31 (2002): 419–47.

de Genova, Nicholas. *Working the Boundaries: Race, Space, and "Illegality" in Mexican Chicago*. Durham, NC: Duke University Press, 2005.

Dela Paz, Chrisee. "Philippines' Back Office Shines in 2015, Exceeds Targets." *Rappler*, February 3, 2016. Accessed October 20, 2017. https://www.rappler.com/business/industries/174-outsourcing/121233-philippines-bpo-ibpap-targets-2015.

Deleuze, Gilles, and Felix Guattari. *A Thousand Plateaus: Capitalism and Schizophrenia*. Minneapolis: University of Minnesota Press, 1987.

DeLillo, Don. *Underworld*. New York: Scribner, 1997.

del Moral, Solsiree. *Negotiating Empire: The Cultural Politics of Schools in Puerto Rico 1898–1952*. Madison: University of Wisconsin Press, 2013.

Deloria, Vine, Jr. *Custer Died for Your Sins: An Indian Manifesto*. Norman: University of Oklahoma Press, 1969.

de Lotbinière, Max. " 'Threat to U.S. Jobs' Shuts USAID Training." *Guardian*, May 15, 2012. Accessed October 20, 2017. https://www.theguardian.com/education/2012/may/05/usaid-jobs-threat.

Dennison, Jean. "Base Structure Report Fiscal Year 2014 Baseline (A Summary of DoD's Real Property Inventory)." Washington, DC, 2014.

Dennison, Jean. *Colonial Entanglement: Constituting a Twenty-First Century Osage Nation*. Chapel Hill: University of North Carolina Press, 2012.

Dennison, Jean. "Whitewashing Indigenous Oklahoma and Chicano Arizona: 21st-Century Legal Mechanisms of Settlement." *PoLAR* 37, no. 3 (2014): 162–80.

Derby, Lauren. "Imperial Secrets: Vampires and Nationhood in Puerto Rico." *Past and Present* 199, no. 3 (2008): 290–312.

Der Derian, James. *Virtuous War: Mapping the Military-Industrial-Media-Entertainment Network*. London: Routledge, 2009.

Derrida, Jacques. *Aporias*. Stanford, CA: Stanford University Press, 1993.

"Dessert-Bridge Will Benefit Tibetan Student." *The Westfield* (N.J.) *Leader*, April 6, 1978, 15. Accessed November 2, 2017. http://www.digifind-it.com/westfield/leader/1907-1979/1978/1978-04-06.pdf.

Diamond, Stanley, Eleanor Leacock, Ashley Montagu, Donald M. Nonini, and Rayna Rapp. "Anthropologists Speak Out on Nuclear Disarmament." *Anthropology News* 25, no. 5 (1984): 5.

Diário Vermelho. "Congresso recebe resultados do plebiscito da ALCA." *CMI Brasil.* September 18, 2002. Accessed August 8, 2017. http://www.midiaindependente.org/en/blue/2002/09/36403.shtml.

Diaz, Vicente M. "Deliberating 'Liberation Day': Identity, History, Memory, and War in Guam." In *Perilous Memories: The Asia-Pacific War(s)*, edited by T. Fujitani, Geoffrey M. White, and Lisa Yoneyama, 155–80. Durham, NC: Duke University Press, 2001.

Diaz, Vicente M. " 'Fight Boys, 'Til the Last . . .': Islandstyle Football and the Remasculinization of Indigeneity in the Militarized American Pacific Islands." In *Pacific Diaspora: Island Peoples in the United States and across the Pacific*, edited by Paul Spickard, Joanne L. Rondilla, and Debbie Hippolite Wright. Honolulu: University of Hawai'i Press, 2002.

"The Diego Garcians," *Washington Post* editorial, September 11, 1975, A22.

DiPrizio, Robert C. *Armed Humanitarians: U.S. Interventions from Northern Iraq to Kosovo.* Baltimore: Johns Hopkins University Press, 2002.

Dirks, Nicholas B., ed. *Colonialism and Culture.* Ann Arbor: University of Michigan Press, 1992.

Doerr, Audrey D. "The Royal Commission on Aboriginal Peoples." *The Canadian Encyclopedia.* 2006. Accessed October 26, 2017. http://thecanadianencyclopedia.ca/en/article/royal-commission-on-aboriginal-peoples/.

Dougherty, Mary, Denise Wilson, and Amy Wu. "Immigration Enforcement Actions: 2004." Department of Homeland Security Office of Immigration Statistics, 2005.

Douglas, Mary. *Purity and Danger: An Analysis of Concepts of Pollution and Taboo.* New York: Praeger, 1966.

Dow, Mark. *American Gulag: Inside U.S. Immigration Prisons.* Berkeley: University of California Press, 2004.

Dow, Mark. "Designed to Punish: Immigrant Detention and Deportation." *Social Research* 74, no. 2 (2007): 533–46.

Duara, Prasenjit. "The Imperialism of 'Free Nations.'" In *Imperial Formations*, edited by Ann Laura Stoler, Carole McGranahan, and Peter Perdue, 211–39. Santa Fe: SAR, 2007.

Du Bois, W. E. B. *The Souls of Black Folk.* Chicago: A. C. McClurg, 1903.

Dudas, Jeffrey R. *The Cultivation of Resentment: Treaty Rights and the New Right.* Stanford, CA: Stanford University Press, 2008.

Dudziak, Mary L. "Desegregation as a Cold War Imperative." In *Critical Race Theory: The Cutting Edge*, edited by Richard Delgado and Jean Stefancic, 106–17. Philadelphia: Temple University Press, 2000.

Dueck, Lorna. "Out of Their Minds for God." *Globe and Mail*, March 2, 2008. Accessed August 8, 2017. https://www.theglobeandmail.com/opinion/out-of-their-minds-for-god/article724502/.

Duggan, Lisa. *Twilight of Equality? Neoliberalism, Cultural Politics, and the Attack on Democracy.* Boston: Beacon, 2004.

Dumas, Lane. *Integrating the Gridiron: Black Civil Rights and American College Football.* Rutgers, NJ: Rutgers University Press, 2009.

Dunn, S. J. "Shore Up the Indian Ocean." *Proceedings* 110, no. 9/979 (1984): 131–36.

Durmo v. Bosnia and Herzegovina, Federation of Bosnia and Herzegovina, CH/02/9842. Human Rights Chamber of Bosnia-Herzegovina, 2003.

Eekelen, Bregje, Jennifer Gonzalez, Bettina Stotzer, and Anna Tsing, eds. *Shock and Awe: War on Words*. Santa Cruz, CA: New Pacific, 2004.

Eiss, Paul. "Hunting for the Virgin: Meat, Money, and Memory in Tetiz, Yucatan." *Cultural Anthropology* 17, no. 3 (2002): 291–330.

Elkins, Caroline, and Susan Pedersen, eds. *Settler Colonialism in the Twentieth Century: Projects, Practices, Legacies*. London: Routledge, 2005.

Eng, David L. *The Feeling of Kinship: Queer Liberalism and the Racialization of Intimacy*. Durham, NC: Duke University Press, 2010.

Engelhardt, Tom. "Baseless Considerations." TomDispatch.com, November 4, 2007. Accessed October 15, 2017. http://www.tomdispatch.com/post/174858.

Engelhardt, Tom. *The End of Victory Culture*. Amherst: University of Massachusetts Press, 2007.

Engelke, Matthew. *A Problem of Presence: Beyond Scripture in an African Church*. Berkeley: University of California, 2007.

Ensarije. "Ilā man yuhmmuhu al-amr." Accessed October 22, 2017. https://web.archive.org/web/20120401181005/http://www.ensarije.com/index.php?id=1132.

Epstein, Rick. "'Barbarianism' Ruled on Sourland Mountain, Historian Says." *TAPinto.net: Your Neighborhood News Online* (2016). Accessed March 27, 2017. https://www.tapinto.net/articles/barbarianism-ruled-on-sourland-mountain-histor.

Erling, Elizabeth. "The Many Names of English: A Discussion of the Variety of Labels Given to the Language in Its Worldwide Role." *English Today* 21, no. 1 (2005): 40–44.

Escobar, Arturo. "Beyond the Third World: Imperial Globality, Global Coloniality and Anti-Globalisation Social Movements." *Third World Quarterly* 25 (2004): 2017–30.

Espiritu, Yen Le. *Body Counts: The Vietnam War and Militarized Refuge(es)*. Berkeley: University of California, 2014.

Essen, L., and J. V. L. Parry. "An Atomic Standard of Frequency and Time Interval." *Nature* 176, no. 4476 (1955): 280–82.

Essoyan, Susan. "Certified Native Hawaiian Role Posted Online with 95,690 Names." *Honolulu Star-Advisor*, July 28, 2015. Accessed July 29, 2017. http://www.staradvertiser.com/2015/07/28/breaking-news/certified-native-hawaiian-roll-posted-online-with-95690-names/.

Estabrook, Robert H. "U.S., Britain Consider Indian Ocean Bases." *Washington Post*, August 29, 1964, A1, A6.

Estrada, Antonio. "Drug Use and HIV Risks among African American, Mexican-American, and Puerto Rican Drug Injectors." *Journal of Psychoactive Drugs* 30 (1998): 247–53.

Etienne, Mona, and Eleanor Leacock, eds. *Women and Colonization*. New York: Praeger, 1980.

Evans-Pritchard, E. E. "Social Anthropology: Past and Present." In *Social Anthropology and Other Essays*, 139–54. New York: Free Press of Glencoe, 1962.

Faludi, Susan. "Broken Promise: How Everyone Got Hawaiians' Homelands Except the Hawaiians." *Wall Street Journal*, September 9, 1991, 1.

Fanon, Frantz. *Black Skin, White Masks*. Translated by Richard Philcox. New York: Grove, 2008.

Fanon, Frantz. *A Dying Colonialism*. Translated by Haakon Chevalier. New York: Grove, 1994.

Fanon, Frantz. *The Wretched of the Earth*. New York: Grove, 1963.

Farmer, Paul. "On Suffering and Structural Violence: A View from Below." In *Social Suffering*, edited by Arthur Kleinman, Veena Das, and Margaret Lock, 261–83. Berkeley: University of California Press, 1997.

Farnam, Julie. *US Immigration Laws under the Threat of Terrorism*. New York: Algora, 2005.

Farquhar, Judith, and Qicheng Zhang. "Biopolitical Beijing: Pleasure, Sovereignty, and Self-Cultivation in China's Capital." *Cultural Anthropology* 20, no. 3 (2005): 303–27.

Fassin, Didier, and Paula Vasquez. "Humanitarian Exception as the Rule: The Political Theology of the 1999 Tragedia in Venezuela." *American Ethnologist* 32, no. 3 (2005): 389–405.

Federal Bureau of Investigation. "Osage Indian Murders." Accessed December 13, 2010. http://foia.fbi.gov/foiaindex/osageind.htm.

Federal-State Task Force on the Hawaiian Homes Commission Act 1983. "Report to United States Secretary of the Interior and the Governor of the State of Hawaii." August 15, 1983. Accessed March 1, 2011. https://www.doi.gov/sites/doi.gov/files/migrated/ohr/upload/Fed-State-Task-Force-on-HHCA-Aug-15-1983.pdf.

Feldman, Allan. "On Cultural Anaesthesia: From Desert Storm to Rodney King." *American Ethnologist* 21, no. 2 (1994): 404–18.

Feldman, Allan. "Securocratic Wars of Public Safety: Globalized Policing as Scopic Regime." *Interventions* 6, no. 3 (2004): 330–50.

Feldman, Gregory. *The Migration Apparatus: Security, Labor, and Policymaking in the European Union*. Stanford, CA: Stanford University Press, 2012.

Feldman, Ilana, and Miriam Ticktin. "Introduction: Government and Humanity." In *In the Name of Humanity: The Government of Threat and Care*, edited by Ilana Feldman and Miriam Ticktin, 1–26. Durham, NC: Duke University Press, 2010.

Fenster, Mark. *Conspiracy Theories: Secrecy and Power in American Culture*. Minneapolis: University of Minnesota Press, 1999.

Ferguson, James. *The Anti-Politics Machine: "Development," Depoliticization, and Bureaucratic Power in Lesotho*. Minneapolis: University of Minnesota Press, 1994.

Ferguson, Niall. *Colossus: The Price of America's Empire*. New York: Penguin, 2004.

Ferguson, R. Brian. "Introduction: Violent Conflict and Control of the State." In *The State, Identity and Violence: Political Disintegration in the Post-Cold War World*, 1–58. London: Routledge, 2003.

Fernos, Antonio. *De San Jerónimo a Paseo Caribe*. San Juan: Ediciones Tal Cual, 2008.

Finkleman, David, John H. Seago, and P. Kenneth Seidelmann. "The Debate over UTC and Leap Seconds." AIAA Guidance, Navigation, and Control Conference, August 2–5, 2010, Toronto. Accessed December 11, 2014. https://www.researchgate.net/profile/David_Finkleman/publication/268057042_The_debate_over_UTC_and_leap_seconds/links/54b3d52c0cf26833efcfd321/The-debate-over-UTC-and-leap-seconds.pdf?origin=publication_list.

Fluri, Jennifer L. "Geopolitics of Gender and Violence from Below." *Political Geography* 28, no. 4 (2009): 259–65.

Forte, Maximilian C., ed. *The New Imperialism*. Vol. 1: *Militarism, Humanism, and Occupation*. Montreal: Alert, 2010.

Fosher, Kerry B. *Under Construction: Making Homeland Security at the Local Level.* Chicago: University of Chicago Press, 2009.

Foucault, Michel. *The Archaeology of Knowledge: And the Discourse on Language.* New York: Pantheon Books, 1972.

Foucault, Michel. *The Birth of Biopolitics: Lectures at the Collège de France, 1978–1979.* Edited by Michel Senellart, translated by Graham Burchell. New York: Palgrave Macmillan, 2008.

Foucault, Michel. *Discipline and Punish: The Birth of the Prison.* New York: Vintage, [1977] 1995.

Foucault, Michel. "Nietzsche, Genealogy, History." In *Language, Counter-Memory, Practice: Selected Writings and Interviews*, edited by D. F. Bouchard, 139–64. Ithaca, NY: Cornell University Press, 1977.

Foucault, Michel, and Jay Miskoweic. "Of Other Spaces." *Diacritics* 16, no. 1 (1986): 22–27.

Frederickson, Kari, and Jane Dailey. *Cold War Dixie: Militarism and Modernization in the American South.* Athens: University of Georgia Press, 2013.

Freeman, Gary. "Client Politics or Populism? Immigration Reform in the United States." In *Controlling a New Migration World*, edited by Virginie Guiraudon and Christian Joppke, 65–96. London: Routledge, 2001.

French, Jan Hoffman. *Legalizing Identities: Becoming Black or Indian in Brazil's Northeast.* Chapel Hill: University of North Carolina Press, 2009.

Frese, Pamela R., and Margaret C. Harrell, eds. *Anthropology and the United States Military: Coming of Age in the Twenty-First Century.* New York: Palgrave Macmillan, 2003.

Freyre, Gilberto. *Brazil: An Interpretation.* New York: Knopf, 1945.

Freyre, Gilberto. *Casa Grande e Senzala: Formação da família brasileira sob o regime da economia patriarcal.* Rio de Janeiro: Maia and Schmidt, 1933.

Friedman, Andrew. *Covert Capital: Landscapes of Denial and the Making of U.S. Empire in the Suburbs of Northern Virginia.* Berkeley: University of California Press, 2013.

Friginal, Eric. *The Language of Outsourced Call Centers: A Corpus-Based Study of Cross-Cultural Interaction.* Philadelphia: John Benjamins Publishing, 2009.

Frost, Roger. "Standards and the Citizen: Contributing to Society—38th World Standards Day." October 14, 2007. Accessed December 11, 2014. http://www.iso.org/iso/news.htm?refid=Ref1079.

Frühstück, Sabine. *Uneasy Warriors: Gender, Memory, and Popular Culture in the Japanese Army.* Berkeley: University of California Press, 2007.

Fry, Peter, Yvonne Maggie, Marcos Chor Maio, Simone Monteiro, and Ricardo Ventura Santos, eds. *Divisões perigosas: Políticas raciais no Brasil contemporâneo.* Rio de Janeiro: Civilização Brasileira, 2007.

Fuchs, Lawrence H. *Hawaii Pono: A Social History.* San Diego: Harcourt Brace Jovanovich, 1961.

Fujitani, T., Geoffrey M. White, and Lisa Yoneyama, eds. *Perilous Memories: The Asia-Pacific War(s).* Durham, NC: Duke University Press, 2001.

Gabriel-Doxtator, Brenda Katlatont, and Arlette Kawanatatie Van den Hende. *At the Woods' Edge: An Anthology of the History of the People of Kanehsatake*. Kanesatake, Canada: Kanesatake Education Centre, 1995.

Gaddis, John Lewis. *The Long Peace: Inquiries into the History of the Cold War*. New York: Oxford University Press, 1989.

Gallup. "Confidence in Institutions." June 7–10, 2012. Accessed August 8, 2017. http://www.gallup.com/poll/1597/confidence-institutions.aspx.

Ganguly, Keya. *States of Exception: Everyday Life and Postcolonial Identity*. Minneapolis: University of Minnesota Press, 2001.

Gardner, Lloyd. *The Case That Never Dies: The Lindbergh Kidnapping*. New Brunswick, NJ: Rutgers University Press, 2012.

Gardner, Lloyd C., Walter F. La Feber, and Thomas J. McCormick. *Creation of the U.S. Empire*. Vols. 1–2, 2nd ed. Chicago: Rand McNally, 1976.

Gell, Alfred. *The Anthropology of Time: Cultural Constructions of Temporal Maps and Images*. Oxford: Berg, 1992.

Gems, Gerald R. *The Athletic Crusade: Sport and American Cultural Imperialism*. Lincoln: University of Nebraska Press, 2006.

Gerges, Fawaz. *The Far Enemy: Why Jihad Went Global*. Cambridge: Cambridge University Press, [2005] 2009.

Gershon, Illana, and Allison Alexy. "Introduction: The Ethics of Disconnection in a Neoliberal Age." *Anthropological Quarterly* 84, no. 4 (2011): 799–980.

Gerson, Joseph. "The Sun Never Sets." In *The Sun Never Sets: Confronting the Network of Foreign U.S. Military Bases*, edited by Joseph Gerson and Bruce Birchard, 3–34. Boston: South End, 1991.

Gessen, Masha. "Russia: The Conspiracy Trap." *New York Review of Books*, March 6, 2017. Accessed August 8, 2017. http://www.nybooks.com/daily/2017/03/06/trump-russia-conspiracy-trap/.

Gherovici, Patricia. *The Puerto Rican Syndrome*. New York: Other, 2003.

Gill, Lesley. *The School of the Americas: Military Training and Political Violence in the Americas*. Durham, NC: Duke University Press, 2004.

Gilroy, Paul. *The Black Atlantic: Modernity and Double Consciousness*. Cambridge, MA: Harvard University Press, 1993.

Gindin, Sam, and Leo Panitch. *The Making of Global Capitalism: The Political Economy of American Empire*. London: Verso, 2012.

The Global Posture Review of United States Military Forces Stationed Overseas. Senate Hearing 108–853, September 23, 2004.

Go, Julian. *American Empire and the Politics of Meaning: Elite Political Cultures in the Philippines and Puerto Rico during U.S. Colonialism*. Durham, NC: Duke University Press, 2008.

Go, Julian. "Introduction: Global Perspective on the U.S. Colonial State in the Philippines." In *The American Colonial State in the Philippines: Global Perspectives*, edited by Julian Go and Anne L. Foster, 1–42. Durham, NC: Duke University Press, 2003.

Go, Julian. *Patterns of Empire: The British and American Empires, 1688 to the Present*. Cambridge: Cambridge University Press, 2011.

Go, Julian, and Anne L. Foster, eds. *The American Colonial State in the Philippines: Global Perspectives*. Durham, NC: Duke University Press, 2003.

Godreau, Isar. *Scripts of Blackness: Race, Cultural Nationalism, and U.S. Colonialism in Puerto Rico.* Chicago: University of Illinois Press, 2015.

Goldstein, Alyosha. *Formations of United States Colonialism.* Durham, NC: Duke University Press, 2015.

Goldstein, Alyosha. "Introduction: Toward a Genealogy of the U.S. Colonial Present." In *Formations of United States Colonialism*, edited by Alyosha Goldstein, 1–30. Durham, NC: Duke University Press, 2015.

Goldstein, Alyosha. "Where the Nation Takes Place: Proprietary Regimes, Antistatism and U.S. Settler Colonialism." *South Atlantic Quarterly* 107, no. 4 (2008): 833–61.

Gonzalez, Roberto J. *American Counterinsurgency: Human Science and the Human Terrain.* Chicago: Prickly Paradigm, 2009.

Gonzalez, Roberto J., ed. *Anthropologists in the Public Sphere: Speaking out on War, Peace, and American Power.* Austin: University of Texas Press, 2004.

Gonzalez, Vernadette V. *Securing Paradise: Tourism and Militarism in Hawai'i and the Philippines.* Durham, NC: Duke University Press, 2013.

Gordon, Linda. "Southeast Asian Refugee Migration to the United States." In *Pacific Bridges: The New Immigration from Asia and the Pacific Islands*, edited by James T. Fawcett and Benjamin V. Carino, 153–73. Staten Island: Center for Migration Studies, 1987.

Gott, Gil. "Imperial Humanitarianism: History of an Arrested Dialectic." In *Moral Imperialism: A Critical Anthology*, edited by Berta Esperanza Hernandez-Truyol, 19–38. New York: New York University Press, 2002.

Gough, Kathleen. "Anthropology and Imperialism." *Economic and Political Weekly* 25, no. 31 (1968): 1705–8.

Gough, Kathleen. " 'Anthropology and Imperialism' Revisited." *Anthropologica* 35, no. 2 (1993): 279–89.

Gough, Kathleen. "New Proposals for Anthropologists." *Current Anthropology* 9, no. 5 (1968): 403–35.

Gough, Kathleen. "Seminar on Debt: The First 5000 Years—Reply." *Crooked Timber*, April 2, 2012. Accessed August 8, 2017. http://crookedtimber.org/2012/04/02/seminar-on-debt-the-first-5000-years-reply/.

Goury, Laurence, and Bettina Migge. *Grammaire du Nengee: Introduction aux langues aluku, ndyuka et pamaka.* Paris: IRD Editions, 2003.

"Gov. Togiola Welcomes Secretary of State Hillary Clinton." Pacific Voyager Forum, November 29, 2010. Accessed October 19, 2017. http://www.ipacific.com/forum/index.php?topic=659.0).

Gow, Peter. "Land, People, and Paper in Western Amazonia." In *The Anthropology of Landscape: Perspectives on Place and Space*, edited by Eric Hirsch and Michael O'Hanlon, 43–63. Oxford: Oxford University Press, 1995.

Grabias, David, and Nicole Newnham, dir. *Sentenced Home.* IndiePix Films, 2006.

Graeber, David. *Debt: The First 5,000 Years.* Brooklyn: Melville House, 2011.

Grandin, Greg. *Empire's Workshop: Latin America, the United States, and the Rise of the New Imperialism.* New York: Metropolitan Books, 2006.

Grandin, Greg. *The Last Colonial Massacre: Latin America in the Cold War.* Durham, NC: Duke University Press, 2004.

Grazia, Victoria de. *Irresistible Empire: America's Advance through Twentieth-Century Europe.* Cambridge, MA: Harvard University Press.

Gregory, Derek. "The Black Flag: Guantánamo Bay and the Space of Exception." *Geografiska Annaler: Series B, Human Geography* 88, no. 4 (2006): 405–27.

Gregory, Derek. *The Colonial Present: Afghanistan, Palestine, Iraq.* Malden, MA: Blackwell, 2004.

Green Korea United. [Noksaek Yŏnhap]. *Fact-Finding Report on 47 Mine Fields in the Border Area* [Chŏpkyŏng Chiyŏk 47gae Chiroejidae Silt'aejosa], 2010.

Grewal, Inderpal. *Transnational America.* Durham, NC: Duke University Press, 2005.

Griswold, Esther Ann. "State Hegemony Writ: International Law and Indigenous Rights." *Political and Legal Anthropology Review* 19, no. 1 (1996): 91–104.

Guevarra, Anna Romina. *Marketing Dreams, Manufacturing Heroes: The Transnational Labor Brokering of Filipino Workers.* New Brunswick, NJ: Rutgers University Press, 2010.

Guha, Ranajit, and Gayatri Chakravorty Spivak, eds. *Selected Subaltern Studies.* Oxford: Oxford University Press, 1988.

Guimarães, Antonio Sérgio Alfredo. "Racial Democracy." In *Imagining Brazil*, edited by Jessé Souza and Valter Sinder, 119–40. Oxford: Lexington Books, 2005.

Gusterson, Hugh. "Anthropology and Militarism." *Annual Review of Anthropology* 36 (2007): 155–75.

Gusterson, Hugh. *Nuclear Rites: A Weapons Laboratory at the End of the Cold War.* Berkeley: University of California Press, 1996.

Gusterson, Hugh. "Project Minerva and the Militarization of Anthropology." *Radical Teacher* 86 (winter 2009): 4–16.

Guttman, Allen. *From Ritual to Record: The Nature of Modern Sports.* New York: Columbia University Press, [1978] 2004.

Guttman, Allen. *Games and Empires: Modern Sports and Cultural Imperialism.* New York: Columbia University Press, 1994.

Gutmann, Matthew. "Military Conscription, Conscientious Objection and Democratic Citizenship in the Americas." In *Conscientious Objection: Resisting Militarized Society*, edited by Özgür Heval Çinar and Coşkun Üsterci, 133–44. London: Zed, 2009.

Gutmann, Matthew, and Catherine Lutz. *Breaking Ranks: Iraq Veterans Speak Out against the War.* Berkeley: University of California Press, 2010.

Gwertzman, Bernard. "McFarlane Took Cake and Bible to Tehran, Ex-C.I.A. Man Says," *New York Times*, January 11, 1987.

Hahm, Kwang Bok. *30 Years of Journeys in the DMZ* [*30 Nyŏn Kanŭi DMZ Kahaeng*]. Seoul: Eastward [Tosŏ Ch'ulp'an], 2007.

Hale, Charles R. *Resistance and Contradiction: Miskitu Indians and the Nicaraguan State, 1894–1987.* Stanford, CA: Stanford University Press, 1994.

Han, Ju Hui Judy. "Beyond Safe Haven: A Critique of Christian Custody of North Korean Migrants in China." *Critical Asian Studies* 45, no. 4 (2013): 533–64.

Han, Ju Hui Judy. "'If You Don't Work, You Don't Eat': Evangelizing Development in Africa." In *Millennium South Korea: Neoliberal Capital and Transnational Movements*, edited by Jesook Song. London: Routledge, 2011.

Han, Ju Hui Judy. "Missionary." *Aether: The Journal of Media Geography* 111 (2008): 58–83.

Han, Ju Hui Judy. "Neither Friends nor Foes: Thoughts on Ethnographic Distance." *Geoforum* 41, no. 1 (2010): 11–14.

Han, Ju Hui Judy. "Our Past, Your Future: Evangelical Missionaries and the Script of Prosperity." In *Territories of Poverty: Rethinking North and South*, edited by Ananya Roy and Emma Shaw Crane, 178–94. Athens: University of Georgia Press, 2015.

Han, Ju Hui Judy. "Reaching the Unreached in the 10/40 Window: The Missionary Geoscience of Race, Difference and Distance." In *Mapping the End Times: American Evangelical Geopolitics and Apocalyptic Visions*, edited by Jason Dittmer and Tristan Sturm, 183–207. Hampshire, UK: Ashgate Publishing, 2010.

Han, Ju Hui Judy. "Urban Megachurches and Contentious Religious Politics in Seoul." In *Handbook of Religion and the Asian City: Aspiration and Urbanization in the Twenty-First Century*, edited by Peter Van der Veer, 133–51. Berkeley: University of California Press, 2015.

Han, Sora. "Bonds of Representation: Race, Law and the Feminine in Post–Civil Rights America." PhD diss., University of California, Santa Cruz, 2006.

Hanchard, Michael. "Acts of Misrecognition: Transnational Black Politics, Anti-Imperialism and the Ethnocentrisms of Pierre Bourdieu and Loïc Wacquant." *Theory, Culture and Society* 20, no. 4 (2003): 5–29.

Hanchard, Michael. *Orpheus and Power: The Movimento Negro of Rio de Janeiro and São Paulo, Brazil, 1945–1988*. Princeton, NJ: Princeton University Press, 1994.

Hansen, Helena. "The 'New Masculinity': Addiction Treatment as a Reconstruction of Gender in Puerto Rican Evangelist Street Ministries." *Social Science and Medicine* 74 (2012): 1721–28.

Haraway, Donna. "Teddy Bear Patriarchy: Taxidermy in the Garden of Eden, New York City, 1908–1936." *Social Text* 11 (winter 1984–85): 20–64.

Hardt, Michael, and Antonio Negri. *Empire*. Cambridge, MA: Harvard University Press, 2000.

Harmon, Alexandra. *Rich Indians: Native People and the Problem of Wealth in American History*. Chapel Hill: University of North Carolina Press, 2010.

Harrison, Faye H., ed. *Decolonizing Anthropology: Moving Further Toward an Anthropology of Liberation*. Washington, DC: Association of Black Anthropologists, 1991.

Hart, Gillian. "Denaturalising Dispossession: Critical Ethnography in the Age of Resurgent Imperialism." *Antipode* 38, no. 5 (2006): 977–1004.

Hartung, William. *Prophets of War: Lockheed Martin and the Making of the Military-Industrial Complex*. New York: Avon, 2011.

Harvey, David. "Between Space and Time: Reflections on the Geographical Imagination." *Annals of the Association of American Geographers* 80 (1990): 418–34.

Harvey, David. *A Brief History of Neoliberalism*. Oxford: Oxford University Press, 2005.

Harvey, David. *The Condition of Postmodernity*. Oxford: Blackwell, 1989.

Harvey, David. *The New Imperialism*. Oxford: Oxford University Press, 2003.

Hasager, Ulla, and Jonathan Friedman. *Hawai'i Return to Nationhood*. Document no. 75. Copenhagen: International Working Group for Indigenous Affairs, 1994.

Havlick, David. "Logics of Change for Military-to-Wildlife Conversions in the United States." *GeoJournal* 69, no. 3 (2007): 151–64.

Hawaii Advisory Committee to the United States Commission on Civil Rights. "A Broken Trust: The Hawaiian Homelands Program: Seventy Years of Failure of the Federal and State Governments to Protect the Civil Rights of Native Hawaiians." 1991.

Hedges, Chris, and Laila al-Arian. *Collateral Damage: America's War against Iraqi Civilians.* New York: Nation Books, 2008.

Hein, Jeremy. *From Vietnam, Laos, and Cambodia: A Refugee Experience in the United States.* New York: Twayne, 1995.

Hellwig, David J. *African-American Reflections on Brazil's Racial Paradise.* Philadelphia: Temple University Press, 1992.

Henig, David. "Iron in the Soil: Living with Military Waste in Bosnia-Herzegovina." *Anthropology Today* 28, no. 1 (2012): 21–23.

Herr, Michael. *Dispatches.* New York: Avon, 1978.

Hersh, Seymour M. "Annals of National Security: The Redirection." *New Yorker,* March 5, 2007. Accessed December 3, 2012. http://www.newyorker.com/reporting/2007/03/05/070305fa_fact_hersh?currentPage=all.

Hesselink, G. *De Maatschappijstad Moengo en haar omgeving.* Amsterdam: Geografisch en Planologisch Instituut van Vrije Universitëit, 1974.

Higate, Paul, and John Hopton. "War, Militarism, and Masculinities." In *Handbook of Studies on Men and Masculinities*, edited by Michael Kimmel, Jeff Hearn, and Raewyn Connell, 432–47. Thousand Oaks, CA: SAGE Publications, 2005.

"Hillary Clinton Shares US Money and Samoan Smiles." *The Samoa Observer,* November 10, 2010.

Hing, Bill Ong. "Deporting Cambodian Refugees: Justice Denied?" *Crime and Delinquency* 51, no. 2 (2005): 265–90.

Hinton, Alexander Laban. *Why Did They Kill? Cambodia in the Shadow of Genocide.* Berkeley: University of California Press, 2005.

Hirsch, Eric. "Introduction: Landscape between Space and Place." In *The Anthropology of Landscape: Perspectives on Space and Place*, edited by Eric Hirsch and Michael O'Hanlon, 1–30. Oxford: Clarendon, 1995.

Ho, Engseng. "Empire through Diasporic Eyes: A View from the Other Boat." *Comparative Studies in Society and History* 46, no. 2 (2004): 210–46.

Ho, Karen. *Liquidated: An Ethnography of Wall Street.* Durham, NC: Duke University Press, 2009.

Hoang, Kimberly. *Dealing in Desire: Asian Ascendancy, Western Decline, and the Hidden Currencies of Global Sex Work.* Berkeley: University of California Press, 2015.

Hoefte, Rosemarijn. *Suriname in the Long Twentieth Century: Domination, Contestation, Globalization.* New York: Palgrave Macmillan, 2013.

Höhn, Maria, and Seungsook Moon, eds. *Over There: Living with the U.S. Military Empire from World War Two to the Present.* Durham, NC: Duke University Press, 2010.

Hokowhitu, Brendan. "'Physical Beings': Stereotypes, Sport and the 'Physical Education' of New Zealand Maori." *Culture, Sport, Society* 6, nos. 2–3 (2003): 192–218.

Hokowhitu, Brendan. "Tackling Maori Masculinity: A Colonial Genealogy of Savagery and Sport." *The Contemporary Pacific* 16, no. 2 (2004): 259–84.

Honey, Martha. *Hostile Acts: US Policy in Costa Rica in the 1980s*. Gainesville: University Press of Florida, 1994.

Hsu, Madeline Y. "Aid Refugee Chinese Intellectuals, Inc., and the Political Uses of Humanitarian Relief, 1952–1962." *Journal of Chinese Overseas* 10, no. 2 (2014): 137–64.

Hudson, Michael. *Super Imperialism: The Origin and Fundamentals of U.S. World Dominance*. New ed. London: Pluto, 2003.

Hume, David. *A Treatise of Human Nature*. Edited by David Fate Norton and Mary J. Norton. Oxford: Oxford University Press, [1739] 2002.

Humphrey, C. "Reassembling Individual Subjects: Events and Decisions in Troubled Times." *Anthropological Theory* 8, no. 4 (2008): 357–80.

Hussain, Nasser. "Beyond Norm and Exception: Guantánamo." *Critical Inquiry* 33, no. 4 (2007): 734–53.

Hutchison, William R. *Errand to the World: American Protestant Thought and Foreign Missions*. Chicago: University of Chicago Press, 1987.

Huttar, G. L., and Huttar, M. L. *Ndyuka: A Descriptive Grammar*. London: Routledge, 1994.

Hwang, Kyu-hak. "Ŏsŏlp'ŭn 'Han'guksik Sŏnkyo,' P'irapŭn Injaeyŏtda [Ill-Prepared 'Korean-Style Mission,' Kidnapping Was a Man-Made Disaster]." *OhMyNews*, August 31, 2007. Accessed August 8, 2017. www.ohmynews.com/nws_web/view/at_pg.aspx?CNTN_CD=A0000431618.

Im, Byeong-sik, and Sook-hui Kwon. "Before Reunification Comes . . . Tasks to Be Completed" [T'ongili Ogi Chŏneh . . . P'urŏya Kwajedŭl]. *Yonhap News*, March 9, 2014.

Imada, Adria L. *Aloha America: Hula Circuits through U.S. Empire*. Durham, NC: Duke University Press, 2012.

Indigenous and Northern Affairs Canada. "Indian Residential School Settlement Agreement." Accessed October 28, 2017. http://www.aadnc-aandc.gc.ca/eng/1100100015576/1100100015577.

Ingold, Tim. *Being Alive: Essays on Movement, Knowledge and Description*. London: Routledge, 2011.

Innes, Robert Alexander. *Elder Brother and the Law of the People: Contemporary Kinship and the Cowessess First Nation*. Winnipeg: University of Manitoba Press, 2013.

Inoue, Masamichi I. *Okinawa and the U.S. Military: Identity Making in the Age of Globalization*. New York: Columbia University Press, 2007.

International Campaign to Ban Landmines. "Landmine and Cluster Munition Monitor." Country Profile: Korea, South, 2013.

Iraq Veterans against the War, Aaron Glantz, and Anthony Swofford. *Winter Soldier, Iraq and Afghanistan: Eyewitness Accounts of the Occupations*. Chicago: Haymarket, 2008.

Isenberg, Andrew. *The Destruction of the Bison*. New York: Cambridge University Press, 2000.

Jamal, Amaney, and Nadine Naber, eds. *Race and Arab Americans after 9/11: From Invisible Citizens to Visible Subjects*. Syracuse, NY: Syracuse University Press, 2007.

James, C. L. R. *Beyond a Boundary*. London: Hutchinson, 1963.

Jenkins, Philip. *The Next Christendom: The Coming of Global Christianity.* Oxford: Oxford University Press, 2002.

Jensen, Richard J. *Reagan at Bergen-Belsen and Bitburg.* College Station: Texas A&M University Press, 2007.

"Jesse Ventura's 9/11 Theory: Dick Cheney 'Allowed It to Happen to Further Their Agenda.'" *CNN*, April 4, 2011. Accessed October 15, 2013. http://piersmorgan.blogs.cnn.com/2011/04/04/jesse-venturas-911-theory-dick-cheney-allowed-it-to-happen-to-further-their-agenda/.

Jimenez, Alberto "Trust in Anthropology." *Anthropological Theory* 11, no. 2 (2011): 177–96.

Johns, Fleur. "Guantánamo Bay and the Annihilation of the Exception." *European Journal of International Law* 16, no. 4 (2005): 613–35.

Johnson, Chalmers. "America's Empire of Bases." TomDispatch.com, January 15, 2004. Accessed August 9, 2017. http://www.tomdispatch.com/post/1181/chalmers_johnson_on_garrisoning_the_planet.

Johnson, Chalmers. *Blowback: The Costs and Consequences of American Empire.* New York: Owl Books, 2000.

Johnson, Chalmers. *The Sorrows of Empire: Militarism, Secrecy, and the End of the Republic.* New York: Metropolitan, 2004.

Johnson, Roy L. Memorandum for Deputy Chief of Naval Operations (Plans & Policy), July 21, 1958. Naval Historical Society, 00 Files, 1958, Box 4, A4–2 Status of Shore Stations.

Johnstone, Patrick, Jason Mandryk, and Robyn Johnstone. *Operation World: When We Pray, God Works.* 21st Century Edition ed. Cumbria, UK: Paternoster Lifestyle, 2001.

Jones, Carla. "Better Women: The Cultural Politics of Gendered Expertise in Indonesia." *American Anthropologist* 112, no. 2 (2010): 270–82.

Jones, Carla. "Whose Stress? Emotion Work in Middle-Class Javanese Homes." *Ethnos* 69, no. 4 (2004): 509–28.

Judt, Tony. "Whose Story Is It? The Cold War in Retrospect." In *Reappraisals: Reflections on the Forgotten Twentieth Century.* New York: Penguin, 2008.

Kaldor, Mary. *The Imaginary War: Interpretation of East-West Conflict in Europe.* Oxford: Blackwell, 1990.

Kamat, Sangeeta. "The Privatization of Public Interest: Theorizing NGO Discourse in a Neoliberal Era." *Review of International Political Economy* 11, no. 1 (2004): 155–76.

Kang, In-chul. *Han'gukŭi Kaesinkyowa Pan'gongjuŭi: Posujŏk Kaesinkyoŭi Chŏngch'ijŏk Haengdongjuŭi T'amgu* [*Protestantism and Anti-Communism in Korea: An Examination of Ideas and Practices of Conservative Protestantism*]. Seoul: Jungsim, 2007.

Kaplan, Amy. *The Anarchy of Empire in the Making of U.S. Culture.* Cambridge, MA: Harvard University Press, 2002.

Kaplan, Amy. "Left Alone with America: The Absence of Empire in the Study of American Culture." In *Cultures of United States Imperialism*, edited by Amy Kaplan and Donald E. Pease, 3–21. Durham, NC: Duke University Press, 1993.

Kaplan, Amy. "Violent Belongings and the Question of Empire Today." Presidential Address to the American Studies Association, Hartford, Connecticut, October 17, 2003. *American Quarterly* 56, no. 1 (2004): 1–18.

Kaplan, Amy. "Where Is Guantánamo?" *American Quarterly* 57 (2005): 831–58.

Kaplan, Amy, and Donald E. Pease, eds. *Cultures of United States Imperialism*. Durham, NC: Duke University Press, 1993.

Kauanui, J. Kēhaulani. "Colonialism in Equality: Hawaiian Sovereignty and the Question of U.S. Civil Rights." *South Atlantic Quarterly* 107, no. 4 (2008): 635–50.

Kauanui, J. Kēhaulani. *Hawaiian Blood: Colonialism and the Politics of Sovereignty and Indigeneity*. Durham, NC: Duke University Press, 2008.

Keane, Webb. *Christian Moderns: Freedom and Fetish in the Mission Encounter*. Berkeley: University of California Press, 2007.

Keeping Families Together Act of 2003. H.R. 3309, 108th Cong, 2003. Accessed February 2, 2012. https://www.congress.gov/bill/108th-congress/house-bill/3309.

Kellogg, Thomas, and Hossam El-Hamalawy. *Black Hole: The Fate of Islamists Rendered to Egypt*. New York: Human Rights Watch, 2005.

Kelly, John D. "Seeking What? Subversion, Situation, and Transvaluation." *Focaal* 64 (2012): 51–60.

Kelly, John D. "U.S. Power, after 9/11 and before It: If Not an Empire, Then What?" *Public Culture* 15, no. 2 (2003): 347–69.

Kelly, John D., Beatrice Jauregui, Sean T. Mitchell, and Jeremy Walton, eds. *Anthropology and Global Counterinsurgency*. Chicago: University of Chicago Press, 2010.

Kent, Noel. *Hawai'i: Islands under the Influence*. 2nd ed. Honolulu: University of Hawai'i Press, 1993.

Keys, Barbara J. *Globalizing Sport: National Rivalry and International Community in the 1930s*. Cambridge, MA: Harvard University Press, 2006.

Kim, Do-hyung. "Floods Prompt Concerns over Buried Mines." *Hangyeoreh* (South Korea), July 30, 2011.

Kim, Eleana J. *Adopted Territory: Transnational Korean Adoptees and the Politics of Belonging*. Durham, NC: Duke University Press, 2010.

Kim, Ha-yŏng. "Ap'ŭgan P'irap, 'Miguk Chŏngbu Much'aegim' 59.3% [59.3% Believe US Government Not Responsible for Hostages in Afghanistan]." *Pressian*, August 6, 2007. Accessed August 9, 2017. www.pressian.com/news/article.html?no=85147.

Kim, Jodi. *Ends of Empire: Asian American Critique and the Cold War*. Minneapolis: University of Minnesota Press, 2010.

Kim, Kevin. "S Koreans Rethink Missionary Work." BBC *News*, August 30, 2007. Accessed August 9, 2017. news.bbc.co.uk/2/hi/south_asia/6969185.stm.

Kim, Ki-ho. "The DMZ as Ecological Repository, in Preparation for Climate Change, Let's Develop Ecotourism Services through Eco-Friendly Landmine Removal" [Saengt'aegye Pogo Dmz, Kihu Pyŏnhwa Taebi Ch'inhwangyŏng Chiroe Chegŏro Chayŏnsaengtae Kwangwang Chawŏnŭro Kaebalhaeya]. *Civil Society Newspaper* [*Simin Sahoe Sinmun*], February 4, 2013.

Kim, Nami. "A Mission to the 'Graveyard of Empires'? Neocolonialism and the Contemporary Evangelical Missions of the Global South." *Mission Studies* 27, no. 1 (2010): 3–23.

Kim, Sangkeun. "Sheer Numbers Do Not Tell the Entire Story: The Challenges of the Korean Missionary Movement from an Ecumenical Perspective." *Ecumenical Review* 57, no. 4 (2005): 463–72.

Kim, Suki. "Asia's Apostles." *Washington Post*, July 25, 2007. Accessed August 9, 2017. www.washingtonpost.com/wp-dyn/content/article/2007/07/24/AR2007072401851.html.

Kim, Sung-Gun. "Korean Christian Zionism: A Sociological Study of Mission." *International Review of Mission* 100, no. 1 (2011): 85–95.

Kimmel, Michael. *Manhood in America: A Cultural History*. Oxford: Oxford University Press, 2005.

Klein, Alan M. *Growing the Game: The Globalization of Major League Baseball*. New Haven, CT: Yale University Press, [2006] 2008.

Klein, Alan M. *Sugarball: The American Game, the Dominican Dream*. New Haven, CT: Yale University Press, 1991.

Klein, Naomi. *The Shock Doctrine: The Rise of Disaster Capitalism*. New York: Metropolitan Books, 2007.

Knaus, John Kenneth. *Orphans of the Cold War: American and the Tibetan Struggle for Survival*. New York: Public Affairs, 1999.

Köbben, A. J. F. "Continuity in Change: Cottica Djuka Society as a Changing System." *Bijdragen tot de Taal-, Land-en Volkenkunde* 124, no. 1 (1968): 147–64.

Köbben, A. J. F. "Unity and Disunity—Cottica Djuka as a Kinship System." *Bijdragen tot de Taal- Land- en Volkenkunde* 123, no. 1 (1967): 10–52.

Koning, Anouk de. "Moengo on Strike: The Politics of Labour in Suriname's Bauxite Industry." *Revista Europea de Estudios Latinoamericanos y del Caribe* 91 (2011): 31–48.

Koning, Anouk de. "Shadows of the Plantation? A Social History of Suriname, a Bauxite Town Moengo." *New West Indian Guide* 85, nos. 3 and 4 (2011): 215–46.

Kornbluh, Peter, and Malcolm Byrne. *The Iran-Contra Scandal: The Declassified History*. New York: New Press, 1993.

Kosek, Jake. "Ecologies of Empire: On the New Uses of the Honeybee." *Cultural Anthropology* 25, no. 4 (2010): 650–78.

Kosek, Jake. *Understories: The Political Life of Forests in Northern New Mexico*. Durham, NC: Duke University Press, 2006.

Kramer, Paul A. *The Blood of Government: Race, Empire, the United States, and the Philippines*. Chapel Hill: University of North Carolina Press, 2006.

Kramer, Paul A. "Race, Empire, and Transnational History." In *Colonial Crucible: Empire in the Making of the Modern American State*, edited by Alfred McCoy and Francisco Scarano, 199–209. Madison: University of Wisconsin Press, 2009.

Krebs, Ronald R. "The Citizen-Soldier Tradition in the United States: Has Its Demise Been Greatly Exaggerated?" *Armed Forces and Society* 36, no. 1 (2009): 153–74.

Kriner, Douglas L., and Francis X. Shen. *The Casualty Gap: The Causes and Consequences of American Wartime Inequalities*. Oxford: Oxford University Press, 2010.

Kristof, Nicholas. "South Korea Extols Some Benefits of Land Mines." *New York Times*, September 3, 1997.

Kundnani, Arun. *The Muslims Are Coming: Islamophobia, Extremism, and the Domestic War on Terror*. London: Verso, 2014.

Kwauk, Christina Ting. "'No Longer Just a Pastime': Sport for Development in Times of Change." *Contemporary Pacific* 26, no. 2 (2014): 303–23.

Kwon, Heonik. *After the Massacre: Commemoration and Consolation in Ha My and My Lai.* Berkeley: University of California Press, 2006.

Kwon, Heonik. *Ghosts of War in Vietnam.* Cambridge: Cambridge University Press, 2008.

Kwon, Heonik. *The Other Cold War.* New York: Columbia University Press, 2010.

Kwon, Soo Ah. *Uncivil Youth: Race, Activism, and Affirmative Governmentality.* Durham, NC: Duke University Press, 2013.

Kyeonggi Province Cultural Foundation. "Research Report on Unification Village: Unification Village People, Stories of Their Lives." Kyeonggi Province Cultural Foundation, 2013.

Lachman, Beth E., A. Wong, and S. A. Reseter. "The Thin Green Line: An Assessment of DoD's Readiness and Environmental Protection Initiative to Buffer Installation Encroachment." Santa Monica, CA: RAND Corporation, 2007.

LaFeber, Walter. "An End to Which Cold War?" In *The End of the Cold War: Its Meaning and Implications*, edited by Michael J. Hogan, 13–19. New York: Cambridge University Press, 1992.

Lake, Eli. "Secret Honors for Cold War Spies." *Washington Times*, May 21, 2009. Accessed January 18, 2013. http://www.washingtontimes.com/news/2009/may/21/cold-war-stalwarts-honored/?page=all.

Lambek, Michael. "Toward an Ethics of the Act." In *Ordinary Ethics: Anthropology, Language, and Action*, edited by Michael Lambek, 39–63. New York: Fordham University Press, 2010.

Lamur, Carlo. *The American Take-Over: Industrial Emergence and Alcoa's Expansion in Guyana and Suriname. With Special Reference to Suriname, 1914–1921.* Leiden: Brill, 1983.

Latour, Bruno. *We Have Never Been Modern.* Translated by Catherine Porter. Cambridge, MA: Harvard University Press, 1993.

Laville, Helen. "The Importance of Being (In)Earnest: Voluntary Associations and the Irony of the State-Private Network during the Early Cold War." In *The US Government, Citizen Groups and the Cold War*, edited by Helen Laville and Hugh Wilford, 47–65. London: Routledge, 2006.

Laville, Helen, and Hugh Wilford, eds. *The US Government, Citizen Groups and the Cold War.* London: Routledge, 2006.

"Law on the Amendments to the Law on Citizenship of Bosnia-Herzegovina." *BH Gazette*, 82/05, November 28, 2005.

Lazaruk, Susan. "77 Year Pedophile Sentenced to 11 Years." *Windspeaker* 13 no. 2 (1995). Accessed November 30, 2015. http://www.ammsa.com/node/20552.

Leddick, R. S. Memorandum for the Record, November 11, 1969. Naval Historical Center, 00 Files, 1969, Box 98, 11000.

Lee, Jin-Kyung. *Service Economies: Militarism, Sex Work, and Migrant Labor in South Korea.* Minneapolis: University of Minnesota Press, 2010.

Lens, Sidney. *Permanent War: The Militarization of America.* New York: Schocken Books, 1987.

Lewis, Oscar. *La Vida: A Puerto Rican Family in the Culture of Poverty.* San Juan: Panther, 1969.

Li, Darryl. "Hunting the 'Out-of-Place Muslim': Sketching the Juridical Architecture of America's 'War on Terror.'" SAMAR: *South Asian Magazine for Action and Reflection,* May 11, 2011. Accessed August 9, 2017. http://samarmagazine.org/archive/articles/355.

Li, Darryl. "A Universal Enemy?: 'Foreign Fighters' and Legal Regimes of Exclusion and Exemption Under the 'Global War on Terror.'" *Columbia Human Rights Law Review* 42, no. 2 (2010): 355–428.

Liisberg, Sune, Esther Oluffa Pedersen, and Anne Line Dalsgard, eds. *Anthropology and Philosophy: Dialogues on Trust and Hope.* New York: Berghahn, 2015.

Lin, Justin Yifu. *Against the Consensus: Reflections on the Great Recession.* Cambridge: Cambridge University Press, 2013.

Lipman, Jana. *Guantánamo: A Working-Class History between Empire and Revolution.* Berkeley: University of California Press, 2009.

Loconto, Allison, and Lawrence Busch. "Standards, Techno-Economic Networks, and Playing Fields: Performing the Global Market Economy." *Review of International Political Economy* 17, no. 3 (2010): 507–36.

Loescher, Gil, and John A. Scanlan. *Calculated Kindness: Refugees and America's Half-Open Door, 1945 to the Present.* New York: Simon and Schuster, 1998.

Loftus, Bethan. "Dominant Culture Interrupted: Recognition, Resentment and the Politics of Change in an English Police Force." *British Journal of Criminology* 48, no. 6 (2008): 756–77.

López, María M., and Nalini Natarajan. "American Colonialism and Puerto Rican 'Criminality.'" *Economic and Political Weekly* 31, no. 33 (1996): 2236–38.

Louis, William Roger, and Ronald Robinson. "The Imperialism of Decolonization." *Journal of Imperial and Commonwealth History* 22, no. 3 (1994): 462–511.

Lucas, George, Jr. *Anthropologists in Arms: The Ethics of Military Anthropology.* Lanham, MD: AltaMira, 2009.

Lugard, Frederick. *The Dual Mandate in British Tropical Africa.* Edinburgh: W. Blackwood and Sons, 1922.

Lutz, Catherine. *The Bases of Empire: The Global Struggle against U.S. Military Posts.* New York: New York University Press, 2009.

Lutz, Catherine. "Empire Is in the Details." *American Ethnologist* 33, no. 4 (2006): 593–611.

Lutz, Catherine. *Homefront: A Military City and the American Twentieth Century.* Boston: Beacon, 2001.

Lutz, Catherine. "Making War at Home in the United States: Militarization and the Current Crisis." *American Anthropologist* 104, no. 3 (2002): 723–35.

Lutz, Catherine. "Military Bases and Ethnographies of the New Militarization." *Anthropology News* 46, no. 1 (2005): 11.

MacKay, Fergus. *Moiwana Zoekt Gerechtigheid: De Strijd Van Een Marrondorp Tegen De Staat Suriname.* Amsterdam: KIT Publishers, 2006.

MacKenzie, Melody Kapilialoha, ed. *Native Hawaiian Rights Handbook.* Honolulu: Native Hawaiian Legal Corporation and the Office of Hawaiian Affairs, 1991.

MacLeish, Kenneth T. *Making War at Fort Hood: Life and Uncertainty in a Military Community.* Princeton, NJ: Princeton University Press, 2005.

Madeley, John. *Diego Garcia: A Contrast to the Falklands.* The Minority Rights Group Report 54. London: Minority Rights Group, 1985.

Magdoff, Harry. *Imperialism without Colonies*. New York: Monthly Review, 2003.

Maguire, Joseph, and Mark Falcous, eds. *Sport and Migration: Borders, Boundaries, and Crossings*. New York: Taylor and Francis, 2012.

Maira, Sunaina. "Belly Dancing, Arab-Face, Orientalist Feminism, and U.S. Empire." *American Quarterly* 60, no. 2 (2008): 317–45.

Maira, Sunaina. "Deporting Radicals, Deporting La Migra: The Hayat Case in Lodi." *Cultural Dynamics* 19, no. 1 (2007): 39–66.

Maira, Sunaina. "'Good' and 'Bad' Muslim Citizens: Feminists, Terrorists, and U.S. Orientalisms." *Feminist Studies* 35, no. 3 (2009): 631–56.

Maira, Sunaina. *Missing: Youth, Citizenship, and Empire after 9/11*. Durham, NC: Duke University Press, 2009.

Maira, Sunaina, and Elisabeth Soep. "Introduction." In *Youthscapes: The Popular, the National, the Global*, edited by Sunaina Maira and Elisabeth Soep, xv–xxxv. Philadelphia: Temple University Press, 2005.

Majumdar, Boria. "Tom Brown Goes Global: The 'Brown' Ethic in Colonial and Post-Colonial India." *International Journal of the History of Sport* 23, no. 5 (2006): 805–20.

Malkki, Liisa. "Speechless Emissaries: Refugees, Humanitarianism, and Dehistoricization." *Cultural Anthropology* 11, no. 3 (1996): 377–404.

Mamdani, Mahmood. *Citizen and Subject: Contemporary Africa and the Legacy of Late Colonialism*. Princeton, NJ: Princeton University Press, 1996.

Mamdani, Mahmood. *Good Muslim, Bad Muslim: America, the Cold War and the Roots of Terror*. New York: Three Leaves, Doubleday, 2004.

Mamdani, Mahmood. "Good Muslim, Bad Muslim: A Political Perspective on Culture and Terrorism." *American Anthropologist* 104, no. 3 (2002): 766–75.

Manalansan, Martin F., IV. *Global Divas: Filipino Gay Men in the Diaspora*. Durham, NC: Duke University Press, 2003.

Mangan, J. *Athleticism in the Victorian and Edwardian Public School: The Emergence and Consolidation of an Educational Ideology*. Cambridge: Cambridge University Press, 1981.

Mangan, J. A. *The Games Ethic and Imperialism: Aspects of the Diffusion of an Ideal*. New York: Viking, 1986.

Mansbridge, Jane J. *Beyond Adversary Democracy*. Chicago: University of Chicago Press, 1983.

Marcus, George. *Ethnography through Thick and Thin*. Princeton, NJ: Princeton University Press, 1998.

Mariner, Joanne. *Ghost Prisoner: Two Years in Secret CIA Detention*. New York: Human Rights Watch, 2007.

Mariscal, George, ed. *Aztlán and Vietnam: Chicano and Chicana Experiences of the War*. Berkeley: University of California Press, 1999.

Mariscal, Jorge. "Homeland Security, Militarism, and the Future of Latinos and Latinas in the United States." *Radical History Review* 93 (fall 2005): 39–52.

Markowitz, W., R. Glenn Hall, L. Essen, and J. V. L. Parry. "Frequency of Cesium in Terms of Ephemeris Time." *Physical Review Letters* 1, no. 3 (1958): 105–7.

Marqués, René. *El puertorriqueño dócil: Literatura y realidad psicológica*. Puerto Rico: Editorial Antillana, 1967.

Martel, James R. *Textual Conspiracies: Walter Benjamin, Idolatry, and Political Theory.* Ann Arbor: University of Michigan Press, 2011.

Marty, Dick. "Alleged Secret Detentions and Unlawful Inter-State Transfers Involving Council of Europe Member States." Strasbourg: Council of Europe, 2006.

Masco, Joseph. "Mutant Ecologies: Radioactive Life in Post–Cold War New Mexico." *Cultural Anthropology* 19, no. 4 (2004): 517–50.

Masco, Joseph. *The Nuclear Borderlands: The Manhattan Project in Post-Cold War New Mexico.* Princeton, NJ: Princeton University Press, 2006.

Masco, Joseph. "'Sensitive but Unclassified': Secrecy and the Counterterrorist State." *Public Culture* 22, no. 3 (2010): 441–67.

Masco, Joseph. *The Theater of Operations: National Security Affect from the Cold War to the War on Terror.* Durham, NC: Duke University Press, 2014.

Maskovsky, Jeff, and Ida Susser. "Introduction: Rethinking America." In *Rethinking America: The Imperial Homeland in the 21st Century*, edited by Jeff Maskovsky and Ida Susser, 1–13. New York: Routledge, 2009.

Mayeda, David T., Lisa Paski, and Meda Chesney-Lind. "'You Gotta Do So Much to Actually Make It': Gender, Ethnicity, and Samoan Youth in Hawaii." *AAPI Nexus* 4, no. 2 (2006): 69–91.

Mazower, Mark. *No Enchanted Palace: The End of Empire and the Ideological Origins of the United Nations.* Princeton, NJ: Princeton University Press, 2009.

Mbembe, Achille. "Necropolitics." *Public Culture* 15, no. 1 (2003): 11–40.

McAlister, Melani. "What Is Your Heart For?: Affect and Internationalism in the Evangelical Public Sphere." *American Literary History* 20, no. 4 (2008): 870–95.

McCaffrey, Katherine. "Environmental Struggle after the Cold War: New Forms of Resistance to the U.S. Military in Vieques, Puerto Rico." In *The Bases of Empire*, edited by Catherine Lutz, 218–42. New York: New York University Press, 2009.

McCaffrey, Katherine. *Military Power and Popular Protest: The U.S. Navy in Vieques, Puerto Rico.* New Brunswick, NJ: Rutgers University Press, 2002.

McCarthy, D. D., and W. J. Klepczynski. "GPS and Leap Seconds—Time to Change?" *GPS World* (1999): 50–57.

McCarthy, Dennis, and P. Kenneth Seidelmann. *Time: From Earth Rotation to Atomic Physics.* Weinheim, Germany: Wiley-VCH, 2009.

McClintock, Anne. *Imperial Leather: Race, Gender, and Sexuality in the Colonial Contest.* New York: Routledge, 1995.

McClintock, Michael. *Instruments of Statecraft: US Guerrilla Warfare, Counterinsurgency, and Counter-Terrorism, 1940–1990.* New York: Pantheon, 1992.

McCoy, Alfred W., and Francisco Scarano, eds. *Colonial Crucible: Empire in the Making of the Modern American State.* Madison: University of Wisconsin Press, 2009.

McDougal, Paul. "U.S. Suspends Controversial Outsourcing Program." *Information Week*, April 23, 2012. Accessed October 20, 2017. https://www.informationweek.com/it-strategy/us-suspends-controversial-outsourcing-training-program/d/d-id/1104010.

McFate, Montgomery. "Anthropology and Counterinsurgency: The Strange Story of Their Curious Relationship." *Military Review* 85, no. 2 (2005): 24.

McGranahan, Carole. *Arrested Histories: Tibet, the CIA, and Memories of a Forgotten War.* Durham, NC: Duke University Press, 2010.

McGranahan, Carole. "Empire out-of-Bounds: Tibet in the Era of Decolonization." In *Imperial Formations*, edited by Ann Laura Stoler, Carole McGranahan, and Peter C. Perdue, 173–209. Santa Fe: SAR, 2007.

McGranahan, Carole. "Truth, Fear, and Lies: Exile Politics and Arrested Histories of the Tibetan Resistance." *Cultural Anthropology* 20, no. 4 (2005): 570–600.

McIndoe, Alistair. "Call Centres Spring Up in Troubled Philippine South." *Straight Times*, May 9, 2009.

Mckiernan-González, John. *Fevered Measures: Public Health and Race at the Texas-Mexico Border, 1848–1942.* Durham, NC: Duke University Press, 2012.

McNeill, J. R., and C. R. Unger. *Environmental Histories of the Cold War.* Cambridge: Cambridge University Press, 2010.

Melo, Lourenço. "Brasil quer entrar no mercado de lançadores de satélites, afirma presidente da AEB." *Agência Brasil*, March 4, 2006. Accessed August 9, 2017. http://www.radiobras.gov.br/materia_i_2004.php?materia=261055&edi.

Mier, Brian. "Alcântara Spaceport: Race, Land Rights and National Sovereignty, an Interview with Sean T. Mitchell." *Brasil Wire*, February 4, 2017. Accessed August 9, 2017. http://www.brasilwire.com/alcantara-spaceport/.

Mignolo, Walter. "Delinking." *Cultural Studies* 21, no. 2 (2007): 449–514.

"Mil hondureños a Irak y Afganistán." *El Heraldo*, May 16, 2005.

Miller, Jim. "The Alberni Residential School Case: Blackwater v Plint." *Indigenous Law Bulletin* 5, no. 12 (2001): 20–21.

Miller, Robert, Jacinta Ruru, Larissa Behrendt, and Tracey Lindberg. *Discovering Indigenous Lands: The Doctrine of Discovery in the English Colonies.* Oxford: Oxford University Press, 2010.

Miller, Ted. "American Football, Samoan Style." ESPN.com, May 28, 2002. Accessed August 1, 2013. http://espn.go.com/gen/s/2002/0527/1387562.html.

Million, Dian. "Telling Secrets: Sex, Power, and Narratives in Indian Residential School Histories." *Canadian Women Studies* 20, no. 2 (2000): 92–104.

Million, Dian. *Therapeutic Nations: Healing in an Age of Indigenous Human Rights.* Tucson: University of Arizona Press, 2013.

Milloy, John. *A National Crime: The Canadian Government and the Residential School System, 1879–1976.* Winnipeg: University of Manitoba Press, 2011.

Mills, David. *Computer Network Time Synchronization.* 2nd ed. Boca Raton: CRC, 2011.

Mir, Shabana. *Muslim American Women on Campus: Undergraduate Social Life and Identity.* Chapel Hill: University of North Carolina Press, 2014.

Mirchandani, Kiran. *Phone Clones: Authenticity Work in the Transnational Service Industry.* Ithaca, NY: Cornell University Press, 2012.

Mitchell, Sean T. "American Dreams and Brazilian Racial Democracy: The Making of Race and Class in Brazil and the United States." *Focaal* 73 (2015): 41–54.

Mitchell, Sean T. *Constellations of Inequality: Space, Race, and Utopia in Brazil.* Chicago: University of Chicago Press, 2017.

Mitchell, Sean T. "Paranoid Styles of Nationalism after the Cold War: Notes from an Invasion of the Amazon." In *Anthropology and Global Counterinsurgency*, edited by John D. Kelly, Beatrice Jauregui, Sean T. Mitchell, and Jeremy Walton, 89–104. Chicago: University of Chicago Press, 2010.

Mitchell, Sean T. "Space, Sovereignty, Inequality: Interpreting the Explosion of Brazil's VLS Rocket." *Journal of Latin American Anthropology* 18, no. 3 (2013): 400–421.

Mitchell, Sean T. "Whitening and Racial Ambiguity: Racialization and Ethnoracial Citizenship in Contemporary Brazil." *African and Black Diaspora: An International Journal* 10, no. 2 (2017): 114–30.

Mitman, Gregg, and Paul Erickson. "Latex and Blood: Science, Markets, and American Empire." *Radical History Review* 107 (spring 2010): 45–73.

Molieri, Jorge Jenkins. *El desafío indígena en Nicaragua: El caso de los miskitos*. Managua: Editorial Vanguardia, 1986.

Monserrat Filho, José. "Testimony at a December 4th Public Hearing before the Brazilian Chamber of Deputies: Debate sobre acordo entre o Brasil e Os Estados Unidos da América sobre salvaguardas tecnológicas relacionadas a lançamentos no Centro de Lançamento de Alcântara." December 4, 2003.

Monserrat Filho, José, and Valnora Leister. "The Discussion in the Brazilian National Congress of the Brazil-USA Agreement on Technology Safeguards Relating to the Use of Alcântara Spaceport." *Revista Brasileira de Direito Aeronáutico e Espacial* 83 (2001).

Moore, John. "The Enduring Reservations of Oklahoma." In *State and Reservation: New Perspectives on Federal Indian Policy*, edited by Robert L. Bee and George P. Castile, 92–109. Tucson: University of Arizona Press, 1992.

Morales, Liliana Cotto. *Desalambrar.* San Juan: Ediciones Tal Cual, 2006.

Morawetz, Nancy. "Rethinking Retroactive Deportation Laws and the Due Process Clause." *New York University Law Review* 73 (1998): 97–161.

Morawetz, Nancy. "Understanding the Impact of the 1996 Deportation Laws and the Limited Scope of Proposed Reforms." *In Defense of the Alien* 23 (2000): 1–30.

Morris, Glenn, and Ward Churchill. "Between a Rock and a Hard Place: Left-wing Revolution, Right-wing Reaction and the Destruction of Indigenous Peoples." *Cultural Survival Quarterly* 11, no. 3 (1987): 17–24.

Morse, Harold. "Home Lands Lawsuit to Be Filed Today, Could Total $100 Million." *Honolulu Star-Bulletin*, December 29, 1999.

Moser, Richard. *The New Winter Soldiers: GI and Veteran Dissent during the Vietnam Era*. New Brunswick, NJ: Rutgers University Press, 1996.

Mosse, George. *The Image of Man: The Creation of Modern Masculinity.* Oxford: Oxford University Press, 1996.

Munn, Nancy. "The Cultural Anthropology of Time: A Critical Essay." *Annual Review of Anthropology* 21 (1992): 93–123.

Munn, Nancy. "Excluded Spaces: The Figure in the Australian Aboriginal Landscape." *Critical Inquiry* 22, no. 3 (1996): 446–65.

Myers, Jim. "Osage Nation, U.S. Settle Legal Battle." *Tulsa World*, last modified October 22, 2011. Accessed November 11, 2011. http://www.tulsaworld.com/news/article.aspx?subjectid=335&articleid=20111022_16_A1_WASHIN293151.

"Naar Moengo II." *De West: Nieuwsblad uit en Voor Suriname*, March 10, 1919.

Naber, Nadine. *Arab America: Gender, Cultural Politics, and Activism.* New York: New York University Press, 2012.

Nader, Laura. "The Phantom Factor: Impact of the Cold War on Anthropology." In *The Cold War and the University: Toward an Intellectual History of the Postwar Years*, edited by Noam Chomsky, 107–48. New York: New Press, 1997.

Nader, Laura. "Up the Anthropologist—Perspectives Gained from Studying Up." In *Reinventing Anthropology*, edited by Dell Hymes, 284–311. Ann Arbor: University of Michigan Press, 1972.

Navaro-Yashın, Yael. *The Make-Believe Space: Affective Geography in a Postwar Polity.* Durham, NC: Duke University Press, 2012.

Negri, Antonio. *Empire and Beyond.* Cambridge: Polity, 2008.

Negrón de Montilla, Aída. *Americanization in Puerto Rico and the Public School System 1900–1930.* Río Piedras: Editorial Universitaria, 1975.

Nelson, Christopher. *Dancing with the Dead: Memory, Performance, and Everyday Life in Postwar Okinawa.* Durham, NC: Duke University Press, 2008.

Nelson, Daniel J. *Defenders or Intruders? The Dilemmas of US Forces in Germany.* Boulder, CO: Westview, 1987.

Nelson, Diane. *Reckoning: The Ends of War in Guatemala.* Durham, NC: Duke University Press, 2009.

Nelson, R. A., D. D. McCarthy, S. Malys, J. Jevine, B. Guinot, H. F. Fliegel, R. L. Beard, and T. R. Bartholomew. "The Leap Second: Its History and Possible Future." *Metrologia* 38, no. 6 (2011): 509–29.

Network of Concerned Anthropologists. *The Counter-Counterinsurgency Manual.* Chicago: University of Chicago Press, 2009.

Newcomb, Simon. *Astronomical Papers Prepared for the Use of the American Ephemeris and Nautical Almanac.* Vol. 6, pt. 1: *Tables of the Sun.* Washington, DC: U.S. Government Printing Office, 1895.

Nguyen, Vinh-Kim. "Antiretroviral Globalism, Biopolitics, and Therapeutic Citizenship." In *Global Assemblages: Technology, Politics, and Ethics as Anthropological Problems*, edited by Aihwa Ong and Stephen J. Collier, 124–44. Malden, MA: Wiley-Blackwell, 2005.

Nichols, Robert Lee. "Contract and Usurpation: Enfranchisement and Racial Governance in Settler Colonial Contexts." In *Theorizing Native Studies*, edited by Audra Simpson and Andrea Smith, 99–121. Durham, NC: Duke University Press, 2014.

Nichols, Robert Lee. "Indigeneity and the Settler Contract Today." *Philosophy and Social Criticism* 39, no. 2 (2013): 1–22.

Nichols, Robert Lee. "Realizing the Social Contract: The Case of Colonialism and Indigenous Peoples." *Contemporary Political Theory* 4, no. 1 (2005): 42–62.

Nietschmann, Bernard Q. "Bruno Gabriel: A Miskito Nationalist and Revolutionary." *Fourth World Journal* 2, no. 3 (1990): 161–84.

Nietschmann, Bernard Q. *United States.* New York: Freedom House, 1989.

Niezen, Ronald. *Truth and Indignation: Canada's Truth and Reconciliation Commission on Indian Residential Schools.* Toronto: University of Toronto Press, 2013.

Nixon, Rob. "Of Land Mines and Cluster Bombs." *Cultural Critique* 67 (2007): 160–74.

Nixon, Rob. *Slow Violence and the Environmentalism of the Poor.* Cambridge, MA: Harvard University Press, 2011.

Nkrumah, Kwame. *Neo-Colonialism: The Last Stage of Imperialism.* New York: International Publishers, 1965.

"Noodles Solve a Tibetan Problem." *Straits Times*, May 27, 1964, 2.

Nugent, David. "Knowledge and Empire: The Social Sciences and United States Imperial Expansion." *Identities* 17, no. 1 (2010): 2–44.

Oak, Sung-Deuk. "The Indigenization of Christianity in Korea: North American Missionaries' Attitudes towards Korean Religions, 1884–1910." PhD dissertation, Boston University School of Theology, 2002.

Obomsawin, Alanis, dir. *Kanehsatake: 270 Years of Resistance*. National Film Board of Canada, 1992.

O'Dwyer, Eliane Cantarino. "Os quilombos e a prática profissional dos antropólogos." In *Quilombos: Identidade étnica e territorialidade*, edited by Eliane Cantarino O'Dwyer, 13–43. Rio de Janeiro: Editora FGV, 2002.

Olson, Kathryn M. "The Controversy over President Reagan's Visit to Bitburg: Strategies of Definition and Redefinition." *Quarterly Journal of Speech* 75, no. 2 (1989): 129–51.

Omandam, Pat. "Report: Annexation Could Be Declared Invalid." *Honolulu Star-Bulletin*, August 11, 1998.

O'Neill, Bruce. "Of Camps, Gulags, and Extraordinary Renditions: Infrastructural Violence in Romania." *Ethnography* 13, no. 4 (2012): 466–86.

Ong, Aihwa. *Flexible Citizenship: The Cultural Logics of Transnationality*. Durham, NC: Duke University Press, 1999.

"On Revising the Official System of Astronomical Constants." In *Constantes fondamentales de l'astronomie*, 19–28. Paris: Centre National de la Recherche Scientifique, 1950.

"On the System of Astronomical Constants." *Astronomical Journal* 53 (1948): 169–79.

Oppenheim, Robert. "On the Locations of Korean War and Cold War Anthropology." *Histories of Anthropology Annual* 4 (2008): 220–59.

Ortega y Gasset, José. *Meditations on Hunting*. Translated by Howard B. Wescott. Belgrade, MT: Wilderness Adventures, 1995.

Ortner, Sherry B. *Making Gender: The Politics and Erotics of Culture*. Boston: Beacon, 1996.

Ottaway, David. "Islanders Were Evicted for U.S. Base." *Washington Post*, September 9, 1975, A1.

Oudschans Dentz, Frederik. "De Bauxietnijverheid en de Stichting van een Nieuwe Stad in Suriname." *De West-Indische Gids* (1921): 481–508.

Ouroussoff, Alexandra. *Wall Street at War: The Secret Struggle for the Global Economy*. Cambridge: Polity, 2010.

Pabón, Carlos. *Nación postmortem: Ensayos sobre los tiempos de insoportable ambigüedad*. San Juan: Ediciones Callejón, 2002.

Paglen, Trevor. *Blank Spots on the Map: The Dark Geography of the Pentagon's Secret World*. New York: Dutton, 2012.

Pak, Ji-ho. "'Chaknyŏn P'yŏnghwach'ukje Yŏllyŏtsŭmyŏn T'alleban Sarajyŏtsŭlgŏt' ['If the Peace Festival Could Have Taken Place Last Year, Taliban Would Have Disappeared']." *News N Joy*, September 16, 2007. Accessed August 9, 2017. www.newsnjoy.us/news/articleView.html?idxno=373.

Pak, Ji-ho. "Yupyŏlnan'gŏn 'Chŏngpu'in'ga 'Int'ŏk'ŏp'in'ga [Is It the 'Government' or 'InterCP' That Is Distinctive?]." *News N Joy*, September 23, 2009. Accessed August 9, 2017. www.newsnjoy.us/news/articleView.html?idxno=1517.

Pakosie, A. R. M. "Orale traditie bij de Bosnegger." OSO—*Tijdschrift voor Economische en Sociale Geografie* [*Journal of economic and social geography*] 8, no. 2 (1989): 159–65.

Pang, Gordon Y. K. "Land You Bought May Actually Be Home Lands." *Honolulu Star-Bulletin*, February 17, 1995, 1, 4.

Park, Edward J. W., and John S. W. Park. *Probationary Americans: Contemporary Immigration Policies and the Shaming of Asian American Communities*. New York: Routledge, 2005.

Parker, Arthur C. *The Constitution of the Five Nations or The Iroquois Book of The Great Law*. Ohsweken, Ontario: Iroqrafts Ltd, [1916] 1991.

Parker, Thomas, and Matsakis, Demetrios. "Time and Frequency Dissemination: Advances in GPS Transfer Techniques." *GPS World* (2004): 32–38.

Pateman, Carole. *Participation and Democratic Theory*. Cambridge: Cambridge University Press, 1970.

Pearce, Roy. *Savagism and Civilization: A Study of the Indian in the American Indian Mind*. Berkeley: University of California Press, 1988.

Pearson, C., P. Coates, and T. Cole. *Militarized Landscapes: From Gettysburg to Salisbury Plain*. New York: Continuum, 2010.

Pease, Donald. *The New American Exceptionalism*. Minneapolis: University of Minnesota Press, 2009.

Pease, Donald. "New Perspectives on U.S. Culture and Imperialism." In *Cultures of United States Imperialism*, edited by Amy Kaplan and Donald Pease, 22–40. Durham, NC: Duke University Press, 1993.

Peck, E. H. "Defence Facilities in the Indian Ocean." U.K. National Archives, May 7, 1965.

Peduzzi, Pedro. "Jobim defende que comunidades quilombolas de Alcântara sejam transferidas." *Agência Brasil*, January 7, 2009. Accessed October 31, 2017. https://noticias.uol.com.br/cotidiano/2009/07/01/ult5772u4544.jhtm.

Pelley, Scott, dir. "American Samoa: Football Island." Episode of *60 Minutes*, CBS, January 14, 2010.

Pereira Junior, Davi. *Quilombolas de Alcântara: Território e conflito*. Manaus: Universidade Federal do Amazônas, 2009.

Pérez, Gina. *Citizen, Student, Soldier: Latino/a Youth, JROTC, and the American Dream*. New York: New York University Press, 2015.

Perlo, Victor. *American Imperialism*. New York: International Publishers, 1951.

Perry, Keisha-Khan. *Black Women against the Land Grab: The Fight for Racial Justice in Brazil*. Minneapolis: University of Minnesota Press, 2013.

Petição Publica Brasil. "ACS—Mudanças já Ou o Destrato do Acordo." 2012. Accessed August 9, 2017. http://www.peticaopublica.com.br/?pi=P2012N31169.

Pierre, Jemima. *The Predicament of Blackness: Postcolonial Ghana and the Politics of Race*. Chicago: University of Chicago Press, 2014.

Pineda, Baron L. *Shipwrecked Identities: Navigating Race on Nicaragua's Miskito Coast*. New Brunswick, NJ: Rutgers University Press, 2006.

Pocock, John. "The Ideal of Citizenship since Ancient Times." In *Theorizing Citizenship*, edited by Ronald Beiner, 29–52. Albany: State University of New York Press, 1995.

Polimé, Thomas S., Stefano Ajintoena, et al. "Petitioners. v. The Republic of Suriname, Respondent—Affidavit of Dr. Thomas Polime Expert Witness." IACHR—Inter-American Court of Human Rights, August 20, 2004.

Polimé, Thomas S., and Bonno Thoden van Velzen. *Vluchtelingen, opstandelingen en andere Bosnegers van Oost-Suriname, 1986–1988*. Leiden: Instituut voor Culturele Antropologie, 1988.

Poster, Winifred. "Who's on the Line? Indian Call Center Agents Pose as Americans for U.S. Outsourced Firms." *Industrial Relations* 46, no. 2 (2007): 271–304.

Postero, Nancy, and Mark Goodale. *Neoliberalism Interrupted: Social Change and Contested Governance in Contemporary Latin America*. Stanford, CA: Stanford University Press, 2013.

Povinelli, Elizabeth A. *The Cunning of Recognition: Indigenous Alterities and Australian Multiculturalism*. Durham, NC: Duke University Press, 2002.

Price, David H. *Cold War Anthropology: The CIA, the Pentagon, and the Growth of Dual-Use Anthropology*. Durham, NC: Duke University Press, 2016.

Price, David H. "Human Terrain Systems, Anthropologists and the War in Afghanistan: A Better Way to Kill?" *Counterpunch*, December 1, 2009. Accessed August 9, 2017. http://www.counterpunch.org/2009/12/01/human-terrain-systems-anthropologists-and-the-war-in-afghanistan.

Price, David H. "Interlopers and Invited Guests: On Anthropology's Witting and Unwitting Links to Intelligence Agencies." *Anthropology Today* 18, no. 6 (2002): 16–21.

Price, David H. *Threatening Anthropology: McCarthyism and the FBI's Surveillance of Activist Anthropologists*. Durham, NC: Duke University Press, 2004.

Price, Richard. *The Convict and the Colonel*. Durham, NC: Duke University Press, 2006.

Price, Richard. *First Time: The Historical Vision of an Afro-American People*. Baltimore: Johns Hopkins University Press, 1983.

Price, Richard. *Rainforest Warriors: Human Rights on Trial*. Philadelphia: University of Pennsylvania Press, 2010.

Price, Richard. *Travels with Tooy: History, Memory, and the African American Imagination*. Chicago: University of Chicago Press, 2007.

Price, Richard, and Sally Price. "Working for the Man: A Saramaka Outlook on Kourou." *New West Indian Guide* 63, nos. 3–4 (1989): 199–207.

Priest, Dana. "Covert Action in Colombia." *Washington Post*, December 21, 2013. Accessed August 9, 2017. http://www.washingtonpost.com/sf/investigative/2013/12/21/covert-action-in-colombia/.

Prucha, Nico. "Online Territories of Terror: Utilizing the Internet for Jihadist Endeavors." *ORIENT* 4 (2011): 43–47.

Public Papers of the Presidents of the United States. *William J. Clinton, Book II*, 1183–86. Washington, DC: U.S. Government Printing Office, 1997.

Pulliam, Sarah. "In the Aftermath of a Kidnapping: The South Korean Missionary Movement Seeks to Mature without Losing Its Zeal." *Christianity Today*, November 7, 2007. Accessed August 9, 2017. www.christianitytoday.com/ct/2007/november/22.64.html.

Quijano, Aníbal. "Coloniality of Power, Eurocentrism, and Latin America." Translated by Michael Ennis. *Nepantla: Views from the South* 1, no. 3 (2000): 533–80.

Quinn, Terry. *From Artefacts to Atoms*. Oxford: Oxford University Press, 2012.

Rabinow, Paul. *Anthropos Today: Reflections on Modern Equipment*. Princeton, NJ: Princeton University Press, 2003.

Rabinow, Paul, George Marcus, James Faubion, and Tobias Reese. *Designs for an Anthropology of the Contemporary*. Durham, NC: Duke University Press, 2008.

Rafael, Vicente. "Translation, American English, and the National Insecurities of Empire." *Social Text 101* 27, no. 4 (2009): 1–23.

Rafael, Vicente. "Translation in Wartime." *Public Culture* 19, no. 2 (2007): 239–46.

Rafael, Vicente. *White Love and Other Events in Filipino History*. Durham, NC: Duke University Press, 2000.

Rafael, Vicente. "White Love: Surveillance and Nationalist Resistance in the U.S. Colonization of the Philippines." In *Cultures of United States Imperialism*, edited by Amy Kaplan and Donald J. Pease, 185–210. Durham, NC: Duke University Press, 1993.

Rai, Amit. *The Rule of Sympathy: Sentiment, Race, and Power, 1750–1850*. New York: Palgrave, 2002.

Rajagopal, Balakrishnan. *International Law from Below: Development, Social Movements and Third World Resistance*. Cambridge: Cambridge University Press, 2003.

Rana, Junaid. *Terrifying Muslims: Race and Labor in the South Asian Diaspora*. Durham, NC: Duke University Press, 2011.

"Rara forma de buscar Nicas para ir a Irak." *El Nuevo Diario*, September 22, 2005.

Razack, Sherene. *Dying from Improvement: Inquests and Inquiries into Indigenous Deaths in Custody*. Toronto: University of Toronto Press, 2015.

Razack, Sherene. "The Murder of Pamela George." In *Race, Space and the Law: Unmapping a White Settler Society*, edited by Sherene Razack, 121–47. Toronto: Between the Lines, 2002.

Reagan, Ronald. "Remarks at a Joint German-American Military Ceremony at Bitburg Air Base in the Federal Republic of Germany." May 5, 1985. Accessed November 13, 2013. http://www.vlib.us/amdocs/texts/reagan051985.html.

Reddy, Chandan. *Freedom with Violence: Race, Sexuality, and the US State*. Durham, NC: Duke University Press, 2011.

Redfield, Peter. *Life in Crisis: The Ethical Journey of Doctors without Borders*. Berkeley: University of California Press, 2013.

Redfield, Peter. *Space in the Tropics: From Convicts to Rockets in French Guiana*. Berkeley: University of California Press, 2000.

Reiger, John. *American Sportsmen and the Origin of Conservation*. Corvallis: Oregon State University Press, 2001.

Reiss, Suzanna. *We Sell Drugs: The Alchemy of U.S. Empire*. Berkeley: University of California Press, 2014.

Remo, Amy R. "IT-BPO sector posted 18.7% revenue growth in 2014." *Philippine Daily Inquirer*, March 19, 2015.

Retort. *Afflicted Powers: Capital and Spectacle in a New Age of War*. London: Verso, 2005.

Richard, Randall. "Banned for Life: Jailed at 17, Kim Ho Ma Can Never Live in America." *AsianWeek*, November 21, 2003. Accessed September 1, 2010. http://www.asianweek.com/2003/11/21/banned-for-life-jailed-at-17-kim-ho-ma-can-never-live-in-america/.

Risério, Antonio. *A utopia brasileira e os movimentos negros*. São Paulo: Editora 34, 2007.

Rivero, Horacio. "Enclosure to memorandum to Chief of Naval Operations, May 21, 1960." Naval History and Heritage Command Archives. 00 Files, 1960, Box 8, 5710.

Rivero, Horacio. "Enclosure to memorandum to Chief of Naval Operations, July 11, 1960." Naval Historical Center, 00 Files, 1960, Box 8, 5710.

Robben, Antonius C. G. M. "Ethnographic Seduction, Transference, and Resistance in Dialogues about Terror and Violence in Argentina." *Ethos* 24, no. 1 (1996): 71–106.

Robben, Antonius C. G. M., ed. *Iraq at a Distance: What Anthropologists Can Teach Us about the War.* Philadelphia: University of Pennsylvania Press, 2009.

Robert, Dana Lee. *Christian Mission: How Christianity Became a World Religion.* Chichester, UK: Wiley-Blackwell, 2009.

Robert, Giovanni. "¿Podemos? . . . y nuestras preguntas." *80grados*, January 21, 2015. Accessed October 20, 2017. http://www.80grados.net/podemos-y-nuestras-preguntas/.

Rodney, Walter. *A History of the Guyanese Working People, 1881–1905.* Baltimore: Johns Hopkins University Press, 1981.

Rodríguez, Dylan. *Suspended Apocalypse: White Supremacy, Genocide, and the Filipino Condition.* Minneapolis: University of Minnesota Press, 2010.

Rodríguez, Nayra, José Vargas Vidot, Juan Panelli, Héctor Colón, Bob Ritchie, and Yasuhiro Yamamura. "GC-MS Confirmation of Xylazine (Rompun), a Veterinary Sedative, in Exchanged Needles." *Drug and Alcohol Dependence* 96, no. 3 (2008): 290–93.

Rodriguez, Robyn. *Migrants for Export: How the Philippine State Brokers Labor to the World.* Minneapolis: University of Minnesota Press, 2010.

"The Role of the Voluntary Agencies in the Tibetan Refugee Relief and Rehabilitation Programme." Travis Fletcher, Field Director, American Emergency Committee for Tibetan Refugees, posted April 18, 1961, to B. A. Garside. Stanford, CA: Hoover Institution Archives.

Román, Madeline. *Narcotráfico: Estado de pánico y pánico del estado. En estado y criminalidad en Puerto Rico: Un abordaje criminológico alternativo.* San Juan: Publicaciones Puertorriqueñas, 1994.

Roosevelt, Theodore. *Hunting Trips of a Ranchman* and *The Wilderness Hunter.* New York: Modern Library, 1998.

Rosaldo, Renato. "Imperialist Nostalgia." *Representations* 26 (1989): 107–22.

Rosario, Melissa. "Intimate Publics: Autoethnographic Meditations on the Micropolitics of Resistance." *Anthropology and Humanism* 39, no. 1 (2014): 36–54.

Roseberry, William. "Understanding Capitalism—Historically, Structurally, Spatially." In *Locating Capitalism in Time and Space*, edited by David Nugent, 61–79. Palo Alto: Stanford University Press, 2002.

Ross, Andrew. *Fast Boat to China: Corporate Flight and the Consequences of Free Trade.* New York: Pantheon, 2006.

Ross, Luana. *Inventing the Savage: The Social Construction of Native American Criminality.* Austin: University of Texas Press, 1998.

Rozakou, Katerina. "The Biopolitics of Hospitality in Greece: Humanitarianism and the Management of Refugees." *American Ethnologist* 39, no. 3 (2012): 562–77.

Ruggie, John. "Territoriality and Beyond: Problematizing Modernity in International Relations." *International Organization* 47, no. 1 (1993): 131–74.

Rutherford, Danilyn. "Sympathy, State Building, and the Experience of Empire." *Cultural Anthropology* 24, no. 1 (2009): 1–32.

Ryan, P. B. "Diego Garcia." *Proceedings* 110, no. 9/979 (1984): 133–38.

Sagapolutele, Fili. "Clinton Rejects U.N. Label 'Colony' for American Samoa." *Samoa News*, November 8, 2010.

Sahlins, Marshall. "The Destruction of Conscience in Vietnam." In *Culture in Practice: Selected Essays*. New York: Zone Books, [1966] 2000.

Said, Edward. *Orientalism*. New York: Vintage, 1978.

Said, Edward. *Out of Place: A Memoir*. New York: Knopf, 1999.

Said, Edward. *The Question of Palestine*. New York: Vintage Books, 1979.

Ṣalāḥ, Muḥammad. *Waqāʾiʿ Sanawāt al-Jihād: Riḥlat al-Afghān al-ʿArab*. Cairo: Khulūd lil-nashr, 2001.

Salahi, Yaman. "Behind the Scenes with Israel's Campus Lobby." *Al Jazeera*, September 26, 2011. Accessed August 9, 2017. http://english.aljazeera.net/indepth/opinion/2011/09/2011923848473148 40.html.

Salaita, Steven. *Israel's Dead Soul*. Philadelphia: Temple University Press, 2011.

Saldaña-Portillo, Maria Josefina. *The Revolutionary Imagination in the Americas in the Age of Development*. Durham, NC: Duke University Press, 2003.

Salesa, Damon. "Samoa's Half-Castes and Some Frontiers of Comparison." In *Haunted by Empire: Geographies of Intimacy in North American History*, edited by Ann L. Stoler, 71–93. Durham, NC: Duke University Press, 2004.

Salgado-Tamayo, Miguel. "La Base de Manta, El Plan Colombia, y los militares ecuatorianos." *Universitas: Revista de Ciencias Sociales y Humanas* (2001): 75–89.

Sanders, Barry. *The Green Zone: The Environmental Costs of Militarism*. Oakland, CA: AK Press, 2009.

Sansone, Livio. *Blackness without Ethnicity: Constructing Race in Brazil*. New York: Palgrave Macmillan, 2003.

Santiago-Valles, Kelvin. *Subject People and Colonial Discourses: Economic Transformation and Social Disorder in Puerto Rico 1898–1947*. Albany: State University of New York Press, 1994.

Saslow, Eli. "Island Hoping: In American Samoa, High School Football Is Seen as the Ultimate Escape." *Washington Post*, August 12, 2007: A1.

Sassen, Saskia. *Globalization and Its Discontents*. New York: W. W. Norton, 1998.

Scahill, Jeremy. *Blackwater: The Rise of the World's Most Powerful Mercenary Army*. New York: Nation Books, 2007.

Schmid, Andre. *Korea between Empires, 1895–1919*. New York: Columbia University Press, 2002.

Schmitt, Carl. *Political Theology: Four Chapters on the Concept of Sovereignty*. Chicago: University of Chicago Press, 2005.

Schwenkel, Christina. "From John McCain to Abu Ghraib: Tortured Bodies and Historical Unaccountability of U.S. Empire." *American Anthropologist* 111, no. 1 (2009): 30–42.

Schwenkel, Christina. "Recombinant History: Transnational Practices of Memory and Knowledge Production in Contemporary Vietnam." *Cultural Anthropology* 21, no. 1 (2006): 3–30.

Schwenkel, Christina. "War Debris in Postwar Society: Managing Risk and Uncertainty in the DMZ." In *Interactions with a Violent Past: Reading Post-Conflict*

Landscapes in Cambodia, Laos, and Vietnam, edited by V. Pholsena and O. Tappe, 135–56. Singapore: NUS Press in association with IRASEC, 2013.

Scott, David. *Conscripts of Modernity: The Tragedy of Colonial Enlightenment*. Durham, NC: Duke University Press, 2004.

Scott, David. *Omens of Adversity: Tragedy, Time, Memory, Justice*. Durham, NC: Duke University Press, 2014.

Scott, Robert. *Limuria: The Lesser Dependencies of Mauritius*. Westport, CT: Greenwood Press, [1961] 1976.

Seago, John, and Mark F. Storz. "UTC Redefinition and Space and Satellite-Tracking Systems." In *Proceedings of the ITU-R SRG Colloquium on the UTC Timescale*. Torino, Italy: IEN Galileo Ferraris, 2003.

Selik, R. M., K. G. Castro, M. Pappaioanou, and J. W. Buehler. "Birthplace and the risk for AIDS among Hispanics in the United States." *American Journal of Public Health* 79, no. 7 (1989): 836–39.

Seng, Jana M. "Cambodian Nationality Law and the Repatriation of Convicted Aliens under the Illegal Immigration Reform and Immigrant Responsibility Act." *Pacific Rim Law and Policy Journal* 10, no. 2 (2001): 443–69.

Sharp, Joanne P. "Geopolitics at the Margins? Reconsidering Genealogies of Critical Geopolitics." *Political Geography* 37 (2013): 20–29.

Shaw, Angel Velasco, and Luis Francia, eds. *Vestiges of War: The Philippine-American War and the Aftermath of an Imperial Dream, 1899–1999*. New York: New York University Press, 2002.

Shehadeh, Raja. *A Rift in Time: Travels of My Ottoman Uncle*. New York: OR Books, 2011.

Sherry, Michael S. *In the Shadows of War: The United States since the 1930s*. New Haven, CT: Yale University Press, 1995.

Shigematsu, Shetsu, and Keith L. Camacho, eds. *Militarized Currents: Towards a Decolonized Future in Asia and the Pacific*. Minneapolis: University of Minnesota Press, 2010.

Shim, Jae Hoon. "God's Work for the Taleban." *Khaleej Times*, September 7, 2007. Accessed August 9, 2017. www.khaleejtimes.com/kt-article-display-1.asp?xfile=data/opinion/2007/September/opinion_September24.xml§ion=opinion.

Shotwell, Alexis. *Against Purity: Living Ethically in Compromised Times*. Minneapolis: University of Minnesota Press, 2016.

Shryock, Andrew. "Cracking Down on Diaspora: Arab Detroit and America's 'War on Terror.'" *Anthropological Quarterly* 73 (2003): 443–62.

Shryock, Andrew, and Sally Howell. "New Images of Arab Detroit: Seeing Otherness and Identity through the Lens of 9/11." *American Anthropologist* 104, no. 3 (2002): 917–22.

Shuck, Peter. *Citizens, Strangers, and In-Betweens*. Boulder, CO: Westview, 1998.

Silva, Noenoe K. *Aloha Betrayed: Native Hawaiian Resistance to U.S. Colonialism*. Durham, NC: Duke University Press, 2004.

Silver, Patricia. "'Then I Do What I Want': Teachers, State, and Empire in 2000." *American Ethnologist* 34, no. 2 (2007): 268–84.

Simpson, Audra. *Mohawk Interruptus: Political Life across the Borders of Settler States*. Durham, NC: Duke University Press, 2014.

Simpson, Audra. "Settlement's Secret." *Cultural Anthropology* 26, no. 2 (2011): 205–17.

Singer, Merrill. "Why Do Puerto Rican Injection Drug Users Inject so Often?" *Anthropology and Medicine* 6, no. 1 (1999): 31–58.

Singer, Merrill, D. Himmelgreen, and R. Dushay, et al. "Variation in Drug Injection Frequency among Out-of-Treatment Drug Users in a National Sample." *American Journal of Drug and Alcohol Abuse* 24, no. 2 (1998): 321–41.

Singh, Bhrigupati, and Naisargi Dave. "On the Killing and Killability of Animals: Nonmoral Thoughts for the Anthropology of Ethics." *Comparative Studies of South Asia, Africa and the Middle East* 35, no. 2 (2015): 232–45.

Singh, Nikhil Pak. *Black Is a Country: Race and the Unfinished Struggle for Democracy.* Cambridge, MA: Harvard University Press, 2004.

Sirin, Selcuk, and Michelle Fine. *Muslim American Youth: Understanding Hyphenated Identities through Multiple Methods.* New York: New York University Press, 2008.

Sluka, Jeffrey A. "Curiouser and Curiouser: Montgomery McFate's Strange Interpretation of the Relationship between Anthropology and Counterinsurgency." *PoLAR: Political and Legal Anthropology Review* 33, no. 1 (2010): 99–115.

Smith, Herbert L. "Landmine and Countermine Warfare: Korea 1950–54." Washington, DC: Department of Defense, Department of the Army, Corps of Engineers, Engineer Agency for Resources Inventories, 1972.

Smith, Neil. *American Empire: Roosevelt's Geographer and the Prelude to Globalization.* Berkeley: University of California Press, 2003.

Smith, Neil. *The Endgame of Globalization.* New York: Routledge, 2005.

Smith, Ross. "Global English: Gift or Curse? The Case against the World's Lingua Franca." *English Today* 21, no. 2 (2005): 56–62.

Snyder, Claire. "The Citizen-Soldier Tradition and Gender Integration of the U.S. Military." *Armed Forces and Society* 29 (2003): 185–204.

Sohn, Jie-ae, and Caroline Faraj. "Pentagon: South Korean Hostage Beheaded." CNN, June 22, 2004. www.edition.cnn.com/2004/WORLD/meast/06/22/iraq.hostage/index.html.

Sontag, Deborah. "In a Homeland Far from Home." *New York Times Magazine*, November 6, 2003, 48–53, 92, 98, 105–6, 108.

Sovuthy, khy. "Ministry Working on Revision of US Repatriation Agreement." *The Cambodia Daily*, March 1, 2017. www.cambodiadaily.com/news/ministry-working-on-revision-of-US-repatriation-agreement-125938.

Sparke, Matthew. *In the Space of Theory: Postfoundational Geographies of the Nation-State.* Minneapolis: University of Minnesota Press, 2005.

Spear, Jeremy, and Robert Pennington. "Polynesian Power: Islanders in Pro Football." *Pacific Islanders in Communications*, 2005.

Spence, Steve. "Cultural Globalization and the US Civil Rights Movement." *Public Culture* 23, no. 3 65 (2011): 551–72.

Spivak, Gayatri C. *An Aesthetic Education in the Era of Globalization.* Cambridge, MA: Harvard University Press, 2012.

Stacewicz, Richard. *Winter Soldiers: An Oral History of the Vietnam Veterans against the War.* New York: Twayne Publishers, 1997.

Stambuk, George. *American Military Forces Abroad: Their Impact on the Western State System.* Columbus: Ohio State University Press, 2012.

Standing Up for Your Rights, Preserving Our Freedom: The Status of Muslim Civil Rights in Northern California, 2013. Santa Clara and Sacramento: Council on American-Islamic Relations, 2013.

Stannard, David. *Before the Horror: The Population of Hawai'i on the Eve of Western Contact*. Honolulu: University of Hawai'i Press, 1989.

Steinmetz, George, ed. *Sociology and Empire: The Imperial Entanglements of a Discipline*. Durham, NC: Duke University Press, 2013.

Stern, Harlan. "Time, Timestamps, and Timescales." In *Requirements for UTC and Civil Timekeeping on Earth*, edited by John H. Seago, Robert L. Seaman, P. Kenneth Seidelmann, and Steven L. Allen. American Astronautical Society Science and Technology Series, vol. 115, 259–65. San Diego: Univelt, 2013.

Stern, Sacha. *Calendars in Antiquity*. Oxford: Oxford University Press, 2012.

Stevenson, Lisa. "The Psychic Life of Biopolitics: Survival, Cooperation, and Inuit Community." *American Ethnologist* 39, no. 3 (2012): 592–613.

Stiglitz, Joseph, and Linda Bilmes. *The Three Trillion Dollar War: The True Cost of the Iraq Conflict*. New York: W. W. Norton, 2008.

Stoler, Ann Laura. "Affective States." In *A Companion to the Anthropology of Politics*, edited by David Nugent and Joan Vincent, 4–20. New York: Wiley, 2004.

Stoler, Ann Laura. *Along the Archival Grain: Epistemic Anxities and Colonial Common Sense*. Princeton, NJ: Princeton University Press, 2008.

Stoler, Ann Laura. *Carnal Knowledge and Imperial Power: Race and the Intimate in Colonial Rule*. Berkeley: University of California Press, 2002.

Stoler, Ann Laura. "Developing Historical Negatives: Race and the (Modernist) Visions of a Colonial State." In *From the Margins: Historical Anthropology and Its Futures*, edited by Brian Keith Axel, 156–66. Durham, NC: Duke University Press, 2002.

Stoler, Ann Laura. *Duress: Imperial Durabilities in Our Times*. Durham, NC: Duke University Press, 2016.

Stoler, Ann Laura. *Haunted by Empire: Geographies of Intimacy in North American History*. Durham, NC: Duke University Press, 2006.

Stoler, Ann Laura. "Imperial Debris: Reflections on Ruins and Ruination." *Cultural Anthropology* 23, no. 2 (2008): 191–219.

Stoler, Ann Laura. "Intimations of Empire: Predicaments of the Tactile and Unseen." In *Haunted by Empire: Geographies of Intimacy in North American History*, edited by Ann Laura Stoler, 1–22. Durham, NC: Duke University Press, 2006.

Stoler, Ann Laura. "Introduction: 'The Rot Remains': From Ruins to Ruination." In *Imperial Debris: On Ruins and Ruination*, edited by Ann Laura Stoler, 1–38. Durham, NC: Duke University Press, 2013.

Stoler, Ann Laura. "On Degrees of Imperial Sovereignty." *Public Culture* 18, no. 1 (2006): 125–46.

Stoler, Ann Laura. *Race and the Education of Desire: Foucault's History of Sexuality and the Colonial Order of Things*. Durham, NC: Duke University Press, 1995.

Stoler, Ann Laura. "Rethinking Colonial Categories: European Communities and the Boundaries of Rule." *Comparative Studies in Society and History* 31, no. 1 (1989): 134–61.

Stoler, Ann Laura. "Sexual Affronts and Racial Frontiers: European Identities and the Cultural Politics of Exclusion in Southeast Asia." *Comparative Studies in Society and History* 34, no. 3 (1992): 514–51.

Stoler, Ann Laura, and David Bond. "Refractions Off Empire: Untimely Comparisons in Harsh Times." *Radical History Review* 95 (2006): 93–107.

Stoler, Ann Laura, and Frederick Cooper. "Between Metropole and Colony: Rethinking a Research Agenda." In *Tensions of Empire: Colonial Cultures in a Bourgeois World*, edited by Frederick Cooper and Ann Laura Stoler, 1–56. Berkeley: University of California Press, 1997.

Stoler, Ann Laura, and Carole McGranahan. "Introduction: Refiguring Imperial Terrains." In *Imperial Formations*, edited by Ann Laura Stoler, Carole McGranahan, and Peter Perdue, 3–44. Santa Fe: SAR, 2007.

Stoler, Ann Laura, Carole McGranahan, and Peter Perdue, eds. *Imperial Formations*. Santa Fe: SAR, 2007.

Strange, Susan. *States and Markets*. 2nd ed. London: Continuum, 1998.

Strathern, Marilyn. "Appendice I. Artifacts of History: Events and the Interpretation of Images." In *Learning to See in Melanesia: Four Lectures Given in the Department of Social Anthropology, Cambridge University, 1993–2008*, 157–78. HAU: Masterclass Series 2, 2013.

Strathern, Marilyn. "On Space and Depth." In *Complexities: Social Studies of Knowledge Practices*, edited by Annemarie Mol and John Law, 88–115. Durham, NC: Duke University Press, 2002.

Strathern, Marilyn. *The Relation: Issues in Complexity and Scale*. Cambridge: Prickly Pear Press, 1995.

Suárez Findlay, Eileen. *Imposing Decency: The Politics of Sexuality and Race in Puerto Rico, 1870–1920*. Durham, NC: Duke University Press, 2000.

Subcommittee of the Committee on Indian Affairs. "Division of Lands and Moneys of the Osage Tribe of Indians: Hearing on H.R. 1478." 58th Congress, 3rd Session, January 20, 1905.

Suskind, Ron. "Faith, Certainty and the Presidency of George W. Bush." *New York Times Magazine*, October 17, 2004.

Svirsky, Marcelo, and Simone Bignall. *Agamben and Colonialism*. Edinburgh: Edinburgh University Press, 2012.

Sweig, Julia E. "What Kind of War for Colombia?" *Foreign Affairs*, September 1 (2002): 122–41.

Swinford, Steven. "Greenwich Mean Time Could Drift to the US, Minister Warns." *Telegraph*, May 14, 2014. Accessed December 11, 2014. http://www.telegraph.co.uk/news/politics/10831974/Greenwich-Mean-Time-could-drift-to-the-US-minister-warns.html.

Syken, Bill. "Football in Paradise." *Sports Illustrated*, November 3, 2003.

Tadiar, Neferti. *Fantasy-Production: Sexual Economies and Other Philippine Consequences for the New World Order*. Manila: Ateneo de Manila University Press, 2004.

Tadiar, Neferti. *Things Fall Away: Philippine Historical Experience and the Makings of Globalization*. Durham, NC: Duke University Press, 2009.

Taussig, Michael. "Culture of Terror—Space of Death: Roger Casement's Putumayo Report and the Explanation of Torture." *Comparative Studies in Society and History* 26, no. 3 (1984): 467–97.

Taussig, Michael. *My Cocaine Museum*. Chicago: University of Chicago Press, 2004.

Taylor, Margaret. "Demore v. Kim: Judicial Deference to Congressional Folly." In *Immigration Stories*, edited by David A. Martin and Peter H. Schuck, 343–76. New York: Foundation, 2005.

Tengan, Ty P. Kawika. "(En)Gendering Colonialism: Masculinities in Hawai'i and Aotearoa." *Cultural Values* 6, no. 3 (2002): 239–56.

Tengan, Ty P. Kawika. *Native Men Remade: Gender and Nation in Contemporary Hawai'i*. Durham, NC: Duke University Press, 2008.

Tengan, Ty P. Kawika. "Re-Membering Panala'au: Masculinities, Nation and Empire in Hawai'i and the Pacific." *The Contemporary Pacific* 20, no. 1 (2008): 27–53.

Terry, Wallace. *Bloods: An Oral History of the Vietnam War by Black Veterans*. New York: Random House, 1984.

Thoden van Velzen, H. U. E. "The Maroon Insurgency: Anthropological Reflections on the Civil War in Suriname." In *Resistance and Rebellion in Suriname: Old and New*, edited by G. Brana-Shute, 159–88. Williamsburg, VA: Department of Anthropology, College of William and Mary 1990.

Thoden van Velzen, H. U. E., and Wilhelmina van Wetering. *The Great Father and the Danger: Religious Cults, Material Forces, and Collective Fantasies in the World of the Surinamese Maroons*. Hawthorne, NY: Foris Publications, 1988.

Thoden van Velzen, H. U. E., and Wilhelmina van Wetering. *In the Shadow of the Oracle: Religion as Politics in a Suriname Maroon Society*. Long Grove, IL: Waveland, 2004.

Torruella, Juan. "The Insular Cases: The Establishment of a Regime of Political Apartheid." *University of Pennsylvania Journal of International Law* 29, no. 2 (2007): 283–347.

Trask, Mililani. *From a Native Daughter: Colonialism and Sovereignty in Hawai'i*. Monroe, ME: Common Courage, 1993.

Trask, Mililani. "The Politics of Oppression." *Hawai'i Return to Nationhood*, IWGIA-Document 75, edited by Ulla Hasager and Jonathan Friedman, 68–87. Copenhagen: IWGIA, 1994.

Trouillot, Michel-Rolph. "The Anthropology of the State in the Age of Globalization: Close Encounters of the Deceptive Kind." *Current Anthropology* 42, no. 1 (2001): 125–38.

Trouillot, Michel-Rolph. *Global Transformations: Anthropology and the Modern World*. New York: Palgrave Macmillan, 2003.

Trouillot, Michel-Rolph. *Silencing the Past: Power and the Production of History*. Boston: Beacon, 1995.

Truth and Reconciliation Commission. Accessed October 27, 2017. http://www.trc.ca/websites/trcinstitution/index.php?p=7.

Tsing, Anna Lowenhaupt. *Friction: An Ethnography of Global Connection*. Princeton, NJ: Princeton University Press, 2005.

Tsing, Anna Lowenhaupt. "Supply Chains and the Human Condition." *Rethinking Marxism: A Journal of Economics, Culture and Society* 21, no. 2 (2009): 148–76.

Tsosie, Rebecca. "Conflict between the Public Trust and the Indian Trust Doctrines: Federal Public Land Policy and Native Indians." *Tulsa Law Review* 39 (2003–4): 271.

Turner, Dale. *This Is Not a Peace Pipe: Towards a Critical Indigenous Philosophy.* Toronto: University of Toronto Press, 2004.

Turse, Nick. "Afghanistan's Base Bonanza: Total Tops Iraq at That War's Height." TomDispatch.com, September 4, 2012. Accessed August 11, 2017. http://www.tomdispatch.com/blog/175588/.

Turse, Nick. "The Pentagon's Planet of Bases." TomDispatch.com, January 9, 2011. Accessed August 9, 2017. http://www.tomdispatch.com/archive/175338/.

Twigg-Smith, Thurston. *Hawaiian Sovereignty: Do the Facts Matter?* Honolulu: Goodale Publishing, 1998.

U.K. Foreign Office. "Steering Committee on International Organisations Presentation of British Indian Ocean Territory in the United Nations." U.K. National Archives, September 8, 1966.

Ung, Loung. *First They Killed My Father: A Daughter of Cambodia Remembers.* New York: HarperCollins, 2000.

United Kingdom of Great Britain and Northern Ireland. "Availability of Certain Indian Ocean Islands for Defense Purposes." Exchange of notes, December 30, 1966.

Uperesa, Fa'anofo Lisaclaire. "Fabled Futures: Migration and Mobility for Samoans in American Football." *Contemporary Pacific* 27, no. 1 (2014): 281–301.

Uperesa, Fa'anofo Lisaclaire. "Seeking New Fields of Labor: Football and Colonial Political Economies in American Samoa." In *Formations of U.S. Colonialism*, edited by Alyosha Goldstein, 207–32. Durham, NC: Duke University Press, 2014.

Uperesa, Fa'anofo Lisaclaire, and Adriana María Garriga-López. "Contested Sovereignties: Puerto Rico and American Samoa." In *Sovereign Acts: Contesting Colonialism across Indigenous Nations and Latinx America*, edited by Frances Negrón-Muntañer, 39–81. Tucson: University of Arizona Press, 2017.

Upstate Citizens for Equality. Accessed October 27, 2017. http://www.upstate-citizens.org/.

U.S. Army Command and General Staff College. *Field Circular 100-20: Low Intensity Conflict.* Fort Leavenworth, KS: U.S. Army Command and General Staff College, July 16, 1986.

U.S. Citizenship and Immigration Services. "Our History." Accessed July 26, 2010. http://www.uscis.gov/history-and-genealogy/our-history/our-history.

U.S. Department of Defense. "Strengthening U.S. Global Defense Posture, Report to Congress." Washington, DC, September 17, 2004.

U.S. Department of State. U.S. Landmine Policy. 2009.

U.S. Department of Veterans Affairs, "Population Tables, Table 1L: VETPOP2011 LIVING VETERANS BY AGE GROUP, GENDER, 2010–2040." Accessed March 5, 2014. http://www.va.gov/vetdata/Veteran_Population.asp.

U.S. Embassy London. Telegram to RUEHCR/Secretary of State, May 10, 1965. Lyndon B. Johnson Presidential Library: NSF, Country File, Box 207, UK Memos vol. IV 5/65–6/65.

U.S. Embassy London. Telegram to Secretary of State, February 27, 1964. Naval Historical Center, 00 Files, 1964, Box 20, 11000/1B.

"U.S. Military Bases and Empire." *Monthly Review*, March 2002. Accessed August 8, 2017. http://www.monthlyreview.org/0302editr.htm.

U.S. National Security Council. *The National Security Strategy of the United States of America.* Washington, DC: Government Printing Office, 2002. https://georgewbush-whitehouse.archives.gov/nsc/nss/2002/.

U.S. Secretary of State. "Responding to Ukrainian Questions Concerning USG Support for Ukrainian-Brazilian SLV Joint Venture at Alcantara." 2009. Wikileaks Cable 09STATE3691_a. *Wikileaks.* Accessed February 9, 2015. https://wikileaks.org/plusd/cables/09STATE3691_a.html.

Uyehara, Mitsuo. *The Ceded Land Trusts, Their Use and Misuse.* Honolulu: Hawaiiana Almanac Publishing Company, 1977.

Veale, Jennifer. "Korean Missionaries under Fire." *Time,* July 27, 2007. Accessed August 9, 2017. www.time.com/time/world/article/0,8599,1647646,00.html.

Ventura, Jesse. *63 Documents the Government Doesn't Want You to Read.* New York: Skyhorse Publishing, 2012.

Vernon, Diane. *Les représentations du corps chez les noirs marrons ndjuka du Surinam et de la Guyane Française.* Paris: Editions de l'ORSTOM, 1992.

Vilas, Carlos M. *Del colonialismo a la autonomía: Modernización capitalista y revolución social en La Costa Atlántica.* Managua: Editorial Nueva Nicaragua, 1990.

Vine, David. *Base Nation: How U.S. Military Bases Abroad Harm America and the World.* New York: Henry Holt, 2015.

Vine, David. *Island of Shame: The Secret History of the U.S. Military Base on Diego Garcia.* Princeton, NJ: Princeton University Press, 2009.

Vine, David. "The Lily-Pad Strategy: How the Pentagon Is Quietly Transforming Its Overseas Base Empire and Creating a Dangerous New Way of War." TomDispatch.com, July 15, 2012. Accessed August 9, 2017. http://www.tomdispatch.com/post/175568/tomgram:_david_vine,_u.s._empire_of_bases_grows/.

Vine, David. "Taking on Empires: Reparations, the Right of Return, and the People of Diego Garcia." In *New Social Movements in the African Diaspora,* edited by Leith Mullings and Manning Marable, 171–91. Hants, UK: Palgrave Macmillan, 2009.

Vine, David. "War and Forced Migration in the Indian Ocean: The U.S. Military Base at Diego Garcia." *International Migration* 42, no. 3 (2004): 111–43.

Viveiros de Castro, E. B. "Exchanging Perspectives: The Transformation of Objects into Subjects in Amerindian Ontologies." *Common Knowledge* 10, no. 3 (2004): 463–84.

VOAnews.com. "São Tomé Sparks American Military Interest." November 12, 2004. Accessed October 30, 2017. https://www.voanews.com/a/a-13-2004-11-12-voa42-66870572/376603.html.

Wacquant, Loïc. "Pugs at Work: Bodily Capital and Bodily Labour among Professional Boxers." *Body and Society* 1, no. 1 (1995): 65–93.

Wade, Peter. "Mestizaje, Multiculturalism, Liberalism and Violence." *Journal of Latin American and Caribbean Ethnic Studies* 11, no. 3 (2016): 323–43.

Wafa, Abdul Waheed. "Cheney Unhurt after Bombing in Afghanistan." *New York Times,* February 27, 2007.

Wainwright, Joel. *Geopiracy: Oaxaca, Militant Empiricism, and Geographic Thought.* New York: Palgrave Macmillan, 2013.

Wakin, Eric. *Anthropology Goes to War: Professional Ethics and Counterinsurgency in Thailand.* Madison: University of Wisconsin Press, 1992.

Waldman, Peter. "A Cold War Coda: Of Severed Heads, Hill Tribe Gratitude." *Wall Street Journal,* January 12, 2000.

Waldron, Jeremy. "Superseding Historic Injustice." *Ethics* 103, no. 1 (1992): 4–28.

Walls, Andrew. *The Cross-Cultural Process in Christian History.* Maryknoll, NY: Orbis Books, 2002.

Walton, Jeremy. "Hungry Wolves, Inclement Storms: Commodified Fantasies of American Imperial Power in Contemporary Turkey." In *Anthropology and Global Counterinsurgency*, edited by John D. Kelly, Beatrice Jauregui, Sean T. Mitchell, and Jeremy Walton, 105–16. Chicago: University of Chicago Press, 2010.

Warner, Roger. *Backfire: The CIA's Secret War in Laos and Its Link to the War in Vietnam.* New York: Simon and Schuster, 1995.

Watterson, John Sayle. *College Football: History, Spectacle, Controversy.* Baltimore: Johns Hopkins University Press, 2000.

Wax, Dustin M., ed. *Anthropology at the Dawn of the Cold War: The Influence of Foundations, McCarthyism and the CIA.* London: Pluto, 2008.

Weheliye, Alexander. *Habeas Viscus: Racializing Assemblages, Biopolitics, and Black Feminist Theories of the Human.* Durham, NC: Duke University Press, 2014.

Weinraub, Bernard. "Reagan Joins Kohl in Brief Memorial at Bitburg Graves." *New York Times*, May 6, 1985.

Weizman, Eyal. *Forensic Architecture: Violence at the Threshold of Detectability.* New York: Zone Books, 2017.

Weltfish, Gene. "Racialism, Colonialism, and World Peace." In *Speaking of Peace*, edited by Daniel S. Gillmore. New York: National Council of the Arts, Sciences, and Professions, 1949.

Westad, Odd Arne. *The Global Cold War: Third World Interventions and the Making of Our Times.* Cambridge: Cambridge University Press, 2005.

Westover, John G. "Combat Support in Korea." Washington, DC: Center of Military History, 1987.

Weyler, Rex. *Blood of the Land: The Government and Corporate War against First Nations.* Gabriola Island, BC: New Catalyst Books, 2007.

Whitehead, John. "Hawai'i: The First and Last Far West?" *Western Historical Quarterly* 23, no. 2 (1992): 153–77.

Wickeri, Philip L., ed. *Scripture, Community, and Mission.* 2nd ed. Hong Kong: Christian Conference of Asia and the Council for World Mission, 2002.

Wik Peoples v. High Court of Australia, 1996, HCA 40.

Wilder, Gary. *Freedom Time: Negritude, Decolonization, and the Future of the World.* Durham, NC: Duke University Press, 2015.

Wilder, Gary. *The French Imperial Nation-State: Negritude and Colonial Humanism between the Two World Wars.* Chicago: University of Chicago Press, 2005.

Wilkins, David. *American Indian Sovereignty and the U.S. Supreme Court: The Masking of Justice.* Austin: University of Texas Press, 1997.

Williams, William Appleman. *Empire as a Way of Life: An Essay on the Causes and Character of America's Present Predicament.* New York: Oxford University Press, [1980] 2007.

Williams, William Appleman. *The Tragedy of American Diplomacy.* Rev. ed. New York: Delta, [1959] 1962.

Wilson, Terry P. *The Underground Reservation: Osage Oil.* Lincoln: University of Nebraska Press, 1985.

Wolf, Eric R. *Europe and the People without History*. Berkeley: University of California Press, 1982.

Wolfe, Patrick. "Settler Colonialism and the Elimination of the Native." *Journal of Genocide Research* 8, no. 4 (2006): 387–409.

Wolfe, Patrick. *Settler Colonialism and the Transformation of Anthropology: The Politics and Poetics of an Ethnographic Event*. London: Cassell, 1999.

Wood, Trish. *What Was Asked of Us: An Oral History of the Iraq War by the Soldiers Who Fought It*. New York: Little, Brown, 2006.

Woolford, Andrew. *The Benevolent Experiment: Indigenous Boarding Schools, Genocide, and Redress in Canada and the United States*. Lincoln: University of Nebraska Press, 2015.

Wright, Melissa. *The Disposable Woman and Other Myths of Global Capitalism*. New York: Routledge, 2006.

Wright, Quincy. *Mandates under the League of Nations*. Chicago: University of Chicago Press, 1930.

Yeh, Emily T. "Tibet and the Problem of Radical Reductionism." *Antipode* 14, no. 5 (2009): 983–1010.

Yi, Mahn-Yol. "Haebang 50 Nyŏn, Han'guk Kyohŏisarŭl Ŏttŏke Pol Kŏssin'ga." *Han'guk kidokkyowa yŏksa* [*History and Christianity in Korea*] 4 (1995): 6–24.

Yoneyama, Lisa. "Liberation under Siege: U.S. Military Occupation and Japanese Women's Enfranchisement." *American Quarterly* 57, no. 3 (2005): 885–910.

Yoo, Yeong-ho. "Unending War: Anti-Personnel Landmines [Kkeutnaji Anŭn Chŏnjaeng, Taein Chiroe]." *T'ongil News*, 2008.

Young, Robert. *Postcolonialism: An Historical Introduction*. Malden, MA: Blackwell, 2001.

Yu, Ch'ae-il. "Han'guk Chŏnjaengkwa Pan'gong Ideologiŭi Chŏngch'ak [Korean War and the Establishment of Anti-Communist Ideology]." *Yŏksa Pip'yŏng* 16 (1992): 139–50.

Yu, Kang-mun. "Irak'ŭsŏ Han'gukin 8 Myŏng Hanttae P'irap [8 Koreans Momentarily Kidnapped in Iraq]." *Hankyoreh*, April 9, 2004. Accessed August 9, 2017. legacy.www.hani.co.kr/section-007003000/2004/04/007003000200404090221099.html.

Contributors

KEVIN K. BIRTH is Professor of Anthropology at Queens College.

JOE BRYAN is Associate Professor of Geography at the University of Colorado.

JOHN F. COLLINS is Associate Professor of Anthropology at Queens College and the CUNY Graduate Center.

JEAN DENNISON is Associate Professor of Anthropology at the University of Washington.

ERIN FITZ-HENRY is Senior Lecturer in Anthropology at the University of Melbourne.

ADRIANA MARÍA GARRIGA-LÓPEZ is Associate Professor of Anthropology at Kalamazoo College in Michigan.

OLÍVIA MARIA GOMES DA CUNHA is Professor of Anthropology at the Museu Nacional, Federal University of Rio de Janeiro.

MATTHEW GUTMANN is Professor of Anthropology at Brown University.

JU HUI JUDY HAN is Assistant Professor of Gender Studies at the University of California, Los Angeles.

J. KĒHAULANI KAUANUI is Professor of American Studies and Anthropology at Wesleyan University.

ELEANA KIM is Associate Professor of Anthropology at the University of California, Irvine.

HEONIK KWON is Professor of Anthropology and Senior Research Fellow at Trinity College, Cambridge University.

SOO AH KWON is Associate Professor of Asian American Studies at the University of Illinois at Urbana-Champaign.

DARRYL LI is Assistant Professor of Anthropology at the University of Chicago.

CATHERINE LUTZ is the Thomas J. Watson Jr. Family Professor of Anthropology and International Studies at Brown University.

SUNAINA MAIRA is Professor of Asian-American Studies at the University of California at Davis.

CAROLE MCGRANAHAN is Associate Professor of Anthropology at the University of Colorado.

SEAN T. MITCHELL is Associate Professor of Anthropology at Rutgers University, Newark.

JAN M. PADIOS is Assistant Professor of American Studies at the University of Maryland, College Park.

MELISSA ROSARIO is an independent scholar who lives and works in Puerto Rico.

AUDRA SIMPSON is Professor of Anthropology at Columbia University.

ANN LAURA STOLER is Willy Brandt Distinguished University Professor of Anthropology and Historical Studies at the New School for Social Research.

FA'ANOFO LISACLAIRE UPERESA is Senior Lecturer in Pacific Studies at the University of Auckland.

DAVID VINE is Associate Professor of Anthropology at American University.

Index